Fodor's 91 Florida

Fodor's Travel Publications, Inc.
New York and London

ISBN 0-679-01907-3

Grateful acknowledgement is made to Alfred A. Knopf, Inc. for permission to reprint excerpts from TROPICAL SPLENDOR: AN ARCHITECTURAL HISTORY OF FLORIDA by Hap Hatton. Copyright © 1987 by Hap Hatton. Reprinted by permission of Alfred A. Knopf, Inc.

Fodor's Florida

Editor: Alison Hoffman
Editorial Contributors: April Athey, Al Burt, Michael Etzkin, Janet Groene, Gordon Groene, Herb Hiller, Ann Hughes, Kathryn Kilgore, George Leposky, Rosalie Leposky, Honey Naylor, Carolyn Price, G. Stuart Smith, Karen Feldman Smith, Joice Veselka, David Wilkening, Fred Wright
Art Director: Fabrizio La Rocca
Cartographer: David Lindroth
Illustrator: Karl Tanner
Cover Photograph: Ed Slater/Southern Stock Photos

Design: Vignelli Associates

Special Sales

Fodor's Travel Publications are available at special discounts for bulk purchases (100 copies or more) for sales promotions or premiums. Special editions, including personalized covers, excerpts of existing guides, and corporate imprints, can be created in large quantities for special needs. For more information write to Special Marketing, Fodor's Travel Publications, 201 E. 50th St., New York, NY 10022. Inquiries from the United Kingdom should be sent to Fodor's Travel Publications, 20 Vauxhall Bridge Rd., London, England SW1V 2SA.

MANUFACTURED IN THE UNITED STATES OF AMERICA

10 9 8 7 6 5 4 3 2 1

Contents

Maps

Foreword

Florida is one of the world's most popular tourist destinations. Visitors from far and near are attracted to the state's sandy beaches, warm and sunny climate, and theme parks such as Disney World. Travelers find Florida rich in historic sites, vast stretches of wildlife preserves, fine restaurants and accommodations to suit every budget. Our Florida writers have put together information on the widest possible range of activities, and within that range present you with selections of events and places that will be safe, worthwhile, and of good value. The descriptions we provide are just enough for you to make your own informed choices from among our selections.

While every care has been taken to assure the accuracy of the information in this guide, the passage of time will always bring change, and, consequently, the publisher cannot accept responsibility for errors that may occur.

All prices and opening times quoted here are based on information available to us at press time. Hours and admission fees may change, however, and the prudent traveler will avoid inconvenience by calling ahead.

Fodor's wants to hear about your travel experiences, both pleasant and unpleasant. When a hotel or restaurant fails to live up to its billing, let us know, and we will investigate.

Send your letters to the editors of Fodor's Travel Publications, 201 E. 50th St., New York, NY 10022

Highlights'91 and Fodor's Choice

Highlights '91

Orlando continues to headline as Florida's most expansive city, and the battle of the studios continues between **Disney-MGM,** which opened in 1989, and 1990's new addition, **Universal Studios Florida.**

Now cinemaphiles visiting Florida get two treats, and the surprises are never ending. In 1990 Disney-MGM announced the arrival of the newest kids in town: the **Muppets.** In 1991 **Muppet Studios** is scheduled to open, featuring a 3-D movie theater and two theme restaurants. Meanwhile, **Nickelodeon,** the children's network, has relocated to the Orlando neighborhood, and kids will be invited to participate in the production of its shows.

Epcot Center is looking forward to "various enhancements" in the upcoming years, and Orlando's big nightlife attraction, **Pleasure Island,** is fighting inflation by lowering its admission prices for 1991.

Prompted by the success of the moderately priced **Caribbean Beach Resort,** Walt Disney World has been hard at work on the **Mississippi River** hotels, including **Port Orleans** and **Dixie Landing Resort.** Meanwhile, around the airport, Orlando welcomes a variety of new hotels, representing every price range. These accommodations should be easily filled, however, with the influx of people who will travel through the **third 24-gate terminal** that opened in late 1990 at the Orlando International Airport.

Orlando's not the only Florida city that's celebrating. After years of renovations, the city of **Miami Beach** has fully recognized the importance of its **Art Deco District.** What began as a controversial attempt at restoration in the early '80s has become an integral part of the city. From all over the world, people come to Florida's **South Beach,** an area now known as a place to flex minds as well as muscles. Renewed by the vitality it enjoyed in the '50s, the area once again flourishes with art galleries, restaurants, bookstores, and the Miami City Ballet.

Miami is welcoming other changes as well. As Cuba continues to undergo its own transitions, Miami's Hispanic community plays a bigger and more dynamic role in Florida's economic and political arenas. **Little Havana** is the pillar of this community and has now taken root in Miami's cultural picture. Unfortunate news for Miami's Coral Gables area is The Biltmore Hotel's foreclosure, which occurred at press time. The community, however, is hopeful that the property will reopen shortly.

Sports is the catchword in southwest Florida, as the region awaits the opening day of the **Minnesota Twins** spring training camp. Scheduled to open in 1991 is Lee County's new 7,500-seat **stadium** in Fort Myers. Another significant event in future sports history, will occur at the Tampa Stadium on January 27, when the city will host the **National Football League's Silver Anniversary Super Bowl XXV.**

Also in early 1991, Tampa's **Lowery Park Zoo** will complete a 12-acre addition, including a new "Florida at Night" building featuring native nocturnal creatures, a manatee research center, and the 8-acre **Lykes Florida Wildlife Center,** where you'll be able to stroll among native plants and animals found from the Panhandle to the Keys.

Key Largo's tightening the bond between nature and technology, too, with a new addition to the **Key Largo Undersea Park.** Plans are underway for the construction of a 280-foot underwater moving sidewalk that will allow visitors a close look at a coral reef and its inhabitants, beneath the surface of a 30-foot-deep lagoon.

Northern Florida continues to welcome those who come to the area in search of "the other Florida." Meanwhile, Florida's cinema industry is taking advantage of the region's diverse settings, as scouts comb the area from its jungle backdrops to its metropolitan skyscrapers.

Fodor's Choice

No two people will agree on what makes a perfect vacation, but it's fun and helpful to know what others think. We hope you'll have a chance to experience some of Fodor's Choices yourself while visiting Florida. For detailed information about each entry, refer to the appropriate chapter in this guidebook.

Sights

The Gulf of Mexico at sunset, particularly at Mallory Square in Key West, where sunset watching is an evening ritual

The boardwalk at Royal Palm Hammock in the Everglades

Art Deco District in Miami Beach

The main span of Sunshine Skyway Bridge, St. Petersburg

The Palm Beach Bicycle Trail along Lake Worth

Gulf of Mexico beaches seen from a fixed-wing glider at Clearwater

White tigers at Busch Gardens, Tampa

Singing Apes of Borneo, Central Florida Zoo, Sanford

IlluminNations in Walt Disney World's Epcot Center, Orlando

The view from the battlements at the Castillo de San Marcos, St. Augustine

San Agustin Antiguo, a restored Spanish colonial village in St. Augustine

Edison's and Ford's homes, with adjoining museum displaying many of their inventions, Fort Myers

The Vizcaya Museum and Gardens in Miami

Hotels

Grand Bay Hotel, Coconut Grove (*Very Expensive*)

Indian River Plantation, Stuart (*Very Expensive*)

Little Palm Island, Little Torch Key (*Very Expensive*)

Marquesa Hotel, Key West (*Very Expensive*)

South Seas Plantation, Captiva Island (*Very Expensive*)

Amelia Island Plantation, Amelia Island (*Expensive–Very Expensive*)

Jacksonville Omni Hotel, Jacksonville (*Expensive–Very Expensive*)

Essex House, Miami Beach (*Expensive–Very Expensive*)

Sandestin Beach Resort, Destin (*Expensive–Very Expensive*)

Peabody Orlando, Orlando (*Expensive–Very Expensive*)

Don CeSar Hotel, St. Petersburg Beach (*Expensive*)

Caribbean Beach Resort, Walt Disney World (*Moderate*)

Casa Rosa Inn, Kissimmee (*Inexpensive*)

Snug Harbor, Amelia Island (*Inexpensive*)

Restaurants

Grand Cafe, Coconut Grove (*Very Expensive*)

Louie's Back Yard, Key West (*Very Expensive*)

Mark's Place, North Miami Beach (*Very Expensive*)

Bern's Steak House, Tampa (*Expensive*)

Chef Allen, North Miami Beach (*Expensive*)

Savannah Moon, Kendall suburb of Miami (*Expensive*)

Topaz Café, Flagler Beach (*Moderate*)

Hy-Vong Vietnamese Cuisine, Little Havana section of Miami (*Moderate*)

Jamie's, Pensacola (*Moderate*)

Flamingo Café, Destin (*Inexpensive–Moderate*)

Homestead, Jacksonville (*Inexpensive*)

Beaches

Crystal Beach Wayside Park

The Fort Pickens area of Gulf Islands National Seashore

John U. Lloyd Beach State Recreation Area, Dania

Pier Park, at the southern tip of Miami Beach and Lummus Park

Sarasota County beaches

Delnor-Wiggins Pass State Recreation Area, Naples

Events

The Boggy Bayou Mullet Festival in October, Niceville

Light Up Orlando in November, Orlando

The ground shaking underfoot as a rocket soars spaceward from Cape Canaveral

King Orange Jamboree Parade preceding the Orange Bowl football game, Miami

Village Wine Festival, each February, Walt Disney World

Carnaval Miami, including the *Calle Oche* Open House, in early March in the Little Havana district of Miami

Coconut Grove and Winter Park arts festivals

Sports

Fishing from the Redington Long Pier, or game fishing for the big ones off the Florida Keys

A jai alai game at any of the many frontons throughout the state

Horse racing at Hialeah

The Orange Bowl Classic football game and its two attendant tennis tournaments, Miami

A round of golf at Key Biscayne Golf Course, which *Golf Digest* calls one of the best in the nation

Golfing at any of the challenging courses around Orlando

After Hours

For local color, a drink at Captain Tony's, the original Sloppy Joe's, Hemingway's favorite bar in Key West

Comedy Corner, Palm Beach

Ragtime Tavern for Dixieland and classic jazz, Atlantic Beach

Tobacco Road bar and restaurant, Miami

Florida

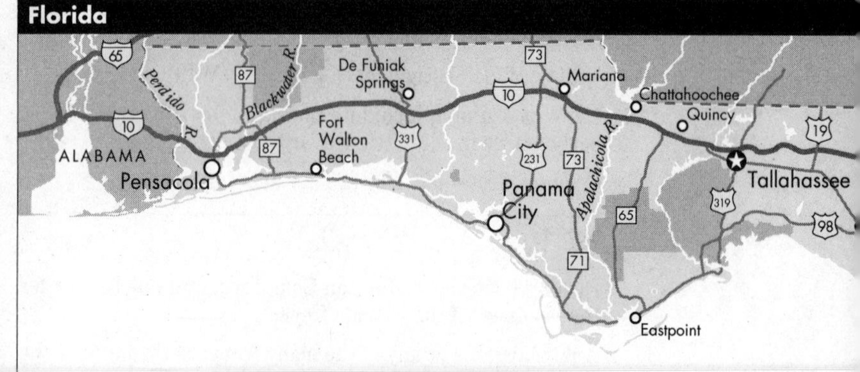

Gulf of Mexico

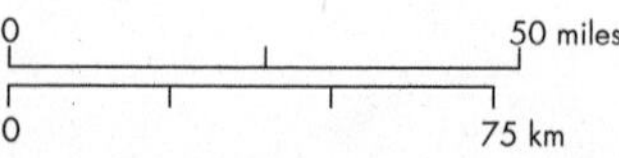

GEORGIA
St. Mary's R.
Amelia Island
Jacksonville
Osceola National Forest
River
Perry
Lake City
St. Johns River
Santa Fe R.
St. Augustine
ATLANTIC OCEAN
Suwannee
Gainesville
Ocala National Forest
Ocala
Daytona Beach
Cedar Keys
Titusville
NASA Kennedy Space Center
Cape Canaveral
Walt Disney World
Orlando
Meritt Island
Tarpon Springs
Melbourne
Tampa
Clearwater
Winter Haven
Florida's Turnpike
Sebastian Inlet Recreation Area
Tampa Bay
St. Petersburg
Vero Beach
Fort Pierce
Manatee R.
Kissimmee R.
Hutchinson Island
Bradenton
Sarasota
Peace R.
Venice
Lake Okeechobee
West Palm Beach
Singer Island
Palm Beach
Caloosahatchee R.
Cape Coral
Fort Myers
Captiva Island
Sanibel Island
Boca Raton
Naples
Fort Lauderdale
Big Cyprus National Preserve
Miami Beach
Miami
Biscayne Bay
Everglades National Park
Cape Sable
Key Largo
Florida Bay
Florida Keys
Key West

World Time Zones

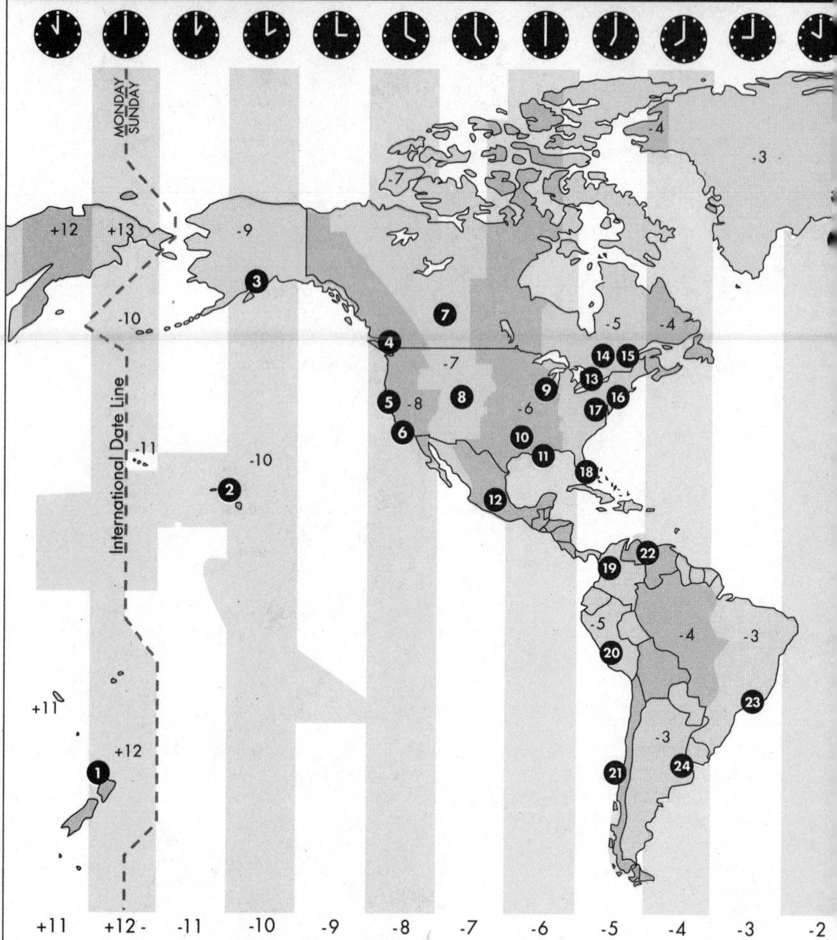

Numbers below vertical bands relate each zone to Greenwich Mean Time (0 hrs.).
Local times frequently differ from these general indications,
as indicated by light-face numbers on map.

Algiers, **29**
Anchorage, **3**
Athens, **41**
Auckland, **1**
Baghdad, **46**
Bangkok, **50**
Beijing, **54**
Berlin, **34**
Bogotá, **19**
Budapest, **37**
Buenos Aires, **24**
Caracas, **22**
Chicago, **9**
Copenhagen, **33**
Dallas, **10**
Delhi, **48**
Denver, **8**
Djakarta, **53**
Dublin, **26**
Edmonton, **7**
Hong Kong, **56**
Honolulu, **2**
Istanbul, **40**
Jerusalem, **42**
Johannesburg, **44**
Lima, **20**
Lisbon, **28**
London (Greenwich), **27**
Los Angeles, **6**
Madrid, **38**
Manila, **57**

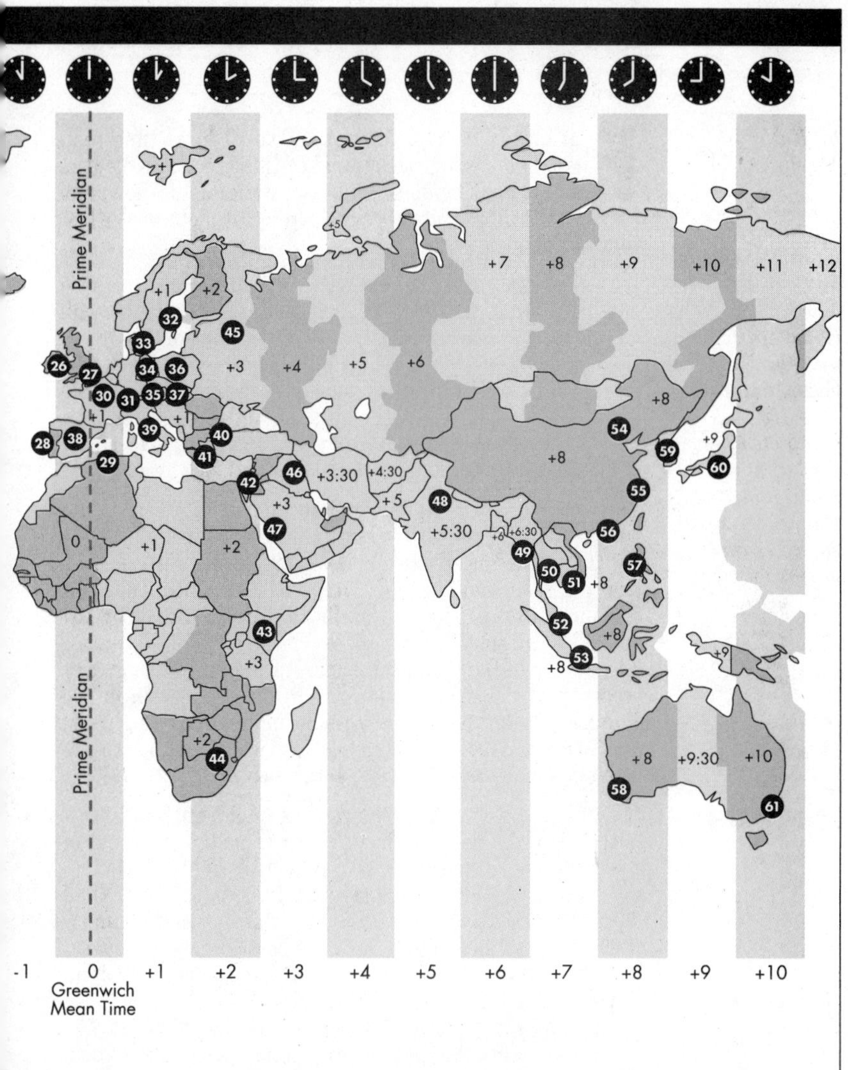

Mecca, **47**
Mexico City, **12**
Miami, **18**
Montreal, **15**
Moscow, **45**
Nairobi, **43**
New Orleans, **11**
New York City, **16**

Ottawa, **14**
Paris, **30**
Perth, **58**
Reykjavík, **25**
Rio de Janeiro, **23**
Rome, **39**
Saigon, **51**

San Francisco, **5**
Santiago, **21**
Seoul, **59**
Shanghai, **55**
Singapore, **52**
Stockholm, **32**
Sydney, **61**
Tokyo, **60**

Toronto, **13**
Vancouver, **4**
Vienna, **35**
Warsaw, **36**
Washington, DC, **17**
Yangon, **49**
Zürich, **31**

Introduction

by Kathryn Kilgore

A freelance journalist, Kathryn Kilgore has worked for The Village Voice *(New York City), and the* Montreal Gazette. *She recently completed her second novel. She has a house in Key West, where she lives and writes for part of each year.*

Florida casts no shadow. A snowbird (part-time resident) in jogging clothes makes this remark to me, the sunburned traveler, while I'm standing on the sunny steps of a small Florida library, holding 10 books on the history of Florida.

I study the snowbird's pale northern profile. He adjusts his sunglasses and continues: Cedar Key is nice; there are still Greek sponge divers at Tarpon Springs; the south edge of the Okefenokee Swamp is certainly worth a trip; don't forget all those empty country roads; and be sure to visit the Everglades. But it's not New England—he shakes his head. You can't feel the past, and you can't see it. The snowbird puts on his Walkman headphones and jogs away.

This traveler plans to drive all around the state, and she isn't ready to agree with this guy. Florida, after all, is bigger than New York State and New Jersey put together. She has just read that the "discovery" of Florida by Ponce de León in 1513 preceded the landing of the Mayflower by 107 years. St. Augustine is the oldest city in the United States. The Seminole Indians, whose ancestors refused to sign any treaty with the white man, still live as they wish in the Everglades and the Big Cypress Swamp. Miami is a glittering Spanish-speaking metropolis, a wide-open door to the Caribbean, Central America, and South America.

It is true, however, that hurricanes, mold, rot, ants, termites, floods, fires, and droughts have made a mess out of the monuments. The earliest architecture in North America has long since rotted away; the Indians left only shell mounds and pottery, and the Spanish left the mere foundations of forts. Although there were homesteads, of course, none has survived the intervening four centuries. As John Rothschild put it in his book *Up for Grabs*, "Historic St. Augustine inadvertently teaches Florida history: 450 years and no proof of occupancy." Still, there's got to be a shadow.

This traveler went to St. Augustine when she was young—in the back seat of her parents' station wagon. She remembers the narrow, peaceful streets of the little town, so different from industrial Jacksonville to its north. She climbed around the Spanish fort, the San Marcos, last rebuilt in 1672: the oldest building in America. She also saw Henry Flagler's fantastic hotels, built in the late 19th century for wealthy northern vacationers, which are among the oldest existing buildings in the state.

Yet in a way, that old snowbird had a point. Florida does feel as though it exists for a different, less serious purpose than does the rest of the country. It always has been a refuge for adventurers, entrepreneurs, and outcasts: conquistadores, both missionaries and gold hunters; escaped slaves and pirates; Seminoles from Georgia; cigar makers from Cuba, sponge divers from Greece; settlers from Minorca and Scandinavia; migrant laborers, refugees from Vietnam: *Marielitos*, who departed from Mariel, Cuba, in 1980, boatpeople from Haiti, retirees, the rich, eccentrics from everywhere, Mickey Mouse from Hollywood—and tourists.

It is also beautiful—a vast, wet, prickly state, empty of people in the center, with hundreds of lakes and huge cattle ranches and horse farms; with red-soil hills to the north, rockets to the east, castles at Orlando, and Confederate town squares near the Georgia border. Fantasy and fish, herons and gators thrive here; panthers still eke it out. The miles of swamps and plains, forests, and lakes outnumber the miles of crowded beaches. Often, even now, only the landscape survives for long, and that, too, floats, blows, or is dredged through changes, making it hard to place the past. The newspapers, even *The New York Times*, run their annual stories on how a hurricane could destroy Florida's high-rise-lined coast. The traveler already knows that this is a land that is still in control of those who live here.

A good way to begin to understand this land is to visit the Citrus Tower, "Florida's showplace for citrus," in Clermont. This traveler rode the elevator to the top of Citrus Tower, where she was supposed to "thrill to the panorama of 17 million citrus trees." What she actually saw were many, many acres of dead twisted branches, trunks, and empty fields, not a living orange tree in sight. This, Florida's finest citrus-growing country, was wiped out by the freeze of 1985 and then by citrus canker. This traveler was surprised, but the natives were sanguine: a killing freeze will occasionally happen. The last one was in 1895, and it resulted in the founding of that frost-free city, Miami. Every hundred years, someone informed the traveler, it's time to move the trees.

Florida is mutable, whimsical, and at odds with itself, the traveler sees. As she begins to read.

On one side of Florida's history are the Indians and the Spanish, and later the Cubans and the Crackers (white farmers). The Spanish-Catholic and Cuban settlers looked to Havana and South America for support; they would have nothing to do with the northern colonies (Cuba is only 90 miles from Florida). The Indians and Crackers stuck to themselves.

On the other side of Florida's history are the slave owners, the hotel builders and land sellers, and the vacationers, all of whom came down from the North and divided the state between them: conquerers who fell for Florida's appeal as a fountain of youth—or at least as a place to begin again.

The poles of Florida now got switched; the northern part became "southern" as it filled with slave-operated plantations and joined the Confederate South. The swampy southern part of Florida gradually became "northern" (as well as Spanish and Caribbean), when pleasure-seeking invaders from the cold, northern states arrived, following the developers' dredges.

The glorification of Florida as the "Sunshine State," friend of the ill and the feeble—and the tourist—has been going on for a long while.

The early Cracker settlers found their country beautiful just as it was: a land of custard apple, moonvine, catfish, and moonshine. These Floridians developed their own attitude toward all the northern invaders. It was spread across the first state flag, which stated, "Let Us Alone."

The Sunshine State has 1,350 miles of coastline, on which the tourist loves to bake whenever possible. It has 10,000 miles of rivers and streams and 7,000 springs and lakes, including the 730-square-mile Lake Okeechobee. It has 12 million residents, making it the fourth largest state in population. It has more than 40 million tourists a year, and the recovering citrus industry produced, in 1988, 130 million boxes of oranges, 51 million boxes of grapefruit, and 799 million gallons of orange juice.

This traveler took off for a trip in her rental car. She explored the city of Miami, ate Cuban food on Calle Ocho, strolled down man-made Miami Beach, looking at the Art Deco hotels. She rode through the Everglades in an airboat driven by a Seminole. She went searching for bears and panthers in Big Cypress Swamp. She drove north through the sugarcane, past the migrant labor camps, the vast Lake Okeechobee. She fished and ate frog legs and then catfish. She drove past miles of cattle on the 35,000-acre Brighton Seminole Reservation. She then went to the west coast, to Sanibel and Captiva islands, walked the beaches, and picked her way among millions of shells. She cruised down to condominium-lined Marco Island, which had changed horribly since the days when her father had brought her there to fish. She struggled back up the coast, caught in a Winnebago spring-flow, and finally got to Sarasota. She visited Ringling's house and museum of Baroque art. She went on to Tampa and stopped among the old Ybor City cigar factories. She drove up to the sponging port in Tarpon Springs and walked through neighborhoods settled by Greeks.

She finally headed toward the quiet country of northern Florida. She went to tiny Cedar Key, with its fishermen's wooden cottages, and slept in a room right over the gulf. She went further off the track, driving small roads out along the bayous, finding fishing villages where she ate delicious shrimp. She entered the Spanish-moss-covered woods and the empty pinelands. She drove on fine county roads, far from the highways, all the way up to pretty Tallahassee.

Then she started back, following the Suwannee River. She meandered into the center of the state and cut through Marjorie Rawlings's rustic Cross Creek. She stopped at Ocala National Forest to swim in a spring and to camp. She dropped over to Lakeland to see all the buildings designed by Frank Lloyd Wright at Florida Southern College, then headed up across the state back to St. Augustine to see Ripley's Believe It or Not Museum. She dawdled down the east coast along the long white shore, passing John D. Rockefeller's last home, at Ormond Beach. She studied the massive old rockets parked along Cape Canaveral. She saw fabulous Addison Mizner houses in Palm Beach. She cut back inland through the orange groves, up to Disney World and Epcot Center, which dip into the collective dream. She went back down the coast again and ambled along the boardwalk at Hollywood. She mailed postcards and set off for the Keys. She went deep-sea fishing and caught a tarpon. As she drove back up to Miami, she began to think about Florida's shadow.

Florida raised itself slightly out of the ocean some 20 million years ago, a swampy newcomer to the continent. It never experienced an ice age, but during the last one it became a popular migrating place, in spite of its rain. It did not take its final shape until 10,000 years ago.

Since the time it was first glimpsed by John Cabot, Florida has always been the object of some sort of land-claim frenzy.

In 1498, the mapmaker Cabot, out exploring for British King Henry VII, sailed down the coast from Labrador and discovered Florida, although it had already been claimed, unseen, by Christopher Columbus for Spain.

Ponce de León, representing Spain, got there second. He first saw La Florida on April 2, 1513, and landed a few days later at what is now St. Augustine. He was looking not for the fountain of youth but for the missing Bimini, where he was supposed to become governor. Finding nothing, he headed down the coast, past Los Martires (as he called the Florida Keys, which looked to him like kneeling martyrs), and up the west coast, stopping at present-day Fort Myers, where he encountered hostile Indians who shouted at him in Spanish. At this, he returned to Puerto Rico. He came back to conquer La Florida in 1521, bringing 200 settlers, including the first Catholic priests, who were supposed to reason with the heathens. The settlement near Charlotte Harbor was soon attacked by Apalachee or Calusa Indians. Ponce de León was wounded by an arrow, and the entire crew removed to Cuba, where he died.

Continuing the Spanish conquest, Pánfilo de Narváez arrived and landed in Tampa Bay in 1528. He immediately headed north, looking for the source of the Indian's gold, little suspecting that the gold he saw the Indians wearing around their necks was actually Spanish gold collected from shipwrecks.

Hernando de Soto came next. He landed at Tampa Bay in 1539 and quickly headed off in search of the same source of gold jewelry, going as far as North Carolina. He died after three years, still looking.

But then the Indians began to lose.

The Spaniard Pedro Menéndez de Aviles founded St. Augustine at long last in 1565. However, Jean Ribaut had established a French settlement at nearby Fort Caroline on the St. Johns River, and the Spanish knew this wouldn't do. Menéndez did not like those card-playing "Lutheran" French, whom he also considered pirates. Therefore, during a hurricane, he and his forces slaughtered them. All that survives of the French settlement are the journals and beautiful drawings of Native Americans done by Ribaut's mapmaker, Jacques le Moyne, who said of the Indians' costumes: "It is wonderful that men so savage should be capable of such tasteful inventions."

In a somewhat serendipitous revenge, England's Sir Francis Drake leveled St. Augustine in 1585. However, St. Augustine was rebuilt and survived (to become the town that Ralph Waldo Emerson, visiting in 1826, found to be full of "lazy desperadoes and land speculators" and that John J. Audubon called "the poorest hole in creation" in 1831).

Meanwhile, by 1560, the Indian population had withered away, as the native people were taken into slavery or died of smallpox, colds, diphtheria, or syphilis. In the 17th century, the total Indian population of 25,000, reduced by more than three-quarters, was tended to by Jesuits and Franciscans at some 50 monasteries.

The Spanish Cubans established "fishing ranchos" south in Calusa territory, and disease killed every Calusa. New British settlers arrived in the 17th century, seized native land, and drove the Timucuans and Apalachees south to their deaths.

By 1763 (when the British first took Florida from Spain in trade for Havana), the native Indians had all vanished. However, Creek Indians and Seminoles (a Creek name for wanderers or renegades), who had been crowded out of Georgia and the Carolinas, came down to replace the native Indians. They made their own land claims, which were soon challenged by the arriviste British/American settlers. Those competing claims eventually resulted in the first, second, and third Seminole wars, during the last of which Andrew Jackson crossed the border into Florida to (among other intentions) "punish" the Indians for living on land that was also claimed by white settlers.

Long before the wars, Florida's genetic pool began growing fast. The Creeks bred with Scots settlers to produce blue-eyed Creeks; the Seminoles kept black slaves and bred with them to produce black Seminoles. The result is that today you can't always guess the background of those you're talking to. In 1764, Londoner Denys Rolle started a colony near Palatka by importing vagrants, beggars, and debtors, who all abandoned him. A Scotsman named Dr. Andrew Turnbull started a colony at New Smyrna in 1768 by importing 1,255 starving Minorcans (and Greeks and Italians), all of whom fled to St. Augustine. The territory was a sort of renegade melting pot.

After America won the revolutionary war, Britain no longer wanted to bother with Florida and traded it back to Spain in 1783.

In 1821, Spain accepted the United States's offer to cancel a $5-million (somewhat bogus) debt in exchange for Florida, and Andrew Jackson again entered Pensacola, this time as governor. His stay was brief. In three months, he left what his wife Rachel called the "vast howling wilderness" and returned to Washington.

In 1830, Congress passed the Removal Law, which required all Indians in the East to be sent west to the Arkansas Territory. A delegation of Seminoles was tricked into signing this white man's treaty, which enraged the Indian Osceola, who pledged, "I will make the white man red with blood." This pledge was the beginning of the Second Seminole War, an affair that cost the white man $40,000 and some 1,500 lives. Osceola was defeated by a U.S. commander's treachery. He was captured during a false truce, and he died of malaria and grief in prison in Charleston, SC, an event that caused the white man to get much bad press in America.

Osceola's successor, Coacoochee, and his people, ragged and starving, soon requested a meeting with the white man. The Seminoles arrived at the parlay dressed in clothes they had stolen, which turned out to be an entire wardrobe of Shakespearean theater costumes. The American military negotiated with Hamlet, Richard III, Horatio, King Lear, and Caliban. Coacoochee said, "The red man's heart will always be free."

In 1842, 3,000 Seminoles were shipped along the "Trail of Tears," across the Mississippi. However, the fighting continued after 1855, when the last Seminole renegade leader, Billy Bowlegs, was caught and sent west. Three hundred of his Seminoles remained forever at large in the Florida swamps. Today their descendants raise cattle and fish, run bingo parlors, and sell trinkets and beads in south-central Florida. In 1976, the Seminoles accepted $16 million (or about 55 cents an acre) for their original 29 million acres of Florida.

Slaveholding Florida became a state in 1845, and five years later the population reached 87,445, of which 39,000 were black slaves who belonged to only 3,000 slave owners. The plantations produced cotton, turpentine, and lumber. The state's first senator, slave owner David Levy Yulee, whose grandfather was the grand vizier to the sultan of Morocco, built Florida's first cross-state railroad in the 1850s, from Fernandina to Cedar Key, laying the tracks for the subsequent land boom.

Florida seceded from the Union in 1861 and became the third state to join the Confederacy. The Civil War cost Florida $20 million and 5,000 lives, and, worse, recovery took a century. The Ku Klux Klan emerged with a vengeance and became a powerful force. Blacks still drank at separate fountains, as they did elsewhere in the South, until the Civil Rights Act of 1964.

Events that tilted Florida toward the tourist market started quietly in the 19th century. In 1844, John Gorrie of Apalachicola invented an ice-making machine and the air conditioner, but nobody paid any attention to him, and his patents ran out. In 1873, Dr. John Wall discovered that mosquitoes carry yellow fever, but nobody paid any attention to him, either. In the 1880s, when the population of Florida reached 270,000, Hamilton Disston came down from Philadelphia, PA, bought four million acres, and began to drain the Caloosahatchee and Kissimmee valleys to make (and sell) a settlers' empire. A Chinese immigrant at Deland, named Lue Gim Gong, invented the frostproof orange, which prospered along the Indian River. In 1871, Gen. Henry Sanford, Lincoln's former ambassador to Belgium, started a citrus plantation and began to import and experiment with every kind of citrus then known. He also brought in an entire colony of Swedes to work the land.

Perhaps the biggest boost to Florida's image came in 1885, when the American Medical Association endorsed Pinellas Point at St. Petersburg as the healthiest spot in the United States. After that, the land race was on. The land boom that began at the turn of the century became madness by the mid-1920s, ebbed through the Great Depression and World War II, then took off again in the 1950s and 1960s. People were—and are—irrationally attracted to the sun.

Ailing 38-year-old Thomas Edison moved from Menlo Park, NJ, to Fort Myers in 1885. There he built the first modern swimming pool in America, and his incandescent lights lit his estate and workshop 30 miles from the Seminoles who were hiding in Big Cypress Swamp.

The year 1885 also saw the influx of Cuban cigar makers into Tampa, attracted from Cuba and the Keys when Vincent Ybor, followed by others, built his Ybor cigar plant.

Ybor spirited his workers away from the labor problems of Key West to this new tax haven after his Key West factory burned. Not much later, sponge divers also deserted Key West for the deep-water sponge beds off Tarpon Springs, in a move initiated by a Greek who recruited deep-water divers from his homeland until there was (and still is) a sizable Greek colony in that city.

After the cigar makers decided to come to Ybor City, the success of their business was guaranteed by Henry Plant, who constructed the Atlantic Coastline Railroad from Richmond, Virginia, to Tampa. Starting in 1884, Plant built the enormous Tampa Bay Hotel, which is modeled on the Alhambra in Grenada, Spain, and has 13 silver Moorish minarets. The guests traveled the long corridors of this hotel by riding in rickshaws. The hotel, worth seeing, now houses a college.

Ybor City became deeply involved in Cuba's effort to free itself from Spain. Money and guns were run, and José Martí came from Cuba to Tampa to raise funds. In 1898, after the U.S.S. *Maine* was blown apart in Havana harbor and the United States entered the Spanish-American War, Plant arranged for Tampa to be the port of embarkation for the 30,000 American troops. The porch of the Tampa Bay Hotel was filled with reporters filing stories on their "rocking-chair war." Winston Churchill was there reporting, and Clara Barton came to set up a Red Cross hospital. Stephen Crane, Frederic Remington, and Richard Harding Davis spent time on this porch. Theodore Roosevelt and his Rough Riders shipped out of Tampa. The end of Spain in the New World was orchestrated from the very shore where Hernando de Soto, conquistador, first landed.

Meanwhile, Henry Morrison Flagler came to visit St. Augustine in income-tax-free Florida. Flagler, a retired Standard Oil baron, was annoyed with St. Augustine's reputation as a place for the sickly and bored by its lack of a decent hotel. In 1885, he started to build. He began with the immense and opulent poured-concrete Ponce de León Hotel, a Moorish-Renaissance monument for the very rich that is still in existence (though no longer a hotel), and followed up with the slightly more frugal Alcazar across the street. Flagler, of course, provided the transportation to his hotels, in the form of the Florida East Coast Railroad, which had an enormous impact on the state. He then continued down the coast, seeking warmth and constructing a series of fantastic hotels to popularize his railroad. Flagler set the tone for the "bastard-Spanish-Moorish-Romanesque-Gothic-Renaissance-bull-market-damn-the-expense" building style, which lasted through the land boom of the 1920s and peaked most elaborately in Addison Mizner's Palm Beach mansions, to which those with the socially necessary private railroad cars traveled. The St. Augustine hotels all closed after half a century when the tourists moved south. But Flagler was south before them, having bought the Ormond Hotel in Ormond Beach in 1890. He built the Royal Poinciana Hotel at Palm Beach in 1893, the largest wooden hotel ever constructed, where Afromobiles (white wicker carts pulled by blacks—competition for Plant's rickshaws) carried the guests about. Palm Beach wasn't even a town when the railroad came through, just a land spit covered by 20,000 coconut palms from a shipwreck.

At the persuasion of Julia Tuttle, who supposedly sent him an orange blossom during the freezing winter of 1894–95 (which had discouraged too many a fragile tourist), Flagler laid his railroad tracks down to the tiny settlement of Miami and incorporated it as a city. By 1896, he had built and opened the Royal Palm Hotel. From Miami, "America's sun porch," Flagler pushed on to Homestead and built the Overseas Railroad to Key West by 1912. (The Overseas Railroad blew away in the hurricane of 1935.) Flagler died in 1913, having been granted a free 2.4 million acres of Florida for his efforts.

In 1912, when millionaire Carl Fisher of Indianapolis came to Miami, all the hotels were on the Miami mainland. Because there was still not much to do, Fisher poked around Biscayne Bay and discovered a mangrove-covered barrier sandbar, where he soon bought land from Quaker avocado farmer John Collins. Fisher applied a dredge to it and came up with the tabula rasa that became Miami Beach, which he began to fill with imported birds, plants, polo fields, golf courses, tennis courts, grandstands, elephants, and picturesque architecture, including the Flamingo Hotel (Spanish-Moorish-Venetian-Arab style) and the Lincoln, Nautilus, King Cole, and Boulevard hotels.

"Carl discovered that sand could hold up a real estate sign, and that was all he wanted it for," said humorist Will Rogers. "Had there been no Carl Fisher, Florida would be known today as the Turpentine State."

In 1925 alone, 481 hotels and apartment buildings rose on Miami Beach. Fisher even built the Dixie Highway from Miami to Michigan. But his flashy bootleg resort was less stable than the competition at Palm Beach; after the land bust and the 1929 stock market crash, Al Capone and others of his ilk moved in. Fisher died broke and an alcoholic.

In 1916, John Deering's architect, the wacky Paul Chalfin, began work on the monstrously imposing Villa Vizcaya in Miami—a kind of Venetian palace with gardens and waterways and a village, furnished in the Medieval-Renaissance-Baroque-Rococo-Neoclassical style. After it was finished, Deering rattled around in Vizcaya alone or with his mother for 10 years until his death. The house and gardens, now restored, are open to the public, for whom there is ample room.

Addison Mizner came to Palm Beach in 1918 to rest his 300-pound frame. The flamboyant self-proclaimed architect, who frequently forgot to include a kitchen or stairs in his plans, soon began his first Palm Beach project, the Everglades Club, which the newspapers called "a little of Seville and the Alhambra, Madeira and Algiers, with Italian lagoon and terrace and garden."

In 1925, right in the middle of the land-sales boom (by which time 2.5 million suckers had rushed to buy their lots), Addison Mizner and his brother Wilson bought 17,500 acres of scrub, which they called Boca Raton. Addison built the Cloister Club and, with Wilson, went into the "surreal" real estate business, immediately selling $26 million of lots.

The scrupulous George Merrick created his beautifully designed Coral Gables (now part of Miami) out of his father's farm. In 1921, he began to sell lots in this, the country's first fully planned, city (with stucco gates and Chinese-and-French-style houses along Venetian canals in the Italian style, with roof tiles removed from houses in Cuba, imported, and reused). Merrick soon hired ex-Secretary of State William Jennings Bryan at $100,000 a year (along with 3,000 other salesmen) to stand by the Venetian pool and sell $150 million worth of property. Before the bust, Merrick had completed the Miami Biltmore Hotel and five international villages, each with houses in a different style: Dutch South African, Chinese, French City, French Country, and French Provincial. He had also established the University of Miami. (The Miami Biltmore reopened in 1987; this ghost-rich towering structure is well worth a visit.)

In the meantime, Florida natives—the white Crackers—farmed, fished, and harvested pines and turpentine to the north and inland. "Conchs" down in the Keys salvaged, caught turtles, rolled cigars, and went broke. Blacks worked at their tenant farms and went to juke joints to listen to music. Marjorie Kinnan Rawlings wrote *The Yearling* on her orange farm at Cross Creek (still there and still mysterious). Zora Neale Hurston of Eatonville, the first all-black community in the United States, wrote *Their Eyes Were Watching God*, about the 1928 hurricane that killed 2,000 people near Lake Okeechobee (there's a handsome WPA-built hurricane monument in Belle Glade). John Ringling, the circus king, set himself up at Sarasota, where he collected fine Baroque art and eventually built his Venetian ducal palazzo, Ca'd'Zan, and his art museum and where, in 1927, he first brought the "Greatest Show on Earth" to its new winter quarters.

The "Tin Can Tourists," back from World War I, arrived from the north in the early 1920s and hit the coasts in their new Fords. At first, they set up tent cities and ate out of cans, but before long they grew interested in owning a piece of the pie. Real estate scam artists, called "binder boys," flooded the state, buying up options on lots that they then resold over and over for a spiraling profit.

Things had gotten out of hand, but they didn't stop. The freeze of 1926 caused a temporary slowdown in the Florida land boom. The cold weather put a lot of people off, as did the crash of 1929, which wiped out the "paper" millionaires. The common people abandoned the small hurricane-swept lots that they'd been ill advised to buy in some impenetrable swamp and went back home. Ernest Hemingway, however, continued to fish off his royalties, down in Key West.

The WPA came to Florida and helped rescue the state from stagnation. Miami Beach's beautiful Streamline, Depression, and Tropical Deco hotels were built during the 1930s and managed to thrive. A steady migration of retirees to Florida also continued through the decade, because land was now cheap and the state still had no state income tax or inheritance tax. Later, many of the elderly ended up living in these same now-downgraded and run-down Art Deco hotels, only to be thrown out in the 1980s when some of the hotels were rescued but the tenants were not.

After World War II, business picked up a bit. By the 1950s, Florida was being redivided again, this time into lots with the kind of tract housing that had been tried successfully by visionaries such as William Levitt of Long Island, who came to Florida and started to build suburbs.

The subdividing continued briskly, and, by the 1960s, it was booming again, led by companies like the giant General Development Corporation, which offered roadless, serviceless land for $50 down, $10 a month, and by the treacherous Gulf American Corporation, which utilized the hard sell to force swamps on customers.

Now we're into visible history. This traveler believes she has glimpsed, but hasn't yet caught, the shadow. So what was she going to tell the snowbird?

She is on her way to meet the snowbird for cocktails. She crosses the bridge to Miami Beach and drives through the dusk down Collins Avenue, toward the Fontainebleau Hotel. That is the Fontainebleau ahead, isn't it? Yes, it is. No, it isn't!

It's even more startling and grandiose than the Fontainebleau she remembers. And it seems they've somehow slightly moved the Fontainebleau. Or else that gateway has distorted the view of the Fontainebleau? From the distance the tourist sees a beautiful Deco arch, beyond which is her destination. But as soon as she decides to drive through this gate, she sees she will crash right into . . . a solid wall. It's the Fontainebleau itself! And this thing before her, it's some sort of mural; it's a fake, a trompe l'oeil of the Fontainebleau Hotel! Painted by some type of trickster.

The traveler slows down. In her mind's eye, Florida's shadow rises over the flimsy suburbs of the 1950s and 1960s and the cement-slab condominiums of the 1970s, which now block the view of Florida's beaches, and further over the alarm-controlled time-shares of the 1980s, where often nobody's home; and on again across those beautiful condominiums on wealthy Brickell Avenue in Miami—the colorful 21-story Atlantis, for instance, the one in the TV series "Miami Vice," the one with the hole in it, the one you can see best from the highway at high speeds. It's like Disney World escaped from Orlando and mutated. Like everything else here, it has the irresistibly playful spirit of a state that won't conform; it's fantastic. And, finally, she understands: that hole, that trompe l'oeil, this is the heart of Florida. Florida plays with shadows.

Conservationist Marjorie Stoneman Douglas wrote that she first saw Florida in 1915 as "lost in the light, as I was, streets, roofs, fringing round-leaved trees over wharves and houseboats, all silent, all asleep. Sea gulls floated in it, white shadows. It caught the pale breasts of pelicans on pilings in dancing nets. Bay or sky, it was all dazzling, diamond-edged."

Catch if it you can.

1 Essential Information

Before You Go

Tourist Information

Contact the **Florida Division of Tourism** for information on tourist attractions and answers to questions about traveling in the state.

In Florida: 126 Van Buren St., Tallahassee 32301, tel. 904/487–1462 or 1463.

In Canada: 150 W. Bloor St., Suite 310, Toronto, Ontario M5S 1M6 2X9, tel. 416/928–3139 or 800/268–3791.

In the United Kingdom: 18/24 Westbourne Grove, 1st floor, London W25RH, tel. 071/727–8854. British travelers can also get assistance from the **U.S. Travel and Tourism Administration** (22 Sackville St., London W1X 2EA, tel. 071/439–7433).

For additional information, contact the regional tourist bureaus and chambers of commerce in the areas you wish to visit (*see* individual chapters for listings).

Tour Groups

If you prefer to leave the driving to someone else, consider a package tour. Although you will have to march to the beat of a tour guide's drum rather than your own, you are likely to save money on airfare, hotels, and ground transportation. For the more experienced or adventurous traveler, a variety of special-interest and independent packages are available. Listed below is a sampling of available options. Check with your travel agent or the Florida Division of Tourism (904/487–1462) for additional resources.

When considering a tour, be sure to find out exactly what expenses are included (particularly tips, taxes, side trips, additional meals, and entertainment); ratings of all hotels on the itinerary and the facilities they offer; cancellation policies for you and for the tour operator; and, if you are traveling alone, the cost for a single supplement. Most tour operators request that bookings be made through a travel agent; there is no additional charge for doing so.

General-Interest Tours

Globus Gateway/Cosmos (150 S. Los Robles Ave., Suite 860, Pasadena, CA 91101, tel. 818/449–0919 or 800/556–5454) offers an Orlando/Bahamas tour. **Domenico Tours** (751 Broadway, Bayonne, NJ 07002, tel. 201/823–8687 or 800/554–TOUR) offers packages to Orlando, Miami Beach, Palm Beach, St. Petersburg, Ft. Lauderdale, and Miami Beach/Bahamas/Walt Disney World. **Casser Tours** (46 W. 43rd St., New York, NY 10036, tel. 212/840–6500 or 800/251–1411) has a "Florida Sunshine" tour that includes Walt Disney World, St. Augustine, Sea World, and Kennedy Space Center. **Tauck Tours** (11 Wilton Rd., Westport, CT 06881, tel. 203/226–6911 or 800/468–2825) offers tours of the resort areas of southern Florida and the Florida Keys, as well as trips to major attractions in central Florida.

Special-Interest Tours

Adventure

Sobek's International Explorers Society (Box 1089, Angels Camp, CA 95222, tel. 209/736–4524) will take you canoeing through the Florida Everglades or island-hopping by sailboat off the Gulf Coast of Florida in their "Adventure Sail Escape." **Wilderness Southeast** (711 Sandtown Rd., Savannah, GA 31410, tel. 912/897-5108) runs rugged trips through the Everglades and places like the Okefenokee Swamp in Georgia. Also available is a four-day trip through central Florida, beginning with canoeing excursions in Ocala National Forest and ending with a snorkeling expedition on the Gulf Coast—this is the only location where tourists can legally swim with the manatees.

Nature Visit the loggerhead turtle on Sanibel Island, off Florida's Gulf Coast, with conservationists in an outing arranged by **Smithsonian Associates Travel Program** (1100 Jefferson Dr. SW, Washington, DC 20560, tel. 202/357-4700). You must pay a $20 fee to become a member of the Smithsonian to take any of the trips offered in the program.

Package Deals for Independent Travelers

American FlyAway Vacations (tel. 800/433-7300) offers city packages with discounts on hotels and car rentals. The airline offers a "Fly and Drive" package to the entire state as well as a number of three- and four-day trips to Orlando and its environs, including Sea World and Disney World. **Delta Air Lines** (tel. 800/872-7786) offers a wide variety of packages in Florida, including trips to Disney World, Daytona, Ft. Lauderdale, Miami, Key West, Tampa, Orlando, Sarasota, Ft. Myers, and Marco Island. **American Express** has similar city packages, with complimentary admission to certain area attractions, available from any American Express office.

Tips for British Travelers

Government Tourist Offices The **United States Travel and Tourism Administration** (22 Sackville St., London W1X 2EA, tel. 071/439-7433) will send brochures and give you advice on your trip to Florida.

Passports and Visas You will need a valid passport (£15) to enter the United States. You do not need a visa so long as you are visiting either on business or pleasure; are staying for less than 90 days; have a return ticket; are flying with a major airline (in effect, all airlines that fly to the United States); and a completed visa waiver form I791 (supplied either at the airport of departure or on the plane and to be handed in on arrival). Otherwise you can obtain a U.S. Visitors Visa either through your travel agent or by post from the **United States Embassy** (Visa and Immigration Dept., 5 Upper Grosvenor St., London W1A 2JB, tel. 071/499-3443). The embassy no longer accepts visa applications made by personal callers. No vaccinations are required.

Customs Visitors of 21 or over can take in 200 cigarettes or 50 cigars or 2 kilograms of tobacco; one U.S. liter of alcohol; and duty-free gifts to a value of $100. Be careful not to try to take in meat or meat products, seeds, plants, fruits, etc. Avoid illegal drugs like the plague.

Returning to Britain you may bring home: (1) 200 cigarettes or 100 cigarillos or 50 cigars or 250 grams of tobacco; (2) two liters of table wine with additional allowances for (a) one liter of alcohol over 22% by volume (38.8 proof, most spirits) or (b) two liters of alcohol under 22% by volume (fortified or sparkling wine); and (3) 60 milliliters of perfume and ¼ liter of toilet water; and (4) other goods up to a value of £32.

Insurance We recommend that you insure yourself to cover health and motoring mishaps through **Europ Assistance** (252 High St., Croydon, Surrey CRO 1NF, tel. 081/680–1234).

It is also wise to take out insurance to cover loss of luggage (though check that this isn't already covered in any existing home-owner's policy). Trip-cancellation insurance is another wise buy. **The Association of British Insurers** (Aldermary House, Queen St., London EC4N 1TT, tel. 071/248–4477) will give comprehensive advice on all aspects of vacation insurance.

Tour Operators Numerous tour operators offer packages to Florida. Here we list just a few; contact your travel agent to find companies best suited to your needs and pocketbook.

Albany Travel (Manchester) Ltd. (Central Buildings, 211 Deansgate, Manchester M3 MNW, tel. 061/833–0202) offers an eight-day "Florida Resorts" tour, organized by its American affiliate, Tauck Tours, featuring southern Florida and the Florida Keys. Prices start from $1095 (£707) per person.

Jetlife Holidays (Suite A, 33 Swanley Centre, Swanley, Kent BR8 7TL has a wide range of vacations to various destinations in Florida.

Poundstretcher (Atlantic House, Hazelwick Ave., Three Bridges, Sussex RH10 1NP, tel. 0293/578022) offers a wide range of fly-drive vacations, golf and tennis vacations, inclusive tours, and cruises, with destinations from Orlando down to Key West.

Thomas Cook Select Holidays (Centurion House, Hertford, Herts. SG14 1BH, tel. 0992–554144) offers seven nights in Orlando starting at £426. Six-night stays at a Holiday Inn in Clearwater start at £473.

Airfares If you want to make your own way to Florida and need a reasonably priced ticket, try the small ads in the daily or Sunday newspapers or in magazines such as *Time Out*. You should be able to pick up something at rock-bottom prices. Be prepared to be flexible about your dates of travel and book as early as possible.

Also check out the APEX tickets offered by the major airlines, which are another good option. As we went to press, round-trip tickets to Orlando and Miami cost about £300. Be sure to ask if there are any hidden extras, since airport taxes and supplements can increase the price dramatically.

Car Rental There are offices of the major car rental companies in most large towns, and you can either make your arrangements before you leave or when you get to your destination.

Avis (Hayes Gate House, Uxbridge Rd., Hayes, Middlesex UB4 0JN, tel. 081/848–8733) offers seven days' rental of, say, a Chevrolet at about £72; extra days start at £16 per day.

Hertz (Radnor House, 1272 London Rd., London SW16 4XW, tel. 081/679–1799) offers an "Affordable America" program. At press time, seven days' rental of a Ford Escort, for example, cost about $185; extra days run about $46 a day. Most rental offers include unlimited mileage, but don't forget to budget for the price of gas, local taxes, and collision insurance. Also check out the fly-drive offers from tour operators and airlines; some good bargains are usually available.

When to Go

Florida is a state for all seasons, although most visitors prefer October-April, particularly in southern Florida.

Winter is the height of the tourist season, when southern Florida is crowded with "snowbirds" fleeing the cold weather in the North. Hotels, bars, discos, restaurants, shops, and attractions are all crowded. Hollywood and Broadway celebrities appear in sophisticated supper clubs, and other performing artists hold the stage at ballets, operas, concerts, and theaters.

During the winter season, the Magic Kingdom at Disney World is more magical than ever, especially from mid-December through January 2, with daily parades and other extravaganzas. The crowds are overwhelming then, too. Winter fairs and festivals, art shows, parades, and fiestas take place in other parts of the state as well. In Tarpon Springs, youths dive for a golden cross during the Epiphany Festival on January 6. And in Tampa, the swashbuckling Gasparilla Festival attracts enormous crowds in mid-winter.

Summer in Florida, as smart budget-minded visitors have discovered, is often hot and very humid, but the season is made bearable along the coast by ocean breezes. Besides, many hotels lower their prices considerably during summer. In the Panhandle, though, summer is the peak season.

Families who want to explore Disney World-Epcot, Sea World, Busch Gardens, and other outstanding attractions will find some crowds in summer—but fewer during the week when children return to school in September.

For the college crowd, **spring** vacation is still the time to congregate in Florida, especially in the Daytona Beach area, and less so now than in recent years in Fort Lauderdale, where city officials, in their effort to have Fort Lauderdale become more of a family resort, no longer indulge young revelers. Also a popular destination among the spring-breakers this year is Panama City Beach.

For senior citizens, September-December are months for discounts to many attractions and hotels in Orlando and along the Pinellas Suncoast in the Tampa Bay area.

Climate What follows are average daily maximum and minimum temperatures for major cities in Florida.

Key West (The Keys)

Jan.	76F	24C	**May**	85F	29C	**Sept.**	90F	32C
	65	18		74	23		77	25
Feb.	76F	24C	**June**	88F	31C	**Oct.**	83F	28C
	67	19		77	25		76	24
Mar.	79F	26C	**July**	90F	32C	**Nov.**	79F	26C
	68	20		79	26		70	21
Apr.	81F	27C	**Aug.**	90F	32C	**Dec.**	76F	24C
	72	22		79	26		67	19

Miami	**Jan.**	74F	23C	**May**	83F	28C	**Sept.**	86F	30C
		63	17		72	22		76	24
	Feb.	76F	24C	**June**	85F	29C	**Oct.**	83F	28C
		63	17		76	24		72	22
	Mar.	77F	25C	**July**	88F	31C	**Nov.**	79F	26C
		65	18		76	24		67	19
	Apr.	79F	26C	**Aug.**	88F	31C	**Dec.**	76F	26C
		68	20		77	25		63	17

Orlando	**Jan.**	70F	21C	**May**	88F	31C	**Sept.**	88F	31C
		49	9		67	19		74	23
	Feb.	72F	22C	**June**	90F	32C	**Oct.**	83F	28C
		54	12		72	22		67	19
	Mar.	76F	24C	**July**	90F	32C	**Nov.**	76F	24C
		56	13		74	23		58	14
	Apr.	81F	27C	**Aug.**	90F	32C	**Dec.**	70F	21C
		63	17		74	23		52	11

Current weather information for over 750 cities around the world may be obtained by calling **WeatherTrak** information service at 900/370–8728 or in TX, 900/575–8728. A taped message will tell you to dial the three-digit access code for the destination you're interested in. The code is either the area code (in the United States) or the first three letters of the foreign city. For a list of all access codes, send a stamped, addressed envelope to Cities, Box 7000, Dallas, TX 75209. For further information, phone 214/869–3035 or 800/247–3282.

Festivals and Seasonal Events

Top seasonal events in Florida include Speed Week's auto racing celebration in Daytona Beach in February; Miami Film Festival in February; Florida Derby Festival from March through April; Sunfest in Palm Beach in May; and Key West's celebration of Hemingway Days in July. For exact dates and details about the following events, call the listed numbers or inquire from local chambers of commerce.

Jan.: Hollywood Sun 'n Fun Festival includes celebrity entertainment and top-notch food (tel. 305/920–3330).
Early Jan.: Polo Season opens at the Palm Beach Polo and Country Club (13198 Forest Hill Blvd., West Palm Beach 33414, tel. 407/793–1440).
Jan. 6: Greek Epiphany Day includes religious celebrations, parades, music, dancing, and feasting at the St. Nicholas Greek Orthodox Cathedral (Box 248, Tarpon Springs 34689, tel. 813/937–3540).
Mid Jan.: Art Deco Weekend spotlights Miami Beach's historic district with an Art Deco street fair, a 1930s-style Moon Over Miami Ball, and live entertainment (661 Washington Ave., Bin L, Miami Beach 33119, tel. 305/672–2014).
Mid-Jan.: Taste of the Grove Food and Music Festival is a popular fund-raiser put on in Coconut Grove's Peacock Park by area restaurants (tel. 305/442–2001).
Late Jan.: South Florida Fair and Exposition takes place in West Palm Beach (General Office, 9067 Southern Blvd., West Palm Beach 33411, tel. 407/793–0333).
Late Jan. or early Feb.: Key Biscayne Art Festival is an annual juried show of 175 talented artists at the entrance to Cape Flor-

ida State Park (Richard Maloy, Key Biscayne Rotary Club, Box 490174, Key Biscayne 33149, tel. 305/361–0775).

Early Feb.–late Feb.: Speed Weeks is a three-week celebration of auto racing that culminates in the famous Daytona 500 in Daytona Beach (Daytona International Speedway, Drawer S, Daytona Beach 32015, tel. 904/253–6711).

Feb–Mar.: Winter Equestrian Festival includes more than 1,000 horses and three grand-prix equestrian events at the Palm Beach Polo and Country Club in West Palm Beach (tel. 407/798–7000).

First weekend in Feb.: Sarasota Classic is a major event on the LPGA tour (Classic, Box 2199, Sarasota 33578).

Early Feb.: Scottish Festival and Games features a variety of events in Key Biscayne (tel. 305/757–6730).

Mid-Feb.: Florida State Fair includes carnival rides and 4-H competitions in Tampa (Box 11766, Tampa 33680, tel. 813/621–7821).

Mid-Feb.: Miami Film Festival is 10 days of international, domestic, and local films sponsored by the Film Society of America (7600 Red Rd., Penthouse Suite, Miami 33157, tel. 305/444–FILM).

Mid-Feb.: Florida Manatee Festival in Crystal River focuses on both the river and the endangered manatee (tel. 904/795–3149).

Mid-Feb.: Florida Citrus Festival and Polk County Fair in Winter Haven showcases the citrus harvest with displays and entertainment (100 Cyprus Gardens Blvd., Winter Haven 33880, tel. 813/293–3175).

Mid-Feb.: Islamorada Sportfishing Festival features a weekend of fishing, arts and crafts, races, and prizes (tel. 305/664–4503).

Mid-Feb.: Coconut Grove Art Festival is the state's largest (tel. 305/447–0401).

Last full weekend in Feb.: Labelle Swamp Cabbage Festival is a salute to the state tree, the cabbage palm (tel. 813/675–0697).

Early Mar.–early Apr.: Florida Derby Festival is a series of cultural, social, artistic, and athletic events in Broward, Dade, and Palm Beach counties (Festival, Box 705, Hallandale 33008, tel. 305/454–8544).

First weekend in Mar.: Sanibel Shell Fair is the largest event of the year on Sanibel Island (tel. 813/472–2155).

Early Mar.: Carnaval Miami is a carnival celebration staged by the Little Havana Tourist Authority (970 S.W. First St., Miami 33130, tel. 305/324–7349).

Early Mar.: Cycle Week is a major motorcycle racing event at Daytona International Speedway that always takes place three weeks after the Daytona 500 (tel. 904/253–6711).

Mid-Mar. and early July: Arcadia All-Florida Championship Rodeo is professional rodeo at its best (Rodeo, Box 1266, Arcadia 33821, tel. 813/494–2014).

Mid-Mar.–Mid-Apr.: Springtime Tallahassee is a major cultural, sporting, and culinary event in the capital (tel. 904/224–5012).

Late Mar.: Azalea Festival is a beauty pageant, arts and crafts show, and parade held in downtown Palatka and Riverfront Park (tel. 904/325–3815).

Late Mar.:Florida International Air Show at the Charlotte County Airport (Bill Graham, 1601 W. Marion Ave., Punta Gorda 33950, tel. 813/639–2788).

Late Mar.: Port Canaveral Seafood Festival requires hearty appetites at Cape Canaveral (tel. 407/459–2200).

Apr.: Arts in April presents a series of visual and performing arts events produced by local independent arts organizations (400 S. Orange Ave., Orlando 32801, tel. 407/849–2221).

Early Apr.: Spring Arts Festival attracts more than 300 artists and craftspeople from across the country to Gainesville (tel. 904/372–1976).

Early Apr.: Bounty of the Sea Seafood Festival in Miami includes a limbo contest, a chowder competition, an Underwater Film Festival, and more (International Oceanographic Foundation/ Planet Ocean, 3979 Rickenbacker Causeway, Miami 33149, tel. 305/361–5786).

Early Apr.–late May: Addison Mizner Festival in Boca Raton celebrates the 1920s in Palm Beach County (tel. 800/242–1774).

Palm Sunday: Blessing of the Fleet is held on the bay front in St. Augustine (tel. 904/829–5681).

Mid-Apr.–mid-May: Water Weeks in Panama City Beach is a spring festival of fishing tournaments, scuba treasure hunts, and sailing regattas (tel. 904/234–6575).

Easter Sunday: Easter Sunrise Service in Orlando is held at Sea World (tel. 407/351–3600).

Late Apr.: River Cities Festival is a three-day event in Miami Springs and Hialeah that focuses attention on the Miami River and the need to keep it clean (tel. 305/887–1515).

Late Apr.-early May: Sun 'n' Fun Festival includes a bathtub regatta, golf tournament, and nighttime parade in Clearwater.

Late Apr.–early May: Conch Republic Celebration in Key West honors the founding fathers of the Conch Republic, "the small island nation of Key West" (tel. 305/294–4440).

First weekend in May: Sunfest includes a wide variety of cultural and sporting events in West Palm Beach (tel. 407/659–5980).

Mid-May: Arabian Nights Festival in Opa-locka is a mix of contemporary and fantasy-inspired entertainment (tel. 305/686–4611).

Mid-May: Pompano Seafood Festival includes one of the nation's premier billfish tournaments, plus area restaurants that showcase their offerings (tel. 305/941–2940).

Mid-May–June: Fiesta of Five Flags in Pensacola celebrates de Luna's landing with dancing and reenactments of the event (tel. 904/433–6512).

First weekend in June: Miami-Bahamas Goombay Festival in Miami's Coconut Grove, celebrates the city's Bahamian heritage (tel. 305/443–7928).

Early–mid-June: Billy Bowlegs Festival in Fort Walton Beach is a week of entertaining activities in memory of a pirate who ruled the area in the late 1700s (tel. 904/244–8191).

July 4: Firecracker Festival in Melbourne is one of the state's most colorful Independence Day celebrations.

Mid-July: Hemingway Days Festival in Key West includes plays, short-story competitions, and a Hemingway look-alike contest (tel. 305/294–4440).

Mid-July: The Greater Jacksonville King Fish Tournament offers a number of cash prizes (tel. 904/241–7127).

Month of Aug.: Boca Festival Days includes many educational, cultural, and recreational activities in Boca Raton (tel. 407/395–4433).

Mid-Aug.: Shark Tournament at Port of the Islands on Marco Island awards prizes for the largest shark in three categories; at Port of the Islands Resort and Marina (Rte. 41, Marco Island 33937, tel. 800/237–4173 or in FL 800/282–3011).

Late Aug.: Worm Fiddler's Day is the biggest day of the year in Caryville (tel. 904/548–5116).
Labor Day Weekend: Florida Pro Surfing Event is held in Sebastian (tel. 407/728–4325).
Early Sept.: Anniversary of the Founding of St. Augustine is held on the grounds of the Mission of Nombre de Dios (tel. 904/829–5681).
Mid- to late Sept.: Festival Miami is three weeks of performing and visual arts sponsored by the University of Miami. (University of Miami School of Music, 6200 San Amaro Dr., Coral Gables 33124, tel. 305/284–3941).
Late Sept.: Pensacola Seafood Festival means food and entertainment in Pensacola (tel. 904/433–6512).
Late Sept.: Miami Boat Show in the Grove draws up to 200,000 people to Coconut Grove in Miami (tel. 305/579–3310).
Oct.: Destin Seafood Festival is a two-day affair where you can sample smoked amberjack, fried mullet, or shark kabobs (tel. 904/837–6241).
Oct.: Banyan Art Festival attracts craftspeople and artists to Coconut Grove (tel. 305/444–7270).
Mid-Oct.: Florida State Chili Cookoff Championship at Port of the Islands Resort in the Everglades means all the chili you can eat (25000 Tamiami Trail East, Naples 33961, tel. 800/237–4173 or in FL 800/282–3011).
Late Oct.: Boggy Bayou Mullet Festival is a three-day hoedown in celebration of the "Twin Cities," Valparaiso/Niceville, and the famed scavenger fish, the mullet (tel. 904/678–1615).
Late Oct.: Fantasy Fest in Key West is an unrestrained Halloween costume party, parade, and town fair (tel. 305/294–4440).
Early Nov.: Light Up Orlando is a street celebration of bands, international foods, and the Queen Kumquat Sashay Parade (tel. 407/363–5800).
Early Nov.: Florida Seafood Festival is Apalachicola's celebration of its seafood staple with oyster-shucking-and-consumption contests and parades (tel. 904/653–8051.)
Early–late Dec.: Winterfest and Boat Show in Fort Lauderdale has a rodeo, shoreline competitions, a Fun Fest for children, and a boat parade and ends with a "Light Up Lauderdale" New Year's Eve bash (tel. 305/522–3983).
Mid-Dec.: Walt Disney World's Very Merry Christmas Parade in the Magic Kingdom (Walt Disney World, Box 10000, Lake Buena Vista 32830–1000).
Mid-Dec.: Christmas Regatta of Lights is a colorful display in St. Augustine (tel. 904/829–5681).
Late Dec.: Coconut Grove King Mango Strut is a parody of the Orange Bowl Parade (tel. 305/858–6253).

What to Pack

Pack light, because porters and luggage trolleys are hard to find. Luggage allowances on domestic flights vary slightly from airline to airline. Most allow three checked pieces and two carryons. In all cases, check-in luggage cannot weigh more than 70 pounds per bag or be larger than 62 inches (length + width + height) and carryons must fit under the seat or in the overhead luggage compartment.

The northern part of the state is much cooler in the winter than is the southern part. Winters are mild in the Orlando area, with daytime temperatures in the 70s and low 80s. But the temperature can dip to the 50s, even in the Keys, so take a sweater or jacket, just in case. Farther north, in the Panhandle area, winters are cool and there's often frost at night.

The Miami area and the Tampa/St. Petersburg area are warm year-round and often extremely humid during the summer months. Be prepared for sudden summer storms, but leave the plastic raincoats at home because they're uncomfortable in the high humidity.

Dress is casual throughout the state, with sundresses, jeans, or walking shorts appropriate during the day. A pair of comfortable walking shoes or sneakers is a must for Disney World. A few of the better restaurants request that men wear jackets and ties, but most do not. Be prepared for air-conditioning bordering on freezing, especially in the Miami/Fort Lauderdale areas.

You can swim in Florida year-round. Be sure to take a sun hat and a good sunscreen because the sun can be fierce, even in the winter.

An extra pair of glasses, contact lenses, or prescription sunglasses is always a good idea; it is important to pack any allergy medication you may need.

Cash Machines

Virtually all U.S. banks belong to a network of ATMs (automatic teller machines), which dispense cash 24 hours a day in cities throughout the country. There are some eight major networks in the United States, the largest of which are **Cirrus,** owned by MasterCard, and **Plus,** affiliated with Visa. Some banks belong to more than one network. These cards are not automatically issued; you have to ask for them. Cards issued by American Express, Visa, and MasterCard may also be used in the ATMs, but the fees are usually higher than the fees on bank cards, and there is a daily interest charge on the "loan," even if monthly bills are paid on time. Each network has a toll-free number you can call to locate machines in a given city. The Cirrus number is 800/424–7787; the Plus number is 800/843–7587. Check with your bank for fees and for the amount of cash you can withdraw per day.

Traveling with Film

If your camera is new, shoot and develop a few rolls before leaving home. Pack some lens tissue and an extra battery for your built-in light meter. Invest about $10 in a skylight filter and screw it onto the front of your lens; it will protect the lens and also reduce haze.

Film doesn't like hot weather. If you're driving in summer, don't store film in the glove compartment or on the shelf under the rear window. Put it behind the front seat on the floor, on the side opposite the exhaust pipe.

On a plane trip, never pack unprocessed film in check-in luggage; if your bags get X-rayed, say goodbye to your pictures. Always carry undeveloped film with you through security and ask to have it inspected by hand. (It helps to isolate your film in a plastic bag, ready for quick inspection.) Inspectors at American airports are required by law to honor requests [for hand in]spection.

The newer airport scanning machines used in all U.S. air[ports] are safe for anything from five to 500 scans, depending on [the] speed of your film. The effects are cumulative; you can put the same roll of film through several scans without worry. After five scans, though, you're asking for trouble.

If your film gets fogged and you want an explanation, send it to the National Association of Photographic Manufacturers (550 Mamaroneck Ave., Harrison, NY 10528). It will try to determine what went wrong. The service is free.

Car Rentals

Florida is a car renter's bazaar, with more discount companies offering more bargains—and more fine print—than anywhere else in the nation. If you're planning to rent a car in Florida, shop around for the best combination rate for car and airfare. Jacksonville, for example, is often somewhat cheaper to fly into than Miami, but Miami's car-rental rate are usually lower than Jacksonville's. In major Florida cities, peak-season rates for a subcompact average around $110 a week, often with unlimited mileage. Some companies advertise peak-season promotional rates as low as $59 a week with unlimited mileage, but only a few cars are available at this rate, and you may have to pay twice as much if you keep the car less than seven days! Some of these companies require you to keep the car in the state and are quick to charge for an extra day when you return a vehicle late.

Avis (tel. 800/331–1212), **Budget** (tel. 800/527–0700), **Dollar** (tel. 800/421–6868), **Hertz** (tel. 800/654–3131), **National** (tel. 800/328–4567), **Sears** (tel. 800/527–0770), and **Thrifty** (tel. 800/367–2277) maintain airport and city locations throughout Florida. So do **Alamo** (tel. 800/327–9633) and **General** (tel. 800/327–7607), which offer some of the state's lowest rates. **Rent-A-Wreck** (tel. 800/221–8282) and **Ugly Duckling** (tel. 800/365–4357) rent used cars throughout the state, usually with more stringent mileage restrictions.

Besides the national rental companies, several regional and local firms offer good deals in major Florida cities. These include **Ajax** (tel. 800/352–2529), **Auto Host** (tel. 800/527–4678), **Payless** (tel. 800/237–2804), **Lindo's** (tel. 800/237–8396), **USA** (tel. 800/872–2277), and **Value** (tel. 800/327–2501). Ajax is a major budget renter in Jacksonville, with three beach offices. In Fort Lauderdale, local companies include **Aapex Thompson** (tel. 305/566–8663), and **Air and Sea** (tel. 305/764–1008). In Orlando, try **Buck An Hour** (tel. 407/273–4000) and **Wheels** (tel. 407/351–6461). Tampa-St. Petersburg companies include **A-Florida Rent-A-Heap** (tel. 813/581–4805) and **Phoenix** (tel. 813/360–6941). In Miami, **A-OK** (tel. 305/633–3313) and **Dolphin** (tel. 305/871–5553) are local budget companies, while **AutoExotica** (tel. 305/871–3686) and **Cars of the Rich and Famous** (tel. 305/945–2737) rent cars fit for a "Miami Vice" set. Down in Key West, try **Tropical Rent-a-Car** (tel. 305/294–8136).

It's always best to know a few essentials *before* you arrive at the car-rental counter. Find out what the collision damage waiver (CDW), usually an $8–$12 daily surcharge, covers and whether your corporate or personal insurance already covers damage to ental car (if so, bring a photocopy of the benefits section ng). More and more companies are now holding renters re- nsible for theft and vandalism damages if they don't buy the W; in response, some credit card and insurance companies extending *their* coverage to rental cars. These include **Ac- s America** (tel. 800/851–2800), **Chase Manhattan Bank Visa rds** (tel. 800/645–7352), and **Dreyfus Consumer Bank Gold and Silver MasterCards** (tel. 800/847–9700). Find out, too, if you must pay for a full tank of gas whether you use it or not, and make sure you get a reservation number.

Traveling with Children

Publications ***Family Travel Times*** is an 8- to 12-page newsletter published 10 times a year by Travel with Your Children (80 Eighth Ave., New York, NY 10011, tel. 212/206–0688). The $35 subscription includes access to back issues and twice-weekly opportunities to call in for specific advice. Send $1 for a sample issue.

Great Vacations with Your Kids: The Complete Guide to Family Vacations in the U.S., second edition, by Dorothy Ann Jordon and Marjorie Adoff Cohen (E. P. Dutton, 2 Park Ave., New York, NY 10016; $12.95) details everything from city vacations to adventure vacations to child-care resources.

Bimonthly publications for parents that are filled with listings of events, resources, and advice are available free at such places as libraries, supermarkets, and museums: ***Florida Parent*** (4331 N. Federal Hwy., Fort Lauderdale 33060, tel. 305/776–3305) covers Palm Beach, Broward, and Dade counties; ***Tampa Bay Family Times*** (Box 17481, Tampa 33682, tel. 813/877–0217) covers Hillsborough County. For a small fee, you can usually have an issue sent to you before your trip.

Hotels Florida may have the highest concentration of hotels with organized children's programs in the United States. The following list gives examples of the kinds of services and activities offered by some of the major chains. It is by no means exhaustive. Be sure to ask about children's programs when you make a reservation.

Club Med (40 W. 57th St., New York, NY 10019, tel. 800/CLUB-MED) opened its new Sandpiper resort village in Port St. Lucie, including a "Baby Club" (4–23 months), "Mini Club" (2 years and up), and "Kids Club" (8 years and up). **Guest Quarters Suite Hotels** (Fort Lauderdale and Tampa locations, tel. 800/424–2900) offers the luxury of two-room suites with kitchen facilities and children's menus in the restaurant. It also allows children under 18 to stay free in the same suite with their parents. Two **Sonesta International Hotels** (tel. 800/343–7170) have children's programs: Sonesta VillHotel Orlando and Sonesta Beach Hotel Key Biscayne. The **Hyatt Regency Grand Cypress** at Orlando (1 Grand Cypress Blvd., Orlando 32819, tel. 407/239–1234 or 800/228–9000) staffs a year-round child-care center for kids 3–12 and organizes summer activities for toddlers through teens. There's a Children's Creative Center at the **Delta Court of Flags** (5715 Major Blvd., Orlando 32819, tel. 407/351–3340). Also look for children's programs at **Marriott's Harbor Beach Resort** (3030 Holiday Dr., Fort Lauderdale 33316, tel. 305/525–4000 or 800/228–9290); The **Stouffer Orlando Resort** (6677 Sea Harbor Dr., Orlando 32821, tel. 407/351–5555 or 800/468–3571); **Amelia Island Plantation Resort** (Rte.

A1A, Amelia Island 32034, tel. 904/261-6161); **Holiday Inn Main Gate East** at Disney World (5678 Space Coast Hwy., Kissimmee 32741, tel. 407/396-4488 or 800/465-4329); and **Marriott's Marco Island Resort** (400 S. Collier Blvd., Marco Island 33937, tel. 813/394-2511 or 800/228-9290). Most **Days Inn** hotels (tel. 800/325-2525) charge only a nominal fee for children under 18 and allow kids 12 and under to eat free (many offer efficiency-type apartments, too).

Condo Rentals See ***The Condo Lux Vacationer's Guide to Condominium Rentals in the Southeast*** by Jill Little (Vintage Books/Random House, New York; $9.95).

Home Exchange Exchanging homes is a surprisingly low-cost way to enjoy a vacation in another part of the country. A good choice for home exchange in the United States is the **Vacation Exchange Club, Inc.**, (12006 111th Ave., Unit 12, Youngstown, AZ 85363, tel. 602/972-2186). The club publishes one directory in February and a supplement in April. Membership is $24.70 per year, for which you receive one listing. A photo costs another $9; listing a second home costs $6.

Getting There On domestic flights, children under 2 who do not occupy a seat travel free. Various discounts apply to children 2-12. Reserve a seat behind the bulkhead of the plane, which offers more legroom and can usually fit a bassinet (supplied by the airline). At the same time, inquire about special children's meals or snacks, offered by most airlines. (See "TWYCH's Airline Guide," in the February 1990 issue of ***Family Travel Times,*** for a rundown of the services offered by 46 airlines; an update is planned for February 1992.) At press time, the FAA was considering two alternatives to the present regulations governing child restraint systems aboard an aircraft. The first alternative would require that air carriers provide children under 40 pounds or 3 years of age with a safety seat; the second alternative would require that air carriers allow the use of safety seats brought on board by parent, guardian, or attendant, provided that a ticket is purchased for the child. For the booklet *Child/Infant Safety Seats Acceptable for Use in Aircraft,* write to the Community and Consumer Liaison Division (APA-400 Federal Aviation Administration, Washington, DC 20591, tel. 202/267-3479).

Hints for Disabled Travelers

The Information Center for Individuals with Disabilities (Fort Point Place, 1st floor, 27-43 Wormwood St., Boston, MA 02117, tel. 617/727-5540) offers useful problem-solving assistance, including lists of travel agents that specialize in tours for the disabled.

Moss Rehabilitation Hospital Travel Information Service (12th St. and Taber Rd., Philadelphia, PA 19141, tel. 215/329-5715) provides information on tourist sights, transportation, and accommodations in destinations around the world. There is a small fee.

Mobility International USA (Box 3551, Eugene, OR 97403, tel. 503/343-1284) is a membership organization with a $20 annual fee offering information on accommodations, organized study, and so forth.

The Society for the Advancement of Travel for the Handicapped (26 Court St., Penthouse Suite, Brooklyn, NY 11242, tel. 718/

858–5483) offers access information. Annual membership costs $40, or $25 for senior travelers and students. Send $1 and a stamped, self-addressed envelope.

The **National Park Service** provides a **Golden Access Passport** free of charge to those who are medically blind or have a permanent disability; the passport covers the entry fee for the holder and anyone accompanying the holder in the same private, noncommercial vehicle and a 50% discount on camping, boat launching, and parking. All charges are covered except lodging. Apply for the passport in person at any national recreation facility that charges an entrance fee; proof of disability is required. For additional information, write to the National Park Service (U.S. Dept. of Interior, 18th and C Sts. NW, Washington, DC 20240).

Information/Referral Numbers for Physically Challenged Visitors is a useful booklet available without charge from the Florida Division of Tourism (Collins Bldg., Room 526, Tallahassee 32399–2000, tel. 904/488–8230).

Greyhound/Trailways (tel. 800/531–5332) will carry a disabled person and companion for the price of a single fare.

Amtrak (tel. 800/USA–RAIL) requests 72 hours' notice to provide redcap service, special seats, or wheelchair assistance at stations equipped to provide this service. All handicapped and elderly passengers are entitled to a 25% discount on regular, discounted coach fares. A special children's handicapped fare is also available, offering qualifying children ages 2–11 a 50% discount on their already discounted children's fare. It should be noted that there are exceptions to these discounts on certain prescribed days with various routes. Always check with Amtrak first. For a free copy of ***Amtrak's Travel Planner,*** a guide to its services for elderly and handicapped travelers, write to Amtrak (National Railroad Corporation, 400 N Capitol St. NW, Washington, DC 20001).

Publications

Twin Peaks Press (Box 129, Vancover, WA 98666, tel. 206/694–2462 or 800/637–2256 for orders only) specializes in books for the disabled. Add $2 postage for the first book; $1 each additional book. ***Travel for the Disabled*** ($9.95) offers a comprehensive list of guidebooks and facilities geared to the disabled. ***Directory of Travel Agencies for the Disabled*** ($12.95) lists more than 350 agencies throughout the world. ***Wheelchair Vagabond*** ($9.95) helps independent travelers plan for extended trips in cars, vans, or campers. Twin Peaks also offers a "Traveling Nurse's Network," which provides registered nurses trained in all medical areas to accompany and assist disabled travelers.

Access to the World: A Travel Guide for the Handicapped, by Louise Weiss, offers tips on travel and accessibility around the world. It is available from Henry Holt & Co. for $12.95 (tel. 800/247–3912, the order number is 0805 001417).

Access America: An Atlas and Guide to the National Parks for Visitors with Disabilities (published by Northern Cartographic, Box 133, Burlington, VT 05402, tel. 802/655–4321) contains detailed information about access for the 37 largest and most visited national parks in the United States. This award-winning book costs $44.95 plus $5 shipping directly from the publisher.

Hints for Older Travelers

The **American Association of Retired Persons** (AARP, 1909 K St. NW, Washington, DC 20049, tel. 202/872-4700) has two programs for independent travelers: (1) the Purchase Privilege Program, which offers discounts on hotels, airfare, car rentals, RV rentals, and sightseeing, and (2) the AARP Motoring Plan, which offers emergency aid (road service) and trip-routing information for an annual fee of $33.95 per person or per married couple. The **AARP Travel Service** also arranges group tours through **American Express Vacations** (Box 5014, Atlanta, GA 30302, tel. 800/241-1700 or in GA, 800/282-0800). AARP members must be 50 or older. Annual dues are $5 per person or per married couple.

If you're planning to use an AARP or other senior-citizen identification card to obtain a reduced hotel rate, mention it at the time you make your reservation, not when you check out. At restaurants, show your card to the maître d' before you're seated, because discounts may be limited to certain set menus, days, or hours. When renting a car, remember that economy cars, priced at promotional rates, may cost less than cars that are available with your ID card.

Travel Industry and Disabled Exchange (TIDE, 5435 Donna Ave., Tarzana, CA 91356, tel. 818/343-6339) is an industry-based organization with a $15-per-person annual membership fee. Members receive a quarterly newsletter and a directory of travel agents for the disabled.

National Council of Senior Citizens (925 15th St. NW, Washington, DC 20005, tel. 202/347-8800) is a nonprofit advocacy group with some 5,000 local clubs across the country. Annual membership is $12 per person or couple. Members receive a monthly newspaper with travel information and an ID for reduced rates on hotels and car rentals.

Mature Outlook (6001 N. Clark St., Chicago, IL 60660, tel. 800/336-6330), a subsidiary of Sears Roebuck & Co., is a travel club for people over 50, offering discounts at Holiday Inns and a bimonthly newsletter. Annual membership is $9.95 per person or per married couple. Instant membership is available at participating Holiday Inns.

Golden Age Passport is a free lifetime pass to all parks, monuments, and recreation areas run by the federal government. People over 62 should pick one up in person at any national park that charges admission. A driver's license or other proof of age is required.

September Days Club (tel. 800/241-5050) is run by the moderately priced **Days Inns of America.** The $12 annual membership fee for individuals or couples over 50 entitles them to reduced car rental rates and reductions of 15%-50% at 95% of the chain's more than 350 motels. Members also receive *Travel Holiday Magazine Quarterly* for updated information and travel articles.

Elderhostel (80 Boylston St., Suite 400, Boston, MA 02116, tel. 617/426-7788) is an innovative educational program for people aged 60 or over (only one member of a traveling couple needs to qualify). Participants live in dorms on 1,200 campuses in the United States and around the world. Mornings are devoted to lectures and seminars, afternoons to sightseeing and field trips. The fee includes room, board, tuition (in the United States and Canada), and round-trip transportation (overseas). Special scholarships are available for those who qualify financially.

Saga International Holidays (120 Boylston St., Boston, MA 02116, tel. 800/343–0273) specializes in group travel for people over age 60. A selection of variously priced tours allows you to choose the package that best meets your needs.

Publications ***The Discount Guide for Travelers Over 55***, by Caroline and Walter Weintz, lists helpful addresses, package tours, reduced-rate car rentals, etc., in the United States and abroad. To order, send $7.95 plus $1.50 shipping and handling to Penguin USA/NAL/Cash Sales (Bergenfield Order Dept., 120 Woodbine St., Bergenfield, NJ 07621, tel. 800/526–0275. Include ISBN 0–525–48358–6).

The Senior Citizen's Guide to Budget Travel in the United States and Canada is available for $4.95 plus shipping from Pilot Books (103 Cooper St., Babylon, NY 11702, tel. 516/422–2225).

Although Florida probably attracts more elderly people than any other state, the state publishes no booklet addressed directly to senior citizens.

Senior-citizen discounts are common throughout Florida, but there are no set standards. Some discounts, like those for prescriptions at the Eckerd Drug chain, require that you fill out a card and register. The best bet is simply to ask whether there is a senior-citizen discount available on your purchase, meal, or hotel stay.

Further Reading

Suspense novels that are rich in details about Florida include Elmore Leonard's *La Brava,* John D. MacDonald's *The Empty Copper Sea,* and Joan Higgins's *A Little Death Music.* Pat Frank's *Alas Babylon* describes a fictional nuclear disaster in Florida.

Marjorie K. Rawlings's classic, *The Yearling,* poignantly portrays life in the brush country, and her *Cross Creek* re-creates the memorable people the author knew from 13 years of living at Cross Creek.

Look for *Snow White and Rose Red* and *Jack and the Beanstalk,* Ed McBain's novels about Matthew Hope, an attorney who practices law in a Florida gulf city. Pat Booth's novel *Palm Beach* describes the glitzy Palm Beach scene.

Other recommended novels include Evelyn Mayerson's *No Enemy But Time; To Have and Have Not,* by Ernest Hemingway; *The Day of the Dolphin,* by Robert Merle; and *Their Eyes Were Watching God,* by Zora Neale Hurston, a tale of life in a black town in northern Florida.

Among the recommended nonfiction books are *Key West Writers and Their Homes,* Lynn Kaufelt's tour of homes of Hemingway, Wallace Stevens, Tennessee Williams, and others; *The Everglades: River of Grass,* by Marjory S. Douglas; *Florida,* by Gloria Jahoda, published as part of the Bicentennial observance; *Miami Alive,* by Ethel Blum; and *Florida's Sandy Beaches,* University Press of Florida.

Arriving and Departing

By Plane

Most major U.S. airlines schedule regular flights into Florida, and some, such as Delta, serve the Florida airports extensively.

Delta, Eastern, and USAir all have regular service into Jacksonville, Daytona Beach, Orlando, Melborne, West Palm Beach, Fort Lauderdale, Miami, Fort Myers, Tampa, Tallahassee, Gainesville, and Key West. Delta also flies into Sarasota, Naples, Pensacola, and Fort Pierce.

Other major airlines that serve the Florida airports include Continental, American, American Trans Air, Northwest, Pan Am, United, and TWA. Many foreign airlines also fly into some of the major airports in Florida; the smaller, out-of-the-way airports are usually accessible through the commuter flights of major domestic carriers.

Packages that combine airfare and vacation activities at special rates are often available through the airlines. For example, Delta (tel. 800/872–7786) offers travel packages to Disney World in Orlando (*see* Package Deals for Independent Travelers).

When booking reservations, keep in mind the distinction between nonstop flights (no stops and no changes), direct flights (no changes of aircraft, but one or more stops), and connecting flights (one or more changes of planes at one or more stops). Connecting flights are often the least expensive, but they are the most time-consuming, and the biggest nuisance.

Smoking New smoking regulations prohibit smoking on all domestic flights under six hours. This rule applies to both domestic and foreign carriers.

Carry-on Luggage Under new rules in effect since January 1988, passengers are usually limited to two carry-on bags. For bags stored under your seat, the maximum dimensions are 9″ × 14″ × 22″. For bags that can be hung in a closet, the maximum dimensions are 4″ × 23″ × 45″. For bags stored in an overhead bin, the maximum dimensions are 10″ × 14″ × 36″. Any item that exceeds the specified dimensions will generally be rejected as a carryon and handled as checked baggage. Keep in mind that an airline can adapt these rules to circumstances; on an especially crowded flight, don't be surprised if you are allowed only one carry-on bag.

In addition to the two carryons, passengers may also bring aboard: a handbag (pocketbook or purse), an overcoat or wrap, an umbrella, a camera, a reasonable amount of reading material, an infant bag, crutches, cane, braces, or other prosthetic device upon which the passenger is dependent, and an infant/child safety seat (depending on space availability).

Note that these regulations are for U.S. airlines only. Foreign airlines generally allow one piece of carry-on luggage in tourist class, in addition to handbags and bags filled with duty-free goods. Passengers in first and business class may also be allowed to carry on one garment bag. It is best to check with your airline ahead of time to find out what their exact rules are regarding carry-on luggage.

Checked Luggage Luggage allowances vary slightly from airline to airline. Many carriers allow three checked pieces; some allow only two. It is best to check before you go. In all cases, check-in luggage cannot weigh more than 70 pounds per piece or be larger than 62 inches (length + width + height).

Lost Luggage On domestic flights, airlines are responsible for lost or damaged property only up to $1,250 per passenger. If you're carrying valuables, either take them with you on the airplane or purchase additional insurance for lost luggage. Some airlines will issue additional luggage insurance when you check in, but many do not. Insurance for lost, damaged, or stolen luggage is available through travel agents or directly through various insurance companies. Two that issue luggage insurance are **Tele-Trip** (Box 31685, 3201 Farnam St., Omaha, NE 68131, tel. 800/228–9792), a subsidiary of Mutual of Omaha, and **The Travelers Insurance Co.** (Ticket and Travel Dept., 1 Tower Sq., Hartford, CT 06183, tel. 203/277–0111 or 800/243–3174). Tele-Trip operates sales booths at airports, and it also issues insurance through travel agents. Tele-Trip will insure checked luggage for up to 180 days at $500–$3,000 valuation. For 1–3 days, the rate for a $500 valuation is $8.25; for 180 days, $100. The Travelers will insure checked or hand luggage at $500–$2,000 valuation per person, also for a maximum of 180 days. Rates for 1–5 days for $500 valuation are $10; for 180 days, $85.

Other companies with comprehensive policies include **Access America Inc.**, a subsidiary of Blue Cross-Blue Shield (Box 807, New York, NY 10163, tel. 800/851–2800) and **Near Services** (450 Prairie Ave., Suite 101, Calumet City, IL 60409, tel. 708/868–6700 or 800/654–6700).

Before you go, itemize the contents of each bag in case you need to file an insurance claim. Be certain to put your home address on each piece of luggage, including carry-on bags. If your luggage is stolen and later recovered, the airline must deliver the luggage to your home free of charge.

By Car

Three major interstates lead to Florida from various parts of the country. I–95 begins in Maine, runs south through New England and the Mid-Atlantic states, and enters Florida just north of Jacksonville. It continues south past Daytona Beach, Vero Beach, Palm Beach, and Fort Lauderdale, eventually ending in Miami.

I–75 begins at the Canadian border in Michigan and runs south through Ohio, Kentucky, Tennessee, and Georgia before entering Florida. The interstate moves through the center of the state before veering west into Tampa. It follows the west coast south to Naples, then crosses the state and ends in Miami.

California and all the most southern states are connected to Florida by I–10. This interstate originates in Los Angeles and moves east through Arizona, New Mexico, Texas, Louisiana, Mississippi, and Alabama before entering Florida at Pensacola on the west coast. I–10 continues straigh part of the state until it terminates in Jac

Speed Limits In Florida the speed limits are 55 mph on 30 mph within city limits and residential the interstates. These limits may vary, so b signs for any changes.

By Train

Amtrak (tel. 800/USA-RAIL) provides service to Orlando, Tampa, Miami, Tallahassee, Jacksonville, and several other major cities in Florida.

By Bus

Greyhound/Trailways passes through practically every major city in Florida, including Jacksonville, Daytona, Orlando, West Palm Beach, Fort Lauderdale, Miami, Sarasota, Tampa, Tallahassee, and Key West. For information about bus schedules and fares, contact your local Greyhound Information Center.

Staying in Florida

Tourist Information

The **Florida Division of Tourism** operates **welcome centers** on I–10, I–75, I–95, U.S. 231 (near Graceville), and in the lobby of the new Capitol in Tallahassee (Department of Commerce, 126 Van Buren St., Tallahassee 32399, tel. 904/487–1462).

Shopping

Malls in Florida are full of nationally franchised shops, major department-store chains, and one-of-a-kind shops catering to a mass audience. Small shops in out-of-the-way places, however, often have the best souvenirs and most special gift items.

Indian Artifacts Indian crafts are abundant, particularly in the southern part of the state, where you'll find billowing dresses and shirts, hand-sewn in striking colors and designs. At the Miccosukee Indian Village, 25 miles west of Miami on the Tamiami Trail (U.S. 41), as well as at the Seminole and Miccosukee reservations in the Everglades, you can also find handcrafted dolls and beaded belts.

Seashells The best shelling in Florida is on the beaches of Sanibel Island off Fort Myers. Shell shops, selling mostly kitsch items, abound throughout Florida. The largest such establishment is The Shell Factory near Fort Myers (*see* Shopping in Chapter 9).

Citrus Fruit Orange juice—Florida's "liquid gold"—is a staple throughout the state. The welcome centers greet visitors with a fresh glass of it and many restaurants squeeze it for you while you watch. Fresh citrus is available most of the year, except in summer. Some groves still give free samples of juice and fruit slices, but many now charge a small fee for a taste.

Don't expect to roam the groves picking your own fruit. Public access was prohibited to limit the spread of a disastrous canker blight that threatened Florida's citrus industry in the mid-1980s.

Two kinds of citrus grow in Florida: the sweeter and more costly Indian River fruit from a thin ribbon of groves along the east coast, and the less-costly fruit from the interior. After killer freezes in 1984, 1985, and 1989 ruined many groves in the Orlando area, the interior growers began planting in warmer areas south and west of Lake Okeechobee.

Citrus is sold in quarter, half, three-quarter, and full bushels. Many shippers offer special gift packages with several varieties of fruit, jellies, and other food items. Some prices include U.S. postage, others may not. Shipping may exceed the cost of the fruit. If you have a choice of citrus packaged in boxes or bags, take the boxes. They are easier to label, are harder to squash, and travel better than the bags.

Malls and Boutiques The Greater Miami area has many look-alike shopping strips and malls with the same retail and discount shops. You'll find finer boutiques in specialty malls such as Mayfair Shops in the Grove (*see* Exploring Coral Gables/Coconut Grove/South Miami in Chapter 3) and the Bal Harbour Shops (9700 Collins Ave., Bal Harbour 33154, tel. 305/866–0311). The half mile of Flagler Street in the heart of downtown Miami is the nation's most important import-export center, where bargain items for international travelers include cameras, electronics, and jewelry (*see* Exploring Downtown Miami in Chapter 3).

Fort Lauderdale's finest shops cluster along six blocks of Las Olas Boulevard (*see* Exploring Fort Lauderdale in Chapter 5) and at the 150-store Galleria At Fort Lauderdale (2414 E. Sunrise Blvd., tel. 305/564–1015).

For the ultimate Florida shopping experience, stroll Palm Beach's Worth Avenue (*see* Shopping in Chapter 6). Here you'll find shops like Gucci and Ralph Lauren tucked between galleries selling ancient Chinese art or Oriental rugs, gourmet restaurants, one-of-a-kind jewelry stores, and chocolatiers.

South of Tampa Bay on Florida's west coast, St. Armand's Circle in Sarasota has many elegant clothing shops and fine restaurants (*see* Shopping in Chapter 9). North of Tampa Bay in Tarpon Springs, you'll enjoy exploring sponge shops and savoring Greek fare along Dodecanese Boulevard.

Shops at the World Showcase in Epcot Center at Walt Disney World offer unusual lines of clothing, decorative items, gifts, and fine wines from many parts of the globe.

To shop and dine in a gracious 19th-century setting, visit the commercial heart of old Pensacola in the Palafox Historic District and the adjoining Seville Historic District centered around Seville Square. At the Quayside Thieves Market (712 S. Palafox St., tel. 904/433–9930), antiques shops and a flea market occupy a historic 19th-century warehouse beside the port. Specialty shops in Pensacola's historic district offer art, Christmas decorations, cookware, fine gifts, linens, and out-of-print books (*see* Exploring Pensacola in Chapter 10).

To travel even farther back in time, stroll the four-block pedestrian zone on Saint George Street in Old St. Augustine. Shoppers are serenaded by street musicians as they pause to window-wish or peer into dimly lit shops to watch craftspeople at work.

Antiques-lovers should explore Micanopy, south of Gainesville off I–75; the Antiques Mall in St. Augustine's Lightner Museum; on U.S. 1 north of Dania Beach Boulevard in Dania; and S.W. 28th Lane and Unity Boulevard in Miami (near the Coconut Grove Metrorail station).

Beaches

No point in Florida is more than 60 miles from saltwater. This long, lean peninsula is bordered by a 526-mile Atlantic coast from Fernandina Beach to Key West and a 792-mile coast along the Gulf of Mexico and Florida Bay from Pensacola to Key West. If you were to stretch Florida's convoluted coast in a straight line, it would extend for about 1,800 miles. What's more, if you add in the perimeter of every island surrounded by saltwater, Florida has about 8,500 miles of tidal shoreline—more than any other state except Alaska. Sand beaches comprise about 1,016 miles of Florida's coastline.

Visitors unaccustomed to strong subtropical sun run a risk of sunburn and heat prostration on Florida beaches, even in winter. The natives go to the beach early in the day or in the late afternoon. If they must be out in direct sun at midday, they limit their sun exposure and strenuous exercise and drink plenty of liquids.

The state owns all beaches below the mean high-tide line, even in front of hotels and private resorts, but gaining access to the public beach can be a problem along much of Florida's coastline. You must pay to enter and/or park at most state, county, and local beachfront parks. Where hotels dominate the beach frontage, public parking may be limited or nonexistent.

Along the Atlantic Coast from the Georgia border south through the Daytona Beach area, the beaches are so broad and firm that you can drive on them. Some beachfront communities in this area charge for the privilege; others provide free beach access for vehicles.

From the Treasure Coast south, erosion has been gnawing away at the beaches. Major beach rehabilitation projects have been completed in Fort Lauderdale, the Sunny Isles area of north Dade County, Miami Beach, and Key Biscayne.

In the Florida Keys, coral reefs and prevailing currents prevent sand from building up to form beaches. The few Keys beaches are small, narrow, and generally have little or no sandy bottom.

On the Gulf Coast, Captiva Island is losing sand to neighboring Sanibel Island, where a stroll beside the water at sunrise or sunset can be a truly sensual experience. Currents bring all sorts of unusual shells onto Sanibel's beach, and scatter sharks' teeth across Venice and Caspersen beaches in south Sarasota County. Siesta Beach in Sarasota County claims to have Florida's softest white sand. At the north end of Longboat Key in Manatee County, accretion has built a magnificent beach in the vicinity of Beer Can Island. Much of that sand came from Coquina Beach and Bradenton Beach, county parks that remain popular despite their dwindling supply of sand. In

Pinellas County, visit Caladesi Island State Park to experience what all the barrier islands used to look like.

In Florida's Panhandle, Gulf Island National Seashore administers 150 miles of beach frontage notable for their sugarlike sand and the impressive dune formations near Fort Walton Beach. Expect the beaches outside Panama City and Pensacola to be crowded on summer weekends.

Participant Sports

Bicycling Bicycling is popular throughout Florida. The terrain is flat in the south and gently rolling along the central ridge and in much of the Panhandle. Most cities of any size have bike-rental shops, which are good sources of information on local bike paths.

Florida's Department of Transportation (DOT) publishes free bicycle trail guides, which you can request from the state bicycle-pedestrian coordinator. (605 Suwannee St., Mail Room Station 19, Tallahassee 32399-0450, tel. 904/488–4640). DOT also sells 11 maps for bicycle trips of 35 to 300 miles. *Maps and Publications, 605 Suwannee St., Mail Room Station 12, Tallahassee 32399-0450, tel. 904/488–9220. Cost: $1 plus 6% sales tax per map.*

For information on local biking events and clubs, contact **Florida Bicycle Associations** (Box 16652, Tampa 33687-6652, tel. 800/FOR BIKE). In Greater Miami, contact Dade County's bicycle-pedestrian coordinator (Office of the County Manager, Metro-Dade Government Center, 111 N.W. 1st St., Suite 910, Miami 33128, tel. 305/375–4507).

Canoeing The best time to canoe in Florida is winter, the dry season, when you're less likely to get caught in a torrential downpour or be eaten alive by mosquitoes.

The Everglades has areas suitable for flat-water wilderness canoeing that are comparable to spots in the Boundary Waters region of Minnesota. Other popular canoeing rivers include the Loxahatchee, Peace, Suwannee, St. Marys, and Santa Fe. A free guide issued by the Florida Department of Natural Resources (DNR), ***Florida Recreational Trails System Canoe Trails,*** describes nearly 950 miles of designated canoe trails along 36 Florida creeks, rivers, and springs (Office of Communications, Marjory Stoneman Douglas Bldg., 3900 Commonwealth Blvd., Tallahassee 32399–3000, tel. 904/488–7326). Contact individual national forests, parks, monuments, reserves, and seashores for information on their canoe trails. Local chambers of commerce have information on canoe trails in county parks.

Two Florida canoe outfitter organizations publish free lists of canoe outfitters who organize canoe trips, rent canoes and canoeing equipment, and help shuttle canoeists' boats and cars. ***Canoe Outpost System*** is a brochure listing eight independent outfitters serving 11 Florida rivers (Rte. 7, Box 301, Arcadia 33821, tel. 813/494–1215). The **Florida Association of Canoe Liveries and Outfitters (FACLO)** publishes a free list of 26 canoe outfitters who organize trips on 28 creeks and rivers (Box 1764, Arcadia 33821).

Fishing When President Bush made his pre-inaugural bonefishing trip to Islamorada in 1989, he was following a time-honored angling tradition. Other celebrities who have come to Florida to cast a hook and line include President Theodore Roosevelt, British statesman Winston Churchill, and novelists Zane Grey and Ernest Hemingway.

In Atlantic and Gulf waters, fishing seasons and other regulations vary by location, and by the number and size of fish of various species that you may catch and retain. For a free copy of the annual ***Florida Fishing Handbook,*** write to the Florida Game and Fresh Water Fish Commission (620 S. Meridian St., Tallahassee 32399-1600, tel. 904/488–1960).

Opportunities for saltwater fishing abound from the Keys all the way up the Atlantic Coast to Georgia and up the Gulf Coast to Alabama. Many seaside communities have fishing piers that charge admission to fishermen (and usually a lower rate to watchers). These piers usually have a bait-and-tackle shop. Write the **Florida Sea Grant Extension Program** for a free list of Florida fishing piers (Rm. G-022, McCarty Hall, University of Florida, Gainesville 32611, tel. 904/392–1771).

Inland, there are more than 7,000 fresh-water lakes to choose from. The largest—448,000-acre **Lake Okeechobee,** the fourth-largest natural lake in the United States—is home to bass, bluegill, speckled perch, and succulent catfish (which the locals call "sharpies"). In addition to the state's many natural fresh-water rivers, South Florida also has an extensive system of flood-control canals. In 1989 scientists found high mercury levels in largemouth bass and warmouth caught in parts of the Everglades in Palm Beach, Broward, and Dade counties, and warned against eating fish from those areas.

It's easy to find a boat-charter service that will take you out into deep water. Some of the best are found in the Panhandle, where small towns like Destin and Fort Walton Beach have huge fleets. The Keys, too, are dotted with charter services, and Key West has a sportfishing and shrimping fleet that you would expect to find in large cities. Depending on your taste, budget, and needs, you can charter anything from an old wooden craft to a luxurious, waterborne palace with state-of-the-art amenities.

Licenses are required for both freshwater and saltwater fishing. The fees for a saltwater fishing license are $30 for nonresidents and $12 for residents. A nonresident seven-day saltwater license is $15. Nonresidents can purchase freshwater fishing licenses good for 10 days ($15) or for one year ($30); residents pay $12 for an annual license. Combined annual freshwater fishing and hunting licenses are also available at $22 for residents.

Golf Except in the heart of the Everglades, you'll never be far from one of Florida's approximately 950 golf courses. Palm Beach County, the state's leading golf locale with 130 golf courses, also hosts the home offices of the National Golf Foundation and the Professional Golfers Association of America.

Many of the best golf courses in Florida allow visitors to play without being members or hotel guests. Thus, you can pretend that you're playing in the annual Doral Ryder Open when you play the deadly 18th hole on the Blue Monster course at the Doral Resort and Country Club in Miami. Walt Disney World's popular Palm Course also is open to public play.

Especially in winter, you should reserve tee-off times in advance. Ask about golf reservations when you make your lodging reservations.

Hunting Hunters in Florida stalk a wide variety of resident game animals and birds, including deer, wild hog, wild turkey, bobwhite quail, ducks, and coots. A plain hunting license costs $11 for Florida residents, $150 for nonresidents, except nonresidents from Alabama who pay $100. A nonresident 10-day hunting license is $25, except for nonresidents from Georgia who pay $121.

Each year in June, the **Florida Game and Fresh Water Fish Commission** announces the dates and hours of the fall hunting seasons for public and private wildlife-management areas. Hunting seasons vary across the state. Where hunting is allowed, you need the landowner's written permission—and you must carry that letter with your hunting license in the field. Trespassing with a weapon is a felony. For a free copy of the annual ***Florida Hunting Handbook,*** contact the game commission (620 Meridian St., Tallahassee 32399–1600, tel. 904/488–4676).

Jogging, Running, and Walking All over Florida, you'll find joggers, runners, and walkers on bike paths and city streets—primarily in the early morning and after working hours in the evening. Some Florida hotels have set up their own running trails; others provide guests with information on measured trails in the vicinity. The first time you run in Florida, be prepared to go a shorter distance than normal because of higher heat and humidity.

Two major Florida festivals include important running races. Each year in December the **Capital Bank Orange Bowl 10K,** one of the state's best-known running events, brings world-class runners to Miami. In April, as part of the Florida Keys annual Conch Republic Days, runners congregate near Marathon on one of the world's most spectacular courses for the **Seven Mile Bridge Run.**

Local running clubs all over the state sponsor weekly public events for joggers, runners, and walkers. For a list of local clubs and events throughout the state, call or send a self-addressed stamped envelope to the **Florida Athletics Congress** (1330 N.W. 6th St., Gainesville 32601, tel. 904/336–2120). For information about events in south Florida contact the 1,500-member **Miami Runners Club** (7920 S.W. 40th St., Miami 33155, tel. 305/227–1500).

Scuba Diving and Snorkling South Florida and the Keys attract most of the divers and snorkelers, but the more than 300 dive shops throughout the state schedule drift, reef, and wreck-diving trips for scuba divers all along Florida's Atlantic and Gulf coasts. The low-tech pleasures of snorkeling can be enjoyed all along the Overseas Highway in the Keys and elsewhere where shallow reefs hug the shore.

Inland in north and central Florida, divers explore more than 100 grottoes, rivers, sinkholes, and springs. In some locations, you can swim with manatees ("sea cows"), which migrate in from the sea to congregate around warm springs during the cool winter months. Ginnie Springs, near Bradford, is one of Florida's most famous springs (Rte. 1, Box 153, High Springs 32643, tel. 904/454–2022 or 800/874–8571). Crystal Lodge Dive

Center in the Econo Lodge (525 N.W. 7th Ave., Crystal River 32629, tel. 904/795–6798) is a popular gateway to river-diving in the Crystal River in central Florida.

Contact the **Dive Industry Association** for a free directory of Florida dive shops. (Teall's Inc., 111 Saguaro La., Marathon 33050, tel. 305/743–3942).

Tennis Many Florida hotels have a resident tennis pro and offer special tennis packages with lessons. Many local park and recreation departments throughout Florida operate modern tennis centers like those at country clubs, and most such centers welcome nonresidents, for a fee. In the Miami area, you can play at the **Biltmore Tennis Center** in Coral Gables, home of the Rolex/Orange Bowl International Tennis Championship or Dade County's **International Tennis Center** on Key Biscayne, home of the Lipton International Players Championships.

For general information and schedules for amateur tournaments, contact the **Florida Tennis Association** (801 N.E. 167th St., Suite 301, North Miami Beach 33162, tel. 305/652–2866).

Trails Trails for biking, canoeing, hiking, and horseback riding are getting new attention in Florida. Contact the **State Trails Coordinator** in the Bureau of Park Planning, Department of Natural Resources (3900 Commonwealth Blvd., Tallahassee 32399, tel. 904/487–4784). Ask for the ***Rails-to-Trails*** brochure, and for ***Parks With Horse Trails,*** among other new publications in 1990.

Parks and Nature Preserves

Although Florida is the fourth most-populous state in the nation, there are 9,711,043 acres of public and private recreation facilities set aside in national forests, parks, monuments, reserves, and seashores; state forests and parks; county parks; and nature preserves owned and managed by private conservation groups.

On holidays and weekends, crowds flock to Florida's most popular parks—even to some on islands that are accessible only by boat. Come early or risk being turned away. Write ahead to ask rangers in the parks, sanctuaries, and preserves about the best season to visit. In winter, northern migratory birds descend on the state. Many resident species breed in the warm summer months, but others (such as the wood stork) time their breeding cycle to the winter dry season. In summer, mosquitoes are voracious and daily afternoon thundershowers add to the state's humidity, but this is when the sea turtles come ashore to lay their eggs and when you're most likely to see frigate birds and other tropical species.

National Parks The federal government maintains no centralized information service for its natural and historic sites in Florida. You must contact each site directly for information on current recreational facilities and hours. To obtain a copy of **Guide and Map of National Parks of U.S.,** which provides park addresses and facilities lists, write to U.S. Government Printing Office, Washington, DC 20402. GPO No. 024005008527. Cost: $1.25 (no tax or postage).

In 1908 the federal government declared the keys around what is now **Fort Jefferson National Monument** in the Dry Tortugas a wildlife sanctuary to protect the sooty tern. **Everglades National Park** was established in 1947. Other natural and historic sites in Florida under federal management include **Big Cypress National Preserve** and **Biscayne National Park** in the Everglades, **Canaveral National Seashore** in central Florida, **Castillo De San Marcos National Monument** in north Florida, **De Soto National Monument** in Bradenton, the 130-acre **Fort Caroline National Memorial** on the St. Johns River in Jacksonville, **Fort Matanzas National Monument** south of St. Augustine, and **Gulf Islands National Seashore** in north Florida.

The federal government operates three national forests in Florida. The **Apalachicola National Forest** encompasses 557,000 acres of pine and hardwoods in two ranger districts across the northern coastal plain (west Apalachicola District; east Wakulla District). The 336,000-acre **Ocala National Forest** includes the sandhills of the Big Scrub (*see* the essay in Chapter 2). Cypress swamps and numerous sinkhole lakes dot the 157,000-acre **Osceola National Forest.**

National wildlife refuges in Florida include the **Great White Heron National Wildlife Refuge** and **National Key Deer Refuge** (in the Keys), **Loxahatchee National Wildlife Refuge** near Palm Beach, **J. N. "Ding" Darling National Wildlife Refuge** in southwest Florida, and **Merritt Island National Wildlife Refuge.** The federal government also operates the **Key Largo National Marine Sanctuary** and **Looe Key National Marine Sanctuary.**

State Parks

The **Florida Department of Natural Resources** is responsible for hundreds of historic buildings, landmarks, nature preserves, and an expanding state park system. When you request a free copy of the ***Florida State Park Guide,*** mention which parts of the state you plan to visit. For information on camping facilities at the state parks, ask for the free ***Florida State Parks, Fees and Facilities*** and ***Florida State Parks Camping Reservation Procedures*** brochures (Marjory Stoneman Douglas Bldg., Room 613, 3900 Commonwealth Blvd., Tallahassee 32399, tel. 904/488–7326.)

Private Nature Preserves

In 1905, Audubon Society warden Guy Bradley died while protecting the egrets nesting at Cuthbert Rookery, in what is now Everglades National Park. Private efforts to preserve Florida's fragile ecosystems continue today, as the **National Audubon Society** and the **Nature Conservancy** acquire and manage sensitive natural areas.

Wood storks nest at the National Audubon Society's **Corkscrew Swamp Sanctuary** near Naples. On Big Pine Key, Audubon has leased acreage without charge to the U.S. Fish and Wildlife Service in the **National Key Deer Refuge.** Audubon also controls more than 65 other Florida properties, including islands, prairies, forests, and swamps. Visitation at these sites is limited. For information, contact National Audubon Society, Sanctuary Director (Miles Wildlife Sanctuary, RR 1, Box 294, West Cornwall Rd., Sharon CT 06069, tel. 203/364–0048).

Five of the preserves managed by the Nature Conservancy are open to the public: **Apalachicola Bluffs & Ravines** in Liberty County, **Blowing Rocks Preserve** (*see* the Treasure Coast section of Chapter 6), the 970-acre **Cummer Sanctuary** in Levy County, the 320-acre **Janet Butterfield Brooks Preserve** near Bristol in Hernando County, the 42-acre **Matanzas Pass Wilderness Preserve** on Estero Island (between Bay and School

Streets east of the 3000 block of Estero Boulevard in Fort Myers Beach) and the **Tiger Creek Preserve** at 225 E. Stuart Ave., Lake Wales in Polk County. Additionally, the 150-acre **Spruce Creek Preserve** in Volusia County is to open in 1991.

For access to these tracts, information on self-guided tour information, and a guide to the Conservancy's holdings contact the Florida Chapter of the Nature Conservancy (1353 Palmetto Ave., Winter Park 32789, tel. 407/628–5887). Visitors are welcome at the Winter Park office and at offices in Key West and Tallahassee. *830 Fleming St., Key West 33040, tel. 305/296–3880. 515-A N. Adams St., Tallahassee 32301, tel. 904/222–0199. Open weekdays 9–5.*

Dining

Florida regional cuisine changes as you move across the state, based on who settled the area and who now operates the restaurants. Look for Minorcan cuisine in St. Augustine, and the traditional Miccosukee and Seminole Indian fried bread, catfish, and frog legs at tribe-owned restaurants in the Everglades. South Florida's diverse assortment of Latin American restaurants offers the distinctive national fare of Argentina, Brazil, Colombia, Cuba, El Salvador, Mexico, Nicaragua, and Puerto Rico as well as West Indian delicacies from the Bahamas, Haiti, and Jamaica.

The influence of earlier Latin settlements remains in Key West and Tampa's Ybor City.

All over Florida, Asian cuisine no longer means just Chinese. Indian, Japanese, Pakistani, Thai, and Vietnamese specialties are now available. Continental cuisine (French, German, Italian, Spanish, and Swiss) is also well represented all over Florida. Many of these restaurants have excellent wine lists. Bern's Steak House in Tampa has the largest wine list in the state—7,000 labels!

Although the better restaurants in all price categories pride themselves on using fresh seafood, in some cases the fish is imported from quite a long distance. Two south Florida seafood pioneers, Joe's Stone Crab Restaurant in Miami Beach and East Coast Fisheries in Miami, still have a steady local supply from their own fish houses in Marathon. In the Florida Keys, many small restaurants specialize in chowder, fritters, salads, and other dishes made with conch (a large shellfish, pronounced "konk").

Every Florida restaurant claims to make the best Key-lime pie. Pastry chefs and restaurant managers take the matter very seriously—they discuss the problems of getting good lime juice and maintaining top quality every day. Traditional Key-lime pie is yellow, not green, with an old-fashioned Graham cracker crust and meringue top. The filling should be tart, and chilled but not frozen. Some restaurants serve their Key-lime pie with a pastry crust; most substitute whipped cream for the more temperamental meringue. Each pie will be a little different. Try several, and make your own choice.

Ratings

Category	Cost*: Major Cities	Cost*: Other Areas
Very Expensive	over $50	over $40
Expensive	$30–$50	$25–$40
Moderate	$15–$30	$10–$25
Inexpensive	under $15	under $10

**per person, excluding drinks, service, and 6% sales tax*

Lodging

Hotels and Motels All the major hotel and motel chains, including Days Inn, Econo Lodge, Hyatt, Hilton, Holiday Inn, Knight's Inn, Marriott, Motel 6, Peabody, Pickett, Quality Inns, Radisson, Ramada, Sheraton, Stouffer, and Westin are represented in Florida. Holiday Inn, Marriott, and Quality Inns operate under a variety of brand names offering varying levels of amenities and prices.

Although many hotels in Florida have affiliated with a chain to get business from its central reservation system, some fine hotels and resorts still remain independent. They include the Brazilian Court and The Breakers in Palm Beach, Chalet Suzanne in Lake Wales, Governors Inn in Tallahassee, and Pier House in Key West.

The Florida Hotel & Motel Association publishes an ***Annual Travel Directory*** which you can obtain without charge at Florida welcome centers or by contacting the **Florida Division of Tourism** (Department of Commerce, 126 Van Buren St., Tallahassee 32399, tel. 904/487–1462). You can also order it from the FH&MA if you send a stamped, addressed No. 10 envelope and $1 for postage and handling (117 W. College Ave., Box 1529, Tallahassee 32301–1529, tel. 904/224–2888).

Ratings

Category	Cost*: Major Cities	Cost*: Other Areas
Very Expensive	$150 peak season $100 off-peak	$100
Expensive	$120–$150 peak season $80–$100 off-peak	$70–$100
Moderate	$80–$120 peak season $50–$80 off-peak	$40–$70
Inexpensive	under $80 peak season under $50 off-peak	under $40

**All prices are for a standard double room, excluding 6% state sales tax and nominal (1%–3%) tourist tax.*

Alternative Lodgings Small inns and guest houses are becoming increasingly numerous and popular in Florida. Many offer the convenience of bed-and-breakfast accommodations in a homelike setting; many, in fact, are in private homes, and the owners treat you almost like a member of the family. **Inn Route, Inc.** (Box 144, Mount Dora 32757, tel. 904/383–8397), a new statewide association of small, architecturally distinctive historic inns, will send you a free brochure published in 1990. You can also order the award-winning ***Guide to the Small and Historic Lodgings of Florida,*** a paperback book updated every two years, most recently in 1990 (Pineapple Press Inc., Drawer 16008, Sarasota 34239, tel. 813/952–1085. Cost: $12.95 plus 6% sales tax).

Bed-and-breakfast referral and reservation agencies in Florida include: **Bed & Breakfast Co., Tropical Florida** (Box 262, Miami 33243, tel. 305/661–3270), **Bed & Breakfast East Coast** (Box 1373, Marathon 33050, tel. 305/743–4118), **Suncoast Accommodations of Florida** (8690 Gulf Blvd., St. Petersburg Beach 33706, tel. 813/360–1753) and **Tallahassee Bed & Breakfast, Inc.** (3023 Windy Hill La., Tallahassee 32308, tel. 904/385–3768).

Camping and RV Facilities

Contact the national parks and forests you plan to visit directly for information on camping facilities (*see* National Parks, above). For information on camping facilities in state parks, contact the Florida Department of Natural Resources (*see* State Parks, above).

The free annual ***Florida Camping Directory*** lists 200 commercial campgrounds in Florida with 50,000 sites. It's available at Florida welcome centers, from the Florida Division of Tourism, and from the **Florida Campground Association** (1638 N. Plaza Dr., Tallahassee 32308–5364, tel. 904/656–8878).

Vacation Ownership Resorts

Vacation ownership resorts sell hotel rooms, condominium apartments, or villas in weekly, monthly, or quarterly increments. The weekly arrangement is most popular; it's often referred to as "interval ownership" or "time sharing." Of more than 2,500 vacation ownership resorts around the world, some 400 are in Florida, with the heaviest concentration in the Disney World/Orlando area. Most vacation ownership resorts are affiliated with one of two major exchange organizations—**Interval International** (6262 Sunset Dr., Penthouse One, South Miami 33143, tel. 305/666–1861 or 800/828–8200) or **Resort Condominiums International** (3502 Woodview Trace, Indianapolis, IN 46268–3131, tel. 317/876–8899 or 800/338–7777). As an owner, you can join your resort's exchange organization and swap your interval for another someplace else in any year when you want a change of scene. Even if you don't own an interval, you can rent at many vacation ownership resorts where unsold intervals remain and/or owners have placed their intervals in a rental program. For rental information, contact the exchange organizations (Interval International, tel. 800/722–1861; Resort Condominiums International, tel. 800/654–5000), the individual resort, or a local real estate broker in the area where you want to rent.

2 Portraits of Florida

In Search of the Real Florida

by April Athey

A freelance writer based in Tallahassee, April Athey has been writing about her home state for magazines and newspapers since 1977. Her work has appeared in many publications, including the New York Times, Chicago Tribune, Christian Science Monitor, Frequent Flyer, *and* Gulfshore Life.

It's hard to imagine a Floridà without a magic kingdom, a spaceport to the stars, interstate highways, or high-rise beachfront hotels. But such a Florida exists, and today the state's natural and historical treasures are being imitated, refurbished, restored, and recognized for their lasting appeal.

Even the state's leader in family entertainment—Walt Disney World—is imitating and popularizing Old Florida with its new Grand Floridian Beach Resort, featuring gabled roofs and Victorian balustrades that were typical of Florida's turn-of-the-century beach resorts. Disney officials say the resort recalls the days when John D. Rockefeller, Thomas Edison, and even President Theodore Roosevelt led the annual winter pilgrimage to Florida's warm shores.

There are those who recall the day when Walt Disney World's fantasy lands and futuristic hotels opened in 1971, setting a technological standard in entertainment that may still be unrivaled. The owners of natural attractions like Silver Springs, Weeki Wachee, and Homosassa Springs struggled to keep the attention of technology-hungry Americans. The lush jungle-lined rivers, exotic wildlife, and crystal-clear spring waters somehow paled in contrast to the make-believe, never-a-dull-moment amusements for which the Disney corporation had become famous. The convenience of a one-stop, no-surprise vacation apparently made real wilderness cruises, beaches, wildlife, and historical attractions passé.

To see and appreciate the real thing, one had to leave the interstate highways and brave a few side roads. Because not many tourists cared to take the road less traveled, many owners of natural attractions were forced to expand their offerings with man-made amusements. If budgets weren't sweet enough to permit this sort of commercialization, the attractions (usually the lesser-known botanical gardens, great homes, and wildlife reserves) saw lean years.

Fortunately, the cycle is coming full circle. Technology-harassed Americans are now looking for the good old days, and Florida is obliging them.

Today, developers of new resorts are focusing attention on the Florida of the 19th century. New resorts not only imitate Old Florida architecture but also, through their landscaping, recall when the only silhouettes scraping

Florida's sky were of stout cabbage palms, mossy oaks, towering cypress, and hardy evergreens.

Maintaining the ecological integrity of the land and its often-endangered inhabitants has become an increasing concern of developers. The Grand Cypress Resort in Orlando was designed to be complemented by a stand of native cypress, and the Registry Resort in Naples nestles at the edge of a 1,000-acre nature preserve, through which a $1-million boardwalk was built to provide access to the beach and protection for the delicate sand dunes.

St. Augustine is the oldest permanent European settlement in the United States—with an extensive historic district to prove it—and was the first Florida resort popularized by Henry Flagler when he brought his Florida East Coast Railroad and friends south for the winter. Key West was the last resort Flagler helped build. His Casa Marina hotel still stands, having been restored and expanded under management by Marriott. The island's "conch houses" also are being restored, and many have been converted into guest houses and restaurants. Flagler also put Palm Beach and its sister, West Palm Beach, on the map. Though his original wooden hotels burned to the ground, his private estate is now the Flagler Museum.

Sharing space with the glinting glass of skyscrapers are the castlelike villas and Old Florida-style homes of former Florida residents. You can tour Ca'd'Zan, the bay-side villa that John Ringling and his wife Mable built, which now is part of the Ringling Museums Complex in Sarasota. Like an oasis in the middle of Miami's asphalt-and-concrete desert, the palatial bay-front estate of John Deering, with its formal gardens and surrounding natural jungles (Vizcaya Museum and Gardens), may be toured daily. Visit Thomas Edison's Winter Home in Fort Myers, and dine out on Cabbage Key, the tiny island accessible by boat (offshore from Captiva)—the retreat of mystery writer Mary Roberts Rinehart. Ormond Beach has reminders of its heyday, when John D. Rockefeller and friends made the riverfront Ormond Hotel a world-renowned wintering spot. Rockefeller eventually built his winter home, The Casements, across the street from the hotel, and both still stand proudly by the shores of the Halifax River, just north of Daytona Beach. The Casements is now an art museum and site of an annual antique-auto show.

Fort Jefferson, the Civil War island fortress on which Samuel Mudd—the physician who treated Lincoln's assassin—was imprisoned, is only a seaplane flight away from tropical Key West. On Key West are the 19th-century fortifications—East and West Martello Towers—one now home to the city's historical museum, and the other the setting of the garden club. Recently excavated and open to the public on Key West is Fort Zachary Taylor. Living-history interpretations are conducted daily at Fort Clinch, a Civil War fortress in Fernandina Beach, and at Fort Foster in Hillsborough State Park, just west of Tampa. Speaking of Tampa, the next time you order a rum and Coke, remember that the concoction was invented there by Teddy Roosevelt's Rough Riders.

In addition to the monuments of recent history, there are the archaeological reminders of Florida's first residents, the aboriginal Indians who greeted European explorers and expatriates. Several state parks preserve treasured archaeological sites, like Hontoon Island on the St. Johns River, Tomoka River State Park, near Daytona Beach (both sites of Timucuan Indian settlements), and Jonathan Dickinson State Park, near the Palm Beaches (site of a Quaker shipwreck and their subsequent imprisonment by Jaega Indians).

These and later Indians left their place names as a lasting legacy—names like Ichetucknee (now a tubing river north of Gainesville), Pensacola, Apalachicola, Tequesta, Kissimmee, Chassahowitzka (a national wildlife refuge near Homosassa Springs), Okeechobee (a 590-square-mile inland lake), Ocala, and Tallahassee (the state capital).

Victorian homes with gingerbread-trimmed wraparound verandas, shaded by sloping tin roofs, are being restored and operated as bed-and-breakfast inns or chic restaurants. Check out K. C. Crump on the River in Homosassa Springs, near Ocala in central Florida, a posh new restaurant in a restored, turn-of-the-century homestead. In Ocala, the newest B&B is the Seven Sisters Inn, which serves gourmet fare. Florida's B&Bs have increased from an estimated five in 1980 to more than 50 in 1988.

Main Street programs are flourishing throughout the state, revitalizing the business/entertainment districts of towns like Winter Park, Orlando, DeLand, and Quincy (in northwest Florida).

Historic hotels and inns, once threatened by wrecking crews, are living new lives. Check out the Heritage in St. Petersburg, a restored, 60-year-old hotel (the original Florida "cracker" home in the backyard now serves as an atrium-greenhouse bar); or book a weekend at Apalachicola's 100-year-old Gibson Inn.

Waterfront redevelopment projects like Miami's Bayside and Jacksonville Landing (Rouse Marketplace developments) are focusing fresh attention on the inlets and bays that once harbored renegade pirates and adventurous pioneers.

Quiet waterfront hamlets, built during the boom in steamboat travel—Sanford and Crescent City are good examples—are beginning to blossom again with the reemergence of riverboat cruising.

Wildlife and wilderness, once overlooked in favor of make-believe amusements, are once again attracting awed attention. In response, Silver Springs turned back the clock with a complete Victorian redesign.

Oddly enough, it may be easier to find an Old Florida vacation experience now than it was 20 years ago.

Though serving to popularize Old Florida, newcomers and their artful imitations are no substitutes for the real thing. The wilderness, wildlife, and historic homes and resorts are already here to enjoy.

Washed by both the Gulf of Mexico and the Atlantic Ocean, Florida seems to be more water than land. Underground freshwater rivers course through the limestone bedrock of its north and central highlands, often boiling to the surface and flowing overland to the sea. A bird's-eye view reveals a peninsula whose upper reaches are dotted and crisscrossed by hundreds of lakes and streams and whose ragged southern borders are home to a vast, shallow river of grass called the Everglades and a maze of mangrove clumps called the Ten Thousand Islands. From the town of Everglades City, on Florida's southwest tip, sightseeing boats meander through the maze of islands, and just off the Tamiami Trail (U.S. 41), on the north-central boundary of Everglades National Park, you can climb the observation deck at Shark Valley Overlook for a good look at the river of grass.

This view, perhaps more than anything, helps to remind people of what Floridians are trying to recapture.

The Florida Scrub

by Al Burt

A roving writer-columnist for The Miami Herald *for the past 15 years, Al Burt specializes in Florida's history, natural habitat, and future. He has written two books on the state—*Becalmed in the Mullet Latitudes *and* Florida: A Place in the Sun. *In 1974, Burt left Miami's city life to make his base in his beloved Scrub Country, near Melrose in north Florida.*

Understanding Florida requires at least some knowledge of the historic Scrub Country, the oldest, the driest, the harshest, and, in some ways, the most delicate part of the state. In water-loving Florida, the Scrub struggles to remain a desert outlaw.

If you have ever walked a beach and observed how the tides and the wind have rolled the sterile sands into a long, graceful dune on which grow a few scraggly, scratchy plants, you may have gotten some idea about Florida's unique Scrub Country and its peculiar beauty.

The Scrub, which once covered most of Florida with bone-dry sandhills, is the legitimate kin to a desert, and it's full of puzzles. The life forms there are persistent, thrifty, and fragile. Once, you could look across the low profile of its vegetation and see odd "islands" of fertility, little oases of tall trees and green life, while all around was the stunted, prickly, vulnerable Scrub growth. They were like oddly matched siblings of nature, growing up side by side, but, by freakish accident, one had been denied its vitamins.

The name came from an early and natural lack of appreciation. It was scrubby country, not like the scenic Florida of the travel books. Except in those "islands," it lacked the towering slash pines and the comfortable shade of large-crowned live oaks and the open landscapes beneath. The Scrub was a place unto itself, with few easy pleasures, and it was not good for conventional farming.

Loving the Scrub came easiest if you grew up with it, if it came naturally to you. Sometimes it became a fierce, protective thing, like a stubbornly loyal Cracker Mama who adored the scrawniest of her children most because it was the misfit.

Flooding rains leached quickly through Scrub sands and left them dry as ever. Rosemary bushes, prickly pears, saw palmettos, sand pines, sandburs, gnarled dwarf oaks, and other scraggly little trees commonly grew there.

The deep sand made it difficult to walk with shoes on. The sands in summer burned the soles of bare feet with temperatures of 135–140 degrees. Everything in the Scrub seemed to scratch and claw at you, fighting for life.

Rattlesnakes loved it. Exotic little creatures (in addition to raccoons, bobcats, and deer), some of them now rare and endangered, made it home—scrub jays, lizards, skinks, gopher frogs and gopher tortoises, exotic mice, red widow spiders, and such.

For years, big patches of the Scrub Country, especially if they were inland and off the main tracks, lay abandoned. If they attracted anyone, it was likely to be the young, who sometimes found the sandhills great places for exploring or play, sliding down them, burrowing into them, and holding beer parties and buggy chases on the tricky sand.

The Scrub did not rebound easily from such use, but nobody cared. The track of a jeep across virgin scrub vegetation might take unaided nature years to erase. That was minor compared with what else happened in the history of the Scrub.

It began when Florida began. The Scrub probably was the first part of Florida to emerge from the ocean, geologists say. Its dunes or sandhills formed under pressures of wind and tides as the ocean levels rose and fell during the ice ages. Great, irregular ridges took shape, almost like terraces. Time altered them into graceful sandhills.

The original Scrub Country became the Central Highlands of Florida, which stretches from east of Gainesville in the north-central part of the state south for some 200 miles and flatten out into the prairies of Lake Okeechobee. In places, the elevation reaches 300 feet.

For Florida, those great sandhills became Sierra Citrus, center of one of its greatest trademark industries. The well-drained Scrub lands were easily cleared and were perfect for oranges—once the growers added fertilizers and artificial irrigation.

You can ride that ridge today in one of the state's most scenic inland drives and imagine the beginning. U.S. 27, a fine highway, rolls up and down those great sandhills, past a series of lakes, along the fringes of Disney World country, and through miles and miles of green and seasonally fragrant citrus groves. (Even though the freezes of recent winters blighted many of them, the scene remains impressive.)

Like smaller versions of the Central Highlands, lesser dunes trailed away to the ocean. All had similar characteristics, but closer to the coast there were subtle changes, particularly if they were close enough to get the windblown ocean spray.

The dunes and the life on them also differed in their northern stretches, where the climate was temperate and subject to more seasonal changes than in southern Florida. In the south, the influence of the Gulf Stream and the more prominent crosswinds from the gulf and the ocean produced an exotic subtropical climate.

Scrub Country was high ground. Water did not collect there, but in strategic or special places development did, especially along the coast. Around the turn of the century, Henry Flagler built his pioneering railroad partially on a high dune ridge running down the east coast. Then he opened up cities like Palm Beach, Miami, and eventually Key West to tourists and development.

For the most part, the Scrub Country was an ugly duckling among Florida real estate developers. Many wanted to use it as raw material or take advantage of its special location, but few perceived it as anything that was uniquely beautiful or valuable in itself. As a result, 90% or more of this original Florida scene no longer exists.

The sand, some of it as fine as sugar, was mined for construction materials. Great areas were leveled for shopping centers and other development. Subdivisions turned dune ripples into square blocks of cottages. Water was piped in, and developers covered these desert sands with St. Augustine grass.

Except for exploiters, the Scrub Country had few advocates. The most notable of them was the writer, Marjorie Kinnan Rawlings, an easterner. Rawlings's work elevated one area of the Scrub into legend.

In 1928, Rawlings fled the rigors of newspaper life in Rochester, NY, and settled in an old Cracker house by an orange grove in an unlikely little village oasis called Cross Creek. She sought inspiration in isolation and frontier surroundings. The creek (between Ocala and Gainesville) was a lane of water connecting two large lakes in north-central Florida.

Her love of the creek and its people expanded to the areas nearby, which included a significant piece of Scrub Country known locally as the Big Scrub. To enrich her knowledge of it, she lived for a while with a family in the Scrub, hunted there, and befriended the Crackers who chose it as a place to live.

Rawlings's novels, particularly *The Yearling*, which won the Pulitzer Prize and then was made into a popular movie, realistically acknowledged but nevertheless romanticized the Big Scrub. She depicted the impoverished Crackers as primitives who lived by their own code—a code that she clearly thought had a noble base.

Rawlings gave the Big Scrub and Florida's Scrub Country a national identity. Within the past few years, her book of essays on Cross Creek and a short story entitled "Gal Young 'Un" also were made into well-received movies. Those films renewed and enlarged Rawlings's loving images of the Cross Creek area and the Big Scrub. Since then, the importance of the Scrub as a unique plant and animal habitat has been recognized. Scientists and conservationists have dedicated themselves to its study and preservation.

Rawlings's books became especially significant because the largest remaining area of Scrub left in Florida, modified though it may be, is the one she idealized. It lies in the central and western portions of the 380,000-acre Ocala National Forest (a multiple-use forest that permits hunting and camping) and still is called the Big Scrub.

The Big Scrub contains the world's largest stand of sand pines. Many of them occur naturally, but, because in some areas the pines were planted in rows so neat that the natural poetry of the forest is altered, some have criticized it as a sand-pine plantation. In either case, both the pines and the patches of dunes, as close as the road shoulders, are visible from the car during a drive through the forest. The area illustrates how sand pines and other scrub vegetation, over time, tend to close and fill in an area, giving it a canopy above and a soil below slowly being altered by collections of natural forest debris, especially leaves, fallen limbs, and root systems. This cycle can change the natural characteristics of the Scrubs, unless fire (the sand pine is highly flammable) or timbering activities interfere. Even so, the Scrub retains its mysteries. Even the foresters cannot always predict with certainty that the Scrub cycle will begin again after a fire.

Most of Florida's Scrub Country is now scattered in bits and pieces around the state. You have to search and guess and inquire locally. Aside from the Ocala forest, a visitor can see examples of it in the Jonathan Dickinson State Park, 13 miles south of Stuart on U.S. 1.

In that same area, you may see from the highway a typical patch of surviving Scrub—a high roadside dune topped by a windswept sand pine, so stressed that it seems picturesquely oriental. The same sand pine, seen in the Ocala Forest, may grow bushy and erect and look like an ideal Christmas tree.

Finding examples of the Scrub elsewhere becomes a matter of travel and identification, of looking for inland dunes left untouched by development. Where there is a low, sandy hill there could be scrub. You can find areas of it down the east coast, from St. Augustine to West Palm Beach, in northeast Florida near the coast and along Rte. AIA, and there are some that sweep back off the Panhandle beaches in northwest Florida. Little of the scrub, however—except that in public parks—has tourist convenience for study and enjoyment. Even in the state and national forests, the sandy footing, the heat, and the numerous insects discourage all but the most hardy explorers.

At least two large tracts are being maintained for scientific research. The University of Florida owns several thousand acres of Scrub east of Gainesville, and the Archbold Biological Station (established in 1941) has 3,800 acres of distinctive Scrub near Lake Placid on the southern slope of the Central Highlands. These are not open for public roaming, however.

One good thing to remember is that, globally, Florida lies in the zone of the great deserts, including the Sahara, so the Scrub is not out of character. Florida began with those ocean sands that bleached into dunes and sandhills and then into the variety that visitors enjoy today.

Remembering the past explains a lot about the true nature of Florida, no matter how wet it looks right now. The Scrub Country reminds us that the makings of a desert are still there, waiting.

Miami Beach Art Deco

by Hap Hatton

Born and raised in Florida, Hap Hatton now lives in New York City, where he is in charge of still photography for PBS station WNET 13. His previous books include The Tent Book *and* The Virgin Homeowner's Handbook.

By 1910 Miami Beach had failed first as a coconut plantation, then as an avocado farm. Now it was being tried as a residential development. It took 10 years to create the present landmass. Carl Fisher, the Hoosier millionaire who financed much of the dredging and land-clearing, envisioned the area as a playground for the wealthy. Interspersed between his opulent hotels were huge estates on lots running 400 feet in from Biscayne Bay. Meanwhile, the southern portion of the barrier island was developed by the Lummus brothers, who plotted smaller lots for a middle-class resort. Scarcely had the dredging begun than the Lummus brothers in 1912 opened the Ocean Beach Realty Company, the first real estate office on the beach. Steady growth was interrupted by World War I, but then Miami Beach took off—until the collapse of the Florida real estate boom and the ensuing Depression.

By 1936, assisted by an expanding tourist industry, south Florida had emerged from the Depression. Hundreds of small hotels and apartment buildings were constructed on the small Lummus lots at the rate of 100 a year until 1941, making Miami Beach one of the few cities in the United States to have a building boom during the Depression. Ernest Hemingway's brother Leicester, also a writer, explains the phenomenon:

During the Depression, people needed to let go. . . . They became wild on Miami Beach. . . . They didn't watch their nickels. . . . [Architects] were determined not to use any older styles like the Spanish. . . . They wanted something modern, so they smoothed out all the Spanish things. They smoothed everything until you got the feeling that life was smooth. The buildings made you feel all clean and new and excited and happy to be there.

The style that prevailed in South Miami Beach was a zesty, crowd-pleasing Art Deco built by a handful of architects and contractors. Many of the architects were not formally trained but freely adapted national design trends to this tropical setting, creating a uniformity in style and scale rarely found in an urban setting. Called Miami Beach Art Deco (the name Tropical Deco has also been applied to the style), this brand of Art Deco was both relatively inexpensive to construct and offered a slick, dramatic, fashionable appearance, while its strong visual tropical symbols—

"Floridiana"—impressed upon visitors the unique charms of the area.

Florida didn't invent the decorative vegetative and animal motifs that dominated the more ornate Miami Beach Art Deco buildings, but it raised them to new stylistic heights with facade bas-reliefs of cast or dyed stone, etched windows, and decorative metalwork on doors and porches.

Flowers, especially voluptuous gladiolus, alluded to the fecund floral paradise. Nymphs and nudes hedonistically stressed sensuous youth and romance. Fountains as well as sunbursts and symbolic zigzag equivalents of rays conjured up the life-renewing natural properties of the climate. Animals such as peacocks, flamingos, greyhounds, herons, and pelicans were chosen for their romantic associations, arabesque shapes, and exaggerated proportions. Originally, most of the buildings were stark white, with trims of azure blue, ocean turquoise, blazing yellow, palm tree green, erotic pink, or purples and mauves that evoked tropical sunsets, bougainvillea, and feelings both sensuous and exotic.

The sense of place is strong among these Deco buildings, leaving no doubt that this is the tropics, far from the cold, gray, sooty, industrial North.

The variances in Miami Beach Art Deco reflected what was occurring economically and architecturally on the national scene. Among others, four prevalent Deco styles comprise Miami Beach Art Deco.

Art Deco. The earliest buildings adapted the original Art Deco style's sharply angular massing with shallow stepped-back facades. Ornate bas-relief panels often framed large central openings. The French love of luxurious, sensuous textures such as crystal, mother-of-pearl, and unusual woods translated into indigenous Florida oolitic limestone, etched glass, stucco, and terrazzo (a cast agglomerate of marble or granite particles in colored and polished cement).

Depression Moderne. By 1937 the mode had shifted to a deco with the more austere look of the reigning International Style. Art Moderne's vertical stucco bands, flat roof with stepped parapet, and facade symmetry were still there, but with an increased horizontal emphasis that would later become dominant in streamlining. Depression Moderne was also readapted for government buildings such as the Miami Beach Post Office, and called PWA Moderne for the Public Works Administration.

Streamlined Moderne. By 1939, a full-blown aerodynamic Moderne featured curved forms, applied racing stripes that accentuated horizontal emphasis, and "eyebrow" shading of the windows with cantilevered slabs to reduce the angle of penetration of the sun. The continuously wrapped stucco surfaces expressed concepts associated with travel and speed. Here the angularity of the originally imported Art Moderne was entirely replaced by soft flowing masses accented with horizontal lines and rows of windows. This phase combined smooth, sweeping curves with straight lines of the machine age in simple, definite, contrasting shapes. Combinations of Cubism's suggestion of dimensionality, Futurism's romance with speed, and Surrealist fantasy are cited as sources of inspiration. This streamlining restored the fun and humor drained by Depression Moderne.

Mannerism. A final development of Miami Beach streamlining was called Resort Mannerism or Mannerist Moderne (from Mannerism, a late 16th-century reaction against the High Renaissance characterized by a deliberate distortion of the existing artistic and architectural repertoire; it gave way to the Baroque, and today the term is associated with the exaggeration and/or distortion of existing themes). Resort Mannerism included Nautical Moderne, with its exaggerated and literal invocations of ships at sea with porthole windows, decklike balconies, and flagstaffs. This mature Moderne emphasized sinuous curves, stylized directional ornament, and bold projections, marking a conscious search by architects both here and in Europe for a unique form to express contemporary modernity. Never a pure style, it even incorporated highlights from the Spanish Mediterranean, such as sloping tile roofs or colored ceramic tiles. The late 1930s film influence brought soaring "trylons" or space-age needles to roofs and facades. This Flash Gordon touch turned the buildings visually into spaceships with Hollywood stage-set lobbies that were also referred to as Cinema Style and Hollywood Style.

Larger Deco hotels did make their appearance, but, by and large, the area known as Old Miami Beach consists of two- and three-story hostelries small in scale and rich in expression. Deco architecture prevailed here later than anywhere else in the country, until World War II abruptly terminated construction. By 1941, most hotels were occupied by the military in training for the war effort. After the war, the area began to decline as Miami Beach continued its development northward.

In 1979, one square mile of Miami Beach became this country's first 20th-century national historic district. It reflects a trend in architecture that took place between the two world wars, when more than 500 Art Deco structures went up in one small area. It is not only the largest and most cohesive concentration of Art Deco buildings in the world but the first historic district that has registered buildings less than 50 years old. It sits on one of the best pieces of real estate in Florida, perhaps on the entire East Coast.

The fight for preservation of these landmarks has raged for years between developers who want to erect more profitable high-rise condominiums and the local Miami Design

Preservation League, founded by Barbara Baer Capitman. A former art historian and now president of the Art Deco Society of Miami, she held her first organizational meeting in 1976 with six people and spoke of the area's potential as "capital of the Art Deco world." Capitman attracted 100 volunteers to survey and research the locality. Then the battle was launched that resulted in tax and zoning incentives for the owners of Deco buildings who preserve their original structures.

Developers fought back and, to block the legislation, lobbied successfully for an ordinance that required 100% owner approval for historic district designations (51% is standard). This ordinance was later struck down when, to avoid costly litigation, Miami Beach changed its ordinance to 51% approval. Some local businessmen see the preservation issue as one of property rights versus government coercion. A few, however, realize that the Art Deco district will yield them long-term beneficial results: It will create a desirable cultural center and provide a sense of identity vital to establishing Miami Beach as a unique city rather than a second-rate Las Vegas.

Because no corresponding local legislation had been passed to protect the district, its designation on the National Register of Historic Places did not prevent demolition of several landmark Art Deco hotels. The turning point came in July of 1986, when Richard Hoberman, president of the Miami Design Preservation League, orchestrated a campaign to secure designation of two key areas: a quarter-mile district covering Ocean Drive/Collins Avenue (from Fifth to Sixteenth streets) as well as Espanola Way, a six-block street that includes a 1920s Spanish theme village. Hoberman packed the city commission chambers with supporters wearing "Deco-pink" ribbons to witness the decisive 6–1 vote. Local designation means that a design review board must approve all renovation work for appropriateness, all new construction must be compatible with surrounding buildings, and—most important—there will be a six-month moratorium on demolition to allow time for other investors to step in. Now prospective developers need not fear that their preservation efforts will be invalidated by high rises, and successful rehabilitation within these two districts should help in the essential designation of additional areas. Things are looking good: Already one developer has turned a million-dollar profit in 10 months by restoring and reselling one of the district's Art Deco hotels. Seven years after federal recognition, the city fathers have finally understood the economic benefits of preservation.

The preservation movement on Miami Beach has generated admiration for Art Deco, and south Florida developers have invested millions of dollars building imitation Deco residential communities for those who want the look of Deco but wish to live outside the troubled inner-city area.

These new homes have much of the generic look of huge housing developments, despite their attempt to blend International Style and Deco. They feature stepped walls and entrances, porthole windows, geometric shapes, and two-tone pastel colors. Builders toned down the bright Deco colors to Necco wafer hues of quiet pastels when a local homeowners' association complained of the bright aqua, peach, and intense pinks. This "switch rather than fight" approach is an attempt to sidestep the complex problems of gentrification. The buildings themselves mark a rejection of International Style anonymity, a recognition of the value of Art Deco, and a positive trend in Miami's search for its own architectural identity.

Meanwhile, in the Deco District the tax credits to be obtained by rehabilitating these architectural treasures have brought developers into the area, and dozens of hotels and apartment houses are being refurbished. The small hotels average 60 to 120 rooms, many having been converted to "pullmanettes" (rooms with kitchenettes). For the past quarter-century these have been popular with mostly Jewish and Eastern European retirees, and a decade ago more than half of the south Beach population was 65 or older. With retirement communities now proliferating in south Florida, for about a decade Miami Beach has ceased to be a destination point for the elderly, and now the percentage is less than one-quarter.

By its nature, rehabilitation means modernization and deviation from original design schemes, and nowhere is this more apparent than in color restoration. The original white with vivid color accents has been rejected in favor of a palette of Post-Modern cake-icing pastels now associated with the former television series "Miami Vice." Leonard Horowitz, the designer who introduced these colors, rationalized that because the neighborhood had deteriorated and much of the original vegetation had died, there was justification for using a plethora of color. Finally, white is being reintroduced.

The buildings of the Miami Beach Historical District chronicle more than a decade of historic cultural change and served the emotional needs of the public in a time of national crisis. No orthodox academic style has accomplished this. Whatever their historical significance or their eventual evaluation as art, these Miami Art Deco habitations are built to the human scale where the desires of the people are met rather than dictated to by sociological or aesthetic theory. Such a value in buildings has generally been condescended to or given mere lip service by respected architects who consider the tastes of the public beneath contempt. Yet the art of living cannot be measured by formal architectural standards of purity or style, only by the pleasure of the time and place. Miami Beach Art Deco created this quality of life with consummate success.

Today, the buildings still hold magic for visitors and inhabitants. Although the romance is slightly tarnished by peeling facades, and idealistic dreams have succumbed to more jaded views, there is still a sense of desire and expectation in the air. There is a glamour about these buildings that invites thoughts of moonlit walks on sparkling beaches, movie-screen romances, dancing under starry skies. There is a sadness, too, of once-vital dreams lost, either demolished or covered over with gaudy wallpaper and wall-to-wall carpeting. But this special fantasy of Florida still twinkles seductively among the vast pile of urban mediocrity that threatens to engulf the Miami Beach Deco District.

3 Miami

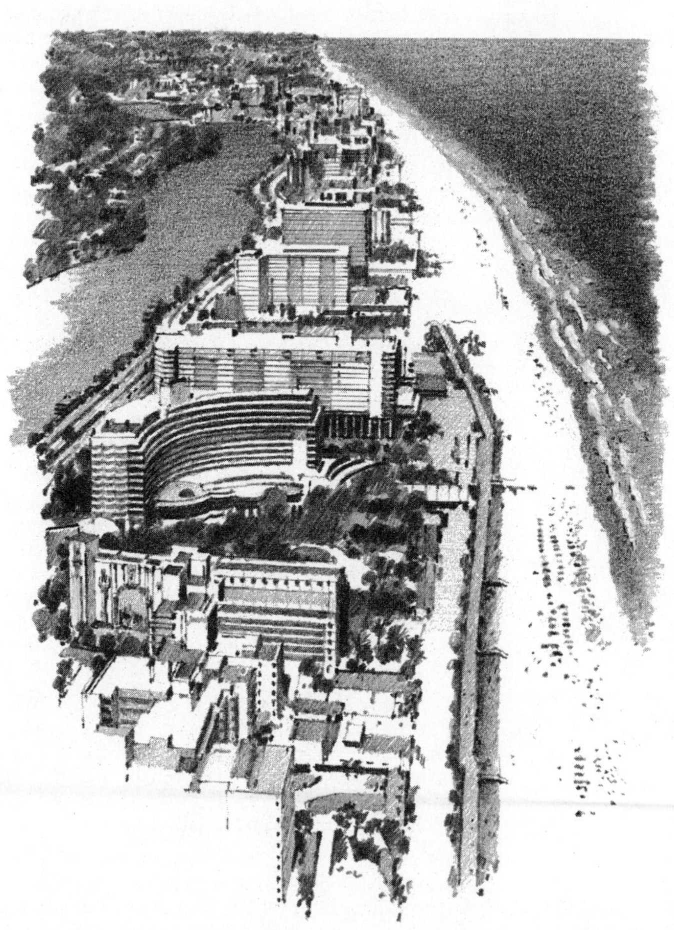

Introduction

by George and Rosalie Leposky

A husband-wife team, George and Rosalie Leposky are veteran Florida travel writers. Their articles have appeared in some 100 newspapers and consumer magazines throughout North America. They also write for trade publications in the travel and hospitality field, including Hotel & Resort Industry *and* Lodging. *The Leposkys live in the Coconut Grove section of Miami.*

What they say about Miami is true. The city *is* different. Miami is different from what it once was and it's different from other cities. Once a sleepy southern resort town, Miami today is a burgeoning giant of international commerce and finance as well as a place to find pleasure and relaxation. Like all big cities, Miami inspires the first-time visitor with hopes and dreams. Also as in other cities, many of these hopes and dreams can be sidetracked by crime and violence.

Miami's natural difference can be detected when you fly into the city. Clinging to a thin ribbon of dry land between the marshy Everglades and the Atlantic Ocean, Miami remains vulnerable to its perennial mosquitoes, periodic flooding, and potential devastation by hurricanes. These perils give life in Miami a flavor of urgency, a compulsion to prosper and party before the dream ends.

Miami may be the wrong place for a city, but it's the right place for a crossroads. Long before Spain's gold-laden treasure ships passed offshore in the Gulf Stream, the Calusa Indians who lived here had begun to trade with their mainland neighbors to the north and their island brethren to the south. Repeating this prehistoric pattern, many U.S. and multinational companies now locate their Latin American headquarters in Greater Miami because no other city can match its airline connections to the Western Hemisphere.

That same ease of access, coupled with a congenial climate, attracts hordes of Latin tourists—especially in Miami's steamy summer months (South America's winter), when domestic visitors from the northern United States are less in evidence.

Access and climate also explain why Miami has become what *Newsweek* calls "America's Casablanca." Whenever a Latin American or Caribbean government erupts in revolution and economic chaos, the inevitable refugees flock inexorably to Miami (where they open restaurants). Even without a revolution, Miami's cosmopolitan character and entrepreneurial spirit attract other immigrants from all over the world.

Today, more than 45% of Greater Miami's population is Hispanic—the majority from Cuba, with significant populations from Colombia, El Salvador, Nicaragua, and Panama. About 150,000 French- and Creole-speaking Haitians also live in Greater Miami, as do Brazilians, Germans, Greeks, Iranians, Israelis, Italians, Jamaicans, Lebanese, Malaysians, Russian Jews, Swedes, and more—a veritable Babel of tongues. Most either know or are trying to learn English. You can help them by speaking slowly and distinctly.

Try not to think of Miami as a melting pot. Where ethnic and cultural diversity are the norm, there's less pressure to conform. Miamians practice matter-of-factly the customs they brought here—much to the consternation of other Miamians whose customs differ. The community wrestles constantly with these tensions and sensitivities.

As a big city, Miami has its share of crime, violence, and drug trafficking—but not the pervasive lawlessness lately portrayed on made-for-TV movies and reruns of "Miami Vice." You probably won't find the city's seamy underside unless you go looking for it.

What you will find just by coming to Miami is a multicultural metropolis that works and plays with vigor and that welcomes you to share its celebration of diversity.

Arriving and Departing by Plane

Airport **Miami International Airport (MIA),** six miles west of downtown Miami, is Greater Miami's only commercial airport. MIA has the nation's second-largest volume of international passenger and cargo traffic. MIA's busiest hours, when flight delays may occur, are 11 AM–8 PM.

MIA contains 108 aircraft gates along seven concourses. During 1990 renovations were completed on concourse H. Moving walkways were installed between concourses B and H on the third level, and from parking garages to concourses D and F.

When you fly out of MIA, plan to check in 55 minutes before departure for a domestic flight and 90 minutes before departure for an international flight. Services for international travelers include 24-hour multilingual information and paging phones and foreign currency conversion booths throughout the terminal. An information booth with multilingual staff and 24-hour currency exchange are at Concourse E.

Between the Airport and Center City

By Bus

Metrobus. The county's Metrobus system has one benefit—its modest cost—if you're willing to put up with the inconveniences of infrequent service, scruffy equipment, and the circuitous path that many routes follow. *Tel. 305/638–6700. Fare: $1 (exact change), transfers 25¢.*

Greyhound/Trailways. You can take a Greyhound bus from the Metrobus depot at MIA to Homestead and the Florida Keys or to other Greyhound stations in Greater Miami *(see* Arriving and Departing by Bus, below).

By Taxi

For trips originating at MIA or the Port of Miami, a $1 toll is added to the meter fare—except for the flat-fare trips described below. You'll pay a $12 flat fare between MIA and the Port of Miami, in either direction.

For taxi service from the airport to destinations in the immediate vicinity, ask a uniformed county taxi dispatcher to call an **ARTS (Airport Region Taxi Service)** cab for you. These special blue cabs will offer you a short-haul flat fare.

SuperShuttle vans transport passengers between MIA and local hotels, the Port of Miami, and even individual residences on a 24-hour basis. The company's service area extends from Palm Beach to Monroe County (including the Lower Keys). Drivers provide narration en route. It's best to make reservations 24 hours before departure, although the firm will try to arrange pickups within Dade County on as little as four hours' notice. *For information and reservations from inside MIA, tel. 305/871–8488. Reservations outside MIA, tel. 305/871–2000 (Dade and Monroe counties) or 305/674–1700 (Broward and Palm Beach counties). Pet transport fee: $5. Lower rate for 2nd passenger in same party for many destinations. Children under 2 ride free with parents. AE, MC, V.*

By Limousine **Bayshore Limousine** has chauffeur-driven four-door town cars and stretch limousines available on demand at MIA or through the 24-hour reservation service. It serves Miami, Fort Lauderdale, Palm Beach, and the Keys. *11485 S.W. 87th Ave., Miami, tel. 305/253–9046, 325–3851, or 858–5888. AE, MC, V.*

Arriving and Departing by Car, Train, and Bus

By Car The main highways into Greater Miami from the north are Florida's Turnpike (toll) and I–95. In Broward County (the next county north), you'll encounter major delays throughout 1990 from construction to widen the highway.

Delays on roads into Miami from other directions are most likely on weekends, when recreational traffic is the heaviest. From the northwest, take I–75 or U.S. 27 into town. From the Everglades to the west, use the Tamiami Trail (U.S. 41). From the south, use U.S. 1 and the Homestead Extension of Florida's Turnpike.

Rental Cars Six rental-car firms—**Avis Rent-a-Car, Dollar Rent-a-Car, General Rent-a-Car, Hertz Rent-a-Car, National Rent-a-Car,** and **Value Rent-a-Car**—have booths near the baggage claim area on MIA's lower level—a convenience when you arrive.

By Train **Amtrak's** two trains between Miami and New York City, the *Silver Meteor* and *Silver Star*, make different stops along the way. Each has a daily Miami arrival and departure.

Amtrak's "All Aboard" fare is the most economical way to travel to Florida, if you have time to meet the length-of-stay requirements. Trains run full all year, except in October and May. For the best fare, contact Amtrak as soon as you decide to take a trip. Ask for Amtrak's 1991 travel planner. *Amtrak Station, 8303 N.W. 37th Ave., Miami 33147. General office tel. 305/835–1200, passenger service tel. 305/835–1225. Advance reservations required. Reservations: Amtrak Customer Relations, 400 N. Capitol St., NW, Washington, DC 20001, tel. U.S. 800/USA-RAIL, Canada 800/4AMTRAK.*

Tri-Rail commuter trains connect Miami with Broward and Palm Beach weekdays. Call for schedule and details on weekly and monthly passes. *Tel. 305/728–8445 or 800/TRI–RAIL. Suite 801, 1 River Plaza, 305 S. Andrews Ave., Fort Lauderdale, FL 33301.*

By Bus **Greyhound/Trailways** buses stop at seven bus stations in Greater Miami. *99 N.E. 4th St., Miami, tel. 305/374–6160. No reservations.*

Getting around Miami

Greater Miami resembles Los Angeles in its urban sprawl and traffic congestion. You'll need a car to visit many of the attractions and points of interest listed in this book. Some are accessible via public transportation.

A department of county government, the Metro-Dade Transit Agency, runs the public transportation system. It consists of 450 Metrobuses on 67 routes, the 21-mile Metrorail elevated rapid transit system, and the 1.9-mile Metromover in downtown Miami. Free maps, schedules, and a First-Time Rider's Kit are available. *6601 N.W. 72nd Ave., Miami 33166. Maps by*

Mail, tel. 305/638-6137. For route information, tel. 305/638-6700 daily 6 AM–11 PM. Fare $1, transfers 25¢, exact change only.

By Train Metrorail runs from downtown Miami north to Hialeah and south along U.S. 1 to Dadeland. *Service every 7½ minutes in peak hours, 15–30 minutes other times. Weekdays 6AM–midnight, weekends 6:30 AM–6:30 PM. Runs until midnight for special events such as the Orange Bowl parade. Fare: $1.*

Metromover's two loops circle downtown Miami, linking major hotels, office buildings, and shopping areas *(see* Exploring Downtown Miami, below). *Service every 90 seconds. Weekdays 6:30 AM–midnight, weekends 8:30 AM–midnight. Later for special events. Fare 25¢.*

By Bus Metrobus stops are marked by blue-and-green signs with a bus logo and route information. The frequency of service varies widely. Obtain specific schedule information in advance for the routes you want to ride. *Tel. 305/638-6700.*

By Taxicab There are some 1,700 taxicabs in Dade County. Fares are $1 for the first ⅙ mile, 20¢ for each additional ⅙ mile; waiting time 20¢ for the first 1⅗ minutes, 20¢ for each additional ⅘ minute. No additional charge for extra passengers, luggage, or road and bridge tolls. Taxi companies with dispatch service are **Central Taxicab Service** (tel. 305/534-0694), **Diamond Cab Company** (tel. 305/545-7575), **Magic City Cab Company** (tel. 305/757-5523), **Metro Taxicab Company** (tel. 305/888-8888), **Society Cab Company** (tel. 305/757-5523), **Super Yellow Cab Company** (tel. 305/885-5555), **Tropical Taxicab Company** (tel. 305/945-1025), and **Yellow Cab Company** (tel. 305/444-4444).

By Car Finding your way around Greater Miami is easy if you know how the numbering system works. Miami is laid out on a grid with four quadrants—northeast, northwest, southeast, and southwest—which meet at Miami Avenue and Flagler Street. Miami Avenue separates east from west and Flagler Street separates north from south. *Avenues* and *courts* run north-south; *streets, terraces,* and *ways* run east-west. *Roads* run diagonally, northwest-southeast.

Many named streets also bear numbers. For example, Unity Boulevard is N.W. and S.W. 27th Avenue, LeJeune Road is N.W. and S.W. 42nd Avenue. However, named streets that depart markedly from the grid, such as Biscayne Boulevard and Brickell Avenue, have no corresponding numerical designations. Dade County and most other municipalities follow the Miami numbering system.

In Miami Beach, *avenues* run north-south; *streets,* east-west. Numbers rise along the beach from south to north and from the Atlantic Ocean in the east to Biscayne Bay in the west.

In Coral Gables, all streets bear names. Coral Gables uses the Miami numbering system for north-south addresses but begins counting east-west addresses westward from Douglas Road (S.W. 37th Ave.).

Hialeah has its own grid. Palm Avenue separates east from west; Hialeah Drive separates north from south. *Avenues* run north-south and *streets* east-west. Numbered streets and avenues are designated west, east, or southeast.

Important Addresses and Numbers

Tourist Information The Greater Miami Convention and Visitors Bureau plans to open tourist information centers in downtown Miami, Miami Beach, Homestead-Florida City, and Miami International Airport. Contact the bureau for locations and hours or to request information by mail.

Visitor Services, Greater Miami Convention and Visitors Bureau (701 Brickell Ave., Suite 2700, Miami 33131, tel. 305/539–3063).

Chambers of Commerce Greater Miami has a central chamber—the Greater Miami Chamber of Commerce (1601 Biscayne Blvd., Miami 33132, tel. 305/350–7700)—as well as more than 20 local chambers of commerce, each promoting its individual community. Most maintain racks of brochures on tourist information in their offices and will send you information about their community.

Coconut Grove Chamber of Commerce (2820 McFarlane Rd., Coconut Grove 33133, tel. 305/444–7270).
Coral Gables Chamber of Commerce (50 Aragon Ave., Coral Gables 33134, tel. 305/446–1657).
Gold Coast Chamber of Commerce (1100 Kane Concourse, Suite 210, Bay Harbor Islands 33154, tel. 305/866–6020). Serves the beach communities of Bal Harbour, Bay Harbor Islands, Golden Beach, North Bay Village, Sunny Isles, and Surfside.
Key Biscayne Chamber of Commerce (Key Biscayne Bank Bldg., 95 W. McIntyre St., Key Biscayne 33149, tel. 305/361–5207).
Miami Beach Chamber of Commerce (1920 Meridian Ave., Miami Beach 33139, tel. 305/672–1270).
South Miami Chamber of Commerce (6410 S.W. 80th St., South Miami 33143, tel. 305/661–1621).

Tickets **Ticketmaster.** You can use this service to order tickets for performing arts and sports events by telephone. A service fee is added to the price of the ticket. *Tel. 800/446–3939 or tel. 305/358–5885 (Dade), 305/523–3309 (Broward), or 407/839–3900 (Palm Beach). MC, V.*

Emergencies Dial 911 for **police** and **ambulance.** You can dial free from pay phones.

Telecommunication lines for the hearing impaired are used by hearing-impaired travelers with telecommunication devices (TDD) to reach TDD-equipped public services:

Fire/Police/Medical/Rescue (tel. 305/595–4749 TDD)
Operator and Directory Assistance (tel. 800/855–1155 TDD)
Deaf Services of Miami (5455 SW 8th St., Room 255, Miami, tel. 305/444–2211 TDD or voice 305/444–2266). Operates 24 hours. Relays calls to help the hearing-impaired contact people who hear and speak normally.

Ambulance **Randle Eastern Ambulance Service Inc.** Serves Greater Miami. Meets air ambulances and takes patients to hospitals. Services include advanced life-support systems. *35 S.W. 27th Ave., Miami 33135, tel. 305/642–6400. Open 24 hrs. AE, MC, V.*

Hospitals The following hospitals have 24-hour emergency rooms:

Miami Beach: *Mt. Sinai Medical Center* (4300 Alton Rd., Miami Beach, tel. 305/674–2121; physician referral, tel. 674–2273). Just off Julia Tuttle Causeway (I–195).

St. Francis Hospital (250 W. 63rd St., Miami Beach, tel. 305/868–5000; physician referral, tel. 305/868–2728). Near Collins Ave. and north end of Alton Rd.

Central: *University of Miami/Jackson Memorial Medical Center.* Includes Jackson Memorial Hospital, a county hospital with Greater Miami's only trauma center. Near Dolphin Expressway. Metrorail stops a block away. *1611 N.W. 12th Ave., Miami, tel. 305/325–7429. Emergency room, tel. 305/549–6901. Interpreter service, tel. 305/549–6316. Patient relations, tel. 305/549–7341. Physician referral, tel. 305/547–5757.*

Mercy Hospital (3663 S. Miami Ave., Coconut Grove, tel. 305/854–4400; physician referral, tel. 305/285–2929). Greater Miami's only hospital with an emergency boat dock.

Miami Children's Hospital (6125 S.W. 31st St., tel. 305/666–6511; physician referral, ext. 2563).

South: *Baptist Hospital of Miami* (8900 N. Kendall Dr., Miami, tel. 305/596–1960; physician referral, tel. 305/596–6557).

24-Hour Pharmacies

Of the nearly 300 pharmacies in Greater Miami, only three are open 24 hours a day. Most pharmacies open at 8 or 9 AM and close between 9 PM and midnight. Many pharmacies offer local delivery service.

Eckerd Drugs. 1825 Miami Gardens Dr. N.E. (185th St.), North Miami Beach, tel. 305/932–5740 and 9031 S.W. 107th Ave., Miami, tel. 305/274–6776.

Walgreens. 5731 Bird Rd., Miami, tel. 305/666–0757.

Physician Referral Services

Dade County Medical Association (1501 N.W. N. River Dr., Miami, tel. 305/324–8717). Office open weekdays 9–5 for medical referral.

East Coast District Dental Society (420 S. Dixie Hwy., Suite 2E, Coral Gables, tel. 305/667–3647). Office open weekdays 9 AM–4:30 PM for dental referral. Services include general dentistry, endodontics, periodontics, and oral surgery.

Guided Tours

Orientation Tours

Old Town Trolley of Miami. Ninety-minute narrated tours of Miami leave Bayside Marketplace every half hour between 9 and 4:30. *Box 12985, Miami 33101, tel. 305/374–8687. Miami tour: $12 adults, $4 children 3–12. No credit cards.*

Special-Interest Tours

Boat Tours

Heritage of Miami II. Miami's official tall ship, an 85-foot steel traditional sailing schooner docks at Bayside Marina. Carries up to 49 passengers for day sailing, sleeps 16; children and cameras welcome. Ice and ice chest on board, soft drinks for sale; bring your own food. Standard Biscayne Bay day trip lasts two hours. Reservations recommended. *3145 Virginia St., Coconut Grove 33133, tel. 305/442–9697. Sails daily, weather permitting. Cost: $10 adults, $5 children under 12.*

Island Queen. Ninety-passenger tour boat docks at the Hyatt Regency Hotel's patio dock, 400 S.E. 2nd Ave., Miami. Two-hour narrated tours of Port of Miami and Millionaires' Row. *Tel. 305/379–5119. Tours daily. Cost: $10 adults, $5 children.*

Nikko Gold Coast Cruises. Three 150-passenger boats based at

Haulover Park Marina specialize in water tours to major Greater Miami attractions. *10800 Collins Ave., Miami Beach, tel. 305/945–5461. Tours daily to Bayside Marketplace, $9 adults, $5 children under 13.*

History Tours **Art Deco District Tour.** Meet your guide at 10:30 AM Saturday at 661 Washington Avenue, the **Miami Design Preservation League's** welcome center, for a 90-minute tour. Wear comfortable shoes and bring a hat. Also available is the League's *Art Deco District Guide*, a book with six detailed walking or driving tours of the square-mile Art Deco District on Miami Beach. *Bin L, Miami Beach 33119, tel. 305/672–2014. Cost: $5 for tour, $6 for book.*

Historical Museum of Southern Florida. Guided tours available in English or Spanish. **Museum Tour** covers the exhibits, which survey 10,000 years of Miami-area history; includes 15-minute slide show. The **Curator's Cabinet Tour** combines the Museum Tour with a look behind the scenes at departments that visitors seldom see, including a research center with 500,000 photos and the cataloging and conservation departments. The museum also conducts tours throughout the Greater Miami area. *101 W. Flagler St., Miami, tel. 305/375–1492.*

Prof. Paul George. Explore Miami's history with a professional historian on a four-hour walking tour of downtown. Paul George is a history professor at Florida Atlantic University and the University of Miami and immediate past-president of the Florida Historical Society. His tour begins on the north bank of the Miami River behind the Hyatt Regency Hotel, 400 S.E. 2nd Ave. Wear comfortable walking shoes and a hat. Sat. 9 AM–1 PM and by appointment. George also gives 3½-hour walking tours of historic Coconut Grove, Coral Gables, Little Havana, Miami's old City Cemetery, the Miami Beach Art Deco District, and downtown Fort Lauderdale. *1345 S.W. 14th St., Miami, tel. 305/858–6021. Cost: $9 adults, $6 children 7–14, under 7 free.*

Rickshaw Tours **Majestic Rickshaw.** Look for rickshaws along Main Highway in Coconut Grove's Village Center (Box 0174, Coconut Grove 33233–0174, tel. 305/443–6571). Nightly 8 PM–2 AM in Coconut Grove. Rickshaw holds two adults. $3 per person for 10-minute ride through Coconut Grove, $6 per person for 20-minute lovers' moonlight ride down to Biscayne Bay. No credit cards.

Exploring Downtown Miami

Numbers in the margin correspond with points of interest on the Downtown Miami map.

Orientation From a distance you see downtown Miami's future—a 21st-century skyline already stroking the clouds with sleek fingers of steel and glass. By day, this icon of commerce and technology sparkles in the strong subtropical sun; at night, it basks in the man-made glow of floodlights.

On the streets downtown, you encounter a polyglot present. Staid-suited lawyers and bankers share the sidewalks with Hispanic merchants wearing open-neck, intricately embroidered shirts called *guayaberas*. Fruit merchants sell their wares from pushcarts. European youths with backpacks stroll the streets. Foreign businessmen haggle over prices in import-export shops. You hear Arabic, Chinese, Creole, French,

German, Hebrew, Hindi, Japanese, Portuguese, Spanish, Swedish, Yiddish, and even a little English now and then.

With effort, you can find remnants of downtown Miami's past, though still less this year than last, when two venerable hotels, the McAlister and the Columbus, were demolished. Most of the city's "old" downtown buildings date from only the 1920s and 1930s—an incongruity if you're from someplace that counts its past in centuries. Remember that Miami is a young city, incorporated in 1896 with just 3,000 residents. A Junior League book, *Historic Downtown Miami*, locates and describes 27 elderly structures in and near downtown, including 21 you can see in a two-hour self-guided walking tour of slightly more than a mile.

Touring Downtown Miami

Parking downtown is inconvenient and expensive. If you're staying elsewhere in the area, leave your car at an outlying Metrorail station and take the train downtown. Metromover, a separate light-rail mass-transit system, circles the heart of the city on twin elevated loops.

No part of the downtown tour is more than two blocks from one of Metromover's nine stations. We've organized the tour around those stations, so you can ride Metromover directly to the downtown attractions that interest you most.

1 When you get off the Metrorail train at **Government Center**
2 **Station,** notice the **Dade County Courthouse** (73 W. Flagler St.). It's the building to the east with a pyramid at its peak, where turkey vultures roost in winter. Built in 1928, it was once the tallest building south of Washington, D.C.

3 As you leave the Metrorail station, you'll enter **Metro-Dade Center,** the county government's 30-story office building. Designed by architect Hugh Stubbins, it opened in 1985.

Across N.W. 1st Street from Metro-Dade Center stands the
4 **Metro-Dade Cultural Center** (101 W. Flagler St.), opened in 1983. The 3.3-acre complex is a Mediterranean expression of architect Philip Johnson's postmodern style. An elevated plaza provides a serene haven from the city's pulsations and a superb setting for festivals and outdoor performances.

The Center for the Fine Arts is an art museum in the tradition of the European *kunsthalle* (exhibition gallery). With no permanent collection, it organizes and borrows temporary exhibitions on many artistic themes. Shows scheduled for early 1991 include prints by Edvard Muench, and for sping and summer, "Printed Symbols," by Jasper Johns, organized by the Walker Art Gallery in Minneapolis, and "Landscapes" from the Metropolitan Museum of Art. *Tel. 305/375–1700. Open Tues.–Sat. 10–5, Thurs. 10–9, Sun. noon–5. Admission: $3 adults, $2.50 senior citizens, $2 children 6–12, under 6 free. Donations Tues.*

The Historical Museum of Southern Florida is a regional museum that interprets the human experience in southern Florida from prehistory to the present. Artifacts on permanent display include Tequesta and Seminole Indian ceramics, clothing, and tools; a 1920 streetcar; and an original edition of Audubon's *Birds of America. Tel. 305/375–1492. Open Mon.–Sat. 10–5, Thurs. 10–9, Sun. noon–5. Admission: $3 adults, $2 children 6–12, under 6 free. Donations Mon.*

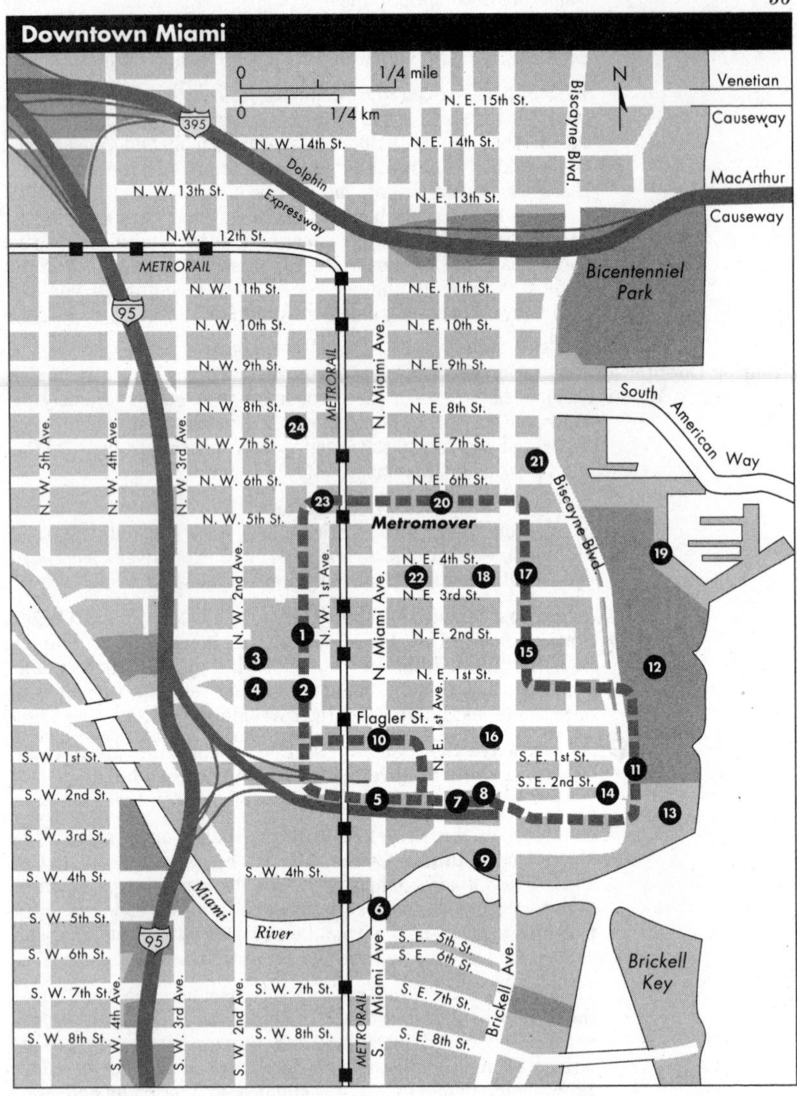

Bayfront Park, **12**
Bayfront Park Station, **11**
Bayside Marketplace, **19**
CenTrust Tower, **8**
College Bayside Station, **17**
Dade County Courthouse, **2**
Edcom Station, **20**
First St. Station, **15**
Ft. Dallas Park Station, **5**
Freedom Tower, **21**
Government Center Station, **1**
Gusman Center, **16**
Hotel Inter-Continental Miami, **13**
James L. Knight International Center, **9**
Knight Center Station, **7**
Metro-Dade Center, **3**
Metro-Dade Cultural Center, **4**
Miami Arena, **24**
Miami Ave. Bridge, **6**
Miami Ave. Station, **10**
Miami-Dade Community College, **18**
Southeast Financial Center, **14**
State Plaza/Arena Station, **23**
U.S. Courthouse, **22**

The Main Public Library has 700,000 volumes and a computerized card catalog. Inside the entrance, look up at the rotunda mural, where artist Edward Ruscha interpreted a quotation from Shakespeare: "Words without thought never to heaven go." You'll find art exhibits in the auditorium and second-floor lobby. *Tel. 305/375–BOOK. Open Mon.–Sat. 9–5, Thurs. 9–9, Sun. 1–5. Closed Sun. May–mid-Oct.*

At Government Center Station, you can also transfer to Metromover's inner and outer loops through downtown. We've listed the stations and their attractions in sequence along the outer loop.

5 The first stop is **Ft. Dallas Park Station.** If you disembark here,
6 you're a block from the **Miami Ave. Bridge,** one of 11 bridges on the river that open to let ships pass. From the bridge approach, watch freighters, tugboats, research vessels, and luxury yachts ply this busy waterway.

Time Out Stroll across the bridge to **Tobacco Road** for some liquid refreshment and a sandwich or snack. Built in 1912, this friendly neighborhood pub was a speakeasy during Prohibition. *626 S. Miami Ave., tel. 305/374–1198. Open weekdays 11:30 AM–5 AM, weekends 1 PM–5 AM. Lunch weekdays 11:30–2:30. Dinner Sun.–Thurs. AE, DC.*

---

7 The next Metromover stop, **Knight Center Station,** nestles in-
8 side the **CenTrust Tower** (100 S.E. 1st St.), a wedge-shape 47-story skyscraper designed by I. M. Pei & Partners. The building is brilliantly illuminated at night. Inside the CenTrust
9 Tower, follow signs to the **James L. Knight International Center** (400 S.E. 2nd Ave., tel. 305/372–0929), a convention and concert hall adjoining the Hyatt Regency Hotel.

At the Knight Center Station, you can transfer to the inner
10 loop and ride one stop to the **Miami Avenue Station,** a block south of **Flagler Street,** downtown Miami's commercial spine. Like most such thoroughfares, Flagler Street lost business in recent years to suburban malls—but unlike most, it found a new lease on life. Today, the half-mile of Flagler Street from Biscayne Boulevard to the Dade County Courthouse is the most important import-export center in the United States. Its stores and arcades supply much of the world with automotive parts, audio and video equipment, medical equipment and supplies, photographic equipment, clothing, and jewelry.

Time Out Walk three blocks north to **The Eating Place,** an open-air Jamaican restaurant as authentic as Kingston. The jukebox pours reggae onto Miami Avenue while waitresses pour the native beer, Red Stripe, which goes well with the oxtail stew or curried goat. *240 N. Miami Ave., tel. 305/375–0156. No credit cards.*

---

11 If you stay on the outer loop, you'll come next to **Bayfront Park**
12 **Station**, opposite **Claude and Mildred Pepper Bayfront Park,** which extends from Biscayne Boulevard east to the edge of the bay. Japanese sculptor Isamu Noguchi redesigned the park just before his death in 1989; it now includes a memorial to the *Challenger* astronauts, an amphitheater, and a fountain honoring the late Florida congressman Claude Pepper and his wife.
13 Just south of Bayfront Park, the lobby of the **Hotel Inter-Conti-**

nental Miami (100 Chopin Plaza) contains *The Spindle*, a huge sculpture by Henry Moore.

West of Bayfront Park Station stands the tallest building in
14 Florida, the 55-story **Southeast Financial Center** (200 S. Biscayne Blvd.), with towering royal palms in its one-acre Palm Court plaza beneath a steel-and-glass space frame.

15 The next Metromover stop, **First Street Station,** places you a
16 block north of Flagler Street and the **Gusman Center for the Performing Arts,** an ornate former movie palace restored as a concert hall. Gusman Center resembles a Moorish courtyard with twinkling stars in the sky. Performances there include the Miami City Ballet, directed by Edward Villella, and the New World Symphony, a unique, advanced-training orchestra led by Michael Tilson Thomas. *Gusman Center: 174 E. Flagler St., Miami 33131. Box office tel. 305/372–0925; ballet: 905 Lincoln Rd., Miami Beach 33139, tel. 305/532–4880; symphony: 555 Lincoln Rd., Miami Beach 33139, tel. 305/673–3330.*

17 The **College/Bayside Station** Metromover stop serves the down-
18 town campus of **Miami-Dade Community College,** where you'll enjoy browsing through two fine galleries. The Frances Wolfson Art Gallery on the fifth floor houses traveling exhibitions of contemporary art. *300 N.E. 2nd Ave., tel. 305/347–3278. Open weekdays 9–5:30. Admission free.*

College/Bayside Station is also the most convenient Metro-
19 mover stop for **Bayside Marketplace,** a waterside entertainment and shopping center built by The Rouse Company, between Bayfront Park and the entrance to the Port of Miami. Bayside's 235,000 square feet of retail space include 150 specialty shops, pushcarts in the center's Pier 5 area, conventional restaurants, and a fast-food court with some 20 vendors. The center adjoins the 208-slip Miamarina, where you can see luxurious yachts moored and ride in an authentic 36-foot-long Venetian gondola. Street performers entertain free throughout the day and evening. *401 Biscayne Blvd., tel. 305/577–3344, for gondola rides 305/529–7178. Open Mon.–Sat. 10–10, Sun. noon–8.*

As Metromover rounds the curve between College/Bayside
20 21 Station and **Edcom Station,** look northeast to see **Freedom Tower** (600 Biscayne Blvd.), where the Cuban Refugee Center processed more than 500,000 Cubans who entered the United States to flee Fidel Castro's regime in the 1960s. Built in 1925 for the *Miami Daily News*, this imposing Spanish-baroque structure was inspired by the Giralda, an 800-year-old bell tower in Seville, Spain. After years as a derelict, Freedom Tower was renovated in 1988. To see it up close, walk north from Edcom Station to N.E. 6th Street, then two blocks east to Biscayne Boulevard.

A two-block walk south from Edcom Station will bring you to
22 the **U.S. Courthouse,** a handsome keystone building erected in 1931 as Miami's main post office. Go to the second-floor central courtroom to see *Law Guides Florida Progress*, a huge depression-era mural by artist Denman Fink. *300 N.E. 1st Ave. Building open weekdays 8:30–5; during those hours, security guards will open courtroom on request. No cameras or tape recorders allowed in building.*

23 24 From **State Plaza/Arena Station,** walk two blocks north on N.W. 1st Avenue to the new **Miami Arena** (721 N.W. 1st Ave., tel. 305/530–4400), home of the Miami Heat, a National Basketball Association team. Other sports and entertainment events take place at the arena, which is also one block east of the Overtown Metrorail Station.

Just across the Miami River from downtown, a canyon of tall buildings lines **Brickell Avenue,** a southward extension of S.E. 2nd Avenue that begins in front of the Hyatt Regency Hotel (400 S.E. 2nd Ave.). For the best views, drive Brickell Avenue from north to south. You'll pass the largest concentration of international banking offices in the United States.

South of S.E. 15th Street, several architecturally interesting condominiums rise between Brickell Avenue and Biscayne Bay. Israeli artist Yacov Agam painted the rainbow-hued exterior of **Villa Regina** (1581 Brickell Ave.). Arquitectonica, a nationally prominent architectural firm based in Miami, designed three of these buildings: **The Palace** (1541 Brickell Ave.), **The Imperial** (1627 Brickell Ave.), and **The Atlantis** (2025 Brickell Ave.). The 20-story Atlantis, where a palm tree grows in a hole in the building between the 12th and 16th floors, formed a backdrop for the opening credits of the television show "Miami Vice."

At S.E. 25th Road, turn right, follow signs to **I–95,** and return to downtown Miami on one of the world's most scenic urban highways. I–95 parallels Brickell Avenue and soars 75 feet above the Miami River, offering a superb view of the downtown skyline. At night, the CenTrust Tower is awash with light, and, on the adjoining Metrorail bridge, a neon rainbow glows—Rockne Krebs's 3,600-foot-long light sculpture, *The Miami Line*. Just beyond the river, take the Biscayne Boulevard exit back to S.E. 2nd Avenue in front of the Hyatt Regency Hotel.

Exploring Miami Beach

Numbers in the margin correspond with points of interest on the Miami Beach map.

Orientation Most visitors to the Greater Miami area don't realize that Miami and Miami Beach are separate cities. Miami, on the mainland, is south Florida's commercial hub. Miami Beach, on 17 islands offshore in Biscayne Bay, is sometimes considered America's Riviera, luring refugees from winter to its warm sunshine, sandy beaches, and graceful palms.

In 1912, what would become Miami Beach was little more than a sandspit in the bay. Then Carl Graham Fisher, a millionaire promoter who built the Indianapolis Speedway, began to pour much of his fortune into developing the island city.

Ever since, Miami Beach has experienced successive waves of boom and bust—thriving in the early 1920s and the years just after World War II, but also enduring the devastating 1926 hurricane, the Great Depression, travel restrictions during World War II, and an invasion of criminals released from Cuba during the 1980 Mariel boatlift.

Today, a renaissance is under way as Miami Beach revels in the architectural heritage of its mile-square Art Deco District.

About 650 significant buildings in the district are listed on the National Register of Historic Places.

The term Art Deco describes the modern architecture that emerged in the 1920s and 1930s. Its forms are eclectic, drawn from nature (including birds, butterflies, and flowers); from ancient Aztec, Mayan, Babylonian, Chaldean, Egyptian, and Hebrew designs; and from the streamlined, aerodynamic shapes of modern transportation and industrial machinery. For detailed information on touring the Art Deco District, contact the Miami Design Preservation League (*see* Guided Tours, above).

Driving Tour of Miami Beach

In our exploration, we direct you from the mainland to Miami Beach and through a cross section of the Art Deco District and the elegant residential neighborhood surrounding the La Gorce Country Club.

From the mainland, cross the **MacArthur Causeway** (Rte. 41) to Miami Beach. To reach the causeway from downtown Miami, turn east off Biscayne Boulevard north of N.E. 11th Street. From I–95, turn east onto I–395. The eastbound Dolphin Expressway (Rte. 836) becomes I–395 east of the I–95 interchange. As you approach the MacArthur Causeway bridge across the Intracoastal Waterway, *The Miami Herald* building looms above Biscayne Bay on your left.

1 Cross the bridge to **Watson Island,** created by dredging in 1931. Make the first left turn to the **Japanese Garden,** which has stone lanterns, a rock garden, and an eight-ton, eight-foot-tall statue of Hotei, Japanese god of prosperity. Industrialist Kiyoshi Ichimura gave the one-acre garden to the City of Miami in 1961 as an expression of friendship. It was restored in 1988.

East of Watson Island, the causeway leaves Miami and enters
2 Miami Beach. On the left, you'll pass the bridge to **Palm and**
3 **Hibiscus islands** and then the bridge to **Star Island.** Past and present celebrities who have lived on these islands include Al Capone (93 Palm Ave., Palm Island), author Damon Runyon (271 Hibiscus Island), and TV star Don Johnson (8 Star Island).

East of Star Island, the causeway mounts a high bridge. Look
4 left to see an island with an obelisk, the **Flagler Memorial Monument.** The memorial honors Henry M. Flagler, who built the Florida East Coast Railroad to Miami, opening south Florida to tourism and commerce.

5 Just beyond the bridge, turn right onto Alton Road past the **Miami Beach Marina** (300 Alton Rd., tel. 305/673–6000), where dive boats depart for artificial reefs offshore in the Atlantic Ocean.

Continue to the foot of Alton Road, turn left on Biscayne
6 Street, then go right at Washington Avenue to enter **South Pointe Park** (1 Washington Ave.). From the 50-yard Sunshine Pier, which adjoins the mile-long jetty at the mouth of Government Cut, you can fish while watching huge ships pass. No bait or tackle is available in the park. Other facilities include two observation towers, and volleyball courts.

When you leave the park, take Washington Avenue north. On
the northwest corner of Washington Avenue and 5th Street,
Cassius Clay (now Muhammad Ali) prepared for his champion-
7 ship bouts in the **Fifth Street Gym.** You can visit to watch young

Art Deco District, **8**
Bass Museum of Art, **15**
Espanola Way, **9**
Fifth Street Gym, **7**
Flagler Memorial, **4**
Fontainebleau Hilton, **16**
Hibiscus Island, **3**
Hotel National, **14**
Jackie Gleason Theater, **13**
La Gorce Country Club, **17**
Lincoln Rd. Arts District, **10**
Miami Beach City Hall, **11**
Miami Beach Convention Center, **12**
Miami Beach Marina, **5**
Palm Island, **2**
South Pointe Park, **6**
Watson Island, **1**

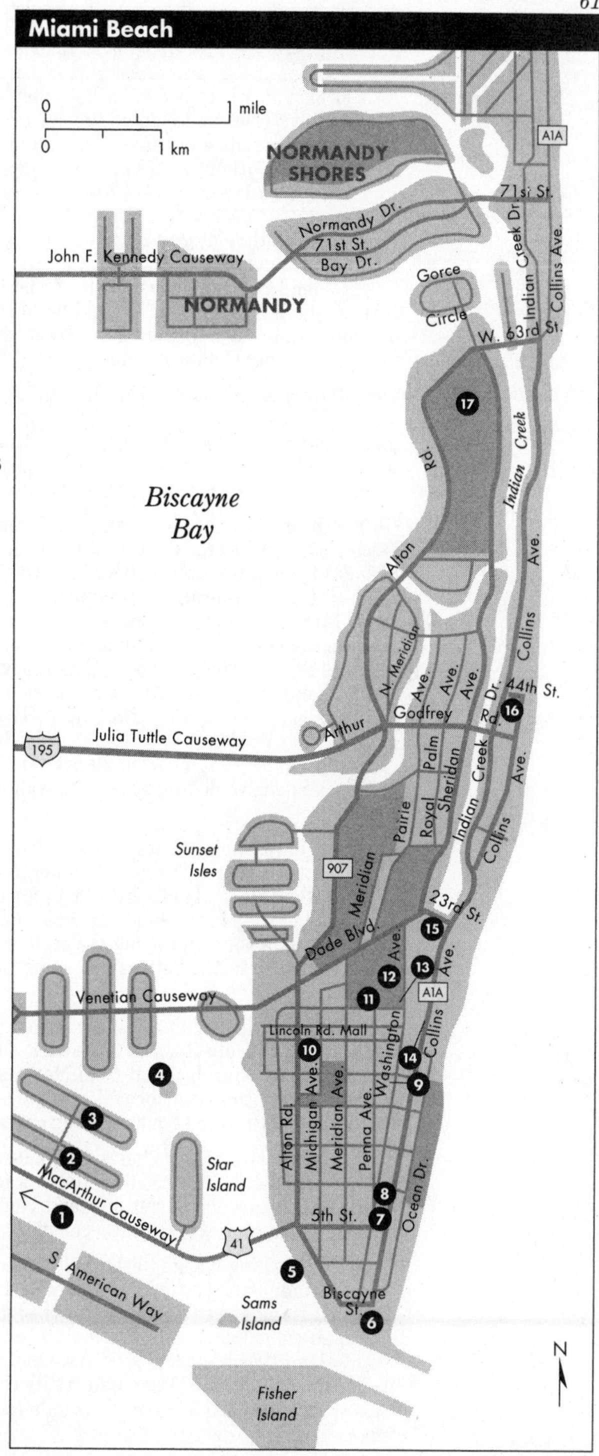

boxers train. *501 Washington Ave., tel. 674–8481. Open Mon.–Sat. 8–7, Sun. 8–2. Admission: $1 to look, $3 to train.*

Time Out A block east on 5th Street and a block north on Collins Avenue, Albert Starr's **Nature's Garden Bakery** makes delicious kosher special-diet breads and cakes. Try the millet cookies and the apple strudel without salt, sweetener, eggs, or yeast. *600 Collins Ave., tel. 305/534–1877. Closed Fri. afternoon and Sat.*

Return to 5th Street, go a block east to Ocean Drive, and turn
8 left. A block north at 6th Street, the **Art Deco District** begins. Take Ocean Drive north past a line of pastel-hued Art Deco hotels on your left and palm-fringed Lummus Park and the beach on your right. Turn left on 15th Street, and left again at the next corner onto Collins Avenue.

Now drive along the Art Deco District's two main commercial streets. Take Collins Avenue south, turn right at 5th Street, and right again at the next corner onto **Washington Avenue,** an intriguing mixture of delicatessens, produce markets, and stores selling Jewish religious books and artifacts.

Go north on Washington Avenue and you'll come to the **Art Deco District Welcome Center** (661 Washington Ave., tel. 305/672–2014, open weekdays 10–6, Sat. 10–5; for more information, *see* Guided Tours). Continuing on Washington Avenue, go
9 past 14th Street to **Espanola Way,** a narrow street of Mediterranean-revival buildings constructed in 1925 and frequented through the years by artists and writers. In the 1930s, Cuban bandleader Desi Arnaz performed in the Village Tavern, now part of the **Clay Hotel & AYH International Youth Hostel** (1438 Washington Ave., tel. 305/534–2988). The hostel caters to young visitors from all over the world who seek secure, inexpensive lodgings within walking distance of the beach.

Turn left onto Espanola Way, go five blocks to Jefferson Avenue, and turn right. Three blocks north of Espanola Way is **Lincoln Road Mall,** a landscaped shopping thoroughfare known during its heyday in the 1950s as "Fifth Avenue of the South." Trams shuttle shoppers along the mall, which is closed to all other vehicular traffic between Washington Avenue and Alton Road.

Park in the municipal lot a half-block north of the mall to stroll
10 through the **Lincoln Road Arts District,** where three blocks of storefronts on Lincoln Road from Meridian Avenue to Lenox Avenue have been transformed into galleries, studios, classrooms, and art-related boutiques and cafes.

The arts district also includes the 500-seat **Colony Theater** (1040 Lincoln Rd., tel. 305/674–1026), a former movie house. Now it's a city-owned performing arts center featuring dance, drama, music, and experimental cinema.

From the parking lot, go to the first main street north of Lincoln Road Mall and turn right. You're on 17th Street, recently renamed **Hank Meyer Boulevard** for the local publicist who encouraged comedian Jackie Gleason to broadcast his TV show from Miami Beach in the 1950s. Two blocks east on your left,
11 beside the entrance to **Miami Beach City Hall** (1700 Convention Center Dr., tel. 305/673–7030), stands *Red Sea Road,* a huge red sculpture by Barbara Neijna.

12 Also to your left is the **Miami Beach Convention Center** (1901
Convention Center Dr., tel. 305/673–7311), doubled in size in
1988 to 1.1 million square feet of exhibit space.

Continuing two more blocks east, admire another large
13 sculpture, *Mermaid*, by Roy Lichtenstein, in front of **Jackie
Gleason Theater of the Performing Arts** (1700 Washington Ave.,
tel. 305/673–8300), where Gleason's TV show once originated.
Now the 3,000-seat theater hosts touring Broadway shows and
classical concert performers. Near the sculpture, stars appear-
ing in the theater since 1984 have left their footprints and
signatures in concrete. This **Walk of the Stars** includes George
Abbott, Julie Andrews, Leslie Caron, Carol Channing, and Edward Villella.

Go two more blocks east on Hank Meyer Boulevard to Collins
Avenue, toward three of the largest Art Deco hotels, built in
the 1940s with streamlined tower forms reflecting the 20th century's transportation revolution: The round dome atop the
14 tower of the 11-story **Hotel National** (1677 Collins Ave., tel.
305/532–2311) resembles a balloon. The tower at the 12-story
Delano Hotel (1685 Collins Ave., tel. 305/538–7881) sports fins
suggesting the wings of an airplane or a Buck Rogers spaceship. The 11-story **Ritz Plaza** (1701 Collins Ave., tel. 305/534–
3500) rises to a cylindrical tower resembling a submarine periscope.

Turn left on Collins Avenue. At 21st Street, turn left beside the
Miami Beach Public Library in Collins Park, go two blocks to
15 Park Avenue, and turn right. You're approaching the **Bass Museum of Art,** with a diverse collection of European art,
including *The Holy Family,* a painting by Peter Paul Rubens;
The Tournament, a 16th-century Flemish tapestry; and works
by Albrecht Dürer and Henri de Toulouse-Lautrec. Park behind the museum and walk around to the entrance past massive
tropical baobab trees. *2121 Park Ave., tel. 305/673–7530. Open
Tues.–Sat. 10–5, Sun. 1–5. Admission: $2 adults, $1 students
with ID, children 16 and under free. Donations Tues.*

Return on 21st Street or 22nd Street to Collins Avenue and
turn left. As you drive north, a triumphal archway looms
ahead, framing a majestic white building set in lush vegetation
beside a waterfall and tropical lagoon. This vista is an
illusion—a 13,000-square-foot outdoor mural on an exterior
16 wall of the **Fontainebleau Hilton Resort and Spa** (4441 Collins
Ave., tel. 305/538–2000). Artist Richard Haas designed the
mural to illustrate how the hotel and its rock-grotto swimming
pool would look behind the wall. Locals call the 1,206-room hotel "Big Blue." It's the giant of Miami Beach, with 190,000
square feet of meeting and exhibit space.

Go left on 65th Street, turn left again at the next corner onto
Indian Creek Drive, and right at 63rd Street, which leads into
Alton Road, a winding, landscaped boulevard of gracious
17 homes styled along Art Deco lines. You'll pass the **La Gorce
Country Club** (5685 Alton Rd. tel. 305/866–4421), which devel-
oper Carl Fisher built and named for his friend Oliver La
Gorce, then president of the National Geographic Society.

To return to the mainland on the MacArthur Causeway, stay on Alton Road south to 5th Street, then turn right.

Exploring Little Havana

Numbers in the margin correspond with points of interest on the Miami, Coral Gables, and Key Biscayne map.

Orientation Thirty years ago, the tidal wave of Cubans fleeing the Castro regime flooded an older neighborhood just west of downtown Miami with refugees. This area became known as Little Havana. Today, with a half-million Cubans widely dispersed throughout Greater Miami, Little Havana remains a magnet for Cubans and Anglos alike. They come to experience the flavor of traditional Cuban culture.

That culture, of course, functions in Spanish. Many Little Havana residents and shopkeepers speak almost no English. If you don't speak Spanish, point and smile to communicate.

Touring Little Havana Begin this tour in downtown Miami, westbound on Flagler Street. Cross the Miami River to Little Havana, and park near Flagler Street and Ronald Reagan Avenue (S.W. 12th Ave.) to explore a thriving commercial district.

Continue west on Flagler Street to Teddy Roosevelt Avenue
1 (S.W. 17th Ave.) and pause at **Plaza de la Cubanidad,** on the southwest corner. Red-brick sidewalks surround a fountain and monument with a quotation from José Martí, a leader in Cuba's struggle for independence from Spain: "*Las palmas son novias que esperan.*" (The palm trees are girlfriends who will wait.)

Turn left at Douglas Road (S.W. 37th Ave.), drive south to
2 **Calle Ocho** (S.W. 8th St.), and turn left again. You are now on the main commercial thoroughfare of Little Havana.

Time Out For a total sensory experience, have a snack or meal at **Versailles,** a popular Cuban restaurant. Etched-glass mirrors lining its walls amplify bright lights and the roar of rapid-fire Spanish. Most of the servers don't speak English; you order by pointing to a number on the menu (choice of English or Spanish menus). Specialties include *palomilla,* a flat beefsteak; *ropa vieja* (literally, old clothes), a shredded-beef dish in tomato sauce; and *arroz con pollo,* chicken and yellow rice. *3555 S.W. 8th St., tel. 305/445–7614. Open Sun.–Thurs. 8 AM–2 AM, Fri. 8 AM–3:30 AM, Sat. 8 AM–4:30 AM. AE, CB, DC, MC, V.*

East of Unity Boulevard (S.W. 27th Ave.), Calle Ocho becomes a one-way street eastbound through the heart of Little Havana, where every block deserves exploration. If your time is limited, we suggest the three-block stretch from S.W. 14th Avenue to S.W. 11th Avenue. Parking is more ample west of Ronald Reagan Avenue (S.W. 12th Ave.).

At Calle Ocho and Memorial Boulevard (S.W. 13th Ave.)
3 stands the **Brigade 2506 Memorial,** commemorating the victims of the unsuccessful 1961 Bay of Pigs invasion of Cuba by an exile force. An eternal flame burns atop a simple stone monument with the inscription: "*Cuba—A Los Martires de La Brigada de Asalto Abril 17 de 1961.*" The monument also bears a shield with the Brigade 2506 emblem, a Cuban flag superimposed on a cross. Walk a block south on Memorial Boulevard from the Brigade 2506 Memorial to see other monuments relevant to Cuban history, including a statue of José Martí.

When you return to your car, drive five blocks south on Ronald
4 Reagan Avenue to the **Cuban Museum of Art and Culture.** Created by Cuban exiles to preserve and interpret the cultural heritage of their homeland, the museum has expanded its focus to embrace the entire Hispanic art community. In 1989, some artists who had previously exhibited in Havana were invited to show here. This policy, however, is under scrutiny by the patronage; at this time funding for 1991 is uncertain. If the museum remains open, it will continue its policy of mounting temporary exhibitions and showing works from its small permanent collection. *1300 S.W. 12th Ave., tel. 305/858-8006. Open Wed.-Fri. 10-5, weekends 1-5. Donation requested.*

To return to downtown Miami, take Ronald Reagan Avenue back north to S.W. 8th Street, turn right, go east to Miami Avenue or Brickell Avenue, turn left, and go north across the Miami River.

Exploring Coral Gables/Coconut Grove/ South Miami

Orientation This tour directs you through three separate communities, each unique in character. Two of them, Coral Gables and South Miami, are independent suburbs. The third, Coconut Grove, was annexed to the City of Miami in 1925 but still retains a distinctive personality.

Coral Gables, a planned community of broad boulevards and Spanish Mediterranean architecture, justifiably calls itself "The City Beautiful." Developer George E. Merrick began selling Coral Gables lots in 1921 and incorporated the city in 1925. He named most of the streets for Spanish explorers, cities, and provinces. Street names are at ground level beside each intersection on whitewashed concrete cornerstones.

The 1926 hurricane and the Great Depression prevented Merrick from fulfilling many aspects of his plan. The city languished until after World War II but then grew rapidly. Today, Coral Gables has a population of about 43,000. In its bustling downtown, many multinational companies maintain headquarters or regional offices.

A pioneer farming community that grew into a suburb, South Miami today retains small-town charm, despite an oversized shopping mall called The Bakery Centre, constructed on the former site of Holsum Bakery.

Coconut Grove is south Florida's oldest settlement, inhabited as early as 1834 and established by 1873, two decades before Miami. Its early settlers included Bahamian blacks, "conchs" from Key West, and New England intellectuals. They built a community that attracted artists, writers, and scientists to establish winter homes. By the end of World War I, more people listed in *Who's Who* gave addresses in Coconut Grove than anyplace else.

To this day, Coconut Grove reflects the pioneers' eclectic origins. Posh estates mingle with rustic cottages, modest frame homes, and starkly modern dwellings—often on the same block. To keep Coconut Grove a village in a jungle, residents lavish affection on exotic plantings while battling to protect remaining native vegetation.

Miami, Coral Gables, and Key Biscayne

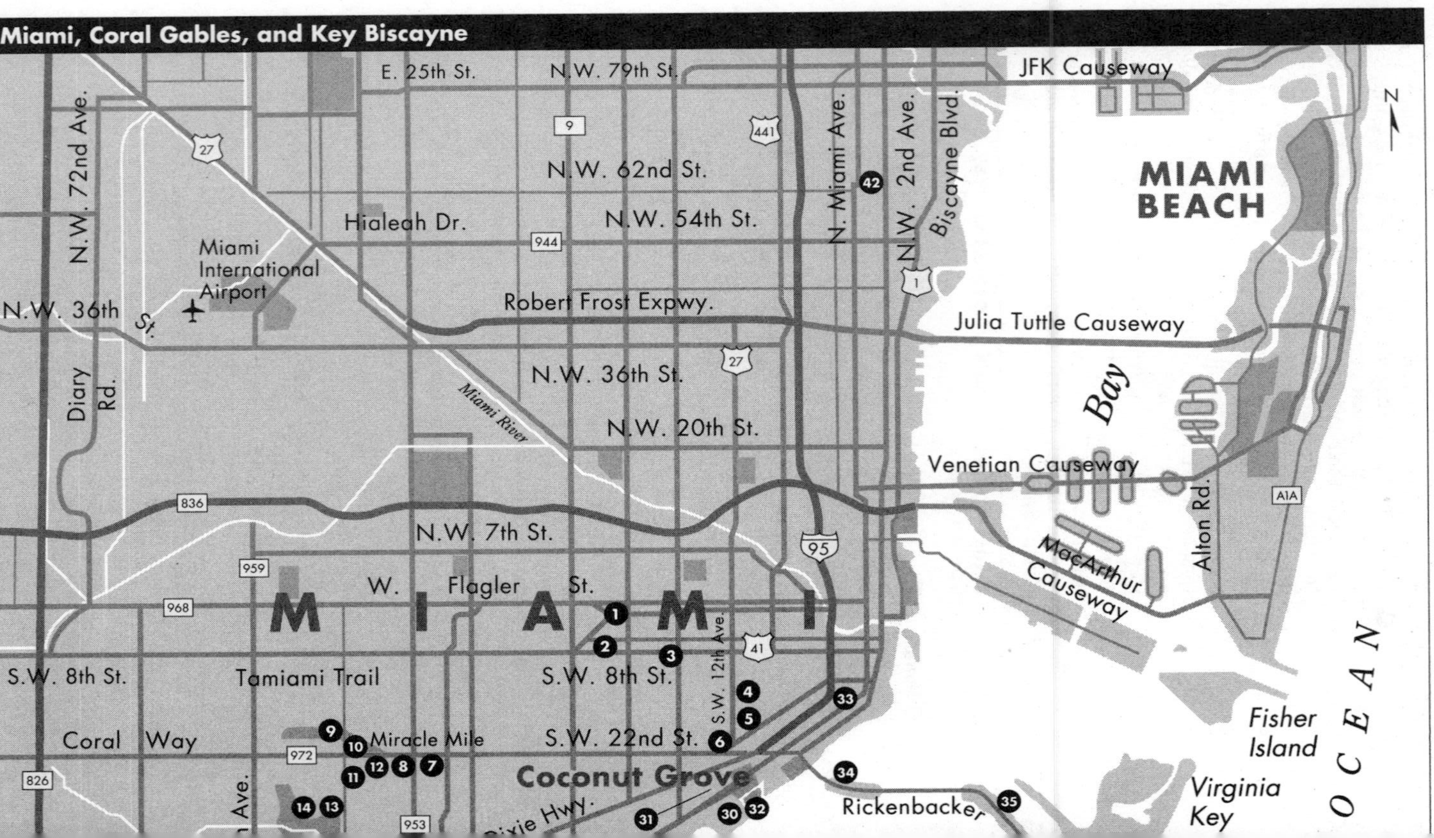

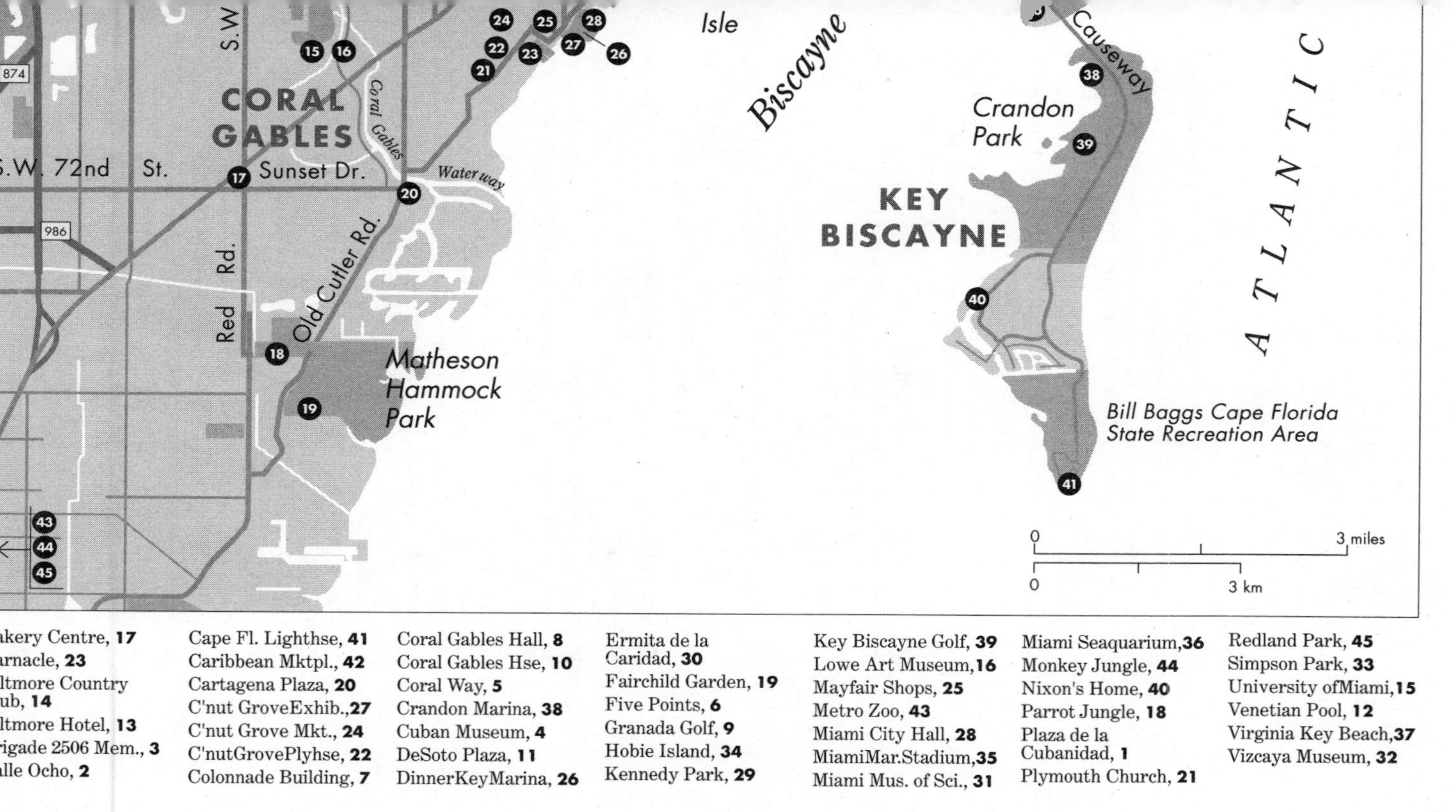

Bakery Centre, **17**
Barnacle, **23**
Biltmore Country Club, **14**
Biltmore Hotel, **13**
Brigade 2506 Mem., **3**
Calle Ocho, **2**
Cape Fl. Lighthse, **41**
Caribbean Mktpl., **42**
Cartagena Plaza, **20**
C'nut GroveExhib.,**27**
C'nut Grove Mkt., **24**
C'nutGrovePlyhse, **22**
Colonnade Building, **7**
Coral Gables Hall, **8**
Coral Gables Hse, **10**
Coral Way, **5**
Crandon Marina, **38**
Cuban Museum, **4**
DeSoto Plaza, **11**
DinnerKeyMarina, **26**
Ermita de la Caridad, **30**
Fairchild Garden, **19**
Five Points, **6**
Granada Golf, **9**
Hobie Island, **34**
Kennedy Park, **29**
Key Biscayne Golf, **39**
Lowe Art Museum,**16**
Mayfair Shops, **25**
Metro Zoo, **43**
Miami City Hall, **28**
MiamiMar.Stadium,**35**
Miami Mus. of Sci., **31**
Miami Seaquarium,**36**
Monkey Jungle, **44**
Nixon's Home, **40**
Parrot Jungle, **18**
Plaza de la Cubanidad, **1**
Plymouth Church, **21**
Redland Park, **45**
Simpson Park, **33**
University ofMiami,**15**
Venetian Pool, **12**
Virginia Key Beach,**37**
Vizcaya Museum, **32**

The historic center of the Village of Coconut Grove went through a hippie period in the 1960s, laid-back funkiness in the 1970s, and a teenybopper invasion in the early 1980s. Today, the tone is increasingly upscale, mellow, and sophisticated—a congenial mix of struggling art-cinema and traditional theater, galleries, boutiques, elegant restaurants, and bars and sidewalk cafes where the literati hang out.

Two Junior League books, *Historic Coral Gables* and *Historic Coconut Grove*, give directions for self-guided walking tours.

Driving Tour

This tour begins in downtown Miami. Go south on S.E. 2nd Avenue, which becomes Brickell Avenue and crosses the Miami
5 River. Half a mile south of the river, turn right onto **Coral Way,** which at this point is S.W. 13th Street. Within half a mile, Coral Way doglegs left under I–95 and becomes S.W. 3rd Avenue. It
6 continues another mile to a complex intersection, **Five Points,** and doglegs right to become S.W. 22nd Avenue.

Along the S.W. 3rd Avenue and S.W. 22nd Avenue segments of Coral Way, banyan trees planted in the median strip in 1929 arch over the roadway. The banyans end at the Miami/Coral Gables boundary, where **Miracle Mile** begins. This four-block stretch of Coral Way, from Douglas Road (37th Ave.) to Le Jeune Road (42nd Ave.) in the heart of downtown Coral Gables, is really a half-mile long. To stroll the full mile, walk up one side and down the other. Miracle Mile's 160 shops range from chain restaurants and shoe stores to posh boutiques and beauty salons. The stores are numbered from 1 to 399. As you go west, numbers and quality both increase. Request a complete directory from the Miracle Mile Merchants' Association (220 Miracle Mile, Suite 218, Coral Gables 33134, tel. 305/445–0591).

7 **The Colonnade Building** (133–169 Miracle Mile, Coral Gables) on Miracle Mile once housed George Merrick's sales office. Its rotunda bears an ornamental frieze and a Spanish-tile roof 75 feet above street level. The Colonnade Building has been restored and connected to the new 13-story Colonnade Hotel and an office building that echoes the rotunda's roofline.

The ornate Spanish Renaissance structure facing Miracle Mile
8 just west of Le Jeune Road is **Coral Gables City Hall,** opened in 1928. It has a three-tier tower topped with a clock and a 500-pound bell. Inside the bell tower, a mural by artist Denman Fink depicts the four seasons. *405 Biltmore Way, Coral Gables, tel. 305/442–6400. Open weekdays 8–5.*

Follow Coral Way west of Le Jeune Road to the right of City
9 Hall. You'll pass the **Granada Golf Course** (2001 Granada Blvd., Coral Gables, tel. 305/442–6484), one of two public courses in Coral Gables.

One block west of the golf course, turn right on Toledo Street to
10 park behind **Coral Gables House,** George Merrick's boyhood home. The city acquired the dwelling in 1976 and restored its 1920s appearance. It contains Merrick family furnishings and artifacts. *907 Coral Way, Coral Gables, tel. 305/442–6593. Open Sun. and Wed. 1–4. Admission: $1 adults, 50¢ children.*

Return to Coral Way, turn right, then left at the first stoplight. Now you're southbound on Granada Boulevard, approaching
11 **DeSoto Plaza and Fountain,** a classical column on a pedestal with water flowing from the mouths of four sculptured faces.

The closed eyes of the face looking west symbolize the day's end. Denman Fink designed the fountain in the early 1920s.

Follow the traffic circle almost completely around the fountain to northeast-bound DeSoto Boulevard. On your right in the
12 next block is **Venetian Pool,** a unique municipal swimming pool transformed from a rock quarry. *2701 DeSoto Blvd., Coral Gables, tel. 305/442–6483. Summer hours: weekdays 11–7:30, weekends 10–4:30; winter hours: Tues.–Fri. 11–4, weekends 10–4:30. Admission (nonresident): $2.85 adults, $1.14 children under 13. Free parking across DeSoto Blvd.*

From the pool, go around the block with right turns onto Almeria Avenue, Toledo Street, and Sevilla Avenue. You'll return to the DeSoto Fountain and take DeSoto Boulevard southeast to
13 emerge in front of **The Biltmore Hotel** (1200 Anastasia Ave., Coral Gables, tel. 305/445–1926). Like the Freedom Tower in downtown Miami, the Biltmore's 26-story tower is a replica of the Giralda Tower in Seville, Spain.

The Biltmore opened in January 1926 as the centerpiece of George Merrick's planned city. It suffered financially during the Great Depression, became a veterans' hospital during World War II, and stood vacant from 1968 to 1986. After extensive restoration, renovation, and reopening, the hotel has again closed, but should reopen shortly. (*See* Highlights for details.)

Inside, the lobby's vaulted ceiling and gargoyles, the two ballrooms' impressive chandeliers and intricately painted ceilings, and the open courtyard's fountain and gracious proportions exude luxury. A second-floor promenade overlooks the 18-hole Biltmore Golf Course, now a public course known for its scenic and competitive layout, and the largest hotel pool in the United States, with a capacity of 1.25 million gallons.

Just west of The Biltmore Hotel stands a separate building,
14 **The Biltmore Country Club,** which the city restored in the late 1970s. It's a richly ornamented beaux arts-style structure with a superb colonnade and courtyard. On its ground floor are facilities for golfers. In the former club lounge, lately Le Biltmore Restaurant, meeting rooms include one lofty space paneled with veneer from 60 species of trees. In 1989 the structure was reincorporated into **The Biltmore Hotel,** of which it was an original part.

From the hotel, turn right on Anastasia Avenue, go east to Granada Boulevard, and turn right. Continue south on Granada Boulevard over a bridge across the **Coral Gables Waterway,** which connects the grounds of The Biltmore Hotel with Biscayne Bay. In the hotel's heyday, Venetian gondolas plied the waterway, bringing guests to a bayside beach.

At Ponce de León Boulevard, turn right. On your left is Metrorail's Stonehenge-like concrete structure, and on your
15 right, the **University of Miami**'s 260-acre main campus. With about 18,000 full-time, part-time, and noncredit students, UM is the largest private university in the Southeast.

Turn right at the first stoplight to enter the campus and park in
16 the lot on your right designated for visitors to UM's **Lowe Art Museum.** The Lowe's permanent collection of 8,000 works includes Renaissance and Baroque art, American paintings, Latin American art, and Navajo and Pueblo Indian textiles and baskets. The museum also hosts traveling exhibitions. *1301*

Stanford Dr., Coral Gables, tel. 305/284–3535 for recorded information, 305/284–3536 for museum office. Open all year Sun. 12–5, Tues.–Sat. 10–5. Admission: $2 adults, $1 students and seniors, children under 16 free.

Now exit the UM campus on Stanford Drive, pass under Metrorail, and cross Dixie Highway. Just beyond the Burger King on your right, bear right onto Maynada Street. Turn right at the next stoplight onto **Sunset Drive.** Fine old homes and mature trees line this officially designated "historic and scenic road" that leads to and through downtown South Miami.

On the northwest corner of Sunset Drive and Red Road (57th Ave.), note the pink building with a mural on which an alligator seems ready to devour a horrified man. This trompe l'oeil fantasy, *South Florida Cascade,* by illusionary artist Richard Haas,
17 highlights the main entrance to **The Bakery Centre** (5701 Sunset Dr., South Miami, tel. 305/662–4155).

On the third level of The Bakery Centre, the **Miami Youth Museum** features cultural arts exhibits, hands-on displays, and activities to enhance a child's creativity and inspire interest in artistic careers. *5701 Sunset Dr., South Miami, tel. 305/661–ARTS. Open weekdays 10–5, weekends noon–5. Admission: $3 adults, senior citizens and children under 2 free.*

Go south on Red Road and turn right just before Killian Drive
18 (S.W. 112th St.) into the grounds of **Parrot Jungle,** where more than 1,100 exotic birds are on display. Many of the parrots, macaws, and cockatoos fly free, but they'll come to you for seeds, which you can purchase from old-fashioned gumball machines. Attend a trained-bird show, watch baby birds in training, and pose for photos with colorful macaws perched on your arms. The "jungle" is a natural hammock surrounding a sinkhole. Stroll among orchids and other flowering plants nestled among ferns, bald-cypress trees, and massive live oaks. Also see the cactus garden and Flamingo Lake, with a breeding population of 75 Caribbean flamingos. Opened in 1936, Parrot Jungle is one of Greater Miami's oldest and most popular commercial tourist attractions. *11000 S.W. 57th Ave., Miami, tel. 305/666–7834. Open daily 9:30–6. Admission: $10.50 adults, $5.25 children 3–12.*

From Parrot Jungle, take Red Road ⅓ mile south and turn left at Old Cutler Road, which curves north along the uplands of
19 south Florida's coastal ridge. Visit 83-acre **Fairchild Tropical Garden,** the largest tropical botanical garden in the continental United States. *10901 Old Cutler Rd., Coral Gables, tel. 305/667–1651. Open daily except Christmas 9:30–4:30. Admission: $4 adults, children under 13 free with parents. Hourly tram rides, $1 adults, 50¢ children under 13.*

North of the garden, Old Cutler Road traverses Dade County's oldest and most scenic park, **Matheson Hammock Park.** The Civilian Conservation Corps developed the 100-acre tract of upland and mangrove swamp in the 1930s on land donated by a local pioneer, Commodore J. W. Matheson. The park's most popular feature is a bathing beach, where the tide flushes a saltwater "atoll" pool through four gates. *9610 Old Cutler Rd., Coral Gables, tel. 305/666–6979. Park open 6 AM–sundown. Pool lifeguards on duty winter 7:30 AM–6 PM, summer 7:30 AM–7 PM. Parking fee for beach and marina $2 per car, $5 per car with trailer. Limited upland parking free.*

20 Continue north on Old Cutler Road to **Cartagena Plaza,** cross the Le Jeune Road bridge over the waterway, and turn right at the first stoplight onto Ingraham Highway. Four blocks later, you're back in the City of Miami, at the south end of Coconut Grove. Follow Ingraham Highway to Douglas Road and turn right at the next stoplight onto Main Highway. You're following old pioneer trails that today remain narrow roads shaded by a canopy of towering trees.

One block past the stoplight at Royal Palm Avenue, turn left
21 onto Devon Road in front of **Plymouth Congregational Church.** Opened in 1917, this handsome coral-rock structure resembles a Mexican mission church. The front door, of hand-carved walnut and oak with original wrought-iron fittings, came from an early 17th-century monastery in the Pyrenees. A hole in the lower right side of the door gives the church cat access to mice. *3400 Devon Rd., Coconut Grove, tel. 305/444–6521. Ask at the office to go inside the church, weekdays 9–4:30. Services Sun. 10 AM.*

When you leave the church, go around the block opposite the church. Turn left from Devon Road onto Hibiscus Street, left again onto Royal Palm Avenue, and left at the stoplight onto Main Highway.

You're now headed for the historic **Village of Coconut Grove,** a trendy commercial district with red-brick sidewalks and more than 300 restaurants, stores, and art galleries.

Parking can be a problem in the village—especially on weekend evenings, when police direct traffic and prohibit turns at some intersections to prevent gridlock. Be prepared to walk several blocks from the periphery into the heart of the Grove.

As you enter the village center, note the apricot-hued Spanish
22 rococo **Coconut Grove Playhouse** to your left. Built in 1926 as a movie theater, it became a legitimate theater in 1956 and is now owned by the State of Florida. The playhouse presents Broadway-bound plays and musical reviews and experimental productions in its 1,100-seat main theater and 100-seat cabaret-style Encore Room. *3500 Main Hwy., Coconut Grove, tel. 305/442–4000 to box office; tel. 305/442–2662 to administrative office. Parking lot: $2 during the day, $4 at night.*

Benches and a shelter opposite the playhouse mark the en-
23 trance to **The Barnacle,** a pioneer residence that is now a state historic site. Commodore Ralph Munroe built The Barnacle in 1891. Its broad, sloping roof and deeply recessed verandas channel sea breezes into the house. A central stairwell and rooftop vent allow hot air to escape. Many furnishings are original. While living at The Barnacle, Munroe built shoal-draft sailboats. One such craft, the ketch *Micco,* is on display. *3485 Main Hwy., Coconut Grove, tel. 305/448–9445. Open for tours only Thurs.–Mon. 9, 10:30, 1, and 2:30; closed Tues. and Wed. Admission: $1 adults, 50¢ children under 12. Reservations for groups of 8 or more; others meet ranger at entrance gate.*

Time Out Turn left at the next street, Commodore Plaza, and pause. **To Market/To Market,** a French gourmet cafe, features 16 kinds of muffins and a superb Greek-style salad bulging with brine-soaked olives and feta cheese. Other fare includes quiches, pâtés, sandwiches, cheeses, French pastries, American-style breakfasts, wine, beer, and soft drinks. On weekend mornings, locals bicycle in for a croissant-and-eggs brunch and a chat with the neighbors. *3195 Commodore Plaza, Coconut Grove, tel. 305/446–6090. Open Sun.–Thurs. 7 AM–10PM, Fri. and Sat. 7 AM–midnight. Inside and outdoor service and carryouts available. MC, V.*

---

24 If your timing is right, visit the **Coconut Grove Farmers Market,** a laid-back, Brigadoon-like happening that appears as if by magic each Saturday on a vacant lot. To get there from Commodore Plaza, go north to Grand Avenue, cross McDonald Avenue (S.W. 32nd Ave.), and go a block west to Margaret Street. Vendors set up outdoor stands to offer home-grown tropical fruits and vegetables (including organic produce), honey, seafoods, macrobiotic foods, and ethnic fare from the Caribbean, the Middle East, and Southeast Asia. Nonfood items for sale include plants, handicrafts, candles, jewelry, and homemade clothing. A masseur plies his trade, musicians play, and the Hare Krishnas come to chant. People-watching is half the fun. *Open Sat. 8–3.*

Now return to the heart of the village center. Then take Grand
25 Avenue a block east to Virginia Street and enter **Mayfair Shops in the Grove,** an exclusive open-air mall with a small high-fashion branch of Burdines department store and 74 other upscale shops. The 181 rooms of Mayfair House, a luxury hotel, surround the mall's southern section. As you stroll through Mayfair, admire its fountains, copper sculptures, and lavish Romanesque ornamentation formed in concrete. The design recalls a classic building in Chicago, The Rookery—with good reason. Frank Lloyd Wright, who remodeled The Rookery in 1905, taught Mayfair's architect, Kenneth Treister. *2911 Grand Ave., Coconut Grove, tel. 305/448–1700. Open Mon., Thurs., and Fri. 10–9; Tues., Wed., and Sat. 10–7; Sun. noon–5:30.*

Leaving the village center, take McFarlane Road east from its intersection with Grand Avenue and Main Highway. Peacock Park, site of the first hotel in southeast Florida, is on your
26 right. Ahead, seabirds soar and sailboats ride at anchor in **Dinner KeyMarina** (3400 Pan American Dr., Coconut Grove, tel. 305/579–6980), named for a small island where early settlers held picnics. With 581 moorings, it's Greater Miami's largest marina.

McFarlane Road turns left onto South Bayshore Drive. Turn right at the first stoplight onto Unity Boulevard (S.W. 27th Ave.), and go east into a parking lot that serves the marina and
27 the 105,000-square-foot **Coconut Grove Exhibition Center** (2700 S. Bayshore Dr., Coconut Grove, tel. 305/579–3310), where antique, boat, and home-furnishings shows are held.

28 At the northeast corner of the lot is **Miami City Hall,** which was built in 1934 as the terminal for the Pan American Airways seaplane base at Dinner Key. The building retains its nautical-style art-deco trim. *3500 Pan American Dr., Coconut Grove, tel. 305/579–6040. Open weekdays 8–5.*

From City Hall, drive west on Pan American Drive toward South Bayshore Drive, with its pyramidlike Grand Bay Hotel.
29 Turn right on South Bayshore Drive, and go north past **Kennedy Park.** Leave your car in the park's lot north of Kirk Street and walk toward the water. From a footbridge over the mouth

of a small tidal creek, you'll enjoy an unobstructed view across Biscayne Bay to Key Biscayne. Film crews use the park often to make commercials and Italian westerns.

Continue north on South Bayshore Drive to Fair Isle Street and turn right. You're approaching **Grove Isle,** a 26-acre island with a 49-room hotel, high-rise apartments, and a private club. Developer Martin Z. Margulies displays selections from his extensive private art collection in the lobbies. Along a walk beside the bay stand massive sculptures by modern luminaries, including Alexander Calder, Jean Dubuffet, Willem de Kooning, Alexander Liberman, and Isamu Noguchi. *4 Grove Isle Dr., Coconut Grove, tel. 305/250–4000. Phone the club's membership office, weekdays 9–5, and mention* Fodor's Florida 1991 *to obtain a free guest pass.*

Return to South Bayshore Drive, turn right, and go north past the entrance to Mercy Hospital, where South Bayshore Drive becomes South Miami Avenue. At the next stoplight beyond the hospital, turn right on a private road that goes past St.
30 Kieran's Church to **Ermita de La Caridad**—Our Lady of Charity Shrine—a conical building 90 feet high and 80 feet wide overlooking the bay so worshipers face toward Cuba. A mural above the shrine's altar depicts Cuba's history. *3609 S. Miami Ave., Coconut Grove, tel. 305/854–2404. Open daily 9–9.*

Return to South Miami Avenue, turn right, go about
31 three-tenths of a mile, and turn left to the **Miami Museum of Science and Space Transit Planetarium.** This is a participatory museum, chock-full of sound, gravity, and electricity displays for children and adults alike to manipulate and marvel at. A wildlife center houses native Florida snakes, turtles and tortoises, birds of prey, and large wading birds. *3280 S. Miami Ave., Miami, tel. 305/854–4247; 24-hour Cosmic Hotline for planetarium show times and prices, 305/854–2222. Open daily 10–6. Admission to museum: $5 adults, $3.50 children; to planetarium shows $5 adults, $2.50 children and seniors; to laser light shows $6 adults, $3 children and seniors.*

32 Across South Miami Avenue is the entrance to **Vizcaya Museum and Gardens,** an estate with an Italian Renaissance-style villa built in 1912–16 as the winter residence of Chicago industrialist James Deering. The house and gardens overlook Biscayne Bay on a 30-acre tract that includes a native hammock and more than 10 acres of formal gardens and fountains. You can leave your car in the Museum of Science lot and walk across the street or drive across and park in Vizcaya's own lot.

The house contains 34 rooms of antique furniture, plus paintings, sculpture, and other decorative arts. These objects date from the 15th through the 19th centuries, representing the Renaissance, Baroque, Rococo, and Neoclassic styles. *3251 S. Miami Ave., Miami, tel. 305/579–2813 (recording) or 305/579–2808. House open 9:30–4:30; ticket booth open to 4:30, garden to 5:30. Admission: $8.50 adults, $4 children 6–18. Guided tours available, group tours by appointment.*

As you leave Vizcaya, turn north (left from the Museum of Science lot, right from the Vizcaya lot) onto South Miami Avenue.
33 Continue to 17th Road and turn left to **Simpson Park.** Enjoy a fragment of the dense tropical jungle—large gumbo-limbo trees, marlberry, banyans, and black calabash—that once covered the entire five miles from downtown Miami to Coconut

Grove. You'll get a rare glimpse of how things were before the high-rises towered. Avoid the park during summer when mosquitoes whine as incessently today as they did 100 years ago. You may follow South Miami Avenue the rest of the way downtown or go back two stoplights and turn left to the entrance to the Rickenbacker Causeway and Key Biscayne.

Exploring Virginia Key and Key Biscayne

Orientation Government Cut and the Port of Miami separate the dense urban fabric of Miami Beach from Greater Miami's playground islands, Virginia Key, and Key Biscayne. Parks occupy much of both keys, providing congenial upland with facilities for basking on the beach, golf, tennis, softball, and picnicking—plus uninviting but ecologically valuable stretches of dense mangrove swamp. Also on the keys are several marinas, an assortment of water-oriented tourist attractions, and the laid-back village where Richard Nixon set up his presidential vacation compound.

Driving Tour To reach Virginia Key and Key Biscayne, take the **Rickenbacker Causeway** across Biscayne Bay from the mainland at Brickell Avenue and S.W. 26th Road, about two miles south of downtown Miami. A fitness pathway for biking and jogging parallels the causeway. In 1990 a new bike lane was added in each direction of the causeway from the new high bridge to the village of Key Biscayne. An older and somewhat uprooted path still meanders as a scenic alternative through pine forests and marsh, and here and there through parking lots. *Toll: $1 per car, bicycles and pedestrians free.*

About 200 feet east of the tollgate (just across the first low
34 bridge), you can rent windsurfing equipment on **Hobie Island.** *Sailboards Miami, Box 16, Key Biscayne, tel. 305/361–SAIL. Open daily 9:30–dusk. Cost: $12 per hour; $39 for a 2-hr windsurfing lesson.*

The **Old Rickenbacker Causeway Bridge,** built in 1947, is now a fishing pier. The west stub begins about a mile from the tollgate. Park near its entrance and walk past fishermen tending their lines to the gap where the center draw span across the Intracoastal Waterway was removed. There you can watch boat traffic pass through the channel, pelicans and other seabirds soar and dive, and porpoises cavort in the bay.

The new high-level **William M. Powell Bridge** rises 75 feet above the water to eliminate the need for a draw span. The panoramic view from the top encompasses the bay, keys, port, and downtown skyscrapers, with Miami Beach and the Atlantic Ocean in the distance. The speed limit is 45 mph, and you can't stop on the bridge, so park in the fishing pier lot and walk up.

35 Next along the causeway stands the 6,538-seat **Miami Marine Stadium** (3601 Rickenbacker Causeway, Miami, tel. 305/361–6732), where summer pop concerts take place and name entertainers occasionally perform throughout the year. You can join the audience on land in the stadium or on a boat anchored just offshore. Fourth of July concertgoers enjoy a spectacular fireworks display that is visible for miles up and down the bay.

36 Down the causeway from Marine Stadium at the **Miami Seaquarium,** Lolita, a killer whale, cavorts in a huge tank. She performs three times a day, as do sea lions and dolphins in sepa-

rate shows. Exhibits include a shark pool, 250,000-gallon tropical reef aquarium, and manatees. *4400 Rickenbacker Causeway, Miami, tel. 305/361–5705; recorded information, 305/361–5703. Open daily 9:30–6:30. Admission: $13.95 adults, $11.95 senior citizens, $9.95 children 3–12.*

Opposite the causeway from the Seaquarium, a road leads
37 north to **Virginia Key Beach,** a City of Miami park, with a two-mile stretch of oceanfront, shelters, barbecue grills, ball fields, nature trails, and a fishing area. Ask for directions at the entrance gate. *Cost: $2 per car.*

From Virginia Key, the causeway crosses **Bear Cut** to the north end of Key Biscayne, where it becomes Crandon Boulevard.
38 The **Crandon Park Marina,** behind Sundays on the Bay Restaurant, sells bait and tackle. *4000 Crandon Blvd., Key Biscayne, tel. 361–1161. Open 7–5 weekdays, 7–6 weekends.*

Beyond the marina, Crandon Boulevard bisects 1,211-acre **Crandon Park.** Turnouts on your left lead to four parking lots, adjacent picnic areas, ball fields, and 3.3 miles of beach. *Open daily 8 AM–sunset. Parking: $2 per car.*

39 On your right are entrances to the **Key Biscayne Golf Course** and the **International Tennis Center.**

From the traffic circle at the south end of Crandon Park, Crandon Boulevard continues for two miles through the developed portion of Key Biscayne. You'll come back that way, but
40 first detour to the site of **President Nixon's home** (485 W. Matheson Dr.). Turn right at the first stoplight onto Harbor Drive, go about a mile, and turn right at Matheson Drive. A later owner enlarged and totally changed Nixon's home.

Emerging from West Matheson Drive, turn right onto Harbor Drive and go about a mile south to Mashta Drive, and follow Mashta Drive east past Harbor Drive to Crandon Boulevard, and turn right.

You are approaching the entrance to **Bill Baggs Cape Florida State Recreation Area,** named for a crusading newspaper editor whose efforts prompted the state to create this 406-acre park. The park includes 1¼ miles of beach and a seawall along Biscayne Bay where fishermen catch bonefish, grouper, jack, snapper, and snook. There is a nature trail with native plants now rare on Key Biscayne.

Also in the park is the oldest structure in south Florida, the
41 **Cape Florida Lighthouse,** erected in 1825 to help ships avoid the shallows and reefs offshore. In 1836 a band of Seminole Indians attacked the lighthouse and killed the keeper's helper. You can no longer climb the 122 steps to the top of the 95-foot-tall lighthouse because the structure awaits about $1 million in repairs —a sum that Dade Heritage Trust, the local preservation society, is endeavoring to raise. *1200 S. Crandon Blvd., Key Biscayne, tel. 305/361–5811. Park open all year 8–sunset. Lighthouse tours daily except Tues. at 10:30, 1, 2:30, and 3:30. Admission to park: $1 per vehicle with driver, 50¢ per passenger, children under 6 free; to lighthouse and keeper's residence: $1 per person.*

When you leave Cape Florida, follow Crandon Boulevard back to Crandon Park through Key Biscayne's commercial center, a mixture of posh shops and stores catering to the needs of the neighborhood. On your way back to the mainland, pause as you approach the Powell Bridge to admire the downtown Miami skyline. At night, the brightly lit Centrust Building looks from this angle like a clipper ship running under full sail before the breeze.

Exploring Little Haiti

Of the nearly 150,000 Haitians who have settled in Greater Miami, some 60,000 live in Little Haiti, a 200-block area on Miami's northeast side. More than 350 small Haitian businesses operate in Little Haiti.

For many Haitians, English is a third language. French is Haiti's official language, but much day-to-day conversation takes place in Creole, a French-based patois. Smiling and pointing will bridge any language barrier you may encounter.

This tour takes you through the Miami Design District on the margin of Little Haiti, then along two main thoroughfares that form the spine of the Haitian community. The tour begins in downtown Miami. Take Biscayne Boulevard north to N.E. 36th Street, turn left, go about four-tenths of a mile west to North Miami Avenue. Turn right, and go north through the **Miami Design District,** where about 225 wholesale stores, showrooms, and galleries feature interior furnishings and decorative arts.

Little Haiti begins immediately north of the Design District in an area with some of Miami's oldest dwellings, dating from the dawn of the 20th century through the 1920s land-boom era. Drive the side streets to see elegant Mediterranean-style homes, and bungalows with distinctive coral-rock trim.

Return to North Miami Avenue and go north. A half-block east on 54th Street is the tiny storefront office of the **Haitian Refugee Center** (32 N.E. 54th St., tel. 305/757–8538), a focal point of political activity in the Haitian community.

Continue north on North Miami Avenue past the former Cuban consulate, a pretentious Caribbean-Colonial mansion that is now the clinic of Haitian physician Lucien Albert (5811 N. Miami Ave., tel. 305/758–2700).

North of 85th Street, cross the Little River Canal into **El Portal,** a tiny suburban village of modest homes where more than a quarter of the property is now Haitian-owned. Turn right on N.E. 87th Street and right again on N.E. 2nd Avenue. You are now southbound on Little Haiti's main commercial street.

Time Out Stop for Haitian breads and cakes made with coconut and other tropical ingredients at **Baptiste Bakery.** *7488 N.E. 2nd Ave., tel. 756–1119. Open 8–8.*

Along N.E. 2nd Avenue between 79th Street and 45th Street, rows of storefronts in faded pastels reflect a first effort by area merchants to dress up their neighborhood and attract outsiders.

42 More successful is the **Caribbean Marketplace**, which the Haitian Task Force (an economic development organization) opened in 1990. Its 25 merchants sell tropical fruits and vegeta-

bles, handmade baskets, and Haitian art and craft items. *Tel. 305/758–8708, 5927 N.E. 2nd Ave., Miami.*

This concludes the Little Haiti tour. To return to downtown Miami, take N.E. 2nd Avenue south to N.E. 35th Street, turn left, go east one block to Biscayne Boulevard, and turn right to go south.

Exploring South Dade

This tour directs you to major attractions in the suburbs southwest of Dade County's urban core. A Junior League book, *Historic South Dade,* locates and describes 40 historic structures and attractions in a South Dade County driving tour.

From downtown Miami, take the Dolphin Expressway (Rte. 836) west to the Palmetto Expressway (Rte. 826) southbound. Bear left south of Bird Road (S.W. 40th St.) onto the Don Shula Expressway (Rte. 874). Exit westbound onto Killian Drive (S.W. 104th St.) and go west to Lindgren Road (S.W. 137th Ave.). Turn left and go south to S.W. 128th Street, the entrance to the Tamiami Airport and **Weeks Air Museum,** where aircraft on display include a World War I-vintage Sopwith Camel (of Snoopy fame), and a B–17 Flying Fortress bomber and P–51 Mustang from World War II. *14710 S.W. 128th St., tel. 305/233–5197. Open daily 10–5. Admission: $4 adults, $3 seniors, $2 children 12 and under.*

Continue south on Lindgren Road to Coral Reef Drive (S.W.
43 152nd St.). Turn left and go east to **Metro Zoo** and the **Gold Coast Railroad Museum.**

Metro Zoo covers 295 acres and is cageless; animals roam free on islands surrounded by moats. In "Wings of Asia," a 1.5-acre aviary, hundreds of exotic birds from southeast Asia fly through a rain forest beneath a protective net enclosure. The zoo has 3 miles of walkways, a monorail with four stations, and an open-air amphitheater for concerts. Paws, a petting zoo for children, opened in 1989. *12400 Coral Reef Dr. (S.W. 152nd St.), tel. 305/251–0400 for recorded information. Gates open daily 9:30–4. Park closes at 5:30. Admission: $8 adults, $4 children 3–12. Admission includes monorail tickets. AE. No credit cards at snack bar.*

The railroad museum's collection includes a 1949 Silver Crescent dome car; and the *Ferdinand Magellan,* the only Pullman car ever constructed specifically for U.S. presidents, used by Roosevelt, Truman, Eisenhower, and Reagan. *12450 Coral Reef Dr. (S.W. 152nd St.), tel. 305/253–0063. Open weekdays 10–3, weekends 10–5. Train rides weekends, holidays. Phone for details.*

Return to Coral Reef Drive, turn right (east) to the Homestead Extension of Florida's Turnpike, take the turnpike south, exit at Hainlin Mill Drive (S.W. 216th St.), and turn right. Cross South Dixie Highway (U.S. 1), go 3 miles west, and turn right
44 into **Monkey Jungle,** home to more than 4,000 monkeys representing 35 species—including orangutans from Borneo and Sumatra, golden lion tamarins from Brazil, and brown lemurs from Madagascar. Performing monkey shows begin at 10 AM and run continuously at 45-minute intervals. The walkways of this 30-acre attraction are caged; the monkeys roam free. *14805 Hainlin Mill Dr. (S.W. 216 St.), tel. 305/235–1611. Open daily*

9:30–5. Admission: $8.75 adults, $7.75 seniors, $4.75 children 5–12. AE, MC.

Continue west on Hainlin Mill Drive to Krome Avenue (S.W. 177th Ave.). Cross Krome to Redland Road (S.W. 187th Ave.). Turn left to Coconut Palm Drive (S.W. 248th St.). You are at
45 the **Redland Fruit & Spice Park,** a Dade County treasure since 1944, when it was established as a 20-acre showcase of tropical fruits and vegetables. More than 500 varieties of exotic fruits, herbs, spices, and nuts from throughout the world grow here, including poisonous plants. There are 50 varieties of bananas, 40 varieties of grapes, and 100 varieties of citrus. A gourmet and fruit shop offers many varieties of produce, jellies, seeds, aromatic teas, and reference books. Remarkably, admission is free. *24801 S.W. 187th Ave. (Redland Rd.), tel. 305/247–5727. Open daily 10–5. No credit cards.*

Drive east on Coconut Palm Drive (S.W. 248th St.) to Newton Road (S.W. 157th Ave.). Turn right and go south to **Orchid Jungle,** where you can stroll under live-oak trees to see orchids, ferns, bromeliads, and anthuriums, and peer through the windows of an orchid-cloning laboratory. *26715 S.W. 157th Ave., Homestead, tel. 305/247–4824, in FL 800/344–2457, or elsewhere in US 800/327–2832. Open daily 8:30–5:30. Admission: $5 adults, $4 senior citizens, and children 13–17, $1.50 children 6–12.*

Continue south on Newton Road to South Dixie Highway (U.S. 1), and turn left. Almost immediately, you'll find **Coral Castle of Florida** on your right. It was built by Edward Leedskalnin, a Latvian immigrant, between 1920 and 1940. The 3-acre castle has a 9-ton gate a child can open, an accurate working sundial, and a telescope of coral rock aimed at the North Star. *28655 South Dixie Hwy., Homestead, tel. 305/248–6344. Open daily 9–9. Admission: $7.25 adults, $4.50 children 6–12. MC, V.*

To return to downtown Miami after leaving Coral Castle, take South Dixie Highway to Biscayne Drive (S.W. 288th St.) and go east to the turnpike. Take the turnpike back to the Don Shula Expressway (Rte. 874), which leads to the Palmetto Expressway (Rte. 826), which leads in turn to the Dolphin Expressway (Rte. 836).

Miami for Free

Concerts **PACE** (Performing Arts for Community and Education, tel. 305/681–1470) supports free concerts in parks and cultural and religious institutions throughout the Greater Miami area.

University of Miami School of Music (tel. 305/284–6477) offers many free concerts at the Coral Gables campus.

Museums Some museums are free all the time. Others have donation days, when you may pay as much or as little as you wish. *(See* Exploring for free-admission policies at major museums.)

Views Ride an elevator to the 18th floor of the new Metro-Dade Center to enjoy spectacular views east to Miami Beach and Biscayne Bay and west to the Orange Bowl and Miami International Airport. *Open weekdays 8–5* (*see* Exploring Downtown Miami, above).

What to See and Do with Children

Greater Miami is a family-oriented vacation destination. Most of the major hotels can provide access to baby-sitting for young children. Although the area lacks major theme parks, families stay occupied with visits to the beach, zoo, and museums. Activities for teenagers are most prevalent on the beaches during spring break but occur throughout the year.

Family Activities

Dade County Youth Fair and Exposition. For 18 days at the end of March each year, Greater Miami's only amusement park comes to life at the Dade County Youth Fair at the 260-acre Youth Fair site surrounded by Tamiami Park. The fairgrounds features a mile-long midway with over 80 amusement and thrill rides. The world's largest youth fair displays 50,000 student exhibits in 30 categories, including science projects and farm animals and equipment. Professional entertainers perform daily on seven stages. If you buy something at a local Publix supermarket, you'll get a gate pass good for free admission on Thursdays. *S.W. 11th Ave. at Coral Way (24th St.), Miami, tel. 305/223–7060. Open weekdays 4–11, weekends, 10 AM–11 PM. Admission: $4 adults, $3 children 6–12.*

Shopping

Except in the heart of the Everglades, visitors to the Greater Miami area are never more than 15 minutes away from a major shopping area. Downtown Miami long ago ceased to be the community's central shopping hub. Today Dade County has more than a dozen major malls, an international free zone, and hundreds of miles of commercial streets lined with storefronts and small neighborhood shopping centers. Many of these local shopping areas have an ethnic flavor, catering primarily to one of Greater Miami's immigrant cultures.

In the Latin neighborhoods, children's stores sell *vestidos* (party dresses) made of organza and lace. Men's stores sell the *guayabera*, a pleated, embroidered shirt that replaces the tie and jacket in much of the tropics. Traditional bridal shops display formal dresses that Latin families buy or rent for a daughter's *quince*, a lavish 15th-birthday celebration.

No standard store hours exist in Greater Miami. Phone ahead. When you shop, expect to pay Florida's 6% sales tax unless you have the store ship your goods out of Florida.

Shopping Districts

Fashion District

Greater Miami is the fashion marketplace for the southeastern United States, the Caribbean, and Latin America. Many of the 500 garment manufacturers in Miami and Hialeah sell their clothing locally, in more than 30 factory outlets and discount fashion stores in the Miami Fashion District, east of I-95 along 5th Avenue from 29th Street to 25th Street. Most stores in the district are open 9–5 Monday–Saturday and accept credit cards.

Miami Free Zone

The Miami Free Zone (MFZ) is an international wholesale trade center where the U.S. Customs Service supervises the exhibition and sales space. You can buy goods duty-free for export or pay duty on goods released for domestic use. More than 140 companies sell products from 75 countries, including aviation equipment, chemicals, clothing, computers, cosmetics, electronics, liquor, and perfumes. The 51-acre MFZ is five minutes west of Miami International Airport off the Dolphin Expressway (Rte. 836), and about 20 minutes from the Port of Miami. *Miami Free Zone, 2305 N.W. 107th Ave., tel. 305/591–4300. Open weekdays 9–5.*

Cauley Square A tearoom and craft, antiques, and clothing shops now occupy this complex of clapboard, coral-rock, and stucco buildings erected 1907–20 for railroad workers who built and maintained the line to Key West. Turn right off U.S. 1 at S.W. 224th Street. *22400 Old Dixie Hwy., Goulds, tel. 305/258–3543. Open Mon.–Sat. 10–4:30, Sun. from Thanksgiving to Christmas Eve 12–5.*

Books Greater Miami's best English-language bookstore, **Books & Books, Inc.,** specializes in books on the arts, architecture, Floridiana, and contemporary and classical literature. Collectors enjoy browsing through the rare-book room upstairs, which doubles as a photography gallery. Frequent poetry readings and book signings. *296 Aragon Ave., Coral Gables, tel. 305/442–4408, and 933 Lincoln Rd. (Sterling Bldg.), Miami Beach, tel. 305/532–3222. Coral Gables store open weekdays 10–8, Sat. 10–7, Sun. noon–5. Miami Beach store open Mon.–Thurs. 10–9, Fri. and Sat. 10–midnight, sun. noon–5. AE, MC, V.*

Children's Books and Toys The friendly staff at **A Likely Story** will help you choose books and educational toys that are appropriate to your child's interests and stage of development. *5740 Sunset Dr., South Miami, tel. 305/667–3730. Open Mon.–Sat. 10–5. MC, V.*

Wine The largest retail collection of fine wines in Florida is at **Foremost Sunset Corners,** home of the Miami chapter of **Les Amis du Vin.** Catalog available. *8701 Sunset Dr., Miami 33173, tel. 305/271–8492. Open Mon.–Sat. 8 AM–9:45 PM. MC, V.*

Beaches

Miami Beach From Haulover Cut to Government Cut, a broad sandy beach extends for 10 continuous miles. Amazingly, it's a man-made beach—a marvel of modern engineering to repair the ravages of nature.

Along this stretch, erosion had all but eliminated the beach by the mid-1970s. Waves threatened to undermine the seawalls of hotels and apartment towers. From 1977 to 1981, the U.S. Army Corps of Engineers spent $51.5 million to pump tons of sand from offshore, restoring the beach to a 300-foot width. Between 21st and 46th streets, Miami Beach built boardwalks and protective walk-overs atop a sand dune landscaped with sea oats, sea grape, and other native plants whose roots keep the sand from blowing away.

The new beach lures residents and visitors alike to swim and stroll. More than 7 million people visit the 7.1 miles of beaches within the Miami Beach city limits annually. The other 2.9 miles are in Surfside and Bal Harbour. Here's a guide to where kindred spirits gather:

The best windsurfing on Miami Beach occurs at First Street, just north of the Government Cut jetty, and at 21st Street. You can also windsurf at Penrod's windsurfing area in Lummus Park at 10th Street and in the vicinity of 3rd, 14th, and 21st streets. Lifeguards discourage windsurfing from 79th Street to 87th Street.

From 1st Street to 14th Street, senior citizens predominate early in the day. Later, a younger crowd appears, including family groups who flock to the new children's play areas in Lummus Park, between Ocean Drive and the beach at 5th and 14th streets.

The beaches opposite the Art Deco District, between 6th Street and 21st Street, attract a diverse clientele of locals and tourists from Europe and Asia. In this area, in an effort to satisfy foreign visitors, city officials don't enforce the law against female bathers going topless as long as everyone on the beach behaves with decorum. Topless bathing also occurs from 35th to 42nd streets. Gays tend to gather at 21st Street.

University of Miami students like the stretch of beach along Millionaires' Row, around 46th Street, where the big hotels have outdoor concession stands on the beach.

If you like a quiet beach experience, go to 35th, 53rd, or 64th streets. Tired young professionals there seek solitude to read a book. Paradoxically, young mothers like to bring their children to these beaches. The two groups coexist nicely.

French-Canadians frequent the 72nd Street beach.

High-school groups gather at 1st, 10th, 14th, and 85th streets for pickup games of volleyball and football.

During the winter, the wealthy condominium crowd clusters on the beach from 96th Street to 103rd Street in Bal Harbour.

City of Miami Beach beaches are open daily with lifeguards, winter 8–5, summer 9–6. Bal Harbour and Surfside have no lifeguards, beaches open daily 24 hours. Beaches free in all three communities; metered parking nearby.

County Park Beaches Metropolitan Dade County operates beaches at several of its major parks. Each county park operates on its own schedule that varies from day to day and season to season. Phone the park you want to visit for current hours and information on special events.

Crandon Park. Atlantic Ocean beach, popular with young Hispanics and with family groups of all ethnic backgrounds. *4000 Crandon Park Blvd., Key Biscayne, tel. 305/361–5421. Open daily 8–sunset. Admission: $2 per car.*

Haulover Beach Park. Atlantic Ocean beach. A good place to be alone. Lightly used compared to other public beaches, except on weekends and in the peak tourist season, when it attracts a diverse crowd. *10800 Collins Ave., Miami, tel. 305/947–3525. Open daily 7 AM–10 PM. Admission: $2 per car.*

Cape Florida **Bill Baggs Cape Florida State Recreation Area** (*see* Exploring Virginia Key and Key Biscayne, above).

Sports and Outdoor Activities

Miami's subtropical climate is paradise for active people, a place where refugees from the frozen north can enjoy warm-weather outdoor sports, such as boating, swimming, and golf, all year long. During Miami's hot, humid summers, people avoid the sun's strongest rays by playing early or late in the day. We've listed below some of the most popular individual and group sports activities.

Spa The **Doral Saturnia International Spa Resort** opened in 1987 on the grounds of the Doral Resort and Country Club. Formal Italian gardens contain the spa pool and a special waterfall under which guests can enjoy natural hydromassage from the gentle pounding of falling water. The spa's 100-foot-high atrium accommodates a 5,000-pound bronze staircase railing created in 1920 by French architect Alexandre Gustave Eiffel and fabricated by artist Edgar Brandt for Paris's Bon Marché department store. The spa combines mud baths and other European pampering techniques with state-of-the-art American fitness and exercise programs. A one-day sampler is available. *8755 N.W. 36th St., Miami 33178, tel. 305/593–6030. 48 suites. Facilities: 4 exercise studios (2 with spring-loaded floors), 2 outdoor heated swimming pools, indoor heated pool, David fitness equipment, beauty salon, 2 restaurants. AE, CB, DC, MC, V.*

Water Sports
Marinas

Listed below are the major marinas in Greater Miami. The dock masters at these marinas can provide information on other marine services you may need. Also ask the dock masters for *Teall's Tides and Guides, Miami-Dade County*, and other local nautical publications.

The U.S. Customs Service requires boats of less than five tons that enter the country along Florida's Atlantic Coast south of Sebastian Inlet to report to designated marinas and call U.S. Customs on a direct phone line. The phones, located outside marina buildings, are accessible 24 hours a day. U.S. Customs phones in Greater Miami are at Haulover Marina and Watson Island Marina (both listed below).

Dinner Key Marina. Operated by City of Miami. Facilities include dockage with space for transients and a boat ramp. *3400 Pan American Dr., Coconut Grove, tel. 305/579–6980. Open daily 7 AM–11 PM.*

Haulover Park Marina. Operated by county lessee. Facilities include a bait-and-tackle shop, marine gas station, and boat launch. *10800 Collins Ave., Miami Beach, tel. 305/944–9647. Open weekdays 7 AM–5 PM, weekends 7 AM–6 PM.*

Watson Island Marina. City of Miami marina. Facilities include bait and tackle, boat ramp, and fuel. When the marina is busy, it stays open until all boaters are helped. *1050 MacArthur Causeway, Miami, tel. 305/371–2378. Open Mon.–Thurs. 8 AM–7:30 PM, Fri.–Sun. 7 AM–10 PM.*

Sailing Dinner Key and the Coconut Grove waterfront remain the center of sailing in Greater Miami, although sailboat moorings and rentals are located along other parts of the bay and up the Miami River.

Windsurfing **Penrod's.** You can rent Hobie Cats, Windsurfers, and surfboards. *1001 Ocean Dr., Miami Beach, tel. 305/538–1111. Open daily 10–sunset.*

Sailboards Miami. (tel. 305/361–7245).

Diving Summer diving conditions in greater Miami equal or exceed the best of those in the Caribbean. Winter diving can be adversely affected when cold fronts come through. Dive-boat schedules vary with the season and with local weather conditions.

Fowey, Triumph, Long, and Emerald Reefs all are shallow 10–15-foot dives that are good for snorkelers and beginning divers. These reefs are on the edge of the continental shelf, a quarter of a mile from depths greater than 100 feet. You can also paddle around the tangled prop roots of the mangrove trees that line Florida's coastline, peering at the fish, crabs, and other onshore creatures that hide there.

Dive Boats and Instruction. Look for instructors who are affiliated with PADI (Professional Association of Dive Instructors) or NAUI (National Association of Underwater Instructors).

Divers Paradise Corp (4000 Crandon Blvd., Key Biscayne, tel. 305/361–DIVE). Complete dive shop and diving charter service, including equipment rental and scuba instruction. PADI affiliation.

Omega Diving International. Private instruction throughout Greater Miami. Equipment consultation and specialty courses, including instructor training and underwater photography. PADI affiliation. *8420 S.W. 133 Ave., Miami, tel. 305/385–0779 or 800/255–1966. Open daily 8–6.*

Diver's Dream. This all-purpose dive shop is located right at the Miami Beach marina. *1290 5th St., Miami Beach 33139, tel. 305/534–7710. Open Mon.–Sat. 10 AM–7 PM. Beach store open weekdays 9 AM–7 PM, weekends 7 AM–6 PM.*

Tennis Greater Miami has more than 60 private and public tennis centers, of which 11 are open to the public. All public tennis courts charge nonresidents an hourly fee.

Florida Tennis Association (801 N.E. 167th St., Suite 301, North Miami Beach 33162, tel. 305/652–2866). Contact for amateur tournament information.

Coral Gables **Biltmore Tennis Center.** Ten well-maintained hard courts. Site of annual Orange Bowl Junior International Tennis Tournament for children 18 and under in December. *1150 Anastasia Ave., tel. 305/442–6565. Open weekdays 8 AM–10 PM, weekends 8–8. Nonresident day rate $4.30, night rate $5 per person per hour.*

Miami Beach **Flamingo Tennis Center.** Has 20 well-maintained clay courts. Site of the Rolex-Orange Bowl Junior International Tennis Tournament for teenagers 18 and under. *1000 12th St., tel. 305/673–7761. Open weekdays 8 AM–9 PM, weekends 8–6. Cost: day $2.12, night $2.65 per person per hour.*

Metropolitan Dade County **International Tennis Center.** Has 17 Laykold Cushion Plus hard courts, four lighted. Reservations necessary for night play. Closed to public play for about two weeks before and after the annual Lipton International Players Championships in March. *7300 Crandon Blvd., Key Biscayne, tel. 305/361–8633. Open daily 8 AM–10 PM. Cost: weekdays $3, weeknights $4, weekend days $4, weekend nights $5 per person per hour. Rental rackets $5 per hour.*

Spectator Sports

Greater Miami offers a broad variety of spectator sports events, including such popular pastimes as football and baseball, and more specialized events, such as boat racing and rugby. Major stadium and arena diagrams appear in the Community Interest Pages of the telephone directory. However, the community lacks a central clearinghouse for sports information and ticket sales.

You can find daily listings of local sports events on page 3 of *The Miami Herald* sports section. The weekend section on Friday carries detailed schedules and coverage of spectator sports. The *Herald* provides a recorded "sports line" message with a brief selection of major sports scores (tel. 305/376–3505).

Orange Bowl Festival. The activities of the annual Orange Bowl and Junior Orange Festival take place early November-late February. Best-known for its **King Orange Jamboree Parade** and the **Federal Express/Orange Bowl Football Classic,** the festival also includes two tennis tournaments: the **Rolex-Orange Bowl International Tennis Championships** for top amateur national and international tennis players 16 and under, and an international tournament for players 14 and under.

Other Orange Bowl sports events include a regatta series for university and professional sailors, a 5-km run in Coral Gables, the **Orange Bowl 10-km Race** on the 6.2-mile Grand Prix course, the annual **American Savings/Orange Bowl Marathon,** which draws over 2,500 runners, and soccer games. *For tickets and a calendar of events: Tickets, Orange Bowl Committee, Box 350748, Miami 33135, tel. 305/642–5211.*

The **Junior Orange Bowl Festival** takes place during November and December, featuring 19 athletic events, including bowling and a sports competition for physically disabled athletes, as well as creative arts competitions. *Junior Orange Bowl Committee, 1390 S. Dixie Hwy., Coral Gables 33146, tel. 305/662–1210.*

Auto Racing

Hialeah Speedway. The Greater Miami area's only independent raceway holds stock-car races on a ⅓-mile asphalt speedway in a 5,000-seat stadium. Five divisions of stock cars run weekly. The Marion Edwards, Jr., Memorial Race for late-model stock cars is in November. Located on U.S. 27, ¼ mile east of Palmetto Expressway (Rte. 826). *3300 W. Okeechobee Rd., Hialeah, tel. 305/821–6644. Open every Sat. late Jan.–early Dec. Gates open 6 PM, racing 7:30–11. Admission: $10 adults, $1 children, under 12 free.*

Grand Prix of Miami. Held in February for the Camel GT Championship on a 1.9-mile, E-shape track in downtown Miami, south of MacArthur Causeway and east of Biscayne Boulevard. Drivers race three hours; the winner completes the most laps. Sanctioned by International Motor Sports Association (IMSA). *Miami Motor Sports, Inc., 7254 S.W. 48th St., Miami 33155, tel. 305/662–5660. Tickets available from Miami Motor Sports, Inc., tel. 305/665–RACE or 800/233–RACE or Ticketmaster* (*see* Important Addresses and Numbers, above).

Baseball

University of Miami Hurricanes. The baseball Hurricanes play home games in the 5,000-seat Mark Light Stadium, at 1 Hurricane Drive on UM's Coral Gables campus. The Hurricanes were the 1982 and 1985 NCAA baseball champions and are perennial contenders. *University of Miami Athletic Department, Box 248167, Coral Gables 33124, tel. 305/284–2655 or 800/GO-CANES. Open weekdays 8–6, Sat. 10–2. Season: 45 home games Feb.–May, day games 2 PM, night games 7:30. AE, MC, V.*

Basketball **Miami Heat.** Third 41 home game season November–May for Miami's National Basketball Association team. *Tickets: Miami Arena, Miami 33136–4102, tel. 305/577–HEAT or Ticketmaster (see* Important Addresses and Numbers, above). **University of Miami Hurricanes.** Games are held in the Miami Arena. *University of Miami Athletic Department, Box 248167, Coral Gables 33124, tel. 305/284–2655, 800/GO-CANES. Open weekdays 8–6, Sat. 10–2. Game time 7:30. AE, MC, V.*

Dog Racing The Biscayne Kennel Club, the Flagler Dog Track in Greater Miami, and Hollywood Greyhound Park in Fort Lauderdale divide the annual racing calendar. Check with the individual tracks for dates. **Biscayne Kennel Club.** Greyhounds chase a mechanical rabbit around illuminated fountains in the track's infield. Near I-95 at N.W. 115th Street. *320 N.W. 115th St., Miami Shores, tel. 305/754–3484. Season: May–June and Sept.–Oct. Admission: table seats $1, grandstand $1, clubhouse $2. Parking 50¢–$2.*

Flagler Dog Track. Inner-city track in the middle of Little Havana, five minutes east of Miami International Airport off Dolphin Expressway (Rte. 836) and Douglas Road (N.W. 37th Ave.). *401 N.W. 38th Ct., Miami, tel. 305/649–3000. Open July–Sept. and late Oct.–Christmas. Dates may fluctuate; call ahead for exact times. General admission $1, clubhouse $2, parking 50¢–$2.*

Football **Miami Dolphins.** President Tim Robbie took over for his dad in late 1989 after the curmudgeonly Joe Robbie passed away. Not, however, before he gave Miami a state-of-the-art football arena—Joe Robbie Stadium—that he named for himself. If major league baseball comes to Miami, this is where it will be played.

JRS, as the stadium is called, has 73,000 seats and a grass playing-field surface with built-in drainage under the sod to carry off rainwater. It's on a 160-acre site, 16 miles northwest of downtown Miami, one mile south of the Dade-Broward county line, accessible from I-95 and Florida's Turnpike. On game days, the Metro-Dade Transit Authority runs buses to the stadium. Bus information, tel. 305/638–6700.

Dolphins tickets: *Miami Dolphins, Joe Robbie Stadium, 2269 N.W. 199th St., Miami 33056, tel. 305/620–2578. Open weekdays 10–6. Also available through Ticketmaster (*see *Important Addresses and Numbers, above).*

University of Miami Hurricanes. The Hurricanes, winners of the 1987 and 1989 national college football championship, play home games in the Orange Bowl, near the Dolphin Expressway (Rte. 836) just west of downtown Miami. *1400 N.W. 4th St., tel. 305/579–6971. Game time 4 PM (unless changed for the convenience of the TV networks). Schedule and tickets: University of Miami Athletic Department, Box 248167, Coral Gables 33124, tel. 305/284–2655 or 800/GO-CANES. Open weekdays 8–6, Sat. 10–2.*

Horse Racing **Calder Race Course.** Opened in 1971, Calder is Florida's largest glass-enclosed, air-conditioned sports facility. This means that Calder actually has two racing seasons, one in fall or winter, another in spring or summer. Contact the track for this year's dates. In April, Calder holds the Tropical Park Derby for three-year-olds, the last major race in Florida before the Kentucky Derby. On the Dade-Broward county line near I-95 and the Hallandale Beach Boulevard exit., ¾ mile from Joe Robbie Stadium. *21001 N.W. 27th Ave., Miami, tel. 305/625–1311. Gates open 11 AM, post time 1 PM, races end about 5:30. General admission $2, clubhouse $4, programs 50¢, parking $1–$3.*

Hialeah Park. A superb setting for Thoroughbred racing, Hialeah's 228 acres of meticulously landscaped grounds surround paddocks and a clubhouse built in a classic French-Mediterranean style. Since it opened in 1925, Hialeah Park has survived hurricanes, but is slowly succumbing to changing population trends which have seen the racetrack crowd steadily move north and east, away from Hialeah. The 1989 season was dismal for this grand old park, making uncertain the future of racing here. Typically during the racing season, the gates open early Sunday mornings for breakfast at Hialeah Park. Admission is free. You can watch the horses work out, explore Hialeah's gardens, munch on breakfast fare of tolerable palatability, and admire the park's breeding flock of 600 Cuban flamingos.

When racing is not in session, Hialeah Park opens daily for free tours 10–4:30. Metrorail's Hialeah Station is on the grounds of Hialeah Park. *2200 E. 4th Ave., Hialeah, tel. 305/885–8000. Admission: grandstand $1, clubhouse $2, parking $1.50–$4 during racing season.*

Jai Alai **Miami Jai-Alai Fronton.** This game, invented in the Basque region of northern Spain, is the world's fastest. Jai alai balls, called *pelotas*, have been clocked at speeds exceeding 170 mph. The game is played in a 176-foot-long court called a *fronton*. Players climb the walls to catch the ball in a *cesta*—a woven basket—with an attached glove. You bet on a team to win or on the order in which teams will finish. Built in 1926, Miami Jai-Alai is the oldest fronton in America. Each evening, it presents 13 games—14 on Friday and Saturday—some singles, some doubles. Located a mile east of Miami International Airport. *3500 N.W. 37th Ave., Miami, tel. 305/633–6400. Open nightly late Nov.–early Sept. except Sun. and Tues., 7:10–midnight. Matinees Mon., Wed., and Sat. noon–5. Admission: $1, clubhouse $5. Dinner available.*

Rugby Without a large corporate organization, a regular office staff, or even a permanent home field, local rugby players have organized themselves into two regular teams. Although one team is called the *University of Miami Rugby Team*, it is not part of the university. The other is the *Miami Tridents*. Weekly throughout the year, a local rugby team plays a visiting team from a 16-team Florida league, from the Caribbean, or from a foreign ship in port. Both local teams participate each August in an annual tournament. Games Saturday 2 PM. *Holy Rosary Church, 9500 S.W. 184th St., Perrine. Spectators welcome. Free. For game information, call Bruce Swidarski, 8550 S.W. 126th Terr., Miami 33156, tel. 305/251–3305 (nights).*

Soccer **Miami Sharks.** This American Soccer League team played its first season in spring 1988. The Sharks' 1990 season includes at least 10 regular-season home games and five international exhibition games, all in the stadium at Milander Park (4800 Palm Ave., Hialeah). *Tickets: 240 E. 1st Ave., Suite 208, Hialeah 33010, tel. 305/888–0838 or Ticketmaster* (*see* Important Addresses and Numbers, above).

Tennis **Lipton International Players Championship (LIPC).** Presented by Mitsubishi Electronics, this 10-day spring tournament at the 64-acre International Tennis Center of Key Biscayne is the fourth largest in the world in terms of attendance. The two main professional tennis organizations—Association of Tennis Professionals and Women's International Tennis Association—helped create this tournament and own part of it. *7300 Crandon Blvd., Key Biscayne, tel. for tickets 305/361–5252 or Ticketmaster (see* Important Addresses and Numbers, above).

Dining

by Rosalie Leposky

You can eat your way around the world in Greater Miami, enjoying just about any kind of cuisine imaginable in every price category. The rich mix of nationalities here encourages individual restaurateurs and chefs to retain their culinary roots. Thus, Miami offers not just Latin fare but dishes distinctive to Spain, Cuba, Nicaragua, and other Hispanic countries; not just Oriental fare but specialties of China, India, Thailand, Vietnam, and other Asian cultures.

And don't neglect American fare just because it's not "foreign." Miami today is a center for innovation in regional cuisine and in combinations reflecting the diversity of domestic climates and cultures.

The most highly recommended restaurants in each price category are indicated by a star ★.

Category	Cost*
Very Expensive	over $55
Expensive	$35–$55
Moderate	$15–$35
Inexpensive	under $15

**per person, excluding drinks, service, and 6% sales tax*

The following credit card abbreviations are used: AE, American Express; CB, Carte Blanche; DC, Diners Club; MC, MasterCard; V, Visa.

American
Coral Gables

Aragon Cafe. If George Merrick, the founder of Coral Gables, entered the bar of Aragon Cafe, he would see on display some of his mother's hand-painted china and silver and portraits of his sisters and wife on the dining room walls. In this new restaurant designed to look old and classy, subdued lighting emanates from gaslight-style chandeliers and etched-glass wall lights. The menu emphasizes fresh fish and reflects Merrick's desire to recreate the best of the Mediterranean in a Florida setting. Specialties include seafood minestrone made with shrimp, scallops, clams, new potatoes, carrots, and kidney and green beans; grilled goat cheese in banana leaves; grilled Florida dolphin with native starfruit sauce; and tuna steak au poivre in a mushroom-based sauce of peppercorns and cream. Dessert offerings include a white chocolate terrine with pistachio sauce. *180 Aragon Ave. in the Colonnade Hotel, Coral Gables 33134, tel. 305/448–9966. Jacket required. Reservations advised. No lunch Sat., closed Sun. Free valet parking. AE, DC, MC, V. Expensive.*

Downtown Miami ★ **The Pavillon Grill.** By day a private club, the Pavillon Grill becomes a gourmet restaurant at night. The mahogany, jade marble, and leather appointments of its salon and dining room exude the conservative classiness of an English private club. A harpist plays. The attentive staff serves regional American fare, including items that are low in calories, cholesterol, and sodium for diners who are on restricted diets. Specialties include marinated confit of duck and red Hawaiian papaya, grilled wild mushrooms, Pacific salmon pillows, cherry smoked lamb chops. The menu changes often. *100 Chopin Plaza, tel. 305/577–1000, ext. 4494 or 4462. Jacket required. Reservations required. Closed Sun. AE, CB, DC, MC, V. Very Expensive.*

Kendall (S.W. Suburb) **Savannah Moon.** Though you drive up to a typical shopping center, Savannah Moon's door leads to the foyer of a Southern mansion, complete with formal staircase. In the second-floor dining room, bentwood chairs, hanging plants, shuttered windows, sheer curtains, and original Audubon engravings suggest a tidewater inn. Evening and late-night entertainment —mellow blues, conservative jazz—makes the place popular with suburban professionals. This restaurant gives a nouvelle-cuisine twist to traditional Low Country coastal fare. Specialties include jambalaya (red rice with Creole sauce, chicken, shrimp, escargot, and Texas sausage); lamb with orange mint sauce; and a dessert cart groaning with delights such as Kirsch-toasted almond cake, and southern bread pudding with nuts and raisins. *13505 South Dixie Hwy., tel. 305/238–8868. Dress: neat but casual. Reservations advised. No lunch weekends. AE, CB, DC, MC, V. Expensive.*

Shorty's Bar-B-Q. Shorty Allen opened his barbecue restaurant in 1951 in a log cabin. Parents bring their teenage children to show them where mom and dad ate on their honeymoon. Huge fans circulate fresh air through the single screened dining room, where you dine family-style at long picnic tables. The walls display an assortment of cowboy hats, horns, saddles, an ox yoke, and heads of boar and caribou. Specialties include barbecued pork ribs, chicken, and pork steak slow cooked over hickory logs and drenched in Shorty's own warm, spicy sauce, and side orders of tangy baked beans with big chunks of pork, corn on the cob, and coleslaw. *9200 South Dixie Hwy., tel. 305/665–5732. A second location opened in 1989 at 5989 South University Dr., Davie, tel. 305/680–9900. Dress: informal. Reservations not accepted. Closed Thanksgiving and Christmas. No credit cards. Inexpensive.*

Miami Beach ★ **The News Cafe.** Owner Mark Soyka, who trained on the cosmopolitan beach scene in Tel Aviv, is right on the money here with quick, friendly waiters and waitresses who don't hurry the guests who are here to shmooze or the intellects who are wrapped up in Tolstoy picked out of the book rack. Open to the salt breeze, looking onto the beach, this is the hippest joint on Ocean Drive. With a little of this, and a little of that—bagels, pâtés, chocolate fondue—come here for a snack, light meal or aperitif. *800 Ocean Dr., tel. 305/538–6397. Dress: casual. No reservations. AE, CB, DC, MC, V. Inexpensive.*

North Miami Beach ★ **Chef Allen's.** In an art-deco world of glass block, neon trim, and fresh flowers, your gaze nonetheless remains riveted on the kitchen. Chef Allen Susser designed it with a picture window, 25 feet wide, so you can watch him create new American masterpieces almost too pretty to eat. Specialties include mesquite-grilled rare tuna with glazed onions and cranberry chutney; and lamb medallions with pine nuts and wilted spinach garnished with goat cheese. Desserts include white-chocolate macadamia nut torte, chocolate pizza, and a sugar junkie's delight—scoops of chocolate, raspberry, caramel, and pistachio ice cream floating in caramel sauce. Fine wines by the glass from a wine bar. *19088 N.E. 29th Ave., tel. 305/935–2900. Dress: informal weekdays, jacket required weekends. Reservations accepted. No lunch weekends. AE, MC, V. Expensive.*

★ **Mark's Place.** Owner/chef Mark Militello cooks *nouvelle* American regional fare in a special oak-burning oven imported from Genoa, behind a display case where you can admire the evening's selections of fish and meat awaiting preparation. The menu changes nightly, based on the availability of fresh ingredients. Typical selections include sea scallops and asparagus sautéed in butter and chardonnay with fresh basil, oregano, and thyme; wild mushrooms (shiitake, tree oyster, chanterelles, angel trumpets, and brown hedgehog) roasted in the oak oven and served with grilled olive and walnut bread; whole yellowtail snapper with oriental ginger, black bean sauce, and a garnish of edible pansies; and cobia filet sautéed in brown butter mixed with orange segments, fresh mint, and bourbon. Desserts include chocolate espresso torte with a hazelnut crust and a warm apple tart with homemade vanilla and caramel sauce. *2286 N.E. 123rd St., North Miami 33181, tel. 305/893–6888. Dress: neat but casual. Reservations advised. Closed Thanksgiving and Christmas. No lunch weekends. AE, DC, MC, V. Very Expensive.*

West Dade

★ **Shula's.** Surrounded by memorabilia of coach Don Shula's perfect 1972 season with the Miami Dolphins, you can drink or dine in this shrine for the NFL-obsessed. The certified black angus beef is almost an afterthought to the icons that include quarterback Earl Morall's rocking chair, assistant coach Howard Schnellenberger's pipe, the autographed playbook from President Nixon to coach Shula. The Sports Ticker fills in for any gaps in conversation, likewise in season the weekly stat sheets of all NFL games. Ladies room mirrors the Orange Bowl locker room where the magic took place, with pictures of the beefy perfect-season squad. Otherwise it's steaks, prime rib, and fish (including dolphin) in a woody, fireplace-cheered, and cedar-shingle setting, not to mention it's on the grounds of Miami Lakes. *15400 NW 77th Ave., tel. 305/822–2325. Dress: neat but casual. Reservations advised. AE, CB, DC, MC, V. Moderate–Expensive.*

Chinese
Key Biscayne

Two Dragons. Robert Chow and his staff run this place like a small family restaurant, serving a Chinese cuisine with all ingredients fresh and prepared to order. Specialties include a Cantonese seafood nest (shrimp, scallops, and crabmeat with Chinese vegetables in a nest of crisp noodles), an orange beef Mandarin, and Szechuan eggplant with a spicy garlic-mustard sauce guaranteed to clear the sinuses. Dine in an intimate pagodalike booth behind hanging curtains of wooden beads or at an open table overlooking an outdoor Oriental garden. A Japanese steak house—the "second dragon"—serves Teppanyaki-style cuisine at six cooking tables in a separate room. *Sonesta Beach Hotel, 350 Ocean Dr., tel. 305/361–2021. Dress: neat but casual. Dinner only. Reservations advised. Closed 2 weeks in Sept. AE, CB, DC, MC, V. Moderate.*

Miami Area Dining

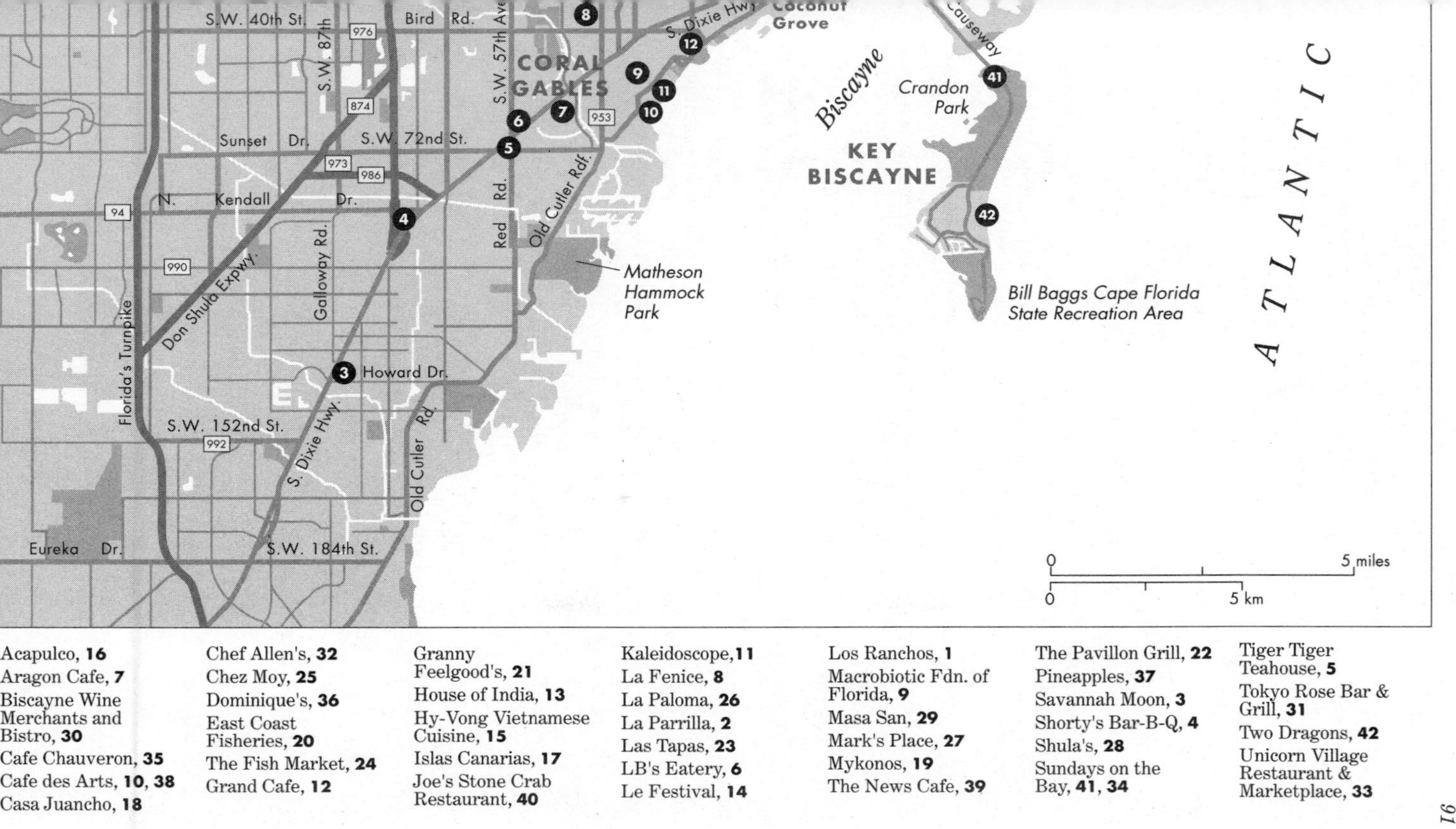
S.W. 40th St.
Bird Rd.
S.W. 87th
S.W. 57th Ave
Coconut Grove
S. Dixie Hwy
CORAL GABLES
Biscayne
Crandon Park
Causeway
KEY BISCAYNE
ATLANTIC
Sunset Dr.
S.W. 72nd St.
N. Kendall Dr.
Red Rd.
Old Cutler Rdf.
Matheson Hammock Park
Bill Baggs Cape Florida State Recreation Area
Galloway Rd.
Don Shula Expwy.
Florida's Turnpike
Howard Dr.
S.W. 152nd St.
S. Dixie Hwy.
Old Cutler Rd.
Eureka Dr.
S.W. 184th St.
976
874
953
973
986
94
990
992
0
5 miles
0
5 km
Acapulco, 16
Aragon Cafe, 7
Biscayne Wine Merchants and Bistro, 30
Cafe Chauveron, 35
Cafe des Arts, 10, 38
Casa Juancho, 18
Chef Allen's, 32
Chez Moy, 25
Dominique's, 36
East Coast Fisheries, 20
The Fish Market, 24
Grand Cafe, 12
Granny Feelgood's, 21
House of India, 13
Hy-Vong Vietnamese Cuisine, 15
Islas Canarias, 17
Joe's Stone Crab Restaurant, 40
Kaleidoscope, 11
La Fenice, 8
La Paloma, 26
La Parrilla, 2
Las Tapas, 23
LB's Eatery, 6
Le Festival, 14
Los Ranchos, 1
Macrobiotic Fdn. of Florida, 9
Masa San, 29
Mark's Place, 27
Mykonos, 19
The News Cafe, 39
The Pavillon Grill, 22
Pineapples, 37
Savannah Moon, 3
Shorty's Bar-B-Q, 4
Shula's, 28
Sundays on the Bay, 41, 34
Tiger Tiger Teahouse, 5
Tokyo Rose Bar & Grill, 31
Two Dragons, 42
Unicorn Village Restaurant & Marketplace, 33

South Miami **Tiger Tiger Teahouse.** Design awards have been bestowed on Tiger Tiger's contemporary Chinese decor, with its embroidered silk panels depicting fierce tigers and its elegant rosewood chairs with jade cushions. Specialties include Peking duck (available without advance notice), lean and succulent beneath crisp orange-glazed skin, wrapped with plum sauce in wheat pancakes; hot, spicy Szechuan beef, marinated in sherry and spices, then stir-fried with Chinese vegetables; honey-garlic chicken; and creamy-smooth litchi ice cream. Unlimited appetizer bar with all entrées; lunch buffet ($4.49) weekdays only, serving ribs, fish, chicken, and salads. *The Bakery Centre, 5785 Sunset Dr., tel. 305/665–5660. Dress: casual. Reservations accepted. Closed for lunch Sun., and on Thanksgiving. AE, CB, DC, MC, V. Inexpensive–Moderate.*

Continental

Coconut Grove

★ **Grand Cafe.** Understated elegance at all hours is the Grand Cafe's hallmark—a bilevel room with pink tablecloths and floral bouquets, sunbathed by day, dim and intimate after dark. Japanese-born, French-trained executive chef Katsuo Sugiura creates "international" cuisine, combining ingredients from all over the world in pleasing presentations that intrigue the palate. Specialties include black linguini (colored with squid ink); fresh smoked salmon; a superbly rich she-crab soup with roe, sherry, and cayenne pepper; "boned" Maine lobster presented in the shape of a lobster, with artichokes and a cream sauce of vermouth and saffron. Dessert specialties include a white-chocolate and pistachio mousse with blackberry sauce and Beaujolais essence. The menu changes frequently. *2669 S. Bayshore Dr., tel. 305/858–9600. Jacket preferred. Reservations advised. AE, DC, MC, V. Very Expensive.*

Kaleidoscope Restaurant. The tropical ambience here extends to a choice of indoor or outdoor seating—all in air-conditioned comfort, because fans blow cold air around a glass-roofed terrace overlooking a landscaped courtyard. Specialties include veal Oscar, and the chef's own fresh apple strudel. *3112 Commodore Plaza, tel. 305/446–5010. Dress: casual. Reservations advised. AE, CB, DC, MC, V. Moderate.*

North Miami **Biscayne Wine Merchants and Bistro.** In this 35-seat retail beer and wine store with a deli counter, strangers often become friends while sharing tables and sampling the merchandise. Owners Jan Sitko and Esther Flores stock over 300 wines (sold by the glass or bottle) and over 70 brands of beer. The menu changes daily but always includes bean and cream soups. Typical fare may include chicken Crustaces (a chicken breast stuffed with leeks, dill, and crab with a light dill sauce) and daily fresh fish specials such as amberjack, dolphin, shark, snapper, swordtail, and wahoo. Sitko and Flores like to create new dishes with fresh herbs, spices, fruits, and vegetables. One favorite is a tangy-sweet sauce with jalapeno and citrus. *12953 Biscayne Blvd., North Miami, tel. 305/899–1997. Dress: informal. No reservations. Closed Thanksgiving, Christmas, and New Year's Day, sometimes other holidays. No lunch Sun. AE, MC, V. Moderate.*

La Paloma. This fine Swiss Continental restaurant offers a total sensory experience: fine food, impeccable service, and the ambience of an art museum. In sideboards and cases throughout, owners Werner and Maria Staub display ornate European antiques that they have spent decades collecting. The treasures include Bacarrat crystal, Limoges china, Meissen porcelains, and Sevres clocks. The staff speak Spanish,

French, German, Portuguese, or Arabic. Specialties include fresh local fish and seafood; Norwegian salmon Caroline (poached, served on a bed of spinach with hollandaise sauce); Wiener schnitzel; lamb chops à la *diable* (coated with bread crumbs, mustard, garlic, and herbs) passion-fruit sorbet; and kiwi soufflé with raspberry sauce. *10999 Biscayne Blvd., tel. 305/891–0505. Jacket advised. Reservations advised. Closed Mon., July, and part of Aug. AE, MC, V. Expensive.*

Cuban
Little Havana

Islas Canarias. A gathering place for Cuban poets, pop music stars, and media personalities. Wall murals depict a Canary Islands street scene and an indigenous dragon tree *(Dracaena draco)*. The menu includes such Canary Islands dishes as baked lamb, ham hocks with boiled potatoes, and *tortilla Española* (a Spanish omelet with onions and chorizo, a spicy sausage), as well as Cuban standards, including palomilla steak, and fried kingfish. Don't miss the three superb varieties of homemade chips—potato, malanga, and plantain. Islas Canarias has another location in Westchester at Coral Way and S.W. 137th Ave. *285 N.W. Unity Blvd. (N.W. 27th Ave.), tel. 305/649–0440. Dress: informal. No reservations. Open Christmas Eve and New Year's Eve to 6 PM. No credit cards. Inexpensive.*

Family Style
Coral Gables

LB's Eatery. Town and gown meet at this sprout-laden haven a half-block from the University of Miami's baseball stadium. Kitschy food-related posters plaster the walls. Relaxed atmosphere, low prices, no waiters. You order at the counter and pick up your food when called. Vegetarians thrive on LB's salads and daily meatless entrées, such as lasagna and moussaka. Famous for Saturday night lobster. (If you plan to come after 8, call ahead to reserve a lobster.) Other specialties include barbecued baby-back ribs, lime chicken, croissant sandwiches, and carrot cake. *5813 Ponce de León Blvd., tel. 305/661–7091. Dress: informal. No reservations. Closed Sun. No credit cards. Inexpensive.*

French
Coral Gables

Le Festival. The modest canopied entrance to this classical French restaurant understates the elegance within. Decor includes etched-glass filigree mirrors and light pink walls. Specialties include appetizers of salmon mousse, baked oysters with garlic butter, and lobster in champagne sauce en croute; rack of lamb (for two), and medallions of veal with two sauces—a pungent, creamy lime sauce and a dark port-wine sauce with mushrooms. Entrées come with real french-fried potatoes. Don't pass up dessert here; the mousses and soufflés are positively decadent. *2120 Salzedo St., tel. 305/442–8545. Dress: neat but casual. Reservations required for dinner, and for lunch parties of 5 or more. Lunch weekdays, closed Sat. noon, all day Sun., and Sept.–Oct. AE, MC, V. Expensive.*

Miami Beach
★

Cafe Chauveron. André Chauveron traces his cafe's roots to Cafe Chambord, which his father began in New York in 1935 on the block where the Citicorp Building now stands. A Florida institution since 1972, Cafe Chauveron serves classical French cuisine in rooms decorated with original paintings and wood paneling. The atmosphere is hushed, the service superb. Mounted pheasants guard the wine cabinet. Specialties include wild duck and pheasant pâté, filet of sole *bonne femme*, frogs' legs Provençale, sautéed veal chop Bercy (white wine and shallots) with braised endive, and dessert soufflés flambéed at tableside. *9561 E. Bay Harbor Dr., tel. 305/866–8779. Jacket* *required. Reservations advised. Closed Aug.–Sept. AE, CB, DC, MC, V. Very Expensive.*

Cafe des Arts. Enjoy French-provincial cuisine in an art-deco setting amid tropical plants, antiques, and an art gallery that changes every six to eight weeks. Indoor and outdoor seating. Specialties include smoked-salmon pasta with artichokes, mushrooms, and brie sauce; roast duck in grape sauce; and quail salad. *918 Ocean Dr., tel. 305/534–6267. In 1989, a second location was opened at 3138 Commodore Plaza, Coconut Grove, tel. 305/446–3634. Dress: casual. Reservations advised. AE, CB, DC, MC, V. No lunch, closed Mon. and 2 weeks in Aug. Moderate.*

★ **Dominique's.** Woodwork and mirrors from a Vanderbilt home and other demolished New York mansions create an intimate setting for a unique nouvelle-cuisine dining experience. Specialties include exotic appetizers, such as buffalo sausage, sautéed alligator tail, and rattlesnake-meat salad; rack of lamb (which accounts for 35% of the restaurant's total sales) and fresh seafood; and an extensive wine list. The restaurant also serves brunch on Sunday. *Alexander Hotel, 5225 Collins Ave., tel. 305/865–6500. Jacket required. Reservations advised. AE, CB, DC, MC, V. Very Expensive.*

Greek
Southwest Miami

Mykonos. A family restaurant serving typical Greek fare since 1974 in a Spartan setting—a single 74-seat room adorned with Greek travel posters. Specialties include gyro; moussaka; marinated lamb and chicken; calamari (squid) and octopus sautéed in wine and onions; and sumptuous Greek salads thick with feta cheese and briny olives. *1201 Coral Way, tel. 305/856–3140. Dress: informal. Reservations accepted for dinner. AE. Open Sun. at 5 PM. Closed Christmas Eve, New Year's Eve, New Year's Day. Belly dancing Sat. evening. Inexpensive.*

Haitian
Little Haiti

Chez Moy. Seating is outside on a shaded patio or in a pleasant room with oak tables and high-backed chairs. Specialties include *grillot* (pork boiled, then fried with spices); fried or boiled fish; stewed goat; and conch with garlic and hot pepper. Try a tropical fruit drink such as sweet sop (also called *anon* or *cachiman)* or sour sop (also called *guanabana* or *corrosol)* blended with milk and sugar, and sweet potato pie for dessert. *1 N.W. 54th St., tel. 305/756–7540. Dress: casual. No reservations. No smoking. MC, V. Inexpensive.*

Indian
Coral Gables
★

House of India. The haunting strains of sitar music lull diners at this popular spot in Coral Gables. Vegetarian and nonvegetarian specialties include hot coconut soup with cardamom, milk, rose water, and sugar; curried goat; and authentic chicken tandoori, cooked in a clay oven. The weekday luncheon buffet is a good bargain. Another location in Fort Lauderdale is at 3060 N. Andrews Ave., tel. 305/566–5666. *22 Merrick Way, tel. 305/444–2348. Dress: casual. Weekend reservations accepted. Closed Sun. lunch, Labor Day, Christmas. AE, MC, V. Moderate.*

Italian
Coral Gables

La Fenice. The restaurant is named for the Venice opera house that rose, phoenixlike, from the ashes of an earlier structure after an 1831 fire; and it is decorated with paintings of St. Mark's Square in Venice, ornate mahogany chairs from Padua, a four-tier fountain, and stained-glass windows. Specialties include rigatoni in creamy vodka sauce topped with caviar; veal scallopini sautéed with Gorgonzola cheese, cream sauce, and mushrooms; and poached salmon with a sauce of sweet red peppers pureed with lemon juice. *2728 Ponce de León Blvd., tel. 305/445–6603. Dress: neat but casual. Reservations advised. AE, MC, V. Lunch weekdays, dinner nightly. Closed Christmas Day. Moderate.*

Japanese-American
North Miami

Tokyo Rose Bar & Grill. Starkly modern decor—neon lights against a minimalist black-and-white backdrop—complements the menu concept of contemporary Japanese fare. While nibbling on boiled soybeans, you choose from an extensive à la carte menu or a selection of daily Japanese- and American-style specials. Typical offerings include California *maki*, a *nori* (dried seaweed) roll with crab, avocado, and cucumber served with *wasabi* (horseradish) and ginger; Kamikaze salad, a conch salad with cucumber and a spicy Korean-style hot pepper dressing; Ginza strip, rare sirloin marinated in vinegar and sesame; Kaizoku, a pasta dish with calamari, scallops, and shrimp in white wine sauce; Tokyo's salmon, prepared with Japanese mayo, flying fish eggs *(masago)*, onions, and lemon butter; and fresh Japanese desserts with coconut-flour crust. *13400 Biscayne Blvd., North Miami 33181, tel. 305/945–7782. Dress: neat but casual. Reservations advised. No lunch. Live jazz by Kenny Millions Fri. and Sat. AE, MC, V. Moderate.*

Japanese

Masa-San. Owner Masa Yamazaki, a Tokyo native who came to the University of Miami in 1971 to study marketing, opened this traditional Japanese restaurant in 1980. It's in a Japanese-style building with a high wood ceiling, rice-paper windows, a tropical fish aquarium, and an 18-seat sushi bar. All sushi is made to order, depending on what Japanese and local fish are available. Try cobia (a species of sea catfish) in sashimi and sushi. Specialties include smoked freshwater eel sushi; *wakame* (Japanese seaweed) with dried squid, herring eggs, ginger, and cucumber; *kombu* (seaweed) with ponzu sauce (soy sauce, vinegar, sweet cooking wine, anon juice, sesame seeds, and scallions); Chinese shark's-fin soup garnished with whole hard-boiled quail eggs; *harumaki*, a Japanese-style eggroll containing bean sprouts, broccoli, cabbage, carrots, celery, and onions; *komochi-age*, deep fried mushroom with seafood stuffing; tempura with a light, crisp batter; and teriyaki. *19355 N.W. 2nd Ave. (U.S. 441), Miami 33169, tel. 305/651–7782. Dress: neat but casual. Reservations advised. No lunch weekends. Closed July 4 and Thanksgiving. AE, DC, MC, V. Moderate.*

Mexican
Little Havana

Acapulco. Authentic Mexican cuisine in an intimate 70-seat room with adobe walls, wooden beams, tabletops of Mexican tiles, and sombreros and serapes on the walls. As soon as you sit down, a waiter descends on you with a free, ample supply of *totopos*, homemade corn chips served hot and crunchy, salt free, with a fiery *pico de gallo* sauce. Specialties include a rich, chunky guacamole; *carnitas asadas* (marinated pork chunks in lemon and butter sauce); *mole poblano* (chicken in chocolate sauce); shrimp and rice in a cherry wine sauce; and combination platters of tacos, burritos, and enchiladas. *727 N.W. Unity Blvd. (N.W. 27th Ave.), tel. 305/642–6961. Dress: informal. Weekend reservations required. AE, CB, DC, MC, V. Inexpensive.*

Natural
Coconut Grove

Macrobiotic Foundation of Florida. All-natural meals are prepared fresh daily with organic vegetables, seeds, grains, and fruits to balance acid and alkaline, Yin and Yang. Even if you don't share this philosophy, the people are nice and the food is tasty. Meals are served boardinghouse-style at long tables in a former church parish house. Specialties include miso soup, whole grains, pasta primavera, and *arame* (an edible seaweed). International Night, on Friday, features cuisine of a different country each week. *3291 Franklin Ave., tel. 305/448–6625. Dress: casual. Reservations required. No smoking. Sunday brunch. Closed for lunch Sat. and dinner Mon., Wed., and Sun. MC, V. Moderate.*

Downtown Miami **Granny Feelgood's.** "Granny" is a shrewd gentleman named Irving Field, who caters to health-conscious lawyers, office workers, and cruise-ship crews at five locations. Since 1989 Jack Osman has owned the original Granny's, and with Irving plans to franchise locations outside Miami. So far no drop in quality downtown. Specialties include chicken salad with raisins, apples, and cinnamon; spinach fettuccine with pine nuts; grilled tofu; apple crumb cake; and carrot cake. *190 S.E. 1st Ave., tel. 305/358–6233. Dress: casual. No reservations. No smoking. AE, MC, V. Closed Sun. Inexpensive.*

Miami Beach **Pineapples.** Art-deco pink pervades this health-food store and restaurant. Specialties include Chinese egg rolls; lasagna filled with tofu and mushrooms; spinach fettuccine with feta cheese, fresh garlic, walnuts, and cream sauce; and salads with a full-flavored Italian-style dressing. *530 Arthur Godfrey Rd., tel. 305/532–9731. Dress: casual. No reservations. No smoking. AE, MC, V. Moderate.*

North Miami Beach ★ **Unicorn Village Restaurant & Marketplace.** Ten years after opening a 1960s-style health food store and restaurant, in 1990 Terry Dalton relocated his top-notch natural foods restaurant to the in-town Water Place Village. Now with 350 seats (up from the original 80), the restaurant caters to vegetarian and nonvegetarian diners. In an outdoor setting of free-form ponds and fountains by a bayfront dock, or in a plant-filled, natural woods interior under three-story-high wood-beamed ceilings sun-bright with skylights, guests enjoy spinach lasagna, a Tuscan vegetable sautée with Italian seasonings, grilled honey-mustard chicken, wok-barbecued shrimp, spicy seafood cakes, fish, Coleman natural beef, and the Unicorn's spring roll of uncooked veggies wrapped in a thin rice paper with cellophane noodles. The food market is the largest natural foods source in south Florida and features desserts all baked on premises. *3565 N.E. 207th St., tel. 305/933–3663. Dress: casual. No reservations. No smoking. MC, V. Moderate.*

Nicaraguan

Little Managua **La Parrilla.** Ten miles west of downtown Miami, about 60,000 Nicaraguans have moved into the Fontainebleau Park subdivision and the tiny suburban town of Sweetwater. Typical of their fare are the beef and fish at La Parilla (Spanish for "the grille"), where hanging plants and sloping barrel-tile roofs above the booths create a rural ambience. An adjoining bar is popular with Nicaraguan *contras*. Specialties include *gallos pintos* (red beans and rice); *chicharron* (fried pork with yucca); and *pargo a la Tipitapa*, baby red snapper fried and served whole in Creole sauce with onions and peppers. *9611 W. Flagler St., tel. 305/553–4419. Dress: casual. Reservations accepted. AE, CB, DC, MC, V. Moderate.*

Los Ranchos. Julio Somoza, owner of Los Ranchos and nephew of Nicaragua's late president, Anastasio Somoza, fled to south Florida in 1979. Somoza sustains a tradition begun 30 years ago in Managua, when the original Los Ranchos instilled in Nicaraguan palates a love of Argentine-style beef—lean, grass-fed tenderloin with *chimichurri*, a green sauce of chopped parsley, garlic, oil, vinegar, and other spices. Nicaragua's own sauces are a tomato-based marinara and the fiery *cebollitas encurtidas*, with slices of jalapeño pepper and onion pickled in vinegar. Specialties include *chorizo* (sausage); *cuajada con maduro* (skim cheese with fried bananas); and shrimp sautéed in butter and topped with a creamy jalapeño sauce. *125 S.W. 107th Ave., tel. 305/221–9367. Also at Bayside Marketplace. Dress: casual. Reservations advised, especially on weekends. AE, CB, DC, MC, V. Closed Christmas Eve, New Year's Day. Moderate.*

Seafood
Downtown Miami

East Coast Fisheries. This family-owned restaurant and retail fish market on the Miami River features fresh Florida seafood from its own 38-boat fleet in the Keys. From tables along the second-floor balcony railing, watch the cooks prepare your dinner in the open kitchen below. Specialties include a complimentary fish-pâté appetizer, blackened pompano with owner David Swartz's personal herb-and-spice recipe, lightly breaded fried grouper, and a homemade Key-lime pie so rich it tastes like ice cream. *360 W. Flagler St., tel. 305/373–5515. Dress: casual. Beer and wine only. AE, MC, V. Moderate.*

The Fish Market. Tucked away in a corner of the Omni International Hotel's lobby, this fine restaurant boasts waiters fluent in French, German, and Spanish and a kitchen staff fluent in seafood's complexities. The menu changes with availability of fresh fish, fruits, and vegetables. Typical menu items include sautéed dolphin in a basil-perfumed olive oil; filet of pompano; pan-baked red snapper; and Florida lobster tail. Daily seafood specials may include bluefish, dolphin, lemon sole, marlin, pompano, puppy shark, redfish, sea bass, sea trout, and tuna. Desserts include chocolate Key lime pie with a Graham-cracker crust and pistachio chocolate terrine with orange cream sauce. *Biscayne Blvd. at 16th St., 33132, tel. 305/374–0000. Jacket required. Reservations accepted. No lunch Sat.; closed Sun. Free valet parking. AE, DC, MC, V. Expensive.*

Key Biscayne

Sundays on the Bay. Two locations overlook the water—the Crandon Park Marina at Key Biscayne and the Intracoastal Waterway at Haulover. Both have inside dining and outdoor decks, bars, live bands playing reggae and top 40 hits nightly, and an energetic young serving staff. Specialties from an extensive seafood menu include conch fritters, conch chowder (tomato-based, served with sherry and Tabasco sauce), and baked grouper topped with crabmeat and shrimp scampi. *Key Biscayne: 5420 Crandon Blvd., tel. 305/361–6777; Haulover Beach Park: 10880 Collins Ave., tel. 305/945–5115. Dress: casual. Reservations accepted; advised for Sun. brunch. AE, CB, DC, MC, V. Moderate.*

Miami Beach
★

Joe's Stone Crab Restaurant. A south Florida tradition since 1913, Joe's is a family restaurant in its fourth generation. You go to wait, people watch, and finally settle down to an ample à la carte menu. Joe's serves about a ton of stone crab claws a day, with drawn butter, lemon wedges, and a piquant mustard sauce (recipe available). Popular side orders include a vinegary coleslaw, salad with a brisk house vinaigrette dressing, creamed garlic spinach, french-fried onion rings and eggplant, and hash brown potatoes. Save room for dessert—a slice of Key-lime pie with graham cracker crust and real whipped cream or apple pie with a crumb-pecan topping. *227 Biscayne St., tel. 305/673–0365. Dress: casual, but no T-shirts, tank tops, or shorts. No reservations. To minimize wait, come for lunch before 11:30, for dinner before 5 or after 9. Closed May 15–Oct. 15. AE, CB, DC, MC, V. Moderate.*

Spanish
Downtown Miami

Las Tapas. *Tapas*—"little dishes"—come in appetizer-size portions to give you a variety of tastes during a single meal. Specialties include *la tostada* (smoked salmon on melba toast, topped with a dollop of sour cream, across which are laid baby eels, black caviar, capers, and chopped onion) and *samfaina con lomo* (eggplant, zucchini, green pepper, onions, tomato, and garlic sautéed with two thin, delicately flavored slices of fresh boneless pork loin). Also available are soups, salads, sandwiches, and standard dinners. *Bayside Marketplace, 401 Biscayne Blvd., tel. 305/372–2737. Dress: casual. Reservations for large parties only. AE, CB, DC, MC, V. Moderate.*

Little Havana
★

Casa Juancho. A meeting place for the movers and shakers of Miami's Cuban community, Casa Juancho serves a cross section of Spanish regional cuisines. The interior recalls old Castile: brown brick, rough-hewn dark timbers, and walls adorned with colorful Talavera platters. Strolling Spanish balladeers will serenade you. Specialties include *cochinillo Segoviano* (roast suckling pig), and *parrillada de mariscos* (fish, shrimps, squid, and scallops grilled in a light garlic sauce) from the Pontevedra region of northwest Spain. For dessert, the *crema Catalana* has a delectable crust of burnt caramel atop a rich pastry custard. The wine list includes fine labels from Spain's Rioja region. *2436 S.W. 8th St., tel. 305/642–2452. Dress: jacket and tie required. Reservations advised; not accepted after 8 PM Fri. and Sat. Closed Christmas Eve. AE, CB, DC, MC, V. Expensive.*

Vietnamese
Little Havana
★

Hy-Vong Vietnamese Cuisine. Under new ownership since 1989, the same magic continues to pour forth from the tiny kitchen of this 36-seat restaurant as it has since 1980. Now the word is out, so come before 7 PM to avoid a long wait. Specialties include spring rolls, a Vietnamese version of an egg roll, with ground pork, cellophane noodles, and black mushrooms wrapped in homemade rice paper; a whole fish panfried with *nuoc man* (a garlic-lime fish sauce); and thinly sliced pork, barbecued with sesame seeds and fish sauce, served with bean sprouts, rice noodles, and slivers of carrots, almonds, and peanuts. *3458 S.W. 8th St., tel. 305/446–3674. Dress casual. Reservations accepted for 5 or more. Closed Mon., American and Vietnamese/Chinese New Years, and 2 weeks in Aug. No smoking. No credit cards. Moderate.*

Lodging

Few urban areas can match Greater Miami's diversity of hotel accommodations. The area has hundreds of hotels and motels with lodgings in all price categories, from $8 for a night in a dormitory-style hostel bed to $2,000 for a night in the luxurious presidential suite atop a posh downtown hotel.

As recently as the 1960s, many hotels in Greater Miami opened only in the winter to accommodate Yankee "snowbirds." Now most stay open all year. In summer, they cater to business travelers and to vacationers from the American South and

Latin America who find Miami quite congenial despite the heat, humidity, and intense thunderstorms almost every afternoon.

Although some hotels (especially on the mainland) have adopted year-round rates, many still adjust their rates to reflect the ebb and flow of seasonal demand. The peak occurs in winter, with only a slight dip in summer when families with schoolchildren take vacations. You'll find the best values between Easter and Memorial Day (a delightful time in Miami but a difficult time for many people to travel), and in September and October (the height of hurricane season).

The list that follows is a representative selection of the best hotels and motels, organized geographically.

The rate categories in the list are based on the all-year or peak-season price; off-peak rates may be a category or two lower.

The most highly recommended places in each price category are indicated by a star ★.

Category	Cost*
Very Expensive	over $120
Expensive	$90–$120
Moderate	$50–$90
Inexpensive	under $50

**All prices are for a standard double room, excluding 6% state sales tax and nominal tourist tax.*

The following credit card abbreviations are used: AE, American Express; CB, Carte Blanche; DC, Diners Club; MC, MasterCard; V, Visa.

Coconut Grove

Doubletree Hotel at Coconut Grove. This high rise with a bay view was built in 1970 and renovated in 1988. Rooms are large, most with balcony, comfortable chairs, armoires, original artwork. Choice of a mauve or turquoise color scheme. Best rooms are on upper floors with bay views. Homemade chocolate-chip cookies are offered to arriving guests. *2649 S. Bayshore Dr., Coconut Grove 33133, tel. 305/858–2500 or 800/528–0444. 190 rooms with bath, including 32 nonsmoker rooms, and 3 rooms for handicapped guests. Facilities: outdoor freshwater pool, 2 tennis courts, restaurant, bar. Guests have access to Casablanca, a private club on the top floor. AE, CB, DC, MC, V. Expensive.*

★ **Grand Bay Hotel.** This modern high rise overlooks Biscayne Bay; rooms have traditional furnishings and original art. The building's stairstep facade, like a Mayan pyramid, gives each room facing the bay a private terrace. Best views, at the northeast corner, include downtown Miami. The staff pays meticulous attention to guests' desires. Only slightly more special than most rooms is 814, Luciano Pavarotti's two-level suite with a baby-grand piano, circular staircase, and canopied king-size bed. You can rent it when he's not there. *2669 S. Bayshore Dr., Coconut Grove 33133, tel. 305/858–9600. 181 rooms with bath, including 49 suites, 20 nonsmoker rooms. Facilities: outdoor pool, hot tub, health club, saunas, masseur, afternoon tea* *in lobby, gourmet restaurant, lounge, poolside bar. AE, CB, DC, MC, V. Very Expensive.*

★ **Grove Isle.** This luxurious mid-rise urban resort sits on a 26-acre island and adjoins the equally posh condominium apartment towers and private club. Developer Martin Margulies displays selections from his extensive private art collection on the premises *(see* Exploring Coconut Grove, above). The oversized rooms have patios, bay views, ceiling fans, and tropical decor with area rugs and Spanish tiles. The rooms with the most light and best bay view are 201–205. *4 Grove Isle Dr., Coconut Grove 33133, tel. 305/858–8300 or 800/858–8300. 49 rooms with bath, including 9 suites. Facilities: outdoor freshwater pool and whirlpool; 12 tennis courts; 85-slip marina; 40-ft. sailboat that guests can charter; health spa with saunas and steam rooms, Nautilus equipment, masseur and masseuse, running track around the island; in-room refreshment bar and coffee maker; free cable TV; free movies in room; complimentary Continental breakfast; restaurant with indoor and outdoor seating. AE, CB, DC, MC, V. Very Expensive.*

Mayfair House. This European-style luxury hotel sits within an exclusive open-air shopping mall *(see* Exploring Coconut Grove, above). Public areas have Tiffany windows, polished mahogany, marble walls and floors, and imported ceramics and crystal. A glassed-in elevator whisks you to the corridor on your floor—a balcony overlooking the mall's central fountains and walkways. In all suites, outdoor terraces face the street, screened from view by vegetation and wood latticework. Each has a Japanese hot tub on the balcony or a Roman tub in the bathroom. Otherwise, each suite is unique in size and furnishings. Sunset (Room 505) is one of 48 suites with antique pianos. Some aspects of the building's design are quirky; you can get lost looking for the ballroom or restaurant, and, in many rooms, you must stand in the bathtub to turn on the water. The worst suite for sleeping is Featherfern (Room 356), from which you can hear the band one floor below in the club. *3000 Florida Ave., Coconut Grove 33133, tel. 305/441–0000 or 800/433–4555. 181 suites, including 22 nonsmoker suites. Facilities: rooftop recreation area with sauna in a barrel, small outdoor freshwater swimming pool, and snack bar; preferred shopper card for discounts in mall shops; complimentary airport limousine service (must be requested one week in advance). AE, CB, DC, MC, V. Very Expensive.*

Coral Gables

The Biltmore Hotel. A historic high rise built in 1926, the Biltmore was restored and renovated in 1986 and reopened as a luxury hotel, although it recently went into foreclosure. (*See* Highlights for details.) Upper-floor rooms facing north and east toward the airport, downtown Miami, and Biscayne Bay have the most spectacular views. *1200 Anastasia Ave., Coral Gables 33134, tel. 305/445–1926 or 800/445–2586. 275 rooms with bath, including 45 suites. Facilities: 18-hole championship golf course, 10 lighted tennis courts, health spa with sauna, pool, restaurant, coffee shop, lounge. AE, CB, DC, MC, V. Very Expensive.*

★ **The Colonnade Hotel.** The twin 13-story towers of this $65-million hotel, office, and shopping complex dominate the heart of Coral Gables, echoing architecturally the adjoining two-story Corinthian-style rotunda on Miracle Mile from which 1920s developer George Merrick sold lots in his fledgling city. Merrick's family provided old photos, paintings, and other heirlooms that are on display throughout the hotel. The oversize rooms come in 26 different floor plans, each with a sitting area, built-in armoires, and traditional furnishings of mahogany. The hospitality bars have marble counters and gold-plated faucets with 1920s-style ceramic handles. The pool is on a 10th-floor terrace, which offers a magnificent view south toward Biscayne Bay. *180 Aragon Ave., Coral Gables 33134, tel. 305/441–2600 or 800/533–1337. 157 rooms, including 17 suites, 18 nonsmoker rooms, and 4 rooms for handicapped guests. Facilities: outdoor heated pool with 2 saunas, Nautilus exercise equipment, 24-hr room service, 2 restaurants. AE, DC, MC, V. Very Expensive.*

★ **Hotel Place St. Michel.** Historic low-rise urban hotel built in 1926 and restored 1981–86. Art nouveau chandeliers suspended from vaulted ceilings grace the public areas of this intimate jewel in the heart of downtown Coral Gables. Paddle fans circulate the air, filled with the scent of fresh flowers. Each room has its own dimension, personality, and imported antiques from England, Scotland, and France. *162 Alcazar Ave., Coral Gables 33134, tel. 305/444–1666 or 800/247–8526. 28 rooms with bath, including 3 suites. Facilities: welcome basket of fruit and cheese in every room, Continental breakfast, restaurant, lounge, French snack shop. AE, CB, DC, MC, V. Expensive.*

★ **Hyatt Regency Coral Gables.** This urban high rise caters to business travelers. Opened in 1987, the hotel is part of a megastructure that includes two office towers. The entire structure follows the area tradition of Spanish Mediterranean architecture, with tile roofs, white-frame casement windows, and pink-stucco exterior. The hotel's interior decor of pastel hues and antique-style furnishings gives a comfortable, residential feel to the rooms and public areas. The best rooms face the pool; the worst face north toward the airport. *501 Alhambra Plaza, Coral Gables 33134, tel. 305/441–1234. 242 rooms with bath, including 50 suites, 45 nonsmoker rooms. Facilities: 2,900-sq.-ft. ballroom, restaurant, lounge, fifth-floor pool, outdoor whirlpool, health club with Nautilus equipment, Life Cycles, sauna, and steam rooms. AE, CB, DC, MC, V. Very Expensive.*

Downtown Miami

★ **Hotel Inter-Continental Miami.** Stand on the fifth-floor recreation plaza and gaze up at this granite 34-story monolith that appears to be arching over you. This optical illusion aside, the Inter-Continental deals in congenial realities. The grain in the lobby's marble floor matches that in *The Spindle*, a massive centerpiece sculpture by Henry Moore. With all that marble, the lobby could easily look like a mausoleum—and did before the addition of palm trees, colorful umbrellas, and oversize wicker chairs and tables. Atop a five-story atrium, a skylight lets the afternoon sun pour in. The triangular hotel tower offers bay, port, and city views that improve with height. *100 Chopin Plaza, Miami 33131, tel. 305/577–1000 or 800/327–0200. 645 rooms with bath, including 34 suites, 48 nonsmoker rooms; corner rooms have extra-wide doors for handicapped guests. Facilities: outdoor heated freshwater pool beside the bay, 2 lighted clay tennis courts, 2 indoor racquetball courts, ¼-mile jogging track with rubber surface, in-room minibar, restaurants, nightclub, lounge. AE, CB, DC, MC, V. Very Expensive.*

Hyatt Regency Miami. This centrally located, 24-story conven-

Miami Area Lodging

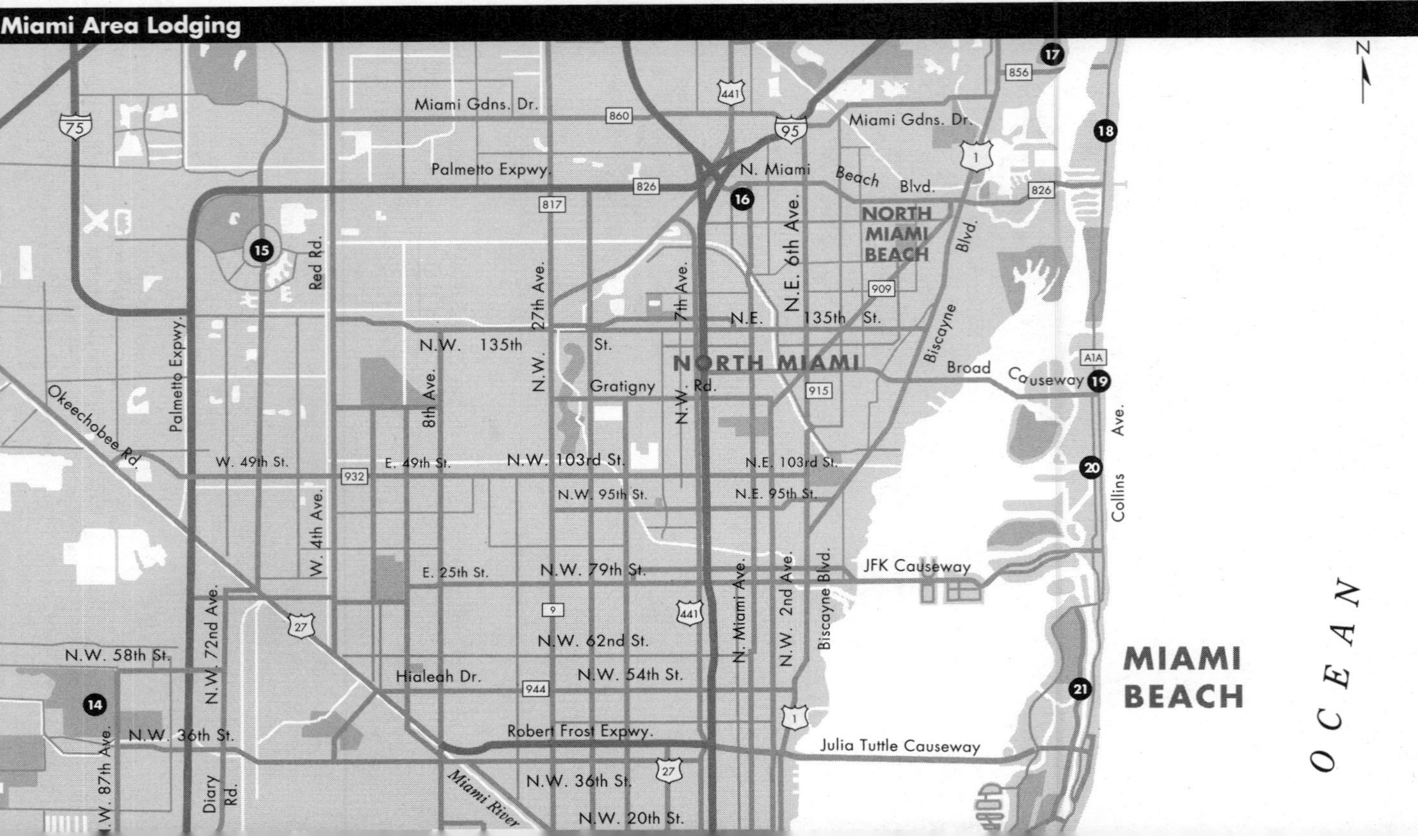

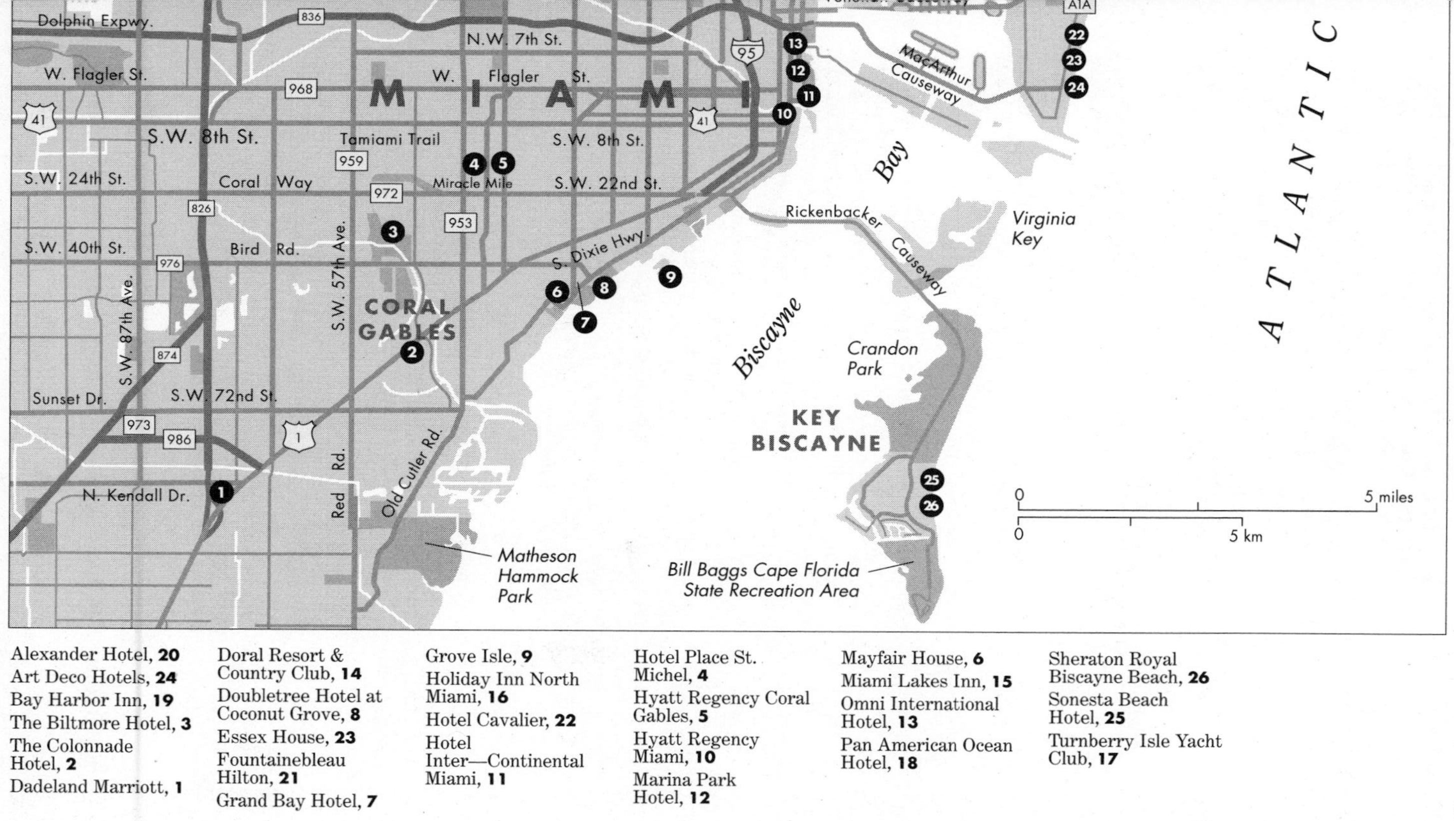

Alexander Hotel, **20**
Art Deco Hotels, **24**
Bay Harbor Inn, **19**
The Biltmore Hotel, **3**
The Colonnade Hotel, **2**
Dadeland Marriott, **1**
Doral Resort & Country Club, **14**
Doubletree Hotel at Coconut Grove, **8**
Essex House, **23**
Fountainebleau Hilton, **21**
Grand Bay Hotel, **7**
Grove Isle, **9**
Holiday Inn North Miami, **16**
Hotel Cavalier, **22**
Hotel Inter—Continental Miami, **11**
Hotel Place St. Michel, **4**
Hyatt Regency Coral Gables, **5**
Hyatt Regency Miami, **10**
Marina Park Hotel, **12**
Mayfair House, **6**
Miami Lakes Inn, **15**
Omni International Hotel, **13**
Pan American Ocean Hotel, **18**
Sheraton Royal Biscayne Beach, **26**
Sonesta Beach Hotel, **25**
Turnberry Isle Yacht Club, **17**

tion hotel adjoins the James L. Knight International Center (*see* Exploring Downtown Miami, above). It nestles beside the Brickell Avenue Bridge on the north bank of the Miami River. From its lower lobby, you can watch tugboats, freighters, and pleasure craft ply the river. The best rooms are on the upper floors, facing east toward Biscayne Bay. A $7-million renovation is underway; room renovations will begin in 1991. *400 S.E. 2nd Ave., Miami 33131, tel. 305/358–1234 or 800/228–9000. 615 rooms with bath, 25 suites, 43 nonsmoker rooms, 17 rooms for handicapped guests. Facilities: outdoor freshwater swimming pool; health club with sauna; in-room safes; in-house pay-TV movies, 2 restaurants, and a lounge. AE, CB, DC, MC, V. Very Expensive.*

Marina Park Hotel. Centrally located, this mid-rise is owned by a French chain. The lobby is paver-tiled, brick, and wicker-full. Rooms have an attractive pastel color scheme with rattan and wicker furnishings, soft mattresses, and trilingual TV. The best views are from east rooms that overlook Bayside and the Port of Miami. *340 Biscayne Blvd., Miami 33132, tel. 305/371–4400 or 800/327–6565. 200 rooms with bath, including 25 suites. Facilities: pool, restaurant, bar. AE, CB, DC, MC, V. Moderate.*

Omni International Hotel. A 20-story hotel built in 1977, the Omni stands atop a 10.5-acre shopping and entertainment complex that includes Maas Brothers/Jordan Marsh and J. C. Penney department stores, 120 specialty shops, the Children's Workshop child-care center, and a hand-made Italian wood carousel. The lowest hotel floor is five stories up; rooms on upper floors have spectacular views of downtown Miami and Biscayne Bay. A $1.25-million room renovation in 1987 eschewed tropical-chic in favor of more traditional decor, with a blue-and-tan color scheme and mahogany furniture in many rooms. *1601 Biscayne Blvd., Miami 33132, tel. 305/374–0000 or 800/THE-OMNI. 535 rooms, including 50 suites, 25 nonsmoker rooms, and 1 room for handicapped guests. Facilities: outdoor heated pool on a terrace 5 stories above the street, lobby bar, terrace cafe, restaurant (The Fish Market), access to nearby health club and spa. AE, DC, MC, V. Very Expensive.*

Kendall

Dadeland Marriott. Catering to business travelers, this 24-story hotel is part of a megastructure that includes the Datran Center office building and the southernmost Metrorail station, Dadeland South. Within walking distance of Dadeland Mall, the hotel has a four-story atrium overlooking the Datran Center's lobby and its extensive sculpture collection. The hotel's contemporary decor, in corals and light greens, incorporates Asian accents. All rooms have desks and good reading lights. The best rooms face the city on the upper floors; 717 and 719 have glass doors opening to the pool. The worst room, 805, overlooks the roof of the exercise room. *9090 Dadeland Blvd., Miami 33156, tel. 305/663–1035 or 800/228–9290. 305 rooms with bath, including 2 suites, nonsmoker floor with 15 rooms, 4 rooms for handicapped guests. Facilities: outdoor heated freshwater pool, Jacuzzi, whirlpool, sauna, exercise room, restaurant, lounge, complimentary airport transportation. AE, DC, MC, V. Very Expensive.*

Key Biscayne

Sheraton Royal Biscayne Beach Resort and Racquet Club. Art-deco pinks, wicker furniture, and chattering macaws and cockatoos in the lobby set the tone for this three-story beachfront resort set amid the waving fronds of coconut palms. Built in

1952 and restored in 1985, this laid-back place has managed to keep its casual demeanor even after starring as a "Miami Vice" set. All rooms have garden and bay views; most have terraces. *555 Ocean Dr., Key Biscayne 33149, tel. 305/361–5775. 192 rooms with bath, including 4 suites with ocean view, 15 junior suites with kitchenette, 15 nonsmoker rooms. Facilities: a ¼-mile of ocean beachfront; 2 outdoor freshwater heated pools; children's wading pool and playground; 10 tennis courts (4 lighted); sailboats, windsurfers, Hobie Cats, aquabikes, snorkeling kits, and bicycles for rent; pay-TV movies, unisex beauty salon; restaurants; and lounge. AE, CB, DC, MC, V. Very Expensive.*

★ **Sonesta Beach Hotel & Tennis Club.** Built in 1969, this eight-story beachfront resort underwent a $5-million renovation in 1985. Tropical hues focus attention on museum-quality modern art by prominent painters and sculptors. Don't miss Andy Warhol's five drawings of rock star Mick Jagger in the hotel's disco bar, Desires. The best rooms face the ocean on the eighth floor, a "club floor" with a small lobby and bar where breakfast is served. *350 Ocean Dr., Key Biscayne 33149, tel. 305/361–2021 or 800/SONESTA. 300 rooms with bath, including 12 suites and 13 villas (3-, 4-, and 5-bedroom homes with full kitchens and screened-in pools). Facilities: 750 feet of ocean beachfront; outdoor freshwater heated Olympic-size pool and whirlpool; 10 tennis courts (3 lighted); health center with Jacuzzi, dry and hot steam rooms, aerobic dance floor, weight room, massage room, and tanning room; gift shops; restaurants, snack bar, deli, disco lounge. AE, CB, DC, MC, V. Very Expensive.*

Miami Beach

★ **Alexander Hotel.** Newly remodeled throughout, with antique furnishings and original art in every suite, this 16-story hotel offers ocean and bay views from every room. Rooms facing south have the best views. A computer keeps track of the mattresses, so you can request the degree of firmness you prefer. *5225 Collins Ave., Miami Beach 33140, tel. 305/865–6500. 212 suites, each with two baths. Facilities: ocean beach, 2 outdoor heated freshwater pools, 4 poolside Jacuzzis, cabanas, Sunfishes and catamarans for rent, Dominique's gourmet restaurant, and coffee shop. AE, DC, MC, V. Expensive.*

Art Deco Hotels. A trio of restored three-story hotels facing the beach are under common ownership and management. The **Hotel Cardozo** dates from 1939, the **Hotel Carlyle** from 1941, and the **Hotel Leslie** from 1937. All three are attractively decorated in art-deco pinks, whites, and grays. Many contain original walnut furniture, restored and refinished. Rooms are comfortable but small; inspect your room before registering to assure that it meets your needs. Air-conditioning has been installed, but most of the time you won't need it—especially in rooms facing the water, where a sea breeze usually blows. *1244 Ocean Dr., Miami Beach 33139, tel. 305/534–2135 or 800/338–9076. 168 rooms with bath, including 15 suites. Facilities: restaurants, bars with live entertainment in the Carlyle and Cardozo. AE, CB, DC, MC, V. Moderate.*

Bay Harbor Inn. Down-home hospitality in the most affluent zip code in the county. Retired Washington lawyer Sandy Lankler and his wife Celeste operate this 35-room lodging in two sections—two moods. The buildings are new, but townside the furnishings are antiques. Townside is the oldest building in Bay Harbor Islands, vaguely Georgian but dating only to 1940.

Behind triple sets of French doors under fan windows, the lobby is full of oaken desks, handmills, grandfather clocks, historical maps, and potted plants. Rooms are antique-filled and no two are alike. Along Indian Creek the inn incorporates the former Albert Pick Hotella, a shipshape tropical-style set of rooms on two floors off loggias surrounded by palms with all rooms facing the water. Mid-century modern here, and chintz. Two restaurants include The Palms townside, and the Seafood Garden creekside. *9660 East Bay Harbor Dr., Miami Beach 33154, tel. 305/868–4141. 35 rooms with bath, including 12 suites. Facilities: outdoor freshwater pool, 2 restaurants, lounge. Complimentary Continental breakfast and champagne tea. AE, CB, DC, MC, V. Expensive.*

★ **Essex House.** After 18 months and $3 million for acquiring and fixing up her little property, Patricia Murphy has revived the stylishness and the creature comforts that made this the premiere lodging of the Art Deco era. It was all here to start: designed by architect Henry Hohauser, Everglades mural by Earl LaPan. Here are the ziggurat arches, the hieroglyph-style ironwork, etched glass panels of flamingos under the palms, five-foot rose medallion Chinese urns. Hallways have recessed showcases with original deco sculptures. The original 66 rooms from 1938 are now 41, plus four petite suites, six grand. A self-styled "spoiled brat" from Newport, Patricia lavishes the amenities: complete turndown service with clothes hung and shoes polished, designer linens and towels, all feather-and-down pillows and sofa rolls, and individually controlled air conditioning and central heat plus ceiling fans. Best of all, the rooms are soundproofed, otherwise unheard of in beach properties of the Thirties. Smallest rooms are yellow-themed and face north. Best are the two-room oceanview suites: 305 and 308, and 205 and 208. Fresh flowers are given to guests who have made reservations. Evian water is free and so is the Continental breakfast. *1001 Collins Ave., Miami Beach 33131, tel. 305/534–2700, 800/55–ESSEX. 51 rooms and suites with bath. Facilities: freshwater pool, breakfast room. No smoking in rooms. AE, MC, V. Expensive–Very Expensive.*

Fontainebleau Hilton Resort and Spa. The Miami area's foremost convention hotel boasts an opulent lobby with massive chandeliers, a sweeping staircase, and new meeting rooms in art-deco hues. There are always some rooms in the hotel that are under renovation. You can request a '50s look or one that's contemporary. Upper-floor rooms in the Chateau Building have the best views. *4441 Collins Ave., Miami Beach 33140, tel. 305/538–2000. 1,206 rooms with bath, including 60 suites, 55 nonsmoker rooms. Facilities: ocean beach with 30 cabanas, windsurfing, parasailing, Hobie Cats, volleyball, 2 outdoor pools (one fresh, one salt), 3 whirlpool baths, 7 lighted tennis courts, health club with exercise classes, saunas, marina, free children's activities, 12 restaurants and lounges, Tropigala nightclub. AE, CB, DC, MC, V. Very Expensive.*

★ **Hotel Cavalier.** Rooms in this three-story beachfront hotel have period maple furnishings, new baths, and air-conditioning. The Cavalier is popular with the film and fashion industry; many guests are artists, models, photographers, and writers. The best rooms face the ocean; the worst are on the ground floor, rear south, where the garbage truck goes by in the morning. *1320 Ocean Dr., Miami Beach 33139, tel. 305/534–2135 or 800/338–9076. 44 rooms with bath, including 2 suites. Facilities: Evian water and flowers in all rooms, Continental breakfast in* *lobby each morning, airport pickup available. AE, CB, MC, V. Expensive–Very Expensive.*

★ **Pan American Ocean Hotel, A Radisson Resort.** This beach hotel sits back from Collins Avenue behind a refreshing garden of coconut palms and seasonal flowers. It first opened in 1954, but a complete renovation took place in 1988–89. The best view faces the ocean from rooms 330, 332, and 333 on the third floor of the north wing. Direct-north and south–facing rooms have only a sliver view of ocean or bay. *17875 Collins Ave., Miami Beach 33160, tel. 305/932–1100 or 800/327–5678. 146 rooms, including 4 suites, Inquire about rooms for handicapped guests available part of the year. Facilities: 400 ft of Atlantic Ocean beach, outdoor heated pool, 4 hard-surface tennis courts, tennis pro and pro shop, 2 shuffleboard courts, 9-hole putting green, beauty salon, coffee shop, pool gazebo bar, terrace lounge and oceanfront restaurant, ping-pong room, video game room, card room, free shuttle service to Bal Harbor and Aventura shopping malls, coin-operated laundry room, refrigerators in all rooms. AE, CB, DC, MC, V. Very Expensive.*

North Dade **Holiday Inn North Miami—Golden Glades.** A mid-rise suburban hotel at a major highway interchange, this hotel is 2 miles from the beach, from Calder Race Course, and from Joe Robbie Stadium (where the Miami Dolphins football team plays home games). A 1987 renovation gave public areas modern furnishings and mauve, peach, and purple wallpaper. Rooms have a green-and-white color scheme with oak furniture. Local police patrol the premises nightly. *148 N.W. 167th St., Miami 33169, tel. 305/949–1441 or 800/HOLIDAY. 163 rooms with bath, including 18 nonsmoker rooms, 12 lady executive rooms, 1 room for handicapped guests. Facilities: outdoor freshwater pool, children's pool, outdoor exercise area for aerobics, in-room refreshment center, restaurant, and lounge. AE, CB, DC, MC, V. Moderate.*

★ **Turnberry Isle Yacht and Country Club.** Part of an upscale condominium community on a 300-acre bayfront site, Turnberry is 12 miles north of downtown Miami. Choose from the European-style Marina Hotel or the Country Club Hotel beside the golf course. Rooms are oversize, with light woods and earth-tone colors at the inn, a nautical-blue motif at the hotel, large curving terraces, Jacuzzis, honor bar, and in-room safes. *19735 Turnberry Way, North Miami Beach 33163, tel. 305/932–6200. 370 rooms with bath, including 47 suites. Facilities: Ocean Club with 250 feet of private beach frontage, diving gear, Windsurfers and Hobie Cats for rent, and complimentary shuttle service to the hotel; 3 outdoor freshwater pools; 24 tennis courts (18 lighted) 2 18-hole golf courses; helipad; marina with moorings for 117 boats up to 150 ft.; full-service spa with physician, nutritionist, saunas, steam rooms, whirlpools, facials, herbal wraps, Nautilus exercise equipment, indoor racquetball courts, and jogging course; 5 private restaurants, lounge, nightly entertainment. AE, CB, DC, MC, V. Very Expensive.*

West Dade **Doral Resort & Country Club.** Millions of airline passengers annually peer down upon this 2,400-acre jewel of an inland golf and tennis resort while fastening their seat belts. It's 4 miles west of Miami International Airport and consists of eight separate three- and four-story lodges nestled beside the golf links. A renovation completed in 1988 gave the resort a tropical theme, with light pastels, wicker, and teak furniture. All guest rooms have minibars; most have private balconies or terraces with views of the golf courses or tennis courts. This is the site of the Doral Ryder Open Tournament, played on the Doral "Blue Monster" golf course. *4400 N.W. 87th Ave., Miami 33178, tel. 305/592–2000. 650 rooms with bath, including 94 suites. Facilities: five 18-hole golf courses, and a 9-hole, par-3 executive course; pro shop and boutique; 15 tennis courts (4 lighted), five Olympic-size heated outdoor freshwater pool; 24-stall equestrian center, offers riding instruction; 3-mi jogging and bike path; bicycle rentals; lake fishing; restaurants and lounges; transportation to beach. AE, CB, DC, MC, V. Very Expensive.*

Miami Lakes Inn, Athletic Club, Golf Resort. This low-rise suburban resort is part of a planned town developed by Florida Senator Bob Graham's family about 14 miles northwest of downtown Miami. The golf resort opened in 1962 and added two wings in 1978. Its decor is English-traditional throughout, rich in leather and wood. All rooms have balconies. The inn opened in 1983 with a typically Florida-tropic look—light pastel hues and furniture of wicker and light wood. In both locations, the best rooms are near the lobby for convenient access; the worst are near the elevators. *Main St., Miami Lakes 33014, tel. 305/821–1150. 310 rooms with bath, including 32 suites. Facilities: 2 outdoor freshwater pools; 9 lighted tennis courts; golf (18-hole par-72 course, lighted 18-hole par-54 executive course, golf school); saunas, steam rooms, and whirlpools; 8 indoor racquetball courts; Nautilus fitness center; full-size gym for volleyball and basketball; aerobics classes; restaurants and lounges; shopping discount at Main St. shops. AE, CB, DC, MC, V. Very Expensive.*

The Arts

Performing arts aficionados in Greater Miami will tell you they survive quite nicely despite the area's historic inability to support a professional symphony orchestra. In recent years, this community has begun to write a new chapter in its performing arts history.

The New World Symphony, a unique advanced-training orchestra, marks its fourth season in 1991. The fledgling Miami City Ballet has risen rapidly to international prominence in its five-year existence. The opera company ranks with the nation's best, and a venerable chamber music series brings renowned ensembles to perform here. Several churches and synagogues also run classical music series with international performers.

In theater, Miami offers English-speaking audiences an assortment of professional, collegiate, and amateur productions of musicals, comedy, and drama. Spanish theater also is active.

In the cinema world, the Miami Film Festival attracts more than 45,000 people annually to screenings of new films from all over the world—including some made here.

Arts Information. Greater Miami's English-language daily newspaper, *The Miami Herald*, publishes information on the performing arts in its Weekend Section on Friday and the Lively Arts Section on Sunday. Phone ahead to confirm details before you go.

If you read Spanish, check *El Nuevo Herald* (a Spanish version of *The Miami Herald*) or *Diario Las Americas* (the area's largest independent Spanish-language paper) for information on the Spanish theater and a smattering of general performing arts news.

Other good sources of information on the performing arts are the calendar in *Miami Today*, a free weekly newspaper available each Thursday in downtown Miami, Coconut Grove, and Coral Gables; and *New Times*, a free weekly distributed throughout Dade County each Wednesday.

Miami's Official Guide to the Arts is a pocket-size monthly publication covering music of all kinds, from the classics to rock, and art gallery openings, theater, and major cultural events in Greater Miami, Broward, and Palm Beach. Editor Margo Morrison tries to be encylopedic and does a good job. Sold at newsstands and at all major hotels all over Greater Miami. *Tel. 305/854–1790. 9–5. Annual subscription $15, individual copy $2. No credit cards.*

WTMI (93.1 FM) provides concert information on its Cultural Arts Line (tel. 305/550–9393).

Ballet

Miami City Ballet. Florida's first major fully professional resident ballet company. Edward Villella, the artistic director, was principal dancer of the New York City Ballet under George Balanchine. Now the Miami City Ballet re-creates the Balanchine repertoire and has begun to introduce new works of its own. Miami City Ballet performances are at Gusman Center for the Performing Arts. Demonstrations of works in progress are at the 800-seat Lincoln Theater in Miami Beach. Villella narrates the children's and works-in-progress programs. *905 Lincoln Rd., Miami Beach 33139, tel. 305/532–7713. Season: Oct.–May. AE, MC, V. Ticketmaster (see* Important Addresses and Numbers, above).

Cinema

The Miami Film Festival. During eight days in February, new films from all over the world are screened in the Gusman Center for the Performing Arts. Tickets and schedule: *444 Brickell Ave., Miami 33131, tel. 305/377–3456. AE, MC, V. Ticketmaster (see* Important Addresses and Numbers, above).

Concerts

Concert Association of Greater Miami. A not-for-profit organization, directed by Judith Drucker, this is the South's largest presenter of classical artists. Ticket and program information: *555 Hank Meyer Blvd. (17th St.), Miami Beach 33139, tel. 305/532–3491. AE, MC, V.*

Friends of Chamber Music (44 W. Flagler St., Miami 33130, tel. 305/372–2975) presents an annual series of chamber concerts by internationally known guest ensembles, such as the Beaux Arts Trio, I Musici, and the Julliard String Quartet.

Drama

Check *Miami's Official Guide to the Arts* for a complete English-language theater schedule. Traveling companies come and go; amateur groups form, perform, and disband. Listed below are the more enduring groups of Greater Miami's drama scene.

Coconut Grove Playhouse. Arnold Mittelman, artistic director, stages Broadway-bound plays and musical reviews and experimental productions. *3500 Main Hwy., Coconut Grove 33133, tel. 305/442–4000. AE, MC, V.*

Ring Theater. The University of Miami's Department of Theatre Arts presents four complete plays a year in this 311-seat hall. *University of Miami, 1312 Miller Dr., Coral Gables 33124, tel. 305/284–3355. AE, MC, V.*

Opera **Greater Miami Opera.** Miami's resident opera company has the seventh-largest operating budget of any American opera organization. It presents two complete casts for five operas in the Dade County Auditorium. The International Series brings such luminaries as Placido Domingo and Luciano Pavarotti; the National Series features rising young singers in the principal roles, with the same sets and chorus, but with more modest ticket prices. All operas are sung in their original language, with titles in English projected onto a screen above the stage. *1200 Coral Way, Miami 33145, tel. 305/854–7890. AE, MC, V. Ticketmaster* (see *Important Addresses and Numbers, above).*

Symphony **New World Symphony.** Although Greater Miami still has no resident symphony orchestra, the New World Symphony, conducted by Michael Tilson Thomas, helps to fill the void. It's a unique phenomenon, a national advanced-training orchestra for musicians aged 22–30 who have finished their academic studies and need performing experience in a professional setting before moving on to a permanent job. *541 Lincoln Rd., Miami Beach 33139, box office tel. 305/673–3331, main office 305/673–3330. AE, CB, DC, MC, V. Season: Oct.–Apr. Ticketmaster* (*see* Important Addresses and Numbers, above).

Theaters Greater Miami lacks a modern performing arts center. Every auditorium and theater in town suffers from a shortage of space on and off the stage, and some have acoustical problems.

Dade County Auditorium (2901 W. Flagler St., Miami 33135, tel. 305/545–3395) satisfies patrons with 2,497 comfortable seats, good sight lines, and acceptable acoustics. Performers grumble at its shortcomings. The lack of a proper orchestra pit frustrates the Greater Miami Opera Association, and storage space is so minimal that between performances the opera company must keep its paraphernalia outside the hall in trailers.

Jackie Gleason Theater of the Performing Arts (1700 Washington Ave., Miami Beach 33119, tel. 305/673–7311 for information; 305/673–8300 for ticket sales for the Broadway Series), with 3,000 seats, has visibility and acoustics problems. Many top performers reportedly won't play here; many patrons are outspoken about not attending.

Gusman Center for the Performing Arts (174 E. Flagler St., Miami 33131, tel. 305/372–0925). In downtown Miami, the center has 1,700 seats made for sardines—and the best acoustics in town. An ornate former movie palace, the hall resembles a Moorish courtyard. Lights twinkle, starlike, from the ceiling. Musicians dread Gusman because they must carry everything they need in and out for each performance.

Gusman Concert Hall (1314 Miller Dr., Coral Gables 33124, tel. 305/284–2438). This 600-seat hall on the University of Miami's Coral Gables campus has good acoustics, and plenty of room for UM's basketball players to stretch their legs. Parking is a problem when school is in session.

Hirschfeld Theatre. Situated in the Castle Hotel and Resort, this 850-seat restored former cabaret once hosted Jackie Gleason and Rowan and Martin. Nine musicals are produced in two seasons, fall-winter and summer, annually. *5445 Collins Ave., Miami Beach 33140, tel. 305/865–PLAY. AE, DC, MC, V.*

Spanish Theater Spanish theater prospers, although many companies have short lives. About 20 Spanish companies perform light comedy, puppetry, vaudeville, and political satire. To locate them, read the Spanish newspapers. When you phone, be prepared for a conversation in Spanish. Most of the box-office personnel don't speak English.

Teatro Avante (Hyatt Regency Miami, 400 SE 2nd Ave., Miami, tel. 305/858–4155). Three to six productions are staged annually in the 442-seat James L. Knight International Center. A Hispanic theater festival is held each May.

Prometeo. This theater has produced three to four bilingual Spanish-English plays a year for 16 years. *Miami-Dade Community College, New World Center Campus, 300 N.E. 2nd Ave., Miami, tel. 305/347–3263. Admission free. Call for invitation.*

Teatro de Bellas Artes. A 255-seat theater on Calle Ocho, Little Havana's main commercial street, Teatro de Bellas Artes presents eight Spanish plays and musicals a year. *Dramas Fri.–Sat. 9 PM and Sun. 3 PM. Musical comedy Sat. midnight and Sun. 9 PM. Recitals Sun. 6 PM. 2173 S.W. 8th St., Miami, tel. 305/325–0515. No credit cards.*

Nightlife

Greater Miami has no concentration of night spots like Bourbon Street in New Orleans or Rush Street in Chicago, but nightlife thrives throughout the Miami area in scattered locations, including Miami Beach, Little Haiti, Little Havana, Coconut Grove, the fringes of downtown Miami, and south-suburban Kendall. Individual clubs offer jazz, various forms of rock-and-roll, and top 40 sounds on different nights of the week. Some clubs refuse entrance to anyone under 21; others set the age limit at 25.

For current information, see the Weekend Section in the Friday edition of *The Miami Herald;* the calendar in *Miami Today*, a free weekly newspaper available each Thursday in downtown Miami, Coconut Grove, and Coral Gables; and *New Times*, a free weekly distributed throughout Dade County each Wednesday.

Love 94 (WLVE, 93.9 FM) sponsors a concert line with information on touring groups of all kinds, except classical (tel. 305/654–9436). Blues Hot Line lists local blues clubs and bars (tel. 305/666–6656). Jazz Hot Line lists local jazz programs (tel. 305/382–3938).

On Miami Beach, where the sounds of jazz and reggae spill into the streets, fashion models and photographers frequent the lobby bars of small Art Deco hotels.

Throughout the Greater Miami area, bars and cocktail lounges in larger hotels operate discos nightly, with live entertainment on weekends. Many hotels extend their bars into open-air courtyards, where patrons dine and dance under the stars throughout the year.

Bars **Churchill's Hideaway.** This enclave of Anglicism in Little Haiti is popular with cruise-line employees and international sports fans. Its satellite dish picks up BBC news programs, and a Sharp Six System VHS plays foreign-format tapes of international soccer and rugby games. Four English beers on tap, 40 kinds of imported bottled beers. Pub grub. Four dart boards. The outdoor bar in back came from an old Playboy Club on Biscayne Boulevard. Not for the unadventurous. Entertainment on weekends. *5501 N.E. 2nd Ave., Miami, tel. 305/757–1807. Open Mon.–Sat. 10 AM–2 AM, Sun. noon–2 AM. No credit cards.*

Hungry Sailor. This small English-style pub run by Englishman Dave Harris is decorated with nautical charts, marine flags, and flotsam and jetsam. It's Coconut Grove's answer to *the pub* with six English/Irish ales and beers on tap plus 16 various bottled brews. The "Sailor" serves traditional Caribbean conch chowder and other island tidbits, as well as the traditional salty inducements to "have another one." Live entertainment nightly: folk, jazz, or reggae. *3064½ Grand Ave., Coconut Grove, tel. 305/444–9359. Open 11:30 AM–2:30 AM. AE, CB, DC, MC, V.*

Mac's Club Deuce. This South Miami Beach gem shows off top international models who pop in to have a drink, shoot some pool. All you get late at night are minipizzas, but the pizzazz lasts, akin to that of the bar scene in *Star Wars*, they'll tell you. One of the best. *222 14th St., Miami Beach, tel. 305/673–9537. Open daily 8 AM–5 AM. No credit cards.*

Stuart's Bar-Lounge. Named for its owner and located in the Hotel Place St. Michel, Stuart's is an original Coral Gables hostelry built in 1926. *Esquire* called Stuart's one of the best new bars of 1987. It is decorated with beveled mirrors, mahogany paneling, French posters, pictures of old Coral Gables, and art-nouveau lighting. Live jazz on weekends. *162 Alcazar Ave., Coral Gables, tel. 305/444–1666. Open Mon.–Sat. 5 PM–12:30 AM, Sun. 6 PM–12:30 AM. AE, CB, DC, MC, V.*

Taurus Steak House. The bar, built in 1922 of native cypress, nightly draws an over-30 singles crowd that drifts outside to a patio. A band plays on weekends. Lunch and dinner. *3540 Main Hwy., Coconut Grove, tel. 305/448–0633. Open daily 5 PM–1 AM, to 4 AM Fri. and Sat. AE, DC, MC, V.*

Tobacco Road. This bar, opened in 1912, holds Miami's oldest liquor license. Upstairs, in space occupied by a speakeasy during Prohibition, local and national blues bands perform Friday and Saturday and in scheduled weeknight concerts. The bar draws a diverse clientele from all over south Florida. *626 S. Miami Ave., Miami, tel. 305/374–1198. Open weekdays 11:30 AM–5 AM, weekends 1 PM–5 AM. Lunch served weekdays. Dinner served Sun.–Thurs. AE, DC.*

Tropics International Restaurant. Music from right-on jazz to rhythm-and-blues, and no cover charge, make Tropics worth popping into. This Memphis-style bar was created by Victor Farinas, one of Miami's top nouveau designers. And if the heat's up, bring your suit and take a dip in the pool. Caribbean menu. *960 Ocean Dr., Miami Beach, tel. 305/531–5335. Open daily 5 PM–3 AM. AE, CB, DC, MC, V.*

Comedy Clubs

Uncle Funny's Comedy Clubs. This 1990s version of vaudeville comedy thrives with humor that's adult, but not obscene. Two acts per show; new performers each week. *Dadeland Marriott Hotel, 9090 S. Dadeland Blvd., Kendall, tel. 305/670–2022. Shows Wed., Thurs., 9 PM; Fri. 9 and 11 PM; Sat. 8 PM, 10 PM, and midnight; Sun., 8 PM. Also at Holiday Inn-Calder, 21485 N.W. 27th Ave., Miami, tel. 305/624–7266. Shows Thurs. and Sun. 9 PM, Fri. and Sat. 9 and 11 PM. Closed Mon.–Wed. Both* *suggest reservations. Cover charge and drink minimum. AE (accepted at door only). CB, DC, MC, V.*

Disco/Rock Clubs

Stringfellows. Opened in May 1989, Peter Stringfellow's Coconut Grove club has been attracting guests from international artistic, business, and social circles, many of whom are already familiar with Stringfellow's other clubs in London and New York. Guests enter through green glass doors decorated with an etched-glass butterfly crest and ascend to the club's second-floor restaurant and nightclub. The restaurant, decorated with art-deco furnishings, pink tablecloths, and fresh orchids, features well-prepared international cuisine. A dinner-hour trio plays jazz. The nightclub, which opens at 11:30, features rock music pumped through a state-of-the-art sound system and a sophisticated light system capable of producing hundreds of variations. *3390 Mary St., Miami 33133, tel. 305/446–7555. Reservations advised. Club cover charge: $10 Tues.–Thurs., $15 Fri., $20 Sat. Closed Sun., Mon., and Christmas. A la carte menu served 8 PM–2:30 AM, late-night supper from 2:30–4 AM. Club open 11:30 PM–5 AM. AE, DC, MC, V.*

Stefano's of Key Biscayne. Live band performs nightly, 7–11 PM. Then this northern Italian restaurant becomes a disco, complete with wood dance floor. *24 Crandon Blvd., Key Biscayne, tel. 305/361–7007. Open 5 PM–5 AM nightly. AE, CB, DC, MC, V.*

Club Nu. The decor at this club changes every three to four months. A large New York–style nightclub with separate champagne room and dining area, this spot attracts a fashion-conscious under-30 crowd, many in bizarre garb. Large terrazzo dance floor. *245 22nd St., Miami Beach 33139, tel. 305/672–0068. Open Wed.–Sun. 10 PM–5 AM. CB, DC, MC, V.*

Nightclubs

Les Violins Supper Club. This standby has been owned for 26 years by the Cachaidora-Currais family, who ran a club and restaurant in Havana. The club's ceiling rises 10 feet during two nightly Las Vegas–style reviews, reminiscent of old Busby Berkeley movies. Live dance band. Wood dance floor. Dinner. *1751 Biscayne Blvd., Miami, tel. 305/371–8668. Open 7 PM. Closes Tues.–Thurs. and Sun. 1 AM, Fri. 2 AM, Sat. 3 AM. Closed Mon. Reservations advised. AE, CB, DC, MC, V.*

Club Tropigala at La Ronde in the Fontainebleau Hilton Hotel. A seven-level round room decorated with orchids, banana leaves, and philodendrons to resemble a tropical jungle, this club is operated by owners of Les Violins. Two bands play Latin music for dancing on the wood floor. Two live costumed shows nightly. Dinner. Long wait for valet parking. *4441 Collins Ave., Miami Beach, tel. 305/672–7469. Open Wed.–Sun. 7 PM–4 AM. Reservations advised. AE, CB, DC, MC, V.*

4 The Everglades

Introduction

by George and Rosalie Leposky

Greater Miami is the only metropolitan area in the United States with two national parks in its backyard: Everglades and Biscayne. Both have image problems.

Because Everglades is famous, people come expecting a spectacle like the mountainous western parks. What they see is a wide expanse of saw grass that at first glance looks frustratingly like a midwestern wheat field. In sea-girded Biscayne, you need a boat and snorkel or scuba gear.

At least these parks are easy to reach. You can drive to either one from downtown Miami in an hour, and their main entrances are just 21 miles apart. Between them sits Homestead, a bustling agricultural city of 25,000.

The creation of Everglades National Park in 1947 made many people in Homestead unhappy. The farmers wanted to plow much of the land that came under the park service's protection.

Today, Homestead views the park, the newer Biscayne National Park, and the town's gateway position vis-à-vis the Florida Keys, more enthusiastically as it turns itself into a tourist center. New motels, shopping centers, and restaurants have opened; old ones are sprucing up. City officials have created a historic district downtown to promote restoration of Homestead's commercial heart. It's all an effort to house, feed, and amuse many of the million visitors who will explore the Everglades in 1991—and the 30,000 hardy souls who will discover Biscayne.

If you intend to spend just one day at Everglades National Park, take the 38-mile main park road from the Main Visitor Center to Flamingo to see a cross section of the park's ecosystems: hardwood hammock (tree islands), freshwater prairie, pineland, freshwater slough, cypress, coastal prairie, mangrove, and marine/estuarine.

At Shark Valley, on the park's northern edge, a 14-mile tram ride takes you to an observation tower overlooking the "river of grass" (*see* Guided Tours, below).

The Gulf Coast and Key Largo ranger stations and the Flamingo Visitor Center offer access to the mangroves and marine habitats—Gulf Coast in the Ten Thousand Islands region along the Gulf of Mexico near Everglades City; Flamingo and Key Largo in Florida Bay. You can take tour boat rides from Everglades City and Flamingo through this ecosystem (*see* Guided Tours, below) and hire a fishing guide to show you where the big ones bite (*see* Participant Sports, below).

Biscayne National Park encompasses almost 274 square miles, of which 96% are under water. Biscayne includes 18 miles of inhospitable mangrove shoreline on the mainland and 45 mangrove-fringed barrier islands seven miles to the east across Biscayne Bay. The bay is a lobster sanctuary and a nursery for fish, sponges, and crabs. Manatees and sea turtles also frequent its warm, shallow waters.

The islands (called keys) are fossilized coral reefs that emerged from the sea when glaciers trapped much of the world's water supply during the Ice Age. Today, a tropical hardwood forest grows in the crevices of these rocky keys.

East of the keys, coral reefs 3 miles seaward attract divers and snorkelers (*see* Participant Sports, below). Biscayne is the only national park in the continental United States with living coral reefs and is the nation's largest marine park.

The park boundary encompasses the continental shelf to a depth of 60 feet. East of that boundary, the shelf falls rapidly away to a depth of 400 feet at the edge of the Gulf Stream.

Getting Around

By Plane

Commercial Flights. **Miami International Airport** (MIA) is the closest commercial airport to Everglades National Park and Biscayne National Park. It's 34 miles from Homestead and 83 miles from the Flamingo resort in Everglades National Park.

By Car From the north, the main highways to Homestead-Florida City are U.S. 1, the Homestead Extension of the Florida Turnpike, and Krome Avenue (Rte. 997).

From Miami to Biscayne National Park, take the turnpike extension to the Tallahassee Road (S.W. 137th Ave.) exit, turn left, and go south. Turn left at North Canal Drive (S.W. 328th St.), go east, and follow signs to park headquarters at Convoy Point. The park is about 30 miles from downtown Miami.

From Homestead to Biscayne National Park, take U.S. 1 or Krome Avenue (Rte. 997) to Lucy Street (S.E. 8th St.). Turn east. Lucy Street becomes North Canal Drive (S.W. 328th St.). Follow signs about 8 miles to the park headquarters.

From Homestead to Everglades National Park's Main Visitor Center and Flamingo, take U.S. 1 or Krome Avenue (Rte. 997) south to Florida City. Turn right (west) onto Rte. 9336. Follow signs to the park entrance. The Main Visitor Center is 11 miles from Homestead; Flamingo is 49 miles from Homestead.

To reach the north end of Everglades National Park, take U.S. 41 (the Tamiami Trail) west from Miami. It's 40 miles to the Shark Valley Information Center and 83 miles to the Gulf Coast Ranger Station at Everglades City.

To reach the south end of Everglades National Park in the Florida Keys, take U.S. 1 south from Homestead. It's 27 miles to the Key Largo Ranger Station (between Mile Markers 98 and 99 on the Overseas Hwy.).

Rental Cars **Homestead Rent-a-Car** (tel. 305/248-8352 or 305/257-2525). Rental cars also available at MIA.

By Van **Super Shuttle.** 11-passenger air-conditioned vans operate between MIA and Homestead. Service on demand from MIA; go to Super Shuttle booth outside most luggage areas on lower level. 24-hour advance reservation requested returning to MIA. *Tel. 305/871-2000. 24-hr daily service. $18–$25 per person depending on zip code in Homestead, $8–$10 each additional person traveling together. AE, DC, MC, V.*

By Bus **Metrobus.** Route 1A runs from Homestead to MIA only during peak weekday hours: 6:30–9 AM and 4–6:30 PM.

Greyhound/Trailways operates two trips daily north and south from MIA (*see* Arriving and Departing in Chapter 3).

By Taxi **Homestead Yellow Cab Company.** Service in Homestead-Florida City area. Full service to and from Flamingo and the tour boats in Biscayne National Park. Service from Homestead to MIA; *416 N.E. 1st Rd., Homestead, tel. 305/247–7777. No credit cards.*

By Boat **U.S. Customs.** The nearest U.S. Customs phones to the two national parks are at **Watson Island Marina** (1050 MacArthur Causeway, Miami, tel. 305/371–2378), about 25 nautical miles to Biscayne National Park headquarters, 50 nautical miles to Flamingo; and **Tavernier Creek Marina** (Mile Marker 90.5, U.S. 1, Tavernier, tel. 305/252–0194 from Miami, 305/852–5854 from the Keys), about 48 nautical miles to Biscayne National Park headquarters, 25 nautical miles to Flamingo.

Scenic Drives **Main road to Flamingo in Everglades National Park.** It's 38 road miles from the Main Visitor Center to Flamingo, across six distinct ecosystems (with access from the road to two others). Highlights of the trip include a dwarf cypress forest, the ecotone (transition zone) between saw grass and mangrove forest, and a wealth of wading birds at Mrazek and Coot Bay ponds. Boardwalks and trails along the main road and several short spurs allow you to see the Everglades without getting your feet wet. Well-written interpretive signs en route will help you understand this diverse wilderness.

Tamiami Trail. U.S. 41 from Miami to the Gulf Coast crosses the Everglades and the Big Cypress National Preserve. Highlights of the trip include sweeping views across the saw grass to the Shark River Slough, a visit to the Miccosukee Indian Reservation, and the Big Cypress National Preserve's variegated pattern of wet prairies, ponds, marshes, sloughs, and strands. It's 83 miles to the Gulf Coast Ranger Station at Everglades City.

Guided Tours

Tours of Everglades National Park and Biscayne National Park typically focus on native wildlife, plants, and park history. Concessionaires operate the Everglades tram tours and the boat cruises in both parks.

In addition, the National Park Service organizes a variety of free programs at Everglades National Park. Ask a ranger for the daily schedule.

Orientation Tours **All Florida Adventure Tours.** All-day narrated 250-mile tour of south Florida wetlands, through the Big Cypress National Preserve to Everglades City and Chokoloskee Island, and Corkscrew. *11137 North Kendall Dr., D105, Miami 33176, tel. 305/270–0219. Tours Tues. and Sat. Cost: $69.50 adults, $49.50 children. No credit cards.*

Special-Interest Tours
Airboat Rides

Buffalo Tiger's Florida Everglades Airboat Ride. The former chairman of the Miccosukee tribe will take you on a 40-minute airboat ride through the Everglades, with a stop at an old Indian camp. Opportunities to watch birds, turtles, and alligators. *Tour location: 12 mi west of Krome Ave., 20 mi west of the Miami city limits (Rte. 997), tel. 305/559–5250. Open daily 9–6. Cost: $7 adults, $5 children under 10. No credit cards.*

Coopertown Airboat Ride. Chuck Norris filmed *Invasion U.S.A.* here. A 30-minute airboat ride through the Everglades saw grass to visit two hammocks (subtropical hardwood forests) and alligator holes. Bird-watching opportunities. *Tour location: S.W. 8th St., 5 mi west of Krome Ave., 15 mi west of Miami city limits, tel. 305/226-6048. Open daily 8 AM–dusk. Cost: $7 per person for 3 or more; minimum $18 for the boat. No credit cards.*

Everglades Air Boat Tours. A four-mile, 30-minute tour of the River of Grass leaves every half hour. *Tour location: 40351 S.W. 192nd Ave., tel. 305/AIRBOAT. Open daily 9–5. Cost: $7.50 adults, $6.50 senior citizens, $3.50 children 4–12, under 4 free. No credit cards.*

Boat Tours

Biscayne National Park Tour Boats. You'll ride to Biscayne National Park's living coral reefs 10 miles offshore on a 53-foot glass-bottom boat. A separate tour to Elliott Key visitor center, on a barrier island 7 miles offshore across Biscayne Bay, is conducted only in winter when mosquitoes are less active. *Tour location: East end of North Canal Dr. (S.W. 328th St.), Homestead, tel. 305/247–2400. Office open daily 8:30–6. Phone for daily schedule. Glass-bottom boat cost: $15.50 adults, $8.50 children, $21 snorkelers. Elliott Key tour Sun. only at 1:30 PM, prices same as for glass-bottom boat tour. Reservations required. AE, MC, V.*

Back Country Tour. A two-hour cruise from Flamingo Lodge Marina & Outpost Resort aboard a 40-passenger pontoon boat covers 12–15 miles through tropical estuaries fringed with impenetrable mangrove forests. You may see manatees, dolphins, sharks, alligators, and many species of bird life, including bald eagles. *Tour location: Flamingo Marina, Flamingo, tel. 305/253–2241 or 813/695–3101. Cruises daily. Phone for schedule. Reservations accepted. Tour admission: $9 adults, $4.50 children 6–12. AE, DC, MC, V.*

Everglades National Park Boat Tours. Sammy Hamilton operates three separate 14-mile tours through the Ten Thousand Islands region along the Gulf of Mexico on the western margin of the park. *Tour location: at Everglades National Park's Gulf Coast Ranger Station on Rte. 29, about 3 mi south of U.S. 41 (Tamiami Trail), tel. 813/695–2591 or in FL 800/445–7724. Office open daily 8:30–4:30. Phone for schedule. No credit cards.*

Florida Bay Cruise. A 90-minute tour of Florida Bay from Flamingo Lodge Marina & Outpost Resort aboard *Bald Eagle*, a 100-passenger pontoon boat. The tour offers a close look at bird life on rookery islands in the bay and on sandbars during low tide. In winter, you're likely to see white pelicans; in summer, magnificent frigatebirds. Also offers backcountry and sunset tours. *Tour location: Flamingo Marina, Flamingo, tel. 305/253–2241 or 813/695–3101. Cruises daily. Phone for schedule. Reservations accepted. Cost: $6.75 adults, $3.50 children 6–12. AE, DC, MC, V.*

Florida Boat Tours. Back-country tours outside Everglades National Park in Everglades City area. Runs three 24-passenger airboats for 30-minute rides, 48-passenger pontoon boat for one-hour cruise. Boats are Coast Guard approved. *Tel. 813/695–4400 or in FL 800/282–9194. Phone for schedule. Cost: $10 adults, $5 children 3–10. MC, V.*

Tram Tours

Wilderness Tram Tour. Snake Bight is an indentation in the Florida Bay shoreline near Flamingo. You can go there aboard a 48-passenger screened tram on this two-hour tour through a mangrove forest and a coastal prairie to a 100-yard boardwalk over the mud flats at the edge of the bight. It's a good birding spot. Tram operates subject to mosquito, weather, and trail conditions. Driver has insect repellent on board. *Departs from Flamingo Lodge gift shop 10:30 AM, 1:30 and 3:30, tel. 305/253–2241 or 813/695–3101. Reservations accepted. Cost: $7 adults, $3.50 children 6–12. AE, CB, DC, MC, V.*

Shark Valley Tram Tours. The trams take a new 15-mile loop road, which is elevated, has 200 culverts, and is considerably less flood prone when the summer rains come. Propane-powered trams travel into the interior, stopping at a 50-foot observation tower on the site of an oil well drilled in the 1940s. From atop the tower, you'll view the Everglades' vast "river of grass" sweeping south toward the Gulf of Mexico. The trams are covered but have open sides, so carry rain gear. *Tour location: Shark Valley entrance to Everglades National Park, 40 mi west of Miami off U.S. 41 (Tamiami Trail), tel. 305/221–8455. Open daily all year 9–4. Reservations recommended Dec.–Mar. Cost: $6.36 adults, $3.18 children, $5.75 senior citizens. No credit cards.*

Personal Guides

Flamingo Lodge Marina & Outpost Resort. Captains of charter fishing boats are available to give individual tours out of Flamingo. Make reservations several weeks in advance through the marina store. *TW Services Inc., Everglades National Park, Box 428, Flamingo 33030, tel. 305/253–2241 or 813/695–3101. Nov. 1–Apr. 30 (except Christmas week). Cost: $215 a day, $140 a half day per person. AE, CB, DC, MC, V.*

Important Addresses and Numbers

Tourist Information

South Dade Visitors Information Center. *100 U.S. 1, Florida City 33034, tel. 305/245–9180. Open daily 8–6.*

Greater Homestead-Florida City Chamber of Commerce. (650 U.S. 1, Homestead 33030, tel. 305/247–2332).

Emergencies

Homestead, Florida City, and unincorporated Dade County use the same emergency number, 911. You can dial free from pay phones.

In the national parks, the rangers perform police, fire, and medical-emergency functions. Look for the rangers at park visitor centers and information stations, or phone the park switchboards: *Biscayne* (tel. 305/247–2044); *Everglades* (tel. 305/247–6211).

Hospitals

James Archer Smith Hospital. 24-hour emergency room. *160 N.W. 13th St., Homestead, tel. 305/248–3232. Physician referral service, tel. 305/248–DOCS.*

Marine Phone Numbers

Biscayne National Park (tel. 305/247–2044). Rangers staff Elliott Key Visitor Center and Adams Key Information Center around the clock and can call the mainland on ship-to-shore radio. Park headquarters on Convoy Point open daily 8–5.

Florida Marine Patrol. Law-enforcement arm of the Florida Department of Natural Resources. Boating emergencies: *24-hour tel. 305/325–3346*. Natural resource violations, including marine fishery laws, mangrove cuttings, manatee reports, filling of wetlands. *For 24-hour Resource Alert Hot Line, tel. 800/342–1821, nonemergencies 305/325–3346.*

National Weather Service. National Hurricane Center office in Coral Gables supplies local forecasts. *Open weekdays 7:30–5, tel. 305/665–0429. For 24-hr weather recording, tel. 305/661–5065.*

U.S. Coast Guard **Miami Beach Coast Guard Base** (tel. 305/535–4314 or 305/535–4315, VHF-FM Channel 16). Local marine emergencies, search-and-rescue, and reporting of navigation hazards.

Exploring Biscayne National Park

Numbers in the margin correspond with points of interest on the Everglades and Biscayne National Parks map.

Because 96% of Biscayne National Park's acreage is under water, you must take a boat ride to visit most of it and snorkel or scuba dive to appreciate it fully. If you don't have your own boat, a concessionaire will take you to the coral reefs 10 miles offshore. These dome-shape patch reefs—some the size of a student's desk, others as broad as a large parking lot—rely on the delicate balance of temperature, depth, light, and water quality that the park was created to maintain.

A diverse population of colorful fish flits through the reefs: angelfish, gobies, grunts, parrot fish, pork fish, wrasses, and many more.

From December through April, when the mosquito population is relatively quiescent, you can comfortably explore several of the mangrove-fringed barrier islands 7 miles offshore. Tropical hardwood forests cloak the upper reaches of these fossilized coral reefs.

The list below describes the facilities at each of Biscayne National Park's visitor service areas, and also at the Metro-Dade County parks within the national park's boundaries.

1 **Adams Key Information Station.** Boat dock, picnic area, rest rooms, short nature trail. Ranger station has ship-to-shore radio contact with mainland. Day use only.

2 **Boca Chita Key.** Mark C. Honeywell, former president of Minneapolis' Honeywell Co., bought this island in 1937 and built the ornamental lighthouse, rainwater catchment cisterns, a wall, and other buildings of coral rock. There is a boat dock, picnic area, and rest rooms. Lighthouse open on occasion; ask rangers.

3 **Convoy Point Information Station.** Park headquarters. Small visitor center and outdoor kiosk with bulletin boards. Launching ramp for canoes and small boats. Boardwalk over shallow water near shore to jetty and path along jetty. Picnic area. Dock where you board tour boats to reefs and Elliott Key. *At east end of North Canal Dr. (S.W. 328th St.), Homestead, tel. 305/247–2044. Open Dec.–Apr. weekdays 8–5, weekends 9–5:30; May–Nov. weekdays 10–4, weekends 10–6. Admission free.*

4 **Elliott Key Visitor Center.** Indoor exhibit area on second floor displays coral, sponges, and sea-turtle shells on a "touching table" that children especially enjoy. A screened enclosure under

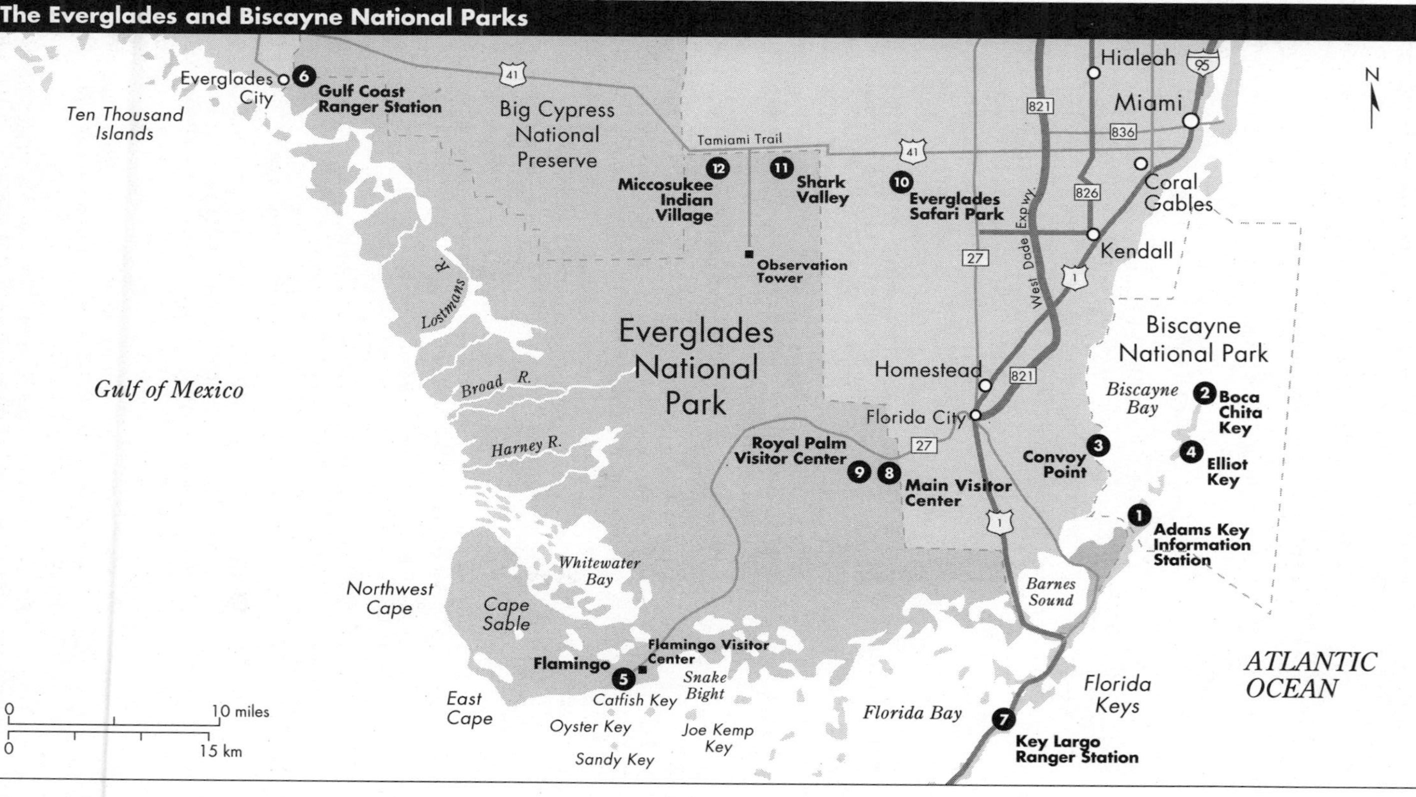
The Everglades and Biscayne National Parks
Everglades City
6 Gulf Coast Ranger Station
Ten Thousand Islands
41
Big Cypress National Preserve
Tamiami Trail
12 Miccosukee Indian Village
11 Shark Valley
Observation Tower
10 Everglades Safari Park
Hialeah
95
Miami
821
836
826
Coral Gables
Kendall
27
1
West Dade Exp wy.
N
Lostmans R.
Everglades National Park
Biscayne National Park
Gulf of Mexico
Broad R.
Harney R.
Homestead
Florida City
Biscayne Bay
2 Boca Chita Key
3 Convoy Point
4 Elliot Key
9 Royal Palm Visitor Center
8 Main Visitor Center
1 Adams Key Information Station
Whitewater Bay
Northwest Cape
Cape Sable
Barnes Sound
Flamingo Visitor Center
5 Flamingo
Snake Bight
Catfish Key
East Cape
Oyster Key
Joe Kemp Key
Sandy Key
Florida Bay
7 Key Largo Ranger Station
Florida Keys
ATLANTIC OCEAN
0 10 miles
0 15 km

the exhibit area houses picnic tables, bulletin boards, and a slide show. *Open weekends and holidays only 10–4.*

Sands Key. Back-country camping allowed; no facilities.

Exploring the Everglades

Winter is the best time to visit Everglades National Park. Temperatures and mosquito activity are moderate. Low water levels concentrate the resident wildlife around sloughs that retain water all year. Migratory birds swell the avian population. Winter is also the busiest time in the park. Make reservations and expect crowds at Flamingo, the main visitor center, and Royal Palm—the most popular visitor service areas.

In spring the weather turns increasingly hot and dry. After Easter, fewer visitors come, and tours and facilities are less crowded. Migratory birds depart, and you must look harder to see wildlife. Be especially careful with campfires and matches; this is when the wildfire prone saw-grass prairies and pinelands are most vulnerable.

Summer brings intense sun and billowing clouds that unleash torrents of rain on the Everglades. Thunderstorms roll in almost every afternoon, bringing the park 90% of its annual 60-inch rainfall from June through October. Water levels rise. Wildlife disperses. Mosquitoes hatch, swarm, and descend on you in voracious clouds. It's a good time to stay away, although some brave souls do come to explore. Europeans constitute 80% of the summer visitors.

Summer in south Florida lingers until mid-October, when the first cold front sweeps through. The rains cease, water levels start to fall, and the ground begins to dry out. Wildlife moves toward the sloughs. Flocks of migratory birds and tourists swoop in, as the cycle of seasons builds once more to the winter peak activity.

Whenever you come, we urge you to experience the real Everglades by getting your feet wet—but most people who visit the park won't do that. Boat tours at Everglades City and Flamingo, a tram ride at Shark Valley, and boardwalks at several locations along the main park road allow you to see the Everglades with dry feet.

The list below describes the facilities at each of the park's visitor service areas.

5 **Flamingo.** Museum, lodge, restaurant, lounge, gift shop, marina, and campground. *Mailing address: Box 279, Homestead 33030, tel. 305/247–6211 (Park Service), tel. 305/253–2241 (Everglades Lodge). Visitor center open daily 8–5.*

6 **Gulf Coast Ranger Station.** Visitor center, where back-country campers pick up required free permits; exhibits; gift shop. *Follow Everglades National Park signs from Tamiami Trail (U.S. 41) south on Rte. 29, tel. 813/695–3311. Open daily winter 8–5, reduced hours in summer. Admission free.*

7 **Key Largo Ranger Station.** No exhibits. *98710 Overseas Hwy., Key Largo, tel. 305/852–5119. Not always staffed; phone ahead. Admission free.*

8 **Main Visitor Center.** Exhibits, film, bookstore, park headquarters. *11 mi west of Homestead on Rte. 9336, tel. 305/247–6211.*

Visitor center open 8–5. Park open 24 hrs. Admission: $5 per car (good for 7 days); $3 per person on foot, bicycle, or motorcycle; senior citizens over 62 free.

9 **Royal Palm Visitor Center.** Anhinga Trail boardwalk, Gumbo Limbo Trail through hammock, museum, bookstore, vending machines. *Tel. 305/247–6211. Open 8–4:30, with a half hour off for lunch.*

10 **Everglades Safari Park.** This package diversion includes an airboat ride, jungle trail, observation platform, alligator wrestling, wildlife museum, gift shop, and restaurant. *9 mi west of Krome Ave., 17 mi west of Miami city limits, on Tamiami Trail (U.S. 41), tel. 305/226–6923 or 305/223–3804. Open daily 8:30–5. Admission: $10 adults, $5 children under 12. No credit cards.*

11 **Shark Valley.** Tram tour, ¼-mile boardwalk, hiking trails, rotating exhibits, bookstore. *Box 42, Ochopee 33943, tel. 305/221–8776. Open daily 8:30–6. Admission: $3 per car, $1 per person on foot, bicycle, or motorcycle (good for 7 days); senior citizens over 62 free. Show Shark Valley admission receipt at Main Visitor Center and pay only the difference there.*

12 **Miccosukee Indian Village.** Near the Shark Valley entrance to Everglades National Park, the Miccosukee tribe operates an Indian village as a tourist attraction. You can watch Indian families cooking and making clothes, dolls, beadwork, and baskets. You'll also see an alligator-wrestling demonstration. The village has a boardwalk and a museum. *On Tamiami Trail (U.S. 41) 40 mi west of Miami. Mailing address: Box 440021, Miami 33144, tel. 305/223–8380. Open daily 9–5. Admission: $5 adults, $3.50 children. Airboat rides: $6 for 30-min trip to another Indian camp on an island in the heart of the Everglades.*

Shopping

Biscayne National Park

Biscayne National Park Tour Boats. T-shirts, snorkeling and diving gear, snacks, and information on Biscayne National Park are available at park headquarters north of the canal. A dive shop van with air compressor is parked south of the canal at Homestead Bayfront Park. *Tel. 305/247–2400. Open daily. Office open 8:30–5:30. AE, MC, V.*

Everglades National Park

Flamingo Lodge Marina & Outpost Resort. The gift shop sells mosquito repellent, Everglades guides, popular novels, T-shirts, souvenirs, and artwork (*see* Participant Sports, below). *Tel. 305/253–2241 or 813/695–3101. Open daily Nov.–Apr. 8–5, Jan.–Mar., 8–8. AE, CB, DC, MC, V.*

Florida City

Robert is Here. A remarkable fruit stand. Robert grows and sells (in season) any tropical fruit that will grow near Everglades National Park. *19200 Palm Dr. (S.W. 344th St.), tel. 305/246–1592. Open daily 8–7. No credit cards.*

Homestead

Homestead's main shopping streets are Homestead Boulevard (U.S. 1), Krome Avenue (Rte. 997), and Campbell Drive (S.W. 312th St., N.E. 8th St.). Shopping centers with major department stores are 10–20 miles north of Homestead along South Dixie Highway (U.S. 1).

Sports and Outdoor Activities

Most of the sports and recreational opportunities in Everglades National Park and Biscayne National Park are related in some way to water or nature study, or both. Even on land, be prepared to get your feet wet on the region's marshy hiking trails. In summer, save your outdoor activities for early or late in the day to avoid the sun's strongest rays and use a sunscreen. Carry mosquito repellent at any time of year.

Water Sports

Boating

Carry aboard the proper *NOAA Nautical Charts* before you cast off to explore the waters of the parks. The charts cost $13.25 each. They are sold at many marine stores in south Florida, at the Convoy Point Visitor Center in Biscayne National Park, and in Flamingo Marina.

Waterway Guide (southern regional edition) is an annual publication of *Marine Buyers' Guide*, which many boaters use as a guide to these waters. Bookstores all over south Florida sell it, or you can order it directly from the publisher. *Communications Channels, Book Department, 6255 Barfield Rd., Atlanta, GA 30328, tel. 800/233–3359. Cost: $25.95 plus $3 shipping and handling.*

Canoeing

The subtropical wilderness of southern Florida is a mecca for flat-water paddlers. In winter, you'll find the best canoeing that the two parks can offer. Temperatures are moderate, rainfall is minimal, and the mosquitoes are tolerable.

Before you paddle into the back country and camp overnight, get a required free permit from the rangers in the park where you plan to canoe (at Convoy Point, Elliott Key, and Adams Key for Biscayne; at Everglades City or Flamingo for Everglades. The Biscayne permit isn't valid for Everglades, and vice versa).

You don't need a permit for day trips, but tell someone where you're going and when you expect to return. Getting lost out there is easy, and spending the night without proper gear can be unpleasant, if not dangerous.

At Biscayne, you can explore five creeks through the mangrove wilderness within 1½ miles of park headquarters at Convoy Point.

Everglades has six well-marked canoe trails in the Flamingo area, including the southern end of the 100-mile Wilderness Waterway from Flamingo to Everglades City. North American Canoe Tours in Everglades City runs a seven-hour shuttle service to haul people, cars, and canoes 151 road-miles between Everglades City and Flamingo.

The vendors listed below all rent aluminum canoes. Most have 17-foot Grummans. Bring your own cushions.

Biscayne National Park Tour Boats. At Convoy Point in Biscayne National Park. *Tel. 305/247–2400. Office open daily 8:30–5:30. Cost: $5 per hr, $17.50 for 4 hrs, $22.50 per day. No launch fee. AE, MC, V.*

Everglades National Park Boat Tours. Gulf Coast Ranger Station in Everglades City. *Tel. 813/695–2591, in FL 800/445–7724. Open daily 8:30–4:30. Cost: $10 per half day, $15 per day; Flamingo-Everglades City shuttle is operated by North Amer-*

ica Canoe Tours at Glades Haven and costs $110 with their canoe or $135 with your own. No credit cards.

North America Canoe Tours at Glades Haven. This outfitter rents canoes and runs guided Everglades trips approved by the National Park Service. *800 S.E. Copeland Ave., Box 5038, Everglades City 33929, tel. 813/695–4666. Open daily 7 AM–9 PM; guided trips Nov. 1–Mar. 31. Canoes $20 the first day, $10 per day thereafter. Outfitter in 1990 opened a bed-and-breakfast in Everglades City called The Ivey House. Inquire for rates. No children under age 8 on guided tours. No pets in park campsites. Reservations required. MC, V.*

Marinas Listed below are the major marinas serving the two parks. The dock masters at these marinas can provide information on other marine services you may need.

Black Point Marina. A new 155-acre Metro-Dade County Park with a hurricane-safe harbor basin, 5 miles north of Homestead Bayfront Park. Facilities include storage racks for 300 boats, 178 wet slips, 10 ramps, fuel, a bait-and-tackle shop, canoe-launching ramp, power-boat rentals, police station, and outside grill serving lunch and dinner, with bar. Shrimp fleet docks at the park. At east end of Coconut Palm Drive (S.W. 248th St.). From Florida's Turnpike, exit at S.W. 112th Avenue, go 2 blocks north, and turn east on Coconut Palm Drive. *24775 S.W. 87th Ave., Naranja, tel. 305/258–4092. Open Mon.–Wed. 6 AM–9 PM, Thurs.–Sun. 6 AM–1 AM. AE, MC, V.*

Marine Management. At Black Point Marina. Rents 15- to 20-foot open fishermen boats and bow riders. *Tel. 305/258–3500. Open daily 7–6 winter, 7–7 summer. Closed Christmas. MC, V.*

Pirate's Spa Marina. Just west of Black Point Park entrance. Shrimp boats dock along canal. Facilities include boat hoist, wet and dry storage, fuel, bait and tackle, and boat rental. *8701 Coconut Palm Dr. (S.W. 248th St.), Naranja, tel. 305/257–5100. Open weekdays 7 AM–sundown, weekends open 6 AM. No credit cards.*

Flamingo Lodge Marina & Outpost Resort. Fifty-slip marina rents 40 canoes, 10 power skiffs, 5 houseboats, and several private boats available for charter. There are two ramps, one for Florida Bay, the other for Whitewater Bay and the back country. The hoist across the plug dam separating Florida Bay from the Buttonwood Canal can take boats up to 26 feet long. A small marina store sells food, camping supplies, bait and tackle, and automobile and boat fuel. *Tel. 305/253–2241 from Miami, 813/695–3101 from Gulf Coast. Open winter 6 AM–7 PM, summer 7–6. AE, DC, MC, V.*

Homestead Bait and Tackle. Facilities include dock and wet slips, fuel, bait and tackle, ice, boat hoist, and ramp. The marina is near Homestead Bayfront Park's tidal swimming area and concessions. *North Canal Dr., Homestead, tel. 305/245–2273. Open daily weekdays 7–5, weekends 7–6. MC, V.*

Diving

Dive Boats and Instruction

Biscayne National Park Tour Boats. This is the official concessionaire for Biscayne National Park. The center provides equipment for dive trips and sells equipment. Snorkeling and scuba trips include about 4 hours on the reefs. *Reef Rover IV and V*, aluminum dive boats, each carries up to 49 passengers. The resort course and private instruction lead to full certification. *Office and dive boat at Convoy Point. Mailing address: Box 1270, Homestead 33030, tel. 305/247–2400. Open daily*

8:30–6. Snorkeling and scuba trips daily 1:30–5 PM; group charters any day. Cost: $19.81 snorkeling, $24.52 scuba. Reservations required. Children welcome. AE, MC, V.

Pirate's Cove Dive Center. This is the last dive store north of the Keys, and it rents, sells, and repairs diving equipment. Staff teaches all sport-diving classes, including resort course, deep diver, and underwater photography. The center does not have a boat; instead they use dive boats at Homestead Bayfront Park. NAUI and PADI affiliation. *116 N. Homestead Blvd., Homestead 33030, tel. 305/248–1808. Open weekdays 9–6, Sat. 8–6, Sun. 8–4. Open to 7:30 May–Sept., around the clock during annual 4-day sport divers' lobster season (in July or Aug.). AE, DC, MC, V.*

Fishing The rangers in the two parks enforce all state fishing laws and a few of their own. Ask at each park's visitor centers for that park's specific regulations.

Swimming **Homestead Bayfront Park.** This saltwater atoll pool, adjacent to Biscayne Bay, which is flushed by tidal action, is popular with local family groups and teenagers. *N. Canal Dr., Homestead, tel. 305/247–1543. Open daily, 7 AM to sundown. Admission: $2 per car.*

Elliott Key. Boaters like to anchor off Elliott Key's 30-foot-wide sandy beach, the only beach in Biscayne National Park. It's about a mile north of the harbor on the west (bay) side of the key.

Bicycling and Hiking **Biscayne National Park.** Elliott Key's resident rangers lead informal nature walks on a 1½-mile nature trail.

You can also walk the length of the seven-mile key along a rough path that developers bulldozed before the park was created.

Everglades National Park. Shark Valley's concessionaire has rental bicycles. You may ride or hike along the Loop Road, a 15-mile round-trip. Yield right of way to trams. *Shark Valley Tram Tours, Box 1729, Tamiami Station, Miami 33144, tel. 305/221–8455. Rentals daily 8:30–3, return bicycles by 4. Cost: $1.50 per hr. No reservations. No credit cards.*

Ask the rangers for *Foot and Canoe Trails of the Flamingo Area*, a leaflet that also lists bike trails. Inquire about water levels and insect conditions before you go. Get a free backcountry permit if you plan to camp overnight.

Dining

Although the two parks are wilderness areas, there are restaurants within a short drive of all park entrances: between Miami and Shark Valley along the Tamiami Trail (U.S. 41), in the Homestead-Florida City area, in Everglades City, and in the Keys along the Overseas Highway (U.S. 1). The only food service in either park is at Flamingo in the Everglades.

The list below is a selection of independent restaurants on the Tamiami Trail, in the Homestead-Florida City area, and at Flamingo. Many of these establishments will pack picnic fare that you can take to the parks. (You can also find fast-food establishments with carryout service on the Tamiami Trail and in Homestead-Florida City.) The most highly recommended restaurants are indicated with a star ★.

Category	Cost*
Very Expensive	over $60
Expensive	$40–$60
Moderate	$20–$40
Inexpensive	under $20

**per person, excluding drinks, service, and 6% sales tax*

The following credit card abbreviations are used: AE, American Express; CB, Carte Blanche; DC, Diners Club; MC, MasterCard; V, Visa.

Flamingo
American

Flamingo Restaurant. The view from this three-tier dining room on the second floor of the Flamingo Visitor Center will knock your socks off. Picture windows overlook Florida Bay, giving you a bird's-eye view (almost) of soaring eagles, gulls, pelicans, terns, and vultures. Try to dine at low tide when flocks of birds gather on a sandbar just offshore. Specialties include a flavorful, mildly spiced conch chowder; teriyaki chicken breast; and pork loin roasted Cuban-style with garlic and lime. The tastiest choices, however, are the seafood. If marlin is on the dinner menu, order it fried so that the moisture and flavor of the dark, chewy meat are retained. Picnic baskets available. They will cook the fish you catch if you clean it at the marina. *At Flamingo Visitor Center in Everglades National Park, Flamingo, tel. 305/253–2241 from Miami, 813/695–3101 from Gulf Coast. Dress: casual. Reservations required for dinner. AE, MC, V. Closed early May–mid-Oct. (The snack bar at the marina store stays open all year.) Moderate.*

Florida City
Mixed Menu
★

Richard Accursio's Capri Restaurant and **King Richard's Room.** This is where locals dine out—business groups at lunch, the Rotary Club each Wednesday at noon, and families at night. Specialties include pizza with light, crunchy crusts and ample toppings; mild, meaty conch chowder; mussels in garlic-cream or marinara sauce; Caesar salad with lots of cheese and anchovies; antipasto with a homemade, vinegary Italian dressing; pasta shells stuffed with rigatoni cheese in tomato sauce; yellowtail snapper Française; and Key-lime pie with plenty of real Key lime juice. *935 N. Krome Ave., Florida City, tel. 305/247–1542. Dress: Capri casual, jacket and tie required in King Richard's. Reservations advised. AE, MC, V. Closed Sun. except Mother's Day and Christmas. Inexpensive.*

Seafood
★

Captain Bob's. The Greek family who owns this restaurant has a list of more than 800 ways to prepare seafood. Specialties include snapper wrapped in phyllo dough in dill velouté sauce and sea trout senator, with sliced almonds, mushrooms, scallions, and sherry-lemon butter sauce. Save room for the Key-lime pie. *326 S.E. 1st Ave., Florida City, tel. 305/247–8988. Dress: casual. Reservations accepted. AE, CB, DC, MC, V. Open daily, beginning with breakfast at 6 AM. Inexpensive.*

Homestead
American

Downtown Bar and Outdoor Cafe. A south Florida interpretation of a New Orleans courtyard restaurant, complete with a wrought-iron gate and live entertainment. Specialties include Buffalo chicken wings (hot or mild) with celery and blue-cheese dip; blackened or grilled dolphin or grouper from the Keys; raspberry nut cake; and refreshingly tart lemonade. *28 S. Krome Ave., Homestead, tel. 305/245–8266. Dress: casual.*

Reservations accepted. AE, MC, V. Closed Easter, Thanksgiving, Christmas. Inexpensive.

Potlikker's. This southern country-style restaurant takes its name from the broth—*pot liquor*—left over from the boiling of greens. Live plants dangle from open rafters in the lofty pine-lined dining room. Specialties include fried Okeechobee catfish, with Cajun spicing in a cornmeal-matzo-meal breading; fresh-carved roast turkey with homemade dressing, and at least 11 different vegetables to serve with lunch and dinner entrées. For dessert, try Key-lime pie—four inches tall and frozen; it tastes great if you dawdle over dessert while it thaws. *591 Washington Ave., Homestead, tel. 305/248–0835. Dress: casual. No reservations. MC, V. Closed Christmas Day. Inexpensive.*

Mexican **El Toro Taco.** The Hernandez family came to the United States from San Luis Potosí, Mexico, to pick crops. They opened this Homestead-area institution in 1971. They make salt-free tortillas and nacho chips with corn from Texas that they cook and grind themselves. The cilantro-dominated salsa is mild for American tastes; if you like more fire on your tongue, ask for a side dish of minced jalapeño peppers to mix in. Specialties include chile rellenos (green peppers stuffed with meaty chunks of ground beef and topped with three kinds of cheese), and chicken *fajitas* (chunks of chicken marinated in vinegar and spices, charbroiled with onions and peppers, and served with tortillas and salsa). Bring your own beer and wine; the staff will keep it cold for you and supply lemon for your Corona beer. *1 S. Krome Ave., Homestead, tel. 305/245–5576. Dress: casual. No reservations. No credit cards. Closed Christmas Day and Dec. 26. Inexpensive.*

Seafood **The Seafood Feast Restaurant.** Bob and Julie Cisco gave up a steak-house franchise to open this all-you-can-eat seafood buffet. It features shrimp, crabs' legs, frogs' legs, several choices of fish, salads, breads, and desserts. Specialties include Cajun-style crawfish from Louisiana, garlic crabs, steamed mussels, and oysters on the half shell (on request). *27835 S. Dixie Hwy., Naranja (3½ mi northeast of downtown Homestead), tel. 305/246–1445. Dress: casual. No reservations. No alcohol on premises. AE, MC, V. Moderate.*

Tamiami Trail

American **The Pit Bar-B-Q.** This place will overwork your salivary glands with its intense aroma of barbecue and blackjack oak smoke. You order at the counter, then come when called to pick up your food. Specialties include barbecued chicken and ribs with a tangy sauce, french fries, coleslaw, and a fried biscuit, and catfish, frogs' legs, and shrimp breaded and deep-fried in vegetable oil. *16400 S.W. 8th St., Miami, tel. 305/226–2272. Dress: casual. No reservations. MC, V. Closed Christmas Day. Inexpensive.*

American Indian **Miccosukee Restaurant.** Murals with Indian themes depict women cooking and men engaged in a powwow. Specialties include catfish and frogs' legs breaded and deep-fried in peanut oil, Indian fry bread (a flour-and-water dough deep-fried in peanut oil), pumpkin bread, Indian burger (ground beef browned, rolled in fry bread dough, and deep-fried), and Indian taco (fry bread with chili, lettuce, tomato, and shredded cheddar cheese on top). *On Tamiami Trail, near the Shark Valley entrance to Everglades National Park, tel. 305/223–8380,* *ext. 332. Dress: casual. No reservations. AE, CB, DC, MC, V. Inexpensive.*

Floridian **Coopertown Restaurant.** A rustic 30-seat restaurant full of Floridiana, including alligator skulls, stuffed alligator heads, alligator accessories (belts, key chains, and the like). Specialties include alligator and frogs' legs, breaded and deep-fried in vegetable oil, available for breakfast, lunch, or dinner. *22700 S.W. 8th St., Miami, tel. 305/226-6048. Dress: casual. No reservations. No credit cards. Inexpensive.*

Lodging

Many visitors to the two parks stay in the big-city portion of Greater Miami and spend a day visiting one or both of the parks. For serious outdoors people, such a schedule consumes too much time in traffic and leaves too little time for nature-study and recreation.

At Shark Valley, due west of Miami, you have no choice. Only the Miccosukee Indians live there; there is no motel.

Southwest of Miami, Homestead has become a bedroom community for both parks. You'll find well-kept older properties and shiny new ones, chain motels, and independents. Prices tend to be somewhat lower than in the Miami area.

Hotel and motel accommodations are available on the Gulf Coast at Everglades City and Naples.

The list below is a representative selection of hotels and motels in the Homestead area. Also included are the only lodgings inside either park. The rate categories in the list are based on the all-year or peak-season price; off-peak rates may be a category or two lower.

Category	Cost*
Very Expensive	over $120
Expensive	$90–$120
Moderate	$50–$90
Inexpensive	under $50

**per room, double occupancy, without 6% state sales tax and modest resort tax*

The following credit card abbreviations are used. AE, American Express; CB, Carte Blanche; DC, Diners Club; MC, MasterCard; V, Visa.

Flamingo Lodge Marina & Outpost Resort. This rustic low-rise wilderness resort, the only lodging inside Everglades National Park, is a strip of tentative civilization 300 yards wide and 1½ miles long. Accommodations are basic but attractive and well kept. An amiable staff with a sense of humor helps you become accustomed to alligators bellowing in the sewage-treatment pond down the road, raccoons roaming the pool enclosure at night, and the flock of ibis grazing on the lawn. The rooms have wood-paneled walls, contemporary furniture, floral bedspreads, and art prints of flamingos and egrets on the walls. Most bathrooms are near the door, so you won't track mud all over the room. Television reception has been improved with addition of a satellite dish, but you don't come here to watch TV. All motel rooms face Florida Bay but don't necessarily overlook it. The cottages are in a wooded area on the margin of a coastal prairie. Ask about reserving tours, skiffs, and canoes when you make reservations. Also inquire about the new 100-passenger tour boat for day and sunset cruises. *Box 428, Flamingo 33030, tel. 305/253–2241 from Miami, 813/695–3101 from Gulf Coast. 121 units with bath, including 101 motel rooms, one 2-bath suite for up to 8 people, 24 kitchenette cottages (2 for handicapped guests). Facilities: screened outdoor freshwater pool, restaurant, lounge, marina, marina store with snack bar, gift shop, coin laundry. AE, CB, DC, MC, V. Lodge, marina, and marina store open all year; restaurant, lounge, and gift shop closed May 1–Oct. 31. Moderate.*

Holiday Inn. Low-rise motel on a commercial strip. The best rooms look out on the landscaped pool and adjoining Banana Bar. Rooms have contemporary walnut furnishings and firm, bouncy mattresses. *990 N. Homestead Blvd., Homestead 33030, tel. 305/247–7020 or 800/HOLIDAY. 139 rooms with bath. Facilities: outdoor freshwater pool, restaurant and lounge with nightly entertainment, poolside bar, cable TV, massage shower heads. AE, CB, DC, MC, V. Moderate.*

Knights Inn. This low-rise motel opened in 1987 on a commercial strip next door to a McDonald's. Beds are a foot longer than normal, and the mattresses are firm. The inn is decorated in English half-timber style, inside and out. *401 U.S. 1, Florida City 33034, tel. 305/245–2800. 100 rooms, 11 fully equipped kitchenettes, 27 for handicapped guests. Facilities: outdoor freshwater pool, free HBO and TV movies, free ice, free local phone calls, coffee bar in lobby, security at night. AE, CB, DC, MC, V. Moderate.*

Park Royal Inn. This low-rise motel on a commercial strip has rooms with rough wood walls, flowered bedspreads, blue or gray carpet, gray chairs and dressers, and lamps with a shell or pelican design. No closet, very small clothes rack. *100 U.S. 1, Florida City 33034, tel. 305/247–3200 or 800/521–6004. 160-unit motel, 7 rooms for handicapped guests. Facilities: outdoor freshwater pool, minirefrigerator in each room, color TV, phone. AE, CB, DC, MC, V. Moderate.*

Camping

Biscayne National Park

You can camp on designated keys 7 miles offshore at primitive sites or in the back country. Carry all your food, water, and supplies onto the keys, and carry all trash off when you leave. Bring plenty of insect repellent. *Free. No reservations. No ferry or marina services. For back-country camping, obtain a required free permit from rangers at Adams Key, Convoy Point, or Elliott Key.*

Everglades National Park

All campgrounds are primitive, with no water or electricity. Come early to get a good site, especially in winter. Bring plenty of insect repellent. *Admission: $7 per site in winter, free in summer. Stay limited to 14 days Nov. 1–Apr. 30. Check-out time 10 AM. Register at campground. Open all year.*

Long Pine Key. 108 campsites, drinking water, sewage dump station.

Flamingo. 235 drive-in sites, 60 walk-in sites, drinking water, cold-water showers, and sewage dump station.

Back country. 34 designated sites, most with chickees (raised wood platforms with thatch roofs). All have chemical toilets.

Carry all your food, water, and supplies in; carry out all trash. Get free permit from rangers at Everglades City or Flamingo. Permits issued for a specific site. Capacity and length of stay limited.

5 Fort Lauderdale

Introduction

If you think of Fort Lauderdale only as a spring-break mecca for collegians seeking sun, suds, and surf, your knowledge is both fragmentary and out of date. The 1960 film, *Where the Boys Are,* attracted hordes of young people to the city's beaches but now the center of spring-break activity has shifted north to Daytona Beach.

Fort Lauderdale today emphasizes year-round family tourism focused on a wide assortment of sports and recreational activities, an extensive cultural calendar, artistic and historic attractions, and fine shopping and dining opportunities.

Sandwiched between Miami to the south and Palm Beach to the north along southeast Florida's Gold Coast, Fort Lauderdale is the county seat of Broward County. The county encompasses 1,197 square miles—17 square miles less than the state of Rhode Island. Broward County has 23 miles of Atlantic Ocean beach frontage, and it extends 50 miles inland to the west. A coastal ridge rising in places to 25 feet above sea level separates the coastal lowlands from the interior lowlands of the Everglades.

Broward County is named for Napoleon Bonaparte Broward, Florida's governor 1905–09. His drainage schemes around the turn of the century opened much of the marshy Everglades region for farming, ranching, and settlement. In fact, the first successful efforts at large-scale Everglades drainage took place within Broward County's boundaries.

Fort Lauderdale's first known white settler, Charles Lewis, established a plantation along the New River in 1793. The city is named for a fort that Major William Lauderdale built at the river's mouth in 1838 during the Seminole Indian wars.

The area was still a remote frontier when Frank Stranahan arrived in 1892 to operate an overnight camp on the river. Stranahan began trading with the Indians in 1901 and built a store, which later became his residence. It's now a museum.

Fort Lauderdale incorporated in 1911 with just 175 residents, but it grew rapidly during the Florida boom of the 1920s. Today the city's population of 160,000 remains relatively stable, while suburban areas bulge with growth. Broward County's population is expected to exceed 1.35 million—more than double its 1970 population of 620,000. The county has become a haven for retirees; more than a third of the new arrivals are over the age of 55.

New homes, offices, and shopping centers have filled in the gaps between older communities along the coastal ridge. Now they're marching west along I–75, I–595, and the Sawgrass Expressway, transforming the Everglades. Meanwhile, Fort Lauderdale is building skyscrapers downtown to cement its position as the county's financial and commercial hub.

Broward County is developing a concentration of clean high-technology industries, including computer manufacturing, data processing, and electronics. Port Everglades, a major deep-water seaport, handles refined petroleum products and general cargo. A cruise terminal at Port Everglades caters to luxury liners, leaving the mass-market cruise business to the Port of Miami.

To accommodate the traffic that comes with all this growth, the Florida Department of Transportation is expanding Broward County's road system. During 1990, construction on I–95 and I–595 created gridlock during rush hours. Tri-Rail, a tri-county commuter train running through Broward County from Miami to West Palm Beach, takes some cars off the highways, but you should still expect traffic delays and allow extra time to move around the county in 1991.

Even when you're stuck in traffic, you can still enjoy Broward County's near-ideal weather. The average temperature is 75 degrees (winter average 66 degrees, summer average 84 degrees). Rainfall averages 65 inches a year, with 60% of the total occurring in afternoon thunderstorms June–October. The warm, relatively dry winters help to give the county about 3,000 hours of sunshine a year.

Arriving and Departing by Plane

Airport **Fort Lauderdale-Hollywood International Airport (FLHIA),** (tel. 305/357–6100), four miles south of downtown Fort Lauderdale, is Broward County's major airline terminal. To get there off I–95, take the I–595 east exit to U.S. 1 and follow the signs to the airport entrance.

Between the Airport and Center City Broward Transit's bus route No. 1 operates between the airport and its main terminal at N.W. 1st Street and 1st Avenue in the center of Fort Lauderdale. The fare is 75 cents. Limousine service is available from **Airport Express** (tel. 305/527–8690) to all parts of Broward County. Fares range from $6 to $13 or more per person, depending on distance. Fares to most Fort Lauderdale beach hotels are in the $6–$8 range. Pickup points are at each of the new terminals.

Arriving and Departing by Car, Train, and Bus

By Car The access highways to Broward County from the north or south are Florida's Turnpike, I–95, U.S. 1, and U.S. 441; for a more scenic—and slower—drive, Rte. A1A, which generally parallels the beach area. The primary access road to Broward County from the west is I–595, paralleled by Rte. 84.

By Train **Amtrak** provides daily service to Broward County, with stops at Hollywood, Fort Lauderdale, and Deerfield Beach. *Fort Lauderdale station, 200 S.W. 21st Terr., tel. 305/463–8251; reservations, tel. 800/872–7245.*

Tri-Rail, which connects Broward, Dade, and Palm Beach counties, has six stations in Broward. All stations are west of I–95. *Tel. 305/728–8445 or 800/TRI-RAIL (in Dade, Broward, and Palm Beach counties).*

By Bus **Greyhound/Trailways** (513 N.E. 3rd St., Ft. Lauderdale, tel. 305/764–6551 or 800/872–6242).

Getting Around

By Car In 1988 the Florida Department of Transportation (FDOT) began to build the last stage of the I–595/Port Everglades Expressway Project, which runs east-west through the middle of Broward County. By 1991, 15 interchanges will be improved and local roads will be linked to I–595, which follows the Rte. 84 corridor from I–75 east to the port.

At the same time, I–95 is being widened, disrupting north-south traffic for 46 miles from Yamato Road, in southern Palm Beach County, through Broward County to Rte. 836, in northern Dade County.

If you're driving into Florida, stop at a visitor center near the state line for a traveler advisory card on the current status of I–95 construction. Ask for current information on travel time and alternative routes.

FDOT officials urge you to take Florida's Turnpike or the Sawgrass Expressway through Broward County to avoid I–95. A new interchange at S.W. 10th Street in Deerfield Beach connects the Sawgrass Expressway directly to I–95. Other alternatives include crowded local roads such as A1A, U.S. 1, U.S. 441, and University Drive (Rte. 817).

Listen to radio traffic reports on the status of I–95 construction. Your hotel clerk should know which stations have them.

Try to avoid driving anywhere in Broward County—and especially on I–95—in the morning and evening rush hours (7–9 AM and 3–6 PM). Allow plenty of time to get where you're going, be patient, and stay calm. South Florida drivers can be among the world's worst.

FDOT has set up a consumer service organization to issue free publications and to provide traffic reports by phone. *Gold Coast Commuter Services, 6261 N.W. 6th Way, Suite 100, Fort Lauderdale, tel. 305/771–9500 or in FL 800/234–7433. Open 8–5.*

By Bus **Broward County Mass Transit** serves the entire county. The fare is 75¢ plus 10¢ for a transfer, with some bus routes starting as early as 5 AM; some continuing to 10 PM. Call for route information (tel. 305/357–8400). There are also special seven-day tourist passes for $8 that are good for unlimited use on all county buses. These are available at most major hotels and at Broward County libraries.

By Taxi It's difficult to hail a taxi on the street; sometimes you can pick one up at a major hotel. Otherwise, phone ahead. Fares are not cheap; meters run at the rate of $2.20 for the first mile and $1.50 for each additional mile. The major company serving the area is **Yellow Cab** (tel. 305/565–5400).

By Water Taxi **Water Taxi** (tel. 305/565–5507) provides service along the Intracoastal Waterway between Port Everglades and Commercial Boulevard 10 AM–2 AM. The boats stop at 30 restaurants, hotels, and nightclubs; the fare is $3.75 one way, all-day pass $10.75.

Important Addresses and Numbers

Tourist Information The main office of the Greater Fort Lauderdale Convention & Visitors Bureau (tel. 305/765–4466) is at 500 E. Broward Boulevard, Suite 104. The office is open weekdays 8:30–5. The Greater Fort Lauderdale Chamber of Commerce (tel. 305/462–6000) is at 208 S.E. 3rd Ave., 33301. Other communities in Broward County also have individual chambers of commerce, including Dania (Box 838, Dania 33004, tel. 305/927–3377), Hollywood (330 N. Federal Hwy., Hollywood 33020, tel. 305/920–3330), Oakland Park–Wilton Manors (181 N.E. 32nd Ct., Oakland Park 33334, tel. 305/564–8300), and Pompano Beach (2200 E. Atlantic Blvd., Pompano Beach 33062, tel. 305/941–2940).

Tickets Call **Ticketmaster** to order tickets for performing arts and sports events (tel. 305/523–3309). MC, V.

Emergencies Dial 911 for **police** and **ambulance** in an emergency.

Poison Control (tel. 800/282–3171).

Hospitals. The following hospitals have a 24-hour emergency room: **Holy Cross Hospital** (4725 N. Federal Hwy., Fort Lauderdale, tel. 305/771–8000; physician referral, tel. 305/776–3223) and **Broward General Medical Center** (1600 S. Andrews Ave., Fort Lauderdale, tel. 305/355–4400; physician referral, tel. 305/355–4888).

24-Hour Pharmacies. Eckerd Drug (1385 S.E. 17th St., Fort Lauderdale, tel. 305/525–8173; and 154 University Dr., Pembroke Pines, tel. 305/432–5510). **Walgreens** (2855 Stirling Rd., Fort Lauderdale, tel. 305/981–1104; 761 S.E. 17th St., Fort Lauderdale, tel. 305/467–5448; and 289 S. Federal Hwy., Deerfield Beach, tel. 305/481–2993).

Telecommunications for the Hearing-Impaired. United Hearing and Deaf Services (4850 W. Oakland Park Blvd., Suite 207, Lauderdale Lakes, tel. 305/731–7208).

Guided Tours

The Voyager Sightseeing Train offers a city tram tour. *600 Seabreeze Blvd., Fort Lauderdale, tel. 305/463–0401 (Broward County), tel. 305/944–4669 (Dade County).*

The ***Jungle Queen,*** built to resemble an old-time steamboat, travels day and night up the New River through the heart of Fort Lauderdale. Dinner cruises are available. The same company sends boats to Miami's Bayside Marketplace. All cruises leave from the Bahia Mar dock on Rte. A1A. *Tel. 305/462–5596 (Broward County), 305/947–6597 (Dade County).*

The ***Paddlewheel Queen,*** a flat-bottom luncheon and sightseeing cruise boat, visits major spots along Fort Lauderdale's Intracoastal Waterway. Four sailings daily. *2950 N.E. 30th St., a block south of Oakland Park Boulevard Bridge, 2 blocks west of Rte. A1A, tel. 305/564–7659. AE, MC, V.*

Exploring Fort Lauderdale

Numbers in the margin correspond with points of interest on the Fort Lauderdale Area map.

Central Fort Lauderdale is diverse, picturesque, and surprisingly compact. Within a few blocks you'll find modern high-rise office buildings; a historic district with museums, restaurants, and antiques shops; a scenic riverfront drive; upscale shopping; and the only vehicular tunnel in Florida—all within 2 miles of the beach.

This tour begins on the beach at Las Olas Boulevard and Rte. A1A. Go north on Rte. A1A along **the beach,** with hotels, restaurants, and shops on your left, the ocean on your right. Turn
1 left at Sunrise Boulevard, then right into **Hugh Taylor Birch**

Fort Lauderdale Area

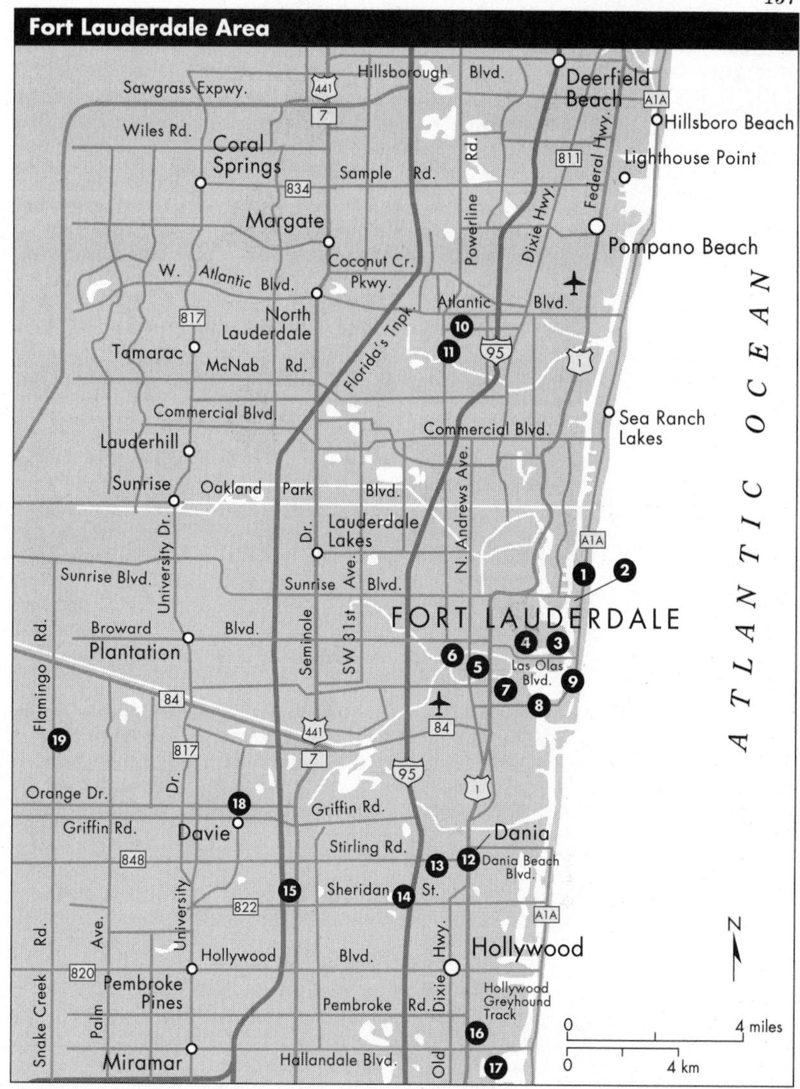

Atlantis, **13**
Bonnet House, **2**
Brooks Memorial Causeway, **8**
Broward County Museum of Archaeology, **6**
Dania Jai-Alai Palace, **12**
Davie Rodeo Complex, **18**
Flamingo Gardens, **19**
Gulfstream Park Race Track, **17**
Hollywood Dog Track, **16**
Hugh Taylor Birch State Recreation Area, **1**
The Isles, **3**
Ocean World, **7**
Pompano Harness Track, **10**
Quiet Waters Park, **11**
River Walk, **5**
Seminole Native Village, **15**
Stranahan House, **4**
Swimming Hall of Fame Museum, **9**
Topeekeegee Park, **14**

State Recreation Area. Amid the 180-acre park's tropical greenery, you can stroll along a nature trail, picnic, play volleyball, pitch horseshoes, ride a rental bike or paddleboats, and canoe. *3109 E. Sunrise Blvd., tel. 305/564–4521; concessions tel. 305/564–4572. Open 8–sundown. Ranger-guided nature walks Fri. 10:30. Admission: $1 per car and driver, 50¢ per passenger; (out of state): $2 per car and driver, $1 per passenger.*

Leaving the park, cross Sunrise Boulevard south anytime but
2 winter and visit the **Bonnet House.** This lyrical house built by
artist Frederic Bartlett is on land he was given by his father-in-law, Hugh Taylor Birch. The house and its subtropical 35-acre estate has since been donated to the Florida Trust for Historic Preservation. From May through November the house is open to visitors with its original works of art, including whimsically carved animals, a swan pond, and, most of all, its tranquility. *900 N. Birch Rd., tel. 305/563–5393. Reservations required. Admission $7.50 adults, $5 seniors, children under 6 free.*

Leaving Bonnet House, go south on Birch Road to Las Olas
Boulevard, turn right, and cross the Intracoastal Waterway.
3 You're now westbound through **The Isles,** Fort Lauderdale's
most expensive and prestigious neighborhood, where the homes line a series of canals with large yachts beside the seawalls. When you reach the mainland, Las Olas becomes an upscale shopping street with Spanish-Colonial buildings housing high-fashion boutiques, jewelry shops, and art galleries. The heart of the **Las Olas Shopping District** is from S.E. 11th Avenue to S.E. 6th Avenue.

4 Turn left on S.E. 6th Avenue, and visit **Stranahan House,** home of pioneer businessman Frank Stranahan. He arrived in 1892 and began trading with the Seminole Indians. In 1901 he built this building as a store, and later made it his home. Now it's a museum with many of the Stranahans' furnishings on display. *1 Stranahan Pl. (S.E. 6th Ave.), tel. 305/524–4736. Open Wed., Fri., Sat. 10–4. Admission: $3, $2 children under 12.*

Return to Las Olas Boulevard, go to S.W. 1st Avenue, and turn
left beside the *News & Sun-Sentinel* building. Go a block south
to New River Drive, where you can park and stroll a portion of
5 the palm-lined **River Walk,** a linear park with walkways and
sidewalk cafes along both banks of the New River. As part of a $44-million redevelopment program, Fort Lauderdale is improving and extending the River Walk. Unlike the Miami River, which carries a heavy load of commercial shipping, New River traffic is primarily recreational yachts and tour boats. Return to Las Olas, turn left, and go to the **Museum of Art,** which features a major collection of works from the CoBrA (Copenhagen, Brussels, and Amsterdam) movement, plus American Indian, pre-Columbian, West African, and Oceanic ethnographic art. Edward Larabee Barnes designed the museum building, which opened in 1986. *1 E. Las Olas Blvd., tel. 305/525–5500. Open Tues. 11–9, Wed.–Sat. 10–5, Sun. noon–5. Admission: $3.25 adults, $2.75 seniors, $1.25 students, free under 12. Free 1-hr highlight tours Tues. noon and 6:30 PM, Wed.–Fri, noon, Sat, Sun. 2 PM. Parking nearby in municipal garage.*

Go west on Las Olas Boulevard to S.W. 1st Avenue, and stop at
6 the **Broward County Museum of Archaeology.** Featured here
are a 2,000-year-old skeleton of a Tequesta Indian girl, remains

of Ice Age mammals, a diorama of Indian life, and information on archaeological techniques. Special shows display artifacts of African, pre-Columbian, and other cultures. *203 S.W. 1st Ave., tel. 305/525–8778. Open Tues.–Sat. 10–4, Sun. 1–4. Admission: $1 adults, 50¢ children and seniors.*

Take S.W. 1st Avenue north to S.W. 2nd Street, turn left, cross the Florida East Coast Railway tracks, and turn left onto S.W. 2nd Avenue. You're now in **Himmarshee Village,** an eight-square-block historic district. Park and walk to explore several fascinating museums.

The **Fort Lauderdale Historical Society Museum** surveys the city's history from the Seminole Indian era to World War II. A model in the lobby depicts old Fort Lauderdale. The building also houses a research library and a bookstore. *219 S.W. 2nd Ave., tel. 305/463–4431. Open Tues.–Sat. 10–4, Sun. 1–4. Admission by donation.*

The **Discovery Center** includes a science museum in the three-story **New River Inn,** Fort Lauderdale's first hotel, and a pioneer residence museum in the restored **King-Cromartie House.** The Discovery Center Museum is a child-oriented place with hands-on exhibits that explore optical illusions and bend rays of light, an insect zoo, a glass-front beehive, a loom, a computer center, and a small planetarium. Changing exhibits are also displayed at the old McCrory Store (2335 S. Andrews Ave.), part of the expanding Discovery Center that in 1992 will move into larger space opposite the downtown Performing Arts Center. *229 and 231 S.W. 2nd Ave., tel. 305/462–4115. Open Tues.–Fri. and Sun. noon–5; Sat. and holidays 10–5. Museum closed Mon. Admission (includes both museums): $3, $5 for the McCrory site as well, children under 3 free.*

A brick drive between the King-Cromartie House and the New River Inn brings you one block west to S.W. 3rd Avenue. On your left is the **Bryan House,** a 1904 dwelling which is now a Chart House restaurant.

Go north on S.W. 3rd Avenue past an assortment of antique shops and restaurants in old commercial buildings that are also part of the Himmarshee Village historic district. At Broward Boulevard, turn right and go east to Federal Highway (U.S. 1). Turn right and go south through the **Henry E. Kinney Tunnel,** named for a founder of Fort Lauderdale; it dips beneath Las Olas Boulevard and the New River.

Continue south on Federal Highway to S.W. 17th Street, then
7 turn left. About a mile east is the entrance to **Ocean World.** Continuous shows daily feature trained dolphins and sea lions. Display tanks hold sharks, sea turtles, alligators, and river otters. You can feed and pet a dolphin here. *1701 S.E. 17th St., tel. 305/525–6611. Open 10–6, last show starts 4:15. Admission: $8.95 adults, $6.95 children 4–12, under 4 free. Boat tour admission: $5 adults, $4 children 4–12, under 4 free.*

8 Go east on S.E. 17th Street across the **Brooks Memorial Causeway** over the Intracoastal Waterway, and bear left onto Seabreeze Boulevard (Rte. A1A). You'll pass through a neighborhood of older homes set in lush vegetation before emerging at the south end of Fort Lauderdale's beachfront strip. On your left at **Bahia Mar Resort & Yachting Center,** novelist John McDonald's fictional hero, Travis McGee, is honored with a

plaque at the marina where he allegedly docked his houseboat (*see* Lodging, below). *801 Seabreeze Blvd., tel. 305/764–2233 or 800/327–8154.*

9 Three blocks north, visit the **Swimming Hall of Fame Museum,** featuring photos, medals, and other souvenirs from major swimming events around the world. Included are memorabilia from Johnny Weissmuller, Mark Spitz, and other swimming champions. An Olympic-size pool hosts special events and is open to the public for swimming at other times. *501 Seabreeze Blvd., museum tel. 305/462–6536, pool tel. 305/523–0994. Open Mon.–Sat. 10–5, Sun. 11–4. Museum admission: $3 adults, $2 children 6–21 and seniors, $5 family. Pool admission: $3 nonresident adults, $2 nonresident students, $1 resident students, military, senior citizens.*

This concludes the central Fort Lauderdale tour. To return to the starting point, continue north on Seabreeze Boulevard to Las Olas Boulevard.

Exploring Broward

Time Out To start a brief exploration of the North Broward, take I–95 North to Cypress Creek Road. Turn west 2 miles to 21st Avenue, then right on 21st to the first light, right again onto 20th Avenue, and right to the end of the street. On your left in a warehouse district is **Acme Smoked Fish** where redolent of New York's East Side you're among deli mavens relishing the smoked salmon, whitefish, and herrings. Acme also sells deli meats and crackers so you can nosh while soaking up the atmosphere. *6704 N.W. 20th Ave., tel. 305/974–8100. Open Tues.–Sat. 9–4. No credit cards.*

Return to I–95 and go north to the Atlantic Boulevard exit and go west to Power Line Road, which will lead you to the popular
10 **Pompano Harness Track.** The Top 'O The Park restaurant overlooks the finish line. Post time: 7:30; call for dates, tel. 305/972–2000.

11 A unique water skiing cableway is at **Quiet Waters Park,** just north of the racetrack, on Power Line Road. **Ski Rixen** offers lessons for beginners, plus skis and life vests. A cable pulls the skiers. If you're skilled enough, there are all sorts of variations to the two-hand, two-ski way of skimming across the water. *Tel. 305/360–1315. Open weekdays 10–sunset, weekends 9:30–sunset. Admission: weekdays free, weekends 50¢. Children under 5 free.*

Exploring Southern Broward

In southern Broward County, an exploration can include native Indian crafts and lifestyles, high-stakes pari-mutuel wagering, and a unique natural park, all within the same driving loop.

12 Start with the **Dania Jai-Alai Palace** (301 E. Dania Beach Blvd., Dania, tel. 305/428–7766), offering one of the fastest games on the planet from early November through April.

Take Dania Beach Boulevard west to U.S. 1, turn left, go south
13 to Stirling Road, turn right, and go west to **Atlantis,** one of the world's largest water-theme parks. It has 2 million gallons of

water in 45 pools and water slides up to seven stories high, plus water ski shows, and children's entertainment. Highlights include a wave pool and an activity pool with trollies, slides, and rope ladders. Riders on Thunderball, the steepest water slide, reach speeds near 40 mph. The park sets minimum and maximum height requirements for participants in some activities. *2700 Stirling Rd., Box 2128, Hollywood, tel. 305/926–1000. Summer hours 10 AM–10 PM; phone for hours at other times of year. Admission: $11.95 adults, $4.95 seniors over 55, $9.95 children 3–11.*

Take I-95 south to the Sheridan Street exit, then west to
14 **Topeekeegee Yugnee Park.** Rentals include sailboats, Windsurfers, paddleboats, and canoes. *Tel. 305/985–1980. Open daily sunrise–sunset. Admission weekends and holidays: $1 car and driver, 50¢ each passenger, children under 6 free.*

Take Sheridan Street west to U.S. 441/Rte. 7, turn right, and
15 go north through the **Seminole Native Village,** a reservation of the never-conquered Seminole Indian tribe. The Indians sell native arts and crafts and run a high-stakes bingo parlor (4150 N. Rte. 7, tel. 305/961–5140 or 305/961–3220). Three bingo games daily; call recording for information. Continue north to **Anhinga Indian Museum and Art Gallery,** where Joe Dan and Virginia Osceola display a collection of artifacts from the Seminoles and other American Indian tribes. They also sell contemporary Indian art and craft objects. *5791 S. Rte. 7, tel. 305/581–8411. Open daily 9–6. V.*

Take U.S. 441/Rte. 7 south to Pembroke Road and go east to
16 Federal Highway to the **Hollywood Dog Track** (831 S. Federal Highway, Hallandale, tel. 305/454–7000). Call for race dates.

17 Take Federal Highway south to **Gulfstream Park Race Track** (901 S. Federal Hwy., tel. 305/454–7000), home of the Florida Derby, one of the southeast's foremost horse racing events. Call for race dates.

Exploring Inland

Between the coastal cities and the watery wilderness of the Everglades, urban sprawl is rapidly devouring Broward County's citrus groves and cow pastures. If you go inland, you can still find vestiges of the county's agricultural past.

18 The **Davie Rodeo Complex** at Orange Drive and Davie Road (6591 S.W. 45th St., Davie 33314, tel. 305/797–1166) holds rodeos in March and December. Just north on Davie Road is the **Buehler Planetarium,** where star-studded skies are on view regardless of the weather. *On the Central Campus of Broward Community College, 3501 S.W. Davie Rd., tel. 305/475–6680 (recording) or 305/475–6681. Call for feature times and special family shows. Admission: $2.50 adults, $1.50 children and seniors. Reservations required.*

Take Davie Road south past Orange Drive, cross the South New River Canal, and turn right on Griffin Road. Go west to **Spykes Grove & Tropical Gardens,** where the entire family can hop aboard a tractor-pulled tram for a 15-minute tour of working citrus groves. *7250 Griffin Rd., tel. 305/583–1987. Tours hourly. Open daily Oct.–June 9–5:30. Admission free.*

Head west on Griffin Road and turn right onto Flamingo Road
19 to **Flamingo Gardens.** There are crocodiles, alligators, monkeys, pink flamingoes, and other exotic birds, along with a petting zoo, a mini botanical garden, 60 acres of orange groves, antique car and historical museums, and a tram ride. *3750 Flamingo Rd., tel. 305/473-2955. Open daily 9–5. Admission: $6.50 adults, $3.25 children 4–14. Seniors and AAA members 20% discount.*

Return to Griffin Road and go west until the road ends at the edge of the Everglades. There you'll find **Everglades Holiday Park and Campground,** which offers a 45-minute narrated airboat tour and an alligator-wrestling show featuring Seminole Indians. The park has a 100-space campground that accommodates recreational vehicles and tents. *21940 Griffin Rd., Ft. Lauderdale 33332, tel. 305/434-8111 (Broward County), 305/621-2009 (Miami). Tour: $12 adults, $6 children, under 3 free. MC, V.*

Fort Lauderdale for Free

Manatees During the winter, manatees frolic in the warm-water discharge from Florida Power & Light Company's Port Everglades power plant. The massive marine mammals, which may be 15 feet long and weigh three-quarters of a ton, are susceptible to cold and congregate around the outfall when the temperature in local waters falls below 68 degrees.

An observation deck at the plant's intake pipe is open to the public, without charge, at all times. There you may see angelfish, reef fish, and sea turtles as well as manatees. Take Rte. 84 east to its end inside the port, turn right at Eisenhower Boulevard, and look on your right near some railroad tracks for the observation deck and a nearby parking area.

What to See and Do with Children

Butterfly World. This attraction in Tradewinds Park South is a screened-in tropical rain forest on 2.8 acres of land, where thousands of caterpillars pupate and emerge as butterflies. Up to 150 species flit through the shrubbery. Many are so tame they will land on you. Best time to go is in the afternoon; school groups fill the place in the mornings. *3600 W. Sample Rd., Coconut Creek, tel. 305/977-4400. Open Mon.–Sat 9–5, Sun. 1–5. Admission: $6 adults, $4 children 3–12, $5 senior citizens.*

Shopping

Shopping Districts **Major malls:** *Galleria Mall* on Sunrise Boulevard, just west of the Intracoastal Waterway, occupies more than one million square feet and includes Neiman-Marcus, Lord & Taylor, Saks Fifth Avenue, and Brooks Brothers (mall open 10–9 Mon.–Sat., noon–5:30 Sun.). *Oceanwalk* in the Hollywood Beach Hotel (101 N. Ocean Dr., Hollywood) is in a seashore environment with shops, restaurants, food, and entertainment. The building is a historic landmark.

Antiques: More than 75 dealers line U.S. 1 (Federal Hwy.) in Dania, a half mile south of the Fort Lauderdale International Airport and a half mile north of Hollywood. Open 10–5 every day but Sunday. Exit Griffin Road East off I–95.

Boutiques and Specialty Shops: *Las Olas Boulevard.* From S.E. 5th Avenue to a block east of the Himmarshee Canal. A tree-lined boulevard with a divided grassy median and bricked crosswalks, with some of the finest shops in Fort Lauderdale.

Beaches

The Fort Lauderdale area boasts an average temperature of 75.5 degrees and 25 miles of oceanfront beach. Parking is readily available, often at parking meters. At the southern end of Broward County, **John U. Lloyd Beach State Recreation Area** (6503 N. Ocean Dr., Dania) offers a beach for swimmers and sunners, but also 251 acres of mangroves, picnic facilities, fishing, and canoeing. *Open 8 AM–sunset. Park tel. 305/923–2833. Admission: nonresident $2 car and driver, $1 per passenger. Concessions tel. 305/922–7320. Open: weekdays 9–3, weekends 9–4. Canoes not rented at low tide.*

Throughout Broward County, each municipality along the Atlantic has its own public beach area. Hollywood also has a 2.5-mile boardwalk, edged with shops and eateries. Dania, Pompano Beach, Deerfield Beach, and Lauderdale-by-the-Sea have fishing piers in addition to the beaches. The most crowded portion of beach in this area is along the **Fort Lauderdale "Strip,"** which runs from Las Olas Boulevard north to Sunrise Boulevard.

In past years, there have been some serious oil spills and dumpings by freighters and tankers at sea, and the gunk has washed ashore in globules and become mixed with the beach sand. The problem has been somewhat eased, but some hotels still include a tar-removal packet with the toilet amenities. If you're concerned, ask at the desk of your hotel or motel.

Participant Sports

Biking Bicycling is popular throughout Greater Fort Lauderdale. Young children should ride accompanied by their parents because of heavy traffic and older drivers who have difficulty seeing children on low bicycles. Some south Florida auto drivers resent bike riders. Ride defensively to avoid being pushed off the road.

Diving Good diving can be enjoyed within 20 minutes of shore along Broward County's 25-mile coast. Among the most popular of the county's 80 dive sites is the 2-mile-wide, 23-mile-long Fort Lauderdale Reef.

South of Port Everglades Inlet, experienced divers can explore Barracuda and Hammerhead reefs. North of the port, three parallel coral reefs extend most of the way to the Palm Beach County line. The reef closest to shore comes within 100 yards of the beach a block north of Commercial Boulevard; the most distant is in 100 feet of water about a mile offshore. Snorkelers and beginning divers should stay on the first reef.

Dive Boats and Instruction All **Force E** stores rent scuba and snorkeling equipment. Instruction is available at all skill levels. Dive boat charters are available. *2700 E. Atlantic Blvd., Pompano Beach, tel. 407/943–3483 or 800/527–8660 (answered by West Palm Beach store). 2104 W. Oakland Park Blvd., Oakland Park, tel. 305/*

735–6227. Open winter weekdays 10–8:30, Sat. 8–7, Sun. 8–4, summer weekdays 8 AM–9 PM, Sat. 8–7, Sun. 8–4. Hours same as Pompano Beach store.

Spas If you watch "Lifestyles of the Rich and Famous" on TV, you'll recognize the names of Greater Fort Lauderdale's two world-famous spas, the Bonaventure Resort & Spa and Palm-Aire Spa Resort. At each resort, women comprise 75%–80% of the spa clientele.

Both resorts offer single-day spa privileges to nonguests. Price and availability of services vary with seasonal demand; resort guests have priority. At each resort, day users may receive a body massage, exercise class, facials, herbal wrap, spa-cuisine lunch, and other spa facilities and services.

Bring your own sneakers and socks. The spa provides everything else you'll need. Each spa will help you design a personal exercise-and-diet program tied to your lifestyle at home. If you already have an exercise program, bring it with you. If you have a medical problem, bring a letter from your doctor.

Bonaventure Resort and Spa (250 Racquet Club Rd., Fort Lauderdale, tel. 305/389–3300) is part of a hotel and convention complex near the Sawgrass Expressway interchange with I-595 in western Broward County. Complimentary caffeine-free herbal teas served in the morning, fresh fruit in the afternoon. Staff nutritionist follows American Heart Association and American Cancer Society guidelines, and can accommodate macrobiotic and vegetarian diets. Full-service beauty salon open to the public.

Palm-Aire Spa Resort (2501 Palm-Aire Drive N., Pompano Beach, tel. 305/972–3300 or 800/327–4960). This health, fitness and stress-reduction spa offers exercise activities, personal treatments, and calorie-controlled meals. It's 15 minutes from downtown Fort Lauderdale.

Spectator Sports

Baseball The New York Yankees hold spring training in 7,000-seat Fort Lauderdale Stadium (5301 N.W. 12th Ave., Fort Lauderdale, tel. 305/776–1921).

Rugby The Fort Lauderdale Knights play rough and ready on the green at Holiday Park. *Off of Federal Hwy., 2 blocks south of Sunrise Blvd., Fort Lauderdale, tel. 305/561–5263 for a recorded message. Games Sept.–Apr. Sat. 2 PM. Admission free.*

Dining

The list below is a representative selection of independent restaurants in Fort Lauderdale and Broward County, organized geographically, and by type of cuisine within each region of the county. Unless otherwise noted, they serve lunch and dinner.

The most highly recommended restaurants are indicated by a star ★.

The following credit card abbreviations are used: AE, American Express; CB, Carte Blanche; DC, Diners Club; MC, MasterCard; and V, Visa.

Category	Cost*
Very Expensive	over $55
Expensive	$35–$55
Moderate	$15–$35
Inexpensive	under $15

**per person, excluding drinks, service, and 6% sales tax*

American **Bimini Boatyard.** With sky-high sloped roof, loads of windows, and paddlefans, this is a rarity among architecturally distinctive restaurants: inexpensive menu, ambience, and a quality bar. Try the Anchor Steam with a loaf of Bimini bread or side of potato skins or buffalo chicken wings. Heartier fare? Go for the *fettuccine al salmone affumicato* (smoked salmon, capers, whole-grain mustard, white wine, cream, and leeks). The extensive menu includes salads, burgers, and dishes from the cookbooks of the Bahamas, Jamaica, and Indonesia (grilled chicken breast with peanut sauce). The restaurant is on the 15th Street canal, and there is seating outside where the yachts tie up, or in. There's high-energy reggae on weekends. *1555 SE 17th St., tel. 305/525–7400. Dress: casual. Reservations accepted for groups. Limited menu after 11. Closed Christmas. AE, MC, V. Inexpensive–Moderate.*

★ **Cafe Max.** As you enter Cafe Max, you're greeted by the aroma of fragrant spices issuing from the open theater kitchen. The decor includes art deco-style black wood chairs, original artwork, and cut flowers. Booth seating is best; the tables are quite close together. Owner-chef Oliver Saucy combines the best of new American cuisine with traditional *escoffier* cooking. Specialties include Anaheim chili peppers stuffed with Monterey Jack cheese; mushroom duxelles served with goat-cheese sauce; duck and smoked mozzarella ravioli with sun-dried tomatoes and basil butter; soft-shell crab with fresh tomato-jicama relish; and grilled veal chops. Daily chocolate dessert specials include hazelnut chocolate cappuccino torte and white-chocolate mousse pie with fresh raspberries. Other desserts include fresh fruit sorbets and homemade ice cream served with sauce *anglaise* and fresh raspberries. *2601 E. Atlantic Blvd., Pompano Beach, tel. 305/782–0606. Jacket preferred. Reservations advised. Dinner only. AE, DC, MC, V. Expensive.*

The Garden. Coral-rock walls, earth-tone rattan furnishings, and terraced seating give this restaurant in the Bonaventure Resort and Spa an inviting, outdoorsy appearance. It's a relaxed family restaurant, catering primarily to a resort clientele but welcoming others as well. Specialties include seafood salad appetizer (shrimp, crab, scallops) served with mustard sauce on a bed of greens, veal Milanese (medallion of veal sautéed in egg batter, with a sauce containing tomatoes, ham, mushrooms, dill pickles, and cream), and tall cheesecake (chocolate, marble, blueberry, strawberry, and plain). *250 Racquet Club Rd., tel. 305/389–3300 or 800/327–8090. Dress: casual. No Reservations. AE, DC, MC, V. Moderate.*

Shorty's Bar-B-Q. A clone of the original Shorty's on U.S. 1 in Miami, opened at the request of a loyal Broward following. The food's the same, and the decor resembles the original log cabin with long wooden tables—but the new building is air-conditioned! *5989 S. University Dr., Davie 33028, tel. 305/680–*

Fort Lauderdale Area Dining and Lodging

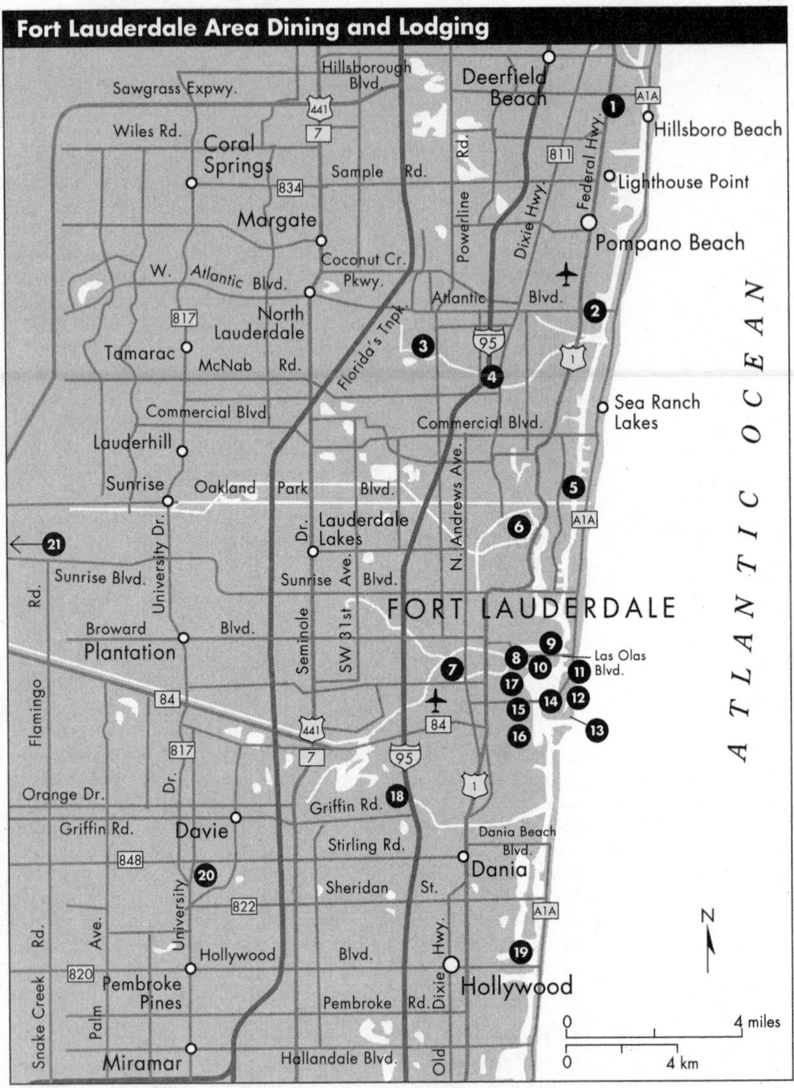

Lodging

Bahia Mar Resort & Yachting Center, **11**

Bonaventure Resort and Spa, **21**

Di Vito by the Sea, **19**

Fort Lauderdale Marriott Hotel & Marina, **17**

Lago Mar Restaurant Hotel Club, **13**

Marriott's Harbor Beach Resort, **12**

Palm-Aire Spa/Resort, **3**

Pier 66 Hotel and Marina, **14**

Riverside Hotel, **8**

Westin Cyprus Creek, **4**

Dining

Bimini Boatyard, **15**

Cafe Max, **2**

Casa Vecchia, **9**

Don Artùro, **18**

Down Under, **5**

The Garden, **21**

Grainary Cafe, **1**

Joe Bel-Air's, **16**

Old Florida Seafood House, **6**

Renaissance Seafood Grill, **21**

Santa Lucia, **10**

Shirttail Charlie's, **7**

Shorty's Bar-B-Q, **20**

Spa Restaurant, **21**

9900. Dress: casual. No reservations. Closed Christmas and Thanksgiving. No credit cards. Inexpensive.

Continental **Down Under.** When Al Kocab and Leonce Picot opened Down Under in 1968, the Australian government sent them a boomerang as a gift. The name actually describes the restaurant's location, below a bridge approach at the edge of the Intracoastal Waterway. The two-story structure was built to look old, with walls of antique brick deliberately laid off-plumb. Specialties include fresh Belon oysters and littleneck clams from Maine; Florida blue crab cakes; Brutus salad (Down Under's version of Caesar salad); fresh Idaho trout lightly sautéed and topped with Florida blue crab and hollandaise sauce; and Florida lobster and stone crab in season. Desserts include Key-lime pie with meringue, crème brûlée, and pecan squares. *3000 E. Oakland Park Blvd., tel. 305/563–4123. Jacket preferred. Reservations advised. AE, CB, MC, V. Expensive.*

Cuban **Don Arturo.** Waiters in tuxedos belie the friendly style of this family-run, romantically lit restaurant popular with the courthouse crowd. It's four stoplights west of I–95 just north of Davie Boulevard. Avoid the party room that's near a noisy service area. If you're new to Cuban food, try the tri-steak sampler (chicken filet, palomilla steak, and pork filet), or one of the dinners for two, such as the *zarzuela de mariscos* (assorted seafood and fish smothered in tangy Spanish red sauce). Wash it down with the homemade sangria. English is widely spoken here. *1998 S.W. 27th Ave., tel. 305/584–7966. Dress: neat but casual. Reservations accepted. Closed July 4th, Thanksgiving, Christmas, New Year's Day. AE, CB, DC, MC, V. Moderate.*

Diner ★ **Joe Bel-Air's.** This place is wacko—from the wisecracking waitresses and the oddball location smack in the middle of the port compound, to the signs and memorabilia adorning the walls. Formerly a strip joint and country-western bar, it's now a '50s diner with favorites like meat loaf and mashed potatoes, roast pork loin, malts, cherry Cokes slid down the counter or plopped on the lacquered tables at shiny blue vinyl banquettes. They grind their own coffee beans, use filtered water, serve pure cream, and everything's homemade, including real whipped cream. You'll probably need to stand in line to get in, but Joe's is a must. *1717 Eisenhower Blvd., tel. 305/463–JOES. Dress: casual. No reservations. Closed Christmas Eve and Christmas Day. AE, MC, V. Inexpensive.*

Italian ★ **Casa Vecchia.** This old house (*casa vecchia*) stands beside the Intracoastal Waterway, surrounded by a formal garden where you can watch boats cruise past. The garden also grows herbs that flavor the restaurant's fare. Casa Vecchia was built in the late 1930s. Diners are encouraged to roam through the building to admire antique furnishings and original statuary and paintings. Spanish tiles decorate Casa Vecchia's walls and many tabletops. Specialties include cannelloni, fettuccine funghi (mushroom-flavored noodles tossed with butter, basil, and porcini), and *granchio* Casa Vecchia (Maryland lump crabmeat served with scallions, a splash of cognac, and red linguine). Desserts include full-flavored sorbets of fresh seasonal fruit prepared on the premises and *zabaglione freddo alla frutta* (cold sabayon with Grand Marnier and fresh fruit). *209 N.*

Birch Rd., tel. 305/463–7575. Jacket preferred. Reservations advised. AE, CB, MC, V. Expensive.

Santa Lucia. "You gotta taste the ocean," says owner/chef Angelo Ciampa, 41 years in restaurants, who now draws packed houses to his little 12-table storefront restaurant next to the fashionable Riverside Hotel on Las Olas Boulevard. The place smells like it ought to at home: pungent with a lot of subtle wafts. Try the *tuna carpaccio* (fresh tuna with capers, olive oil, parmesan cheese, and fresh Italian parsley) or the *rigatoni à la Rusia* (tomato, garlic, hot pepper, parmesan, and basil with a splash of vodka). The *zuccotto* (a homemade sponge cake), is made with whipped cream, liqueurs, roasted pine nuts, almonds, and walnuts. Ask for the Moretti beer, a full-bodied Italian gift to the world. Or choose from a half dozen Italian wines. *602 E. Las Olas Blvd., tel. 305/525–9530. Dress: neat but casual. Reservations advised. No lunch. Closed Mon. in summer; closed July. AE, MC, V. Expensive.*

Natural

Grainary Cafe. Although this place is hard to find, it's worth the effort: It's eight blocks south of Hillsboro Boulevard behind Dirty Harry's in the Palm Plaza on the west side of Federal Highway. It's just a plain storefront with only 12 tables, but there are always fresh flowers, local art on the walls, and a dedication to quality. Try Bhudda's favorite, fresh garden veggies and garlic sautéed and served over a bed of brown rice topped with melted cheddar or mozzarella, with tofu or tempeh; or the West Indian fish and vegetable sauté served hot and spicy or mild and plain. You can get a rice burger with marinara or tahini or a bean and veggie burrito in a corn tortilla with salsa. *847 S. Federal Hwy., Deerfield Beach, tel. 305/360–0824. Dress: casual. Reservations accepted. BYOB. AE, MC, V. Inexpensive.*

Spa Restaurant. In the Bonaventure Resort and Spa, this 70-seat restaurant caters primarily to spa guests. Menus state the number of calories in each item. Tropical pastels and white rattan furniture seem to match the healthful, low-calorie natural fare prepared in a separate kitchen by chefs attuned to special dietary needs. Specialties include cream of cauliflower soup, a broad variety of salads, medallions of turkey Santa Barbara with a tangy-sweet apricot-lingonberry sauce, peach cobbler topped with granola, and strawberry-rhubarb crustless pie. *250 Racquet Club Rd., tel. 305/389–3300 or 800/327–8090. Dress: casual. Breakfast, lunch, dinner. Reservations advised. Closed last 2 weeks in Aug. AE, DC, MC, V. Moderate.*

Seafood

Old Florida Seafood House. Plain on atmosphere, friendly on price. Owner Bob Wickline has run this traditional seafood restaurant since 1978 with a West Virginian's eye toward giving value for money so he keeps his trade. Nothing's frozen, nothing portion-controlled. He'll bring out a whole swordfish to show that it's fresh or take you to the cutting room with him. Best recommendation: Local waiters, waitresses, bartenders, and fellow restaurateurs all patronize the place. Not gourmet, just good. Try the veal Gustav (sautéed veal topped with a lobster tail), and a snapper New Orleans (sautéed with mushrooms and artichokes, laced with a light brown sauce). There's usually a 30-minute wait weekends. *1414 N.E. 26th St., Wilton Manors, tel. 305/566–1044. Dress: neat but casual. No Sat. lunch. Closed Thanksgiving. AE, MC, V. Moderate.*

★ **Shirttail Charlie's.** You can watch the world go by from the outdoor deck or upstairs dining room of Shirttail Charlie's. Boats glide up and down the New River. Sunday–Thursday diners may take a free 45-minute after-dinner cruise on the *Cavalier*, which chugs upriver past an alleged Al Capone speakeasy. Charlie's itself is built to look old, with 1920s blue-and-white five-sided tile on a floor that leans toward the water. The menu reflects Caribbean cuisine. Specialties include an alligator-tail appetizer served with Tortuga sauce (a béarnaise with turtle broth and sherry); conch served four ways; crab balls; shark bites; blackened tuna with Dijon mustard sauce; crunchy coconut shrimp with a not-too-sweet piña colada sauce; and a superbly tart Key-lime pie with graham cracker-crust. *400 S.W. 3rd Ave., tel. 305/463–3474. Jacket preferred upstairs, casual downstairs. Reservations advised upstairs. AE, MC, V. Moderate.*

Seafood **Renaissance Seafood Grill.** This gourmet restaurant, in the Bonaventure Resort and Spa, five-star-rated by the Confrérie de la Chaine des Rôtisseurs, features mesquite-grilled seafood and California cuisine with Florida adaptations. You dine in a rain forest, with views of a waterfall surrounded by palm and ficus trees, ferns and blooming flowers, and a pond with variegated foot-long carp. Specialties include chilled cream of avocado and cucumber soup; hot cream of poblano pepper soup with chunks of brie; a spinach-and-bean sprout salad with pickled eggs and rosemary vinaigrette dressing; whole wheat fettuccine sautéed with chunks of Maine lobster, scallops, and chives in a lobster sauce; mako shark in a lime-parsley-butter sauce. *250 Racquet Club Rd., tel. 305/389–3300 or 800/327–8090. Jacket preferred. Reservations required. AE, DC, MC, V. Dinner only. Expensive.*

Lodging

In Fort Lauderdale, Pompano Beach, and the Hollywood-Hallandale area, dozens of hotels line the Atlantic Ocean beaches. You can find accommodations ranging from economy motels to opulent luxury hotels with posh, pricey suites.

Inland, the major chain hotels along I–95 north and south of the airport cater primarily to business travelers and overnight visitors en route to somewhere else.

Wherever you plan to stay in Broward County, reservations are a good idea throughout the year. Tourists from the northern United States and Canada fill up the hotels from Thanksgiving through Easter. In summer, southerners and Europeans create a second season that's almost as busy.

The list below is a representative selection of hotels and motels, organized geographically. The rate categories in the list are based on the all-year or peak-season price; off-peak rates may be a category or two lower.

The most highly recommended hotels are indicated by a star ★.

Category	Cost*
Very Expensive	over $120
Expensive	$90–$120

Moderate	$50–$90
Inexpensive	under $50

**All prices are for a standard double room, excluding 6% state sales tax and nominal tourist tax.*

The following credit card abbreviations are used: AE, American Express; CB, Carte Blanche; DC, Diners Club; MC, MasterCard; V, Visa.

Bahia Mar Resort & Yachting Center (a Clarion hotel). Naval architect J.H. Phillpot designed the Bahia Mar marina in 1949; it was the first in Fort Lauderdale to accommodate boats longer than 30 feet. Travis McGee, fictional hero of mystery author John McDonald, "lived" at Bahia Mar aboard a boat called *The Busted Flush.* Two months after McDonald died in December 1986, the Literary Landmark Association dedicated a plaque at slip F-18 in memory of McDonald and McGee. Ironically, McDonald never stayed on the premises. Marina wing rooms are furnished in tropical decor; tower rooms have a soft blue-white color scheme. Upper floors of the 16-story tower provide spectacular views of the ocean and Intracoastal Waterway. *801 Seabreeze Blvd., 33316, tel. 305/764–2233 or 800/327–8154. 298 rooms with bath, including 9 suites, 30 nonsmoker rooms, 3 rooms for handicapped guests. Facilities: outdoor freshwater pool, 350-slip marina where 15 deep-sea-fishing charter boats dock, power-boating and sailing instruction, dive boat and shop, 4 tennis courts, restaurants, conference center, shopping arcade. AE, CB, DC, MC, V. Expensive.*

Bonaventure Resort and Spa. Mid-rise resort with spa and conference center on 1,250 acres, 17 miles west of Fort Lauderdale. The hotel lobby is light and airy, with colorful angelfish and a cuddly-looking sand shark in a large aquarium just inside the front entrance. All guest rooms are in nine four-story buildings. Room views look out on the pools, lake, and golf courses. Bathroom amenities include bidets in many rooms, heat lamps, and full-size bath towels. *250 Racquet Club Rd., 33326, tel. 305/389–3300 or 800/327–8090. 504 rooms, including 8 suites. Facilities: 5 outdoor solar-heated freshwater pools; 2 18-hole golf courses; 24 tennis courts, 43,000-square-foot spa with separate facilities for men and women (see* Participant Sports, above*); canoes, paddleboats, and a small sailboat on a half-mile-long lake that winds through the resort; bicycles and bicycle paths, saddle club, bowling alley, roller-skating rink, 4 restaurants, 2 lounges. AE, DC, MC, V. Expensive.*

Di Vito By the Sea. This eccentric low-rise beachfront hotel was built by Anthony Di Vito to express his love for his wife and exalt their Italian origins. Its architecture incorporates a reproduction of the Leaning Tower of Pisa with sea-horses, mermaids, and friezes with mythological heroes. Most guests rent by the week. There is no lobby, just an office and a patio facing the boardwalk in front of the building. *3500 N. Surf Rd., Hollywood 33019, tel. 305/929–7227. 20 rooms with bath, 4 yearly-rental apartments in an adjoining building. Facilities: 200 feet of beach frontage, efficiency kitchen in some rooms. No credit cards. Moderate.*

Fort Lauderdale Marriott Hotel & Marina. This hotel's 13-story tower beside the Intracoastal Waterway commands a striking view of the beach and the entrance to Port Everglades. Most rooms have balconies overlooking the water and standard Marriott furnishings in natural dark woods with pink, mauve, and green fabrics and wall coverings. An $8-million renovation was completed at the end of 1988 that included updating three-quarters of the guest rooms. *1881 S.E. 17th St., 33316, tel. 305/463–4000 or 800/228–9290. 583 rooms with bath, including 19 suites, 26 nonsmoker rooms, 17 rooms for handicapped guests. Facilities: outdoor freshwater pool and whirlpool, free shuttle to beach, 32-slip marina for yachts up to 200 feet long, 4 tennis courts, fitness center, game room, in-room minibars and safes, pay-TV movies, AE, CB, DC, MC, V. Very Expensive.*

Lago Mar Resort Hotel & Club. The Banks family has owned this sprawling resort since the early 1950s. Under Walter Banks it draws lots of customers back again because of the easygoing management style that leaves guests feeling they're in a much smaller place. After a half-dozen expansions in different architectural styles, the eclectic look helps make guests feel they're in their own compound. Everyone shares the broad beach in this Harbor Beach section of the city, which is cut off from the rowdiness that sometimes affects the beachfront farther north. If you like a larger room, ask for a newer wing, although you'll pay less for the older. *1700 S. Ocean Lane, 33310, tel. 305/523–6511 or 800/255–5246. On the ocean just south of 17th St. causeway. 180 rooms with bath, including 135 suites. Facilities: 2 outdoor heated pools, 4 tennis courts, 2 volleyball courts, miniature golf, putting green, room service. AE, CB, DC, MC, V. Very Expensive.*

Marriott's Harbor Beach Resort. Fort Lauderdale's only AAA-rated five-diamond hotel is a 14-story tower on 16 acres of oceanfront. Built in 1984, its guest rooms were renovated in 1989. The free-form pool has a cascading waterfall. Room furnishings are light wood with mauve, pink, blue, and green hues; each room has a balcony facing either the ocean or the Intracoastal Waterway. *3030 Holiday Dr., 33316, tel. 305/525–4000 or 800/228–9290. 624 rooms with bath, including 36 suites, 45 nonsmoker rooms, 7 rooms for handicapped guests. Facilities: 1,100 ft of beach frontage, cabanas, windsurfing, Hobie cats, 65-foot catamaran, parasailing, outdoor heated freshwater pool and whirlpool, 5 tennis courts, fitness center, men's and women's saunas, masseuse, 3 boutiques, 5 restaurants, 3 lounges, in-room minibars, HBO, TV movies. AE, DC, MC, V. Very Expensive.*

Palm-Aire Spa Resort. This mid-rise resort with spa and conference center on 1,500 acres 15 miles north of Fort Lauderdale is lushly landscaped, and planters on each terrace make the four-story main building resemble a hanging garden. The rooms have big closets, a separate dressing alcove, and choice of soft or firm pillows. *2501 Palm-Aire Dr. N, Pompano Beach 33069. tel. 305/972–3300 or 800/327–4960. 192 rooms with bath and private terrace, 4 outdoor freshwater pools, 5 golf courses, half-mile jogging trail with exercise stations, 37 lighted tennis courts, Continental and spa restaurants, boutique. AE, DC, MC, V. Very Expensive.*

★ **Pier 66 Resort and Marina.** Phillips Petroleum built Fort Lauderdale's original high-rise luxury hotel on the eastern bank of the Intracoastal Waterway. An octagonal rooftop cocktail lounge rotates slowly, offering patrons a spectacular view. Rooms are attractively furnished in tropical pastels. *2301 S.E. 17th St., 33316, tel. 305/525–6666, 800/432–1956 (FL) 800/327–3796 (rest of US). 388 rooms with bath, including 8 suites. Fa-*

cilities: water taxi and van shuttle to beach, outdoor freshwater pool, heated Jacuzzi, full-service marina with 142 wet slips for boats up to 200 ft long, scuba diving, snorkling, parasailing, small boat rentals, waterskiing, fishing and sailing yacht charters, 2 clay tennis courts, indoor and outdoor health clubs with saunas and exercise equipment, massage therapy. AE, CB, DC, MC, V. Very Expensive.

★ **Riverside Hotel.** This six-story hotel, on Fort Lauderdale's most fashionable shopping thoroughfare, was built in 1936, and was extensively remodeled in 1987. An attentive staff includes many veterans of two decades or more. Each room is unique, with antique oak furnishings, framed French prints on the walls, in-room refrigerators, and European-style baths. Best rooms face south, overlooking the New River; worst rooms, where you can hear the elevator, are the 36 series. *620 E. Las Olas Blvd., 33301, tel. 305/467–0671, 800/421–7666 (FL), 800/325–3280 (rest of US). 117 rooms with bath, including 5 suites, 15 nonsmoker rooms. Facilities: kidney-shaped heated outdoor freshwater pool beside the New River, 540 ft of dock with mooring space available by advance reservation, volleyball court, 2 restaurants, poolside bar. AE, DC, MC. Expensive.*

Westin Cypress Creek. Built in 1986, this high-rise business hotel is in Radice Corporate Park, a suburban office complex surrounding a lagoon with a fountain in the center. The hotel's three-story atrium lobby was inspired by the Great Temple at Karnak, Egypt; eight weathered-looking concrete columns with a rough pink-stucco finish rise to a skylight through which you can see the building's facade. Best rooms are on the 14th and 15th floors, where concierge service includes a Continental breakfast and a cocktail hour. *400 Corporate Dr., 33334, tel. 305/772–1331 or 800/228–3000. 294 rooms with bath, including 35 suites, 34 nonsmoker rooms, 19 rooms for handicapped guests. Facilities: outdoor heated freshwater pool and Jacuzzi, poolside bar with lunchtime barbecue, health club with Nautilus equipment, men's and women's saunas, jogging trail, 3 restaurants, 2 lounges, in-room minibars. AE, CB, DC, MC, V. Very Expensive.*

The Arts and Nightlife

For the most complete weekly listing of events, read the "Showtime!" entertainment insert and events calendar in the Friday *Fort Lauderdale News/Sun Sentinel*.

Tickets are sold at individual box offices and through Ticketmaster, a computerized statewide sales system (tel. 305/523–3309 in Broward County).

The Arts

Theater

Sunrise Musical Theatre (5555 N.W. 95th Ave., Sunrise, tel. 305/741–7300) stages Broadway musicals, some dramatic plays with name stars, and concerts by well-known singers throughout the year. The theater is 14 miles west of Fort Lauderdale Beach via Commercial Boulevard.

Concerts

Bailey Concert Hall is a popular place for classical music concerts, dance, drama, and other performing arts activities, especially October–April. *On the Central Campus of Broward Community College, 3501 S.W. Davie Rd., tel. 305/475–6884 for reservations.*

The Philharmonic Orchestra of Florida, south Florida's only fully professional orchestra, is Broward-based but performs in eight locations in Broward, Dade, and Palm Beach counties. It offers a variety of series and individual-performance tickets; write for schedule. *1430 N. Federal Hwy., 33304, tel. 305/561-2997 (Dade County), 305/945-5180 (Broward County), 407/392-5443 (Boca Raton), 407/659-0331 (Palm Beach), 800/446-3939 (Ticketmaster statewide). Office open weekdays 9–5. AE, MC, V.*

The Fort Lauderdale Opera Guild presents the current production of the Greater Miami Opera in War Memorial Auditorium (800 N.E. 8th St.). For tickets, contact the Guild office. *333 S.W. 2nd St., 33312, tel. 305/728-9700. Office open weekdays 9–5.*

Nightlife

Bars and Nightclubs

Musician Exchange Downtown Cafe. This 200-seat club features an eclectic mix of blues, jazz, and rock-and-roll, with reggae on Sundays. Performers include local bands as well as leading musicians like Donovan, John Lee Hooker, Laura Nyro, Carmen McCrae, and Stan Getz. *729 W. Sunrise Blvd., 305/764-1912. Admission price varies with show. National big-name acts Fri. and Sat. Call for schedule and reservations.*

Shirttail Charlie's Downstairs Bar. A scenic place to have a beer or snack and watch boat traffic on the New River through downtown Fort Lauderdale. No entertainment. Informal. *400 S.W. 3rd Ave., tel. 305/463-3474. Open Mon.–Sat. 11:30–10, Sun. 11:30–9.*

Peppers. High-energy nightclub with art-deco decor in Westin Cypress Creek Hotel. Features rock-and-roll DJs most weekend nights, with videos produced in-house. Wood dance floor, pool table. *400 Corporate Dr., tel. 305/772-1331. Open Mon.–Thurs. 5 PM–1:30 AM. Fri.–Sat. 7 PM–1:30 AM. No cover or minimum.*

Comedy Clubs

The Comic Strip. Stand-up comedians from New York work surrounded by framed old newspaper funnies—Katzenjammer Kids, Superman, Prince Valiant, L'il Orphan Annie, Hubert, etc. Full restaurant menu, two-drink minimum, alcoholic and nonalcoholic beverages. *1432 N. Federal Hwy., tel. 305/565-8887. Showtime Sun.–Fri. 9:30, Sat. 9 and 11:15. Subject to change on holidays.*

Country/Western

Do-Da's Country Music Emporium. The Frontier Room seats 800 at buckboard tables and has a 2,100-square-foot wood dance floor; the smaller pecky-board Tennessee Room seats 100. Glass-and-brick arches enclose the Tex-Mex dining area, Steak House. The shoot-'em-down corral bar in the Frontier Room has an old-fashioned barber chair. Free international buffet during happy hour, weekdays 4:30–8 PM. *700 S. U.S. 441, Plantation, tel. 305/791-1477. Open 4 PM–4 AM. Live country/western music, with name bands nightly from 8 PM–3 AM.*

6 Palm Beach

Introduction

Wealth has its privileges. That's the continuing reality of Palm Beach. Those privileges include the finest homes, cars, food, wine, furniture, jewelry, art, clothing, and toys that money can buy—and the right to stare back at the tourists who visit this elegant barrier-island enclave 70 miles north of Miami.

Henry Morrison Flagler created Palm Beach in 1894. Earlier he helped John D. Rockefeller establish the Standard Oil Company, then retired and put his money into Florida railroads and real estate. He bought a small railroad between Jacksonville and St. Augustine and extended it southward. Eventually it was called the Florida East Coast Railroad. Along the rail line he built hotels to generate traffic, including a huge wooden structure, the 2,000-room Royal Poinciana, beside a tidal bay called Lake Worth.

Flagler created an international high-society resort at Palm Beach, attracting the affluent for the Season, December 15 to Washington's Birthday (Feb. 22). Then they departed for Europe, extolling Palm Beach's virtues and collecting great art to ship back to the mansions they were building on the island.

A workman told Flagler that people liked to picnic along the beach "down by the breakers," so he built a second hotel there in 1896. It burned, was rebuilt, and burned again. The third structure to bear the name The Breakers rose in 1926 and stands today as the grande dame of Palm Beach hostelries.

Socialites and celebrities still flock to The Breakers for charity galas. They browse in the stores along Worth Avenue, regarded as one of the world's classiest shopping districts. They swim on secluded beaches that are nominally public but lack convenient parking and access points. They pedal the world's most beautiful bicycle path beside Lake Worth. And what they do, *you* can do—if you can afford it.

Despite its prominence and affluence, the Town of Palm Beach occupies far less than 1% of the land area of Palm Beach County, which is 521 square miles larger than the state of Delaware and is a remarkably diverse political jurisdiction.

West Palm Beach, on the mainland across Lake Worth from Palm Beach, is the city Flagler built to house Palm Beach's servants; today it's the county seat and commercial center of Palm Beach County, with a population of about 70,000.

Lantana, to the south, has a large Finnish population. Delray Beach began as an artists' retreat and a small settlement of Japanese farmers, including George Morikami, who donated the land for the beautiful Morikami Museum of Japanese Culture to the county park system (4000 Morikami Park Rd., Delray Beach 33446; tel. 407/495–0233. Open Tues.–Sun. 10–5. Closed Easter, Thanksgiving, Christmas, New Year's Day. Donation). Boca Raton, an upscale community developed by pioneer architect Addison Mizner as a showcase for his Spanish Revival style, retains much of its 1920s ambience through strict zoning.

To the north, Palm Beach Gardens is a golf center, home of the Professional Golfer's Association. Jupiter boasts the Jupiter

Theater and a dune-fringed beach that remains largely free of intrusive development.

Many visitors to Palm Beach County don't realize that it extends 50 miles inland to encompass the southeastern quadrant of 448,000-acre Lake Okeechobee, the fourth-largest natural lake in the United States. Its bass and perch attract fishermen; catfish devotees prize the hearty flavor of succulent Okeechobee "sharpies."

Marinas at Pahokee and Belle Glade provide lake access. In Lake Harbor, about as far west as you can go in Palm Beach County, the state is restoring a lock and lock master's house built early in the 20th century on the Miami Canal.

Palm Beach County is also the main gateway to the Treasure Coast, consisting of Martin, St. Lucie, and Indian River counties along the Atlantic Coast to the north.

Arriving and Departing by Plane

Airport **Palm Beach International Airport (PBIA)** (Congress Ave. and Belvedere Rd., West Palm Beach, tel. 407/683–9400) opened its new $59 million, 24-gate terminal in 1988. It now handles almost six million passengers a year and will add up to 24 more gates by 1993.

Between the Airport and City Center Route No. 10 of **Tri-Rail Commuter Bus Service** joins PBIA and Tri-Rail's Palm Beach Airport station during weekday rush hours only. For schedule, call 800/TRI–RAIL. For connections with CoTran (Palm Beach County Transportation Authority) routes, call 407/686–4560 or 407/686–4555 in Palm Beach, 407/272–6350 in Boca Raton–Delray Beach.

Palm Beach Transportation (tel. 407/689–4222) provides taxi and limousine service from PBIA. Reserve at least a day in advance for a limousine.

Arriving and Departing by Train and Car

By Train **Amtrak** (201 S. Tamarind Ave., West Palm Beach, tel. 800/872–7245 or 407/832–6169) connects West Palm Beach with cities along Florida's east coast daily.

Tri-Rail has six stations in Palm Beach County. For details, tel. 800/TRI–RAIL or 305/728–8445.

By Car Most visitors explore Palm Beach County by car. I–95 runs north-south, to link West Palm Beach with Miami and Fort Lauderdale to the south. To get to central Palm Beach, exit at Belvedere Road or Okeechobee Boulevard. Southern Boulevard (U.S. 98) runs east-west. From West Palm Beach, take I–95 south to Boca Raton and Delray Beach, north to Palm Beach Gardens and Jupiter.

Getting Around

By Bus CoTran buses require exact change (80¢, 40¢ for seniors and handicapped persons, plus 15¢ for a transfer). Service is provided from 6 AM to 9 PM, with individual route variations. For details, tel. 407/686–4560 or 407/686–4555 (Palm Beach), 407/272–6350 (Boca Raton-Delray Beach).

By Taxi **Palm Beach Transportation** (tel. 407/689–4222). Cab meters start at $1.25. Each mile is $1.50. Some cabs may charge more.

Important Addresses and Numbers

Tourist Information **Palm Beach County Convention & Visitors Bureau** (1555 Palm Beach Lakes Blvd., Suite 204, West Palm Beach 33401, tel. 407/471–3995) is open weekdays 8:30–5.

Chamber of Commerce of the Palm Beaches (401 N. Flagler Dr., West Palm Beach 33401, tel. 407/833–3711) is open weekdays 8:30–5.

Palm Beach Chamber of Commerce (45 Cocoanut Row, Palm Beach 33480, tel. 407/655–3282) is open weekdays 9–5.

Deaf Service Center of Palm Beach County (5730 Corporate Way, Suite 210, West Palm Beach 33407, TDD tel. 407/478–3904; toll-free from south Palm Beach County tel. 407/392–6444, voice tel. 407/478–3903) is open weekdays 8–4:30; Christmas–New Year's Day 10–3.

Tickets Call **Ticketmaster** to order tickets for performing arts and sports events. *Tel. 407/839–3900. MC, V.*

Emergencies Dial 911 for **police** and **ambulance** in an emergency.

Hospitals Two hospitals in West Palm Beach with 24-hour emergency rooms are **Good Samaritan Hospital** (Flagler Dr. and Palm Beach Lakes Blvd., tel. 407/655–5511; doctor-referral, tel. 407/650–6240) and **St. Mary's Hospital** (901 45th St., tel. 407/844–6300; doctor-referral, tel. 407/881–2929).

24-Hour Pharmacies **Eckerd Drugs** (3343 S. Congress Ave., Palm Springs, southwest of West Palm Beach, tel. 407/965–3367). **Walgreen Drugs** (1688 Congress Ave., Palm Springs, tel. 407/968–8211).

Exploring Palm Beach and West Palm Beach

Numbers in the margin correspond with points of interest on the Palm Beach and West Palm Beach map.

Palm Beach is an island community 12 miles long and no more than a quarter-mile across at its widest point. Three bridges connect Palm Beach to West Palm Beach and the rest of the world. This tour takes you through both communities.

Begin at Royal Palm Way and County Road in the center of Palm Beach. Go north on County Road past the Episcopal
1 church, **Bethesda-by-the-Sea,** built in 1927 by the first Protestant congregation in southeast Florida. Inspiring stained-glass windows and a lofty, vaulted sanctuary grace its Spanish-Gothic design. A stone bridge with an ornamental tile border spans the pond; bubbling fountains feed it. *141 South County Rd., Palm Beach, tel. 407/655–4554. Gardens open 8–5. Services Sun. 8, 9, and 11 AM in winter, 8 and 10 June–Aug.; phone for weekday schedule.*

2 Continue north on County Road past **The Breakers** (1 S. County Rd., Palm Beach), an ornate Italian renaissance hotel built in 1926 by railroad magnate Henry M. Flagler's widow to replace an earlier hotel, which burned (*see* Lodging, below). Explore the elegant public spaces—especially on a Sunday morning, when you can enjoy the largest champagne brunch in Florida at The Beach Club.

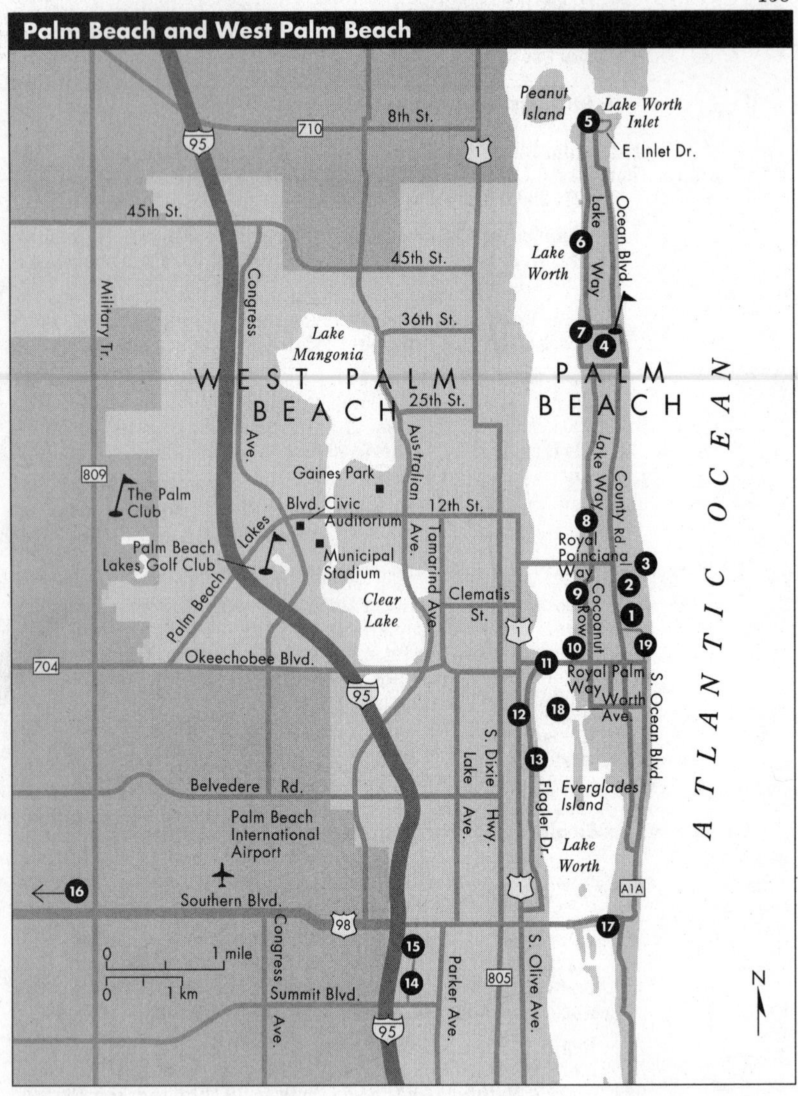

Ann Norton Sculpture Gardens, **13**
Bethesda-by-the-Sea, **1**
The Breakers, **2**
Canyon of Palm Beach, **7**
Dreher Park Zoo, **14**
E. Inlet Drive, **5**
Lion Country Safari, **16**
Mar-A-Lago, **17**
Norton Gallery of Art, **12**
Palm Beach Bicycle Trail, **6**
Palm Beach Biltmore Hotel, **8**
Palm Beach Country Club, **4**
Palm Beach Post Office, **3**
Public Beach, **19**
Royal Palm Bridge, **11**
Society of the Four Arts, **10**
South Florida Science Museum, **15**
Whitehall, **9**
Worth Ave., **18**

Continue north on County Road to Royal Poinciana Way. Go in-
3 side the **Palm Beach Post Office** to see the murals depicting
Seminole Indians in the Everglades and royal and coconut
palms. *95 N. County Rd., Palm Beach, tel. 407/832–0633 or
407/832–1867. Open weekdays 8:30–5.*

Continue north on County Road to the north end of the island,
4 past the very-private **Palm Beach Country Club** and a neighborhood of expansive (and expensive) estates.

5 You must turn around at **E. Inlet Drive,** the northern tip of the
island, where a dock offers a view of Lake Worth Inlet, the U.S.
Coast Guard Reservation on Peanut Island, and the Port of
Palm Beach across Lake Worth on the mainland. Observe the
no-parking signs; Palm Beach police will issue tickets.

Turn south and make the first right onto Indian Road, then the
first left onto Lake Way. You'll return to the center of town
through an area of newer mansions, past the posh, private Sail-
6 fish Club. Lake Way parallels the **Palm Beach Bicycle Trail**
along the shoreline of Lake Worth, a palm-fringed path
through the backyards of some of the world's priciest homes.
Watch on your right for metal posts topped with a swatch of
white paint, marking narrow public-access walkways between
houses from the street to the bike path.

Lake Way runs into Country Club Road, which takes you
7 through the **Canyon of Palm Beach,** a road cut about 25 feet
deep through a ridge of sandstone and oolite limestone.

As you emerge from the canyon, turn right onto Lake Way and
continue south. Lake Way becomes Bradley Place. You'll pass
8 the **Palm Beach Biltmore Hotel,** now a condominium. Another
flamboyant landmark of the Florida boom, it cost $7 million to
build and opened in 1927 with 543 rooms.

As you cross Royal Poinciana Way, Bradley Place becomes Co-
9 coanut Row. Stop at **Whitehall,** the palatial 73-room mansion
that Henry M. Flagler built in 1901 for his third wife, Mary Lily
Kenan. After the couple died, the mansion was turned into a
hotel. In 1960, Flagler's granddaughter, Jean Flagler
Matthews, bought the building. She turned it into a museum,
with many of the original furnishings on display. The art collection includes a Gainsborough portrait of a girl with a pink sash,
displayed in the music room near a 1,200-pipe organ. Exhibits
also depict the history of the Florida East Coast Railroad.
Flagler's personal railroad car, "The Rambler," is parked behind the building. A tour by well-informed guides takes about
an hour; afterwards, you may browse on your own. *Cocoanut
Row at Whitehall Way, Palm Beach, tel. 407/655–2833. Open
Tues.–Sat. 10–5, Sun. noon–5; closed Mon. Admission: $3.50
adults, $1.25 children.*

Continue south on Cocoanut Row to Royal Palm Way. Turn
10 right and then right again onto the grounds of the **Society of the
Four Arts.** This 55-year-old cultural and educational institution
is privately endowed and incorporates an exhibition hall for
art, concerts, films, and lectures; a library open without
charge; 13 distinct gardens, and the Philip Hulitar Sculpture
Garden. *Four Arts Plaza, tel. 407/655–7226. Exhibitions and
programs, Dec.–Apr. 22, Mon.–Sat. 10–5, Sun. 2–5. Library
open Nov.–Apr., Mon.–Sat. 10–5; May–Oct., weekdays 10–5.
Gardens open Nov.–Apr., Mon.–Sat. 10–5; Jan.–Apr. 15,*

Sun. 2:30–5; May–Oct., weekdays 10–5. Admission: $15 concerts, $10 lectures, $2.50 Friday films, $1 young people's programs; exhibitions: suggested donation $2; Sun. art films and gallery talks, free. Concert and lecture tickets for nonmembers may be purchased one week in advance. Tickets for Fri. films available at time of showing.

Continue west on Royal Palm Way across the Royal Park
Bridge into West Palm Beach. On the mainland side, turn left
onto Flagler Drive, which runs along the west shore of Lake
11 Worth. A half-mile south of the **Royal Palm Bridge,** turn right
onto Actaeon Street, which is the north edge of a sloping mall
12 leading up to the **Norton Gallery of Art.**

Founded in 1941 by steel magnate Ralph H. Norton, the Norton Gallery boasts an extensive permanent collection of 19th- and 20th-century American and European paintings with emphasis on 19th-century French Impressionists, Chinese bronze and jade sculptures, a sublime outdoor patio with sculptures on display in a tropical garden, and a library housing more than 3,000 art books and periodicals. The Norton also secures many of the best traveling exhibits to reach south Florida. *1451 S. Olive Ave., West Palm Beach, tel. 407/832–5194. Open Tues.–Sat. 10–5, Sun. 1–5. Admission free; donation requested.*

Return to Flagler Drive, go a half-mile south to Barcelona
13 Road, and turn right again. You're at the entrance to the **Ann
Norton Sculpture Gardens,** a monument to the late American sculptor Ann Weaver Norton, second wife of Norton Gallery founder Ralph H. Norton. In three distinct areas of the 3-acre grounds, the art park displays seven granite figures and six brick megaliths. Plantings were designed by Norton, an environmentalist, to attract native birdlife. Native plants include 150 different kinds of palms. Other sculptures in bronze, marble, and wood are on display in Norton's studio. *253 Barcelona Rd., West Palm Beach, tel. 407/832–5328. Open Tues.–Sat. noon–4 or by appointment. Admission: $2 adults, children under 12 free.*

Return again to Flagler Drive and continue south to Southern
Boulevard (U.S. 98). Turn right and go west almost a mile, turn
left onto Parker Avenue, and go south about a mile. Turn right
onto Summit Boulevard, and right again at the next stoplight
14 into the parking lot at the **Dreher Park Zoo.** The 29-acre zoo has
nearly 300 animals representing 100 different species, including an endangered Florida panther. Of special interest are the reptile collection and the petting zoo. *1301 Summit Blvd., West Palm Beach, tel. 407/585–2197 (recording) or 407/533–0887. Open daily 9–5. Closed Thanksgiving and Christmas. Admission: $5 adults, $4 seniors over 60, $3 children 3–12.*

15 About a quarter-mile from the zoo is the **South Florida Science
Museum.** Here you'll find hands-on exhibits, aquarium displays with touch-tank demonstrations and feedings daily at 4 PM, planetarium shows, and a chance to observe the heavens Friday nights through the most powerful telescope in south Florida (weather permitting). *4801 Dreher Trail N, West Palm Beach, tel. 407/832–1988. Open Tues.–Sun. 10–5, Fri. 6:30–10 PM. Admission varies according to exhibit: $3–$5 adults, $2.50–$4 seniors over 62, $1.50 children 4–12; laser show $2 extra. Planetarium admission: $1.75 extra.*

Leaving the science museum, retrace your path on Summit Boulevard and Parker Avenue to Southern Boulevard (Rte.
16 80), turn left, and go about 16 miles west to **Lion Country Safari,** where you drive (with car windows closed) on eight miles of paved roads through a 500-acre cageless zoo where 1,000 wild animals roam free. Lions, elephants, white rhinoceroses, giraffes, zebras, antelopes, chimpanzees, and ostriches are among the species in residence. Try to go early in the day, before the park gets crowded. If you have a convertible or a new car on which you don't want animals to climb, the park will rent you a zebra-stripe, air-conditioned sedan. An adjacent KOA campground offers campers a park discount. *Box 16066, West Palm Beach 33416, tel. 407/793–1084. Open daily 9:30–5:30. Admission: $11.95 adults, $9.95 children 3–16, $8.55 seniors over 65, under 3 free; car rental $5 per hour.*

Returning to town on Southern Boulevard, look for the Italian-
17 ate towers of **Mar-A-Lago** (1100 S. Ocean Blvd.) silhouetted against the sky as you cross the bridge to Palm Beach. Mar-A-Lago, the former estate of breakfast-food heiress Marjorie Meriweather Post, is now owned by real estate magnate Donald Trump. It's closed to the public, but you can catch a glimpse as you drive past.

Turn north on Ocean Boulevard, one of Florida's most scenic drives. The road follows the dune top, with the beach falling away to surging surf on your right, and some of Palm Beach's most opulent mansions on your left. You will pass the east end
18 of **Worth Avenue,** regarded by many as the world's classiest shopping street (*see* Shopping, below).

19 As you approach Worth Avenue, the **public beach** begins. Parking meters along Ocean Drive between Worth Avenue and Royal Palm Way signify the only stretch of beach in Palm Beach with convenient public access.

This concludes the tour. To return to its starting point, turn left on Royal Palm Way and go one block west to County Road.

What to See and Do with Children

Gumbo Limbo Nature Center. At this unusual nature center, you can stroll a 1,628-foot boardwalk through a dense tropical forest and climb a 50-foot tower to overlook the tree canopy. The forest is a coastal hammock, with tropical species growing north of the tropics. One tree species you're sure to see is the gumbo-limbo, often called "the tourist tree" because of its red, peeling bark. A new *Coastal Park Plant Guide* has been published ($4) for Gumbo Limbo, James Rutherford, Red Reef, and Spanish River parks that details the parks' flora, with photos and brief text keyed to numbered posts along the trails. In the nature center building, a diorama depicts the nest of a loggerhead sea turtle along the nearby beach. The center's staff leads guided turtle walks to the beach to see nesting mothers come ashore and lay their eggs. *1801 N. Ocean Blvd., Boca Raton, tel. 407/338–1473. Open Mon.–Sat. 9–4. Admission free. Turtle walks early June–late July Mon.–Thurs. 9 PM–12:30 AM. Admission: $3. Reservations required.*

Off the Beaten Track

Arthur R. Marshall Loxahatchee National Wildlife Refuge Loxahatchee Refuge is 221 square miles of saw-grass marshes, wet prairies, sloughs, and tree islands. You go there to stroll the nature trails, see alligators and birds (including the rare snail kite). You can also fish for bass and panfish, ride an airboat, or paddle your own canoe through this watery wilderness. Loxahatchee refuge was renamed in memory of Art Marshall, a Florida environmental scientist instrumental in Everglades preservation efforts. *Refuge entrance fee: $3 per car, $1 per pedestrian. Open ½ hr before sunrise–½ hr after sunset.*

The refuge has three access points, each with its own facilities and services:

Headquarters The ranger at the visitor center will show a seven-minute slide presentation on request. Walk both nature trails—a boardwalk through a dense cypress swamp, and a marsh nature trail to a 20-foot-tall observation tower overlooking a pond. A 7-mile canoe trail starts at the boat-launching ramp here. *Entrance off U.S. 441 between Boynton Blvd. (Rte. 804) and Atlantic Ave. (Rte. 806), west of Boynton Beach. Mailing address: Rte. 1, Box 278, Boynton Beach 33437–9741, tel. 407/732–3684 or 407/734– 8303.*

Hillsboro Recreation Area A concessionaire offers airboat rides, boat rentals, guide services, and a store with snacks, fishing tackle, and bait. The airboat ride lasts a half hour, in a 20-passenger craft with a Cadillac engine. The driver will take you into the middle of the Everglades, then shut off the engine and explain the unique ecosystem around you. *Entrance off U.S. 441 on Lox Rd. (Rte. 827), 12 mi south of Headquarters and west of Boca Raton. Loxahatchee Recreation, Inc., Rte. 1, Box 642–S, Pompano Beach 33060, tel. 305/426–2474. Concessionaire open 6 AM–30 min before park closing. Airboat rides 9–4:30, $7.50 adults, $4 children under 11, under 3 free. Rental for 14-ft boat with outboard engine $27.50 for 5 hours, $13.75 evening special for last 3 daylight hours; for rowboat, $10 for 5 hours. Fishing and hunting guide $150 per half-day, $200 per day. MC, V.*

20-Mile Bend Recreation Area Boat ramp and fishing area at north end of refuge. *Entrance off U.S. 98 and 441, due west of West Palm Beach. No services.*

Shopping

Worth Avenue One of the world's last strongholds for quality shopping, Worth Avenue runs a quarter-mile east–west across Palm Beach, from the beach to Lake Worth.

The street has more than 250 shops. The 300 block, with a maze of Italianate villas designed by Addison Mizner, retains a quaint charm. The 100 and 200 blocks are more overtly commercial. Most merchants open at 9:30 or 10 AM, and close at 5:30 or 6 PM. Summer hours may be shorter.

Parking on and around Worth Avenue is quite limited. On-street parking has a one- or two-hour limit, strictly enforced. An alternative is Apollo Valet Parking at Hibiscus and Peruvian avenues, a block off Worth Avenue. Merchants will stamp your parking ticket if you buy something (or if you look like a prospective customer); each stamp is good for an hour of free parking.

Apollo's parking deal is just one reason to look presentable when you tour Worth Avenue. Come dressed to feel comfortable, blend in, and indulge your fantasies.

The Worth Avenue Association has strict rules to keep the street classy; no renovations are allowed from October to May, and special sales are limited to 21 consecutive days anytime between April and October.

Many "name" stores associated with fine shopping have a presence on Worth Avenue, including Brooks Brothers, Cartier, Elizabeth Arden, Gucci, Pierre Deux, Saks Fifth Avenue, and Van Cleef & Arpels. No other street in the world has such a dense concentration of these upscale firms—and they tend to send their best merchandise to Worth Avenue to appeal to the discerning tastes of their Palm Beach clientele.

Beaches

The best beaches in Palm Beach County are in the Jupiter area, on Singer Island, and in Boca Raton. Surfing isn't a major draw for this portion of the Atlantic, but wading and surf diving into the shallow waves are.

Participant Sports

Biking Because of traffic, bicycle with caution while on city and county roads. A nice bike path is in **John D. MacArthur Park** (alongside PGA Blvd.) as it runs east toward Singer Island. Rentals are available at **Palm Beach Bicycle Trail Shop,** *223 Sunrise Ave., Palm Beach, tel. 407/659–4583. Open daily 9–5:30. AE, MC, V.*

Diving You can drift-dive or anchor-dive along Palm Beach County's 47-mile Atlantic Coast. Drift divers take advantage of the Gulf Stream's strong currents and proximity to shore—sometimes less than a mile. A group of divers joined by nylon line may drift across coral reefs with the current; one member of the group carries a large, orange float that the charter-boat captain can follow. Drift diving works best from Boynton Beach north. South of Boynton Beach, where the Gulf Stream is farther from shore, diving from an anchored boat is more popular.

Dive Boats and Instruction The following **Force E** stores rent scuba and snorkeling equipment and have PADI affiliation. Instruction available at all skill levels. Dive-boat charters are also available.

1399 N. Military Trail, West Palm Beach, tel. 407/471–2676 or 800/527–8660. Open winter weekdays 10–8:30, summer weekdays 9–8:30, Sat. 8–7, Sun. 8–4.

155 E. Blue Heron Blvd., Riviera Beach, tel. 407/845–2333. Open weekdays year-round. 8–6:30, Sat. 6:30–6:30, Sun. 6:30–4:30.

39 S. Ocean Blvd., Delray Beach, tel. 407/272–0311. Open daily 10–6.

877 E. Palmetto Park Rd., Boca Raton, tel. 407/368–0555. Hours same as West Palm Beach store.

7166 Beracasa Way, Boca Raton, tel. 407/395–4407. Hours same as West Palm Beach store.

Fishing Palm Beach County is fisherfolks' heaven, from deep-sea strikes of fighting sailfish and wahoo to the bass, speckled perch, and bluegill of Lake Okeechobee. In between there are numerous fishing piers, bridges, and waterways where pompano, sheepshead, snapper, and grouper are likely catches. Representative of the fleets and marinas are:

Deep Sea Fishing **B-Love Fleet.** *314 E. Ocean Ave., Lantana, tel. 407/588–7612. Mornings at 8; afternoons at 1; evenings at 7. $17 per person includes rod, reel, bait.*

Lake Fishing **Slim's Fish Camp.** *Drawer 250, Belle Glade 33430, tel. 407/996–8750 or 407/996–3844. Guided tour 1 or 2 people $185 per day. Boat rental $35 per day. License required: non-Florida resident 7-day permit $16.50, 1-year permit $31.50; Florida resident 1-year permit $13.50.*

J-Mark Fish Camp. *Box 2225, Belle Glade 33430, tel. 407/996–5357. Guided tour 1 or 2 people $200 per day. Boat rental $35 per day (sunrise–sunset). License required.*

Golf There are more than 130 public, private, and semiprivate golf courses in the Palm Beach County area. The **PGA Sheraton Resort** west of the city, has one of the most famous golf courses in the area (*see* Lodging, below).

Hunting **Holey Land Wildlife Management Area.** You can hunt deer, wild hog, raccoon, possum, coyote, and skunk on this 35,350-acre state preserve. Access at Palm Beach/Broward County Line off U.S. Highway 27. At the larger **J.W. Corbett Wildlife Management Area,** (tel. 407/683–0748). 57,892 acres, also run by the state, you can hunt deer, wild hog, squirrel, and quail in season. Access off Indiantown Road and Beeline Highway, west of Jupiter. For information on licensing, call the Florida Game and Fresh Water Fish Commission.

Spas **Hippocrates Health Institute** (1443 Palmdale Ct., West Palm Beach, tel. 407/471–8876 or 407/471–8868), was founded in Boston in 1963 by Ann Wigmore and moved to its present 10-acre site in 1987. Guests receive complete examinations by traditional and alternative health-care professionals. Personalized programs include juice fasts and the eating of raw foods.

Spectator Sports

The *Palm Beach Post's* weekly "TGIF" section on Fridays carries information on sports activities.

Baseball The **Atlanta Braves** and the **Montreal Expos** both conduct spring training in West Palm Beach's Municipal Stadium, which is also home to the Palm Beach Expos, a Class-A team in the Florida State League. *1610 Palm Beach Lakes Blvd., Box 3087, West Palm Beach 33402, stadium tel. 407/683–6012. Expos tickets: Box 3566, West Palm Beach 33402, tel. 407/689–9121, AE, MC. Braves tickets: Box 2619, West Palm Beach 33402, tel. 407/683–6100. No credit cards.*

Greyhound Racing **Palm Beach Kennel Club** opened in 1932 and has 3,000 free seats. Dine in the Paddock Dining Room or watch and eat on the Terrace. Call for schedule. *1111 N. Congress Ave., Palm Beach 33409, tel. 407/683–2222. Admission: 50¢ general admission, $2 dining rooms. Free parking.*

Jai Alai

Palm Beach Jai Alai. This jai alai fronton is the site of two world records: for the largest payoff ever, $988,325; and for the fastest ball ever thrown, 188 mph. *1415 45th St., West Palm Beach, ¼ mi east of I-95 off exit 54, tel. 407/844–2444 or 407/427–0009 (toll-free south to Pompano Beach). Admission: 50¢ to $5. Free parking. Sala Del Toro Restaurant. Open: Sept. to July. Schedule changes seasonally. No cameras.*

Equestrian Sports and Polo

Palm Beach county is the home of three major polo organizations. Seventy miles north in Vero Beach, the **Windsor Polo and Beach Club** held its first polo match in February 1989. Although only the affluent can support a four-member polo team, admission is free for some games and priced reasonably for others. If you like horses and want to rub elbows with the rich and famous, dress like the locals in tweeds or a good golf shirt and khakis and spend an afternoon watching some of the world's best professional polo players.

Polo teams play under a handicap system in which the U.S. Polo Association ranks each player's skills; a team's total handicap reflects its members' individual handicaps. The best players have a 10-goal handicap. The average polo game lasts about 90 minutes. Each game consists of six periods or chukkers of 7½ minutes each.

Gulf Stream Polo Club, the oldest club in Palm Beach, began in the 1920s and plays medium-goal polo (for teams with handicaps of 8–16 goals). It has six polo fields. *4550 Polo Rd., Lake Worth 33467, tel. 407/965–2057. Play Dec.–April. Games Fri. 3 PM and Sun. 1 PM. Admission free.*

Royal Palm Polo, founded in 1959 by Oklahoma oilman John T. Oxley, has a total sports complex open to the public. It includes seven polo fields with two stadiums, a fitness center with 13 clay tennis courts, racquetball courts, a pool, and three restaurants. The complex is home to the $100,000 International Gold Cup Tournament. *6300 Clint Moore Rd., Boca Raton 33496, tel. 407/994–1876. Winter season Jan.–Apr. Summer season June–Oct. Games Sun. 1 and 3 PM. General admission $5, box seats $15, $3 children and students.*

Palm Beach Polo and Country Club. Started in 1979, this is the site each April of the $100,000 Cadillac World Cup competition (*see* Lodging, below). *Stadium address: 13198 Forest Hill, West Palm Beach, 33414, tel. 407/798–7605. Games Sun. 3 PM. General admission reserve $10, lower level $14, upper level $17. AE, MC, V.*

Rugby

Boca Raton Rugby Club practices on Tuesday and Thursday nights. Home games are played Saturday 2 PM at Boca Raton's Lake Wyman Park. *For information, contact Allerton "Bing" Towne, president, Florida Rugby Football Clubs, 1580 S.W. 6th Ave., Boca Raton 33486, tel. 407/451–0800 weekdays or 407/395–4259 weekends and nights.*

Dining

The list below is a representative selection of independent restaurants in Palm Beach County, organized geographically, and by type of cuisine within each region of the county. Unless otherwise noted, they serve lunch and dinner.

The most highly recommended restaurants are indicated by a star ★.

Category	Cost*
Very Expensive	over $55
Expensive	$35–$55
Moderate	$15–$35
Inexpensive	under $15

**per person, excluding drinks, service, and 6% sales tax*

The following credit card abbreviations are used: AE, American Express; CB, Carte Blanche; DC, Diners Club; MC, MasterCard; V, Visa.

Boca Raton
Continental

Gazebo Cafe. The locals who patronize this popular restaurant know where it is, even though there is no sign. You'll probably circle the block three times. Look for the Barnett Bank in Sun Plaza, a block north of Spanish River Drive. Once you find the place, await your table in the open kitchen where Greek-born owner-chef William Sellas and his staff perform a gastronomic ballet. The main dining room has a high noise level. You may be happier in the smaller back dining room. Specialties include lump crabmeat with an excellent glaze of Mornay sauce on a marinated artichoke bottom; spinach salad with *fresh* heart of palm, egg white, bacon, croutons, mushrooms, fruit garnish, and a dressing of olive oil and Dijon mustard; Paul Sellas's (the chef's young son) "classic" bouillabaisse with Maine lobster, shrimp, scallops, clams, and mussels topped with julienne vegetables in a robust broth flavored with garlic, saffron, and tomatoes; and raspberries with a Grand Marnier-Sabayon sauce. The staff can accommodate travelers in seven languages. *4199 N. Federal Hwy., Boca Raton, tel. 407/395–6033. Jacket preferred. Reservations advised. Closed Sun. except New Year's Eve through Mother's Day. AE, DC, MC, V. Moderate.*

French
★

La Vieille Maison. This elegant French restaurant occupies a two-story dwelling, which architect Addison Mizner may have designed. The structure dates from the 1920s, hence the name, which means old house. It has been renovated repeatedly, but it retains features typical of Mizner's work. Closets and cubbyholes have become intimate private dining rooms. You may order from a fixed-price or an à la carte menu throughout the year; in summer, a separate fixed-price menu available Sunday through Thursday offers a sampling of the other two at a more modest price. Specialties include *pompano aux pecans* (pompano filets sautéed in butter strewn with pecans under a creamy chardonnay sauce) and *l'endive Cyrille* (smoked salmon, onions, and Belgian endive with light vinaigrette). Dessert specialties include *crêpe soufflé au citron* and a chocolate tart. *770 E. Palmetto Park Rd., tel. 407/391–6701 in Boca Raton, 407/737–5677 in Delray Beach and Palm Beach, 305/421–7370 in Ft. Lauderdale. Jacket required. Reservations required. Closed Memorial Day, Labor Day, July 4th, AE, CB, MC, V. Expensive.*

Soul Food

Tom's Place. "This place is a blessing from God," says the sign over the fireplace, to which you'll add, "Amen!" That's in between mouthfuls of sauce-slathered ribs and chicken cooked in a peppery mustard sauce over hickory and oak. Tom Wright purely brings it on—pork chop sandwich to sweet potato pie.

You'll want to leave with a bottle or two of Tom's BBQ sauce: $2.95/pint, $5.90/quart. You'll come back the way Mr. T has, like Sugar Ray Leonard, Joe Frazier, and a rush of NFL pro players. You can bet the place is family run. *7251 N. Federal Hwy., tel. 407/947–0920. Dress: neat but casual. No reservations. Closed Sun., Mon., Thanksgiving, Christmas, and for a month around Sept. No credit cards. Inexpensive.*

Jupiter
American

Lighthouse Restaurant. Still another family eatery thrives on the Gold Coast. Next year it'll be 60 years old, and one cook's been here more than half that time. You'll see the same familiar faces at the counter drinking coffee at 6 AM and midnight. House specialties include roast turkey with giblet gravy, leg of lamb with mint jelly, fresh ham with applesauce, Yankee pot roast, deep-fried Okeechobee catfish, prime rib. "They love my meat loaf and biscuits," manager for 12 years Renée Jordan says. "But I keep 'em in suspense. They never know when I'm gonna have it." You can get breakfast 24 hours a day, Sunday dinner at noon. The same people operate the Jupiter Crab Company next door. Zealously nautical, California-rustic, the Lighthouse has two parrots who greet you at the door while you wait with a numbered balloon for your table. *1510 U.S. 1, tel. 407/746–4811. Dress: casual. No reservations. Beer and wine only. Closed Chirstmas Eve and 1 Sun. night a month (call ahead). MC, V. Inexpensive.*

Lake Worth
American
★

John G's. About the only time the line lets up here is when the restaurant closes. Otherwise, there's little to complain about: certainly not the service, the patrons, the price, or the noise. The menu is as big as the crowd: eggs every which way, including a UN of ethnic omelets; big fruit platters; sandwich board superstars; grilled burgers and seafood. The Greek shrimp (seven at recent count) come on fresh linguine topped by feta. Decor is not the thing: a big, open room with tables and counter seats under nautical bric-a-brac. *On the beach, Lake Worth Casino, tel. 407/585–9860. Dress: casual. No reservations. No dinner. No credit cards. Closed Christmas. Inexpensive.*

Palm Beach
American

Chuck & Harold's. Boxer Larry Holmes and thespians Brooke Shields and Burt Reynolds are among the celebrities who frequent this combination power-lunch bar, celebrity sidewalk cafe, and nocturnal big-band/jazz garden restaurant. A blue-and-yellow tent on pulleys rolls back in good weather to expose the garden to the elements. Local businesspeople wheel and deal at lunch in the bar area while quaffing Bass ale and Harp on tap. Locals who want to be part of the scenery frequent the front-porch area, next to pots of red and white begonias mounted along the sidewalk rail. Specialties include a mildly spiced conch chowder with a rich flavor and a liberal supply of conch; an onion-crunchy gazpacho with croutons, a cucumber spear, and a dollop of sour cream; a *frittata* (an omelet of bacon, spinach, pepperocini, potatoes, smoked mozzarella, and fresh tomato salsa); and a tangy Key-lime pie with a graham cracker crust and a squeezable lime slice for even more tartness. *207 Royal Poinciana Way, tel. 407/659–1440. Dress: neat but casual. Reservations advised. AE, CB, DC, MC, V. Moderate.*

Dempsey's. A New York–style Irish pub under the palms: green baize, plaid café curtains, brass rods, burgundy banquettes, *Ring Magazine* covers, open beams, paddlefans, sculpted horse heads, mounted hat racks, horse prints, and antique coach lanterns. George Dempsey was a Florida horse rancher until he entered the restaurant business 13 years ago.

This place is packed, noisy, and as electric as Black Friday at the stock exchange when major sports events are on the big TV. Along with much socializing, people put away plates of chicken hash Dempsey (with a dash of Scotch), shad roe, prime rib, and hot apple pie. You go for the scene. Dempsey is knock-out champ at making it. *50 Cocoanut Row, tel. 407/835–0400. Dress: neat but casual. Reservations advised for 6 or more. AE, MC, V. Closed Christmas. Moderate.*

Continental **The Breakers.** The main hotel dining area at The Breakers consists of the elegant Florentine Dining Room, decorated with fine 15th-century Flemish tapestries; the adjoining Celebrity Aisle where the maître d' seats his most honored guests; and the Circle Dining Room, with a huge circular skylight framing a bronze-and-crystal Venetian chandelier. Specialties include rack of lamb Dijonnaise; salmon *en croûte* with spinach, herbs and sauce Véronique (a grape sauce); *vacherin glacé* (praline-flavored ice cream encased in fresh whipped cream and frozen in a baked meringue base); and Key-lime pie. The Breakers also serves less formally at its Beach Club, where locals flock for the most sumptuous Sunday champagne brunch in Florida, and at the Fairway Cafe in the golf-course clubhouse. *1 S. County Rd., tel. 407/655–6611 or 800/833–3141. Jacket and tie required. Reservations required. AE, CB, DC, MC, V. Expensive.*

Deli **TooJay's.** Offering Jewish deli food with California accents, daily specials include matzoh ball soup, corned beef on homemade, hand-sliced rye, killer cake with five chocolates, and homemade whipped cream. On the high holy days look for carrot *tzimmes* (a sweet compote), beef brisket with gravy, potato pancakes, and roast chicken. Naturally, Hebrew National kosher salami layered with onions, muenster cheese, cole slaw, and Russian dressing on rye or pumpernickel is a house favorite. There's also dill-chicken; seafood with crabmeat, shrimp, and sour cream; and for the vegetarians, hummus, tabouleh, and a wheatberry salad. It's fast and busy with wise-cracking waitresses. The decor is bright, with a high, open packing-crate board ceiling, and windows overlooking the gardens. *313 Royal Poinciana Plaza, tel. 407/659–7232. Dress: casual but neat. Beer and wine only. No reservations. Closed Yom Kippur, Christmas. AE, DC, MC, V. Inexpensive.*

French **Jo's.** This is an intimate, candlelit bistro with flowers on pink cloths, greenery against lattice backdrops, and, after eight years, a well-rehearsed menu. The three-soup sampler has been tried and true: buttery lobster bisque, potage St. Germain (green pea soup), and beef consommé. Osso bucco is ever on the chalkboard, served with rice and vegetables. The half roast duckling (boned) with orange demiglaze is never rare but always moist. For dessert try the fresh apple *tarte tatin* or fresh raspberries Josephine with Grand Marnier. Jo's is tucked off County Road behind the Church Mouse Thrift Shop. *200 Chilian Ave., tel. 407/659–6776. Jacket required. Reservations advised. Dinner only. Closed Sun. in Sept., and Christmas. Expensive.*

Petite Marmite. Former British secret service agent Frederick Danielski, the inspiration for Bogart's Rick in *Casablanca,* has breathed new life into this Palm Beach landmark for good dining. New value, too, thanks to prix fixe dinners that range from the low- to mid-$20s depending on season, including choice of soup, house salad, chef's choice of entrée, dessert, and coffee. Chef's choice? Might be angel hair pasta with veal and prosciutto in a parmesan-basil cream sauce, grilled dolphin, or linguine with red or white clam sauce. Maintaining the country French look with brick, balloon chintz curtains, and flowers in season, the charm is topped with the entertainment of a small combo band in the evenings. *313 Worth Ave., tel. 407/655–0550. Jacket required for dinner. Reservations advised. Closed Labor Day through Sept., and off-season Sun. AE, DC, MC, V. Moderate–Expensive.*

International ★

The Dining Room. Since it opened in 1926, this formal hotel dining room in the Brazilian Court has been a favorite with the Palm Beach elite. The 94-seat dining room, with Romanesque arches and a sunny yellow color scheme, opens onto the outdoor Fountain Court. David Woodward, executive chef, uses only fresh ingredients and prepares all sauces from scratch. Specialties include Brazilian black-bean soup, a hotel standard throughout its history; warm Maine lobster with black bean and ginger relish; escallop of salmon with a smoked-salmon crust served with a mint and parsley sauce; roast rack of baby lamb with a timbale of spinach and sweet garlic; flan; and chocolate-and-pistacchio truffle cake. *301 Australian Ave., tel. 407/655–7740. Jacket and tie required. Reservations required. AE, CB, DC, MC, V. Expensive.*

Seafood

Charley's Crab. Audubon bird prints, fresh flowers, and French posters accent the walls of this restaurant across the street from the beach. During the season, the dinner line forms early. The raw bar in front is noisy and crowded, the back dining rooms more relaxed. Menus change daily. Specialties include 8–10 daily fresh fish specials. *456 S. Ocean Blvd., tel. 407/659–1500. Dress: casual. Reservations advised. AE, DC, MC, V. Expensive.*

Palm Beach Gardens
Continental

The Explorers. You sit in red leather hobnail chairs at tables lit with small brass and glass lanterns. The à la carte menu includes a variety of international and American regional preparations. Specialties include a fresh sushi appetizer with soy, wasabi, and pickled ginger; loin of deer with lingonberry conserve; and almond snow eggs, an egg-shaped meringue poached in almond cream, plated between three-fruit coulis (boysenberry, mango, and tamarillo) and garnished with a nest of butter caramel. The Explorers Wine Club meets monthly for wine and food tastings and is open to the public for a one-time $5 membership. Contact the club for a schedule of events. *400 Ave. of the Champions, tel. 407/627–2000. Jacket required. Reservations advised. Closed Sun.–Mon. May–Sept. AE, MC, V. Expensive.*

West Palm Beach
Northern Italian

Brasseria La Capannina. A virtuoso range of satisfactions from lunchtime pizza by the slice to formal dining by the fountain. The pizza, out of a wood-burning oven, is thin and crisp, and is available to-go along with market-deli fare from sandwiches to Italian pasta. Extensive à la carte dinners feature the local yellowtail baked with white wine, parsley, and garlic; rigatoni alla vodka with caviar; and double-cut veal chops Milanese (pounded thin and breaded). The indoor dining room, with etched-glass elegance, overlooks Lake Worth. *777 S. Flagler Dr., tel. 407/766–3770. Jacket required. Reservations advised. Closed Sat. lunch and Sun. Mother's Day–Thanksgiving. AE, MC, V. Expensive.*

Lodging

The list below is a representative selection of hotels and motels in Palm Beach County. The rate categories in the list are based on the all-year or peak-season price; off-peak rates may be a category or two lower.

The most highly recommended hotels are indicated by a star ★.

Category	Cost*
Very Expensive	over $120
Expensive	$90–$120
Moderate	$50–$90
Inexpensive	under $50

**All prices are for a standard double room, excluding 6% state sales tax and nominal tourist tax.*

The following credit card abbreviations are used: AE, American Express; CB, Carte Blanche; DC, Diners Club; MC, MasterCard; V, Visa.

Very Expensive

Boca Raton Resort & Club. Architect and socialite Addison Mizner designed and built the original. The tower was added in 1961, the ultramodern Boca Beach Club, in 1981. Room rates during the winter season are based on the modified American plan (including breakfast and dinner). The rooms in the older buildings tend to be smaller and cozily traditional; those in the newer buildings are light, airy and contemporary in color schemes and furnishings. *501 E. Camino Real, Boca Raton 33432, tel. 407/395–3000 or 800/327–0101. 1,000 rooms: 100 in the original 1926 Cloister Inn, 333 in the 1931 addition, 235 in the 27-story Tower Building, 212 in the Boca Beach Club, 120 in the Golf Villas. Facilities: 1½ mi of beach, 4 outdoor freshwater pools, 22 tennis courts (2 lighted), health spa, 23-slip marina, fishing and sailing charters, 7 restaurants, 3 lounges, in-room safes. AE, DC, MC, V.*

★ **Brazilian Court.** Built in 1926, the Brazilian Court received new owners and an extensive renovation in 1984–85. The yellow Mediterranean-style buildings still surround a pair of courtyards, where much of the original landscaping survives today. An open loggia with ceiling beams of exposed pecky cypress was enclosed to provide a gracious European-style lobby. A concierge at an antique desk greets you for check-in. All guest rooms feature brass-plated plumbing fixtures, firm mattresses, and valances above the beds and windows. However, no two rooms are alike. *301 Australian Ave., Palm Beach 33480, tel. 407/655–7740 or 800/351–5656. 134 rooms with bath, including 6 suites, rooms for nonsmokers and handicapped guests. Facilities: outdoor heated freshwater pool, cable TV, 2 restaurants, lounge, 24-hr room service. AE, CB, DC, MC, V.*

★ **The Breakers.** This historic seven-story oceanfront resort hotel, built in 1926 and enlarged in 1968, is currently undergoing renovation. At this palatial Italian Renaissance structure, cupids wrestle alligators in the Florentine fountain in front of the main entrance. Inside the lofty lobby, your eyes rise to majestic ceiling vaults and frescoes. The hotel's proud tradition of formality remains. After 7 PM, men and boys must wear jackets and ties in the public areas. (Ties are optional in summer.) The new room decor comes in two color schemes: cool greens and soft pinks in an orchid-patterned English cotton chintz fabric; the other is in blue, with a floral and ribbon chintz. Both designs include white plantation shutters and wall coverings, Chinese porcelain table lamps, and original 1920s furniture restored to its period appearance. The original building has 15 different sizes and shapes of rooms. If you prefer more space, ask to be placed in the newer addition. *1 S. County Rd., Palm Beach 33480, tel. 407/655–6611 or 800/833–3141. 528 rooms with bath, including 40 suites. Facilities: ½ mi of beachfront, outdoor heated freshwater pool, 19 tennis courts, 2 golf courses, health club with Keiser and Nautilus equipment, men's and women's saunas, lawn bowling, croquet, shuffleboard, shopping arcade with upscale boutiques, 3 restaurants, lounge. AE, CB, DC, MC, V.*

The Colony. The Phil Brinkman mural that depicted turn-of-the-century Palm Beach in the lobby is gone. But then so too are the Duke and Duchess of Windsor who often stayed, and John Lennon (once turned away from the dining room because he arrived tieless). No change in location, still a block from Worth Avenue, and one of the Palm Beach legends since its completion in 1947. But big change completed in 1990 has transformed the lobby into a Park Avenue salon of plush white silks, chandeliers, scenic oils, and a baby grand piano. Some 80 of the 106 rooms and suites have also metamorphosed from tropical pastels to cool neutrals. Left undone and to be avoided are the little servant-size rooms with unfortunate rooftop views. New dining room features include an open display kitchen, and by the pool, a tiki bar and outdoor grill for casual outdoor dining. Low-rise maisonettes built in mid-1950s, and apartments from the 1960s are across the street. *155 Hammon Ave., Palm Beach 33480, tel. 407/655–5430, fax 407/659–1793. 106 rooms, including 36 suites and apartments. Facilities: outdoor heated freshwater pool, restaurant serves 3 meals daily, dancing nightly with live band, beauty parlor. AE, MC, V.*

PGA National Resort. This sportsperson's mecca at PGA National Golf Club underwent a $1.8-million renovation in 1987–88 by an interior designer who likes mauve, peach, and aqua. The resort is headquarters for the Professional Golfer's Association and the U.S. Croquet Association, and hosts many major golf, tennis, and croquet tournaments. *400 Ave. of the Champions, Palm Beach Gardens 33418, tel. 407/627–2000 or 800/325–3535. 413 rooms with bath, including 25 suites, 36 nonsmoker rooms, 14 rooms for handicapped guests, 80 2-bedroom, 2-bath cottages with fully equipped kitchen. Facilities: 5 golf courses, 19 tennis courts (10 lighted), 5 croquet courts, 6 indoor racquetball courts, outdoor freshwater pool, sand beach on 26-acre lake, sailboats and aquacycles for rent, fitness center, sauna, whirlpool, aerobic dance studio, 4 restaurants, 2 lounges, in-room minibars and safes. AE, DC, MC, V.*

Palm Beach Polo and Country Club. Individual villas and condominiums are available in this exclusive 2,200-acre resort where Britain's Prince Charles comes to play polo. Arrange to rent a dwelling closest to the sports activity that interests you: polo, tennis, or golf. Each residence is uniquely designed and furnished by its owner according to standards of quality set by the resort. *13198 Forest Hill Blvd., West Palm Beach 33414, tel. 407/798–7000 or 800/432–4151. 140 privately owned villas* *and condominiums available for rental when the owners are away. Facilities: 10 outdoor freshwater pools, 24 tennis courts, two 18-hole golf courses and one 9-hole course, men's and women's saunas, 10 polo fields, equestrian trails through a nature preserve, 5 stable barns, 2 lighted croquet lawns, squash and racquetball courts, sculling equipment and instruction, 5 dining rooms. AE, DC, MC, V.*

Expensive ★ **The Jupiter Beach Hilton.** This high-rise oceanfront resort hotel is frequented by celebrities and sea turtles. The sea turtles come ashore each summer to lay their eggs in the sand along this stretch of unspoiled beach. The Jupiter Beach Hilton's beach director leads turtle walks at night to look for nesting mothers. In the morning, he collects the eggs in a holding pen by the beach hut to protect them from predators. When the eggs hatch, he helps the baby turtles dig out and guards them as they scramble into the surf. Human guests are at least as well-pampered by a friendly and efficient staff. The nine-story hotel has interior decor of sophisticated informality. The lobby suggests Singapore, with wicker and bamboo furniture, whitewashed wood floors, white ceiling fans, and a plethora of palms, orchids, and other tropical plants. *Indiantown Rd. and Rte. A1A, Jupiter 33477, tel. 407/746–2511, in FL 800/432–1420, elsewhere in the USA 800/821–8791, in Canada 800/228–8810. 197 rooms with bath, including 4 suites, 26 nonsmoker rooms, 2 rooms for handicapped guests. Facilities: outdoor heated freshwater pool, 400 ft of beachfront, 60 cabanas, snorkeling, windsurfing, lighted tennis court, poolside snack bar, boutique, fitness center, restaurant, lounge, cable TV, in-room minibars. AE, CB, DC, MC, V.*

Bed-and-Breakfast Rated Moderate–Expensive, the bed-and-breakfast has become a popular alternative to pricey Palm Beach County accommodations. For the entire county, contact *Open House Bed & Breakfast, Box 3025, Palm Beach 33480, tel. 407/842–5190.*

The Arts and Nightlife

The *Palm Beach Post*, in its "TGIF" entertainment insert on Fridays, lists all events for the weekend, including concerts. Admission to some cultural events is free or by donation.

Nightclub **Banana Max.** They have nights when anyone in a skirt—including men—gets $1 off admission. Monday is live reggae, Thursday night is break-the-ice dating. All the time it's disco with video screens, state-of-the-art psychedelic lights, and a casinolike mood. Free happy hour buffet with sliced meats, cheese, and salad bar 5–8 PM. *200 N. Federal Hwy., across from the Jupiter Mall, tel. 407/744–6600 or 407/744–7301. Mon.–Thurs. 5 PM–2 AM, Fri. 5 PM–3 AM, Sat. 7 PM–3 AM, Sun. 7 PM–2 AM. No cover Sun., Mon.; $2 Tues.–Thurs.; $3 Fri., Sat.*

Performing Arts Center **Mizner Park** (Box 1695, Boca Raton 33429), a cultural center between Federal Highway and Mizner Boulevard, is scheduled to open by 1991. It will house a performing arts complex; art, science, and children's museums; and a specialty shopping center.

Theater **Caldwell Theatre Company.** This professional equity regional theater, part of the Florida State Theater system, moved to a temporary site in 1989 while awaiting completion of permanent quarters in the new Mizner Center. *7887 N. Federal Hwy., Boca Raton 33487, tel. 407/368–7509 (Boca Raton), 407/832–2989 (Palm Beach), 305/462–5433 (Broward County).*

Royal Palm Dinner Theater. Equity cast performs five or six contemporary musicals each year. *303 Golfview Dr., Royal Palm Plaza, Boca Raton 33432, tel. 407/426–2211 or in FL, 800/841–6725. Tues.–Sat. 8 PM, Sun. 6 PM, Wed. and Sat. matinees 2 PM. AE, MC, V.*

Excursion: Treasure Coast

Numbers in the margin correspond with points of interest on the Treasure Coast map.

This excursion north from **Palm Beach** through the Treasure Coast counties of Martin, St. Lucie, and Indian River traverses an area that was remote and sparsely populated as recently as the late 1970s. Resort and leisure-oriented residential development has swollen its population. If you plan to stay overnight or dine at a good restaurant, reservations are a must.

The interior of all three counties is largely devoted to citrus production, and also cattle ranching in rangelands of pine-and-palmetto scrub. St. Lucie and Indian River counties also contain the upper reaches of the vast St. Johns Marsh, headwaters of the largest northward-flowing river in the United States. If you take Florida's Turnpike from Palm Beach north to the Orlando–Disney World area, you will dip into the edge of St. Johns Marsh about eight miles north of the Fort Pierce exit. Along the coast, the broad expanse of the Indian River (actually a tidal lagoon) separates the barrier islands from the mainland. It's a sheltered route for boaters on the Intracoastal Waterway, a nursery for the young of many saltwater game fish species, and a natural radiator keeping frost away from the tender orange and grapefruit trees that grow near its banks.

Completion of I–95's missing link from Palm Beach Gardens to Fort Pierce in 1987 eliminated the Treasure Coast's last vestiges of relative seclusion. Hotels, restaurants, and shopping malls already crowd the corridor from I–95 to the beach throughout the 70-mile stretch from Palm Beach north to Vero Beach. The Treasure Coast has become another link in the chain of municipalities that some Floridians call "the city of U.S. 1."

Of special interest in this area are the sea turtles that come ashore at night from April to August to lay their eggs on the beaches. Conservation groups, chambers of commerce, and resorts organize turtle-watches, which you may join.

Exploring Treasure Coast

1 This tour takes you north from **Palm Beach** along the coast as far as Sebastian Inlet, but you can break away at any intermediate point and return to Palm Beach on I–95.

2 From downtown **West Palm Beach,** take U.S. 1 about 5 miles north to Blue Heron Boulevard (Rte. A1A) in Riviera Beach, turn right, and cross the **Jerry Thomas Bridge** onto Singer Island. Sightseeing boats depart from **Phil Foster Park** on the island side of the bridge.

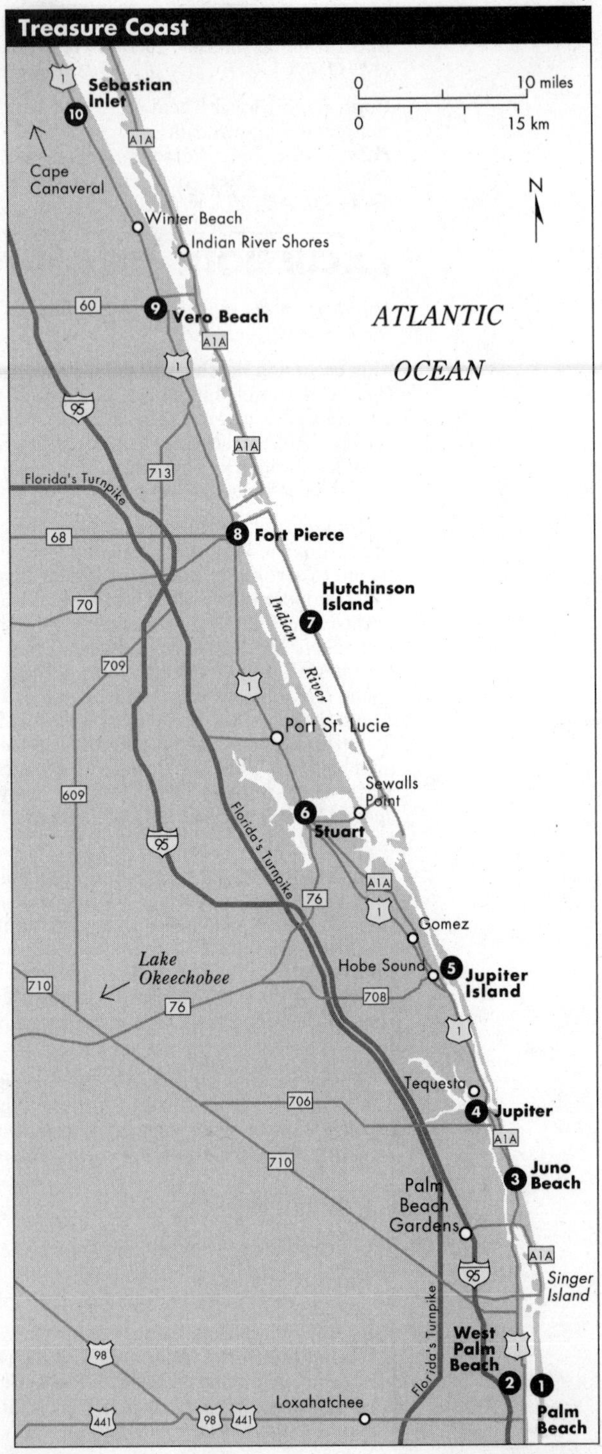
Treasure Coast
0
10 miles
0
15 km
N
ATLANTIC
OCEAN
Sebastian Inlet
10
Cape Canaveral
Winter Beach
Indian River Shores
9 Vero Beach
Florida's Turnpike
8 Fort Pierce
Hutchinson Island
7
Indian River
Port St. Lucie
Sewalls Point
6 Stuart
Florida's Turnpike
Gomez
Hobe Sound
5 Jupiter Island
Lake Okeechobee
Tequesta
4 Jupiter
3 Juno Beach
Palm Beach Gardens
Singer Island
West Palm Beach
2
1 Palm Beach
Loxahatchee
Florida's Turnpike
A1A
1
60
95
713
68
70
709
609
76
708
706
710
98
441

Continue on Rte. A1A as it turns north onto Ocean Boulevard, past hotels and high-rise condominiums to **Ocean Reef Park** (3900 N. Ocean Dr., Riviera Beach, tel. 407/842–6905), a snorkeling spot where the reefs are close to shore in shallow water. You may see angelfish, sergeant-majors, rays, robin fish, and occasionally a Florida lobster (actually a species of saltwater crayfish). Wear canvas sneakers and cloth gloves.

Go north on Rte. A1A to **John D. MacArthur State Park** (10900 Rte. A1A, North Palm Beach, tel. 407/627–6097), which offers more good snorkeling along almost 2 miles of beach, and access to the mangrove swamps in the upper reaches of Lake Worth.

North of MacArthur State Park, Rte. A1A rejoins U.S. 1, then
3 veers east again 1½ miles north at **Juno Beach.** Take Rte. A1A north to the **Loggerhead Park Marine Life Center of Juno Beach,** established by Eleanor N. Fletcher, "the turtle lady of Juno Beach." Museum displays interpret the sea turtles' natural history; hatchlings are raised in saltwater tanks, tagged and released into the surf. The museum conducts guided turtle watches June 1–July 15, at the height of the nesting season. Also on view are displays of coastal natural history, sharks, whales, and shells, and there are saltwater aquariums. *1111 Ocean Dr., but enter on U.S. 1, on the west side of the park, Juno Beach, tel. 407/627–8280. Open Tues.–Sat. 10–3. Admission free.*

4 From Juno Beach north to **Jupiter,** Rte. A1A runs for almost 4 miles atop the beachfront dunes. West of the road, about half the land is undeveloped, with endangered native plant communities. The road veers away from the dunes at **Carlin Park** (400 Rte. A1A, Jupiter, tel. 407/964–4420), which provides beach frontage, covered picnic pavilions, hiking trails, a baseball diamond, tot-lot, six tennis courts, and fishing sites. The Park Galley, serving snacks and burgers, is usually open daily 10:30–5.

At the northwest corner of Indiantown Road and Rte. A1A is **The Jupiter Theater** (formerly the Burt Reynolds Jupiter Theater). Reynolds grew up in Jupiter; his father was Palm Beach County sheriff. More than 150 Broadway and Hollywood stars have performed here since the theater opened in 1979. In 1989 Reynolds gave the theater to Palm Beach Community College. It is now run as a not-for-profit regional theater. *1001 E. Indiantown Rd., Jupiter, tel. 407/746–5566.*

Leave the theater grounds on Indiantown Road, go west to U.S. 1, and turn right. About a mile north on Jupiter Island, turn right into Burt Reynolds Park to visit the **Loxahatchee Historical Society Museum.** Permanent exhibits completed in 1990 emphasize Seminole Indians, the steamboat era, pioneer life on the Loxahatchee River, shipwrecks, railroads and modern-day development. A pioneer dwelling at the mouth of the river, the Dubois Home, is open Sunday 1–3:30; ask for directions at the museum. *805 N. U.S. 1, Box 1506, Jupiter, tel. 407/747–6639. Open Tues.–Fri. 10–3, weekends noon–3, closed Mon. Donation.*

Continue north on U.S. 1 across the Loxahatchee River. The 105-foot-tall **Jupiter Lighthouse,** east of the bridge, is the oldest structure in Palm Beach County, built 1855–59. To reach the lighthouse and a small museum of local history on the ground floor, turn east on Route 707, then take the first right into Lighthouse Park. *No phone. Donation. Open Sun. noon–2:30.*

5 Take Rte. 707 north from the lighthouse onto **Jupiter Island.** Just north of the Martin County line, stop at the Nature Conservancy's 73-acre **Blowing Rocks Preserve,** with plant communities native to beachfront dune, strand (the landward side of the dunes), marsh, and hammock (tropical hardwood forest). Sea grape, cabbage palms, saw palmetto, and sea oats help to anchor the dunes. The floral beauty of Indian blanket, dune sunflower, and goldenrod carpets the ground. You may see pelicans, seagulls, ospreys, redbellied and pileated woodpeckers, and a profusion of warblers in spring and fall. A trail takes you over the dune to the beach. At high tide, spray shoots up through holes in the largest Anastasia limestone outcropping on the Atlantic Coast. At dead low tide, you can walk on the seaward side of the rocks and peer into caves and solution holes. Best time to go is early morning, before the crowds. The parking lot holds just 18 cars, with room for three cars to wait; Jupiter Island police will ticket cars parked along the road shoulder. *Box 3795, Tequesta, tel. 407/575–2297. Open 6–5. Admission by donation. No food, drinks, ice chests, pets, or spearfishing allowed. No rest rooms.*

Continue north through the town of Jupiter Island, a posh community where President Bush's mother and many other notables dwell in estates screened from the road by dense vegetation. At the north end of Jupiter Island, **Hobe Sound National Wildlife Refuge** has a 3½-mile beach where turtles nest and shells wash ashore in abundance. On the mainland at refuge headquarters, visit the **Elizabeth W. Kirby Interpretive Center.** Take Rte. 707 and County Road 708 through the town of Hobe Sound to U.S. 1, then turn left and go about 2 miles south. The center is on the left (east) side of the highway. An adjacent ½-mile trail winds through a forest of sand pine and scrub oak —one of Florida's most unusual and endangered plant communities. *13640 S.E. Federal Hwy., Hobe Sound 33455, refuge tel. 407/546–6141, nature center tel. 407/546–2067. Trail always open. Nature center open weekdays 9–11 and 1–3, group tours by appointment.*

From the interpretive center, go south 2½ miles to the entrance to **Jonathan Dickinson State Park.** Follow signs to Hobe Mountain, an ancient dune topped with a tower where you'll have a panoramic view across the park's 10,284 acres of varied terrain. It encompasses sand pine, slash pine, and palmetto flatwoods, mangrove river swamp, and the winding upper northwest fork of the Loxahatchee River, which is part of the federal government's wild and scenic rivers program and populated by manatees in winter and alligators all year. *14800 S.E. Federal Hwy., Hobe Sound, tel. 407/546–2771. Open daily 8–sundown. Admission: $1 driver, 50¢ per passenger. Facilities: bicycle and hiking trails, campground, snack bar. Contact State Vending Corp., 16450 S.E. Federal Hwy., Hobe Sound 33455, tel. 407/746–1466 for information and reservations on cabins, rental canoes and rowboats. 2-hr narrated river cruise: $9 adults, $4 children under 12.*

Return to U.S. 1 and proceed north. Quality of life values are
6 most apparent in **Stuart,** the county seat, undergoing downtown revival that is making this one-time fishing village of
about 20,000 residents a magnet for people who want to live and

work in a small-town atmosphere. Strict architectural and zoning standards are guiding civic renewal in the older section of Stuart. In 1989 construction of a riverwalk began with a ¼-mile portion running from City Hall to Youth Center Park. In 1990 a platform stage with 160 seats was installed along the river at the end of St. Lucie Street, and still more portions of the riverwalk will go up in 1991. By 1994 the 5-mile walk curving along the St. Lucie River will be completed. Early 20th-century buildings have been converted into museums, office buildings, and art spaces, and the Lyric Theater has been revived for performing and community events. Various means of transportation are planned, including shuttle trams, horse-and-carriage rides, and paddleboat rentals. Among the restaurants that have reopened on West Osceola Street, in the heart of downtown, is the **Thirsty Whale** (265 West Osceola St., tel. 407/220–2157), with a sidewalk deck under tall oaks edged onto the street.

7 Continue north on Rte. A1A to **Hutchinson Island.** Stop at the pastel-pink **Elliott Museum,** built in 1961 in honor of inventor Sterling Elliott. On display is an early model of his Elliott Addressing Machine, forerunner of today's Addressograph machines. Elliott also invented a four-wheel bicycle, the quadricycle; the mechanism that makes its wheels turn is the basis of the automobile differential. In addition to Elliott's inventions, the museum features antique automobiles, dolls and toys, and fixtures from an early general store, blacksmith shop, and apothecary shop. Children enjoy feeding coins to a voracious collection of 19th-century mechanical banks. *825 N.E. Ocean Blvd., Stuart, tel. 407/225–1961. Open daily 1–4. Admission: $2.50 adults, 50¢ children 6–13, under 6 free.*

Across the street from the Elliott Museum is the expanding **Coastal Science Center** (890 N.E. Ocean Blvd., Stuart 34996, tel. 407/225–0505) of the Florida Oceanographic Society. Its nearly 40-acre site combines a coastal hardwood hammock and mangrove forest. So far, resources include temporary displays about coastal ecology, a library program, and an interpretive nature trail. A visitor center is expected to be completed late in 1991.

A mile south of the Elliott Museum stands the **House of Refuge Museum,** built in 1875 and now restored to its original appearance. It's one of 10 such structures erected by the U.S. Life Saving Service (an ancestor of the Coast Guard) to aid stranded sailors along Florida's then-remote Atlantic Coast. The keeper here patrolled the beach looking for shipwreck victims whose vessels foundered on Gilbert's Bar, an offshore reef. Exhibits include antique lifesaving equipment, maps, ships' logs, artifacts from nearby wrecks, boatmaking tools, and six tanks of local fish from the ocean and the Indian River. A 35-foot watchtower in the front yard was used during World War II by submarine spotters. *301 S.E. MacArthur Blvd., Stuart, tel. 407/225–1875. Open Tues.–Sun. 1–4, closed Mon. and holidays. Admission: $1 adults, 50¢ children 6–13, under 6 free.*

Just south of the House of Refuge Museum, at the southern tip of Hutchinson Island, is **Bathtub Beach,** a public facility ideal for visitors with children because the waters are shallow for about 300 feet offshore and usually calm. At low tides bathers can walk to the reef. Facilities include rest rooms and showers.

Continue up Rte. A1A as far as the Jensen Beach Bridge. Cut
back to the mainland and turn right on Indian River Drive, Rte.
707. This scenic road full of curves and dips follows the route of
early-20th-century pineapple plantations. In Fort Pierce, turn
right over the South Beach Causeway Bridge. On the east side,
take the first road left onto the grounds of the **St. Lucie County**
8 **Historical Museum.** Enter through a replica of the old **Fort**
Pierce FEC Railroad Station. Among exhibits and early-20th-
century memorabilia are photos and murals of Indian River
Drive, along which you've just driven. *414 Seaway Dr., Fort*
Pierce, tel. 407/464-6635. Open Tues.–Sat. 10–4, Sun.
noon–4. Admission: $1 adults, 50¢ children 6–12, under 6 free.

Recross South Beach Causeway Bridge west, turn right onto U.S. 1 north to Webster College. **Mel Fisher's Treasure Exhibit**—affiliated with the same treasure salvor's museum in Key West (*see* Exploring in Chapter 7)—is located in a storefront behind Webster College in a commercial development between U.S. 1 and Old Dixie Highway. Displays here are salvaged from a 1715 Spanish fleet located by Fisher in nearby offshore waters. Treasures include a 70-pound silver bar, gold and pearl crucifixes, an emerald cross, gold toothpicks, and a gold cup with stone-mounted center said to detect poison. A small store sells gold coins, books, cards, and promotional items. *Treasure Coast Business Park, 2141 Old Dixie Hwy., Fort Pierce 34946, tel. 407/465-1715. Open Tues.–Sun. 10–5. Admission: $1, children under 7 free.*

From here, backtrack to Rte. A1A and turn east across North Beach Causeway. About a mile east, as you approach the ocean, Rte. A1A turns left. Go right instead to visit **Fort Pierce Inlet State Recreation Area,** where a sand bottom creates the Treasure Coast's safest surfing conditions and a nature trail winds through a coastal hammock.

North on Rte. A1A at Pepper Park is the **UDT-Seal Museum,** beside the beach where more than 3,000 Navy frogmen trained during World War II. The museum traces the exploits of Navy divers from the 1944 Normandy invasion through Korea, Vietnam, and astronaut landings at sea. *Box 1117, Ft. Pierce, tel. 407/464-FROG (3764). Open Wed.–Sun. 10–4. Admission: $1 adults, 50¢ children 6–11, under 6 free.*

Within a mile north of Pepper Beach, turn left to the parking lot for the **Jack Island wildlife refuge,** accessible only by footbridge. The 1-mile Marsh Rabbit Trail across the island traverses a mangrove swamp to a 30-foot observation tower overlooking the Indian River. You'll see ospreys, brown pelicans, great blue herons, ibis, and other water birds.

9 Return to Rte. A1A and go north to **Vero Beach,** an affluent city of about 30,000; retirees comprise half the winter population. In the exclusive Riomar Bay section, north of the 17th Street Bridge, "canopy roads" shaded by massive live oaks cross the barrier island between Rte. A1A and Ocean Drive. **Painted Bunting Lane,** a typical canopy road, is lined with elegant homes—many dating from the 1920s.

The city provides beach-access parks with boardwalks and steps bridging the foredune. (Open daily 7 AM–10 PM, admission free.) From shore, snorkelers and divers can swim out to explore reefs 100–300 feet off the beach. Summer offers the best diving conditions. At low tide you can see the boiler and other remains of an iron-screw steamer, *Breconshire*, which foundered in 1894 on a reef just south of Beachland Boulevard.

Along Ocean Drive near Beachland Boulevard, a specialty shopping area includes art galleries, antique stores, and upscale clothing stores. Also in this area is **The Driftwood Inn Resort** (3150 Ocean Dr., Vero Beach, tel. 407/231–0550), a unique beachfront hotel and restaurant built in the 1930s by Waldo Sexton, an eccentric plow salesman from Indiana. He used driftwood and other scavenged lumber as well as art treasures salvaged from Palm Beach mansions torn down during the Depression.

Well-endowed cultural life in Vero Beach centers around the twin arts facilities in Riverside Park. In the 633-seat **Riverside Theatre** (400 Beachland Blvd., Vero Beach, 32964, tel. 407/231–6990), the resident Equity troupe performs six shows a season and hosts road shows and visiting performers as well as a children's theater program. **The Center for the Arts** (3001 Riverside Park Dr., tel. 407/231–0707) connected by a walkway, was opened in 1986. The center, which operates the largest museum art school in Florida and houses a collection of 20th-century American art and contemporary Florida sculpture, presents films, concerts, humanities lectures, seminars, and a year-round program of local and visiting exhibitions.

Continue north on Rte. A1A past the John's Island development. Turn left onto Old Winter Beach Road. The pavement turns to hard-packed dirt as the road curves north. This is the old **Jungle Trail.** Portions of the trail along the Indian River are still undeveloped and provide a glimpse of yesteryear Florida surrounded by palms and moss-covered oaks. Turn right on the paved Wabasso Beach Road (Rte. 510) to A1A. Turn left and
10 proceed 7 miles to **Sebastian Inlet.** The high bridge offers spectacular views as it connects the two sides of the 576-acre **State Recreation Area.** A vast stacking of fisherfolk clambers on jetties, walls, and piers. Swimming and driftwood collecting are also popular. A concession is open daily from 7:30 AM to about 5:30 or 6 PM, serving fast food, bait and tackle, apparel, and souvenirs.

Return via Rte. A1A to the Wabasso Beach Road, turn right, and continue via Rtes. 510 and 512 to I–95, turning south to complete the tour.

Spectator Sports

Baseball The **Los Angeles Dodgers** train each March in the 6,000-seat Holman Dodgertown Stadium at 3901 26th St., near the Municipal Airport. *Box 2887, Vero Beach 32960, tel. 407/569–4900 or 800/334–PLAY.*

The **New York Mets** hold spring training in the 7,300-seat St. Lucie County Sport Complex, home stadium for the Florida League's St. Lucie Mets. A new exit—Exit 63–B, St. Lucie West Blvd., off I–95—was opened in 1989. Take it east to Peacock Boulevard, where the stadium is located. *525 N.W. Peacock Blvd., Box 8808, Port St. Lucie 34986, tel. 407/879–7378 or 407/340–0440.*

Polo **Windsor Polo and Beach Club.** Geoffrey and Jorie Kent's new polo club featured England's Prince Charles in a special charity game, the Prince of Wales Cup, when it opened in February of

1989. The 1991 season runs from mid-January to early April. Charity events benefit the international Friends of Conservation, of which Prince Charles is a patron. *9300 North A1A, Suite 201, Vero Beach 32963, tel. 407/589–9800 or 800/233–POLO.*

Dining

The list below is a representative selection of restaurants on the Treasure Coast, organized geographically, and by type of cuisine within each community. Unless otherwise noted, they serve lunch and dinner.

Highly recommended restaurants in each price category are indicated by a star ★.

Category	Cost*
Very Expensive	over $55
Expensive	$35–$55
Moderate	$15–$35
Inexpensive	under $15

**Average cost of a 3-course dinner, per person, excluding drinks, service, and 6% sales tax.*

The following credit card abbreviations are used: AE, American Express; CB, Carte Blanche; DC, Diners Club; MC, MasterCard; and V, Visa.

Stuart
American

The Emporium. Indian River Plantation's coffee shop is an old-fashioned soda fountain and grill that also serves hearty breakfasts. Specialties include eggs Benedict, omelets, and fresh-baked pastries. *555 N.E. Ocean Blvd., Hutchinson Island, tel. 407/225–3700. Dress: informal. No reservations. AE, DC, MC, V. Inexpensive.*

The Porch. This casual indoor/outdoor restaurant overlooks the tennis courts at Indian River Plantation. Specialties include hearty clam chowder, a daily quiche, fried calamari, and two daily selections of fresh fish. *555 N.E. Ocean Blvd., Hutchinson Island, tel. 407/225–3700. Dress: informal. No reservations. AE, DC, MC, V. Inexpensive.*

Continental

★ **The Inlet.** This intimate 60-seat restaurant in the heart of Indian River Plantation features fine dining on gold-rimmed plates in a setting of ethereal pinks and earth tones. Specialties include oysters Rockefeller, creamy lobster bisque with cognac, steak Diane, and fresh snapper. *555 N.E. Ocean Blvd., Hutchinson Island, tel. 407/225–3700. Jacket and tie required. Reservations required. AE, DC, MC, V. No lunch. Closed Sun. Open July–Sept. Fri.–Sat. only. Expensive.*

★ **Scalawags.** Part of Indian River Plantation's new hotel complex, Scalawags can seat you on a terrace overlooking the marina, in a dining room decorated with original paintings of Florida birds, or in a private 20-seat wine room. Specialties include Caribbean conch soup, sea scallops with fresh dill sauce, seafood ravioli, and rack of lamb. The Sunday champagne brunch is superb. *555 N.E. Ocean Blvd., Hutchinson Island, tel. 407/225–3700. Jacket required. Reservations required. AE, DC, MC, V. Dinner only May–Sept. Expensive.*

Seafood ★ **Mahoney's Oyster Bar.** Mike Mahoney ensures the personal scale by limiting what he buys to what he can carry on his bike. Well, the beer's trucked in—real stuff like Guinness, Harp, and Molson on draft. Choose from 12 tables and banquettes, or sit at the 14-stool bar, where Mike's got 13 hot sauces lined up to go with the oysters, clams, and shrimp stew. A chalkboard lists items like sardines and greens on toast, with green onions, red pepper ring, and parsley and a basic pub salad. Decor consists of wind socks, oars, fish traps and nets, charts, and a couple worshipful paintings of Mike and his bar, and another of Chief Osceola. *201 St. Lucie Ave., tel. 407/286–9757. Dress: casual. No reservations. Beer and wine only. Closed Sun.–Wed. and major holidays, and Aug.–Sept. No credit cards. Inexpensive.*

Sewalls Point
Delicatessen **Harbour Bay Gourmet & Cafe.** Jeffrey Schagrin in sneakers and shorts runs this upscale deli/cafe with the nonstop pace of a cycling courier on commissions. Go for the *cervelat* (salami with garlic and whole peppercorns), *sopressata* (Italian country-style salami with peppercorns), and sun-dried tomato and provolone on French bread, the turkey and gruyére grilled on sourdough (all the breads are homemade) with curry mayonnaise. Less? Try the pâté *de maison* with herbed mustard on French bread served with crisp *cornichons* (baby pickles). Start with top American Anchor Steam or top British Sam Smith beer. Finish with a decadent mix of Heathbar cookies, milk chocolate, and macadamia nuts, an Irish Cream, a *café framboise*, or a frothy cappuccino. Tables are upstairs, retail shop down. *Sewalls Point in the Harbour Bay Plaza, tel. 407/286–WINE. Dress: neat but casual. Reservations accepted. MC, V. Inexpensive–Moderate.*

Jensen Beach
American **Palace Cafe.** Twelve tables anchor buoyant eccentricity that otherwise fills the two-story 1908 building with a rafter art gallery, a clutter of figureheads, hanging plants, odd lamps, and murals. The grouper, calf's liver, or boneless breast of duck will satisfy, but if you're only out *aprés-diner*, so will the brie and fruit, shrimp cocktail, or desserts. Thursday through Sunday a jazz duo performs live. *1897 NE Jensen Beach Blvd., tel. 407/334–7767. Dress: neat but casual. No reservations. Beer and wine. No Sun. lunch. Closed all holidays. MC, V. Moderate.*

Continental **11 Maple Street.** Cracker elegant, this 13-table restaurant sits two blocks off the railroad tracks and stands gourmets agog. Everything's from scratch, including a walnut bread with melted fontina cheese appetizer. Gazpacho simmered with grilled Maine lobster, chipotle chilis, and avocado is both smooth and snappy. The shrimp pasta is made with sun-dried tomatoes, vermouth, and herbs fresh from the garden. The mesquite-grilled duck is crispy, moist, and wild with mushrooms under a Madeira cream sauce. While you wait for dinner, prepared to order, you can indulge with beer and wine on the tropical porch or in the flower garden. Hanging plants lushly dangle from open beams, while cane, local art, brick walls and floors, paddlefans, stained glass hangings, and chalkboards create the fine ambience. *3224 Maple Ave., tel. 407/334–7714. Dress: neat but casual. Reservations required. Dinner only. Closed Mon.–Tues.; June–Aug. Mon.–Wed. MC, V. Moderate.*

Seafood ★ **Conchy Joe's.** This classic Florida stilt-house full of antique fish mounts, gator hides, and snakeskins dates from the late 1920s, though Conchy Joe's, like a hermit crab sidling into a new shell, only sidled up in '83. Up from West Palm Beach for the relaxed atmosphere of Jensen Beach, they say. Still feels utterly island where, under a huge Seminole-built *chickee* with a palm through the roof, you get the freshest Florida seafoods from a menu that changes daily—though some things never change: grouper marsala, the house specialty; broiled sea scallops; fried cracked conch. Try the rummy drinks with names like Goombay Smash, Bahama Mama, and Jamaica Wind, while you listen to steel band calypsos Thursday through Sunday nights. *3945 N. Indian River Dr., tel. 407/334–1131. Dress casual. No reservations. Closed Thanksgiving, Christmas, New Year's Day, Superbowl Sun. AE, MC, V. Moderate.*

Mangrove Mattie's. This upscale rustic spot on Fort Pierce inlet for 11 years has dazzling views and imaginative decor with food to match. Try the shrimp brochette Key Largo, sizzled with garlic and butter; or the tile St. Lucie, a pan sautéed filet with crabmeat, green onions, and croutons in a beurre blanc sauce. Seating is under high open-beam ceilings with a roll-down canvas and plastic tarps in case of rain, or in a California-carpentered lounge full of greenery and track lighting with paddlefans of fabric and etched glass. Complimentary raw bar with drinks Thursday and Friday 5–7 PM. *1640 Seaway Dr., tel. 407/466–1044. Dress: neat but casual. Reservations advised for 5 or more. AE, MC, V. Closed Christmas. Moderate.*

Fort Pierce *Seafood* **Theo Thudpucker's Raw Bar.** Businesspeople dressed for work mingle here with people off the beach in bathing suits. Specialties include oyster stew, smoked fish spread, conch salad and fritters, soft-shell crabs, fresh catfish, and alligator tail. *2025 Seaway Dr. (South Jetty), tel. 407/465–1078. Dress: informal. No reservations. No credit cards. Closed Christmas, Easter, Mother's Day, and Thanksgiving. Inexpensive.*

Vero Beach *Continental* ★ **The Black Pearl.** This small, intimate restaurant (19 tables) with pink, and green art deco furnishings offers entrées that combine fresh local ingredients with the best of the Continental tradition. Specialties include chilled leek-and-watercress soup, hearty conch-and-crab chowder, feta cheese and spinach fritters, mesquite-grilled swordfish, and dolphin brushed with lime juice and olive oil. *1409 Rte. A1A, tel. 407/234–4426. Reservations advised. AE, MC, V. Dinner only. Closed Christmas, New Year's Day, and July 4th. Moderate.*

French **Chez Yannick.** Chef Yannick has moved on, but chef Wilner Pompée who opened this country French restaurant with him six years ago maintains the classical tradition. An older, conservative clientele favors the cream of lobster soup, lobster ravioli, hearts of palm salad with a hot vinaigrette sauce, the dover sole, rack of lamb, tournedos with truffles and Madeira sauce. The intimate Chandelier Room features draped ceilings, a wood-burning fireplace, and a 13-foot-high, 84-light electric-adapted chandelier that hung during the gaslight era in the Boston Opera House. The country look is in the paver floors, pastel walls, and poolside gardens, where cocktails can be served. *1601 S. Ocean Dr., in the Riviera Motel, tel. 407/234–4115. Jacket advised. Reservations advised. AE, MC, V. Closed Christmas, New Year's Day. Moderate.*

Seafood **Ocean Grill.** Opened as a hamburger shack in 1938, the Ocean Grill has since been refurbished and outfitted with antiques—Tiffany lamps, wrought-iron chandeliers, and Beanie Backus paintings of pirates and Seminole Indians. The menu has also changed with the times and now includes black bean soup, crisp onion rings, jumbo lump crabmeat salad, at least three kinds of fresh fish every day, prime rib, and a tart Key-lime pie. *Sexton Plaza (Beachland Blvd. east of Ocean Dr.), tel. 407/231–5409. Reservations accepted for parties of 5 or more. AE, MC, V. Dinner only. Closed Superbowl Sun. Moderate.*

Lodging

The list below is a representative selection of hotels and guest houses on the Treasure Coast. The rate categories in the list are based on the all-year or peak-season price; off-peak rates may be a category or two lower.

Highly recommended lodgings in each price category are indicated by a star ★.

Category	Cost*
Very Expensive	over $120
Expensive	$90–$120
Moderate	$50–$90
Inexpensive	under $50

**All prices are for a standard double room; excluding 6% state sales tax and nominal tourist tax.*

The following credit card abbreviations are used: AE, American Express; CB, Carte Blanche; DC, Diners Club; MC, MasterCard; and V, Visa.

Stuart ★ **Indian River Plantation.** Situated on a 192-acre tract of land on Hutchinson Island, this resort includes a three-story luxury hotel that is an architectural gem in the Victorian Beach Revival style, with tin roofs, shaded verandas, pink stucco, and much latticework. Some 70 new condos are scheduled to open by 1991. *555 N.E. Ocean Blvd., Hutchinson Island, 34996, tel. 407/225–3700 or 800/444–1432. 200 hotel rooms with bath, including 10 rooms for handicapped guests; 54 1- and 2-bedroom oceanfront condominium apartments with full kitchens. Facilities: 3 pools, outdoor spa, 13 tennis courts, golf course, 77-slip marina, power boat and jet-ski rentals, 5 restaurants. AE, DC, MC, V. Very Expensive.*

Guest House **The Homeplace.** The house was built in 1913 by pioneer Sam Matthews who contracted much of the early town construction for railroad developer Henry Flagler. To preserve the house, present-day developer Jim Smith moved it from Frazier Creek to Creekside Common. The new riverwalk will wrap around the property. Smith's wife Jean Bell has restored the house to its early look, from hardwood floors to fluffy pillows. Fern-filled dining and sun rooms, full of chintz-covered cushioned wicker, overlook a pool and patio. Three guest rooms are Captain's Quarters, Opal's Room, and Prissy's Place. *501 Akron Ave., Stuart 34994, tel. 407/220–9148. 3 rooms with bath. Facilities: pool, spa. No credit cards. Moderate–Expensive.*

Vero Beach

The Pickett Suite Resort. Built in 1986, this five-story rose stucco hotel on Ocean Drive provides easy access to Vero Beach's specialty shops and boutiques. First-floor rooms have patios opening onto the pool. *3500 Ocean Dr., 32963, tel. 407/231–5666 or 800/742–5388. 55 1- and 2-bedroom suites with bath. Facilities: pool, outdoor pool bar/restaurant, TV, movie rentals. All suites with balconies and ocean views, in-room refrigerators stocked with complimentary candy bars, juices, snacks, sodas; coffeemakers; VCRs. AE, DC, MC, V. Very Expensive.*

7 The Florida Keys

Introduction

by George and Rosalie Leposky

The Florida Keys are a wilderness of flowering jungles and shimmering seas, a jade pendant of mangrove-fringed islands dangling toward the tropics. The Florida Keys are also a 110-mile traffic jam lined with garish billboards, hamburger stands, shopping centers, motels, and trailer courts. Unfortunately, you can't have one without the other. A river of tourist dollars gushes southward along the only highway—U.S. 1—to Key West. Many residents of Monroe County live by diverting some of that river's green flow to their own pockets, in ways that have in spots blighted the Keys' fragile beauty—at least on the 31 islands linked to the mainland by the 42 bridges of the Overseas Highway.

As you drive down U.S. 1 through the islands, the silvery blue and green Atlantic, with its great living reef, is on your left, and Florida Bay, the Gulf of Mexico and the back country are on your right. At points the ocean and the gulf are 10 miles apart; on the narrowest landfill islands, they are separated only by the road.

The Overseas Highway varies from a frustrating traffic-clogged trap to a mystical pathway skimming across the sea. There are more islands than you will be able to remember. Follow the little green mile markers by the side of U.S. 1, and even if you lose track of the names of the islands, you won't get lost.

There are many things to do along the way, but first you have to remind yourself to get off the highway, which is lined with junk and has the seductive power of keeping you to itself. Once you leave this road, you can rent a boat and find a secluded anchorage at which to fish, swim, and marvel at the sun, sea, and sky. To the south in the Atlantic, you can dive to spectacular coral reefs or pursue dolphin, blue marlin, and other deep-water game fish. Along the Florida Bay coastline you can seek out the bonefish, snapper, snook, and tarpon that lurk in the grass flats and in the shallow, winding channels of the back country.

Along the reefs and among the islands are over 600 kinds of fish. Diminutive deer and pale raccoons, related to but distinct from their mainland cousins, inhabit the Lower Keys. And throughout the islands you'll find such exotic West Indian plants as Jamaica dogwood, pigeon plum, poisonwood, satinwood, and silver and thatch palms, as well as tropical birds like the great white heron, mangrove cuckoo, roseate spoonbill, and white-crowned pigeon.

Another Keys attraction is the weather: in the winter it's typically 10 degrees warmer in the Keys than on the mainland; in the summer it's usually 10 degrees cooler. The Keys also get substantially less rain, around 30 inches annually compared to 55–60 inches in Miami and the Everglades. Most of the rain falls in brief, vigorous thunderstorms on summer afternoons. In winter, continental cold fronts occasionally stall over the Keys, dragging temperatures down to the 40s.

The Keys were only sparsely populated until the early 20th century. In 1905, however, railroad magnate Henry Flagler began building the overseas extension of his east coast Florida railroad south from Homestead to Key West. His goal was to establish a rail link to the steamships that sailed between Key

West and Havana, just 90 miles away across the Straits of Florida. The railroad arrived at Key West in 1912 and remained a lifeline of commerce until the Labor Day hurricane of 1935 washed out much of its roadbed. For three years thereafter, the only way in and out of Key West was by boat. The Overseas Highway, built over the railroad's old roadbeds and bridges, was completed in 1938.

Although on the surface the Keys seem homogenous to most mainlanders, they are actually quite varied in terms of population and ambience. Most of the residents of the Upper Keys, which extend from Key Largo to Long Key Channel, moved to Florida from the Northeast and Midwest; many are retirees. Most of the work force is employed by the tourism and service industries. Key Largo, the largest of the keys and the one closest to the mainland, is becoming a bedroom community for Homestead, South Dade, and even the southern reaches of Miami. In the Middle Keys, from Long Key Channel through Marathon to Seven Mile Bridge, fishing and related services dominate the economy. Most residents are the children and grandchildren of migrants from other southern states. The Lower Keys from Seven Mile Bridge down to Key West have a diverse population: native "Conchs" (white Key Westers, many of whom trace their ancestry to the Bahamas), freshwater Conchs (longtime residents who migrated from somewhere else years ago), gays (who now make up at least 20% of Key West's citizenry), Bahamians, Hispanics (primarily Cubans), recent refugees from the urban sprawl of Miami and Fort Lauderdale, transient Navy and Air Force personnel, students waiting tables, and a miscellaneous assortment of vagabonds, drifters, and dropouts in search of refuge at the end of the road.

Arriving and Departing

By Plane

Shuttle and connecting flights go to **Key West International Airport** (S. Roosevelt Blvd., tel. 305/296–5439) from the Miami and Orlando International airports. From Miami, you can fly direct to Key West on American Eagle, Continental Express, Eastern Express, and USAir. From Fort Lauderdale-Hollywood you can fly direct on Delta ComAir. From Orlando you must change planes in Miami unless you fly with Delta ComAir, which has limited nonstop service to Key West as well as connecting service through Fort Lauderdale-Hollywood.

Six carriers provide direct service between Miami and **Marathon Airport** (MM 52, BS, 9000 Overseas Hwy., tel. 305/743–2996): Airways International (tel. 305/743–0500), Air Sunshine (tel. 305/743–8755), American Eagle (tel. 800/433–7300), Continental Express (tel. 800/525–0280), Delta ComAir (tel. 305/743–5782), and Eastern Express (tel. 800/327–8376).

Between Miami and the Keys

The Airporter. Scheduled van and bus service is available from the lower level of MIA's Concourse E to major hotels in Key Largo ($22 per person) and Islamorada ($25 per person). *797 S. Homestead Blvd., Homestead 33030, tel. 305/247–8874 (Miami); 305/247–8874 or 305/247–8877 (Keys). Reservations required.*

Island Taxi. Meets arriving flights at MIA. Reservations are required 24 hours in advance for arrivals, one hour for departures. Accompanied children ride free. *Tel. 305/852–9700 (Upper Keys), 305/743–0077 (Middle Keys), 305/872–4404 (Lower Keys). Fare from airport to destination: $150 for 1 or 2* *persons; or $4 for first 2 mi, then $1.50 per mi in Key Largo and Islamorada; $3 for first 2 mi, then $1 per mi Marathon.*

By Car If you want to avoid Miami traffic on the way to the Keys, take the Homestead Extension of Florida's Turnpike; although it's a toll road that carries a lot of commuter traffic, it's still the fastest way to go. From MIA, take LeJeune Road (SW 42nd Ave.) south, turn west on the Dolphin Expressway (Rte. 836) to the turnpike, then go south to the turnpike's southern end. If you prefer traffic to tolls, take LeJeune Road south to U.S. 1 and turn right.

Just south of Florida City, the turnpike joins U.S. 1 and the Overseas Highway begins. Once you cross the Jewfish Creek bridge at the north end of Key Largo, you're officially in the Keys.

From Florida City, you can also reach Key Largo on Card South Road. Go 13 miles south to the Card Sound Bridge (toll: $1), which offers a spectacular view of blue water and mangrove-fringed bays (and of Florida Power & Light Company's hulking Turkey Point nuclear power plant in the distance to your left). At low tide, flocks of herons, ibis, and other birds frequent the mud flats on the margin of the sound. Beyond the bridge, on north Key Largo, the road traverses a mangrove swamp with ponds and inlets harboring the exceedingly rare Florida crocodile. At the only stop sign, turn right onto Route 905, which cuts through some of the Keys' few remaining large tracts of tropical hardwood jungle. You'll rejoin U.S. 1 in north Key Largo 31 miles from Florida City.

Car Rentals All six of the rental-car firms with booths inside Miami International Airport also have outlets in Key West, which means you can drive into the Keys and fly out. Don't fly into Key West and drive out; the rental firms have substantial drop charges to leave a Key West car in Miami. Avis and Hertz also serve Marathon Airport.

Enterprise Rent-A-Car has offices at MIA, several Keys locations, and participating hotels in the Keys where you can pick up and drop off cars when the offices are closed. You can rent a car from Enterprise at MIA and return it there, or leave it in the Keys for a drop charge. *Tel. 305/576–1300 or 800/325–8007 (Miami); 305/451–3998 (Key Largo). Open weekdays 8–6, Sat. 9–noon. AE, DC, MC, V.*

By Bus **Greyhound/Trailways.** Buses traveling between Miami and Key West make 10 scheduled stops, but you can flag down a bus anywhere along the route. *Tel. 305/374–7222 (Miami) for schedule; 24-hr Miami Greyhound Station, tel. 305/871–1810; Big Pine Key, tel. 305/872–4022; Key West, 615½ Duval St., tel. 305/296–9072. No reservations.*

By Boat Boaters can travel to Key West either along the Intracoastal Waterway through Florida Bay, or along the Atlantic Coast. The Keys are full of marinas that welcome transient visitors, but they don't have enough slips for everyone who wants to visit the area. Make reservations in advance, and ask about channel and dockage depth—many Key marinas are quite shallow.

Florida Marine Patrol (MM 49, OS, 2835 Overseas Hwy., Marathon, tel. 305/743–6542).

Coast Guard Group Key West provides 24-hour monitoring of VHF-FM Channel 16. Safety and weather information is broadcast at 7 AM and 5 PM Eastern Standard time on VHF-FM Channel 16 and 22A. *Key West 33040, tel. 305/292–8727. 3 stations in the Keys: Islamorada, tel. 305/664–4404; Marathon, tel. 305/743–6778; Key West, tel. 305/292–8856.*

Getting Around

The only address many people have is a mile marker (MM) number. The markers themselves are small green rectangular signs along the side of the Overseas Highway (U.S. 1). They begin with MM 126 a mile south of Florida City and end with MM 0 on the corner of Fleming and Whitehead streets in Key West. Keys residents also use the abbreviation BS for the Bay Side of U.S. 1, and OS for the Atlantic Ocean Side of the highway.

Florida Visitor Centers and the Florida Department of Commerce distribute *Florida's Official Transportation Map* free. Write to Florida Department of Commerce (Collins Bldg., Tallahassee 32304).

The best road map for the Florida Keys is published by the Homestead/Florida City Chamber of Commerce. You can obtain a copy at the Tropical Everglades Visitor Center in Florida City, or by mail. *160 U.S. Hwy. 1, Florida City 33034, tel. 305/245–9180. Open daily 8–6. Map costs $2.*

Throughout the Keys, the local chambers of commerce, marinas, and dive shops will offer you the local **Teall's Guide**—a land and nautical map—for $1, which goes to build mooring buoys to protect living coral reefs from boat anchors. The separate guides that used to cover Miami to Key Largo, John Pennekamp Coral Reef State Park and Key Largo National Marine Sanctuary, the Middle Keys, and Marathon-Key West are now in a 12″×18″ complete Florida packet that costs $14.95, postage included. Order from Teall's Florida Guides (111 Saguaro Ln., Marathon 33050, tel. 305/743–3942).

By Car The 18-mile stretch of U.S. 1 from Florida City to Key Largo is a hazardous two-lane road with heavy traffic (especially on weekends) and only two passing zones. Try to drive it in daylight, and be patient day or night. The Overseas Highway is four lanes wide in Key Largo, Marathon, and Stock Island (just north of Key West), but narrow and crowded elsewhere. Expect delays behind large tractor-trailer trucks, cars towing boats, and rubbernecking tourists. Allow at least five hours from Florida City to Key West on a good day. After midnight, you can make the trip in three hours—but then you miss the scenery.

In Key West's Old Town, parking is scarce and costly ($1.25 per hour, $6 maximum at Mallory Square). Use a taxicab, bicycle, moped, or your feet to get around. Elsewhere in the Keys, however, having a car is crucial. Gas prices are higher in the Keys than on the mainland. Fill your tank in Miami and top it off in Florida City.

By Bus The **City of Key West Port and Transit Authority** operates two bus lines: Mallory Square (counterclockwise around the island) and Old Town (clockwise around the island). A free Shopping Center Shuttle (Key Plaza to Searstown) may be resumed. *Tel. 305/292–8165 or 292–8164. Exact fare: 75¢; monthly pass, $20.*

By Taxi **Island Taxi** offers 24-hour service from Key Largo to Boca Chica Key. Accompanied children ride free. There is no service to downtown Key West. *Tel. 305/852–9700 (Upper Keys), 305/743–0077 (Middle Keys), 305/872–4404 (Lower Keys). Fare: $4 for first 2 mi, then $1.50 per mi in Key Largo and Islamorada; $3 for first 2 mi, then $1 per mi in Marathon.*

Maxi-Taxi Sun Cab System (tel. 305/294–2222 or 305/296–7777) provides 24-hour service in Key West and also operates **Carriage Trade Limousine Service** (tel. 305/296–0000). Airport van service: $4 per person; cab service: $4.50 per person. Local metered service, $1.40 first ½-mi, 35¢ each additional ¼-mi. Inquire for group and zone rates. Limousine tours by 1980 stretch Cadillac: $40 per hour, minimum 3 hrs.

Important Addresses and Numbers

Tourist Information **Florida Keys & Key West Visitors Bureau** (Box 1147, Key West 33041, tel. 305/296–3811 or 800/FLA–KEYS). Ask for their free accommodations guide.

Local chambers of commerce in Key Largo, Islamorada, Marathon, and Key West have visitor centers with information on accommodations, recreation, restaurants, and special events:

Key Largo Chamber of Commerce (MM 103.4, BS, 103400 Overseas Hwy., Key Largo 33037, tel. 305/451–1414 or 800/822–1088).

Islamorada Chamber of Commerce (MM 82.6, BS, Box 915, Islamorada 33036, tel. 305/664–4503 or 800/FAB–KEYS).

Greater Marathon Chamber of Commerce (MM 48.7, BS, 3330 Overseas Hwy., Marathon 33050, tel. 305/743–5417 or 800/842–9580).

Lower Keys Chamber of Commerce (MM 30.5, OS, Drawer 511, Big Pine Key 33043, tel. 305/872–2411 or 800/872–3222).

Greater Key West Chamber of Commerce (402 Wall St., Key West 33041, tel. 305/294–2587 or 800/648–6269).

Emergencies Dial 911 for **ambulance** and **police.**

Hospitals The following hospitals have 24-hour emergency rooms: **Mariners Hospital** (MM 88.5, BS, 50 High Point Rd., Tavernier, Plantation Key 33070; physician-referral service, tel. 305/852–9222), **Fishermen's Hospital** (MM 48.7, OS, 3301 Overseas Hwy., Marathon, tel. 305/743–5533), **De Poo Hospital** (1200 Kennedy Dr., Key West 33040, tel. 305/294–4692 or 294–5183), and **Florida Keys Memorial Hospital** (MM5, BS, 5900 Junior College Rd., Stock Island, tel. 305/294–5531).

Late-Night Pharmacies The Keys have no 24-hour pharmacies. Hospital pharmacists will help with emergencies after regular retail business hours.

Guided Tours

Orientation Tours **The Conch Tour Train.** This 90-minute narrated tour of Key West travels 14 miles through Old Town and around the island. The driver pauses frequently to discuss points of historical interest and to chat with friends. *Boarding Locations: Mallory Sq. Depot on the half hour, Roosevelt Blvd. Depot just north of the Quality Inn on the hour; tel. 305/294–5161. Runs daily 9–4. Fare: $10 adults, $3 children. No credit cards.*

Old Town Trolley. Key West has 11 trackless trolley-style buses that run every 30 minutes. The trolleys are smaller than the Conch Tour Train and go places the train won't fit. The narrated trolley tour lasts 90 minutes, passes more than 100 points of interest, and makes 16 stops all around the island. You may disembark at any stop and reboard a later trolley. *1910 N. Roosevelt Blvd., Key West 33040, tel. 305/296–6688. Runs 9 AM–4:30 PM. Admission: $11 adults, $5 children. MC, V.*

Special-Interest Tours

Canoe Tours

Canoeing Nature Tours. Stan Becker leads a full-day 5-mile canoe and hiking trip in the Key Deer National Wildlife Refuge. The trip includes three hours in canoes and four hours exploring Watson Hammock on Big Pine Key. *MM 28, BS, Box 62, Big Pine Key 33043, tel. 305/872–2620. Reservation required. Children welcome; no pets. Box lunch provided. 9 AM–4 PM. Fee: $60 per person.*

Sunset and Harbor Boat Tours

Residents and tourists alike flock to west-facing restaurants, hotel docks, and bars to watch the glowing orbsink into the sea. Hundreds of people gather on Key West's Mallory Square Dock, where street performers and food vendors vie with the sunset for your attention. Throughout the keys, many motor yacht and sailboat captains take paying passengers on sunset cruises. Contact local chambers of commerce and hotels for information.

M/V *Miss Key West* offers a one-hour narrated cruise that explores Key West's harbor up to a half-mile from shore. The 45-passenger, 45-foot motor yacht passes Trumbo Point Navy Base, home of all six of the Navy's hydrofoil guided-missile destroyers. The sundown cruise includes live music. A morning cruise seeks dolphins, sea turtles, and birds. *Zero Duval St. (booth in front of Ocean Key House), tel. 305/296–8865, in FL 800/231–9864, rest of U.S. 800/231–9864. Open 8 AM–11 PM. Tours: 10 AM, noon, 2 PM, 4 PM, and sundown. Admission: harbor and sunset cruise $8 adults, children under 12 free; dolphin watch and nature trip, $10 adults, children under 12 free. AE, MC, V.*

Walking Tours

Pelican Path is a free walking guide to Key West published by the **Old Island Restoration Foundation.** The tour discusses the history and architecture of 43 structures along 25 blocks of 12 Old Town streets. Pick up a copy at the Key West Chamber of Commerce.

Solares Hill's Walking and Biking Guide to Old Key West, by local historian Sharon Wells, contains eight walking tours of the city and a short tour of the Key West cemetery. Free copies are available from Key West Chamber of Commerce, many hotels and stores.

Exploring the Florida Keys

Attractions are listed by island or by mile marker (MM) number.

Numbers in the margin correspond with points of interest on the Florida Keys map.

The Upper Keys

This tour begins on Key Largo, the northeasternmost of the Florida Keys accessible by road. The tour assumes that you have come south from Florida City on **Card Sound Road** (Rte. 5). If you take the Overseas Highway (U.S. 1) south from Florida City, you can begin the tour with John Pennekamp Coral Reef State Park.

Cross the **Card Sound Bridge** onto **North Key Largo**, where Card Sound Road forms the eastern boundary of **Crocodile Lakes National Wildlife Refuge.** In the refuge dwell some 300 to 500 crocodiles, the largest single concentration of these shy, elusive reptiles in North America. There's no visitor center here—just 6,800 acres of mangrove swamp and adjoining upland jungle. For your best chance to see a crocodile, park on the shoulder of Card Sound Road and scan the ponds along the road with binoculars. In winter, crocodiles often haul out and sun themselves on the banks farthest from the road. Don't leave the road shoulder; you could disturb tern nests on the nearby spoil banks or aggravate the rattlesnakes.

Take Card Sound Road to Route 905, turn right, and drive for 10 miles through **Key Largo Hammock**, the largest remaining stand of the vast West Indian tropical hardwood forest that once covered most of the upland areas in the Florida Keys. The state and federal governments are busy acquiring as much of the hammock as they can to protect it from further development, and they hope to establish visitor centers and nature trails. For now, it's best to admire this wilderness from the road. According to law-enforcement officials, this may be the most dangerous place in the United States, a haven for modern-day pirates and witches. The "pirates" are drug smugglers who land their cargo along the ocean shore or drop it into the forest from low-flying planes. The "witches" are practitioners of voodoo, *santeria*, and other occult rituals. What's more, this jungle is full of poisonous plants. The most dangerous, the manchineel or "devil tree," has a toxin so potent that rainwater falling on its leaves and then onto a person's skin can cause sores that resist healing. Florida's first tourist, explorer Juan Ponce de León, died in 1521 from a superficial wound inflicted by an Indian arrowhead dipped in manchineel sap.

Time Out Pause for a drink at the **Caribbean Club**, a friendly neighborhood bar on a historic site. Scenes from *Key Largo*, the 1948 Bogart-Bacall movie, were filmed in the original Caribbean Club, which burned down in the 1950s. *MM 104, BS, Key Largo, tel. 305/451–9970. Open daily 7 AM–4 AM. Closed Christmas. No credit cards.*

Continue on U.S. 1 to Transylvania Avenue (MM 103.2) and turn left to visit the **Key Largo Undersea Park.** This commercial attraction is affiliated with the nonprofit **Marine Resources Development Foundation**, which shares its terrestrial and underwater site. The park's family attractions include a museum devoted to the history of man and sea, tanks for growing sea sprouts (a species of edible red algae), an air-conditioned grotto theater with a 13-minute multimedia slide show, and a gift shop. Through high-tech two-way communications the audience can interact with divers in the 30-foot-deep lagoon where guides lead scuba and snorkel tours. Installation of an underwater 280-foot moving sidewalk encased by a clear tube should be completed in 1991 making an underwater museum available to nondivers. Visitors are also invited to the oceanside campus marine lab, where underwater research is conducted. *Key Largo Undersea Park, 51 Shoreland Dr., Box 787, Key Largo, tel. 305/451–1139 or 800/858–7119. Open daily 9–5:30. Theater ad-*

mission: $8 adults, $6 children; scuba program fee, including tanks and gear: $35; snorkel program fee, including gear: $12 adults, $10 children 16 and under accompanied by adult.

1 Return to U.S. 1, turn left, and left again into **John Pennekamp Coral Reef State Park.** The primary attraction here is diving on the offshore coral reefs (*see* Sports and Outdoor Activities, below), but even a landlubber can appreciate the superb interpretive aquarium in the park's visitor center. A huge central tank holds angelfish, stingrays, and Florida spiny lobsters. There's also a touch tank where you can fondle starfish, sponges, and various species of bivalves. A concessionaire rents canoes and sailboats and offers boat trips to the reef. The park also includes a nature trail through a mangrove forest, a swimming beach, picnic shelters, a snack bar, a gift shop, and a campground. *MM 102.5, OS, Key Largo, tel. 305/451–1202. Open daily 8 AM–sunset. Admission: Florida residents $1.50 car and driver, $1 per passenger; out-of-state visitors $2.50 car and driver, $1.50 per passenger; children under 6 free.*

Return to U.S. 1 and turn left. At MM 100, turn left again into the parking lot of the Holiday Inn Key Largo Resort. In the adjoining Key Largo Harbor Marina you'll find the ***African Queen,*** the steam-powered workboat on which Katharine Hepburn and Humphrey Bogart rode in their movie of the same name. The 30-foot craft was built in England in 1912. James W. Hendricks, an attorney from Kentucky who owns the resort, bought the boat in 1982 and lovingly restored her. Hendricks also owns and displays at the resort the *Thayer IV*, a 22-foot mahogany Chris Craft built in 1951 and used by Ms. Hepburn and Henry Fonda in Fonda's last film, *On Golden Pond.*

Continuing south on U.S. 1 you'll cross **Plantation Key** (MM 93–87), named for the plantings of limes, pineapples, and tomatoes
2 cultivated here at the turn of the century. Next comes **Windley Key,** notable for **Theater of the Sea,** where seven dolphins, two sea lions, and an extensive collection of tropical fish swim in the pits of a 1907 railroad quarry. Allow at least two hours to attend the dolphin and sea lion shows and visit all the exhibits, which include a "bottomless" boat ride, touch tank, shark-feeding pool, and a 300-gallon "living reef" aquarium with invertebrates and small reef fishes. *MM 84.5, OS, Box 407, Islamorada, tel. 305/664–2431. Admission: $10.25 adults, $5.50 children 4–12. Open daily 9:30 AM–4 PM. Swim with dolphins (30-min orientation and 30 min in the water): $50. Reservations required with 50% deposit, minimum age 13, mask and swim fins recommended, life vests optional. Video or still photos: $49.95 additional. AE, MC, V.*

Watch for the **Hurricane Memorial** (MM 82) beside the highway. It marks the mass grave of 423 victims of the 1935 Labor Day hurricane. Many of those who perished were veterans who had been working on the Overseas Highway; they died when a tidal surge overturned a train sent to evacuate them. The art deco-style monument depicts wind-driven waves and palms bowing before the storm's fury.

Time Out Stop at **Green Turtle Seafood Market & Cannery** on Upper Matecumbe Key. Owner Henry Rosenthal, who also operates the nearby **Green Turtle Inn** (*see* Dining, below), cans five kinds of chowder—turtle, conch, Manhattan clam, New England clam, and New England fish—plus turtle consommé and Key-

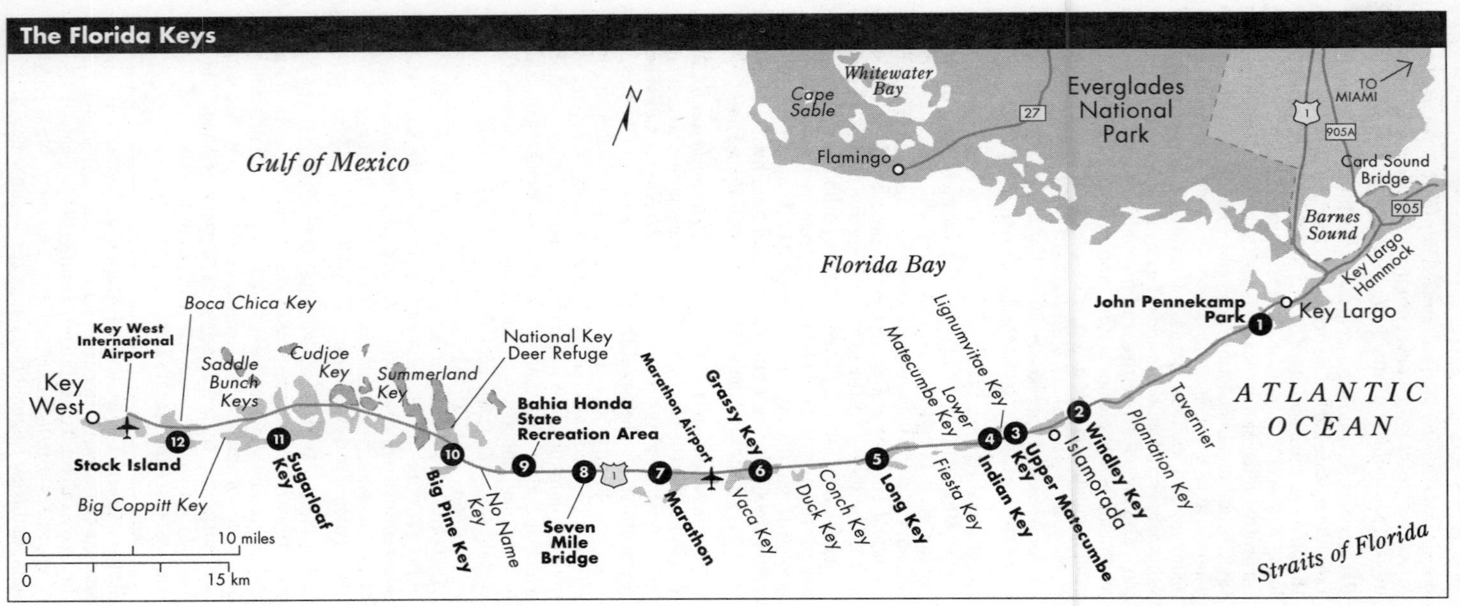

The Florida Keys
Whitewater Bay
Cape Sable
Everglades National Park
27
TO MIAMI
1
905A
Card Sound Bridge
905
Barnes Sound
Gulf of Mexico
N
Flamingo
Florida Bay
Key Largo Hammock
John Pennekamp Park
Key Largo
ATLANTIC OCEAN
Boca Chica Key
Key West International Airport
Saddle Bunch Keys
Cudjoe Key
Summerland Key
National Key Deer Refuge
Key West
Stock Island
Big Coppitt Key
Sugarloaf Key
Big Pine Key
No Name Key
Bahia Honda State Recreation Area
Seven Mile Bridge
Marathon Airport
Marathon
Grassy Key
Vaca Key
Duck Key
Conch Key
Long Key
Fiesta Key
Lower Matecumbe Key
Lignumvitae Key
Indian Key
Upper Matecumbe Key
Islamorada
Windley Key
Plantation Key
Tavernier
Straits of Florida
0
10 miles
0
15 km

lime pie filling. If the cannery is running when you visit, he'll show you the operation. Most of the fresh seafood on sale is local, right off the boats that dock behind the building, but the market also sells Key West shrimp, blue crabs from Maryland and Argentina, and oysters from Apalachicola Bay in north Florida. *MM 81.5, OS, Islamorada, tel. 305/664–4918. Open Tues.–Sun. 8–6.*

---

3 At the lower tip of **Upper Matecumbe Key,** stop at the **International Fishing Museum** in Bud n' Mary's Marina. The museum contains a collection of antique fishing tackle and a video library with information on fishing activities, fishery conservation, and the natural history of various species of local fishes. The videos don't circulate, but you can watch them in the museum. The museum staff can also help you find a charter captain for deep-sea or back-country fishing. *MM 79.5, OS. For information, contact Bob Epstein, 124 Gardenia St., Tavernier 33070, tel. 305/664–2767 (office), 305/852–8813 (home). Open Mon.–Wed., Fri., Sat. noon–5; hours may change. Admission free.*

4 The dock on **Indian Key Fill** at MM 78, BS, is the closest point on the Overseas Highway to three unusual state parks accessible only by water. The newest of these parks, dedicated in 1989, is **San Pedro Underwater Archaeological Preserve** (*see* Sports and Outdoor Activities, below). State-operated boat tours aboard the M. V. *Monroe* will take you to the other two, **Indian Key State Historic Site** (OS) and **Lignumvitae Key State Botanical Site** (BS). Indian Key was a county seat town and shipwrecker's station until an Indian attack wiped out the settlement in 1840. Dr. Henry Perrine, a noted botanist, was killed in the raid. Today you'll see his plants overgrowing the town's ruins. A virgin hardwood forest still cloaks Lignumvitae Key, punctuated only by the home and gardens that chemical magnate William Matheson built as a private retreat in 1919. *MM 78. For information and tour boat reservations, contact Long Key State Recreation Area, Box 776, Long Key, tel. 305/664–4815. Indian Key open daily 8 AM–sunset; Lignumvitae Key open Thurs.–Mon. with 1-hr guided tour (admission: $1 adults, children under 6 free) at 10:30 AM, 1 and 2:30 PM for visitors from private boats. State tour boat admission: $6 adults, $3 children under 12, for 3-hr tours Thurs.–Mon. to Indian Key, 8:30 AM, to Lignumvitae Key, 1:30 PM.*

5 Return to U.S. 1 and turn right. Continue down to **Long Key** (MM 69), where you'll pass a tract of undisturbed forest on the right (BS) just below MM 67. Watch for a historical marker partially obscured by foliage. Pull off the road here and explore **Layton Trail,** named after Del Layton, who incorporated the city of Layton in 1963 and served as its mayor until his death in 1987. The marker relates the history of the Long Key Viaduct, the first major bridge on the rail line, and the Long Key Fishing Club that Henry Flagler established nearby in 1906. Zane Grey, the noted western novelist, was president of the club. It consisted of a lodge, guest cottages, and storehouses—all obliterated by the 1935 hurricane. The clearly marked trail leads through the tropical hardwood forest to a rocky Florida Bay shoreline overlooking shallow grass flats offshore.

Less than a mile below Layton Trail, turn left into **Long Key State Recreation Area,** then left again to the parking area for the **Golden Orb Trail.** This trail leads onto a boardwalk through a mangrove swamp alongside a lagoon where many herons and other water birds congregate in winter. The park also has a campground, a picnic area, a canoe trail through a tidal lagoon, and a not-very-sandy beach fronting on a broad expanse of shallow grass flats. Instead of a pail and shovel, bring a mask and snorkel here to observe the marine life in this rich nursery area. *Box 776, Long Key, tel. 305/664–4815. Open daily 8 AM–sunset. Admission: Florida residents $1.50 car and driver, $1 per passenger; out-of-state visitors $2.50 car and driver, $1.50 per passenger.*

The Middle Keys

Below Long Key, the Overseas Highway crosses Long Key Channel on a new highway bridge beside the railroad's **Long Key Viaduct.** The second-longest bridge on the rail line, this two-mile-long structure has 222 reinforced-concrete arches. It ends at **Conch Key** (MM 63), a tiny fishing and retirement community. Below Conch Key, the causeway on your left at MM 61 leads to **Duck Key,** an upscale residential community where **Hawk's Cay Resort** (*see* Lodging, below) offers hotel guests a swim-with-the-dolphins experience at its Zoovet Dolphin Center.

6 Next comes **Grassy Key** (MM 59). Watch on the right for the **Dolphin Research Center** and the 35-foot-long concrete sculpture of the dolphin Theresa and her offspring Nat outside the former home of Milton Santini, creator of the original *Flipper* movie. The 16 dolphins here today are free to leave and return to the fenced area that protects them from boaters and predators. *MM 59, BS, Box Dolphin, Marathon Shores, tel. 305/289–0002. Admission: $5 donation. Visitor center open Wed.–Sun. 9 AM–3 PM, closed Christmas, New Years, and Thanksgiving. Walking tours at 9:30 and 10 AM, 12:30, and 2 PM. Swim with dolphins (20 min) $65. Children 5–12 swim with an accompanying, paying adult (also $65). Reserve for dolphin swim on the first day of the month before the month you plan to be in the Keys.*

Continuing down U.S. 1, you'll pass the road to **Key Colony Beach** (MM 54, OS), an incorporated city developed in the 1950s as a retirement community. It has a golf course and boating fa-
7 cilities. Soon after, you'll cross a bridge onto **Vaca Key** and enter **Marathon** (MM 53–47), the commercial hub of the Middle Keys. Marathon is notorious for perpetual road construction along U.S. 1, which has resulted in the disappearance of mile markers beside the road. You must navigate here by means of numbered cross streets.

On your right (BS) at 55th Street is **Crane Point Hammock,** a 63-acre tract that includes the world's last undisturbed thatch-palm hammock. The Florida Keys Land Trust, a private, nonprofit conservation group, paid $1.2 million to acquire the property in 1988. Early in 1990 the Trust opened **The Museum of Natural History of the Florida Keys** as the first phase of educational facilities planned for the hammock. The tract also includes an exotic plant arboretum, an archaeological site, and the remnants of a Bahamian village with the oldest surviving example of Conch-style architecture outside Key West. *MM 50, BS, 5330 Overseas Hwy., Box 536, Marathon 33050, tel. 305/*

743–3900. Open Wed.–Mon. 10:30–6:30, Fri. 10:30–8. Admission: $3.50 adults, $2 senior citizens, $1.20 children 12–17.

Across the Overseas Highway from **Crane Point Hammock,** between the K-Mart and the Marine Bank, Sombrero Beach Road (Rte. 931 East) leads two miles south past Marathon High School to a free county beach on the ocean. **Sombrero Beach** has a modest stretch of sand, some limestone rock ledges at the water's edge, and picnic tables in covered shelters for sun and rain protection. Just offshore is the world's first underwater county park, **Marathon Marine Sanctuary** (*see* Sports and Outdoor Activities, below). Return to the Overseas Highway.

8 As you approach the new **Seven Mile Bridge,** turn right at MM 47 to the entrance to the **Old Seven Mile Bridge.** An engineering marvel in its day, the bridge rested on 546 concrete piers spanning the broad expanse of water that separates the Middle and Lower Keys. Monroe County maintains a 2-mile stretch of the old bridge to provide access to **Pigeon Key** (MM 45), where the county's public schools and community college run marine-science classes in a railroad work camp built around 1908. In 1990 Pigeon Key was placed on the National Register of Historic Places, a status the Old Seven Mile Bridge already enjoyed. Other plans for Pigeon Key include establishing a civic, cultural, and educational facility open to visitors and the restoration of the key to its original look as a railroad camp. In time a tram will bring visitors from Marathon across the old bridge to Pigeon Key. *For information, contact James Lewis, Chairman, Pigeon Key Advisory Authority, 2945 Overseas Hwy., Marathon 33050, tel. 305/743–6040.*

Return to U.S. 1 and proceed across the new **Seven Mile Bridge** (actually only 6.79 miles long!). Built between 1980 and 1982 at a cost of $45 million, the new Seven Mile Bridge is the world's longest segmental bridge, with 39 expansion joints separating its cement sections. Each April marathon runners gather in Marathon for the annual Seven Mile Bridge Run.

The Lower Keys

9 At **Bahia Honda State Recreation Area** (MM 36.5) on Bahia Honda Key, you'll find a sandy beach most of the time. Lateral drift builds up the beach in summer; winter storms whisk away much of the sand. The park's Silver Palm Trail leads you through a dense tropical forest where you can see rare West Indian plants, including the Geiger tree, sea lavendar, Key spider lily, bay cedar, thatch and silver palms, and several species found nowhere else in the Florida Keys: the West Indies satinwood, Catesbaea, Jamaica morning glory, and wild dilly. The park also includes a campground, cabins, gift shop, snack bar, marina, and dive shop offering snorkel trips to offshore reefs. *MM 36.5, OS, Rte. 1, Box 782, Big Pine Key, tel. 305/872–2353. Open daily 8 AM–sunset. Admission: Florida residents $1.50 car and driver, $1 per passenger; out-of-state visitors $2.50 car and driver, $1.50 per passenger; children under 6 free.*

Cross the Bahia Honda Bridge and continue past Spanish Har-
10 bor Key and Spanish Harbor Channel onto **Big Pine Key** (MM
32–30), where prominent signs warn drivers to be on the lookout for Key deer. Every year cars kill 50 to 60 of the delicate
creatures. A subspecies of the Virginia white-tailed deer, Key
deer once ranged throughout the Lower and Middle Keys, but

hunting and habitat destruction reduced the population to fewer than 50 in 1947. Under protection in the **National Key Deer Refuge** since 1954, the deer herd grew to about 750 by the early 1970s. The government owns only about a third of Big Pine Key, however, and as the human population on the remaining land grew during the 1980s, the deer herd declined again until today only 250 to 300 remain.

To visit the refuge, turn right at the stoplight, then bear left at the fork onto Key Deer Boulevard (Rte. 940). Pass Road Prison No. 426 and a fire tower on the way to Watson Boulevard, then turn left and go about a mile to the **Refuge Headquarters** to see interpretive displays and obtain brochures.

The best place to see Key deer is on **No Name Key,** a sparsely populated island just east of Big Pine Key. To get there, take Watson Boulevard east to Wilder Road, and turn left. You'll go 2 miles from Key Deer Boulevard to the middle of the Bogie Channel Bridge, which links Big Pine and No Name Keys, and 1½ miles from there across No Name Key. If you get out of your car at the end of the road to walk around, close all doors and windows to keep raccoons from wandering in. Deer may turn up along this road at any time of day—especially in early morning and late afternoon. Admire their beauty, but don't try to feed them—it's against the law. To resume your journey, take Wilder Road back to Key Deer Boulevard at the fork just before the stoplight on U.S. 1. Turn right at the stoplight, and continue on down the Keys across **Big Torch, Middle Torch,** and **Little Torch Keys** (named for the torchwood tree, which settlers used for kindling because it burns easily even when green). Next comes **Ramrod Key** (MM 27.5), a base for divers in **Looe Key National Marine Sanctuary** 5 miles offshore (*see* Sports and Outdoor Activities, below).

11 On **Lower Sugarloaf Key** (MM 20), you'll find the Sugar Loaf Lodge (MM 17, BS), an attractive motel known for its performing dolphin named Sugar, who lives in a lagoon behind the restaurant (*see* Lodging, below). Follow the paved road northwest from the motel for a half mile past an airstrip, and keep going on an unpaved spur. There, in bleak, gravel-strewn surroundings, you'll find a reconstruction of R. C. Perky's **bat tower.** Perky, an early real estate promoter, built the tower in 1929 to attract mosquito-eating bats, but no bats ever roosted in it.

Continue on through the Saddlebunch Keys and Big Coppitt Key to **Boca Chica Key** (MM 10), site of the Key West Naval Air Station. You may hear the roar of jet fighter planes in this vicin-
12 ity. At last you reach **Stock Island** (MM 5), the gateway to Key West. Pass the 18-hole **Key West Resort Golf Course,** then turn right onto Junior College Road and pause at the **Key West Botanical Garden,** where the Key West Garden Club has labeled an extensive assortment of native and exotic tropical trees.

Key West

Numbers in the margin correspond with points of interest on the Key West map.

In April 1982, the U.S. Border Patrol threw a roadblock across the Overseas Highway just south of Florida City to catch drug runners and illegal aliens. Traffic backed up for miles as Border

Patrol agents searched vehicles and demanded that the occupants prove U.S. citizenship. City officials in Key West, outraged at being treated like foreigners by the federal government, staged a mock secession and formed their own "nation," the so-called Conch Republic. They hoisted a flag and distributed mock border passes, visas, and Conch currency. The embarrassed Border Patrol dismantled its roadblock, and now an annual festival recalls the secessionists' victorious exploits.

The episode exemplifies Key West's odd station in life. Situated 150 miles from Miami and just 90 miles from Havana, this tropical island city has always maintained its strong sense of detachment, even after it was connected to the rest of the United States—by the railroad in 1912 and by the Overseas Highway in 1938. The U.S. government acquired Key West from Spain in 1819 along with the rest of Florida. The Spanish had named the island Cayo Hueso (Bone Key) in honor of Indian skeletons they found on its shores. In 1822, Uncle Sam sent Commodore David S. Porter to the Keys to chase pirates away.

For three decades, the primary industry in Key West was "wrecking"—rescuing people and salvaging cargo from ships that foundered on the nearby reefs. (According to some reports, when business was slow, the wreckers hung out lights to lure ships aground). Their business declined after 1852, when the federal government began building lighthouses along the reefs.

In 1845 the Army started to construct Fort Taylor, which held Key West for the Union during the Civil War. After the war, an influx of Cuban dissidents unhappy with Spain's rule brought the cigar industry to Key West. Fishing, shrimping, and sponge-gathering became important industries, and a pineapple-canning factory opened. Major military installations were established during the Spanish-American War and World War I. Through much of the 19th century and into the second decade of the 20th, Key West was Florida's wealthiest city in per-capita terms.

In the 1920s the local economy began to unravel. Modern ships no longer needed to stop in Key West for provisions, the cigar industry moved to Tampa, Hawaii dominated the pineapple industry, and the sponges succumbed to a blight. Then the depression hit, and even the military moved out. By 1934 half the population was on relief. The city defaulted on its bond payments, and the Federal Emergency Relief Administration took over the city and county governments.

Federal officials began promoting Key West as a tourist destination. They attracted 40,000 visitors during the 1934–35 winter season. Then the 1935 Labor Day hurricane struck the Middle Keys, sparing Key West but wiping out the railroad and the tourist trade. For three years, until the Overseas Highway opened, the only way in and out of town was by boat.

Ever since, Key West's fortunes have waxed and waned with the vagaries of world affairs. An important naval center during World War II and the Korean conflict, the island remains a strategic listening post on the doorstep of Fidel Castro's Cuba. Although the Navy shut down its submarine base at Truman Annex and sold the property to a real-estate developer, the nearby Boca Chica Naval Air Station and other military installations remain active.

As the military scaled back, city officials looked to tourism again to take up the slack. Even before it tried, Key West had much to sell—superb frost-free weather with an average temperature of 79°F, quaint 19th-century architecture, and a laid-back lifestyle. Promoters have fostered fine restaurants, galleries and shops, and new museums to interpret the city's intriguing past. There's also a growing calendar of artistic and cultural events and a lengthening list of annual festivals—including the Conch Republic celebration in April, Hemingway Days in July, and a Halloween Fantasy Fest rivaling the New Orleans Mardi Gras.

Gentrification is in the breeze. New city rules say no to retail T-shirt displays on sidewalks, and to amplified sound spilling out of open-air bars. Sundown revelry at Mallory Square is threatened by cruise ships which may be sanctioned at the pier even if that means blocking the sunset. Ironically, the taming of Key West comes on the watch of Capt. Tony Tarracino, longtime saloon keeper until just a year before his 1989 mayoral election. The fate of the reforms remains to be seen, so stay tuned. In the meantime, begin this tour at Front and Duval streets, near the Pier House hotel and Ocean Key House. Start
1 by going west on Front Street to **Mallory Square,** named for Stephen Mallory, secretary of the Confederate Navy, who later owned the Mallory Steamship Line. On the nearby **Mallory Dock,** a nightly sunset celebration draws street performers, food vendors, and thousands of onlookers.

2 Facing Mallory Square is the **Key West Aquarium,** which features hundreds of brightly colored tropical fish and other fascinating sea creatures from the waters around Key West. A touch tank enables visitors to handle starfish, sea cucumbers, horseshoe and hermit crabs, even horse and queen conchs—living totems of the Conch Republic. Built in 1934 by the Works Progress Administration as the world's first open-air aquarium, the building has been enclosed for all-weather viewing. *1 Whitehead St., tel. 305/296–2051. Open daily, 10–6 (10–7 in winter). Guided tours in winter every hour on the hour; other times of year 11 AM, 1, 3, 4:30; shark feeding on every tour. Admission: $5 adults, $2.50 children 8–15.*

Return to Front Street and turn right to **Clinton Place,** where a Civil War memorial to Union soldiers stands in a triangle formed by the intersection of Front, Greene, and Whitehead streets. On your right is the **U.S. Post Office and Customs House,** a Romanesque Revival structure designed by prominent local architect William Kerr and completed in 1891. Tour guides claim that federal bureaucrats required the roof to have a steep pitch so it wouldn't collect snow.

3 On your left is the **Mel Fisher Maritime Heritage Society Museum,** which displays gold and silver bars, coins, jewelry, and other artifacts recovered in 1985 from the Spanish treasure ships *Nuestra Señora de Atocha* and *Santa Margarita.* The two galleons foundered in a hurricane in 1622 near the Marquesas Keys, 40 miles west of Key West. In the museum you can lift a gold bar weighing 6.3 Troy pounds and see a 77.76-carat natural emerald crystal worth almost $250,000. One display replicates the hold of the *Atocha,* with smooth ballast stones, silver bars, and copper ingots for casting cannons and balls. A 20-minute video shows treasure being recovered from the wrecks. *200 Greene St., tel. 305/294–2633. Open daily 10–6;*

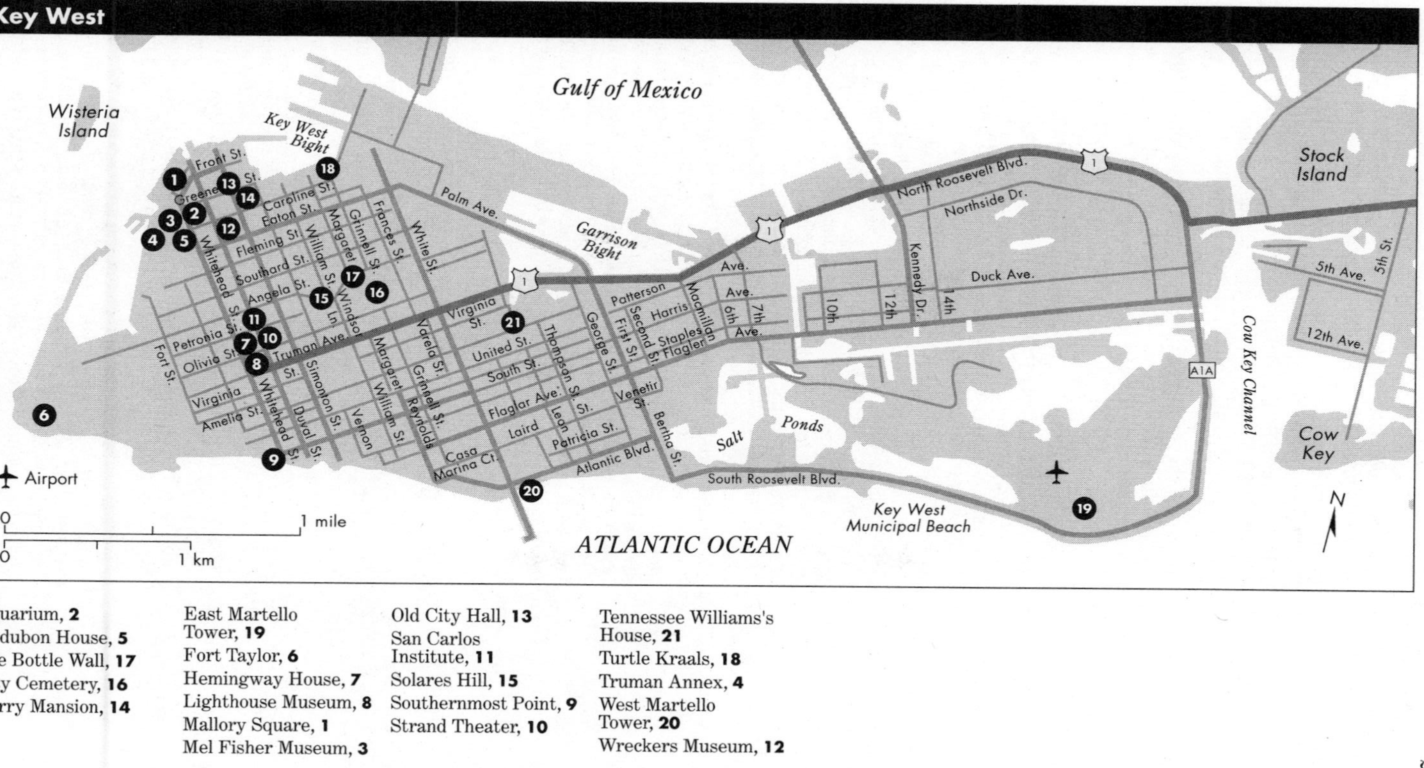

Aquarium, **2**
Audubon House, **5**
The Bottle Wall, **17**
City Cemetery, **16**
Curry Mansion, **14**
East Martello Tower, **19**
Fort Taylor, **6**
Hemingway House, **7**
Lighthouse Museum, **8**
Mallory Square, **1**
Mel Fisher Museum, **3**
Old City Hall, **13**
San Carlos Institute, **11**
Solares Hill, **15**
Southernmost Point, **9**
Strand Theater, **10**
Tennessee Williams's House, **21**
Turtle Kraals, **18**
Truman Annex, **4**
West Martello Tower, **20**
Wreckers Museum, **12**

Christmas and New Year's Day 10–2; last video showing 4:30, last ticket sold 5:15. Museum admission: $5 adults, $4 military and Conch Train and trolley passengers with ticket stub, $1 children 6–12.

Mel Fisher's museum occupies a former navy storehouse that
4 he bought from Pritam Singh, the developer of **Truman Annex** (Key West 33040, tel. 305/296–5601), a decommissioned navy base. An American who embraced the Sikh religion, Singh speaks gently of his hope to "engender different forms of interaction" on the 103 acres the government sold him in 1986 for $17.25 million. Singh is making good on his promise that people of modest means will be able to rub elbows with the wealthy in his planned development. Bicyclists and pedestrians are welcome every day from 8 AM to sunset on the grounds of the Truman Annex. Visitors can tour the Little White House Museum where memorabilia are being collected of President Truman and other prominent visitors including Presidents Kennedy and Nixon and English Prime Minister Harold MacMillan. Also near ready to open is a restaurant downstairs in the 1891 Customs House—a National Landmark which is now the yacht club.

Among the first condominiums to sell out at the property were the 160 in the Shipyard section. They sold at below market rates that were mandated by a Key West growth management ordinance to supply much-needed worker housing. Singh has kept 16 original structures (including six Victorian-style officers' houses) and several warehouses with 30,000 square feet of rentable space for art studios. New construction includes 93 condominiums in two waterfront complexes adjoining the deep-water harbor where submarines docked during World War II, 63 condominium town houses in four compounds, 60 single-family homes, a shopping village, and The Ritz-Carlton Hotel. Two presidential suites are upstairs of the museum which the hotel will rent to guests. On nearby Sunset Island—formerly Tank Island—Singh is building 25 luxurious houses. A ferry service will provide access to a mainland dock where there will be 82 boat slips and 40 additional moorings. Part of Sunset Island will be open to the public for a fee as a high-quality recreation area with a beach, tennis center, concert pavilion, and perhaps an environmental center and aviary. The Ritz-Carlton Hotel is expected to open in 1992. *For up-to-date information, call the public relations office, tel. 305/296–5601.*

From Mel Fisher's museum, cross Whitehead Street to visit
5 the **Audubon House and Gardens.** A museum in this three-story dwelling built in the mid-1840s commemorates ornithologist John James Audubon's 1832 visit to Key West. On display are several rooms of period antiques and a large collection of Audubon engravings. A 12-minute video in the upstairs gallery describes Audubon's travels, and an exquisite collection of porcelains of American birds and foliage by Dorothy Doughty is on display. In 1989 a children's room was opened, furnished in 18th- and 19th-century antiques. *205 Whitehead St., tel. 305/294–2116. Open daily 9:30–5. Admission: $4.50 adults, $1 children 6–12.*

Continue up Whitehead Street past **Pigeonhouse Patio Restaurant & Bar** (301 Whitehead St., tel. 305/296–9600). This building was the first headquarters of Pan American World Airways, the first U.S. airline to operate scheduled international air service. The inaugural flight took off from Key West

International Airport on Oct. 28, 1927. Passengers paid $9.95 for the 90-mile, 80-minute flight from Key West to Havana aboard *The General Machado*, a Fokker F-7 trimotor.

6 Turn right onto Southard Street and follow the signs to the **Fort Zachary Taylor State Historic Site.** Built between 1845 and 1866, the fort served as a base for the Union blockade of Confederate shipping during the Civil War. More than 1,500 Confederate vessels captured while trying to run the blockade were brought to Key West's harbor and detained under the fort's guns. What you will see at Fort Taylor today is a fort within a fort. In 1989 a moat was dug to suggest how the fort originally looked when it was surrounded by water. In 1898 the army built poured-concrete gun emplacements for the Spanish-American War atop remnants of the original brick structure, burying the largest collection of Civil War cannons in the U.S. They are now being excavated and preserved for display. The concrete has been painted black as it was 90 years ago to absorb the muzzle flash and avoid disclosing the position of hideaway cannons that rolled forward to fire and then withdrew inside the walls. In 1989, the officers' kitchen became a 1,700-square-foot museum. Rangers give guided tours of the fort, including the museum. Since 1989 the addition of sand has made the beach. Snorkeling is excellent here because of an artificial reef, except when the wind blows south-southwest and muddies the water. Look for a new concession stand on the beach this winter. *Box 289, tel. 305/292–6713. Park open daily 8–sunset, fort open 8–5. Free 90-min tour daily at 2PM. Admission: Florida residents $1.50 car and driver, $1 per passenger; out-of-state visitors $2.50 car and driver, $1.50 per passenger; children under 6 free.*

Time Out Pause for a libation at the **Green Parrot Bar.** Built in 1890, the bar is Key West's oldest, a sometimes-rowdy saloon where locals outnumber the tourists. *601 Whitehead St. (corner of Southard St.), tel. 305/294–6133. Open daily 10 AM–4 AM. No credit cards.*

7 Return to Whitehead Street, turn right, and go three blocks to the **Hemingway House,** now a museum dedicated to the novelist's life and work. Built in 1851, this two-story Spanish Colonial dwelling was the first house in Key West to have running water and a fireplace. Hemingway bought the house in 1931 and wrote about 70% of his life's work here, including *A Farewell to Arms* and *For Whom the Bell Tolls*. Three months after Hemingway died in 1961, local jeweler Bernice Dickson bought the house and its contents from Hemingway's estate and two years later opened it as a museum. Of special interest are the huge bed with a headboard made from a 17th-century Spanish monastery gate, a ceramic cat by Pablo Picasso (a gift to Hemingway from the artist), the handblown Venetian glass chandelier in the dining room, and the swimming pool. The museum staff gives guided tours rich with anecdotes about Hemingway and his family and feeds the 42 feline inhabitants (for the 42 bridges in the Keys), descendents of Hemingway's own 50 cats. Kitten adoptions are possible (for a fee), but there's a five-year waiting list. Tours begin every 10 minutes and take 35–40 minutes; then you're free to explore on your own. *907 Whitehead St., tel. 305/294–1575. Open daily 9–5. Admission: $5 adults, $1 children 6–12.*

Down the block and across the street from Hemingway House
8 is the **Lighthouse Museum,** a 92-foot lighthouse built in 1847 and an adjacent 1887 clapboard house where the keeper lived. Both underwent extensive restoration in 1989. You can climb 98 steps to the top of the lighthouse for a spectacular view. On display in the keeper's quarters are vintage photographs, ship models, nautical charts, military uniforms, and a working submarine periscope. Note especially the old photos of the Key West Naval Air Station and the relics from the battleship U.S.S. *Maine*, which was blown up in Havana Harbor on February 15, 1898, precipitating the Spanish-American War. *938 Whitehead St., tel. 305/294–0012. Open daily 9:30–5. Admission: $3 adults, $1 children 6–12.*

Continue to the foot of Whitehead Street, where a huge con-
9 crete marker proclaims this spot to be the **Southernmost Point** in the United States. Most tourists snapping pictures of each other in front of the marker are oblivious to Key West's real southernmost point, on a nearby navy base off limits to civilians but visible through the fence to your right. Bahamian vendors of shells and straw hats line the sidewalk and blow a conch horn at passing Conch Tour Trains and Old Town Trolleys.

Turn left on South Street. To your right are two dwellings that both claim to be the **Southernmost House**—the Spanish-style home built in the 1940s at 400 South Street by Thelma Strabel, author of *Reap the Wild Wind*, a novel about the wreckers who salvaged ships aground on the reef in Key West's early days, and the adjoining cream-brick Queen Anne mansion at 1400 Duval Street. Neither is open to the public. Take the next right onto Duval Street, which ends at the Atlantic Ocean and the **Southernmost Beach.** *Open daily 7 AM–11 PM. Admission free.*

Time Out **The Eatery,** adjoining the Southernmost Beach, serves carryouts and buffets for breakfast, lunch, and dinner. *Open daily 6 AM–9 PM. MC, V.*

Now go north on Duval Street towards downtown Key West. Pause at the **Cuban Club** (1108 Duval St., tel. 305/296–8997). The original building—a social club for the Cuban community—burned in 1983 and was replaced by shops and luxury condominiums; some of the original facade was retained. Continuing on Duval Street, you'll pass several art galleries from the 1100 block through the 800 block.

Pause to admire the colorful marquee and ornamental facade of
10 the **Strand Theater,** built in 1918 by Cuban craftsmen. After a period as a movie theater, it now offers a variety of live entertainment: reggae, rock-and-roll, etc. *527 Duval St., tel. 305/294–6700 (recording).*

11 Continue on to the **San Carlos Institute,** a Cuban-American heritage center, which houses a museum and research library focusing on the history of Key West and of 19th- and 20th-century Cuban exiles. The San Carlos Institute was founded in 1871 by Cuban immigrants who wanted to preserve their language, customs, and heritage while organizing the struggle for Cuba's independence from Spain. Cuban patriot Jose Martí delivered many famous speeches in Key West from the balcony of the auditorium. Opera star Enrico Caruso sang in the 400-seat hall of the Opera House, which reportedly has the best acous-

tics of any concert hall in the South. The current building was completed in 1924, replacing the original built in 1871 that burned in the Key West fire of 1886, in which two-thirds of the city was destroyed. A second building succumbed to the hurricane of 1919. After Cuba and the United States broke off diplomatic relations in 1961, the building deteriorated. It was saved from demolition when Miami attorney Rafael A. Penalver, Jr., secured a $2.7 million state grant for its restoration. The building is scheduled to be open by 1991. Plans call for hourly film presentations on the history of Key West and of the Cuban community in the United States, as well as nightly performing arts presentations. *516 Duval St. For information, contact Mr. Penalver at 1101 Brickell Ave., Suite 1700, Miami 33131, tel. 305/579–9000 (Miami) or call Key West Directory Assistance for local phone number. Open daily 9–5. Guided tour, concluding with 30-min film. Admission: $2 adults, $1.50 children.*

12 Continue north on Duval Street to the **Wreckers Museum,** which is alleged to be the oldest house in Key West. It was built in 1829 as the home of Francis Watlington, a sea captain and wrecker. He was also a Florida state senator, but resigned to serve in the Confederate Navy during the Civil War. Six of the home's eight rooms are now a museum furnished with 18th- and 19th-century antiques. In an upstairs bedroom is an eight-room miniature dollhouse of Conch architectural design, outfitted with tiny Victorian furniture. *322 Duval St., tel. 305/294–9502. Open daily 10–4; closed Christmas. Admission: $2 adults, 50¢ children 3–12.*

Take Duval Street to Front Street, turn right, go two blocks to Simonton Street, turn right again and go one block to Greene
13 Street to see the **Old City Hall,** which has recently been restored. Designed by William Kerr, the architect also responsible for the Customs House, the Old City Hall opened in 1891. It has a rectangular tower with four clock faces and a fire bell. The ground floor, used as a city market for many years, now houses the **Historic Key West Shipwreck Museum.** Among the displays are relics from the *Isaac Allerton,* built at Portsmouth, New Hampshire, in 1838 and sunk off Key West in 1856. The second floor houses the city commission's meeting room and offices of the city government and the Historic Florida Keys Preservation Board. *516 Greene St., tel. 305/292–9740. Open daily 9–6. Museum admission: $4 adults, $2 children 10–16.*

Return to Simonton Street, go one block south to Caroline
14 Street, and turn right to the **Curry Mansion.** Built in 1899 for Milton Curry, the son of Florida's first millionaire, this 22-room Victorian mansion is an adaptation of a Parisian town house. It has the only widow's walk open to the public in Key West. The owners have restored and redecorated most of the house. Take an unhurried self-guided tour with a comprehensive brochure, which includes floor plans, full of detailed information about the history and contents of the house. *511 Caroline St., tel. 305/294–5349. Open daily 10–5. Admission: $5 adults, $1 children under 12.*

Return to Simonton Street, go south to Angela Street, and turn
15 left. Before you rises **Solares Hill,** the steepest natural grade in Key West. Its summit, the island's loftiest elevation, is 18 feet above sea level.

Now cross Elizabeth Street and bear right onto Windsor Lane
16 to the **City Cemetery.** Turn left onto Passover Lane to the entrance at Margaret Street. Clustered near a flagpole resembling a ship's mast are the graves of 22 sailors killed in the sinking of the battleship U.S.S. *Maine. Open sunrise–sunset. Guided tours weekends 10 AM and 4 PM. Admission free. Tour donation: $5.*

17 At the corner of Margaret and Angela streets, pause at **The Bottle Wall.** Hundreds of bottles from vintage champagne to ketchup have been mortared into a homespun work of art that's equally practical. Carolyn Gorton Fuller says she's done it so the dazzle keeps vehicles from missing the curve and crashing into her house. The first wall built 16 years ago went down in a firetruck crash. Note one of the doorsteps of Ms. Fuller's Conch house: the headstone for a grave—in place, she says, when she bought the house.

18 Go up Margaret Street to the harbor docks and visit the **Turtle Kraals,** where the Florida Marine Conservancy runs a hospital for sea creatures. Biologist Linda Bohl maintains a touch tank with horseshoe crabs, sea anemones, sea urchins, and other benign beasts you can fondle—but keep your fingers away from Hawkeye and Gonzo, a churlish pair of 150-pound, 31-year-old hawksbill turtles. A fish pond on the premises gives you a good look at live denizens of local waters, including barracuda, bluefish, lemon and nurse sharks, and yellowtail snapper. *1 Land's End Village, tel. 305/294–2640. Open 11 AM–1 AM weekdays, weekends noon–1 AM. Admission free; donations accepted.*

Return to Margaret Street and go one block south to Eaton Street, turn left and continue east past White Street, where Eaton Street doglegs to the right into Palm Avenue. You'll cross a causeway and bridge across a corner of **Garrison Bight Yacht Basin,** where many charter-fishing boats dock.

Turn left onto North Roosevelt Boulevard (U.S. 1) and go east. Past the turnoff to Stock Island at the east end of Key West, North Roosevelt Boulevard becomes South Roosevelt Boulevard and turns west. On your left is a small community of houseboats. On your right, just past the entrance to Key West
19 International Airport, stands **East Martello Tower,** one of two Civil War forts of similar design overlooking the Atlantic Ocean. The **Key West Art and Historical Society** operates a museum in East Martello's vaulted casemates. The collection includes Stanley Papio's "junk art" sculptures, Cuban primitive artist Mario Sanchez's chiseled and painted wood carvings of historic Key West street scenes, memorabilia from movies shot on location in the Keys, and a display of books by many of the 55 famous writers (including seven Pulitzer Prize winners) who live in Key West. Historical exhibits have been developed to present a chronological history of the Florida Keys and are on display. A circular 48-step staircase in the central tower leads to a platform overlooking the airport and surrounding waters. *3501 S. Roosevelt Blvd., tel. 305/296–6206. Open daily 9:30–5. Admission: $3 adults, $1 children.*

Continue west on South Roosevelt Boulevard past Smathers Beach on your left. To your right are the **salt ponds,** where early residents evaporated seawater to collect salt. The area is now a wildlife sanctuary. Turn right where South Roosevelt Boulevard ends at Bertha Street, then make the first left onto

Atlantic Avenue. Near White Street are **Higgs Memorial Beach**
20 (a Monroe County park) and **West Martello Tower,** a fort built in
1861 and used as a lookout post during the Spanish-American
War. Within its walls the Key West Garden Club maintains an
art gallery and tropical garden. *Tel. 305/294–3210. Open Wed.–
Sun. 10 AM–noon and 1–4 PM. Inquire about Mon. and Tues.
openings. Donations accepted.*

Take White Street nine blocks north to Duncan Street, turn
21 right, and go three blocks to **Tennessee Williams's House** (1431
Duncan St., at the corner of Duncan and Leon Sts.), a modest
Bahamian-style cottage where the playwright lived from 1949
until his death in 1983.

Shopping

Throughout the Keys many strip shopping centers cater to the basic needs of locals and visitors alike. In season, supermarkets and roadside stands sell tropical fruits. Look for Key limes (Apr.–Jan.), guavas (Aug.–Oct.), lychee nuts (June), and sapodillas (Feb.–Mar.).

Key West In Key West's Old Town, you'll find specialty shops with international reputations:

Greenpeace. Opened in 1983, this is the only storefront in Florida operated by Greenpeace, an international conservation organization known for its efforts to prevent the killing of whales and seals. The store sells conservation-oriented educational materials, gift items, and T-shirts. *719 Duval St., tel. 305/296–4442. Open Mon.–Sat. 10–9, Sun. 10–6. AE, MC, V.*

Key West Aloe. A company founded in a garage in 1971, Key West Aloe today produces some 300 perfume, sunscreen, and skin-care products for men and women. When you visit the factory store, you can watch the staff measure and blend ingredients, then fill and seal the containers. *Main store: 524 Front St., tel. 305/294–5592, 800/433–2563 (FL), 800/445–2563 (US). Open daily 9–8. Factory store: Greene and Simonton Sts. Open 9–5, production weekdays 9–5. Free self-guided tour. AE, DC, MC, V.*

Key West Hand Print Fabrics. In the 1960s, Lilly Pulitzer's designs made Key West Hand Print Fabrics famous. Shoppers can watch workers making handprinted fabric on five 50-yard-long tables in the Curry Warehouse, a brick building erected in 1878 to store tobacco. *201 Simonton St., tel. 305/294–9535. Open daily 10–6. AE, MC, V.*

Key West Island Bookstore. You'll find a good selection of books on south Florida here and a rare book room to which you must request admittance. *513 Fleming St., tel. 305/294–2904. Open daily 10–6. AE, MC, V.*

Duval Books and Cards. Owned by the proprietors of Key West Island Bookstore, this shop specializes in new books and greeting cards. *817 Duval St., tel. 305/296–3508. Open Mon.–Sat. 9–9, Sun. 10–5. AE, MC, V.*

Tikal Trading Co. Since 1975, owners George and Barbara Webb have designed, produced, and sold double-stitched women's clothing of hand-woven Guatemalan cotton. *129 Duval St., tel. 305/296–4463. Open Sun.–Thurs. 10–9, Fri. and Sat. 10–10. AE, MC, V.*

The former Singleton Seafood, Inc., shrimp docks and warehouse along Key West Bight have been reincarnated as a row of marinas. One of these, **Key West Seaport,** a nautically oriented shopping area where boat builders work and charter-boat captains have booths to sign up customers. Merchants you might visit include the following:

Lazy Jake's Hammocks. Run by a man who describes himself as Key West's oldest beach bum, this establishment makes and sells hammocks of all shapes and sizes. *205 Elizabeth St., no phone. Open daily 8–5.*

Seafarers Heritage Library and Nautique. A storefront operated by the National Center for Shipwreck Research, Ltd., this shop sells maritime books and gift items. Its staff arranges archaeology dives, seminars, training programs, and other educational activities. *Seaport La., tel. 305/292–1301. Open daily 11–6. MC, V.*

Just east of Key West Seaport is Key West Bight. Popular stores there include the following:

Waterfront Baits & Tackle. (201 William St., tel. 305/292–1961). This store sells bait and fishing gear.

Waterfront Fish Market, Inc. (201 William St., tel. 305/294–8046). Fresh seafood is the draw here.

Waterfront Market. (201 William St., tel. 305/294–8418 or 305/296–0778). This store sells health and gourmet foods, deli items, fresh produce, and salads.

Ever since John James Audubon came to Key West in 1832, artists have flocked to the Florida Keys. Today's flourishing art community provides a rich array of merchandise for galleries throughout the Keys.

The Rain Barrel in Islamorada represents 300 local and national artists and has eight resident artists. *MM 86.7, BS, 86700 Overseas Hwy., Islamorada, tel. 305/852–3084. Open daily 9–5; closed Christmas. AE, MC, V.*

Lane Gallery specializes in lesser-known local artists. *1000 Duval St., Key West, tel. 305/294–0067. Open winter, daily 11–6, in summer, daily noon–6. AE, MC, V.*

Gingerbread Square Gallery, owned by former two-time Key West Mayor Richard Heyman, represents Keys artists who have attained national prominence. *901 Duval St., Key West, tel. 305/296–8900. Open winter, daily 11–6; summer, Thurs.–Mon. AE, MC, V.*

Haitian Art Center sells the works of 175 Haitian artists. *600 Frances St., Key West, tel. 305/296–8932. Open daily 10–6. AE, CB, DC, MC, V.*

Sports and Outdoor Activities

Biking A bike path parallels the Overseas Highway from Key Largo through Tavernier and onto Plantation Key, from MM 106 (at the Route 905 junction) to MM 86 (near the Monroe County Sheriff's Substation). The **Marathon** area is popular with bikers. Some of the best areas include the paths along Aviation Boulevard on the bay side of Marathon Airport; the new four-lane section of the Overseas Highway through Marathon; Sadowski Causeway to Key Colony Beach; Sombrero Beach Road from the Overseas Highway to the Marathon public beach; the roads on Boot Key (across a bridge from Vaca Key on 20th Street, OS); and a 2-mile section of the old Seven Mile

Bridge that remains open to Pigeon Key, where locals like to ride to watch the sunset.

Key West is a cycling town, but many tourists aren't accustomed to driving with so many bikes around, so ride carefully. Some hotels rent bikes to their guests; others will refer you to a nearby bike shop and reserve a bike for you.

Key Largo Bikes stocks adult, children's, and tandem bikes, all single-speed with coaster brakes, and multispeed mountain bikes. *MM 99.4, 99275 Overseas Hwy., Key Largo, tel. 305/451–1910. Open Mon.–Sat. 9:30–5:30. MC, V.*
KCB Bike Shop rents single-speed adult and children's bikes. *MM 53 (11518 Overseas Hwy.), Marathon, tel. 305/289–1670. Open weekdays 8:30–5, Sat. 8:30–2; closed Sun. MC, V.*
Pedal Pushers has moped and bicycle rentals for adults and children. *512 Greene St., Key West, tel. 305/296–8385. Open daily 8–6. No credit cards.*

Camping The State of Florida operates recreational-vehicle and tent campgrounds in **John Pennekamp Coral Reef State Park,** MM 102.5 (Box 487, Key Largo 33037, tel. 305/451–1202); **Long Key State Recreation Area,** MM 67.5 (Box 776, Long Key 33001, tel. 305/664–4815); and **Bahia Honda State Recreation Area,** MM 36.5 (Rte. 1, Box 782, Big Pine Key 33043, tel. 305/872–2353). Bahia Honda also has rental cabins.

The **Florida Campground Association** (1638 N. Plaza Dr., Tallahassee 32308, tel. 904/658–8878) publishes a free annual directory of over 200 member campgrounds in 11 regions. The Keys are in Region L, which lists 12 commercial campgrounds from Key Largo to Key West. The guide is available at Florida Welcome Centers or by mail.

Diving Although there are reefs and wrecks all along the east coast of Florida, the state's most extensive diving grounds are in the Keys. Divers come for the quantity and quality of living coral reefs within six or seven miles of shore, the kaleidoscopic beauty of 650 species of tropical fish, and the adventure of probing wrecked ships that foundered in these seemingly tranquil seas during almost four centuries of exploration and commerce. A popular dive destination is the 9-foot **Christ of the Deep** statue, a gift to the Underwater Society of America from an Italian dive equipment manufacturer. The statue is about 6 miles east-northeast of Key Largo's South Cut in about 25 feet of water. It's a smaller copy of the 50-foot Christ of the Abysses off Genoa, Italy.

Much of the Keys' expanse of coral reefs is protected in federal, state, and county parks and sanctuaries. From Key Biscayne south almost to Key Largo, **Biscayne National Park** (*see* The Everglades in Chapter 4) encompasses most of Biscayne Bay, its barrier islands, and the patch reefs eastward to a depth of 60 feet. Biscayne National Park's southern boundary is the northern boundary of John Pennekamp Coral Reef State Park and Key Largo National Marine Sanctuary.

John Pennekamp Coral Reef State Park encompasses 78 square miles of coral reefs, sea grass beds, and mangrove swamps on the Atlantic Ocean side of Key Largo. The park is 21 miles long and extends to the seaward limit of state jurisdiction three miles offshore. Its reefs contain 40 of the 52 species of coral in the Atlantic Reef System. *MM 102.5, OS. Park admission:*

Florida residents $1.50 car and driver, $1 per passenger; out-of-state residents $2.50 car and driver, $1.50 per passenger. Park open daily 8 AM–sunset. Coral Reef Park Co., a concessionaire, offers glass-bottom boat, scuba, sailing, and snorkeling tours: Box 1560, Key Largo 33037, tel. 305/451–1621, in FL 800/432–2871. Concession open daily 8–5:30. AE, MC, V.

The **Key Largo National Marine Sanctuary** (Box 1083, Key Largo 33037, tel. 305/451–1644) covers 103 square miles of coral reefs from the boundary of John Pennekamp Coral Reef State Park, 3 miles off Key Largo, to a depth of 300 feet some 8 miles offshore. Managed by the National Oceanic and Atmospheric Administration (NOAA), the sanctuary includes Elbow, French, and Molasses reefs; the 1852 Carysfort Lighthouse and its surrounding reefs; Christ of the Deep; Grecian Rocks, Key Largo Rocks, and the torpedoed WW II freighter *Benwood.*

San Pedro Underwater Archaeological Preserve. The state recently established this underwater park in 18 feet of water about a mile off the western tip of Indian Key. The *San Pedro* was part of a Spanish treasure fleet wrecked by a hurricane in 1733. You can get there on the *Coral Sea*, a 40-passenger glass-bottom dive and snorkel boat, from the dive shop at Bud 'n' Mary's Fishing Marina. *MM 79.5 OS, Box 1126, Islamorada, tel. 305/664–2211. 3-hr trips at 9 AM and 1:30 PM. Call for reservations. Cost: $13 adults, $7.50 children under 12. AE, MC, V.*

Marathon Marine Sanctuary. Monroe County recently established its first underwater park off the Middle Keys in Hawk Channel opposite MM 50, OS. It runs from Washerwoman Shoal on the west to navigation marker 48 on the east. The two-square-mile park contains a dozen patch reefs ranging from the size of a house to about an acre. *Greater Marathon Chamber of Commerce, MM 49, BS, 330 Overseas Hwy., Marathon, tel. 305/743–5417 or 800/842–9580.*

National Key Deer Refuge (Box 510, Big Pine Key 33043, tel. 305/872–2239) and **Great White Heron National Wildlife Refuge.** Reefs where the Keys' northern margin drops off into the Gulf of Mexico attract fewer divers than the better-known Atlantic Ocean reefs. A favorite Gulf spot for local divers is the Content Keys, off Big Pine Key (MM 30).

Looe Key National Marine Sanctuary (Rte. 1, Box 782, Big Pine Key 33043, tel. 305/872–4039). Many divers say Looe Key Reef, five miles off Ramrod Key (MM 27.5), is the most beautiful and diverse coral community in the entire region. It has large stands of elkhorn coral on its eastern margin, large purple sea fans, and ample populations of sponges and sea urchins. On its seaward side, it has an almost-vertical dropoff to a depth of 50–90 feet. The reef is named for H.M.S. *Looe*, a British warship wrecked there in 1744.

From shore or from a boat, snorkelers can easily explore grass flats, mangrove roots, and rocks in shallow water, almost anywhere in the Keys. You may see occasional small clusters of coral and fish, mollusks, and other sea creatures. Ask dive shops for snorkeling information and directions. Diving and snorkeling are prohibited around bridges and near certain keys.

Dive shops all over the state organize Keys dives and offer diving instruction. South Florida residents fill dive boats on weekends, so plan to dive Monday through Thursday, when the boats and reefs are less crowded.

Jules Undersea Lodge, the world's first underwater hotel, takes reservations a year in advance from divers who want to stay in its two-room lodge in 30 feet of water. A resort course for new divers is offered. PADI affiliation. *MM 103.2, OS, Box 3330, Key Largo 33037, tel. 305/451–2353. AE, MC, V.*

Dive Shops

All of the dive shops listed below organize dives, fill air tanks, and sell or rent all necessary diving equipment. All have NAUI and/or PADI affiliation.

Quiescence Diving Service, Inc. Six people per boat. *MM 103.5, BS, 103680 Overseas Hwy., Key Largo, tel. 305/451–2440. Open daily 8–6; closed Thanksgiving and Christmas. AE, MC, V.*

Capt. Corky's Diver's World of Key Largo. A reef and wreck diving package is available. Reservations accepted for wreck diving of the *Benwood*, Coast Guard cutters *Bibb* and *Duane*, and French and Molasses reefs. *MM 99.5, OS, Box 1663, Key Largo 33037, tel. 305/451–3200, outside FL 800/445–8231. Open daily 8–5; closed Thanksgiving and Christmas. MC, V.*

Florida Keys Dive Center organizes dives from just south of John Pennekamp Coral Reef State Park to Alligator Light. This center has two Coast Guard-approved dive boats and offers training from introductory scuba through instructor course. Full-day "scuba safari" dives include complimentary on-board box lunch and barbecue afterward at the store. Inquire about 16′–19′ boat rentals. *MM 90.5, OS, 90500 Overseas Hwy., Box 391, Tavernier, tel. 305/852–4599 or 800/433–8946. Open daily 8–5. AE, MC, V.*

Treasure Divers, Inc., a full-service dive shop with instructors, arranges dives to reefs, Spanish galleons, and other wrecks. *MM 85.5, BS, 85500 Overseas Hwy., Islamorada, tel. 305/664–5111 or 800/356–9887. Open daily 8–5. AE, MC, V.*

Hall's Dive Center and Career Institute offers trips to Looe Key, Sombrero Reef, Delta Shoal, Content Key, and Coffins Patch. *MM 48.5, BS, 1994 Overseas Hwy., Marathon, tel. 305/743–5929 or 800/331–4255. Open daily 9–6. AE, MC, V.*

Looe Key Dive Center. This is the dive shop closest to Looe Key National Marine Sanctuary. *MM 27.5, OS, Box 509, Ramrod Key, tel. 305/872–2215. Open daily 7–6. AE, MC, V.*

Captain's Corner. Seven full-time instructors provide dive classes in English, French, German, and Italian. All captains are licensed dive masters. Reservations are accepted for regular reef and wreck diving, spear and lobster fishing, and archaeological and treasure hunting. Also has fishing charters. *Store at 201 William St., Key West, tel. 305/296–8918. Open 8–5. Booth at Zero Duval St., Key West, tel. 305/296–8865, 800/231–9864 (FL), or 800/328–9815 (US). Booth open daily 8 AM–11 PM. AE, MC, V.*

Fishing and Boating

Fishing is popular throughout the Keys. You have a choice of deep-sea fishing on the ocean or the gulf or flat-water fishing in the mangrove-fringed shallows of the backcountry. Each of the areas protected by the state or federal government has its own set of rigorously enforced regulations. Check with your hotel or a local chamber of commerce office to find out what the rules are in the area where you're staying. The same sources can refer you to a reliable charter-boat or party-boat captain who will take you where the right kind of fish are biting.

Glass-bottom boats, which depart daily (weather permitting) from docks throughout the Keys, are popular with visitors who want to admire the reefs without getting wet. If you're prone to seasickness, don't try to look through the glass bottom in rough seas.

Motor yachts, sailboats, Hobie Cats, Windsurfers, canoes, and other water-sports equipment are all available for rent by the day or on a long-term basis. Some hotels have their own rental services; others will refer you to a separate vendor.

Treasure Harbor Charter Yachts on Plantation Key rents bare sailboats, from 25-foot Watkins to a 45-foot Lancer; and powerboats, from a 32-foot Bayliner to a 42-foot Grand Banks. Captains and provisions available. No pets are allowed. *MM 86.5, OS, 200 Treasure Harbor Dr., Islamorada, tel. 305/852–9440 or 800/FLA–BOATS. Open 9–6. Reservations and advance deposit required; minimum 3-day rental; $100 per day captain fee for boats returned elsewhere. MC, V.*

Golf Two of the five golf courses in the Keys are open to the public:

Key Colony Beach Par 3. Nine-hole course near Marathon. *MM 53.5, 8th St., Key Colony Beach, tel. 305/289–1533. Fees: $4.50 9 holes; $3 each additional 9.*
Key West Resort Golf Course. Eighteen-hole course on the bay side of Stock Island. *6450 E. Junior College Rd., Key West, tel. 305/294–5232. Fees: $32.10 18 holes with cart; $23.54 9 holes with cart.*
The other three courses, open only to members and their guests, are the 18-hole **Ocean Reef Club** on Key Largo, the nine-hole, par 3 executive course at **Cheeca Lodge** in Islamorada, and the 18-hole **Sombrero Country Club** course in Marathon.

Beaches

Keys shorelines are either mangrove-fringed marshes or rock outcrops that fall away to mucky grass flats. Most pleasure beaches in the Keys are manmade, with sand imported from the U.S. mainland or the Bahamas. There are public beaches in **John Pennekamp Coral Reef State Park** (MM 102.5), **Long Key State Recreation Area** (MM 67.5), **Sombrero Beach** in Marathon (MM 50), **Bahia Honda State Recreation Area** (MM 36.5), and at many roadside turnouts along the Overseas Highway. Many hotels and motels also have their own small shallow-water beach areas.

When you swim in the Keys, wear an old pair of tennis shoes to protect your feet from rocks, sea-urchin spines, and other potential hazards.

Key West **Smathers Beach** features almost two miles of sand beside South Roosevelt Boulevard. Trucks along the road will rent you rafts, Windsurfers, and other beach "toys."
Higgs Memorial Beach. Near the end of White Street, this is a popular sunbathing spot. A nearby grove of Australian pines provides shade and the **West Martello Tower** provides shelter should a storm suddenly sweep in.

Dog Beach. At Vernon and Waddell streets, this is the only beach in Key West where dogs are allowed.

Southernmost Beach. On the Atlantic Ocean at the foot of Duval Street, this spot is popular with tourists at nearby motels. It has limited parking and a nearby buffet-type restaurant.

Fort Zachary Taylor State Historic Site. The beach here, several hundred yards of shoreline near the western end of Key West, adjoins a picnic area with barbecue grills in a stand of Australian pines. The restoration project begun in 1989 has leveled the beach after much sand erosion. Snorkeling is good except when winds blow from the south-southwest. This beach is relatively uncrowded and attracts more locals than tourists.

Simonton Street Beach. At the north end of Simonton Street, facing the Gulf of Mexico, this is a great place to watch boat traffic in the harbor, but parking here is difficult.

Two hotels in Key West have notable beaches:

Pier House (1 Duval St.) has a beach club for locals and patrons of certain nearby guest houses.

Several hotels allow varying degrees of undress on their beaches. Pier House permits female guests on its beach to go topless, and topless bathing is acceptable at the **Atlantic Shores Motel** (510 South St.). Contrary to popular belief, the rangers at Fort Taylor beach do *not* allow nude bathing.

Dining

by Rosalie Leposky

Don't be misled by the expression *Key-easy*. Denizens of the Florida Keys may be relaxed and wear tropical-casual clothes, but these folks take food seriously. A number of young, talented chefs have settled here in the last few years to enjoy the climate and contribute to the Keys' growing image as a fine-dining center. Best-known among them is Norman Van Aken, who made his reputation at Louie's Backyard. Van Aken's book, *Feast of the Sunlight* (Random House, 1988) describes the delights of Key West's "fusion cuisine," a blend of Florida citrus, seafood, and tropical fruits with Southwestern chilis, herbs, and spices.

The restaurant menus, the rum-based fruit beverages, and even the music reflect the Keys' tropical climate and their proximity to Cuba and other Caribbean islands. The better American and Cuban restaurants serve imaginative and tantalizing dishes that incorporate tropical fruits and vegetables, including avocado, carambola (star fruit), mango, and papaya.

Freshly caught local fish have been on every Keys menu in the past, but that is starting to change. The Keys' growing population has degraded the environment, disrupting fisheries and pricing fishermen out of the local housing market. Because many venerable commercial fish houses have abandoned the business in the past decade, there's a good chance the fish you order in a Keys restaurant may have been caught somewhere else. Since 1985, the U.S. government has protected the queen conch as an endangered species, so any conch you order in the Keys has come fresh-frozen from the Bahamas, Belize, or the Caribbean. Florida lobster and stone crab should be local and fresh from August through March.

Purists will find few examples of authentic Key-lime pie: a yellow lime custard in a Graham-cracker crust with a meringue top. Many restaurants now serve a version made with white-pastry crust and whipped cream, which is easy to prepare and hold for sale. The Pier House's **Market Bistro** and **Pier House Restaurant** serve the real thing with an extra-high meringue.

The list below is a representative selection of independent restaurants in the Keys, organized by mile marker (MM) number in descending order, as you would encounter them when driving down from the mainland. Small restaurants may not follow the hours listed here. Sometimes they close for a day or a week, or cancel lunch for a month or two, just by posting a note on the door.

The most highly recommended restaurants are indicated by a star ★.

Category	**Cost***
Very Expensive	over $55
Expensive	$35–$55
Moderate	$15–$35
Inexpensive	under $15

**per person, excluding service, drinks, tip, 6% state sales tax, and local tourist tax*

The following credit card abbreviations are used: AE, American Express; CB, Carte Blanche; DC, Diners Club; MC, MasterCard; V, Visa.

Florida City

Alabama Jack's. In 1953 Alabama Jack Stratham opened his restaurant on two barges at the end of Card Sound Road, 13 miles south of Homestead in an old fishing community between Card and Barnes sounds. The spot, something of a no-man's-land, belongs to the Keys in spirit thanks to the Card Sound toll bridge, which joined the mainland to upper Key Largo in 1969. Regular customers include Keys fixtures such as balladeer Jimmy Buffett, Sunday bikers, local retirees, boaters who tie up at the restaurant's dock, and anyone else fond of dancing to country-western music and clapping for cloggers. You can also admire the tropical birds cavorting in the nearby mangroves and the occasional crocodile swimming up the canal. Though Jack's been gone since the early '80s, owner Phyllis Sague has kept the favorites, specialties that include peppery homemade crab cakes; crispy-chewy conch fritters; crunchy breaded shrimp; homemade tartar sauce; and a tangy cocktail sauce with horseradish. *58000 Card Sound Rd., Florida City, tel. 305/248–8741 (Miami). Dress: casual. No reservations. Open 8:30–7. Live band Sat.–Sun. 2–7. No credit cards. Moderate.*

Key Largo

Crack'd Conch. Foreign money and patrons' business cards festoon the main dining room, where vertical bamboo stakes support the bar. There's also a screened outdoor porch. Specialties include conch (cracked and in chowder, fritters, and salad), fried alligator, smoked chicken, and 88 kinds of beer. *MM 105, OS, Rte. 1, 105045 Overseas Hwy., tel. 305/451–0732. Dress: casual. No reservations. Open Thurs.–Tues. noon–10; closed Wed.; Tues. from Easter through Memorial Day, and Sept. through Christmas. AE. Moderate.*

Italian Fisherman. White plaster statues of two nude fishermen, a nude goddess, and a clothed Columbus welcome you to the Italian Fisherman. You can dine indoors, but the best seating is on the 250-seat deck overlooking Florida Bay where an audience of seagulls awaits any morsel you may hurl in their direction. An Olympic-size pool and heated Jacuzzi were added in 1990 for sybaritic dining. Chef Joseph Rotonda is particularly adept at pasta and rich tangy marinara sauce. Specialties include hearty minestrone soup with lots of vegetables and fresh garlic bread; linguine *marechiaro* with shrimp, scallops, and clams; and the catch of the day blackened New Orleans–style. *MM 104, BS, tel. 305/451–4471. Dress: casual. Reservations accepted for parties of 10 or more. Closed Christmas and Thanksgiving. AE, DC, M, V. Moderate.*

★ **Mrs. Mac's Kitchen.** Hundreds of beer cans, beer bottles, and expired auto license plates from all over the world decorate the walls of this wood-paneled, open-air restaurant. At lunchtime, the counter and booths fill up early with locals. Regular nightly specials are worth the stop: meatloaf on Monday, barbecue on Tuesday, Italian on Wednesday, and seafood Thursday through Saturday. The chili is always good, and the imported beer of the month is $1.25 a bottle or can. Breakfast served 7–11 AM, Sun. to 2 PM. MM 99.4, Rte. 1, tel. 305/451–3722. *Dress: casual. No reservations. Closed major holidays. No credit cards. Inexpensive.*

Islamorada

★ **Marker 88.** The best seats in chef/owner Andre Mueller's main dining room catch the last glimmers of sunset. Hostesses recite a lengthy list of daily specials and offer you a wine list with over 200 entries. You can get a good steak or veal chop here, but 75% of the food served is seafood. Specialties include a robust conch chowder; banana blueberry bisque; salad Trevisana, made with radicchio, leaf lettuce, Belgium endive, watercress, and sweet-and-sour dill dressing (President Bush's favorite); sautéed conch or alligator steak meunière; grouper Rangoon, served with chunks of papaya, banana, and pineapple in a cinnamon and currant jelly sauce; and Key-lime pie. *MM 88 on Overseas Hwy., BS, Plantation Key, tel. 305/852–9315. Dress: casual. Reservations advised. AE, DC, MC, V. Expensive.*

Whale Harbor Inn. This coral rock building has oyster shells cemented onto the walls and a water mark at the 7-foot mark as a reminder of Hurricane Donna's fury in 1960. Several restaurant employees rode out the storm in the building's lighthouse tower. The main attraction is a 50-foot-long all-you-can-eat buffet, which includes a stir-fry area for wok cookery and a plentiful supply of shrimp, rock shrimp, crayfish, and snow crab legs. The adjoining Dockside Restaurant and Lounge has a raw bar and grill and a catwalk overlooking a marina. *MM 83.5, OS, Upper Matecumbe Key, tel. 305/664–4959. Dress: casual. No reservations. AE, CB, DC, MC, V. Moderate.*

Green Turtle Inn. Photographs of locals and famous visitors dating from 1947 line the walls and stuffed turtle dolls dangle from the ceiling over the bar. Harry Rosenthal, the restaurant's third owner, retains the original menu cover and some of the original dishes. Specialties include a turtle consommé; conch fritters, nicely browned outside, light and fluffy inside; conch salad with vinegar, lime juice, pimiento, and pepper; alligator steak (tail meat) sautéed in an egg batter; and Key-lime pie. Whole pies are available for carry-out. *MM 81.5, OS, tel. 305/664–9031. Dress: casual. No reservations. Closed Mon. and Thanksgiving Day. AE, CB, DC, MC, V. Moderate.*

Marathon

Ship's Pub and Galley. The collection of historic photos on the restaurant walls depict the railroad era in the Keys, the development of Duck Key, and many of the notables who have visited here. Dinners include soup and a 40-item salad bar with all the steamed shrimp you can eat. Specialties include homemade garlic bread, Swiss onion soup, certified New York Angus beef, at least two fish specials, Florida stone crab claws (in season), and mile-high shoofly mudpie, a 6-inch-high coffee ice cream pie with a whipped cream topping. The adjoining lounge has live entertainment and a dance floor. *MM 61, OS, tel. 305/743–7000, ext. 3627. Dress: casual. Reservations accepted. Early bird specials. AE, CB, DC, MC, V. Moderate.*

Grassy Key Dairy Bar. Look for the Dairy Queen-style concrete ice-cream cones near the road. Locals and construction workers stop here for quick lunches. Owner/chefs George and Johnny Eigner are proud of their fresh-daily homemade bread, soups and chowders, fresh seafood, and fresh-cut beef. *MM 58.5, OS, Grassy Key, tel. 305/743–3816. Dress: casual. Reservations accepted. Closed Sun.–Mon. No credit cards. Moderate.*

Herbie's Bar. A local favorite for lunch and dinner since the 1940s, Herbie's has three small rooms with two bars. Indoor diners sit at wood picnic tables or the bar; those in the screened outdoor room use concrete tables. Specialties include spicy conch chowder with chunks of tomato and crisp conch fritters with homemade horseradish sauce. Nightly specials. *MM 50.5, BS, 6350 Overseas Hwy., tel. 305/743–6373. Dress: casual. No reservations. Closed Sun.; closed Mon. Easter–Nov. No credit cards. Inexpensive.*

Kelsey's. The walls in this restaurant at the Faro Blanco Marine Resort are hung with boat paddles inscribed by the regulars and celebrities like Joe Namath and Ted Turner. All entrees here are served with fresh-made yeast rolls brushed with drawn butter and Florida orange honey. Chef David Leeper serves only fresh local seafood and lobster. Specialties include Faro Blanco clambake, a potpourri of native seafood, and grouper gourmet (lightly floured, dipped in egg batter, sautéed in white wine and fresh lemon, and topped with artichoke hearts, mushrooms, and toasted almonds). You can bring your own cleaned and filleted catch for the chef to prepare. Dessert offerings change nightly and may include Mrs. Kelsey's original macadamia pie and Key-lime cheesecake. *MM 48, BS, 1996 Overseas Hwy., tel. 305/743–9018. Dress: casual. Reservations accepted. Dinner only. Closed Mon. AE, MC, V. Moderate.*

Mile 7 Grill. This open-air diner built in 1954 at the Marathon end of Seven Mile Bridge has walls festooned with mounted fish, sponges, and signs describing individual menu items. Specialties include grouper chowder, fresh fish sandwich of the day, and a foot-long chili dog on a toasted sesame roll. *MM 47.5, BS, 1240 Overseas Hwy., tel. 305/743–4481. Open daily for lunch and dinner. Closed Wed.–Thurs., Christmas Eve–first Fri. after New Year's, and when they want to in Aug.–Sept. No credit cards. Inexpensive.*

Cafe Marquesa. Only 15 tables and banquettes, the secret of the cafe's success is its openness in all respects. It is open to innovative cuisine, it has a friendly staff, an open kitchen through a *trompe l'oeil* pantry mural—nothing's snooty about this place. Owners of the hotel now attract locals and visitors alike with affordable meals that include arugala salad with sun-dried tomatoes, fresh mushrooms, corn kernels, and bacon; a delicate, generously served blue corn pasta layered with spinach, mushrooms, red bell peppers, ricotta and parmesan cheeses, with a vegetarian béchamel on a bed of zucchini coulis; grilled shrimp with *piripiri* sauce (a salsa of tomatoes, chilis, garlic, cilantro, and shallots). Limitless helpings of the excellent sesame flatbread with black pepper accompany all meals. For dessert try the fruit tart with kiwi, strawberries, and crème fraîche. *600 Fleming St., tel. 305/292–1244. Dress: neat but casual. Reservations accepted. AE, MC, V. Closed Christmas, New Year's Day. Moderate.*

Key West
American
★

Louie's Backyard. This place is really two restaurants and a bar. The upstairs Cafe at Louie's has a coffered ceiling, an open-theater kitchen, louvered transom windows, and a balcony. Downstairs in Louie's Backyard, the walls are decorated with abstract art and old Key West paintings. Menus in both restaurants change seasonally and include nightly specials. The cafe serves Spanish-Caribbean cuisine. The menu may include pan-charred grouper with a dash of soy sauce, Myers's dark rum, and cracked black pepper; chicken livers pan-fried in olive oil with Spanish sherry vinegar, sweet peppers, red onion, chilies, and celery; and marinated roast pork served with black bean sauce, plantains, slices of red onion, sour cream, and lime. At Louie's Backyard, innovative selections include Bahamian conch chowder with bird-pepper hot sauce and grilled catch of the day with tomato-butter and red-onion marmalade and roasted peppers. *700 Waddell Ave., tel. 305/294–1061. Jacket required. Reservations advised. Dinner only at the cafe. AE, DC, MC, V. Very Expensive.*

Pepe's Cafe and Steak House. Judges, policemen, carpenters, and fishermen rub elbows every morning in their habitual breakfast seats, at three tables and four pine booths under a huge paddlefan. Outdoors are more tables and an open-air bar under a canvas tarp. Pepe's was established downtown in 1919 and moved to the current site in 1962. The specials change nightly: barbecued chicken, pork tenderloin, ribs, potato salad, red or black beans, and corn bread on Sunday; meatloaf on Monday; seafood Tuesday and Wednesday; a full traditional Thanksgiving dinner every Thursday; filet mignon on Friday; and prime rib on Saturday. *806 Caroline St., tel. 305/294–7192. Dress: casual. No reservations. MC, V. Moderate.*

★ **Pier House Restaurant.** Steamships from Havana once docked at this pier jutting out into the Gulf of Mexico. Now it's an elegant place to dine, indoors or out, and to watch boats gliding by in the harbor. At night the restaurant shines lights into the water, attracting schools of brightly colored parrot fish. The menu emphasizes tropical fruits, spices, and fish. Executive Chef Michael Kulow specializes in native seafood prepared to order. Included on the menu are grilled sea scallops with black bean cake and *pico de gallo* (tomato, shallots, cilantro, chopped chayote); lobster ravioli in a creamy pesto sauce and salmon caviar; and a seafood catch prepared with tomatillo vinaigrette and saffron aioli. Ordered specially, a poached yellowtail is served with broccoli flowerets and red peppers triangulated on alternate rounds of yellow and green squash. Even simple food becomes art. Desserts include definition-perfect Key-lime pie with a 5-inch meringue topping, and an apple pie in a phyllo dough formed to look like a milliner's creation with a caramel sauce. *1 Duval St., tel. 305/296–4600, 800/432–3414 (FL), 800/*

327–8340 (U.S.). Dress: neat but casual. Reservations advised. AE, DC, MC, V. Very Expensive.

Cuban **El Siboney.** This family-style restaurant serves traditional Cuban food. Specials include chicken and rice every Friday, oxtail stew with rice and beans on Saturday. Always available are roast pork with *morros* (black beans and white rice) and cassava, paella, and *palomilla* steak. *900 Catherine St., tel. 305/296–4184. Dress: casual. No reservations. Closed Thanksgiving, Christmas, New Year's Day, 2 wks in June. No credit cards. Inexpensive.*

Delicatessen **Market Bistro.** The Pier House's deli and fine-dining snack shop sells the hotel's classic Key-lime pie by the slice, as well as a chocolate decadence: a triple chocolate flourless torte with raspberry sauce and rose petals. A cooler holds a respectable selection of fine wines, champagnes, and beers. Specialties include tropical fruit drinks, sandwiches, salads, gourmet cheeses, pâtés, and homemade pastries. *1 Duval St. in the Pier House, tel. 305/296–4600. Dress: casual. No reservations. AE, DC, MC, V. Moderate.*

French **Cafe des Artistes.** This intimate 75-seat restaurant occupies part of a hotel building constructed in 1935 by C. E. Alfeld, Al Capone's bookkeeper. Haitian paintings and Keys scenes by local artists decorate the walls. Skylights in one of the five rooms are open in good weather, and some seating is available in a secluded courtyard. Executive chef Christian Karcher presents a French interpretation of tropical cuisine, using fresh local seafood and produce and light, flour-free sauces. Specialties include his award-winning lobster "tango-mango," flambéed with Cognac, served with shrimp in a mango-saffron beurre blanc, salade "Jessica" (avocado, hearts of palm, strawberries, and orange-ginger vinaigrette dressing), pear and champagne cream soup with bits of fresh pear, a very light raspberry Cointreau cheesecake, and pear tart with passion fruit ice cream. *1007 Simonton St., tel. 305/294–7100. Dress: neat but casual. Reservations advised. No lunch. AE, MC, V. Moderate–Expensive.*

Seafood ★ **Half Shell Raw Bar.** "Eat It Raw" is the motto, and even off-season the oyster bar keeps shucking. You eat at shellacked blond picnic tables and benches in a shed under ship models, life buoys, mounted dolphin, old license plates. Once a fish market, the Half Shell looks out onto the deep-sea fishing fleet. Eat indoors or out. Specials are chalked on the blackboard: broiled dolphin sandwich, linguine seafood marinara. The same owners operate The Turtle Kraals Restaurant & Bar on the other side of Land's End Village. *Land's End Marina, tel. 305/294–7496. Dress: casual. No reservations. No credit cards. Inexpensive–Moderate.*

The Buttery. The Buttery's waiters have come to be known as buttercups, a nickname they share with the house's special drink, a blended frozen concoction of vodka, Kahlua, amaretto, coconut milk, and cream. Each of the restaurant's six rooms has its own character. The back room with the bar has wood paneling and skylights; a small private dining room in front has green-painted woodwork and floral wallpaper. The front rooms have green carpets and swag lamps, candles in large glass hurricane chimneys, and many plants. Specialties include yellowtail snapper baked with sliced bananas, walnuts, and banana liqueur; steak "Ricardo" (fillets of tenderloin sautéed with mushrooms in Madeira-wine sauce), and chilled Senegalese cream of celery soup made with curry, heavy cream, and mango chutney, and, for dessert, Poor Richard's Super Rich, a creamy blend of Godiva and three other kinds of chocolate in a chocolate piecrust topped with fresh whipped cream, and crushed English walnuts. *1208 Simonton St., tel. 305/294-0717. Dress: neat but casual. Reservations advised. Closed 2–3 wks in Sept. No lunch. AE, CB, DC, MC, V. Moderate.*

Dockside Bar and Raw Bar. When the crowds get too thick on the Mallory Dock at sunset, you can come up here, have a piña colada and a snack, and watch the action from afar. This establishment, on a 200-foot dock behind Ocean Key House, has a limited but flavorful menu: freshly smoked fish, crunchy conch salad, crispy conch fritters, and fresh clams, oysters, and shrimp. Live island music is featured nightly. *Ocean Key House, Zero Duval St., tel. 305/296-7701. Dress: casual. No reservations. AE, CB, DC, MC, V. Inexpensive.*

Lodging

Some hotels in the Keys are historic structures with a charming patina of age; others are just plain old. Salty winds and soil play havoc with anything manmade in the Keys. Constant maintenance is a must, and some hotels and motels don't get it. Inspect your accommodations before checking in. The best rooms in the Keys have a clear bay or ocean view and a deep setback from the Overseas Highway.

The city of Key West offers the greatest variety of lodgings, from large resorts to bed-and-breakfast rooms in private homes. Altogether there are about 4,000 units (including about 1,500 rooms in close to 60 guest houses) as well as approximately 1,800 condominium apartments that are available for daily or weekly rental through their homeowners associations.

Accommodations in the Keys are more expensive than elsewhere in south Florida. In part this is due to the Keys' popularity and ability to command top dollar, but primarily it's because everything used to build and operate a hotel costs more in the Keys. All materials and supplies must be trucked in, and electric and water rates are among the steepest in the nation.

The Florida Keys and Key West Visitors Bureau provides a free accommodations guide (*see* Important Addresses and Numbers, above). The list below is a representative selection of hotels, motels, resorts, and guest houses. In the Upper, Middle, and Lower Keys outside Key West, we've listed hotels, motels, and resorts by mile marker (MM) number in descending order, as you would encounter them when driving down from the mainland.

Category	**Cost***
Very Expensive	over $175
Expensive	$110–$175
Moderate	$75–$110
Inexpensive	under $75

**All prices are for a standard double room, excluding 6% state sales tax and local tourist tax.*

The following credit card abbreviations are used: AE, American Express; CB, Carte Blanche, DC, Diners Club; MC, MasterCard; V, Visa.

Key Largo **Largo Lodge.** No two rooms are the same in this vintage 1950s resort. A tropical garden with palm trees, sea grapes, and orchids surrounds the guest cottages. Late in the day, wild ducks, pelicans, herons, and other birds come looking for a handout from long-time owner Harriet "Hat" Stokes. *MM 101.5, BS, 101740 Overseas Hwy., 33037, tel. 305/451–0424 or 800/IN-THE-SUN. 6 apartments with kitchen, 1 efficiency. Facilities: 200 feet of bay frontage, public phone, boat ramp and 3 slips. No children under 16 or pets. AE, MC, V. Moderate.*

★ **Holiday Inn Key Largo Resort & Marina.** James W. Hendricks, the Kentucky attorney who restored the *African Queen*, completed renovations and new landscaping at this resort at the Key Largo Harbor Marina in 1989. The hotel was built in 1971, and a new wing was added in 1981. Decor includes blond wood furniture and pink-and-green bedspreads. Provides onshore accommodations for guests coming to Jules Undersea Lodge. *MM 100, OS, 99701 Overseas Hwy., 33037, tel. 305/451–2121, 800/HOLIDAY, OR 800/THE KEYS. 132 rooms with bath, including 13 nonsmoker rooms and 2 rooms for handicapped guests. Facilities: 2 pools (1 with waterfall), Jacuzzi, marina with 35 transient spaces, gift shop, dive and glass-bottom tour boats, boat rentals. AE, MC, V. Expensive.*

★ **Marina Del Mar Resort and Marina.** This resort beside the Key Largo Harbor Canal caters to sailors and divers. Two buildings opened in 1986, a third in 1988. All rooms contain original art by local artists Sue, Zita, and Mary Boggs. The best rooms are suites 502, 503 and 504, each of which has a full kitchen and plenty of room for large families or dive groups. The fourth-floor observation deck offers spectacular sunrise and sunset views. Advance reservations are required for boat slips. To find the hotel, turn OS on U.S. 1 by the Texaco station at Laguna Avenue, and left at the first intersection onto Caribbean Boulevard. Marina Del Mar is about 100 yards on the left. *MM 100, OS, Box 1050, 33037, tel. 305/451–4107, 800/253–3483 (FL), 800/451–3483 (US), 800/638–3483 (Canada), or 305/451–4107. 76 rooms with bath, including 8 nonsmoker suites, 16 studios with full kitchens, 16 nonsmoker rooms, and 3 rooms for handicapped guests. Facilities: in-room refrigerators, 40-slip full-service marina, showers and washing machines for marina guests, pool, 2 lighted tennis courts, weight room, washers and dryers on all floors, picnic tables, free Continental breakfast in lobby, restaurant and bar with live nightly entertainment, dive packages, diving and snorkeling charters, fishing charters. No pets. AE, CB, DC, MC, V. Expensive.*

Sunset Cove Motel. Each room has one hard and one soft mattress plus a sleeper sofa, tile floors, and original hand-painted murals. Special discounts are offered to senior citizens and members of conservation groups. *MM 99.5, BS, Box 99, 33037, tel. 305/451–0705. 10 units with bath and a dormitory group house with kitchen for up to 15 people. Facilities: free watersports equipment (canoes, glass-bottom and regular paddleboat, sailboats, trimaran, and Windsurfers), 115-foot fishing pier, boat ramp. No children under 16. No pets. MC, V. Moderate.*

Bay Harbor Lodge. Owner Laszlo Simoga speaks German, Hungarian, and Russian and caters to an international clientele. Situated on two heavily landscaped acres, this resort has a rustic wood lodge and several concrete-block structures. Unit 14, a large efficiency apartment with a deck, has a wood ceiling, original oil paintings, and a dining table made from the hatch cover of a World War II Liberty Ship. *MM 97.5, BS, Rte. 1, Box 35, 33037, tel. 305/852–5695. 12 rooms with bath. Facilities: Jacuzzi, saltwater shower, Olympic weightlifting equipment, individual outdoor barbecues, paddleboat, rowboats, canoes, 2 docks, cable TV, boat and trailer parking. No pets. MC, V. Inexpensive–Moderate.*

Sheraton Key Largo Resort. This four-story hotel is nestled in 12½ acres of coastal hardwood hammock and mangrove swamp. A modern interpretation of traditional Conch architecture, the resort's three-story atrium lobby features a multitude of small glass windowpanes separated by prominent mullions, a Mexican-tile floor, coral-rock walls, and rattan furniture. *MM 97, BS, 97000 Overseas Hwy., 33037, tel. 305/852–5553, 800/325–3535 (US), 800/268–9393 (eastern Canada), or 800/268–9330 (western Canada). 200 rooms with bath, including 10 suites. Facilities: 2 heated pools, 2 lighted tennis courts, 2,000-foot labeled nature trail, sailboat and Windsurfer rental, fishing and dive charters, dive shop, 21-slip dock for hotel guests, minibars, 2 restaurants, 3 lounges, beauty shop. AE, CB, DC, MC, V. Expensive.*

Islamorada

Cheeca Lodge. Reminiscent of Miami Beach in the 1950s, this 27-acre resort on Upper Matecumbe Key appeals to affluent northeasterners who appreciate ostentatious informality. It reopened in 1988 after being closed for 17 months for a $30-million total renovation and expansion. Lobby decor includes cypress beams and Florida keystone floors. Color schemes used for the guest rooms and suites are periwinkle blue, strawberry, and green. All guest units have British Colonial–style furniture with bamboo and wicker headboards and chairs. Ocean Suite 102 features a cathedral ceiling and a screened porch. Fourth-floor rooms in the main lodge open onto a terrace with either an ocean or bay view. *MM 82, Upper Matecumbe Key, Box 527, 33036, tel. 305/664–4651 (Islamorada), or 305/245–3755 (Miami), or 800/327–2888 (US and FL). 203 rooms, including 64 suites, 160 nonsmoker rooms, and 5 rooms for handicapped guests. Facilities: in-room minibar, free golf-cart shuttle service around the resort, 9-hole par-3 executive golf course designed by Jack Nicklaus, 6 lighted tennis courts, 2 heated pools and one saltwater tidal pool, 525-foot fishing pier, 2 restaurants, lounge. Sun. brunch served in the Atlantic's Edge Dining Room. Beach Hut rents Hobie Cats, rafts, snorkeling and fishing gear, parasailing equipment, and power boats. All-year children's program. AE, CB, DC, MC, V. Very Expensive.*

Holiday Isle Resorts and Marina. Situated near Theater of the Sea, this is actually four separate resort motels under common ownership and management—the original Holiday Isle Resorts and Marina, El Capitan, Harbor Lights, and Howard Johnson's. All except El Capitan were renovated in 1988. Each motel in the complex offers variety in price and location. On weekends, the resort is popular with the under-30 set. Harbor Lights, off on its own a half mile up the road, is quieter than the rest. *MM 84.5, OS, Windley Key, 84001 Overseas Hwy., 33036, tel. 305/664–2321, 800/432–2875 (FL), 800/327–7070 (US and Canada). 171 rooms with bath, including 18 suites and 21 effi-*

ciencies, 3 nonsmoker rooms in Howard Johnson's. Facilities: 3 pools, 18-slip marina, 5 restaurants, Wave Runners charter fishing boats, Holiday Princess glass-bottom sightseeing boat; Holiday Isle Watersports, a concessionaire, rents Hobie 14s, jet skis, and sailboats and offers parasailing. No pets. AE, CB, DC, MC, V. Inexpensive–Very Expensive.

Long Key **Lime Tree Bay Resort.** In 1991 look for eight new units with cathedral ceilings and skylights at this steadily improving 2.5-acre resort built in 1972 and now owned by Nick Stefanyshyn. Each room is decorated differently. A palm tree grows through the floor of "The Treehouse," a two-bedroom unit with kitchen that is popular with larger families. You can swim and snorkel in the shallow grass flats just offshore. *MM 68.5, BS, Box 839, Layton, 33001, tel. 305/664–4740. 28 rooms with bath. Facilities: outdoor pool and Jacuzzi, tennis court, power and sailboat rentals, dive boats and charter boats, 2 restaurants. No pets. AE, MC, V. Moderate.*

Marathon ★ **Hawk's Cay Resort.** Morris Lapidus, architect of the Fontainebleau Hilton hotel in Miami Beach, designed this rambling West Indies–style resort, which opened in 1959 as the Indies Inn and Marina. Over the years it has entertained a steady stream of politicians (including Harry Truman, Dwight Eisenhower, and Lyndon Johnson) and film stars who come to relax and be pampered by a friendly, low-key staff. Hawk's Cay retains the comfortable ambience it has always had, even after an $8-million renovation of rooms, public areas, meeting space, and landscaping completed in 1989. The new decor features wickerwork rattan, a sea-green and salmon color scheme, and original contemporary artwork in guest rooms and public areas. Most rooms face the water. New since 1990 are 86 two-bedroom marina villas available to hotel guests; a new health club is scheduled to open in 1991. *MM 61, OS, 33050, tel. 305/743–7000, 800/432–2242 (FL), 800/327–7775 (US). 177 rooms with bath, including 16 suites, 15 rooms for handicapped guests. Facilities: heated pool, 2 whirlpool spas, 1-mi fitness trail, 8 tennis courts, Tim Farwell's Tennis School, use of Sombrero Golf Course in Marathon, 70-slip full-service marina, PADI-certified and handicap diving certified dive boats, Club Nautico boat rentals, fishing and sailing charter boats, Zoovet Dolphin & Sea Lion Center (where guests can swim free with the dolphins and attend free dolphin and sea lion shows), 4 restaurants, complimentary full-breakfast buffet, nightclub, 4 boutique and specialty shops, billiard room, video game room. $10 per child per day for educational and entertainment program. AE, DC, MC, V. Very Expensive.*

Rainbow Bend Fishing Resort. First you notice the shocking-pink exterior, then the well-kept appearance of this 2.7-acre resort built in the late 1950s as a lumberyard and CIA base. Every room is different. A restaurant offering complimentary breakfast overlooks an ample manmade beach, good bonefish flats just a few yards offshore, and a dock with boats available free to guests, except for minimum $4 fuel charge. *MM 58, OS, Grassy Key, Route 1, Box 159, 33050, tel. 305/289–1505. 21 rooms with bath, including 18 suites, and efficiencies. Facilities: heated pool and Jacuzzi, small fishing pier, 4 hrs free use of 15-foot Boston Whaler, free use of sailboats and canoe, complete bait and tackle shop, 2 charter boats, restaurant. AE, MC, V. Expensive.*

Valhalla Beach Resort Motel. Watch for this resort's large sign along the Overseas Highway. The resort itself is a half mile off the road, surrounded by water on three sides. It's a 1950s motel that has been run by the same family for over 20 years. *MM 56.5, OS, Crawl Key, Rte. 1, Box 115, 33050, tel. 305/289–0616. 12 rooms with bath, including 8 efficiencies. Facilities: boat ramp and dock, private beach. No credit cards. Inexpensive.*

Sombrero Resort & Lighthouse Marina. You can choose from marina or pool views in this complex of buildings ranging in height from one to three stories. The original structure built in 1960 was renovated in 1985, and new rooms were opened in 1988 and 1989. Turn OS off the Overseas Highway by the K-Mart onto Sombrero Beach Road, then right at the first corner onto Sombrero Boulevard. The resort is to your left, across from the Sombrero Country Club. *MM 50, OS, 19 Sombrero Blvd., 33050, tel. 305/743–2250 or 800/433–8660. 124 suites. Facilities: pool, sauna, 4 lighted tennis courts, tennis pro and pro shop, ship's store, boat ramp, 54-slip marina, cable and phone hook-ups, shower, rest room, laundry, restaurant, bars. AE, MC, V. Expensive.*

Faro Blanco Marine Resort. Now operated by Westrec Properties of California, this 40-year-old resort, since 1990, incorporates the Boot Key Seaport Resort and stretches from bayside to oceanside. The lighthouse is a Middle Keys landmark that anchors a fine restaurant (*see* **Kelsey's,** in Dining, above) and a mix of lodgings well suited to the Keys. *MM 48, BS, 47.8 OS, 1996 Overseas Highway, 33050, tel. 305/743–9018 or 800/759–3276. 120 units including garden cottages, 21 3-bedroom condominiums, 31 anchored houseboat suites that move in the wind, 1 room for handicapped guests. Facilities: Olympic-size freshwater pool, full-service marina with 100 slips, boat rentals, charter booking services, restaurant, raw bar, grill, ship store, gift shops. Pets welcome for $18 fee and advance reservation. Boat-dockage fee $10 per night. AE, MC, V. Expensive.*

Little Torch Key

★ **Little Palm Island.** The lobby is just off the Overseas Highway on Little Torch Key, but the resort itself is a 3-mile boat ride away on a palm-fringed island at the western end of the Newfound Harbor Keys. There you'll find 14 thatch-roof villas, each with two suites, and two additional suites in the Great House, a cypress fishing lodge built in 1928. Each suite has a Mexican-tile bath and dressing area, beds draped with mosquito netting, and Mexican and Guatemalan wicker and rattan furniture. Built on stilts 9 feet above mean high tide, all villas afford good views of the water. The island is in the middle of Coupon Bight Aquatic Preserve and is the closest point of land to the Looe Key National Marine Sanctuary. *MM 28.5, Overseas Highway, Route 4, Box 1036, 33042, tel. 305/872–2524 or 800/343–8567. 30 suites, 1 for handicapped guests. Facilities: air conditioners, wet bars and stocked refrigerators, room safes, heated lagoon-style pool, sauna, tiki bar, gift shop, restaurant, 12-slip marina for hotel and restaurant guests. Free on-the-hour launch service 7 AM–11 PM. Pickup from Marathon Airport and Key West International Airport, $35 per person round-trip. Guided tours and excursions. Full American plan—breakfast, lunch, dinner, Sun. brunch. Restaurant reservations: 305/872–2551. Call for restrictions. Very Expensive.*

Ramrod Key

Looe Key Reef Resort and Dive Center. The rooms in this two-story divers' motel were refurnished in 1987. In the tiny lobby, the front desk doubles as a package liquor store. Rooms are spartan but comfortable, with firm mattresses and ocean-blue bedspreads and carpets. The least desirable rooms are the three singles without a canal view. Guests can make an appointment for free pickup from the private airstrip on Summerland Key. *MM 27.5, US 1, OS, Box 509, 33042, tel. 305/872–2215. 23 rooms with bath, 1 for handicapped guests. Facilities: air conditioners, cable TV, outdoor pool, dive shop, 400 feet of boat dockage, 2 Coast Guard–certified dive boats, restaurant, poolside tiki bar and raw bar. MC, V. Moderate.*

Lower Sugarloaf Key

Sugar Loaf Lodge. This well-landscaped older motel overlooking mangrove islands and Upper Sugarloaf Sound has one building with soft beds and an eclectic assortment of furniture and another with high ceilings, wall murals, and balconies on the second floor. A friendly dolphin named Sugar inhabits a lagoon just outside the restaurant; diners can watch her perform through a picture window. *MM 17, BS, Box 148, 33044, tel. 305/745–3211. 55 rooms with bath. Facilities: pool, tennis court, 18-hole miniature golf course, restaurant, lounge, free dolphin performances at 9 AM, 1 PM, and 5 PM. AE, CB, DC, MC, V. Moderate.*

Key West

House and Condominium Rentals

Key West Reservation Service makes hotel reservations and helps visitors locate rental properties (condominiums and private homes). *628 Fleming St., Drawer 1689, 33040, tel. 305/294–7713, 800/356–3567 (FL), 800/327–4831 (US). AE, MC, V.*

Property Management of Key West, Inc., offers lease and rental service for condominiums, town houses, and private homes, including renovated Conch homes. *1213 Truman Ave., 33040, tel. 305/296–7744. AE, MC, V.*

Hotels and Motels

★ **The Banyan Resort.** A time-share resort across the street from the Truman Annex, the Banyan Resort includes three Victorian houses, a former cigar factory listed on the National Registry of Historic Places, and three modern buildings in the Victorian style. The award-winning gardens are a tropical cornucopia of avocado, Barbados cherry, eggfruit, papaya, Persian lime, and sapodilla. The rooms have a gray, maroon, and mauve color scheme and rattan and wicker furniture. *323 Whitehead St., 33040, tel. 305/294–9573, 305/296–7786 or 800/225–0639. 38 suites with bath. Facilities: 2 pools (1 heated), 2 Jacuzzis, bar. Call for restrictions. AE, MC, V. Very Expensive.*

Hyatt Key West. A first for Hyatt, this "baby grand" resort consists of three four-story buildings surrounding a tropical piazza. The lobby has a Mexican terra-cotta tile floor and cherry wood fixtures; the room decor employs mint, lilac, peach, and teal blue hues with light-wood dressers and wicker chairs. All rooms except 2209 and 2110 have water views. *601 Front St., 33040, tel. 305/296–9900, 800/228–9001, 800/228–9005 (HI, AK), or 800/233–1234. 120 rooms with bath, including 16 suites, 16 nonsmoker rooms, and 6 rooms for handicapped guests. Facilities: pool, Jacuzzi, hot tub, fitness room, massage studio, small private manmade beach, bicycle and motor scooter rental, 6-slip marina, 60-ft rental ketch. AE, CB, DC, MC, V. Very Expensive.*

Marriott's Casa Marina Resort. Henry Morrison Flagler built La Casa Marina in 1921 at the end of the Florida East Coast Railroad line. New wings were added in 1978 and 1986. The entire 13-acre resort revolves around an outdoor patio and lawn facing the ocean. The lobby has an elegant beamed ceiling, polished wood floor of Dade County pine, and wicker furniture. Rooms are decorated in purple, mauve, and green pastels and prints of fish and Key West scenes. Among the best rooms are the two-bedroom loft suites with balconies facing the ocean, and the lanai rooms on the ground floor of the main building with French doors opening directly onto the lawn. Guest rooms and lobby of the original building were completely refurbished in 1989–90. *1500 Reynolds St., 33040, tel. 305/296–3535, 800/235–4837 (FL), 800/228–9290 (US). 314 rooms with bath, including 63 suites, 16 nonsmoker rooms, 4 rooms for handicapped guests. Facilities: heated pool, whirlpool, 600-ft fishing pier, health club, massage studio and sauna, 3 tennis courts, 2 gift shops, activity center for children, game room, restaurant, poolside bar. Key West Water Sports, a concessionaire, offers deep-sea charter boats, light-tackle fishing, party-boat fishing, Hobie Cats, Sunfish, jet skis, scuba and snorkel trips, bicycle and moped rentals. AE, DC, MC, V. Very Expensive.*

Ocean Key House. This newly refurbished five-story city resort hotel has large and comfortable rooms decorated in tasteful pastel colors and art-deco reproductions. The best rooms, penthouse suites 511 and 512, overlook the Gulf of Mexico. Ocean Key House is the closest hotel to Mallory Square. From its pool deck you can watch the sunset show while quaffing a piña colada from the outdoor bar. *Zero Duval St., 33040, tel. 305/296–7701, 800/231–9864 (FL), 800/328–9815 (US). 100 units with bath, including 52 1-bedroom suites and 16 2-bedroom suites. Suites have fully equipped kitchen, private Jacuzzi, full-size living room/dining room, minibar. Facilities: heated pool, 6 boat slips, dockside raw bar, pool bar, dive shop. AE, CB, DC, MC, V. Expensive.*

★ **Pier House.** This is the catbird seat for touring Key West—just off the intersection of Duval and Front streets and within easy walking distance of Mallory Square and downtown. Yet within the hotel grounds you feel the tranquility of a remote tropical island. New since 1990 is the Caribbean Spa: 22 new rooms and suites with hardwood floors and two-poster plantation beds in each bedroom. Eleven of the baths convert to steam rooms; the others have whirlpool tubs. In the new rooms you are pampered by VCRs and a library of movies and CD players with compact discs. You can also avail yourself of a loofa rub, herbal wrap, or facial; there is also a complete fitness center. Weathered-gray buildings flank a courtyard filled with tall coconut palms and hibiscus blossoms. Locals gather around a thatch-roof shelter at the Beach Club, a tiki bar. The complex's eclectic architecture includes an original Conch house. The entire hotel was renovated in 1989. *1 Duval St., 33040, tel. 305/296–4600, 800/432–3414 (FL), 800/327–8340 (US). 142 rooms with bath, including 33 suites in 5 separate low-rise buildings. Facilities: heated pool, 5 bars, 5 restaurants. AE, MC, V. Expensive.*

Econo Lodge. Half the rooms of this six-story motel face the Gulf of Mexico, the rest face the pool and parking lot. The sixth-floor penthouses have the best view of the Gulf's mangrove islands, grass flats, the nightly sunset, and Mount Trashmore on Stock Island. The rooms are decorated with Key West prints, floral-print bedspreads, and blond-wood furniture. The trackless trolley stops in front of the main entrance. *3820 N. Roosevelt Blvd., 33040, tel. 305/294–5511, 800/533–9378 (FL), 800/446–6900 (US). 143 rooms with bath, including 4 1-bed-*

room suites with kitchenette and 4 penthouses with 2 bedrooms and 1½ baths. Facilities: pool, restaurant, lounge, poolside tiki bar. AE, DC, MC, V. Expensive, but inexpensive off-season. Inquire about seasonal rates.

★ **La Concha Holiday Inn.** This seven-story art deco hotel in the heart of downtown Key West is the city's tallest building. It opened in 1926, was totally renovated and enlarged in 1986, and in 1987 was added to the National Register of Historic Places. Novelist Ernest Hemingway and playwright Tennessee Williams both stayed here. The lobby has a polished floor of pink, mauve, and green marble and a conversation pit with comfortable chairs. Rooms are large and furnished with 1920s-era antiques, lace curtains, and big closets. The restorers kept the old building's original louvered room doors, light globes, and floral trim on the archways. You can enjoy the sunset from "The Top," a restaurant and lounge that overlooks the entire island. *430 Duval St., 33040, tel. 305/296–2991, 800/227–6151 (FL), 800/HOLIDAY (US). 160 rooms with bath, including 2 suites, 18 nonsmoker rooms, and 8 rooms for handicapped guests. Facilities: pool and sun deck, whirlpool, fitness room, restaurant, 3 bars, bicycle and motor scooter rentals. AE, CB, DC, MC, V. Moderate–Expensive.*

★ **The Marquesa Hotel.** Key West architect Thomas Pope supervised the restoration of this four-story 1884 home and added onto it in a compatible style. The lobby resembles a Victorian parlor, with antique furniture, Audubon prints, fresh flowers, and a bowl of apples for nibbles. Rooms have French Provincial furnishings and dotted Swiss curtains. There are marble vanities in some baths, marble floors in others. Continental breakfast is served poolside ($5 extra). *600 Fleming St., 33040, tel. 305/292–1919 or 800/UNWIND–1. 15 rooms with bath. Facilities: heated pool, room service, 24-hr staff, in-room safe, free off-street parking. AE, MC, V. Very Expensive.*

Guest Houses

★ **The Curry Mansion Inn.** Careful dedication to detail by Key West architect Thomas Pope and owners Al and Edith Amsterdam have produced a near-perfect match between the Victorian Curry Mansion (1899) and its modern bed-and-breakfast addition. Each room has a different color scheme of tropical pastels; all rooms have carpeted floors, wicker headboards and furnishings, and quilts from the Cotton Gin Store at MM 94.5 in Tavernier. Rooms 1 and 8 are honeymoon suites with canopy beds and balconies. *511 Caroline St., 33040, tel. 305/294–5349. 15 rooms with bath, 2 rooms for handicapped guests. Facilities: pool, in-room safes, wet bars, wheelchair lift. Guests have privileges at Pier House Beach Club. AE, CB, DC, MC, V. Expensive.*

Eaton Lodge. Long one of Key West's best, Eaton Lodge was sold late in 1989 and has gone through a complete change that has made it even better. New owners are potter–baker–pastry chef Mark Anderson from Edinburgh and artist Val Roy Gerischer from Los Angeles. Mr. Gerischer was head designer for Boehm Porcelain, then was with Lenox China, and the Franklin Mint. His botanical and bird prints, and the partners' antiques lend polish to the eight rooms of the main house and four in adjoining coach house. The gardens are being restored to make them again the prize they were when planted by Dr. Warren, the original owner, more than 100 years ago. He founded the island's garden club. *511 Eaton St., 33040, tel. 305/*

294–3800. 12 rooms with bath. Facilities: whirlpool spa. Airport pickup service in London taxi. MC, V. Very Expensive.

Island City House. This guest house is actually three separate buildings: the vintage-1880s Island City House and Arch House (a former carriage house) and a 1970s reconstruction of an old cigar factory that once stood on the site. Guests share a private tropical garden. *422 William St., 33040, tel. 305/294–5702 or 800/634–8230. 24 parlor suites with bath and kitchen. Facilities: pool, Jacuzzi, bike rental. AE, MC, V. Expensive.*

The Mermaid & The Alligator. This is a homey bed-and-breakfast convenient to the center of town. The original 1904 structure of Dade County pine recently underwent extensive restoration. The Garden Room, the only downstairs room, has Japanese wall hangings, a white paddlefan, and a private doorway to the garden. Upstairs, the Blue Room (also known as the honeymoon suite) has a canopied Charleston four-poster bed with a rice pattern, a Roman-style tub, and a balcony overlooking St. Mary's by the Sea Catholic Church. The South West Suite, under the eaves on the third floor, has the only air conditioner in the house. *729 Truman Ave., 33040, tel. 305/294–1894. 5 rooms with bath. No children under 16. Facilities: heated Jacuzzi. AE, MC, V. Moderate.*

★ **The Watson House.** Small in number of rooms but big in amenities, this guest house provides utmost privacy with Duval Street convenience. It's one block from the bustle but light years from the hassle. Ed Czaplicki with partner Joe Beres has restored the house to its 1860s Bahamian look that guests find caressingly soothing. The three units are the deco Cabana Suite by the two-tier pool gardens, the William Suite on the second floor of the house, and the connecting or private Susan Room. French doors and gingerbread dress up the pristine yellow-and-white exterior. *525 Simonton St., 30040, tel. 305/294–6712. 2 suites with bath and full kitchen, one room with bath. Facilities: heated pool, whirlpool, off-street parking. AE, MC, V. Expensive–Very Expensive.*

The Arts and Nightlife

The Arts

The Keys are more than warm weather and luminous scenery—a vigorous and sophisticated artistic community flourishes here. Key West alone currently claims among its residents 55 full-time writers and 500 painters and craftsmen. Arts organizations in the Keys sponsor many special events, some lasting only a weekend, others spanning an entire season.

The monthly ***Island Navigator,*** Monroe County's only countywide general-interest newspaper, is free at banks, campgrounds, and convenience stores. Its monthly community calendar lists cultural and sports events.

Three free publications covering Key West arts, music, and literature are available at hotels and other high-traffic areas:

The weekly ***Island Life,*** the most current and complete, is published by JBM Publications. *517 Duval St., Suite 200, Key West 33040, tel. 305/294–1616. Subscription by mail: $18/year.* ***Entertainment Key West,*** a biweekly, and ***Solares Hill,*** a monthly community newspaper, are published by Solares Hill Co., Inc. (4 Key Lime Sq., Key West 33040, tel. 305/294–3602). In the Upper and Middle Keys, the weekly ***Free Press*** is available at hotels, motels, and retail outlets. *Box 469, Islamorada 33036, tel. 305/664–2266. Subscription by mail: $3/month.*

Theater

Jan McArt's Cabaret Theater at Mallory Square. In a brick wrecker's warehouse built in 1879 and restored in 1986, Jan McArt has established a 300-seat theater for Equity and nonEquity musical productions. (McArt also operates Jan McArt's Royal Palm Dinner Theater in Boca Raton.) *410 Wall St., Box 4866, Key West, tel. 305/296–2120, 800/346–3240 (FL), or 800/356–8217 (US). Closed Mon. AE, MC, V.*

Red Barn Theater. This nonEquity, 94-seat theater in its 11th year performs dramas and musical comedies, including plays by new playwrights. *319 Duval St., Key West, tel. 305/296–9911. Closed some Mon. No credit cards.*

Waterfront Playhouse. This mid-1850s wrecker's warehouse was converted into an 185-seat nonEquity community theater that specializes in comedy and drama. *Mallory Sq., Key West, tel. 305/294–5015. Open Dec.–May. No credit cards.*

Tennessee Williams Fine Arts Center. A 490-seat theater built in 1980 on Stock Island, BS, the center presents chamber music, dance, jazz concerts, plays (dramatic and musical) with national and international stars, and other performing-arts events. *Florida Keys Community College, 5901 Junior College Rd., Key West, tel. 305/294–6232. Open Nov.–Apr. MC, V.*

Nightlife

Key Largo

Coconuts Restaurant and Bar. The soft island music during dinner changes to top 40 after 10 PM. The outdoor bar at the marina is popular with the under-30 crowd. To find Coconuts from U.S. 1, turn OS at the Texaco station at Laguna Avenue, then left at the first intersection onto Caribbean Boulevard and continue about 100 yards. *MM 100, OS, in the Marina Del Mar Resort and Marina, tel. 305/451–4107. Open weekdays noon–4 AM, weekends 11–4 AM. AE, CB, DC, MC, V.*

Key West

Cafe Exile. When everyone else on Duval Street closes, Cafe Exile is still going strong. You can get an espresso or cappuccino here nearly 24 hours a day—though sometimes not between 4 and 7 AM when the place is being cleaned. The menu is American as Key-lime pie, but the ambience is decidedly Continental—an outdoor courtyard with a white fence, brick sidewalk, banyan trees festooned with white Italian lights, and umbrellas sheltering the tables. The Rum Runner is the most popular drink. There is jazz nightly 8 PM–1 AM; local musicians join the group. An adjoining indoor nightclub, Backstreet at Exile, is open 10 PM–4 AM. *700 Duval St., tel. 305/296–0991. Food service 8 AM–5 AM, bar service 8 AM–4 AM. No credit cards.*

Capt. Tony's Saloon. While tourists flock to Sloppy Joe's, a predominantly local crowd enjoys old-style Key West nightlife at this bar a block away in an 1852 structure first used as a morgue and ice house. Later it was Key West's first telegraph station. It got its name from Capt. Tony Tarracino who sold it in 1988 and was elected mayor of Key West the next year. Old business cards and T-shirts cover the walls and ceiling. Coral Reef, the house drink, contains a secret rum-based formula. Live country and rhythm-and-blues entertainment is featured nightly; Jimmy Buffet got his start here. *428 Greene St., tel. 305/294–1838. Open 11 AM–4 AM. No credit cards.*

Coconuts. This is the southernmost of the Sunshine Comedy Club Network. The room is decorated with photos of nationally known comedians, including Chevy Chase, Bill Murray, and Eddie Murphy. Two veteran stand-up comics perform. *2407 N.*

Roosevelt Blvd., tel. 305/294–8882. Show time: 9 PM Wed.–Sat. Cover charge: $5. AE, MC, V.

Havana Docks Lounge. A high-energy disco club popular with young locals and visitors, this lounge is in the old William R. Porter Docks Shipping Office, now part of the Pier House hotel. The Havana Docks deck is a good place to watch the sun set when Mallory Square gets too crowded. *1 Duval St., tel. 305/296–4600 or 800/432–3414 (FL). Open Sun.–Thurs. 4 PM–2 AM, Fri.–Sat. 4 PM–4 AM, though sometimes closing at 2 AM. AE, MC, V.*

Margaritaville Cafe. This place is owned by Key West resident and MCA recording star Jimmy Buffett, who performs here several times a year. The menu, which changes often, includes Jimmy's grandmother's recipes. The house special drink is, of course, a margarita. *500 Duval St., tel. 305/292–1435. Open 11 AM–4 AM; Sun. 11:30–4 AM. Live music Tues.–Sun. Cover charge for special events. AE, MC, V.*

Sloppy Joe's. Named for its founder, Capt. Joe Russell, Sloppy Joe's started as a speakeasy. Ernest Hemingway liked to gamble in a partitioned club room in back. After Hemingway's death, the original manuscript of *To Have and Have Not*, sections of *Death in the Afternoon, The Fifth Column*, and notes for *A Farewell to Arms* were found among personal papers he had stored at the bar. Decorated with Hemingway memorabilia and marine flags, the bar is popular with tourists and is full and noisy all the time. There is live entertainment from noon to 2 AM by local and touring groups. *201 Duval St., Key West, tel. 305/294–5717. Dress: shoes and shirt required. No reservations. All customers must show proof of age at night. Open 9 AM–4 AM. Usually a $1 cover charge after 8 PM. No credit cards.*

The Top Lounge. Located on the seventh floor of the La Concha Holiday Inn, Key West's tallest building, this is one of the best places from which to view the sunset. The Top features live jazz nightly. *430 Duval St., tel. 305/296–2991 or 800/227–6151 (FL). Open 11 AM–2 AM. AE, CB, DC, MC, V.*

8 Disney World and the Orlando Area

Introduction

by David Wilkening

A freelance writer who lives in Orlando, David Wilkening is a contributing editor of Orlando Magazine. *He writes for several local and national publications, including travel books and travel magazines.*

Orlando, a high-profile city of fast growth boosted by a robust business climate and thriving tourist trade, seems to be an area touched by pixie dust. A magical city. But it was not always that way.

A military outpost was established here in 1838, and the area became known as Fort Gatlin. In 1850, that name gave way to Jernigan, in deference to one of the region's most prosperous residents. It wasn't until 1875 that the one-square-mile-wide city was incorporated as Orlando. There are various theories why the name was chosen, but the most popular is that the new city was named after Orlando Reeves, a soldier killed fighting the Seminole Indians.

Upon its incorporation, Orlando had less than 100 residents. The town had no seaport or major waterway. There was no railroad to spur its growth. There was little to stimulate or sustain any prosperity. But Orlando had a sunny year-round climate. And it had something else—a location in the very center of what would become one of the fastest-growing states in the country.

Citrus and cattle were the dominant industries in Orlando's early years. The English arrived in the mid-1860s, bringing with them tennis, polo, and afternoon tea. The great freezes of 1884 and 1885 virtually ruined the citrus industry, and traditional farming returned. Orlando remained a clean, sleepy, handsome city, known for its lakes and for its sprawling oak trees planted by northerners who wanted to remember the world they had left behind.

In the 1950s, large corporations gave the area a solid business base on which to build. Today, in large part because of Walt Disney World, Orlando is known for its tourism. But it's also a growing center of national and international business activity.

In its graceful and quiet past Orlando enjoyed a small-town pace that earned it the title of "The City Beautiful." The city today is far more metropolitan, even cosmopolitan, but much of the original charm remains. Many residents have homes near the hundreds of clear spring-fed lakes, far from the south Orlando-based tourist corridor. The aroma here is often that of orange blossoms and citrus trees. The city has retained its parklike atmosphere.

The population of the greater metropolitan area that includes Orange, Seminole, and Osceola counties is now approaching one million. Various surveys cite the greater Orlando area as among the fastest growing in the country.

With all its business activity, however, Orlando is better known as the world's Number One tourist destination. Disneyland had long been a successful staple in California when Disney decided, in the early 1960s, to build another theme park in the eastern United States. By 1963, Florida was chosen as the best state. Orlando was chosen for a variety of reasons, including its transportation system and its large amounts of open, available land.

By 1964, property was quietly purchased. Eventually, a huge tract of 28,000 acres was bought. But, it wasn't until late 1965

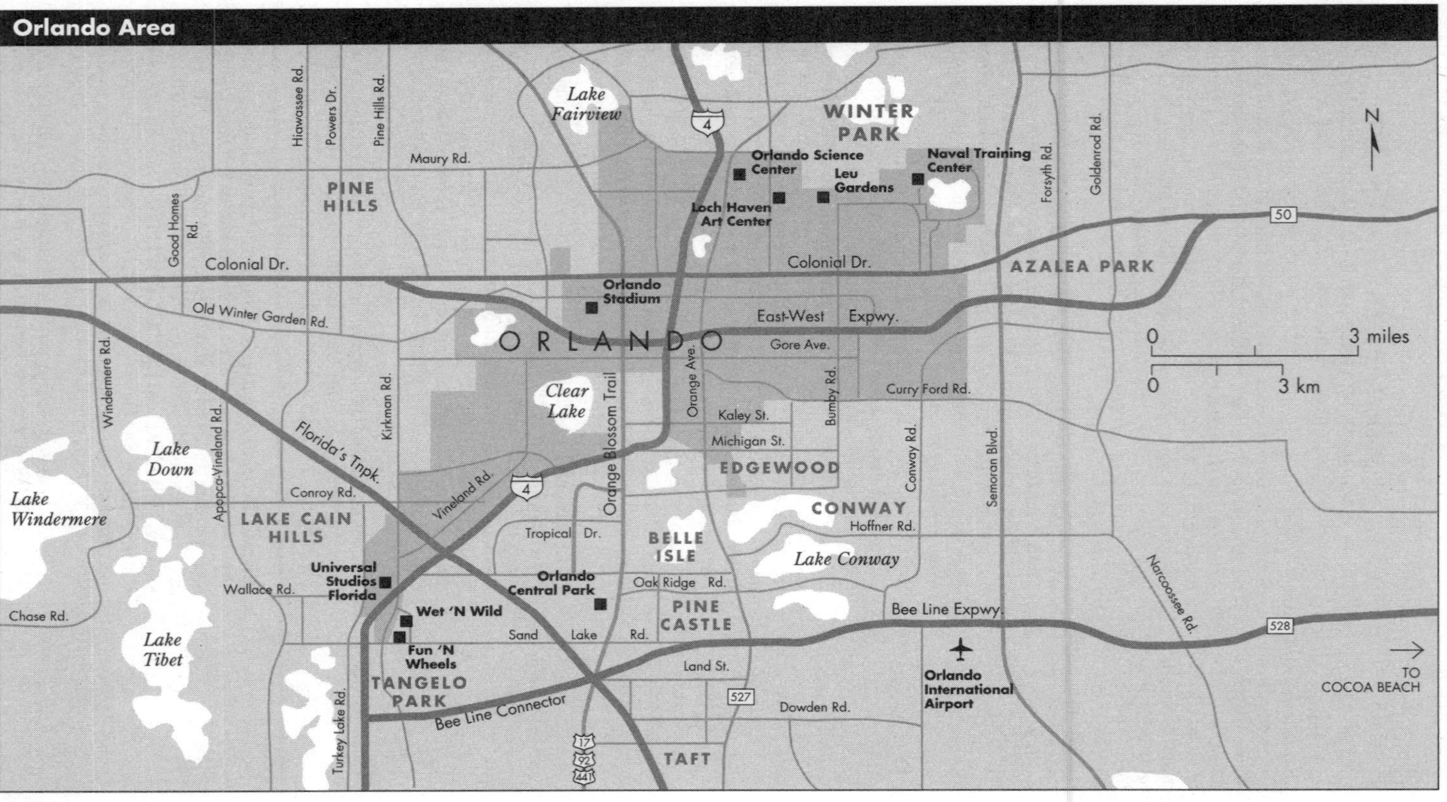
Orlando Area
Lake Fairview
WINTER PARK
Orlando Science Center
Leu Gardens
Naval Training Center
Loch Haven Art Center
Hiawassee Rd.
Powers Dr.
Pine Hills Rd.
Maury Rd.
PINE HILLS
Good Homes Rd.
Forsyth Rd.
Goldenrod Rd.
50
Colonial Dr.
AZALEA PARK
Orlando Stadium
Old Winter Garden Rd.
East-West Expwy.
ORLANDO
Gore Ave.
0 3 miles
0 3 km
N
Windermere Rd.
Apopca-Vineland Rd.
Kirkman Rd.
Clear Lake
Orange Blossom Trail
Orange Ave.
Bumby Rd.
Curry Ford Rd.
Kaley St.
Michigan St.
EDGEWOOD
Conway Rd.
Semoran Blvd.
Lake Down
Florida's Tnpk.
Vineland Rd.
4
Conroy Rd.
CONWAY
Hoffner Rd.
Lake Windermere
LAKE CAIN HILLS
Tropical Dr.
BELLE ISLE
Lake Conway
Narcoossee Rd.
Universal Studios Florida
Orlando Central Park
Oak Ridge Rd.
Wallace Rd.
Chase Rd.
Wet 'N Wild
Sand Lake Rd.
PINE CASTLE
Bee Line Expwy.
528
Lake Tibet
Fun 'N Wheels
Land St.
Orlando International Airport
TO COCOA BEACH
TANGELO PARK
Bee Line Connector
527
Dowden Rd.
Turkey Lake Rd.
17
92
441
TAFT

that news reports leaked out that Disney was buying those parcels of land in anticipation of a large-scale theme park.

The accumulation of the land, often in small parcels purchased by agents working silently for Disney, was a dramatic story in itself. But seeing how the surrounding tourist areas around his California park had suffered rampant commercial sprawl, Disney was determined to buy enough land in Orlando to prevent that from happening again. This time, he would have **control** of the surrounding area.

On November 16, 1965, Walt Disney outlined his dream of an innovative working and living center that would provide a new way of life. He called it Experimental Prototype Community of Tomorrow (EPCOT). The first phase: the Magic Kingdom and a vacation complex. Walt Disney died the next year and never saw his dream come true. But construction began in 1969 on the park, which opened in 1971. New attractions were added continually, and, by the end of the fifth year, almost 11 million visitors annually were parading through the Magic Kingdom.

Plans were announced for another phase of the Disney master plan in 1975. That was EPCOT. On October 1, 1982, Epcot Center, as it is now called, opened its gates. It was not a quiet opening but included a month-long celebration that featured the West Point Glee Club, the 450-piece All American Marching Band, and World Showcase Festival performers representing 23 countries. The Epcot Center that emerged after Disney's death was not the one he envisioned—a living, working community set next to theme parks—apparently because it was later determined that the concept was not practical. But Epcot Center, standing on its own, was an immediate success. Almost 23 million visitors passed through its gates the very first year.

Walt Disney World added Disney-MGM Studios Theme Park in 1989. This park spans 135 acres and offers visitors an opportunity to get behind the scenes and sometimes in front of the cameras at a working movie and television studio reminiscent of Hollywood in the 1930s and '40s.

And for those visitors who want to dip their toes or their fishing lines into the ocean, the Cocoa Beach area is less than an hour from Orlando.

Arriving and Departing

By Plane More than 29 scheduled airlines operate in and out of Orlando's airport, with direct service to more than 100 U.S. cities. At last count, Delta, the official airline of Disney World, had 70 flights to and from the airport every day! Travel packages to Disney World are offered by Delta (tel. 800/872–7786) and Pan Am (tel. 800/843–8687).

Major U.S. airlines that serve Orlando include American, Braniff, British Airways, Continental, Delta, Eastern, Icelandair, KLM, Midway, Northwest, Pan Am, TWA, United, and USAir.

Between the Airport and the Hotels You can catch a public bus between the airport and downtown Orlando, which goes to and from the main terminal of **Tri-County Transit Authority** (438 Woods Ave., Orlando, tel. 407/841–8240). The cost is 75¢. Transfers are 10¢. The downtown area, however, is far from most hotels, so you might want to consider other options. **Airport Limousine Service of Orlando** (tel. 407/423–5566) sends 11-passenger vans to Disney World and along Rte. 192 every 30 minutes. Prices range from $12 one-way for adults and $7 for children 4–11 to $21 round-trip for adults and $11 for children 4–11. **Town & Country Limo** (tel. 407/828–3035) and **First Class Transportation** (tel. 407/578–0022) also offer limousine service between the airport and WDW. The trip takes about 35 minutes. **Suncoast Shuttle** (tel. 407/676–4557; in FL, 800/226–4557 or outside FL, 800/762–5466) services the Cocoa Beach area. One-way fares are $15, round-trip is $28. Suncoast Shuttle also provides round-trip service from the Space Coast to the major attractions. Round-trip to Walt Disney World is $28.

By Taxi Taxis are the fastest way to travel (25–30 minutes to hotels), but the ride won't be cheap. To Walt Disney World hotels or to hotels along West 192, a cab trip will cost about $35 plus tip. To the International Drive area, it will cost about $25 plus tip.

By Car When leaving the airport, a left turn onto the Beeline Expressway (Rte. 528) leads you past Sea World to I–4. A left turn on I–4 takes you to Walt Disney World Village and Epcot Center or to U.S. 192 and the Magic Kingdom entrance. A right turn on I–4 from the Beeline takes you past Highway 482 and into downtown Orlando. A right turn on the Bee Line from the airport takes you to the Atlantic Ocean coast and connects with the three major north–south ocean coast highways: I–95, U.S. 1, and S.R. A1A.

By Train **Amtrak** (tel. 800/USA–RAIL) Autotrain stops at Sanford (600 Persimmon Blvd.), and the passenger service makes stops at Sanford (800 Persimmon Blvd.), Winter Park (150 Morse Blvd.), Orlando (1400 Sligh Blvd.), and then, 20 minutes later, in Kissimmee (416 Pleasant St.).

By Bus Contact **Greyhound/Trailways** (tel. 407/843–7720) or consult your phone book or directory assistance for a local number that will automatically connect you with the national Greyhound/Trailways Information Center.

Getting Around

By Car The most important artery in the Orlando area is **Interstate 4 (I–4),** which many locals simply refer to as "the Expressway." This interstate ties everything together, and you'll invariably receive directions in reference to it. The problem is that I–4 is considered an east-west expressway in our national road system (the even numbers refer to an east-west orientation, the odd numbers to a north-south orientation). I–4 does run from east to west *if* you follow it from the Atlantic Coast to Florida's Gulf of Mexico. But in the Orlando area, I–4 actually runs north-south. Always remember, therefore, that when the signs say east, you are often going north, and when the signs say west, you are often going south. Think north-east and south-west. Another main drag is **International Drive,** which has several major hotels, restaurants, and shopping centers. You can get onto International Drive from I–4 Exits 28, 29, and 30B.

The other main road, Irlo Bronson Memorial Highway (U.S. 192), cuts across I–4 at Exits 25A and 25B. This highway goes through the Kissimmee area and crosses Walt Disney World property.

By Bus If you are staying along International Drive, in Kissimmee, or in Orlando proper, you can take advantage of the limited public bus system, but only to get places locally. To find out which bus to take, ask your hotel clerk or call the Tri-County Transit Authority Information Office (tel. 407/841–8240) during business hours. A transfer will add 10¢ to the regular 75¢ fare.

By Taxi Taxi fares start at $2.45 and cost $1.30 for each mile thereafter. Call **Yellow Cab Co.** (tel. 407/699–9999) or **Town and Country Cab** (tel. 407/828–3035).

Guided Tours

General-Interest Tours **Globus Gateway/Cosmos** (150 S. Los Robles Ave., Suite 860, Pasadena, CA 91101, tel. 818/449–0919 or 800/556–5454) offers a comprehensive eight-day tour that includes entry to Disney World. If you live on the East Coast of the country, **Domenico Tours** (751 Broadway, Bayonne, NJ 07002, tel. 201/823–8687 or 800/554–TOUR) will take you to Orlando via coach tour or direct flight; from the west, it's air only.

Special-Interest Tours **Carnival Cruise Lines.** (Tel. 800/327–7373.) Three- and four-day cruises go to the Bahamas aboard *Carnivale*.

Boat Tours **Rivership Romance.** A 110-foot, triple-decker catamaran takes visitors up the cypress-lined, densely forested St. John's River for either a few hours or a couple of days. The day trips take you through a peaceful, tropical landscape. You may see some interesting wildlife, such as manatees (the endangered sea cows), blue herons, and bald eagles, but most of the time you'll be listening to the silence. The cost ranges from $26.25 to $40 per person ($223 for the overnight trip), including some meals. *Monroe Harbour, 433 N. Palmetto Ave., Sanford (from I–4 take Exit 51 and drive east 4 mi), tel. 407/321–5091 or 800/423–7401. Dress: casual. Reservations required. AE, MC, V. Moderate.*

Balloon Tours **Balloon Flights of Florida.** This Church Street Station event is not cheap, but it's an experience you'll never forget. The flight, led by a balloonist who made the first trip across the Atlantic, is followed by brunch at Lili Marlene's. *124 W. Pine St., Orlando, tel. 407/841–UPUP. $140 per person.*

Rise and Float Balloon Tours. Depart at dawn and indulge yourself with an in-flight champagne breakfast. *5767 Major Blvd., Orlando, tel. 407/352–8191. $250 to $325 per couple.*

Helicopter Tours **J.C. Helicopters.** Sign up for aerial tours of Walt Disney World, Sea World, and other attractions. The flights at dark are spectacular. *Orlando Hyatt Heliport at I–4 and U.S. 192 (next to Walt Disney World), tel. 407/857–7222. Prices start at $35 adults, $20 children.*

Important Addresses and Numbers

Visitors to **Mickey's Kingdom** can direct all inquiries to Walt Disney World (Box 10040, Lake Buena Vista, 32830, Attention: Guest letters, tel. 407/824–4321.) Request a free copy of the *Walt Disney World Vacation Guide.*

For information on the greater Orlando area, contact the **Tourist Information Center** (8445 International Drive, Orlando

32819, tel. 407/363–5871). Open 8-8. Ask for the free *Discover Orlando* guidebook.

Visitors to the Kissimmee area on U.S. 192 can get brochures from the **Kissimmee/St. Cloud Convention and Visitors' Bureau,** 1925 E. Spacecoast Hwy., E. U.S. 192, Kissimmee 32742, tel. 407/847–5000, in FL 800/432–9199, outside FL 800/327–9159.

Visitors can get information from the **Cocoa Beach Area Chamber of Commerce,** 400 Fortenberry Road, Merritt Island, tel. 407/459–2200.

Emergency Dial 911 for **police** and **ambulance** in an emergency.

Doctors Hospital emergency rooms are open 24 hours a day. The most accessible hospital, located in the International Drive area, is the **Orlando Regional Medical Center/Sand Lake Hospital** (9400 Turkey Lake Rd., tel. 407/351–8500).

For hotel-room visits by physicians for minor medical care, contact a mobile minor emergency service called **Housemed** (tel. 407/648–9234 or 407/846–2093 in Kissimmee).

On the coast, **Cape Canaveral Hospital** is on the Highway 520 Causeway between Cocoa Beach and Merritt Island (tel. 407/799–7150).

24-Hour Pharmacies **Eckerd Drugs** (908 Lee Rd., Orlando, tel. 407/644–6908). **Walgreen Drug Store** (2410 E. Colonial Dr., Orlando, tel. 407/894–6781).

Road Service **AAA Emergency Road Service** (tel. 407/896–1166 or 800/824–4432).

Disney World Walt Disney World Information, tel. 407/824–4321.
Accommodations Reservations, tel. 407/W–DISNEY.
Dinner Show Reservations, tel. 407/W–DISNEY.
Walt Disney World Resort Dining/Recreation Information, tel. 407/824–3737.
Tours: Magic Kingdom, Epcot Center, and Disney-MGM, tel. 407/827–8233.
Magic Kingdom Lost and Found, tel. 407/824–4521.
Epcot Center Lost and Found, tel. 407/560–6105.
Disney-MGM Lost and Found, tel. 407/420–4668.
Central Lost and Found, tel. 407/824–4245.
Car Care Center, tel. 407/824–4813.
Western Union at Walt Disney World, tel. 407/824–3456.
Banking Information (Sun Bank), tel. 407/824–5767.
Time and Weather, tel. 407/422–1611.
Walt Disney World Shopping Village Information, tel. 407/828–3058.
KinderCare Child Care, tel. 407/827–5444, private babysitting; 407/827–5437, group sitting.

Exploring Walt Disney World and the Orlando Area

Walt Disney World has its own complete transportation system to get you wherever you want to go. Yet because the property is so extensive—28,000 acres, 98 of them for the Magic Kingdom, 260 for Epcot Center, and another 135 for Disney-MGM—the system can be a bit confusing, even for an experienced visitor. Best-known is the elevated monorail, which connects Walt Disney World's biggest resorts and attractions. There are also extensive bus, motor-launch, and ferry systems. If you are staying at an on-site resort or a Walt Disney World Village hotel or if you hold a combination Magic Kingdom-Epcot Center ticket, transportation is free. If not, you can buy unlimited transportation within Walt Disney World for $2.50 a day.

By Monorail This elevated train of the future operates daily 7:30 AM–11 PM (or until 1 hour after the Magic Kingdom closes). It does not go everywhere. The central connecting station for the monorail is called the **Transportation and Ticket Center** (TTC). One monorail line goes from the TTC to the Magic Kingdom and back in a loop around Seven Seas Lagoon. This line is primarily for visitors who are not guests at the on-site resorts. Another line connects the TTC with the Contemporary Resort, the Magic Kingdom, the Grand Floridian, and the Polynesian. A third line goes directly from the TTC to Epcot Center. The TTC is where you can transfer between the Disney bus system and the monorail. When you get to a monorail station, ask an attendant if you can sit in the conductor's cabin, called "the nose" by the crew.

By Bus Each bus carries a small color-coded or letter-coded pennant on the front and sides. Here's where the buses take you:

Green—Connects Disney Inn and Polynesian Village Resort with the TTC. This line operates every 15 minutes 7 AM–2 AM.

Blue—Connects Fort Wilderness Resort Area with the TTC. These buses operate every eight minutes 7 AM–2 AM.

Green-and-Gold—If the pennant has the letters EC on it, the bus connects Epcot, the Resort Villas, and Disney Village Clubhouse. If the bus has the letters MK on it, it travels only between the TTC and the villas. If the bus has ST/V on it, the bus connects Disney-MGM, Disney Village Marketplace, Pleasure Island, the Resort Villas, and Disney Village Clubhouse. These lines operate every 20 minutes: EC from 8 AM to 2 AM; MK from 7 AM to 2 AM; and ST/V from 8 AM to two hours after Disney-MGM closes.

Red-and-White—Connects Walt Disney World Village Hotel Plaza with the theme parks and Pleasure Island about every 20 minutes beginning at 8 AM and running until two hours after the respective parks close. EC goes to Epcot, MK to the TTC for the Magic Kingdom, and ST goes to Disney-MGM. The V bus connects with Pleasure Island and operates between 6 PM and 2 AM.

Red—Connects TTC, Disney Village Marketplace, Epcot, and Typhoon Lagoon between 8 AM and 2 AM. It includes Pleasure Island from 4 PM to 2:30 AM. The line operates on 15- to 25-minute intervals.

Gold—Connects the Grand Floridian, Polynesian Resort, and Contemporary Resort with the TTC at 15- to 25-minute intervals from 7 AM to 2 AM.

Orange-and-White Stripe—If the pennant has the letters MK on it, the bus connects Caribbean Beach Resort with the TTC from 8 AM until 2 AM. If the bus has the letters EC on it, it connects Epcot and Caribbean Beach Resort from 8 AM to two hours after Epcot closes. If the pennant is ST, the bus connects Caribbean Beach Resort with Disney-MGM from 8 AM to 2 AM. If the letter is V, the bus connects Caribbean Beach Resort with Disney Marketplace and Typhoon Lagoon between 8 AM and 2:30 AM, and includes Pleasure Island from 4 PM to 2:30 AM. These lines run at 15- to 25-minute intervals.

Purple-and-Gold—These buses service the Walt Disney World Swan and the three major parks: EC to Epcot, MK to TTC, and ST to Disney-MGM from 8 AM until two hours after the respective parks close.

Gold-and-Black—The STE bus takes a Disney-MGM, Fort Wilderness, Contemporary Resort route, while the STW bus stops at Disney-MGM, the Polynesian Village, the Grand Floridian, and Disney Inn. Both routes run from 8 AM until two hours after the park closes.

Blue-and-White—The EC connects Disney-MGM with Epcot from 8 AM until two hours after the park closes, and the MK connects Disney-MGM with TTC between 8 AM and 2 AM.

Brown—A Fort Wilderness Transportation Circle line. It connects the Trading Post, Trail Blaze Corral, the Outpost, Loops 600–1300, Loops 2100–2800, and the Meadow Recreation Complex from 7 AM to 2 AM at 15- to 25-minute intervals.

Silver—Another Fort Wilderness Transportation Circle line. It connects Creekside Meadow Group Camping with Loops 300–500 and Loops 1400–2300 from 7:30 AM to 2 AM at 15- to 25-minute intervals.

Orange—The Caribbean Beach Resort internal transportation line operates from 7 AM to 2 AM about every 20 minutes.

Orange (tram)—The tram connects River Country to its parking lot operating during River Country hours. If you are staying at one of the Epcot Center resorts, check with your hotel concierge for new bus routes and schedules.

By Motor Launch These boats depart about every 20 minutes and use color-coded flags to identify their routes. They are for the use of Disney resort guests only, with the exception of day guests with special activity tickets to such places as Discovery Island and River Country.

Blue—Connects the Contemporary Resort with the Fort Wilderness Resort Area and Discovery Island every 15 minutes 9 AM-10 PM.

Gold—Connects the Grand Floridian, Magic Kingdom, and Polynesian Resort at 15- to 25-minute intervals from half an hour before the Magic Kingdom opens until it closes, with pickup only from the Magic Kingdom until the park clears.

Green—Connects the Magic Kingdom, Fort Wilderness Resort Area, and Discovery Island (when it is open) every 20–25 minutes from half an hour before opening until closing time.

By Ferry A ferry service runs across Seven Seas Lagoon connecting the TTC with the Magic Kingdom. They depart from each side of the lagoon about every 12 minutes when the Magic Kingdom is open. They often get you to the Magic Kingdom faster than does the monorail. It is a comfortable ride, gliding over the lagoon's silky waters. Most people heading for the Magic Kingdom opt for the monorail and then take the ferry back at day's end, so if you want to avoid the worst of the lines for both the monorail and ferry, take the opposite tack.

By Water Taxi Plans are for a water taxi to be on line this year connecting the Epcot Center Resorts with Disney-MGM.

By Car If you arrive at either the Magic Kingdom, Epcot, or Disney-MGM by car, there is a $3 parking charge. If you're staying at a Disney World hotel, show your guest ID for free parking. Remember or write down *exactly* where you park; you'll have a long wait before the sea of automobiles has departed and yours is the only one left. Trams make frequent trips between the parking areas and the front gate.

Car Care: If your car won't start or it breaks down in Disney World, the **Car Care Center** (tel. 407/824–4813) near the Toll Plaza to the Magic Kingdom offers emergency road service. Open weekdays 7 AM–5:30 PM. The gas islands stay open 90 minutes after the Magic Kingdom closes. If you need to drop your car off to be serviced, there is free shuttle service around the park.

Admission Visiting Walt Disney World is not cheap, especially if you have a child or two along. There are no discounted family tickets. Fourteen different types of admission tickets are sold in one of two categories—adult, meaning everyone aged 10 and older, and children aged 3–9. Children under age 3 get in free.

The word "ticket" is used by Disney World only to mean a single day's admission to the Magic Kingdom, Epcot, or the Disney-MGM Studios Theme Park. The price is $29 for adults and $23 for children. If you want to spend two or three days visiting the attractions, you have to buy a separate ticket each day. For more than three days, Disney World offers what it calls the All Three Parks Passport, which admits you to all three parks, along with unlimited use of the internal transportation system.

Here is a list of prices. They are subject to change, so call for confirmation.

One-day ticket	$31 adults, $25 children
Four-day passport	$100 adults, $80 children
Five-day passport	$117 adults, $95 children
Annual Pass (new)	$180 adults, $155 children*
Annual Pass (renewal)	$160 adults, $135 children*
Annual Pass (charter renewal)	$140 adults, $115 children*
River Country, one day	$11.75 adults, $9.25 children; *$10.75/ $8.25*
River Country, two days	$17.75 adults, $13.75 children; *$16.75/ $12.75*
River Country annual pass	$50 adults and children
Combined River Country/Discovery Island, one day	$15 adults, $11 children; *$14/$10*

Discovery Island, one day	$7.50 adults, $4 children
Typhoon Lagoon, one day	$17.50 adults, $14 children; *$15.50/ $12.50*
Typhoon Lagoon, two days	$29 adults, $23 children; *$25/$20*
Typhoon Lagoon annual pass	$75 adults and children

*An additional $15 (adults) and $11 (children) entitles passholders to unlimited use of River Country and Discovery Island for the duration of their annual pass.

Italics indicate prices for visitors staying in a Disney World resort or in a resort in the WDW Village Hotel Plaza.

Passports are available for four or five days. They can save you a great deal of money and may be advisable even if you're staying in the area for only two days. Each time you use a Passport, the entry date is stamped on it; the remaining days may be used any time in the future. If you buy a one-day ticket and later decide to extend your visit, you can get full credit for it toward the purchase of any Passport. Exchanges can be made at City Hall in the Magic Kingdom, at Earth Station in Epcot, or at Guest Relations at Disney-MGM. Do this before leaving the park; once you've left, the ticket is worthless.

Tickets and Passports to Walt Disney World and Epcot Center may be purchased at admission booths at the TTC, in on-site or Hotel Plaza resorts (if you're a registered guest), or at the Walt Disney World kiosk on the second floor of the main terminal at Orlando International Airport. If you want to buy tickets before you arrive in Orlando, send a check or money order to Admissions, Walt Disney World, Box 10000, Lake Buena Vista, 32830. Remember, it usually takes four to six weeks for the order to be processed, so write well in advance.

If you want to leave the Magic Kingdom or Epcot Center and return on the same day, be sure to have your hand stamped on the way out. You'll need your ticket *and* the hand stamp to be readmitted.

Operating Hours Hours vary widely throughout the year and change for school and legal holidays. In general, the longest hours are during the summer months, when the Magic Kingdom is open until midnight, Epcot Center is open to 11 PM, and Disney-MGM is open to 9 PM. At other times of year, Epcot Center and Disney-MGM are open until 8 PM, and the Magic Kingdom to 6 PM, with Main Street remaining open until 7. Though each park usually opens at 9 AM, visitors can enter the grounds up to an hour earlier and get a significant head start on the crowds. A good bet for breakfast before 9 AM is the **Crystal Palace** in the Magic Kingdom (turn left at the end of Main St.). For current hours, tel. 407/ 824–4321.

When to Go The busiest days of the week are Monday, Tuesday, and Wednesday. You would think the weekend would be busiest, but it's not. Perhaps everyone tries to beat the crowds by going in the early part of the week, or perhaps vacationers leave on Friday, travel over the weekend, and begin their visits on Mon-

Walt Disney World

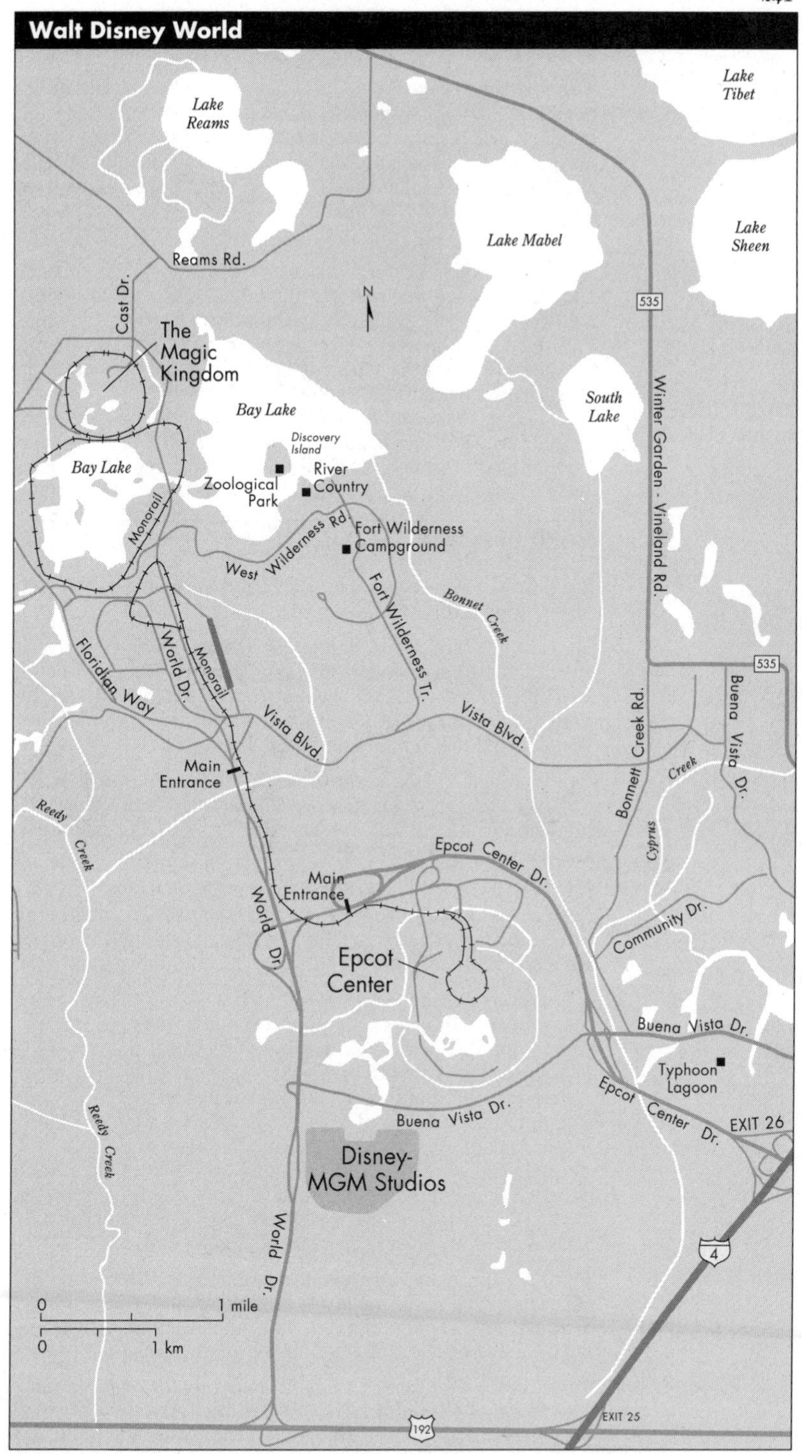

day. Whatever the reason, Friday and Sunday are the slowest days, and Thursdays and Saturdays are only moderately busy.

The best time of the day to be at the parks is in the late afternoon and evening—especially during the summer months and holidays, when the attractions stay open late. It also helps to arrive as soon as the gates open, up to an hour before the "official" opening time. The most crowded time of the year is from Christmas through New Year's Day. The parks are also packed around Easter.

Memorial Day weekend is not only crowded, but hot. Other busy times of the year are mid-June–mid-August, Thanksgiving weekend, the week of Washington's Birthday in mid-February, and the weeks of college spring break in late March. The rest of the year is generally hassle-free, particularly from early September until just before Thanksgiving. The best time of all is from just after Thanksgiving weekend until the beginning of the Christmas holidays. Another excellent time is from early January through the first week of February. If you must go during summer, late August is best.

Magic Kingdom

You'll first see Town Square. City Hall is on your left. The railroad station is directly behind you.

Sprawling before you is Main Street—a shop-filled boulevard with Victorian-style stores, and dining spots. Walk two blocks along Main Street and you'll enter Central Plaza, with **Cinderella Castle** rising directly in front of you. This is the hub of the Kingdom; all the "lands" radiate out from it.

This is as good a place as any to see the daily parade at 3 PM. All Disney's characters are featured in the 20-minute show. In summer and during holidays, there's also an Electrical Parade of giant floats at 9 and 11 PM.

City Hall is a good place to pick up the *Magic Kingdom Guide Book* and a schedule of daily events. It is also the lost-and-found point for property and people. Nearby, beneath the railroad, are lockers where bags and gifts may be stored.

A great way to get an overview of the Kingdom is to hop aboard the railroad and take a 14-minute, 1½-mile ride around the perimeter of the park. You can board at the Victorian-style station you pass beneath to enter Town Square. The only other stations are at Frontierland and Mickey's Starland. The Magic Kingdom is the home of Mickey and Minnie Mouse, Goofy, Pluto, and dozens of other Disney characters. Seen on the streets, they're a child's delight, and even adults beam with pleasure as they shake hands with the fantasies they've grown up with. Characters are always willing to pose for photos. They're most often found next to City Hall.

The Magic Kingdom is divided into seven lands. Stories are told of tourists who spend an entire day in one land, thinking they have seen all the park; don't let that happen to you. The following is a selected list of Magic Kingdom attractions.

Adventureland These soft adventures to far-off lands are among the most crowded in the Kingdom. Visit as late in the afternoon as possible or, better yet, in the evening. Adventureland is the worst place to be in the morning, because other travel guides recommend it as a first stop.

Swiss Family Robinson Treehouse (popular; all ages) is a good way to get some exercise and a panoramic view of the park. Visitors walk up the many-staired tree in single file, a trip that can take up to a half hour.

Jungle Cruise (very popular; all ages) takes visitors along the Nile, across an Amazon jungle, and so on. The tour guide's narration is corny but nevertheless brings laughs. The ride itself takes only 10 minutes, but the line can take as long as an hour. Go during the parade time at 3 PM or after 5 PM. Avoid 10 AM–noon.

Pirates of the Caribbean (very popular; all ages) is a journey through a world of pirate strongholds and treasure-filled dungeons. The Audio-Animatronics pirates are first rate.

Tropical Serenade-Enchanted Tiki Birds (not very popular; for children) was one of the first Audio-Animatronic creations. The show's talking birds are somewhat charming, but the show itself can be confusing because it's difficult to tell what bird is speaking at any time. If you're in a hurry, you can safely skip this one.

Fantasyland This is a land in which storybook dreams come true and children are very much in their element.

There are a few traditional amusement-park rides with Disney themes, such as the Mad Tea Party, where teacups spin around a large teapot. Other favorites are Dumbo the Flying Elephant and a spectacular merry-go-round. There are also several indoor rides that spook and enchant children as they pass through a cartoon world filled with many familiar fairy-tale characters.

20,000 Leagues Under the Sea (very popular; all ages) is an underwater cruise inspired by the Jules Verne novel. Lines move slowly, but how often do you get to ride in a submarine and explore the world beneath the sea?

Frontierland "Frontier Fun" is the theme of this gold-rush town of the Southwest.

Big Thunder Mountain Railroad (very popular) is a scream-inducing roller coaster. Children must be at least 4′2″. For real rollercoaster fans, the ride is somewhat tame, but it's one of two fast rides in Walt Disney World (Space Mountain is the other one). Try to go in the evening when the mountain is lit up and lines are relatively short.

Country Bear Jamboree (moderately popular; for children) is a somewhat dated show with furry bears who sing and dance. A better show is put on at **Diamond Horseshow Jamboree** (popular; all ages)—a live stage show with singing, dancing, and innocently rowdy entertainment. You must make reservations early in the morning at the Hospitality House on Main Street, because there are only five shows daily. The strongest demand is usually for the noon and 1:30 shows. Other performances are at 3, 4:30, and 6 PM.

Tom Sawyer Island (not very popular; all ages) has little to see but offers a happy respite from the crowds on the mainland. Adults can relax at **Aunt Polly's Landing** with lemonade and lunch while the kids scramble up Harper's Mill (a working windmill) or explore the caves and bridges.

Liberty Square

This is a small land adjoining and blending into Frontierland. It's theme is Colonial history and it has a few decent but tame attractions.

Haunted Mansion (very popular; all ages) is the most popular attraction here. The spine-tingling effects, with ghosts, goblins, and graveyards, are realistic and may be too intense for the very young. The best time to go is in the morning when the lines are short. Avoid the noon–4 PM rush.

Liberty Square Riverboats (moderately popular; all ages) take visitors on a quiet, half-mile cruise through the rivers of America, passing Wild West scenes. It's not great entertainment, but it can be a comfortable escape from the crowds and the sun.

Hall of Presidents (moderately popular; adults or mature children) was a sensation when it first opened, but now it seems a bit slow and unexciting. Still, visitors of all ages find it interesting to see the Audio-Animatronics presidents in action. Adults find it educational; young children find it boring.

Mickey's Starland

The newest of Disney's lands, it was called Mickey's Birthdayland when it was built in 1988 to celebrate Mickey Mouse's 60th birthday. Here, in Duckburg, visitors can view some of Mickey's cartoons and films, visit Mickey's house, and meet Mickey for some photos. For parents who don't have the same energy level as their youngsters, here is a good place to rest their feet while children explore a maze, pet young farm animals, or run around the playground.

Mickey's Hollywood Theatre (very popular; younger children). Here is the best opportunity to have your picture taken with Mickey Mouse when you meet him backstage in his dressing room.

Tomorrowland

"Fun in the Future" is the motto of this land. Save it for the future if your time is limited because, except for Space Mountain, its rides are lackluster compared to others in the park. One major problem is that most attractions are sponsored by major corporations, and audiences are bombarded by commercial advertising. Plans are to make over Tomorrowland by 1996, changing it into an "intergalactic spaceport for arriving aliens."

Space Mountain (very popular, children must be at least 3 years old, and children under 7 must be accompanied by an adult) is about the only reason to stop here until the makeover. The space-age roller coaster may never go over 20 miles an hour, but the experience in the dark, with everyone screaming, is thrilling, even for hard-core roller-coaster fans.

American Journeys, including **CircleVision, Carousel of Progress,** and **Mission to Mars** (unpopular; all ages), is a series of 20-minute attractions that may be 20 minutes too long. CircleVision's patriotic look at the landscape of America on nine movie screens is perhaps the best bet.

Grand Prix Raceway (popular) takes children in mini race cars to speeds up to 7 miles per hour. The ride is confining with little room to maneuver your vehicle. Children must be at least age 7 to ride alone, and there are usually long lines.

Epcot Center

Epcot Center is divided almost equally into two distinct areas separated by the 40-acre World Showcase Lagoon. The northern half, which is where the main admission gates are, is filled with the Future World pavilions, sponsored by major American corporations. The southern half is World Showcase, with an entrance through International Gateway next to the France pavilion. If you want to minimize the time spent waiting in line, do the opposite of what most people do. In the morning, visitors head for what's closest, which is Future World, so you should begin at World Showcase. In the afternoon, come back and explore Future World when the crowds have shifted to World Showcase. Evening hours, of course, are the best times for visiting either area.

Visitors who are familiar with the Magic Kingdom find something entirely different at Epcot Center. For one thing, Epcot is twice as large. For another, Epcot's attractions all have an educational dimension. **Future World** explores technological concepts, such as energy and communications, in entertaining ways. **World Showcase** is a series of pavilions in which various nations portray their cultures through a combination of films, exhibits, and seemingly endless shops. Bring a hearty appetite, because ethnic cuisines are featured in each foreign pavilion.

As you enter Epcot Center, you'll pass beneath **Spaceship Earth,** a 17-story sphere that marks the start of Future World. World Showcase is behind Future World. Stop first at Earth Station to pick up a guidebook and entertainment schedule. Also, make reservations for the busy, full-service restaurants here. Remember that it's not unusual for most restaurants to be fully reserved by 10 AM in the peak season. Remember also that guests who are staying in on-site properties can make their reservations ahead of time.

Future World The subjects explored at Future World include the ocean, agriculture, communications, energy, imagination, and transportation.

Communicore East and West (popular; all ages). These two buildings house exhibits by the various sponsoring companies of Epcot Center. The educational computer games are very popular with children.

Horizons (popular; all ages). A journey into the lifestyles of the next century, with robotic-staffed farms, ocean colonies, and space cities.

Journey Into Imagination (popular; for children). Two of the most popular characters, Dreamfinder and Figment, are your guides on a tour of the creative process that depicts how literature and art come from the sparks of ideas. Particularly popular with teenagers is **Captain EO,** a $17-million, 3-D film starring singer Michael Jackson. The experience here is well worth the wait in line, but try to go in the late afternoon when there are fewer people. Also be sure to see the "dancing waters" display in front of the entrance to Captain EO.

Listen to the Land (popular; for adults and mature children). The main event here is a boat ride through the experimental greenhouse that demonstrates how plants may be grown in the future, not only on Earth but in outer space. It's provocative for adults but somewhat dull for children. Those who are interested can arrange to join one of several walking tours. Reservations can be made in the morning on the lower floor, in the corner opposite the boat ride, behind the *Broccoli and Company* kiosk.

The Living Seas (popular; all ages). This is a new attraction and one of the most popular. It's the largest facility ever dedicated to the relationship of humans with the ocean and is sometimes known as the "eighth sea." Visitors take a gondola ride beneath the sea for a dynamic close-up look at marine life in a six-million-gallon aquarium more than four fathoms deep. There are more than 200 varieties of sea life among the 5,000 inhabitants. You can easily spend a half day here.

Spaceship Earth (very popular; all ages). This million-pound silver geosphere is so large that on clear days airline passengers on both coasts of Florida can see it. Inside the dome, visitors take a highly praised journey through the dramatic history of communications, from cave drawings to space-age technology. Visitors see the dome when they first get to Epcot Center and routinely make their way here. You would be well advised to wait until the late afternoon when the crowds have left **Universe of Energy** (very popular; all ages). This is a fast-paced exploration of the forces that fuel our lives and the universe. You'll ride on theater seats through a display on the Earth's beginnings, past battling dinosaurs, through earthquakes, and beneath volcanoes.

Wonders of Life (popular; all ages). The newest pavilion in Future World, which has something to do for all ages housed under a 60-foot gold dome, combines a thrill ride, a theater, exhibits, and hands-on activities while you learn about good health painlessly. Even the food offered in this pavilion is healthful.

World Showcase

World Showcase offers an adventure that is very different from what you will experience in either the world of the future in Epcot Center or the world of fairy tales in the Magic Kingdom. The Showcase presents an ideal image—a Disney version—of life in 11 countries. Native food, entertainment, and wares are on display in each of the pavilions. Most of the nations have done an imaginative and painstaking job of re-creating scale models of their best-known monuments, such as the Eiffel Tower in France, a Mayan temple in Mexico, and a majestic pagoda in Japan. During the day, these structures are impressive enough, but at night, when the darkness inhibits one's ability to judge their size, you get the sense that you are seeing the real thing. It's a wonderful illusion, indeed.

Unlike Future World and the Magic Kingdom, the Showcase doesn't offer amusement-park-type rides (except in Mexico and Norway). Instead, it features breathtaking films, ethnic art, cultural entertainment, Audio-Animatronics presentations, and dozens of fine shops and restaurants featuring national specialties. The most enjoyable diversions in World Showcase are not inside the national pavilions but in front of them. At various times of the day, each pavilion offers some sort of live street show, featuring comedy, song, or dance routines and demonstrations of folk arts and crafts. Don't be shy about trying to improve your foreign-language skills!

The only unfortunate note in this cultural smorgasbord is that with so many shops and restaurants, there seems to be more of an emphasis on commercialism than on education or entertainment. Know in advance that a taste of a nation may mean a bit out of your bank account.

The focal point of World Showcase, on the opposite side of the lagoon from Future World, is the host pavilion, the **American Adventure.** The pavilions of the other countries fan out from the right and left of American Adventure, encircling the lagoon. Going clockwise from the left as you enter World Showcase from Future World are the pavilions of Mexico, Norway, People's Republic of China, Germany, Italy, the United States, Japan, Morocco, France, United Kingdom, and Canada.

Mexico: This tame "boat ride" inside the pavilion is much like rides you have seen in the Magic Kingdom. The major tourist attractions of Mexico are its theme. Windows and doorways are filled with colorful video images, and rooms are full of dancing, costumed puppets, and Audio-Animatronics landscapes that roar, storm, and light up as you journey from the jungles of the Yucatán to the skyline of Mexico City. In front of the pavilion is **Cantina de San Angel**—a fast-food joint and bar that's good for burritos, margaritas, and, at night, a great view of the laser show.

Norway: Visitors take a ride in small Viking vessels through the landscape and history of this Scandinavian country. You can tour a 10th-century Viking Village, sail through a fjord, and experience a storm and the midnight sun. The main spectacle of this pavilion is a re-creation of a 14th-century coastal fortress in Oslo called Akershus.

China: The much-talked about film should not be missed. It is a CircleVision presentation on the landscape of China, taking viewers on a fantastic journey from inner Mongolia to the Tibetan mountains, along the Great Wall, into Beijing, and through some of the most glorious landscape on Earth. The Chinese pavilion also has an art gallery with treasures never before displayed in the West and a wonderful shopping gallery with ivory goods, jade jewelry, hand-painted fans, opulent carpets, and inlaid furniture.

Germany: The main event in this replica of a small Bavarian village is the restaurant's oompah band show, with singers, dancers, and musicians. The indoor village is worth a quick look. There are four shows daily. You'll also find plenty of German wines, sweets, glassware, and porcelain for sale.

Italy: The main attraction is the architecture—a reproduction of St. Mark's Square in Venice, with the Campanile (bell tower) di San Marco as its centerpiece, and, behind it, the elegant and elaborately decorated Doges Palace. Complementing these buildings are Venetian bridges, gondolas, colorful barber poles, and the sculpture of the Lion of St. Mark atop a column. In the plaza of this pavilion, you can watch and participate in a comedy show put on by an Italian theater troupe. The show can be amusing, but only if there is a full, lively audience.

American Adventure: This is a 30-minute Audio-Animatronics show about the development of the United States. The huge, colonial-style theater features the most sophisticated and realistic animatronics characters in Disney World. The show takes visitors from the arrival of the Pilgrims through the revolutionary war, the Civil War, the taming of the West, the two world wars; and so on. The voyage is hosted by Benjamin Franklin and Mark Twain. Some will find the presentation a bit long, even though 30 minutes is not much time to cover 200 years of history. Many people find it inspiringly patriotic, but children may take this opportunity to catch a few winks—the dramatic music often puts them right to sleep.

Directly opposite the American Adventure pavilion, on the lagoon, is the open-air **American Gardens Theatre,** where live, high-energy, all-American shows are performed about four times a day. Show times vary but are posted each day on boards in front of the theater's entrances.

Japan: Elegant landscaping of rocks, streams, trees, and shrubs combines with traditional architecture to create this peaceful and charming pavilion. Inside the *torii* gates are monumental bronze sculptures and a pagoda. Of special interest are the Mitsukoshi Department Store, where lacquered dinnerware, teapots, vases, bonsai trees, and Japanese dolls and toys are for sale, and the Bijutsu-kan Gallery, featuring temporary exhibits of traditional Japanese crafts. The Yakitori House serves inexpensive Japanese fast food in a pleasant garden—a good bet for lunch.

Morocco: This is one of the more spectacular-looking of the pavilions. It has a replica of the Koutoubia Minaret from a famous prayer house in Marrakesh; a gallery of Moroccan art, tapestries, and traditional costumes; and a street with shops selling basketry, leather goods, samovars, and exquisite jewelry. Dancers move to the exotic rhythms of North Africa.

France: This 18-minute film is projected on a five-panel semicircular screen and takes viewers on a romantic tour of France —through the countryside, into the Alps, along the coast, and, of course, into Paris. It is a sophisticated visual adventure with little narration but much lyrical poetry and classical music.

The pavilion itself resembles a French boulevard, lined with shops and cafes. Of special interest are **Tout Pour le Gourmet** and **La Maison du Vin,** two shops featuring French culinary specialties, such as wines, cheeses, mustards, herbs, and pâtés. A little patisserie/boulangerie prepares all kinds of baked goods. Two restaurants, **Bistro de Paris** and **Au Petit Cafe,** are ideal for lunch. Also in this pavilion is an impressive model of the Eiffel Tower that was constructed using Alexandre-Gustave Eiffel's original blueprints.

United Kingdom: On this street from Old London are a variety of architectural styles, from thatch-roof cottages to Tudor and ornate Victorian homes. The city square and rural streets are filled with numerous food, toy, and souvenir shops. The very British **Rose and Crown** pub serves Stilton cheese, ales, and simple English fare. Street artists and a minstrel troupe perform throughout the day.

Canada: A CircleVision film takes its audience into Canada's great outdoors, from the magnificent snow-peaked Rockies, down sprawling Arctic glaciers, and across the plains to Montreal. Peaceful gardens, a rocky gorge, an emporium selling everything from sheepskins to lumberjack shirts and maple syrup, and a cafeteria-style restaurant called **Le Cellier** are other highlights of this quaint pavilion.

Other Attractions in Disney World

Disney-MGM Studios Theme Park Scheduled to open this year at Disney-MGM is the Muppet Studios, which will include a 3-D movie. The park, which started to expand almost as soon as it opened in 1989, added a Muppets parade; Here Come the Muppets, a musical show combining the characters with film; Dick Tracy Musical Revue; and a play area known as the Honey, I Shrunk the Kids Adventure Zone. Among the highlights at the park:

The **Backstage Studio Tour** and the **Animation Tour** are for those who want a close-up, behind-the-scenes look at a real studio. The Backstage Studio Tour takes up to two hours, but half of it is on a tram that will take you through costuming, into a shop where they make scenery, down a backlot "residential" street, into Catastrophe Canyon for a look at special effects, and for a quick glance at more back-lot props before the walking part of the guided tour begins. The walking portion takes in a water effects tank, special-effects workshops, soundstages, post-production work, and a theater showing previews of new movies. The Animation Tour takes visitors step-by-step through the process by looking over the artists' shoulders from a raised, glass-enclosed walkway.

Epic Stunt Spectacular is a live show with real stunt performers. Audience members are selected to join the actors on the set.

The Great Movie Ride begins tamely, like the Magic Kingdom's Pirates of the Caribbean, but soon the guide begins interacting with the Audio-Animatronics characters, and the action picks up to the delight of the younger children.

Star Tours is Disney's most recent simulator thrill ride. Created under the direction of George Lucas, the five 40-seat theaters become spaceships, and you are off to the moon of Endor. Be forewarned: the ride is rough.

Typhoon Lagoon This 50-acre aquatic entertainment complex features the largest water-slide mountain in the world. The mountain is just under 100 feet high, with nine water slides shooting down it into white-water rivers and swirling pools. There are huge wave-making lagoons for swimming and surfing. The water park also includes a Swiss Family Robinson–type tropical island covered with lush greenery, where guests can play at being shipwrecked. A saltwater pool contains a coral reef where snorkelers come mask-to-face with all sorts of Caribbean sea creatures, such as groupers, parrotfish, and even baby sharks. *Typhoon Lagoon, tel. 407/560–4142. Admission: (one-day tickets) $17.50 adults, $14 children 3–9; $15.50 adults, $12.50 children 3–9 who are members of Magic Years Club, Magic Kingdom Club, or resort guests. Admission: (two-day tickets) $29 adults, $23 children 3–9; $25 adults who are members of Magic Years Club, Magic Kingdom Club, or resort guests, $20 children who are members of Magic Years Club, Magic Kingdom Club, or resort guests. Admission: (annual pass) all guests $75.*

River Country In the backwoods setting of the Fort Wilderness Campground Resort, kids can slide, splash, and swim about in an aquatic playground, complete with white water inner-tubing channels and corkscrew water slides that splash down into a 300,000 gallon pond. The pool is heated during the winter, so kids can take a dip here year-round. During the summer, River Country can get very congested, so it's best to come late in the afternoon. *Fort Wilderness Resort, tel. 407/824–2760. Admission: (one-day tickets) $11.75 adults, $9.25 children 3–9, $10.50 adults, $8 children 3–9 Magic Kingdom Club, Magic Years Club, $10.75 adults, $8.25 children 3–9 resort, Lake Buena Vista hotel guests; (two-day tickets) $17.75 adults, $13.75 children 3–9, $16.50 adults, $12.50 children 3–9 Magic Kingdom Club, Magic Years Club, $16.75 adults, $12.75 children 3–9 resort, Lake Buena Vista hotel guests; (annual pass) $50 all resort guests, $45 all Magic Kingdom Club members, $8.50 all Florida residents holding a 3-Season Salute card (May and September only); $15 adults with an annual Worldpassport, $11 children 3–9, and this includes unlimited admission to Discovery Island.*

Discovery Island Covered with exotic flora, small, furry animals, and colorful birdlife, this little island makes a great escape from the man-made tourist attractions of Walt Disney World. Visitors listen to nature as they stroll along winding pathways and across footbridges. Disney did not create these creatures—he just brought them here. Keep an eye out for the Galapagos tortoises, trumpeter swans, scarlet ibis, and bald eagles. Tickets are sold at Fort Wilderness's River Country, at the TTC, at guest service desks in the Disney resorts, and on the island itself. You can get there by watercraft from the Magic Kingdom, Contemporary Resort, Polynesian Village, Grand Floridian, and River Country in Fort Wilderness. *Discovery Island, tel. 407/824–2875. Admission: $7.50 adults, $4 children 3–9. River Country/Discovery Island combination ticket: $15 adults, $11 children 3–9, $13.75 adults, $9.75 children 3–9 Magic Years Club, Magic Kingdom Club, $14 adults, $10 children 3–9 resort, Lake Buena Vista hotel guests.*

The Orlando Area

Numbers in the margin correspond with points of interest on the Orlando Area Attractions map.

1 **Alligatorland Safari Zoo.** More than 1,600 exotic animals and birds in a natural setting. *U.S. 192 between Kissimmee and Walt Disney World, tel. 407/396–1012. Admission: $5 adults, $3.95 children 4–11. Open daily 8:30–dusk.*

2 **Bok Tower Gardens.** A 128-acre garden with pine forests, shady paths, and a bell tower that rings daily at 3 PM. *Between Haines City and Lake Wales off U.S. 27, tel. 813/676–1408. Admission: $3 per person, children under 12 free. Open daily 8–5.*

3 **Central Florida Zoological Park.** A 110-acre zoo. *U.S. 17–92, 1 mi east of I–4 and 4 mi west of Sanford, tel. 407/323–4450. Admission: $5 adults, $2 children 3–12. Open daily, 9–5.*

4 **Cypress Gardens.** Central Florida's original theme park features exotic flowers, waterskiing shows, and bird and alligator shows. *East of Winter Haven off Rte. 540, tel. 813/324–2111.*

Alligatorland Safari Zoo, **1**
Bok Tower Gardens, **2**
Central Florida Zoological Park, **3**
Cypress Gardens, **4**
Fun 'n Wheels, **5**
Gatorland Zoo, **6**
Mystery Fun House, **7**
Places of Learning, **8**
Sea World, **9**
Universal Studios Florida, **10**
Wet 'n Wild, **11**
Xanadu, **12**

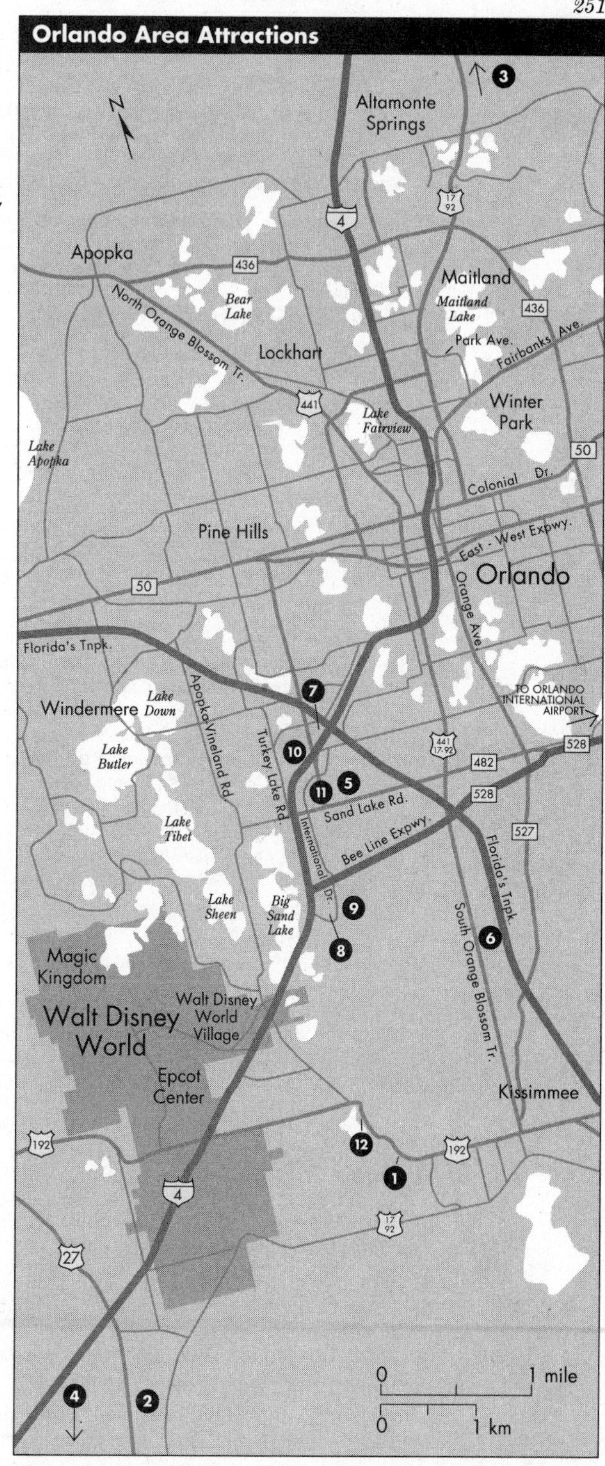

Admission: $17.50 adults, $11.50 children 3–11. Open daily 9–6.

5 **Fun 'n Wheels.** An expensive but active family theme park with go-cart tracks, rides, minigolf course, bumper boats, and cars. *6739 Sand Lake Rd. at International Dr., Orlando, tel. 407/351–5651. No general admission charge. Open Sun. 10 AM–11 PM, Mon.–Thurs. 4–11, Fri. 4–midnight, Sat. 10–midnight.*

6 **Gatorland Zoo.** Thousands of alligators and crocodiles sleeping in the sun are viewed from a walkway. Also snakes, flamingos, monkeys, and other Florida critters. *South of Orlando on U.S. 17–92 near Kissimmee, tel. 407/857–3845. Admission: $6.95 adults, $4.95 children 3–11. Open daily 8 AM–6 PM.*

7 **Mystery Fun House.** Magic mirrors, moving floors, laughing doors, barrels that roll, a shooting arcade—all are favorites with children, though the price is high for not much more than afew minutes' entertainment. *5767 Major Blvd., off Kirkman Rd. near International Dr., tel. 407/351–3355. Admission: $6.95 adults, children under 4 free; $4.95 for Starbase Omega, a laser tag game. Open daily 10–midnight.*

8 **Places of Learning.** Great selection of children's books and educational games. Recommended for the nonbookish, too. *6825 Academic Dr., Orlando, tel. 407/345–1038. Open daily 9–6. Admission free.*

9 **Sea World.** A major theme park celebrating sea life, including popular Baby Shamu and an awesome exhibit that guides you through a shark tank on a moving sidewalk. Marine animals perform in seven major shows. The park also has penguins, tropical fish, otter habitats, walrus training exhibits, botanical gardens, and other educational diversions in a setting more tranquil than that of most theme parks. *Located 10 mi south of Orlando at the intersection of I–4 and the Bee Line Expressway, 7007 Sea World Dr., Orlando, tel. 407/351–3600 or 800/327–2420. Open daily 9–8, with extended summer and holiday hours. Admission: $25.40 adults, $21.15 children 3–11.*

10 **Universal Studios Florida.** The largest working film studio outside Hollywood, Universal opened its doors to tours in the summer of 1990. The tour is patterned after the one at the highly successful attraction in Los Angeles, except the Florida tours have been developed to more fully integrate the tour with studio production facilities, allowing visitors an even closer and more interactive behind-the-scenes look at movie and TV production. Visitors view live shows, participate in movie-themed attractions, and tour back-lot sets. The tour showcases the special-effects magic of creative consultant Steven Spielberg and the animation wizardry of Hanna-Barbera. A **Hard Rock Cafe** is on the premises. *Get off I–4 at Exit 30B and follow the signs. Tel. 407/363–8000. Hours vary seasonally. One-day admission: $29 adults, $23 children 3–11; two-day admission: $49 adults, $39 children 3–11.*

11 **Wet 'n Wild.** Water slides, flumes, lazy rivers, and other water-related activities for swimmers and sunbathers. *6200 International Dr., Orlando, tel. 407/351–3200. Open daily 10–6, except in winter. Admission: $16.95 adults, $14.95 children 3–12, $8.45 adults 55 and over.*

12 **Xanadu.** A dome-shaped home showcasing technological and electronic devices. Guided tours daily. *Located at the intersec-*

tion of U.S. 192 and Rte. 535, Kissimmee, tel. 407/396–1992. Admission: $5.95 adults, $4.95 children 3–12.

Orlando for Free

Citrus World, Inc. Free film showing citrus processing from tree to grocer; free samples. The film is shown every 40 minutes. *U.S. 27S, Lake Wales, about 1 hr south of Orlando, tel. 813/676–1411. Open Nov.–June, weekdays 9–4:30.*

Kissimmee Livestock Market, Inc. Going, going, gone in a real cattle auction, one of the oldest in Florida. *Box 2329, Kissimmee 32742, tel. 407/847–3521. Open Wed. at 1 PM.*

Lake Wales Museum. Railroad memorabilia and area history. *325 S. Scenic Hwy., Lake Wales, tel. 813/676–5443. Open weekdays 9–5, Sat. 10–4.*

Monument of the States. A 50-foot-tall step pyramid built in the 1940s from concrete and stones donated by every state in the union. *Monument St., Lake Front Park, Kissimmee, tel. 407/847–3174.*

Slocum Water Gardens. An extensive display of water plants. *1101 Cypress Gardens, Winter Haven 33880, tel. 813/293–7151. Open weekdays 8–noon and 1–4, Sat. 8–noon.*

Tupperware World Headquarters. Narrated tours and displays depicting the evolution of food storage since the days of the ancient Egyptians. *U.S. 441 south of Orlando near Kissimmee, tel. 417/847–3111. Open weekdays 9–4.*

Water Ski Museum and Hall of Fame. Waterskiing fans will love what is probably the world's largest collection of equipment and memorabilia. *799 Overlook Dr., Winter Haven, tel. 813/324–2472. Open weekdays 10–5.*

The Cocoa Beach Area

Kennedy Space Center Spaceport USA. Free museum exhibits and films are featured, as well as guided bus tours and an IMAX theater film presentation, *The Dream is Alive*, narrated by Walter Cronkite. *Visitors' Center, tel. 407/452–2121. Open daily 9–7. Closed Christmas. Bus tours: $4 adults, $1.75 children 3–12. IMAX theater admission: $2.75 adults, $1.75 children 3–12.*

Off the Beaten Track

Big Tree Park. One of the oldest and largest bald cypress trees in the country is featured in this moss-draped park with picnic tables. *U.S. 17–92 on General Hutchinson Pkwy., Longwood, tel. 407/323–9615. Open weekdays 8–sunset, weekends 9–sunset. Admission free.*

Cassadaga. The mystic's mecca, an eerily tree-shaded village started by Spiritualists. Many of the residents read palms, peer into the future, and relay messages from the world beyond. When the psychics meet from January to March, many of the lectures and seminars are open to the public. Visit anytime. *Located off I–4, 7 miles south of De Land. First Spiritualist Church of Cassadaga, Box 152, Cassadaga 32706, tel. 904/228–2880.*

Hontoon Island State Park. Take a ferry-boat ride to a 1,650-acre park and campground with six rustic cabins, 22 campsites, a floating marina with slips for 54 boats, and an 80-foot observation tower. The park is off Rte. 44 on Hontoon Road. *Hontoon Island, 2309 Riverride Rd., De Land 32720, tel. 904/736–5309.*

Open daily 8 AM–sunset. The ferry operates from 9 AM until an hour before the park closes.

Navy Graduation. Recruit graduation parade every Friday at 9:45 AM. *Orlando Naval Training Center, General Rees Rd., entrance off Corrine Dr., Orlando, tel. 407/646–5054. Admission free.*

Pioneer Settlement for the Creative Arts. Folk museum with demonstrations of day-to-day pioneer lifestyles, a turn-of-the-century country store, and a train depot. *Intersection of U.S. 40 and 17 in De Land, about 40 mi from Orlando, tel. 904/749–2959. Open weekdays 9–4, Sat. 9–2. Admission: $2.50 adults, $1 children under 17.*

Shopping

Altamonte Mall. The largest mall in central Florida was renovated in 1989; a food court was added in 1990; and there are plans for two more anchor stores and a parking garage in 1991. Sears, Maison Blanche, Jordan Marsh, and Burdine's department stores anchor the two-level mall with its 165 specialty shops. *A half mile east of I–4 on Rte. 436 in Altamonte Springs, tel. 407/830–4400. Open Mon.–Sat. 10 AM–9 PM, Sun. noon–5:50 (except holidays).*

Florida Mall. This is a newer, large-scale center in Orlando, closer to the Walt Disney World tourism corridor. More than 160 stores in an enclosed mall that has three distinctive shopping areas—Victorian, Mediterranean, and Art Deco. *On the corner of Sand Lake Rd. (Rte. 482) and S. Orange Blossom Trail and near International Dr., tel. 407/851–6255. Open Mon.–Sat. 10–9, Sun. noon–5:30.*

Flea World. Flea markets are scattered across the Orlando area, but this is the largest and most popular. Well over 1,500 booths, some air-conditioned, offer arts and crafts, auto parts, citrus produce, and so on. *Highway 17–92 between Orlando and Sanford, tel. 407/645–1792. Open Fri., Sat., and Sun. 8–5. Admission free.*

Park Avenue. This is the place to go for fashionable, upscale shopping in Winter Park. Most stores are open weekdays 9–5, but you can window-browse anytime and enjoy the many restaurants and ice cream shops along the avenue. The shops range from the Ralph Lauren Polo Shop to small antiques shops.

Mercado Mediterranean Village. The latest trend in Orlando is "festive retail," where shopping is combined with entertainment. At Mercado, visitors wander along brick streets and browse through more than 50 specialty shops in the atmosphere of a Mediterranean village. Free entertainment nightly. Exotic foods are all under one roof at the International Food Pavilion. *8445 International Dr., tel. 407/345–9337. Open 10–10 daily.*

Old Town. Also in the tourist corridor is this collection of more than 70 specialty shops and restaurants along pedestrian walks. Tethered balloon rides are available. *5770 Spacecoast Pkwy., Kissimmee, tel. 407/396–4888. Open daily 10–10.*

Ron Jon's Surf Shop. They have everything you will need for a day at the beach ranging from their distinctive T-shirts to surfboards. A scuba center at the back of the shop offers equipment, rentals, and lessons. *4151 N. Atlantic Ave., Cocoa Beach, tel. 407/799–8888. Open daily 9 AM–11 PM.*

Walt Disney World. For unusual and sophisticated shopping, try

World Showcase, where each country offers unique native merchandise. Walt Disney World Village in Lake Buena Vista, only 2 miles from Epcot Center and 6 miles from the Magic Kingdom, is a collection of some 20 shops that offer everything from Christmas tree ornaments to Disney memorabilia.

Participant Sports

Bicycling The most scenic bike riding in Orlando is on the property of Walt Disney World, along roads that take you past forests, lakes, golf courses, and Disney's wooded resort villas and campgrounds. Bikes are available for rent at **Caribbean Beach Resort** (tel. 407/934–3400), **Fort Wilderness Bike Barn** (tel. 407/824–2742), and **Walt Disney World Village Villa Center** (tel. 407/824–6947). Bike rental is $3 an hour, $7 per day. In Cocoa Beach, **Ron Jon's Surf Shop** (4151 N. Atlantic Ave., tel. 407/799–8888) has bikes to rent.

Fishing Central Florida is covered with freshwater lakes and rivers teeming with all kinds of fish, from largemouth black bass to perch, catfish, sunfish, and pike.

If you are staying at WDW, **Fort Wilderness Campground** (tel. 407/824–2900) is the starting point for two-hour fishing trips, departing at 8 AM and 3 PM. Boats, equipment, and guide for up to five anglers cost $110.

Lake Tohopekaliga is a popular camping and fishing destination and convenient for most visitors to central Florida. Among the best fishing camps are: **Red's Fish Camp** (4715 Kissimmee Park Rd., St. Cloud, tel. 407/892–8795); **Richardson's Fish Camp** (1550 Scotty's Rd., Kissimmee, tel. 407/846–6540); **Scotty's Fish Camp & Mobil Home Park** (1554 Scotty's Rd., Kissimmee, tel. 407/847–3840); and **East Lake Fish Camp** (3680 E. Boggy Creek Rd., Kissimmee, tel. 407/348–2040).

Bass Challenger Guide (9900 E. Colonial Dr., Orlando, tel. 407/273–8045) rents Ranger boats equipped with drinks and tackle. Transportation can be arranged to and from their location. Half day (1 or 2 persons) from $125, full day from $175.

Bass Bustin' Guide (5935 Swoffield Dr., Orlando, tel. 407/281–0845) provides boat, tackle, transportation, and amenities for bass fishing on local lakes, and it guarantees fish! Half day from $125, full day from $175.

You can deep-sea troll in the Atlantic for blue and white marlin, sailfish, dolphin, king mackerel, tuna, and wahoo. Grouper, red snapper, and amberjack are deep-sea bottom-fishing prizes. Surf casting is popular for pompano, bluefish, flounder, and sea bass. From fishing piers, anglers pull in sheepshead, mackerel, trout, and tarpon. Most Atlantic beach communities have a lighted pier with a bait-and-tackle shop and rest rooms. Deep-sea charters are found at Port Canaveral. Call ahead for prices and reservations. **Cape Marina** (800 Scallop Dr., tel. 407/783–8410); **Miss Cape Canaveral** (630 Glen Cheek Dr., tel. 407/783–5274); **Pelican Princess** (665 Glen Cheek Dr., tel. 407/784–3474).

Golf Many resort hotels let nonguests use their golf facilities. Some hotels are affiliated with a particular country club and offer preferred rates. If you are staying near a resort with facilities you want to use, call and inquire about its policies. Be sure to call in advance to reserve tee times. What follows is a list of the best places that are open to the public.

Golfpac (Box 940490, Maitland, 32794, tel. 407/660–8559) packages golf vacations and prearranges tee times at over 30 courses around Orlando.
Poinciana Golf & Racquet Club (500 Cypress Pkwy., tel. 407/933–5300) has a par-72 course about 18 miles southeast of Walt Disney World.
Walt Disney World's three championship courses—all played by the PGA Tour—are among the busiest and most expensive in the region. Greens fees are $55 for guests staying in Disney World properties; $60 for nonguests; $30 after 3 PM.

Golf lessons are given in small groups at the Disney Inn courses, the Magnolia, and the Palm. Private lessons are available both at these courses and at the Lake Buena Vista Club. There is also a six-hole, 3,058-yard course on artificial turf with natural turf greens for children under 17 ($10) and adults ($13). For private lessons at the Lake Buena Vista Club, phone tel. 407/828–3741. For all other information, phone tel. 407/824–2270.

Grenelefe Golf and Tennis Resort (3200 Rte. 546, Haines City, tel. 813/422–7511; 800/237–9546; in FL, 800/282–7875), about 45 minutes from Orlando, has three 18-hole courses over gentle hills. Make the West Course (18 holes, par 72, 7,325 yards) your first choice. East Course is 6,802 yards, par 72, and the South Course is 6,869 yards, par 71.
Orange Lake Country Club (8085 W. U.S. 192, Kissimmee, tel. 407/239–0000) offers three nine-hole courses and is about five minutes from Walt Disney World's main entrance. The Orange (with a 118-yard island hole) and the Cypress is the most challenging 18-hole combination. All three courses are par 36 and about 3,300 yards.

Other challenging courses open to the public are: **Cocoa Beach Municipal Golf Course** (5000 Tom Warriner Blvd., Cocoa Beach, tel. 407/783–5351, 6,968 yards); **Cypress Creek Country Club** (5353 Vineland Rd., Orlando, tel. 407/425–2319, 6,952 yards); **Hunter's Creek Golf Course** (14401 Sports Club Way, Orlando, tel. 407/240–4653, 7,432 yards); **Timacuan Golf and Country Club** (550 Timacuan Blvd., Lake Mary, tel. 407/321–0010, 7,027 yards); **Turtle Creek Golf Club** (1278 Admiralty Blvd., Rockledge, tel. 407/632–2520, 6,709 yards); **Wedgefield Golf and Country Club** (20550 Maxim Parkway, Orlando, tel. 407/568–2116, 6,378 yards); **MetroWest Country Club** (2100 S. Hiawassee Rd., Orlando, tel. 407/297–0052, 7,051 yards).

Horseback Riding

Grand Cypress Resort Equestrian Center (tel. 407/239–1234) offers hunter/jumper private lessons and riding trails for guided outings. Private lesson $35 an hour, trailside $20 an hour.
Fort Wilderness Campground (tel. 407/W–DISNEY) in Walt Disney World offers tame trail rides through the backwoods and along lakesides. Open to the general public. Call in advance to arrange an outing. Rides at 9, 10:30, noon, 1, and 2. Cost: $12 per person for 45–60 minutes. Children must be over 9.
Poinciana Horse World (tel. 407/847–4343) takes visitors for hour-long rides along old logging trails near Kissimmee. Cost: $14.

Ice Skating

Orlando Ice Skating Palace (3123 W. Colonial Dr., Parkwood Shopping Plaza Orlando, tel. 407/299–5440) isn't the most attractive rink, but if you are homesick for a winter chill, this should do the trick. Open Wed.–Fri. 7:30–10:30 PM, Sat. 12:30–3:30 and 4–7, and Sun. 2–5. Call for additional weekday hours.

Jogging Walt Disney World has several scenic jogging trails. Pick up jogging maps at any Disney resort. **Fort Wilderness** (tel. 407/824–2900) has a 2.3-mile jogging course, with plenty of fresh air and woods, as well as numerous exercise stations along the way.

Tennis For the following courts that aren't first-come, first-served, call to reserve courts.

Disney Inn (tel. 407/824–1469) has two courts, **Lake Buena Vista Club** (tel. 407/828–3741) has three, **Fort Wilderness Campground** has two (first come, first served), the **Disney World Dolphin** (tel. 407/934–4000) has eight, the **Disney World Swan** (tel. 407/934–3000) has eight, and the **Contemporary Resort** (tel. 407/824–3578) has six, where private and group lessons are available. All courts are lighted and open until 10 PM. Racquets may be rented by the hour.

Orange Lake Country Club (8505 W. U.S. 192, Kissimmee, tel. 407/239–2255) has 16 all-weather courts, 10 of them lighted.

Orlando Tennis Center (649 W. Livingston St., tel. 407/849–2646) has 16 lighted courts (nine clay, seven hard), two racquetball courts, and two tennis pros.

The Orlando Vacation Resort (west of I–4 on U.S. 27, tel. 407/394–6171) has 17 asphalt courts open only to guests.

Water Sports Marinas at **Caribbean Beach Resort, Contemporary Resort, Fort Wilderness, Polynesian Village,** and **Walt Disney World Village** rent Sunfish, catamarans, motor-powered pontoon boats, pedal boats, and Water Sprites for the 450-acre Bay Lake, the adjoining 200-acres of the Seven Seas Lagoon, Club Lake, Lake Buena Vista, and Buena Vista Lagoon. The Polynesian Village marina rents outrigger canoes. Fort Wilderness rents canoes. For waterskiing ($65 per hour) reservations, phone 407/824–2222, ext. 2757.

Airboat Rentals (4266 Vine St., Kissimmee, tel. 407/847–3672) rents airboats ($15.99 per hour) and canoes for use on Shingle Creek, with views of giant cypress trees and Spanish moss.

Ski Holidays (13323 Lake Bryan Dr., tel. 407/239–4444) has waterskiing, jetskiing, and parasailing on a private lake next to Walt Disney World. Boat rental: $60 per hour. Also available: wave runners, jet boats, and jetskis. To get there take I–4 to the Lake Buena Vista exit, turn south on Rte. 535 toward Kissimmee. Turn left onto a private dirt road about 300 yards down on the left.

Rent a powerful seven-seater ski boat at **Sanford Boat Rentals** (tel. 407/321–5906, in Florida 800/237–5105, outside Florida 800/692–3414) up the St. Johns River. Bring your own equipment for bass fishing or rent waterski equipment. Houseboats and pontoons are available for day, overnight, weekend, or week-long trips. Pontoon and ski boats $60 for 4 hours; 44-foot houseboat $350 per day, $560 for 2 days, $450 weekends, $900 weekly. Rates vary seasonally.

Go Vacations (2280 Hontoon Dr., DeLand, tel. 800/262–3454 or 904/736–9422) rents luxury houseboats on the St. Johns River.

Among the packages is a $759 weekend deal and a weekly price of $1,295. Rates vary seasonally.

Jetskiing, boardsailing, waterskiing, sailing, and powerboating are popular pastimes on the Atlantic Intracoastal Waterway. Rental equipment is available at **The Water Works** (1891 E. Merritt Island Causeway, Rte. 520, Merritt Island, tel. 407/452-2007).

Spectator Sports

Jai Alai

Orlando-Seminole Jai-Alai. The sport is fun to watch even if you don't bet. *Tel. 407/331-9191. Admission: $1 general, $2 reserved seating. Open May–Jan. at 7:20 nightly except Sun. with noon matinees Mon., Thurs., and Sat.*

Dog Racing

Sanford Orlando Kennel Club (301 Dog Track Rd., Longwood, tel. 407/831-1600) has dog racing and betting nightly except Sun. at 7:30. Matinees Mon., Wed., and Sat. at 1. *Open Dec.–May. Admission: $1.*

Seminole Greyhound Park (2000 Seminola Blvd., Casselberry, tel. 407/699-4510) is a newer track with racing nightly at 7:45 except Sunday. Matinees Mon., Wed., and Sat. at 1 PM. *Open May–Oct. Admission: $1 general, clubhouse $2, children half price.*

Basketball

Orlando Magic (Box 76, Orlando 32802, tel. 407/89-MAGIC) joined the National Basketball Association in the 1989–90 season. The team plays in the new, 15,077-seat Orlando Arena. *Admission: $8–$28. Off I-4 at Amelia, the arena is 2 blocks west of the interstate.*

Baseball

The **Orlando SunRays** are Minnesota's Class AA Southern League affiliate. They play baseball at Tinker Field. *Tel. 407/849-6346. Get off I-4 at Colonial Ave. (Hwy. 50), go west to Tampa Ave. and south on Tampa to the stadium.*

The **Osceola Astros** (tel. 407/933-5500) are Houston's Class A team in the Florida State League. They play at Osceola County Stadium in Kissimmee.

The **Baseball City Royals** (tel. 407/648-5151) are Kansas City's Class-A team in the Florida State League. They play at the former Boardwalk and Baseball complex at I-4 and U.S. 27.

Soccer

Orlando Lions play in the American Soccer League. Games are April through August at Showalter Field in Winter Park, weekends at 7:30 PM. *Tel. 407/240-0769. Admission: $6.*

Dining

If you want to try some local specialties, consider stone crabs, pompano (a mild white fish), Apalachicola oysters, small but tasty Florida lobsters, and conch chowder. Fresh hearts of palm are a treat, too.

The most highly recommended restaurants in each price category are indicated by a star ★.

Category	Cost*
Very Expensive	over $40
Expensive	$30–$40

Moderate	$20–$30
Inexpensive	under $20

**per person, excluding drinks, service, and 6% sales tax*

The following credit card abbreviations are used: AE, American Express; CB, Carte Blanche; DC, Diners Club; MC, MasterCard; V, Visa.

In Epcot Center World Showcase offers some of the finest dining not only in Walt Disney World but in the entire Orlando area. The problem is that the restaurants are often crowded and difficult to book. Many of them are operated by the same people who own internationally famous restaurants in their home countries. The top-of-the-line places, such as those in the French, Italian, and Japanese pavilions, can be expensive, but they are not as pricey as comparable restaurants in large, cosmopolitan cities such as Paris or New York. One good thing about Epcot's restaurants, besides the food, is that most of them have limited-selection children's menus with drastically lower prices, so bringing the kids along to dinner won't break the bank.

Visitors are not expected to go all the way back to their hotels to change and clean up and then return for dinner, so casual dress is expected in all the restaurants, even the finest.

If you want to eat in one of the more popular restaurants, it will be much easier to get a reservation for lunch than for dinner. It won't be quite the same experience, but it will be cheaper. Another way to get a table is to have lunch before noon and dinner before 6 or after 8.

Both lunch and dinner reservations are strongly recommended at all the finer restaurants in Epcot. Unless you are staying at one of the Walt Disney World hotels, you cannot reserve in advance of the day on which you wish to eat, and you can't book by phone. Instead, you must reserve in person at each restaurant or head for Earth Station at the base of Spaceship Earth as soon as you get to Epcot Center. There you will find a bank of computer screens called WorldKey Information. You need to stand in line to get to one of these screens and place the reservation, and the lines form very early. On busy days, most top restaurants are filled within an hour of Epcot's opening time, so you may have to line up at the Epcot admissions booth before opening time and then, once you're through the gate, make a mad dash for the WorldKey computer terminals. If there is a long line when you get to Earth Station, remember that on the far side of Future World, just before the bridge to World Showcase, is an outdoor kiosk with five WorldKey terminals that few people notice. There is also another WorldKey kiosk on the far side of the Port of Entry gift shop, near the boat dock for the water taxi to the Moroccan pavilion. Having made the reservations, you can begin to enjoy your day at Epcot.

If you are a guest at an on-site Walt Disney World resort or at one of the Walt Disney World Village hotels, avoid the battle of the WorldKey by booking a table by phone (tel. 407/824–4000). Remember that if you are staying at one of these resorts, you cannot make a same-day reservation by phone but must book either one or two days in advance between noon and 9 PM. The restaurant will ask to see your resort identification card, so don't leave it in your hotel room. No matter how you book, try to show up at the restaurant a bit early to be sure of getting your table. You can pay with American Express, Visa, MasterCard, or, of course, cash. If you're a guest of a Disney hotel, you can charge the tab to your room.

British **Rose and Crown.** This is a very popular, friendly British pub, where visitors and Disney employees come at the end of the day to knock off a pint of crisp Bass ale or blood-thickening Guinness stout with a few morsels of Stilton cheese. "Wenches" serve up simple pub fare, such as steak-and-kidney pie, beef tenderloin, and fish and chips. The Rose and Crown sits on the shore of the lagoon, so on warm days it's nice to lunch on the patio at the water's edge and enjoy the soft breezes and the homiest atmosphere in Epcot Center. *Moderate.*

French **Bistro de Paris.** Located on the second floor of the French pavilion, above Chefs de France (*see* below), this is a relatively quiet and charming spot for lunch or dinner. The bistro specializes in regional cooking from southern France. A favorite is steamed filet of fresh grouper with tomato, mushrooms, fresh herbs, and white wine sauce, served with rice pilaf. Wines are moderately priced and available by the glass. *Expensive.*

★ **Chefs de France.** Three of France's most famous culinary artists came together to create this French restaurant. The most renowned of the three, Paul Bocuse, operates one restaurant north of Lyon and two in Tokyo and has published several famous books on French cuisine. Another, Gaston Lenôtre, has gained eminence for his pastries and ice creams. The third of this culinary triumvirate, Roger Vergé, operates one of France's most highly rated restaurants, near Cannes. The three don't actually prepare each meal, but they were the ones who created the menu and carefully trained the chefs. Some of their most popular classic dishes are roast duck with prunes and wine sauce; beef filet with fresh ground pepper, raisins, and Armagnac sauce; and filet of grouper topped with salmon-vegetable mousse and baked in puff pastry. *Expensive.*

German **Biergarten.** This popular spot boasts Oktoberfest 365 days a year. Visitors sit at long communal tables and are served by waitresses in typical Bavarian garb. The cheerful—some would say raucous—atmosphere is what one would expect from a place where performers yodel, sing, and dance to the rhythms of an oompah band. The crowd, pounding pitchers of beer or wine while consuming hot pretzels and hearty German fare, is usually pretty active when audience participation is called for and just as active when it is not. *Moderate.*

Italian **L'Originale Alfredo di Roma Ristorante.** This is a World Showcase hot spot, with some of the finest food in Walt Disney World. During dinner, waiters skip around singing Italian songs and bellowing arias. The restaurant is named for the man who invented the now-classic fettuccine Alfredo, a pasta served with a sauce of cream, butter, and loads of freshly grated Parmesan cheese. Another popular dish is *lo Chef Consiglia* (the chef's selections), which consists of an appetizer of spaghetti or fettuccine, a mixed green salad, and a chicken or veal entrée. The most popular veal dish is *piccata di vitello*—veal thinly sliced and panfried with lemon and white wine. *Expensive.*

Japanese **Mitsukoshi.** This isn't just a restaurant, it's a complex of dining areas on the second floor above the Mitsukoshi Department Store. Each of the five dining rooms (on your left as you enter) has four tables, which seat eight and are equipped with a grill on which chefs prepare meats and fish with acrobatic precision. It's an American's idea of the real Japan, but fun nonetheless. *Moderate.*

Mexican **San Angel Inn.** The lush, tropical surroundings—cool, dark, almost surreal—make this one of the most exotic restaurants in Disney World. The ambience is at once romantic and lively. Tables are candlelit, but close together, and the restaurant is open to the pavilion, where folk singers perform and musicians play guitars or marimbas. One of the specialties is *langosta Baja California*—Baja lobster meat, sautéed with tomatoes, onions, olives, Mexican peppers, and white wine, and baked in its shell. Try the margaritas, and, for dessert, don't miss the chocolate Kahlúa mousse pie. *Moderate.*

Moroccan **Restaurant Marrakesh.** Belly dancers and a three-piece Moroccan band set the mood in this exotic restaurant, where you may feel as though you have stumbled onto the set of *Casablanca.* The food is mildly spicy and relatively inexpensive. At lunch, you may want to try the national dish of Morocco, *couscous,* served with garden vegetables. For dinner, try the *bastila,* an appetizer of sweet and spicy pork between many layers of thin pastry, with almonds, saffron, and cinnamon. *Moderate.*

Norwegian **Restaurant Akershus.** Norway's tradition of seafood and cold meat dishes is highlighted at the restaurant's *koldtbord,* or Norwegian buffet. Hosts and hostesses explain the dishes to guests and suggest which ones go together. It is traditional to make several trips to the koldtbord, so there is no need to shovel everything you see onto your plate at one time. The first trip is for appetizers, usually herring prepared in a number of ways. On your next trip choose cold seafood items—try gravlaks, salmon cured with salt, sugar, and dill. Pick up cold salads and meats on your next trip, and then you fill up with hot dishes on your fourth trip, usually a choice of lamb, veal, and venison. Desserts are offered à la carte, including cloudberries, delicate, seasonal fruits that grow on the tundra. There are four dining rooms, seating 220 in an impressive copy of Oslo's famous Akershus Castle. *Moderate.*

The Walt Disney World Area

These are restaurants close to Disney World, situated along International Drive or near Kissimmee, Disney Maingate, or Lake Buena Vista.

American ★ **Chatham's Place.** In this elegant, simple, unpretentious restaurant the Chatham brothers show their skills with such entrées as black grouper with pecan butter, spaghetti à la Grecque, and duck breast, grilled to crispy perfection. It's a small space, and the office building exterior belies what's inside, but this is arguably one of Orlando's best. *7575 Dr. Phillips Blvd., Orlando, tel. 407/345–2992. Dress: informal. Reservations advised. MC, V. Moderate–Expensive.*

Empress Lilly. Disney's 220-foot, 19th-century Mississippi-style riverboat is a popular tourist dining spot at the far end of Walt Disney World Shopping Village, right on Buena Vista Lagoon. The boat is permanently moored; it looks like an elegant old-fashioned Victorian showboat, complete with brass lamps, burgundy velvet love seats, mahogany wood, and several restaurants and lounges. Beef is served in the *Steerman's Quarters* and seafood in *Fisherman's Deck.* Only 5% of the tables are open for reservations, two days in advance. Visitors without reservations should arrive early, add their names to the list, then go and listen to banjo music in the *Baton Rouge Lounge*. The food is as predictable as it is expensive, but dining here can be an enjoyable experience for large families or groups who want a decent meal but do not want to feel inhibited by a stuffy atmosphere. The third restaurant on the showboat is the *Empress Room*, a plush, Victorian dining room filled with gilded reminders of another age. It is a luxurious (if gaudy) setting that might bring out the Rhett Butler or Scarlett O'Hara in you, but you will wish that the food were more palatable, especially at these prices. The menu reads elegantly, featuring such specialties as duck, pheasant, venison, and various seafood dishes, but the food is unlikely to live up to your elegant expectations. *Steerman's Quarters and Fisherman's Deck: Walt Disney World Shopping Village, tel. 407/828–3900. Dress: casual. Only a few reservations accepted. AE, CB, DC, MC, V. Moderate. Empress Room: Jacket required. Reservations required, up to a month in advance. AE, CB, DC, MC, V. Expensive.*

Hard Rock Cafe Orlando. The guitar-shaped structure is at Universal Studios Florida with an entrance from the studio or off the street. Hamburgers, barbecue, and sandwiches are served to the sound of rock music amidst rock memorabilia. *Universal Studios Florida, 5401 S. Kirkman Rd., tel. 407/363–ROLL. Dress: casual. No reservations. AE, MC, V. Inexpensive.*

Cajun/Creole

Royal Orleans. Some of the most authentic Louisiana cooking outside New Orleans is prepared under the direction of the award-winning Cajun chef, "Beany" MacGregor. Specialties include sherried turtle soup and *la truite roulée* (small slivers of trout fillet, shrimp, Louisiana blue crab, and fresh artichoke hearts wrapped in spinach leaves and topped with béarnaise sauce). Fresh seafood and crawfish are flown in daily from Louisiana. *8445 International Dr., Orlando, tel. 407/352–8200. Jacket required. Reservations advised. AE, CB, DC, MC, V. Moderate.*

Chinese

Ming Court. This is no take-out Chinese, but truly fine Oriental-style dining. Although some dishes will seem familiar, creative flairs make each dish unique. Try the jumbo shrimp in lobster sauce flavored with crushed black beans, or the Hunan *kung pao* chicken with peanuts, cashews, and walnuts. Prices may seem high, but the elegant surroundings—glass walls allow you to look out on the pond and floating gardens—make the check worthwhile. *Not far from the Orange County Convention Center. 9188 International Dr., Orlando, tel. 407/351–9988. Dress: casual. Reservations advised. AE, DC, MC, V. Moderate.*

Continental

Dux. In the Peabody Hotel's gourmet restaurant, some creations are innovative, such as the grilled quail with poached quail eggs, served with wild rice in a carrot terrine nest. Others are a trifle self-conscious, like the avocado with sautéed salmon, artichoke chips, and champagne caviar sauce. For an entrée, consider the baked Florida lobster with chanterelle mushrooms, spinach, and champagne sauce. The selection of California wines is outstanding. *Peabody Hotel, 9801 International Dr., Orlando, tel. 407/352–4000. Jacket required. Reservations strongly recommended. AE, CB, DC, MC, V. Expensive.*

La Coquina. This is a hotel restaurant with an emphasis on seafood and serious sauces. One popular meat specialty is loin of lamb with eggplant and goat cheese in grape leaves, served with grilled *polenta* (a type of cornmeal). The best bet here is Sunday brunch—a cornucopia of fruits, vegetables, pastries, pâtés, smoked fish, and a number of dishes cooked before your eyes. The $27 brunch is served with Domaine Chandon champagne; the $52 brunch, with all the Dom Perignon champagne you can consume. If you're hungry and thirsty enough, you just might be able to put them out of business. *Hyatt Regency Grand Cypress Resort, 1 Grand Cypress Blvd., Orlando, tel. 407/239–1234. Jacket required. Reservations suggested. AE, CB, DC, MC, V. Expensive.*

Victoria and Albert's. The prix fixe menu changes daily but always offers a choice among beef, seafood, and poultry. The prices tend to be high, but help pay for the Royal Doulton china, Sambonet silver, Schott-Zweisel crystal, and turn-of-the-century costumes for your servers—a maid and butler named Victoria and Albert. The surroundings and treatment impress more than the food. *Grand Floridian Beach Resort, Walt Disney World, tel. 407/824–2833. Jacket required. Reservations required. AE, MC, V. Very Expensive.*

Indian

Darbar. This lavishly decorated dining room features northern Indian cuisine. In addition to curries and pilafs, Darbar specializes in tandoori cooking—barbecuing with mesquite charcoal in a clay oven. Meats and vegetables are marinated in special sauces overnight and cooked to perfection. If you're not familiar with Indian cuisine, this is a good place to begin. The best bet is the tandoori dinner for two, with different types of lamb and chicken. *7600 Dr. Phillips Blvd., Orlando, tel. 407/345–8128. To get there, take Sand Lake Blvd. (exit 29 off I–4) and head west to the Marketplace Shopping Center (right after the 2nd stoplight). The restaurant is in the shopping center. Dress: casual. Reservations advised on weekends. AE, CB, DC, MC, V. Moderate.*

Italian

★ **Christini's.** For traditional Italian cuisine, this is Orlando's finest. The restaurant is not about to win any awards for decor, but the food couldn't be fresher and the service couldn't be more efficient. The restaurant makes its own pastas daily and serves them with herbs, vegetables, and freshly grated Parmesan. Specialties include fresh fish; a fish soup with lobster, shrimp, and clams; and veal chops with fresh sage. *Intersection of Sand Lake Rd., and Dr. Phillips Blvd., in the Marketplace Shopping Center, tel. 407/345–8770. Jacket required. Reservations recommended. AE, CB, DC, MC, V. Expensive.*

Japanese

★ **Ran-Getsu.** The best Japanese food in town is served in this palatial setting. The atmosphere may seem a bit self-conscious—an American's idea of the Orient—but the food is fresh and carefully prepared. Sit at the curved, dragon's tail-shaped sushi bar for the Matsu platter—an assortment of *nigiri-* and *maki-*style sushis—or, if you are with a group, sit Japanese style at tables overlooking a carp-filled pond and decorative gardens. Specialties are sukiyaki and *shabu-shabu* (thinly sliced beef in a boiling seasoned broth, served with vegetables and prepared at your table). If you feel more adventurous, try the deep-fried alligator tail. *8400 International Dr., Orlando, tel. 407/345–0044. Dress: casual. Reservations accepted. AE, CB, DC, MC, V. Moderate.*

Kosher **Palm Terrace.** This is a kosher restaurant supervised by Rabbi Jakobs of the Orthodox Union. Diners who are not guests at the Hyatt Orlando pay a fixed price of just under $30 (half price, half portions for children) for Shabbos meals. Meals must be prepaid on Friday, and reservations are required one-half hour before candle lighting. Kosher breakfast and lunch items are available next door at the Marketplace Deli from 6 AM to midnight (the Hyatt also has a shul, with services held twice daily). *Hyatt Orlando, 6375 Irlo Bronson Memorial Hwy., Kissimmee, tel. 407/396–1234. Dress: casual. Reservations required. AE, CB, DC, MC, V. Moderate.*

Middle Eastern **Phoenician.** *Hummus, baba ghanouj,* and *lebneh* are just some of the exotic dishes at this small cafe serving authentic Mediterranean and Middle Eastern cuisine. The best bet is to order a tableful of appetizers, *meza,* and sample as many as possible. *7600 Dr. Phillips Blvd., Suite 142, Orlando, tel. 407/345–1001. Dress: casual. No reservations. AE, MC, V. Inexpensive.*

Seafood **Hemingway's.** Located by the pool at the Hyatt Regency Grand Cypress, this restaurant serves all sorts of sea creatures, from conch, scallops, and squid to grouper, pompano, and monkfish. In addition to the regular menu, Hemingway's also has what is called a "Cuisine Naturelle" menu, featuring dishes that are low in fat, calories, sodium, and cholesterol—recipes that are approved by the American Heart Association and Weight Watchers. What more could you want other than a big hot-fudge sundae for dessert? *Hyatt Regency Grand Cypress Resort, 1 Grand Cypress Blvd., Orlando, tel. 407/239–1234. Dress: casual. Reservations suggested. AE, CB, DC, MC, V. Moderate–Expensive.*

Thai **Siam Orchid.** Another in the trend of elegant Oriental restaurants offering fine dining, Siam Orchid is in a gorgeous structure and is a bit off the more beaten path of International Drive. Waitresses, in the attire of their homeland, serve authentic Thai cuisine. Some standouts are the Siam wings appetizer—stuffed chicken wings—and *pla lad prig* (a whole fish, deep-fried and covered with a sauce of red chili, bell peppers, and garlic). If you like your food spicy, ask for it "Thai hot," and grab a fire extinguisher. *7575 Republic Dr., Orlando, tel. 407/351–3935. Dress: casual. AE, DC, MC, V. Moderate.*

24 Hours **Beeline Diner.** This is a slick 1950s-style diner that's always open. It is in the Peabody Hotel, so it's not exactly cheap, but the salads, sandwiches, and griddle foods are tops. A good bet for breakfast or a late-night snack. And for just a little silver, you get to play a lot of old tunes on the jukebox. *Peabody Hotel, 9801 International Dr., Orlando, tel. 407/352–4000. Dress casual. AE, CB, DC, MC, V. Moderate.*

The Orlando Area The following restaurants are in or near the city of Orlando and cater mostly to a local clientele.

American **Jordan's Grove.** This old house was built in 1912 and now holds one of Orlando's most popular restaurants. The menu changes daily and the prix fixe includes choice of soup or salad, appetizer, entree with vegetables, and dessert. Nothing is à la carte. The changing menu allows for some creative flexing in the kitchen, and few people leave unsatisfied. Wine is the only alcoholic beverage served. The list is small but well-planned, featuring mostly American wines from smaller estates. *1300 S. Orlando Ave. (U.S. 17–92), Maitland, tel. 407/628–0020.*

Dress: casual. Reservations advised. AE, DC, MC, V. Moderate–Expensive.

Murphy Jim's. A tiny restaurant packed with charm, Murphy Jim's offers a creative menu served by an attentive staff. Highlights include broiled jumbo shrimp with lime butter and tequila sauce and red snapper doused with pineapple butter. *249 W. Rte. 436, Altamonte Springs, tel. 407/862–1668. Dress: casual. Reservations advised. AE, MC, V. Moderate.*

Chinese
★ **4, 5, 6.** Pedestrian surroundings don't hide well-prepared and well-served traditional dishes, such as steamed sea bass and chicken with snow peas that are served in Chinatown-fashion by cart-pushing waiters. *657 N. Primrose Dr., Orlando, tel. 407/898–1899. Dress: casual. Reservations advised on weekends. Open weekends to 2 AM. AE, CB, DC, MC, V. Inexpensive.*

Continental
★ **Chalet Suzanne.** If you like to drive or are returning from a day at Cypress Gardens, consider dining at this award-winning family-owned country inn and restaurant. It has been expanded bit by bit since it opened in the 1930s. Today, it looks like a small Swiss village—right in the middle of Florida's orange groves. The place settings, china, glasses, chairs, and even the tables are of different sizes, shapes, and origins. Strangely, however, it all works together as the expression of a single sensibility. For an appetizer, try broiled grapefruit. Recommended among the seven entrees are chicken Suzanne, shrimp curry, lobster Newburg, shad roe, and filet mignon. Crêpes Suzanne are a good bet for dessert. The seven-course meals begin at $40. This unlikely back-road country inn should provide one of the most memorable dining experiences one can have in Orlando. *U.S. 27 north of Lake Wales, about 10 mi past Cypress Gardens turnoff, tel. 813/676–6011. Jacket required. Reservations advised. Closed Mon. during summer. AE, CB, DC, MC, V. Expensive.*

★ **Park Plaza Gardens.** To feel part of the Park Avenue crowd, you must dine at Park Plaza Gardens. The dining room is actually a courtyard with a glass roof (contrary to what most people think, Florida is not a great place to dine al fresco), but it feels like you are dining outdoors. Tuxedoed waiters serve such delights as grouper *escovitche* and roast rack of lamb. Atmosphere is high-class but not pretentious. *319 Park Ave. S., Winter Park; tel. 407/645–2475. Dress: neat but casual. Reservations advised. AE, CB, DC, MC, V. Moderate–Expensive.*

★ **Sweet Basil.** Standing apart from other fast-food restaurants, Sweet Basil has a creative cuisine designed to take a little time. Red snapper Provençale and chicken diavolo are standouts. Specialty of the house is the painted desserts. Cheesecakes and pies are served on a vanilla sauce painted with chocolate sauce and raspberry coulis. *1009 W. Vine St., Kissimmee, tel. 407/846–1116. Dress: casual. Reservations accepted. AE, MC, V. Moderate.*

Cuban
★ **Numero Dos.** Cuban cuisine is a Florida staple, and Numero Dos is one of the best places to try it. Black bean soup, dirty rice, chicken with yellow rice, and minced meat are just a few of the specialties of this cuisine. *870 Sermoran Blvd., Casselberry, tel. 407/767–9677. Dress: casual. No reservations. MC, V. Inexpensive.*

French **La Belle Verrière.** Dine among plants and fresh flowers in the glow of Tiffany stained glass. Specialties include leg of lamb and fresh fish dishes in delicate sauces. Save room for the crème caramel or chocolate mousse. *142 S. Park Ave., Winter Park, tel. 407/645–3377. Dress: neat but casual. Reservations advised. Closed Sun. AE, CB, DC, MC, V. Moderate.*

★ **Le Coq au Vin.** The atmosphere here is "Mobile Home Modern", but the traditional French fare is first class. After dining here, you can pride yourself on discovering a place few tourists know about but that is nearly always filled with a friendly Orlando clientele. Owners Louis Perrotte and his wife, Magdalena (the hostess), are a charming couple who give the place its warmth and personality. The specialties include homemade chicken liver pâté, fresh rainbow trout with champagne, and roast Long Island duckling with green peppercorn sauce. For dessert, try the *crème brûlée. 4800 S. Orange Ave., Orlando, tel. 407/851–6980. Dress: casual. Reservations suggested. AE, CB, DC, MC, V. Moderate.*

Italian **Baby Nova.** The name Baby Nova comes from Villa Nova, the restaurant next door. But the baby proved to be such a hit when it opened in 1989 that the owners all but closed down Villa Nova and concentrated on raising their new child. The cuisine is "New Wave Italian," which means that old standards are updated. The interior is fun, with faux granite tabletops, odd-shaped flatware and plates, and high-intensity lighting. *839 N. Orlando Ave. (U.S. 17–92), Winter Park, tel. 407/644–2060. Dress: casual. Reservations for parties of 6 or more. AE, DC, MC, V. Inexpensive–Moderate.*

Mexican ★ **Bee Line Mexican Restaurant.** It looks like another hole-in-the-wall eatery, but the burritos, taco salads, meat *chalupas*, and chili rellenos are among the best in the area. *4542 Hoffner Rd., Orlando (near the airport), tel. 407/857–0566. Dress: casual. No reservations. No credit cards, but checks are accepted. Inexpensive.*

Border Cantina. A new addition to Park Avenue, Border Cantina is trendy Tex-Mex. If you can forgive the pink walls and neon lights in this third-floor restaurant, you won't have any complaints about the food. The Border does fajitas better than you'll find in most places, and the salsa is a fresh, chunky mix that will suit all tastes. *329 Park Ave. S., Winter Park, tel. 407/740–7227. Dress: casual. Reservations accepted for parties of 8 or more. AE, MC, V. Inexpensive–Moderate.*

★ **Paco's.** Good Mexican food in a cheerful but cramped little house. Guacomole is hand mashed from avocados on the premises; so are the refried beans. *1801 W. Fairbanks Ave., Winter Park, tel. 407/629–0149. Dress: casual. No reservations. No credit cards. Inexpensive.*

Pizza **Johnny's Pizza Palace.** Red leather booths are the setting for crisp pizza and a two-crust pie that Chicagoans call a stuffed pizza. Pasta and sandwiches are also on the menu. *4909 Lake Underhill Rd., tel. 407/277–3452. Dress: casual. Reservations not necessary. MC, V. Inexpensive.*

Pizzeria Uno. It's a chain, but when the pizza tastes this good, you can't hold that against it. The decor is early Chicago, a tribute to the franchise's birthplace. The menu includes spinaccoli pizza, which gets its name from the two main ingredients: spinach and broccoli. *55 W. Church St., Orlando, tel. 407/839–1800. Dress: casual. No reservations. AE, MC, V. Inexpensive.*

Rossi's. This is a local pizza joint—a garlic bread pepperoni pizza and a pitcher of Bud or root beer type of spot. The food is not about to win any awards, but Rossi's is a good escape from the tourist/hotel scene, and the price is right. *5919 S. Orange Blossom Trail, Orlando, tel. 407/855–5755. Dress: casual. AE, MC, V. Inexpensive.*

Seafood

Wekiwa Marina Restaurant. Plenty of local color here as customers ranging from three-piece-suited bankers to overall-clad farmers eat catfish, frog legs, and cheese grits in a Cracker-style wooden building on the wharf. *1000 Miami Springs Rd., Longwood (off I–4, about 20 min north of Orlando), tel. 407/862–9640. Dress: casual. Reservations only for large parties. AE, CB, DC, MC, V. Inexpensive.*

Gary's Duck Inn. This long-time Orlando favorite is known for its knotty-pine nautical motif and its fresh shrimp, crab, and fish dishes. This was the model for a seafood chain known as Red Lobster. *3974 S. Orange Blossom Trail, Orlando, tel. 407/843–0270. Dress: casual. Reservations accepted. AE, CB, DC, MC, V. Moderate.*

Steak

Cattle Ranch. If you're hungry and looking for a big, thick, juicy, down-home American steak, then steer for the Cattle Ranch. It's cheap and, if you're insanely hungry, it's free. Just take "The 6-pound Challenge," in which you're given 75 minutes to eat an entire six-pound steak dinner, including salad, potato, and bread. If you can do it, you won't have to pay a dime. If you can't, it will cost you just over $30. There is nothing fancy about this cowboy cafeteria except the steaks that come off the burning orangewood fire. And you won't see another tourist for miles around. *6129 Old Winter Garden Rd., Orlando (5 blocks west of Kirkman Rd.); tel. 407/298–7334. Dress: casual. No reservations. AE, MC, V. Inexpensive.*

Cocoa Beach Area

Moderate prices and fresh seafood are characteristic of Cocoa Beach dining. Here are some favorites.

American

Gatsby's Food and Spirits. This casual waterfront spot serves up prime rib, steaks, and seafood. Early-bird special dinner prices are in effect between 4:30 and 6:30. *480 W. Cocoa Beach Causeway, Cocoa Beach, tel. 407/783–2380. Dress: casual. Reservations advised. AE, CB, DC, MC, V. Moderate.*

Mango Tree Restaurant. Candles, fresh flowers, white linen tablecloths, rattan basket chairs, and eggshell-color walls adorned with tropical watercolors by local artists set a romantic mood at the Mango Tree. The intimate dining room overlooks a garden aviary that is home to exotic doves and pheasants. Try the grouper broiled and topped with scallops, shrimp, and hollandaise sauce. *Cottage Row, 118 N. Atlantic Ave., Cocoa Beach, tel. 407/799–0513. Dress: casual. Reservations advised. AE, MC, V. Expensive.*

Italian

Alma's Italian Restaurant. Five crowded, noisy dining rooms keep the waitresses busy. The specialties of the house are veal marsala and more than 200 imported and domestic wines. *306 N. Orlando Ave., Cocoa Beach, tel. 407/783–1981. Dress: casual. Reservations advised. AE, DC, MC, V. Inexpensive.*

Seafood

Bernard's Surf. Don't come to Bernard's for the view; there are no windows in the two main dining rooms. Come for steaks and local fish and a few unusual dishes like alligator and buffalo. A specialty is Doc Stahl's Skillet, a combination of shrimp, crabmeat, mushrooms, and wild rice sautéed and served in the skillet. *2 S. Atlantic Ave., Cocoa Beach, tel. 407/783–2401. Dress: casual. Reservations advised. AE, DC, MC, V. Closed Christmas. Expensive.*

Lodging

To stay within or outside Walt Disney World—that is the question. The law of inertia seems to keep most Walt Disney World guests within its realm. And if you are coming to Orlando for only a few days and are interested solely in the Magic Kingdom, Epcot Center, and the other Disney attractions, the resorts on Disney property may be right for you. But if you plan to visit other attractions, you should at least consider the alternatives. Let's look at the pros and cons of staying in an on-site hotel. On the positive side, you won't need to drive, and transportation within Disney World will be free. None of the hotels is within the actual confines of the Magic Kingdom or Epcot Center, but transportation is usually quick and efficient. Remember, though, that the monorail serves just three on-site hotels: the Grand Floridian, Contemporary, and Polynesian Village Resorts. If you stay anywhere else you will have to take Disney's bus to the monorail.

If you have kids, they will be able to fend for themselves more easily and stay out of trouble within Walt Disney World. Built with families in mind, rooms in the on-site resorts are large and can as a rule accommodate up to five persons. They offer cable TV with the Disney Channel and a channel providing the latest updates on special daily events.

The thrill—especially for children—of knowing you are actually staying in Walt Disney World may be worth staying here. The hotels offer many of their own special events, such as theme dinner shows and breakfasts at which Disney cartoon characters come to entertain the kids.

As a Disney guest, you get first rights to tee-off times at the busy golf courses, and you are able to call up to two days in advance to make hard-to-get reservations at any of the fine restaurants in Epcot Center. Outsiders can make reservations only by calling while at the park on the day they wish to dine.

As an on-site guest, you also get a transportation pass, and with the proper authorization, it will allow you to charge most meals and purchases made throughout WDW to your room.

On the negative side, hotels with comparable facilities tend to cost more on Disney property than off it. You may have heard that by staying at a Disney hotel you get discounts on multiple-day passports. This is little more than an advertising ploy—unless you consider the savings of a few dollars on hundreds of dollars worth of passports a significant discount. Whatever small savings you may realize will be undercut by the higher cost of staying in an on-site property.

Reservations All on-site accommodations may be booked through the Walt Disney World Central Reservations Office (Box 10100, Suite 300, Lake Buena Vista 32830, tel. 407/W–DISNEY). Reservations must often be made several months in advance and sometimes, for the best rooms during high season, a year in advance. There are always cancellations, of course, so it's worth trying even at the last minute. Keep in mind that Delta Airlines (tel. 800/221–1212) has many rooms allotted to it for its travel packages, so check with Delta, too. Visitors on a tight budget should be aware that many hotels (and attractions) offer discounts up to 40% from September to mid-December.

If the on-site resorts are full, central reservations will automatically try to book a place for you at one of the Walt Disney World Village hotels. Be sure to tell them exactly what you are looking for. You must give a deposit for your first night's stay within three weeks of making your reservation, and you can get a refund if you cancel at least five days before your scheduled stay.

Land packages, including admissions tickets, car rentals, and hotels either on or off Disney property, can be made through Walt Disney Travel Co. (1675 Buena Vista Dr., Lake Buena Vista 32830, tel. 407/828–3255).

Land/air packages, with accommodations both on and off Disney property, can be booked through **Disney Reservation Service** (tel. 800/828–0228).

Ratings The most highly recommended properties in each price category are indicated by a star ★. Rates usually include the price of two children under 18.

Category	Cost*
Very Expensive	over $150
Expensive	$120–$150
Moderate	$65–$120
Inexpensive	under $65

**double room; add 9% taxes or service*

The following credit card abbreviations are used: AE, American Express; CB, Carte Blanche; DC, Diners Club; MC, MasterCard; and V, Visa.

Walt Disney World Hotels Visitors have a choice of staying at (1) hotels that are owned and operated by Disney, (2) hotels that are privately owned but that are located on Disney property, and (3) hotels in the Orlando area.

Let's look at the Disney-run hotels first. In brief, the **Contemporary** seems to be the one that is most crowded with children and conventioneers. Yet it is also the center of action, with the most entertainment, shops, and restaurants.

The **Polynesian Village** is the most popular, particularly with families and couples. It has a relaxed environment with low, tropical buildings and walking paths along the Seven Seas Lagoon. It can be difficult to find a place to be alone, however. The charm of the **Grand Floridian** will survive the crowds. The waterfront location makes it particularly attractive.

The most relaxed and low-key of the hotels is the **Disney Inn.** It is the smallest, and, because it is between two golf courses, it is the quietest. The **Resort Villas** are especially attractive for families or groups of two or more couples. There are four different types of villas in relatively isolated woodland settings. Least formal are the trailer and camp sites that are in an even more wooded setting in the Fort Wilderness Resort area.

Spurred on by the success of its **Caribbean Beach Resort,** WDW is putting the finishing touches on **Port Orleans Resort,** half of the Mississippi River hotels project. When **Dixie Landings** is completed next year, there will be 5,168 moderately priced hotel rooms at WDW.

Four hotels, which were built around a 50-acre lagoon, opened in 1990 and are linked with Epcot by a dazzling boardwalk filled with entertainment, restaurants, and shopping. The **Swan** and the **Dolphin** are whimsical on the outside and luxurious on the inside. The **Yacht Club** and **Beach Club** resorts remind visitors of turn-of-the-century New England and Virginia oceanside resorts.

Reservations sometimes become available at the last minute. For same-day reservations, phone each Disney property directly. For advance reservations, tel. 407/W–DISNEY.

Contemporary Resort Hotel. This high rise in the heart of Walt Disney World has a slick, space-age impersonality. Shops, lounges, and restaurants bustle under the 15-story atrium, creating an urban atmosphere not found in other, more easygoing Disney facilities. The futuristic monorail running right through the lobby contributes to the stark, modernistic mood. Rooms in the front are at a premium because they look out toward the Magic Kingdom. *Central Reservations, Box 10100, Lake Buena Vista 32830, tel. 407/W–DISNEY or 407/824–1000 for same-day reservations. 1,052 rooms. AE, MC, V. Very Expensive.*

Disney Inn. Golfers are "fore" it, of course, but anyone who wants to get away from the crowds will appreciate this hotel once known as the Golf Resort. It's the smallest and quietest resort among the on-site hotels. The golf is world class, but since its name change the inn has also been discovered by couples who want some quiet time (with or without children). The most expensive rooms overlook the pool. Rooms on the first floor have direct access to the pool but can be noisy at times. Rooms with a view of the golf fairways are particularly pleasant. One of the quietest places to eat within Walt Disney World is located here—a restaurant called the Garden Gallery, serving American cuisine. *Central Reservations, Box 10100, Lake Buena Vista 32830, tel. 407/W–DISNEY or 407/824–2200. 288 rooms. AE, MC, V. Expensive–Very Expensive.*

★ **Grand Floridian Beach Resort.** This Palm Beach-style coastal hot spot offers old-fashioned character with all the conveniences of a modern hotel. The gabled red roof, brick chimneys, and long ambling verandahs were built with loving attention to detail. Small touches, such as crystal chandeliers and stained-glass domes, create the feeling of a more sedate and leisurely era. As might be expected from a beach resort, there are all sorts of water sports at the marina. The Floridian also has its own monorail stop that links it to the TTC. Even the resort's monorail station elegantly carries off the Victorian theme. *Central Reservations, Box 10100, Lake Buena Vista 32830, tel. 407/W–DISNEY. AE, MC, V. 900 rooms, including 69 concierge rooms and 12 suites. Very Expensive.*

Polynesian Village Resort. You are supposed to get the feeling that you are on a tropical island when you come here, so everything at The Poly, as it's called, has a South Pacific slant to it. The focal point of the resort is the Great Ceremonial House, where visitors check in. The atrium sets the tone, with its lush tropical atmosphere complete with volcanic rock fountains, blooming orchids, and coconut palms—the whole bit. You might think you were at a resort in Fiji if you didn't notice all the kids running around wearing Mickey Mouse caps.

Stretching from the main building are 11 two- and three-story "longhouses," each of which carries the name of some exotic Pacific Island. All rooms offer two queen-size beds and a small sleeper sofa, and accommodate up to five people. Except for some second-floor rooms, all have a balcony or patio. If you don't like to walk too much and want to be near the main building, with its shops and entertainment, request a room in the Bora Bora or Maui longhouses. For the best view of the Magic Kingdom and the Seven Seas Lagoon, with its sandy palm-trimmed beaches, stay in the Samoa, Moorea, or Tonga.

The least expensive rooms look out at the other buildings, the monorail, and the parking lot across the street. Slightly more expensive are the garden- and pool-view rooms. Rooms overlooking the lagoon are the priciest, but they are also the most peaceful and include a host of upgraded amenities and services that make them among the most sought after in Disney World. Recreational activities center around the hotel's large sandy beach and marina, where you can rent boats for sailing, waterskiing, and fishing. If you can pull together a group of eight, you can even rent an outrigger canoe. The two pools can be overrun by children; you may want to go to the beach for a dip instead. *Central Reservations, Box 10100, Lake Buena Vista 32830, tel. 407/W–DISNEY or 407/824–2000 for same-day reservations. AE, MC, V. 855 rooms. Very Expensive.*

The Caribbean Beach Resort. Like the Polynesian Village Resort, the Caribbean Beach Resort is made up of villages—Aruba, Barbados, Jamaica, Martinique, and Trinidad—all two-story buildings on a 42-acre tropical lake. Each village has its own pool, laundry facility, and stretch of white-sand beach. Bridges over the lake connect the mainland with Parrot Cay, a one-acre island featuring footpaths, bike paths, and children's play areas. There is a 500-seat food court and an adjoining 200-seat lounge. Check-in is at the Custom House, off Buena Vista Drive. *WDW Central Reservations, 10100 Lake Buena Vista 32830, tel. 407/W–DISNEY or 407/934–3400. 1,200 1-bedroom units. AE, MC, V. Moderate.*

Walt Disney World Dolphin. From a distance, this hotel gives the impression of whispered whimsy, but as you get closer it shouts for recognition as another unforgettable Disney landmark. Two 55-foot sea creatures at both ends of the hotel's 14-story rectangular main section, with a 27-story pyramid, make the Sheraton-operated hotel the tallest structure in Walt Disney World. Seashell fountains with cascading waterfalls and large dolphin statues adorn this monstrous building. Seven restaurants, ranging from an ice-cream parlor to one of fine dining, surround the shell-shaped pool. The exterior is painted with a giant mural of banana leaves in coral and green. The rooms are furnished colorfully and amenities include an in-room safe, minibar, and a large vanity area. The best rooms overlook Epcot with a stunning view of IllumiNations. The 12th through 18th floors are Tower Floors and offer special services. Hotel facilities include multilingual concierge service, health club, game room, eight tennis courts, shops, youth hotel, beauty salon, car rental, airlines desk, and swimming in regular

Beach Resort, **27**
Buena Vista Palace, **10**
Caribbean Beach Resort, **29**
Casa Rosa Inn, **19**
Chalet Suzanne, **22**
Contemporary Resort Hotel, **34**
Disney Inn, **32**
Dolphin, **26**
Embassy Suites, **2**
Fort Wilderness, **30**
Grand Cypress Resort, **8**
Grand Floridian Beach Resort, **33**
Grosvenor Resort, **11**
Hilton at WDW Village, **16**
Howard Johnson, **15**
Hyatt Orlando, **21**
Knight's Inn Orlando Maingate West, **24**
Orlando Heritage Inn, **5**
Park Plaza, **1**
Peabody Orlando, **4**
Pickett Suite Resort, **13**
Polynesian Village Resort, **31**
Radisson Inn, **3**
Radisson Inn Maingate, **23**
Ramada Resort Maingate East, **18**
Residence Inn, **20**
Resort Villas, **12**
Royal Plaza, **14**
Sonesta Villa, **6**
Stouffer Orlando Resort, **7**
Swan, **25**
Travelodge, **9**
Vistana, **17**
Yacht Club, **28**

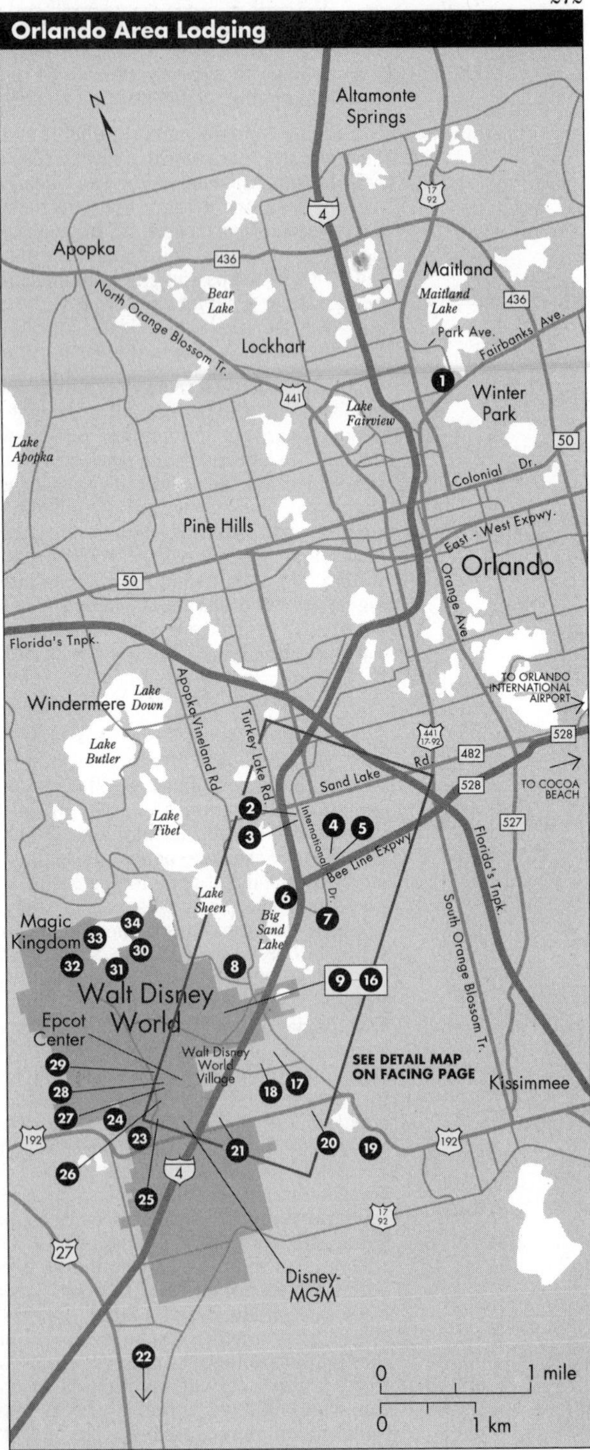

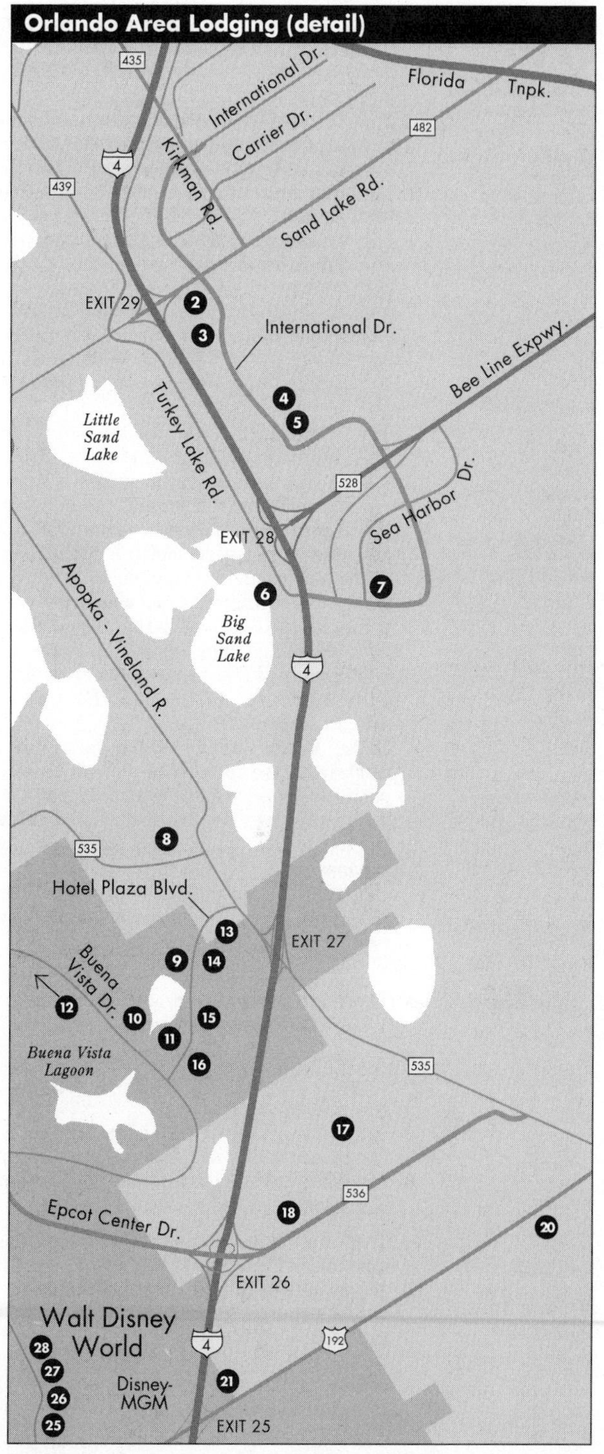
Orlando Area Lodging (detail)
435
International Dr.
Florida
Tnpk.
Carrier Dr.
482
Kirkman Rd.
4
439
Sand Lake Rd.
EXIT 29
2
3
International Dr.
Bee Line Expwy.
4
5
Little Sand Lake
Turkey Lake Rd.
528
Sea Harbor Dr.
EXIT 28
7
6
Apopka - Vineland R.
Big Sand Lake
4
8
535
Hotel Plaza Blvd.
13
EXIT 27
9
14
Buena Vista Dr.
12
10
15
11
Buena Vista Lagoon
16
535
17
536
Epcot Center Dr.
18
20
EXIT 26
Walt Disney World
28
4
192
27
21
Disney-MGM
26
25
EXIT 25

pools, a grotto, or a lake with a white-sand beach. *1500 Epcot Resort Blvd., Lake Buena Vista 32830, tel. 407/934–4000 or 800/325–3535. 1,509 rooms. AE, CB, DC, MC, V. Very Expensive.*

Walt Disney World Swan. Connected by a covered causeway to the Dolphin, the Swan is 12 stories high with two seven-story wings. Two 45-foot swans grace the rooftop, and the exterior of the hotel is painted in waves of aquamarine and coral. Rooms are decorated in a blend of coral, peach, teal, and yellow floral and geometric patterns. Amenities include in-room safe, stocked refrigerator, car rental, youth hotel, baby-sitting service, three restaurants, two lounges, health club, heated pool, tropical grotto, white-sand beach, eight lighted tennis courts, and shops. *1200 Epcot Resort Blvd., Lake Buena Vista 32830, tel. 407/934–3000 or 800/248–SWAN or 800/228–3000. 713 rooms 45 concierge rooms on 11th and 12th floors. AE, CB, DC, MC, V. Very Expensive.*

The Disney Yacht Club was built to resemble a New England seaside summer cottage of the late 1800s. A lighthouse on the pier and evergreens carry out the themed landscaping. Guests cross a wood-plank bridge to the five-story, oyster-gray clapboard resort, which features hardwood floors, rich millwork, and brass in a nautical motif. A replica of a 1902 yacht is docked at the marina and is available for evening cocktail cruises. The resort has restaurants and shops and shares a common public area with the Beach Club that includes a water recreation area with slides and snorkeling, child care, a game arcade, and a health club. *WDW Central Reservations, 10100 Lake Buena Vista 32830, tel. 407/W–DISNEY. 634 rooms, AE, CB, DC, MC, V. Expensive.*

Disney Beach Club looks like the old seaside hotel of the late 1800s with its colorful blue-and-white stick architecture and its patterned concrete walkway that leads to an entrance flanked with palm trees and an ornamented gateway bridge. The distinctive walkway also leads past a croquet lawn to beachside cabanas on a white-sand shore. The Beach Club has its own shops and restaurants, including a setting for an informal clambake, and it shares the commons with the Yacht Club. *WDW Central Reservations, 10100 Lake Buena Vista 32830, tel. 407/W–DISNEY. 580 rooms. AE, CB, DC, MC, V. Expensive.*

The Resort Villas There are a few good reasons why you may prefer the Resort Villas to the resort hotels:

- You are visiting Walt Disney World with your family or with other couples, and you want to stay together and avoid the expense of separate rooms.
- You enjoy the convenience of having your own kitchen and would like to save money by preparing some of your own meals.
- You don't like big, busy hotels, but you appreciate the amenities of a resort.

There are five clusters of villas, each with its own character and ambience. Though they are not quite as plush as rooms in the resort hotels, they are more spacious. Since the villas are not on the monorail, transportation to the parks can be slow, and to get around within the village you may want to use your car or rented golf cart. On the positive side, you have immediate access to great golf, great fishing, shopping, and an active nightlife. Check-in for resort villas is at the entrance to Disney Village Resort. *Disney World Co., Central Reservations,*

10100 Lake Buena Vista 32830, tel. 407/W–DISNEY or 407/827–1100 for same-day reservations.

One- and two-bedroom villas. They were originally built as The Vacation Villas in 1971 but were refurbished in 1986. Each unit has complete living facilities with equipped kitchens and one or two bedrooms. The one-bedroom villas have a king-size bed in one room and a queen-size sofa bed in the living room (accommodating up to four). The two-bedroom units, accommodating up to six, have a king-size bed or two twin beds in each bedroom and a sofa bed in the living room (accommodating as many as six). There are two outdoor pools. *139 1-bedroom units, 87 2-bedroom units. Very Expensive.*

Club Suite Villas. These are the smallest and the least memorable of the villas—and also the least expensive. Built of cedar, they each have one bedroom, a sofa bed, a wet bar, but no kitchen—the only villas that don't. Their size and ambience reflect the needs of business people attending meetings at the nearby Conference Center. Facilities include two outdoor pools, a small game room, a playground, and boat rentals. *61 units. Expensive.*

Two-Bedroom Villas. These villas are built of cedar, like those at Club Suite, but they are more tastefully decorated and very spacious. All have two bedrooms, and a full loft accommodating up to six. They were formerly known as the Fairway Villas because the property is surrounded by several fairways of the Lake Buena Vista Golf Course. Guests may use the pools at the Villa Recreation Center or Disney Village Clubhouse. *64 units. Very Expensive.*

Three-Bedroom Villas. If you really want to get away from it all, this is the place to stay. Isolated within a peaceful, heavily wooded area, these curious villas stand on stilts. You won't exactly feel like Tarzan and Jane in these bungalows, but you may hear some howls late at night. Predictably, this out-of-the-way little forest retreat is popular among young couples.

All "tree houses" accommodate six and have two bedrooms with queen-size beds and a third bedroom with a double bed, kitchen and breakfast bar, living room, and two bathrooms. The third bedroom is on a lower level. There is also a utility room with a washer/dryer. Guests can use nearby pools at the Villa Recreation Center or Disney Village Clubhouse. *60 units. Very Expensive.*

Fort Wilderness. If you want to rough it, stay among 730 acres of woodland, streams, small lakes, and plenty of water activities along the southeastern edge of Bay Lake, at the northern edge of Walt Disney World property.

You can rent a 42-foot-long trailer (accommodating up to six) or a 35-foot trailer (accommodating up to four). Both types have one bedroom, a bath, a full kitchen, air-conditioning, heat, and daily housekeeping services. The trailer sites are spread over 80 forested acres.

For those who are more serious about getting in touch with the great outdoors, there are campsites spread across 21 areas. Some are for visitors' own trailers, complete with electrical outlets, outdoor charcoal grills, private picnic tables, water, and waste disposal. For a real wilderness experience, full maid service is provided. There are also tent sites with water and electricity but not sewage. The most expensive sites (100–700) are nearest the lake. The least expensive (1600–1900) are far from the lake in denser vegetation. If there's a bargain, this is it. Each site accommodates up to 10 people. *Central Reservations, Box 10100, Lake Buena Vista 32830, tel. 407/W-DISNEY, or 407/824–2900 for same-day reservations. Trailers, Moderate; campsites, Inexpensive.*

Lake Buena Vista Village The formal name of this area is Walt Disney World Village Hotel Plaza at Lake Buena Vista, but most people refer to it simply as Hotel Plaza. Aside from the resorts that are actually inside Walt Disney World, these seven hotels are the most popular among visitors to Walt Disney World. This is because the properties publicize themselves as official Walt Disney World Hotels and offer many of the same incentives. Many people believe these hotels are owned by Disney. Not true. They were invited to establish themselves on Disney property, and they pay for the privilege with a percentage of their revenues. Disney does keep a close eye on them, however, to ensure that they maintain certain standards.

Because these hotels are "official," there is a premium on rooms, and rates are somewhat inflated compared with what you can find off the Disney property. Many Disney fans believe, however, that the benefits of staying in these hotels make it worthwhile. You decide.

- You can avoid box-office lines at Magic Kingdom, Epcot Center, and Disney-MGM by buying tickets at your hotel. However, you can also send for these tickets before leaving home. For a four-day passport, you get less than a 2% discount—a savings of only $1.
- You get free rides on Disney World transportation, but so does anyone with a Magic Kingdom/Epcot pass. Though you are very close to Disney World, the bus takes 15–20 minutes just to reach the monorail and runs every 10–15 minutes. Transportation from nonofficial hotels off Disney property is often just as fast.
- You can make telephone reservations for restaurants and dinner shows in Disney World in advance of the general public.
- You can use the tennis and golf facilities. The Hotel Plaza resorts are all part of an attractively landscaped complex. Each has its own restaurants and lounges, and all are within walking distance of the popular Walt Disney World Shopping Village (a pleasant outdoor mall filled with gift shops and restaurants and connected to Pleasure Island, a nighttime entertainment complex).
- All seven hotels are comfortable and convenient, and each has a character of its own. But all are usually crowded with conventions, tour groups, or just a full house of guests.

You can call each hotel's toll-free number for reservations, or you can book rooms at any of them through the **Walt Disney World Central Reservations Office,** Box 10100, Lake Buena Vista 32830, tel. 407/W-DISNEY.

Buena Vista Palace and Palace Suites Resort at Walt Disney World Village. This is the largest of the Hotel Plaza resorts, with one of its towers soaring 27 stories. When you enter its lobby, the hotel seems smaller and quieter than its bold, modern exterior and sprawling parking lots might suggest. Don't be fooled. You have entered on the third floor; when you head down to the ground level, you'll see just how large this place truly is. In 1989 $2 million was spent redecorating guest rooms in the Palace's main hotel. Early this year, a $15 million project—a 200-suite hotel connected to the tower by tropically landscaped walkways, including a covered one, was completed. Resort facilities include a health club, three heated pools, four tennis courts, beauty salon, game room, gift shops, and 10 restaurants and lounges. Rooms on the upper floors are more expensive; the best ones look out toward Epcot Center. Ask for a room in the main tower to avoid the late-night noise from the nightclub that reverberates through the atrium. *1900 Lake Buena Vista Dr., Lake Buena Vista 32830, tel. 407/827–2727 or 800/327–2990, in FL 800/432–2920. 11,029 rooms. AE, CB, DC, MC, V. Expensive–Very Expensive.*

Grosvenor Resort. This attractive hotel is probably the best deal in the neighborhood, with a wealth of facilities and comfortable rooms for a fair price. The former Americana Dutch Resort, it was completely refurbished in British colonial-style and renamed the Grosvenor. Public areas are spacious, with high molded ceilings and columns, warm cheerful colors, and plenty of natural light. Recreational facilities are geared toward the active life and include two heated pools; two lighted tennis courts; racquetball, shuffleboard, basketball, and volleyball courts; a children's playground; and a game room. Rooms are average in size, but colorfully decorated, with a refrigerator/bar and a videocassette player. In the lobby, you may rent movies for the VCR or cameras to make your own videos. *1850 Hotel Plaza Blvd., Lake Buena Vista 32830, tel. 407/828–4444 or 800/624–4109. 629 rooms. AE, CB, DC, MC, V. Moderate–Expensive.*

★ **Hilton at Walt Disney World Village.** The Hilton is generally considered the top hotel in the Village. It is also one of the most expensive. In contrast to the lackluster facade, the interiors are richly decorated with brass and glass and softened with tasteful carpets. Guest rooms sparkle. Rooms are not huge, but they are cozy and contemporary, with high-tech amenities. All are the same size, with a king-size bed, two double beds, or two queen-size beds. The most expensive rooms have views of the shopping village and lake. Rooms overlooking the pool are also desirable. Although all rooms are the same size, they vary dramatically in price by location and floor, as well as by season. The Hilton provides a service that many parents will consider indispensable—a **Youth Hotel** for children aged 3–12. The hotel has full-time supervisors for its playroom, a large-screen TV (with Disney Channel, of course), a six-bed dormitory, and scheduled meals. The Youth Hotel is open daily 4:30 PM–midnight. The cost is $4 per hour. Other facilities include two pools, a health club, two lighted tennis courts, and several outdoor and indoor bars and restaurants, including the popular **American Vineyards,** serving New American cuisine. *1751 Hotel Plaza Blvd., Lake Buena Vista 32830, tel. 407/827–4000 or 800/445–8667. 813 rooms. AE, MC, V. Expensive–Very Expensive.*

Pickett Suite Resort. Walt Disney World is certainly not one to fall behind the current trends in the hotel industry, so it is not surprising that the most recent addition to the Lake Buena Vista neighborhood would be an all-suite hotel. Suites consist of a comfortable living room area and a separate bedroom with two double beds or a king-size bed. With a sofa bed in the living room, a suite can accommodate up to six people, but certainly not all comfortably. The arrangement is convenient for small families who want to avoid the hassle of cots and the expense of two separate rooms. Each unit has a TV in each room (plus a small one in the bathroom!), a stocked refrigerator, a wet bar, a coffee maker and, on request, a microwave oven. The hotel attracts a quiet, family-oriented crowd and few of the noisy conventioneers one finds at the larger, splashier properties. Facilities include a whirlpool spa, heated swimming and wading pools, two tennis courts, a game room, and a children's play area. *2305 Hotel Plaza Blvd., Lake Buena Vista 32830, tel. 407/934–1000 or 800/742–5388. 229 units. AE, CB, DC, MC, V. Expensive–Very Expensive.*

Royal Plaza. From the lobby, this hotel seems a bit dated in comparison with the slick, modern hotels in the neighborhood. But the extremely casual, fun-loving atmosphere makes it popular with families who have young children and teenagers. The rooms are generous in size, the best ones overlooking the pool. If you have any interest in afternoon naps, make sure your room isn't too close to the ground floor. The hotel has several restaurants and bars, a few shops, a hair salon, four lighted tennis courts, a sauna, pool, and putting green. *1905 Hotel Plaza Blvd., Lake Buena Vista 32830, tel. 407/828–2828 or 800/248–7890. 397 rooms. AE, CB, DC, MC, V. Expensive–Very Expensive.*

Howard Johnson Lake Buena Vista. The hotel is popular with young couples and senior citizens. The price and the upgraded, 24-hour Howard Johnson's restaurant make up for the rather plain appearance. There are two heated pools, a wading pool, and a game room. *1805 Hotel Plaza Blvd., Lake Buena Vista 32830, tel. 407/828–8888 or 800/654–2000; in FL, 800/FLORIDA, in NY 800/822–3950. 323 rooms. AE, CB, DC, MC, V. Moderate–Very Expensive.*

Travelodge Hotel Walt Disney World Village. The hotel was recently refurbished, so the lobby and rooms are stylishly decorated, but other than having minibars, the rooms are unexceptional. The pool, playground, and game room are popular with kids; the nightclub on the 18th floor has a beautiful view of Disney World. *2000 Hotel Plaza Blvd., Lake Buena Vista 32830, tel. 407/828–2424, in FL, 800/423–1022, outside FL, 800/348–3765. 325 rooms. AE, CB, DC, MC, V. Expensive.*

Maingate Resorts

Maingate refers to an area full of large hotels that are not affiliated with Walt Disney World but are clustered around its northernmost entrance, just off I–4. These hotels are mostly resort hotels on sprawling properties, catering to Disney World vacationers. All are good-quality hotels with a resort sameness one can find the world over. However, they vary in size and price. As a simple rule of thumb, the bigger the resort and the more extensive the facilities, the more you can expect to pay. If you're looking for a clean, modern room, you cannot go wrong with any of them. All are equally convenient to Walt Disney World, but one may emphasize a particular recreational activity over others. Where you stay may depend on how much time you plan to spend at your hotel or on which stroke—drive or backhand—you feel needs most improving.

★ **Grand Cypress Resort.** If you were to ask someone familiar with the Orlando area which resort is the most spectacular, few would hesitate to name the Grand Cypress. The resort property is so extensive—over 1,500 acres—that guests need a trolley system to get around. There is virtually every activity you can imagine at a resort: a dozen tennis courts, boats of all shapes and varieties, scenic bicycling and jogging trails, a full health club, dozens of horses, a 600,000-gallon, triple-level swimming pool fed by 12 cascading waterfalls, a 45-acre Audubon nature reserve, 45 holes of Jack Nicklaus-designed golf, and a golfing academy for a high-tech analysis of your game. This huge resort has just one drawback: the king-size conventions that it commonly attracts. *1 Grand Cypress Blvd., Orlando 32819, tel. 407/239–1234 or 800/228–9000. 750 rooms. AE, CB, DC, MC, V. Very Expensive.*

Hyatt Orlando Hotel. This is another very large hotel, but without the extensive resort facilities. Instead of a single towering building, the hotel consists of nine two-story buildings in four clusters. Each cluster is a community with its own pool, Jacuzzi, park, and playground at its center. The rooms are spacious but otherwise unmemorable. The lobby and convention center are in a building at the center of the clusters. The lobby is vast and mall-like, with numerous shops and restaurants. One of the restaurants, the **Palm Terrace,** features a full kosher menu supervised by the Orthodox Union. There is also a very good take-out deli, with great picnic snacks for those who are wise enough to avoid the lines and prices at amusement-park fast-food stands. There are a few tennis courts, but not much else in the way of recreation. However, for busy travelers who will be spending most of their time attacking Orlando's attractions, this is a convenient, not-too-expensive headquarters. *6375 W. Irlo Bronson Memorial Hwy., Kissimmee 32746, tel. 407/396–1234; in FL, 800/331–2003; outside FL, 800/544–7178. 946 rooms. AE, CB, DC, MC, V. Moderate.*

Knight's Inn Orlando Maingate West. There's a good selection of rooms here for a budget motel, including rooms with two double beds and efficiency apartments. Nonsmoker rooms are available, and there is a pool. *7475 W. Irlo Bronson Hwy., Kissimmee 32746, tel. 407/396–4200. 120 units. AE, CB, DC, MC, V. Inexpensive.*

Ramada Resort Maingate East at the Parkway. The Ramada may offer the best deal in the neighborhood—a more attractive setting at more competitive prices. It has three lighted tennis courts, a pool with a waterfall, a few shops and restaurants, and a delicatessen for picnickers. The rooms, like the rest of the hotel grounds, are spacious and bright, decked out in tropical and pastel colors. The best rooms, because of the view and light, face the pool. *2900 Parkway Blvd., Kissimmee 32746, tel. 407/396–7000; in FL, 800/255–3939, outside FL, 800/634–4774. 592 rooms. AE, CB, DC, MC, V. Moderate.*

Vistana Resort. Anyone interested in tennis should consider staying at this peaceful time-share resort spread over 50 beautifully landscaped acres. It is also popular with families or groups who are willing to share a spacious, tastefully decorated villa or town house, each with at least two bedrooms and all the facilities of home—a full kitchen, living room, a washer/dryer, and so on. The price may seem high, but considering the number of people each condominiumlike unit can accommodate (up to six or eight), the rates can be a bargain. The 14 clay and all-weather tennis courts can be used without charge. Private or semi-private lessons are available for every type of player. Other facilities include a huge, free-form pool and a full health club. *13800 Vistana Dr., Lake Buena Vista 32830, tel. 407/239–3100 or 800/877–8787. 604 units. AE, CB, DC, MC, V. Very Expensive.*

Orlando Area
International Drive

The International Drive area, referred to by locals as "The Drive" and formally labeled "Florida Center," is a main drag for all sorts of hotels, restaurants, and shopping malls. As you head north along The Drive, the hotels get cheaper, the restaurants turn into fast-food joints, and malls translate into factory outlets. The southern end of The Drive is more classy, but the northern end may be more congenial to your budget—particularly if all you need is a place to put your head at night.

You will be hard pressed to find any structure around here older than you are, even if you are a teenager, because the area has been built up mostly in the past 10 years as an alternative to the Disney properties. For those who are not interested exclusively in Disney World, The Drive is a convenient point of departure for Orlando's countless other attractions. The Drive immediately parallels I–4 (at Exits 28 and 29), so a few minutes' drive north puts you in downtown Orlando, while a few minutes south on I–4 puts you in Disney World.

International Drive showcases such local attractions as Sea World, the labyrinth water-slide park, Wet 'n Wild, and many popular dinner shows. Many veteran Orlando visitors consider The Drive the territory's most comfortable home base, featuring some of the best hotels around.

★ **Peabody Orlando.** From afar, the Peabody looks like a high-rise office building. Don't let its austere exterior scare you away. Once inside, you will discover a very impressive, handsomely designed hotel. If you ignore the soaring numbers in the elevators and the sweeping view from your room, you will never know you are in a 27-story hotel. The Peabody's lobby has rich marble floors and fountains, and the entire hotel is decorated with modern art, giving it much color and flare. The rooms with the best views face Walt Disney World and a sea of orange trees that extends as far as the eye can see. If you want to be pampered, stay in the Peabody Club on the top three floors and enjoy special concierge service. The Peabody has a pool, a health club, and four lighted tennis courts. There are also two fine restaurants. *9801 International Dr., Orlando 32819, tel. 407/352–4000 or 800/PEABODY. 891 rooms. AE, CB, DC, MC, V. Expensive–Very Expensive.*

★ **Sonesta Villa Resort Hotel.** The Sonesta, located off I–4 near International Drive, is a string of multi-unit town houses on a lakefront. Following the lead of the all-suite hotels, the Sonesta "villas" consist of small apartments, some of which are bilevel with a fully equipped kitchenette, dining room/living room area, small patio, and bedroom. The units are comfortable and homey, each with its private, ground-floor entrance. One bonus of staying at the Sonesta is the outdoor facilities, including tennis courts, mini health club, pool, and whirlpools convenient to each villa. Guests can sail and waterski on the lake or offer themselves to the sun on a sandy beach. There is a restaurant and bar, but the only action is the nightly outdoor barbecue buffet. If you want to cook at "home" but are too busy to go shopping, the hotel offers a grocery delivery service. Laundry, however, is self-service. *10000 Turkey Lake Rd., Orlando 32819, tel. 407/352–8051 or 800/343–7170. 384 units. AE, CB, DC, MC, V. Expensive.*

Stouffer Orlando Resort. This first-rate resort was originally the Wyndham Hotel Sea World, until it was sold to the Stouffer chain in 1987. Located directly across the street from Sea

World, this bulky, 10-story building looks more like a Federal Reserve Bank than a comfortable hotel. When you enter, you step into what is billed as the largest atrium lobby in the world. Facilities include six lighted tennis courts, a pool, a whirlpool, a child-care center, a game room, and access to an 18-hole golf course. On the second floor are a Nautilus-equipped fitness center and a beauty salon where you can work off or hide the effects of dinner. Guest rooms are all large and spacious. The most expensive rooms face the atrium, but if you are a light sleeper, ask for a room facing outside to avoid the music and party sounds of conventioneers, which rise through the atrium. *6677 Sea Harbor Dr., Orlando 32821, tel. 407/351–5555, 800/327–6677, or 800/HOTELS–1. 778 rooms. AE, CB, DC, MC, V. Expensive.*

Embassy Suites Hotel at Plaza International. The concept of the all-suite hotel has become very popular in the Orlando area, and the Embassy Suites, a chain hotel, was the first to offer it. All suites have a bedroom and a full living room equipped with wet bar, refrigerator, desk, pull-out sofa, and two TVs. It is a comfortable and economical arrangement, somewhat less expensive than a single room in the top-notch hotels. Because the bedroom can be closed off, it is ideal for small families. The core of the hotel is a wide atrium. It is not nearly as large as the atrium at the Stouffer, but it is much cozier, with a relaxing lounge and a pianist as its centerpieces. The hotel has both an indoor and an outdoor pool, an exercise room with Jacuzzi, sauna, steam room, and game room, but with none of the other recreational facilities that the larger hotels have. *8250 Jamaican Court, Orlando 32819, tel. 407/345–8250 or 800/327–9797. 246 rooms. AE, CB, DC, MC, V. Moderate–Expensive.*

Orlando Heritage Inn. If you are looking for a simple, small hotel with reasonable rates but plenty of deliberate charm, the Heritage is the place to stay. Located next to the towering Peabody, this inn creates the atmosphere of Victorian-style Florida, complete with reproduction turn-of-the-century furnishings, rows of French windows and brass lamps, and a smattering of genuine 19th-century antiques. The guest rooms are decorated with a colonial accent—lace curtains on double French doors, folk-art prints on the walls, and quilted bed covers. The hotel has a small saloon-type lounge, and there is a dinner theater in the large Victorian rotunda several nights a week. With the exception of a pool, there are few facilities. The whole place has a kitsch quaintness, in contrast to the area's other hotels, and a staff that is strong on southern hospitality. *9861 International Dr., Orlando 32819, tel. 407/352–0008 or in FL 800/282–1890 or outside FL 800/447–1890. 150 rooms. AE, CB, DC, MC, V. Moderate.*

Radisson Inn and Aquatic Center. If you want to get in shape while visiting Orlando but want to avoid fancy resort prices, this is the place for you. Radisson is a big, modern, moderately priced hotel offering comfortable rooms (the best ones face the pool), but what makes it truly special are its outstanding athletic facilities. The hotel has a fine outdoor pool, but for those who are serious about swimming, there is also an indoor Aquatic Center with an Olympic-size swimming and diving pool. The center was built for competitive swimming and diving events and has a high-tech Human Performance Lab for personal health assessment. Other hotel facilities include a complete Nautilus center with weights and aerobicycles; tennis, raquetball, and handball courts; a jogging track; aerobics and swimmercise classes; and plenty more, including access to a local country club for golf. *8444 International Dr., Orlando 32819, tel. 407/345–0505 or 800/333–3333. 300 rooms. AE, CB, DC, MC, V. Moderate.*

U.S. 192 Area If you are looking for anything remotely quaint, charming, or sophisticated, head elsewhere. The U.S. 192 strip, formally called Irlo Bronson Memorial Highway and referred to as the Spacecoast Parkway, is generally known as Kissimmee. But whatever you call it, it is an avenue crammed with bargain-basement motels and hotels, inexpensive restaurants, fast-food chains, nickel-and-dime attractions, gas stations, and minimarts. If all you are looking for is a decent room with perhaps a few extras for a manageable price, this is your wonderland. The number of motels here is mind boggling. It is a buyer's market, and room rates start as low as $20 a night—or lower if it is the right time of year and you can cut the right deal. But most rooms will run about $30–$70 a night, depending on the hotel's facilities and its proximity to Disney World. Among the chain hotels are Travelodge, Econolodge, Comfort Inn, Holiday Inn, Radisson, Sheraton, and Best Western.

The Residence Inn. Of the all-suite hotels on U.S. 192, this one is probably the best. It consists of a row of four-unit town houses with private stairway entrances to each suite. One side of the unit faces the highway, the other overlooks an attractive lake, where visitors can sail, waterski, jet ski, and fish. Forty of the units are penthouses, with complete kitchens, small living rooms, loft bedrooms, and even fireplaces. The other units are set up like studio apartments, but they still contain full kitchens and fireplaces. Regular studio suites accommodate two people; double suites accommodate up to four. Both Continental breakfast and a grocery shopping service are complimentary. The price may seem expensive, considering the location, but there is no charge for additional guests, so you can squeeze in the whole family at no extra cost. *4786 W. Irlo Bronson Memorial Hwy., Kissimmee 32746, tel. 407/396–2056; in FL, 800/648–7408; outside FL, 800/468–3027. 160 units. AE, CB, DC, MC, V. Moderate–Expensive.*

Radisson Inn Maingate. Located just a few minutes from the Magic Kingdom's front door, the building is very sleek and modern with cheerful guest rooms, large bathrooms, and plenty of extras for the price. Facilities include a pool, a whirlpool, two lighted tennis courts, and a jogging trail. Not fancy, but sufficient. The best rooms are those with a view of the pool. One floor is reserved for nonsmokers. *7501 W. Irlo Bronson Memorial Hwy., Kissimmee 32746, tel. 407/396–1400 or 800/333–3333. 580 rooms. AE, CB, DC, MC, V. Moderate.*

★ **Casa Rosa Inn.** For simple motel living—no screaming kids or loud music, please—this is your place. The pink, Spanish-style motel does not have much in the way of facilities other than a little pool and free in-room movies, but it is a good, serviceable place to hang your hat. *4600 W. Irlo Bronson Memorial Hwy., Kissimmee 32746, tel. 407/396–2020 or 800/874–1589. 54 rooms. AE, MC, V. Inexpensive.*

Off the Beaten Track Mention should be made of two hotels that are off the beaten track—close enough to be part of the immediate Orlando area, but not so close that they fit into one of our categories.

Winter Park ★ **Park Plaza Hotel.** Located in Orlando's very posh, established suburb of Winter Park, the Park Plaza is an old-fashioned, wood-and-wicker Southern hotel, built in 1922. If you are in need of recreational facilities or special amenities, look elsewhere, but if you are hoping to find real Southern charm and hospitality, this is perhaps the best place in the Orlando area to find it. You are as far from the world of tourism as you can get and still be within a short driving distance of all the major attractions. It is a small, intimate hotel that gives you the feeling that you are a guest in somebody's home. All rooms open up onto one long balcony, covered with ferns, flowers, and wicker furniture. *307 Park Ave. S, Winter Park 32789, tel. 407/647–1072 or 800/228–7220. To get there, drive east on I–4 and exit at Fairbanks Ave. Turn right for 1 mi until you reach Park Ave. The hotel is on your left. 27 rooms. AE, CB, DC, MC, V. Moderate–Expensive.*

Lake Wales **Chalet Suzanne.** You'll find this conversation piece of a hotel in orange-grove territory, in what seems the middle of nowhere. A homemade billboard directs you down a country road that turns into a palm-lined drive. Cobblestone paths lead to a row of chalet-style houses and cabins, complete with balconies and thatch roofing. The Chalet Suzanne has been built bit by unlikely bit over the years, and the furnishings range from the rare and valuable to the garage-sale special. Bathrooms are tiled and have old-fashioned tubs, and wash basins. The most charming rooms face the lake. *U.S. Highway 27S, Drawer AC, Lake Wales 33859, tel. 813/676–6011. To get there, either land your Cessna or Lear jet on the private airstrip, or drive. Go west on I–4 from Orlando to the Rte. 27 exit and head toward Cypress Gardens. The chalet's billboard is past the Cypress Gardens turnoff, just after Lake Wales. 30 rooms. AE, CB, DC, MC, V. Moderate–Expensive.*

Cocoa Beach **Holiday Inn Cocoa Beach Resort.** When two separate beach hotels were redesigned and a promenade park landscaped between them, the Holiday Inn Cocoa Beach Resort was born. It features plush modern public rooms, an Olympic-size heated pool, tennis courts, and private access to the beach. You can choose from a wide selection of accommodations—standard, king, and oceanfront suites; villas; and bilevel lofts—all with in-room movies. Free aerobic workouts are offered, as are planned activities for children. *1300 N. Atlantic Ave., Cocoa Beach 32931, tel. 407/783–2271. 500 rooms. AE, DC, MC, V. Expensive.*

Crossway Inn—A Cocoa Beach Resort. Located across the street from the ocean and within walking distance of at least 16 restaurants, this is a convenient lodging. You can choose from standard double rooms, minisuites, or fully equipped efficiencies—all are clean, comfortable, and decorated in tropical colors. Amenities include a lighted volleyball court, 15-foot "mallet pool" court (you sink the 8-ball with a croquet mallet), children's playground, and an airy Key West–style lounge with rattan furnishings and hand-painted tropical murals. *3901 N. Atlantic Ave., Cocoa Beach 32931, tel. 407/783–2221; in FL, 800/247–2221; outside FL, 800/327–2224. 94 units. AE, DC, MC, V. Inexpensive.*

Pelican Landing Resort On the Ocean. This recently refurbished, two-story beachfront motel conveys a friendly family atmosphere with its oceanfront views and screened porches (available in units 1 and 6). A microwave in each room, boardwalks to the beach, picnic tables, and a gas grill round out the amenities. *1201 S. Atlantic Ave., Cocoa Beach 32931, tel. 407/783–7197. 11 units. MC, V. Inexpensive.*

Nightlife

Walt Disney World

Top of the World. This is Disney's sophisticated nighttime entertainment spot, located on the top floor of the Contemporary Resort. A spirited show called "Broadway at the Top" runs for about an hour after the two nightly seatings for dinner. A cast of high-energy dancers and singers bring to life some of Broadway's greatest hits. A single price includes the show and dinner. Tax, gratuity, and alcoholic drinks are extra. *Contemporary Resort, tel. 407/W–DISNEY. Jacket required. Reservations necessary months in advance. Admission: $42.50 adults, $19.50 children 3–11. Seatings at 6 and 9:15.*

Polynesian Revue and Mickey's Tropical Revue. Put on some comfortable, casual clothes and head over to the Polynesian Village Resort for an outdoor barbecue and a tropical luau, complete with fire jugglers and hula drum dancers. It's a colorful, South Pacific setting and an easygoing evening that families find relaxing and trouble free. There are two shows nightly of the Polynesian Revue and an earlier show for children called Mickey's Tropical Revue, where Disney characters perform decked out in costumes befitting these South Seas surroundings. *Polynesian Village Resort, tel. 407/W–DISNEY. Dress: casual. Reservations necessary, usually months in advance. Polynesian Review: $29 adults, $23 juniors 12–20, and $15 children 3–11. Seatings at 6:45 and 9:30. Mickey's Tropical Revue: adults $25, juniors $20, children $11. Seating at 4:30.*

Hoop-Dee-Doo Revue. This family entertainment dinner show may be corny, but it is also the liveliest and most rollicking. A troupe of jokers called the Pioneer Hall Players stomp their feet, wisecrack, and make merry in this Western mess-hall setting. The chow consists of barbecued ribs, fried chicken, corn on the cob, strawberry shortcake, and all the fixins. There are three shows nightly at Pioneer Hall in the Fort Wilderness area—not the easiest place to get to. *Fort Wilderness Resort, tel. 407/W–DISNEY. Dress: informal. Reservations necessary, sometimes months in advance. For same day reservations, 407/824–2748. Admission: $30 adults, $24 juniors 12–20, $16 children 3–11. Seatings at 5, 7:30, and 10 PM.*

Pleasure Island. There is a single admission charge to this nightlife entertainment complex, which features a comedy club, teenage dance center, rock-and-roller skating-rink disco, numerous restaurants, lounges, shops, and even a 10-screen theater complex. Six themed nightclubs offer everything from swinging jazz to foot-stompin' country and western to the latest pop video hits. It doesn't cost anything to wander around the island, but an admission ticket is required for all clubs except the Baton Rouge Lounge on the *Empress Lilly*. One ticket gets you into all the clubs, but there are some age restrictions. The clubs and their opening hours are: **Adventurers Club,** live performers and special effects, 6:30 PM; **Baton Rouge Lounge,** live jazz and comedy, noon; **Comedy Warehouse,** comedy club, 7 PM; **Mannequins Dance Palace,** dancing to Top-40 music in a high-tech disco, 8 PM; **Neon Armadillo Music Saloon,** live country-and-western music and dancing, 7 PM; **Videopolis East,** rock music videos and dancing for the 13–20 set, no alcoholic beverages sold, 6:30 PM; **XZFR Rockin' Rollerdrome,** dancing to a live band with rollerskating in a multilevel hall, skate rental is extra, weekdays 5 PM., weekends 11 AM; **Orbiter Lounge,** place to go at XZFR's for "Zappy Hour" from 5–7, admission ticket required at 7. *Pleasure Island, tel. 407/934–7781. Dress: informal. Reservations not necessary. Admission: $9.95. Hours: 10 AM–2 AM.*

IllumiNations. You won't want to miss Epcot Center's grand finale, a laser show that takes place along the shores of the World Showcase lagoon, every night just before Epcot closes. It is a show unlike any other. In the middle of the lagoon, laser projections of dancing images move across screens of spraying water. Orchestral music fills the air as multicolored neon lasers streak across the sky, pulsating to the rhythms of the music. Suddenly the night lights up with brilliant fireworks and the lagoon vibrates with the sounds of Tchaikovsky's 1812 Overture. Projections of the Earth's continents transform Spaceship Earth into a luminescent, spinning globe. The lasers used to create these images are powerful enough to project an identical image on a golf ball up to five miles away. The projections are called IllumiNations, and one of them creates a towering Mt. Fuji over the Japan pavilion. When the show is over, the crowds exit as Spaceship Earth continues to revolve. It is a stellar performance that you won't want to miss.

The Orlando Area

Until a few years ago Orlando's nightlife was more like that of Oskaloosa, Iowa, than of a booming tourist haven. But slowly, an after-dark scene has developed, spreading farther and farther beyond the realm of Disney. Orlando entrepreneurs have now caught on that there is a fortune to be had by satisfying the fun-hungry night owls that flock to this city. New night spots open constantly, offering everything from flashy discos to ballroom dancing, country-and-western saloons, Broadway dinner theaters, and even medieval jousting tournaments.

The Arts

If all the fantasyland hype starts to wear thin, and you feel the need for more sophisticated entertainment, check out the local fine arts scene in *Orlando Magazine*, *Center Stage*, or the "Calendar" and "Arts and Entertainment" sections of Friday's and Sunday's *Orlando Sentinel*, available at any newsstand. The price of a ticket to performing arts events in the Orlando area rarely exceeds $10–$12 and is often half that price.

Orlando has an active performing arts agenda of ballet, modern dance, classical music, opera, and theater, much of which takes place at the **Carr Performing Arts Centre** (401 Livingston St., tel. 407/849–2070). This community auditorium presents a different play each month (Wed.–Sat., with Sun. matinees). The Broadway series features performances on the way to Broadway or current road shows.

During the school year, **Rollins College** (tel. 407/646–2233) in Winter Park has a choral and symphonic concert series that is open to the public and usually free. The first week of March, there is a **Bach Music Festival** (tel. 407/646–2110) that has been a Winter Park tradition for over 55 years. Also at the college is the **Annie Russell Theater** (tel. 407/646–2145), which has a regular series of productions.

Across the street from the Peabody Hotel on International Drive is the **Orange County Civic and Convention Center** (tel. 407/345–9800), which hosts many big-name performing artists.

Brevard Community College (1519 Clearlake Rd., Cocoa, tel. 407/632–1111, ext. 3660) each year sponsors the **Lyceum Series,** featuring a lineup of state, national, and international performing groups in the fields of music, theater, and dance.

Surfside Playhouse (Brevard Ave. and S. Fifth St., Cocoa Beach, tel. 407/783–3127), a community theater in operation since 1959, annually produces a season of high-standard performances.

Dinner Shows

Dinner shows have become an immensely popular form of nighttime entertainment around Orlando. A set price usually buys a multiple-course dinner and a theatrical production—a totally escapist experience. The food tends to be predictable—but not the major attractions. Always make reservations in advance, especially on weekends. A lively crowd can be an asset; a show playing to a small audience can be a pathetic and embarrassing sight. What the shows lack in substance and depth, the audience makes up for in color and enthusiasm. The result is an evening of light entertainment, which kids in particular will enjoy.

Arabian Nights. This attraction inside an Arabian Palace (home to eight breeds of horses from around the world) features 60 performing horses, music, special effects, a chariot race, and a four-course dinner. Low-cholesterol meals may be ordered when making reservations. *6225 W. Irlo Bronson Memorial Hwy. (U.S. 192), Kissimmee, tel. in Orlando, 407/239–9223, in Kissimmee, 407/396–7400 or 800/533–6116, in Canada, 800/533–3615. Dress: casual. Reservations required. Admission: $25.95 adults, $16.95 children 3–11. AE, CB, DC, MC, V.*

Mardi Gras. This jazzy, New Orleans–style show is the best of Orlando's dinner attractions. The set menu consists of mixed vegetable soup, tossed salad, buckets of fried chicken, platters of roast beef, apple pie with ice cream, and all the beer, wine, or soda you can drink. It is not an elaborate meal, but it is as good as one can expect from a dinner theater. A New Orleans jazz band plays during dinner, followed by a one-hour cabaret with colorful song-and-dance routines to rhythms of the Caribbean, Latin America, and Dixieland jazz. Although the kids are more likely to vote for the Wild West or medieval shows, adults tend to prefer Mardi Gras because it is more of a restaurant nightclub than a fantasyland. *At the Mercado Mediterranean Village, 8445 International Dr., Orlando, tel. 407/351–5151 or 800/347–5151. Dress: casual. Reservations required. Admission: $27.95 adults, $19.95 children 3–11. AE, CB, DC, MC, V.*

Fort Liberty. Run by the same company that operates Mardi Gras and King Henry's Feast, this dinner show whisks you out to the Wild West. The entertainment is a mixed bag of real Indian dances, foot-stompin' sing-alongs, and acrobatics. A British cowboy shows what he can do with bullwhips and lassos, and a musician plays the 1812 Overture on the tuba and "America the Beautiful" on an old saw (yes, the kind that cuts wood). The show is full of slapstick theatrics and country-western shindigging that children really enjoy. The chow is what you might expect to eat with John Wayne out on the prairie: beef soup, fried chicken, corn on the cob, and pork and beans. You are served by a rowdy chorus of cavalry recruits who keep the food coming and beverages freely pouring. All tables seat 12, so unless you are in a big party, expect to develop pass-the-ketchup relationships. Fort Liberty is a stockade filled with shops and stalls selling gifts and souvenirs with a Western theme. The ambience is set by the photographers snapping photos of visitors dressed in cowboy garb. Forever trying to attract tourists, the Fort Liberty entertainers perform in the courtyard during the day. If the kids are more intent on seeing Marlboro country than you are, go at lunch time (11–2), pick up some fast-food fried chicken for $2, and see many of the acts that are in the dinner show. *5260 Irlo Bronson Memorial Hwy. (U.S. 192), Kissimmee, tel. 407/351-5151 or 800/847-8181. Dress: casual. Reservations required. Admission: $24.95 adults, $16.95 children 3–11. AE, CB, DC, MC, V.*

King Henry's Feast. Driving along the strip of hotels and shopping malls on I-4 or International Drive, you may notice two Tudor-style buildings. One of them is the Econolodge; the other is the home of Orlando's King Henry VIII and his court of 16th-century jesters. The entertainment includes a corny but talented magician, a daring fire-swallowing acrobat, and much singing, dancing, and revelry as King Henry celebrates his birthday and begins his quest for his seventh bride. Saucy wenches, who refer to customers as "me lords" and "me ladies," serve potato-leek soup, salad, chicken and ribs, and all the beer, wine, and soft drinks you can guzzle. Bar drinks are extra. *8984 International Dr., Orlando, tel. 407/351-5151 or 800/347-8181. Dress: casual. Reservations required. Admission: $24.95 adults, $16.95 children 3–11. AE, CB, DC, MC, V.*

Medieval Times. In a huge, modern-medieval manor, visitors enjoy a four-course dinner while watching the struggle of good and evil in a tournament of games, sword fights, and jousting matches, including no less than 30 charging horses and a cast of 75 knights, nobles, and maidens. Sound silly? It is. Yet if you view it through the eyes of your children, this two-hour extravaganza of pageantry and meat-and-potatoes banquet fare can be amusing. Everyone faces forward along narrow banquet tables that are stepped auditorium-style above the tournament. If you and your family traveled the amusement-park route all day and are tired of looking and nagging at each other, you may get some respite, a bit of comic relief, and some vicarious pleasure from a night of crossing lances. *4510 W. Irlo Bronson Memorial Hwy. (U.S. 192), Kissimmee, tel. 407/239-0214 or 407/396-1518, in FL 800/432-0768, outside FL 800/327-4024. Dress: informal. Reservations required. Admission: $25 per person. AE, MC, V.*

Mark Two. This is the only true dinner theater in Orlando, with full Broadway musicals, such as *Oklahoma!*, *My Fair Lady*, *West Side Story* and *South Pacific*, staged through most of the year. During the Christmas holiday season, shorter Broadway musical revues are presented. A buffet and full-service cocktail bar open for business about two hours before the show. The food is nothing to write home about and should not be the reason to pay a visit. The buffet of seafood Newburg, baked whitefish, a variety of meats, and salad bar is only a few notches above cafeteria food. Best bets are the rich desserts that arrive during intermission. The shows are directed by the theater's owner, and the sets, costumes, music, and choreography are all done in-house. The actors are mostly from the Orlando area. It will not be the best performance you will ever see, but it can be a pleasure to hear the scores and see the routines of a favorite old musical while you sit comfortably at your table with a drink in hand. The cost of the show includes your meal. The buffet is served from 6 to 7:30. The performance starts at 8. *Edgewater Center, 3376 Edgewater Dr., Orlando (from I-4, take Exit 44 and go west), tel. 407/843-6275. Dress: casual. Reservations advised. Closed Mon. Moderate. AE, MC, V.*

Church Street Station

This downtown Orlando attraction is a complete entertainment experience. Widely popular among both tourists and locals, it single-handedly began Orlando's metamorphosis from a sleepy town, to the nighttime hot spot it now boasts to be and is on its way to becoming. Unlike much of what you see in Walt Disney World, this place doesn't just look authentic—it *is* authentic. The train on the tracks is an actual 19th-century steam engine, and the whistling calliope was especially rebuilt to blow its original tunes. The buildings have been completely redecorated with collectibles and memorabilia from around the world. You can spend an evening in part of the complex, or you can wander from area to area, soaking up the peculiar characteristics of each. For a single admission price of $14.95 adults or $9.95 children 4–12, you're permitted to wander freely, stay as long as you wish, and do what you want, whether it's drinking, dancing, dining, or people-watching. Food and drink cost extra and are not cheap, but they add to the fun. Parts of the complex are open during the day, but the place is usually quiet then; the pace picks up at night, especially on weekends, with crowds thickest 10–11. *129 W. Church St., Orlando, tel. 407/422-2434. Reservations not necessary. Dress: casual. AE, MC, V.*

Rosie O'Grady's. This is a turn-of-the-century saloon with dark wood, brass trim, a full Dixieland band blaring out of a gazebo, and countertop can-can dancers, tap dancers, and vaudeville singers. Is this a set for *The Music Man* or an evening at the Moulin Rouge? It's difficult to tell at first. The 90-minute shows begin at 7 or 7:30 PM. The last show starts at 11:45. Multidecker sandwiches and hot dogs are sold in the Gay 90s Sandwich Parlour 4:30–11 PM.

Apple Annie's Courtyard. This is a relatively quiet nook that features continuous live folk and bluegrass music from about 8 PM to 2 AM. It's a good place to rest your feet, have a drink, and people-watch. Salads, fruit platters, and exotic drinks are served 11 AM–2 AM.

Lili Marlene's Aviators Pub. Here you have a relaxed, wood-paneled English-pub atmosphere and the finest dining on Church Street. Food is hearty, upscale, and very American—mostly steaks, ribs, and seafood. Prices are not cheap. The walls have biplane-era memorabilia, and a large-scale model aircraft hangs from the ceiling. Open for lunch and dinner until midnight.

Phileas Phogg's Balloon Works. This is a very popular disco filled with young singles over age 21 and a sprinkling of old-timers showing off their moves on the dance floor. It is a good-looking yuppie tourist crowd, leavened with locals. Contemporary dance tunes are played on a sound system that will blow your socks off. The place is jammed by midnight and open until 2 AM. Much of the young crowd feels it is worth the price of admission into the Church Street Station just to be able to come here.

Orchid Garden. Decorative lamps, iron latticework, arched ceilings, and stained-glass windows create a striking Victorian arcade where visitors sit, drink, and listen to first-rate bands pounding out popular tunes from the 1950s to the '80s. Open until 2 AM.

Cracker's Oyster Bar. Located behind the Orchid Garden, Cracker's is a good place to get a quick gumbo or chowder and slam down a few oysters with a beer chaser. It has one of the largest wine cellars in Florida. Open until midnight.

Cheyenne Saloon and Opera House. This is the biggest, fanciest, rootin'-tootin' saloon you may ever see. The former triple-level opera house is covered with moose racks, steer horns, buffalo heads, and Remington rifles; a seven-piece country-and-western band darn near brings the house down. This is a fun crowd to watch, with all the pickin', strummin', fiddlin', hollerin', and do-see-doin'. Make sure you come equipped with your best stompin' shoes, cowboy hat, and catcalls. An upstairs restaurant serves chicken-and-ribs saloon fare. The shows start at 7:30 PM, 11 PM, and 12:45 AM.

Church Street Exchange. The newest addition to the complex, near Church Street Station, is a razzle-dazzle marketplace filled with more than 50 specialty shops and restaurants on the first two floors. The third floor has been taken over by Commander Ragtime's Midway of Fun, Food, and Games. The Exchange is free and open 11 AM–2 AM, although most of the shops close earlier.

Bars and Clubs

The bars and nightclubs have been divided into three sections. The first covers the tourist hotel districts in the Disney area, including Kissimmee, Lake Buena Vista, and International Drive. These places are usually filled with visitors to Disney World. The second section covers the city of Orlando and Winter Park, both of which cater to a more local crowd. The third hits some of the hot spots around Cocoa Beach. Remember that clubs on Disney property are allowed to stay open later than are bars elsewhere, and many of them don't have last call until 2:45 AM.

Disney Area

Little Darlin's Rock n' Roll Palace. Shake, rattle, and roll the night away in this 1950s and '60s nostalgia nightclub. The interior looks like an opera house, with an orchestra-pit dance floor and a huge bandstand stage featuring famous old rock bands that still tour, such as The Drifters, Platters, and Bo Diddley. The crowd is a mix of young and old, singles and couples. The club features a very talented house band that serves up live music seven nights a week. Much of the menu is vintage '50s: Philly hot dogs, cheese-steak sandwiches, banana splits, but there also is prime rib. *Old Town, 5770 Spacecoast Pkwy., Kissimmee 32746, tel. 407/396–6499. Dress: casual. Admission: $8.50, children under 3 free. AE, MC, V.*

Giraffe Lounge. Located inside the Hotel Royal Plaza, Lake Buena Vista (World Village), this flashy disco with spinning, colored lights is usually densely packed on weekends. It is a small place, and classy it ain't, but there's a lot going on, including live bands five nights a week. Happy hour runs daily 4–9:30 PM. Music plays and the bartender pours until 3 AM. *Hotel Royal Plaza, Walt Disney World Village, Lake Buena Vista, tel. 407/828–2828. Dress: casual. Open 4 PM–3 AM. No cover. AE, CB, DC, MC, V.*

The Laughing Kookaburra. A big hotel nightclub with live band music nightly and a serious singles crowd of all ages. The music is loud and the dance floor can get very crowded—a plus for some, a minus for others. The bar serves up 99 brands of beer, plus cocktails. Happy hour with free bar food runs daily 4–8

PM. The band plays six nights a week (off Monday). *Buena Vista Palace Hotel, Walt Disney World Village, Lake Buena Vista, tel. 407/827–2727. Dress: casual. Open 4 PM–3 AM. No cover. AE, CB, DC, MC, V.*

La Cantina. This little bar in the Hotel Royal Plaza has guitar music seven nights a week and a happy hour, Sunday–Thursday, from midnight to 3 AM(!) It's a good thing most visitors are hotel guests—it's hard to get in an accident in an elevator! *Hotel Royal Plaza, tel. 407/828–2828. Open 11 AM–3 AM.*

Bennigan's. A young singles' spot that draws crowds in the early evening and during happy hours, from 4–7 PM and 11 PM–2 AM. It caters mostly to nontourists who work in the area. Food is served almost until closing. *6324 International Dr., Orlando, tel. 407/351–4436. Open 11 AM–2 AM.*

Orlando Area

The nightclubs in Orlando have significantly more character than those in the Disney hotel area. If you have the energy to get in your car, you will probably find these spots more satisfying and less touristy—if you can find them.

J.J. Whispers. A classy, brassy singles crowd flocks to this trendy disco, which tries hard to maintain an image of cosmopolitan class. Expect to mingle with fashion-conscious locals in their tastefully outrageous attire. The club is equally popular with the over-30 set, who listen to music from the 1940s, '50s, and '60s in the Showroom. The young people do what young people do in a massive, multilevel, state-of-the-art disco. J.J.'s has one restaurant serving bar-food fare, and another, a deli, that is open for lunch. It is also home to Bonkerz!, a comedy club. Live entertainment (Tues.–Sun., 8 PM–2 AM) includes all-male and all-female revues and live bands. *5100 Adanson St., Orlando 32804, tel. 407/629–4779. To get there, take I–4 to the Lee Rd. exit and go west for about half a mile on Lee Rd. Watch for a sharp left-hand turn at Adanson St. J.J.'s is located at the end of the Lee Rd. Shopping Center. Dress: tasteful but outrageous —or just a jacket. AE, MC, V. Cover charge: $2 and up.*

Cheek-to-Cheek. Monday nights are a big deal here because of the many big-name performers—mostly contemporary jazz musicians in the Class Act Lounge, and rock and reggae in Cheek-to-Cheek. Past performers have included Al Stewart, Wynton Marsalis, Rita Coolidge, and even Tommy Dorsey. The place can get very crowded; tables are crammed so close together that you will become fast friends, or enemies, with your neighbors. Other nights of the week (Tues.–Sat.) are very popular with the 35–50-year-old crowd, who dance to Top-40s music played by Cheek-to-Cheek's house band. *839 N. Orlando Ave. (U.S. 17–92), tel. 407/644–2060. Open 8 PM–2 AM. Mon. cover charge up to $20. Tues.–Sat. cover charge $4. Closed some Sun.*

Crocodile Club. This bar, inside a restaurant called Bailey's in Winter Park, collects a young, well-dressed college crowd from neighboring Rollins College. The atmosphere is more sophisticated and yuppified than most Orlando bars. Expect to hear Motown and dance to pop. *Bailey's Restaurant, 118 W. Fairbanks Ave., Winter Park, tel. 407/647–8501.*

Sullivan's Trailways Lounge. A very popular place with much right-friendly charm, where people of all ages and many families come to strut their stuff on the largest dance floor in Florida. Even Yankees are welcome in this southern country-and-western dance hall. Big name performers entertain on occasion; local bands play nightly, except Sunday. *1108 S. Orange Blossom Trail (U.S. 441), tel. 407/843–2934. Bands play 9 PM–2 AM. Cover charge: $2 and up.*

Cocoa Beach

Coconuts. The Saturday bikini contests and the April jet-ski rodeo, along with Mr. Muscle contests and dirt-in-the-face volleyball attract the under-40 set to this oceanside night spot. Patrons dance to live music most evenings, and there is a dining area. *2 Minuteman Causeway, tel. 407/784–1422. Dress: no cut-offs. Open Mon.–Sat. 11:30 AM–2 AM, Sun. 11:30 AM–midnight.*

Plum's Lounge/Holiday Inn Cocoa Beach. This lounge features Top 40 music with dancing and live entertainment most nights. There is a beach deck on the ocean and a bar by the pool. *1300 N. Atlantic Ave., Cocoa Beach, tel. 407/783–2271. Dress: neat, but casual. Open Mon.–Sat. 11 AM–1 AM, Sun. noon–midnight.*

Spinnaker's. In this entertainment center on an 800-foot pier extending into the ocean, visitors can find a boutique, fishing bait, and dining ranging from mesquite-grilled alligator snacks at a boardwalk bar to coconut-beer shrimp at the Pier House. *401 Meade Ave., tel. 407/783–7549. Dress: neat but casual. Reservations required. Dinner 5–10 PM. AE, MC, V. Moderate–Expensive.*

9 Southwest Florida

Introduction

by Karen Feldman Smith and G. Stuart Smith

Karen Feldman Smith is the travel editor for the Fort Myers News-Press. *G. Stuart Smith is a reporter for* WBBH-TV *in Fort Myers. Together, they run the Sunshine Syndicate, an organization of writers and photographers based in Florida.*

Tourists and developers are fast discovering a region they formerly raced through in their haste to get to better-known Florida vacation destinations.

Southwest Florida spans some 200 miles and includes a host of diverse cities and towns. That variety satisfies the varied tastes of young singles, families, and older travelers. Sunning, shelling, sailing, and space to breathe characterize vacations on the Gulf Coast.

Although the east coast of Florida may claim most of the state's historic sites there are lower-profile but equally worthy sites to enjoy on the Gulf Coast. There are culturally rich ethnic neighborhoods, soothing natural sanctuaries harboring rare species, hotels from basic to deluxe, and some worthwhile tourist attractions. And, of course, there are the beaches, which stretch along the translucent waters of the Gulf of Mexico.

The sprawling region can be divided into three parts: the Tampa Bay area, encompassing Tampa, St. Petersburg, Tarpon Springs, and Clearwater; the Sarasota area, including Bradenton and Venice; and the Naples/Fort Myers region, from Port Charlotte south to the Everglades below Marco Island.

Getting Around

By Plane

Most major carriers fly into at least one of the area's three major airports, in Tampa, Sarasota, and Fort Myers.

Tampa International (tel. 813/276–3400) is 6 miles from downtown. It is served by Air Canada (tel. 800/422–6232), Air Jamaica (tel. 800/523–5585), American (tel. 800/433–7300), British Airways (tel. 800/247–9297), Cayman (tel. 800/422–9626), Continental (tel. 800/525–0280), Delta (tel. 800/221–1212), Eastern (tel. 800/EASTERN), Midway (tel. 800/621–5700), Northwest (tel. 800/225–2525), Pan Am (tel. 800/221–1111), Piedmont (tel. 800/251–5720), Transworld (tel. 800/221–2000), United (tel. 800/241–6522), and USAir (tel. 800/428–4322).

Sarasota's Airport is **Sarasota-Bradenton** (tel. 813/359–5200), just north of the city. It is served by Air Sunshine (tel. 800/432–1744), American, Continental, Delta, Eastern, Midway, Northwest, Transworld, and United.

The Fort Myers/Naples area's airport is **Southwest Florida Regional Airport** (tel. 813/768–1000), about 12 miles south of Fort Myers, 25 miles north of Naples. It is served by Air Canada, American, Continental, Delta, Eastern, Midway, Northwest, Piedmont, Transworld, United, USAir, and Wardair Canada.

Between the Airport and the Hotels

Major car-rental companies and taxi and limousine companies service all three airports. Many hotels also operate shuttles.

In Tampa, major transportation services include **Central Florida Limousine** (tel. 813/276–3730), serving Hillsborough and Polk counties; **The Limo** (tel. 813/822–3333 in St. Petersburg and Clearwater), serving Pinellas County; and **Florida Suncoast Limousines** (tel. 813/620–3597). Expect taxi fares to be about $9–$12 for most of Hillsborough County and about twice that for Pinellas County.

In Sarasota, transportation includes **Airport Limousine** (tel. 813/355–9645) and **Diplomat Taxi** (tel. 813/366–9822). Both deliver to most parts of the county. An average cab fare is $5–$10.

In Lee County, a taxi ride to downtown Fort Myers or the beaches (Sanibel, Captiva), costs about $25, about twice that to Naples. Other transportation companies include **Airport Limousine** (tel. 813/489–1023), **Aristocat Super Mini-Van Service** (tel. 813/275–7228), **Boca Limousine Service** (tel. 813/936–5466), **Personal Touch Limousines** (tel. 813/549–3643), and **Sanibel Island Limousine** (tel. 813/472–8888).

By Car I-75 spans the region from north to south. Once you cross the border into Florida from Georgia, it should take about three hours to reach Tampa. Add an hour for Sarasota, two to Fort Myers, and three to Naples. Alligator Alley (Rte. 84) links up with I-75 at Naples and runs east to Fort Lauderdale. I-75 is being extended along the Alligator Alley right-of-way; expect construction delays.

U.S. 41 also runs the length of the region and serves as the business district in many communities. It's best to avoid all bridges and U.S. 41 during rush hours, 7–9 AM and 4–6 PM.

Rental car prices can vary dramatically, so it pays to shop around. Major companies serving Southwest Florida include **Alamo** (tel. 800/327–9633), **Avis** (tel. 800/331–1212), **Budget** (tel. 800/527–0700), **Dollar** (tel. 800/421–6868), **Enterprise** (tel. 800/325–8007), **Hertz** (tel. 800/654–3131), **Payless** (tel. 800/237–2804), **Sears** (tel. 800/527–0770), **Thrifty** (tel. 800/367–2277), and **Value** (tel. 800/468–2583).

By Train **Amtrak** (tel. 800/872–7245) connects the Northeast, Midwest, and much of the South to Tampa. From Tampa, Amtrak heads east, across the coast, then up to Jacksonville and points north. Amtrak's Autotrain runs from Lorton, Virginia (near Washington, DC), to Sanford, Florida (near Orlando). In Tampa, the Amtrak station is at 601 N. Nebraska Avenue (tel. 813/221–7600). Within Tampa, the PeopleMover rail line provides transportation between the business district and Harbour Island. Tokens cost 25 cents each way.

By Bus **Greyhound/Trailways** provides service to and throughout the state. Call the nearest office for schedules and fares (Fort Myers, tel. 813/334–1011; St. Petersburg, tel. 813/898–1496; Sarasota, tel. 813/955–5735; and Tampa, tel. 813/229–2112).

Around Tampa, the **Hillsborough Area Regional Transit** (HART), (tel. 813/254–4278, 7 AM–6 PM) system serves most of the county.

In Sarasota, **Sarasota County Area Transit** (SCAT), (tel. 813/951–5850) is the public transit company. The **Lee County Transit System** (tel. 813/939–1303) serves Fort Myers and most of the county.

Scenic Drives **I-275 between St. Petersburg** and **Terra Ceia.** Motorists get a bird's-eye view of bustling Tampa Bay along the Sunshine Skyway and its bright-yellow suspension bridge.

Rte. 679 takes you along two of St. Petersburg's most pristine islands, Cabbage and Mullet keys.

Rte. 789 carries you over several of the coast's slender barrier islands, past miles of green-blue Gulf waters, beaches, and waterfront homes. The road does not connect all the islands, however. It runs from Holmes Beach off the Bradenton coast south to Lido Beach in Sarasota, then begins again on Casey Key south of Osprey and runs south to Nokomis Beach.

Rte. 867 (McGregor Boulevard), Fort Myers's premier road, passes Thomas Edison's winter home and goes southwest toward the beaches. The road is lined with thousands of royal palm trees and many large old homes.

J.N. "Ding" Darling National Wildlife Refuge. Drive along the 5-mile dirt road in Sanibel and, especially at low tide, you may see raccoons; alligators; and birds, such as roseate spoonbills, egrets, ospreys, herons, and anhingas.

Head west on **Mooringline Drive** in Naples for a drive past some of the cushiest coastline property in the state. Mooringline turns south and becomes Gulf Shore Boulevard. Condominiums, shops, hotels, and lots of beaches line this drive.

Just near the end of Gulf Shore Boulevard on Broad Avenue, you can pick up **2nd Street South,** which becomes Gordon Drive. It leads into Port Royale, where million-dollar homes are a dime a dozen. The architecture, landscaping, and statuary that are visible from the road make it a worthwhile expedition.

Guided Tours

Orientation Tours

Around the Town (tel. 813/932–7803) conducts tours for groups of 25 or more in the Tampa Bay area, plus Tarpon Springs and Sarasota, the dog tracks, and area theaters. Try to make reservations several weeks in advance.

Gulf Coast Gray Line (tel. 813/822–3577) makes daily trips from Tampa to Disney World, Epcot Center, Sea World, Busch Gardens, and other attractions.

Travel is Fun Tours of St. Petersburg (tel. 813/821–9479) offers day-long tours to area sights from St. Petersburg.

Boat Tours

Sea Escape Cruises (tel. 800/432–0900) are day-long excursions into the Gulf of Mexico on full-size cruise ships departing from St. Petersburg.

The ***Captain Anderson*** (tel. 813/367–7804) combines sightseeing and dinner cruises from the St. Petersburg Causeway, 3400 Pasadena Ave. It operates from October through May, St. Petersburg Beach.

The Admiral (tel. 813/462–2628) is docked at Clearwater Beach Marina. It runs dinner and sightseeing cruises all year.

The ***Starlite Princess*** (tel. 813/595–1212) is a paddlewheel excursion boat offering three-hour, five-course meals from Hamlin's Landing, Indian Rocks Beach. Old-fashioned boat adds to the fun.

The ***Miss Cortez*** (tel. 813/794–1223) departs from Cortez, just north of Bradenton, every Tuesday, Thursday, and Sunday for Egmont Key, a small abandoned island just north of Anna Maria Island.

Myakka Wildlife Tours (tel. 813/365–0100) is at Myakka River State Park, east of Sarasota on Rte. 72. *The Gator Gal*, a large airboat, conducts one-hour tours of the 29,000-acre wildlife and bird sanctuary. Three trips daily; closed Tuesday.

Epicurean Sailing Charters (tel. 813/964–0708) conducts half-

and full-day cruises from Boca Grande to Useppa Island, Cabbage Key, and other area islands.

King Fisher Cruise Lines (tel. 813/639–0969) offers cruises and island sightseeing around Charlotte Harbor from Fishermen's Village, Punta Gorda.

Babcock Wilderness Adventures (tel. 813/639–4488) conducts guided swamp-buggy tours through the Telegraph Cypress Swamp on the 90,000-acre Crescent B Ranch, south of Punta Gorda. Reservations required.

Everglades Jungle Cruises (tel. 813/334–7474) explores the Caloosahatchee and Orange rivers of Lee County and makes day trips to Lake Okeechobee and two-day trips across the vast inland lake. Has lunch and dinner cruises as well. Trips last three hours to two days. They depart from the Fort Myers Yacht Basin.

Tallship Excursions (tel. 813/463–SAIL) offers tall ship excursions in San Carlos Bay aboard the 80-foot sailboat departing from Fort Myers Beach.

Jammin' Sailboat Cruises (tel. 813/463–3520) offers day and sunset cruises from Fort Myers Beach. Call for reservations.

The Capt. J.P. (tel. 813/334–7474) is a stern paddlewheeler that sails mid-November-mid-April, daily from the Fort Myers Yacht Basin. There are a variety of cruises, from three-hour excursions on the Caloosahatchee River to 12-hour trips to Lake Okeechobee. Brunch, lunch, and dinner-dance cruises also are offered.

Dalis Charter (tel. 813/262–4545) offers half-day fishing and sightseeing trips and sunset cruises. Also available for private cocktail cruises. It's docked at Old Marine Market Place at Tin City (1200 Fifth Ave. S, Naples).

Tiki Boat Tours (tel. 813/262–7577) conducts a variety of tours through the northern section of the Everglades' Ten Thousand Islands, including half-day fishing and shelling expeditions to Keewaydin Island and sightseeing along Naples Bay. Tours start at the dock behind Old Marine Market Place, Naples.

Wooten's Everglades (tel. 813/394–8080) runs a variety of airboat and swamp-buggy tours through the Everglades daily from Wooten's alligator farm, 35 miles east of Naples on U.S. 41.

Eden of the Everglades (tel. 813/695–2800) travels the wilderness wetlands of the Everglades' Ten Thousand Islands, departing from Everglades City in southern Collier County six times daily.

Florida Boat Tours (tel. 813/695–4400) depart from the Captain's Table Resort in Everglades City. The 40-minute tours of the Ten Thousand Islands set off hourly.

By Plane Helicopter tours of the Tampa Bay area and the west coast of Florida are offered by **Suncoast Helicopters** (tel. 813/872–6625), based at Tampa International Airport; and **West Florida Helicopters** (Albert Whitted Airport, tel. 813/823–5200). In the Charlotte Harbor area, sightseeing tours are offered by the **Boca Grande Seaplane Service** (tel. 813/964–0234), 4th and Bayou, Boca Grande.

Important Addresses and Numbers

Tourist Information All the following offices are open weekdays 9–5 and closed on holidays:

Charlotte County Chamber of Commerce (2702 Tamiami Trail, Port Charlotte, tel. 813/627–2222).
Lee County Visitor and Convention Bureau (2180 W. First St., Fort Myers, tel. 813/335–2631 or 800/237–6444).
Sanibel-Captiva Chamber of Commerce (Causeway Rd., Sanibel, tel. 813/472–1080).
Sarasota Convention and Visitors Bureau (655 N. Tamiami Trail, tel. 813/957–1877 or 800/522–9799).

Tampa Bay Area **The Greater Tampa Chamber of Commerce** (801 E. Kennedy Blvd., tel. 813/228–7777). For information on current area events, call the **Visitors Information Department** (tel. 813/223–1111).
Tampa/Hillsborough Convention and Visitors Association (100 S. Ashley, Suite 850, tel. 800/826–8358).
Tarpon Springs Chamber of Commerce (210 S. Pinellas Ave., Suite 120, tel. 813/937–6109).
Treasure Island Chamber of Commerce (152 108th Ave., tel. 813/367–4529).
Greater Clearwater Chamber of Commerce (128 N. Osceola Ave., tel. 813/461–0011).
Greater Dunedin Chamber of Commerce (434 Main St., tel. 813/736–5066).
Gulf Beaches Chamber of Commerce (105 5th Ave., Indian Rocks Beach, tel. 813/595–4575).
Madeira Beach Chamber of Commerce (501 150th Ave., tel. 813/391–7373).
Pinellas Suncoast Tourist Development Council (4625 E. Bay Dr., Suite 109, Clearwater, tel. 813/530–6452).
St. Petersburg Chamber of Commerce (100 2nd Ave. N, tel. 813/821–4069).

Emergencies Dial 911 for **police** or **ambulance** in an emergency.

Hospitals Hospital emergency rooms are open 24 hours. In Tampa: **University Community Hospital** (3100 E. Fletcher Ave.). In St. Petersburg: **Bayfront Medical Center** (701 6th St. S). In Bradenton: **Manatee Memorial Hospital** (206 2nd St. E). In Sarasota: **Sarasota Memorial Hospital** (1700 S. Tamiami Trail, U.S. 41). In Fort Myers: **Lee Memorial Hospital** (2776 Cleveland Ave.). In Naples: **Naples Community** (350 7th St. N).

24-Hour Pharmacy **Eckerd Drugs** (11613 N. Nebraska, Tampa, tel. 813/978–0775).

Exploring Southwest Florida

The Tampa Bay Area

Numbers in the margin correspond with points of interest on the Tampa-St. Petersburg Area map.

Tampa boasts more business suits than any other part of the region. Its port is the country's seventh largest, with phosphate, shrimp, and bananas the primary cargo. The city's shrimp fleet, docked at Hooker's Point, is the state's largest. Industry flourishes as well, with millions of cigars rolled daily, phosphate mined from massive pits, and two major breweries—Busch and Schlitz—producing their wares here.

It's fitting that an area with a thriving international port should also be populated by a wealth of nationalities—Greeks, Scots, Hispanics, and Italians, to name only a few. American Indians were the sole inhabitants of the region for many years (Tampa is an Indian phrase meaning "sticks of fire"). The Spanish explorers Juan Ponce de Léon, Pánfilo de Narváez, and Hernando de Soto passed through in the mid-1500s. The U.S. Army and civilian settlers arrived in 1824; a military presence remains in the form of MacDill Air Force Base, where the U.S. Operations Command is located.

The Cubans brought their cigar-making industry to the area in 1866 and developed Ybor City. This east Tampa suburb is still primarily Cuban but contains a dwindling number of cigar makers.

Tampa does not have a Gulf beach, and Tampa Bay, though lovely to look at, is too polluted for swimming. For that, visitors should head to neighboring St. Petersburg, which sits on a peninsula bordered on three sides by bays and the Gulf of Mexico, filled with pleasure and commercial craft.

North of Tampa, in Tarpon Springs, there has been a large Greek population for decades, since sponge divers from the Dodecanese Islands of Greece moved to the area at the turn of the century. This was the world's largest sponge center during the 1930s. Although a bacterial blight wiped out the sponge beds in the 1940s, the Greeks held on, and the sponge industry has returned, though in lesser force than during its heyday. Today, the Greek influence remains evident in the churches, the restaurants, and, often, in the language spoken on the streets.

The accent is Scottish in Dunedin, just south of Tarpon Springs. Two Scots were responsible for giving the town its Gaelic name in the 1880s. If the sound of bagpipes played by men in kilts appeals to you, head to Dunedin in March or April, when the Highland games and the Dunedin Heather and Thistle holidays pay tribute to the Celtic heritage.

Tampa Tampa is the business and commercial hub of this part of the state, as you'll quickly notice when driving by the busy port. The major north-south route is I-75; if you're heading from Orlando, you'll likely drive in on east-west I-4.

Let's begin a tour of Tampa along that I-4 corridor at Exit 5 (Orient Rd., east of the city). The water tower with an arrow
❶ sticking through it gives it away: this is the **Seminole Indian Village,** which contains a village and museum displaying artifacts of the Seminole Indians, who inhabited Florida long before white settlers arrived. You'll also be treated to alligator wrestling and snake shows. *5221 N. Orient Rd., tel. 813/621–2279. Open Mon.–Sat. 9–5, Sun. noon–5. Admission: $4.50 adults, $3.75 children under 12, $3.50 senior citizens.*

❷ **Ybor City** is Tampa's Cuban melting pot, which thrived on the cigar-making industry at the turn of the century. To get there, take I-4 west to Exit 1 (22nd St.) and go south five blocks to 7th Avenue. You're in the heart of Ybor City, where the smell of cigars—hand-rolled by Cuban refugees—mingles with old-world architecture. Take a stroll past the ornately tiled Columbia Restaurant and the stores lining the street, or step back to the past at **Ybor Square.** The restored cigar factory (1901 13th St.) now is a mall with boutiques, offices, and several restau-

The Admiral, **9**
Busch Gardens, **4**
Cedar Key, **19**
Crystal River, **18**
Fort Desoto Park, **6**
Homosassa Springs Nature World, **16**
John's Pass Village, **7**
Kapok Tree Restaurant, **14**
Museum of Fine Arts, **12**
The Pier, **11**
Salvador Dali Museum, **10**
Seminole Indian Village, **1**
Suncoast Seabird Sanctuary, **8**
Sunken Gardens, **13**
Sunshine Skyway, **5**
Tampa Museum of Art, **3**
Weeki Wachee Spring, **15**
Ybor City, **2**
Yulee Sugar Mill, **17**

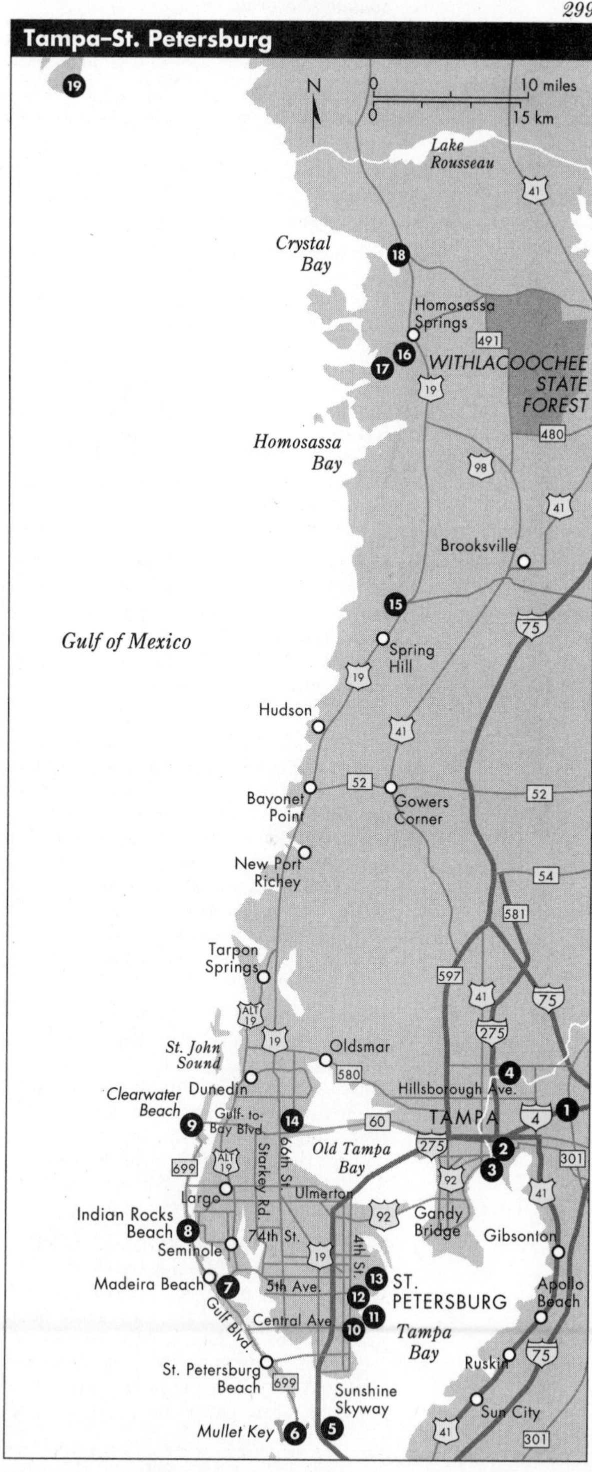

rants. You can watch as artisans continue the local practice of hand rolling cigars.

For something a little more modern, head for the new skyscrapers downtown. From 7th Avenue, go west to Nebraska Avenue and turn left. That will take you to Kennedy Boulevard; turn right and drive a few blocks to the vicinity of Franklin Street. You are now in one of Tampa's booming growth areas, with a pedestrian mall down the center of Franklin Street.

3 A few more blocks to the east you'll find the **Tampa Museum of Art,** near Curtis Hixon Convention Center. Egyptian, Greek, and Roman artifacts are on display, as well as traveling exhibits. *601 Doyle Carlton Dr., tel. 813/223–8128. Open Tues.–Sat. 10–6, Wed. 10–9, Sun. 1–5. Donations accepted.*

4 On another day, enjoy a romp through **Busch Gardens.** A safari simulating a journey to the Dark Continent will let you watch free-roaming zebras, giraffes, rhinos, lions, and more—all from the comfort of a monorail. There are many other rides and attractions in this 300-acre park, so allow at least six hours here. *3000 Busch Blvd. (Rte. 580), 2 mi east of I-275, tel. 813/971–8282. Open daily 9:30–6. All-inclusive admission: $23.95.*

St. Petersburg

St. Petersburg and the Pinellas Suncoast form the thumb of the hand jutting out of the west coast, holding in Tampa Bay. I-275 crosses the bay from Tampa through the heart of the city and then crosses the bay again at the Sunshine Skyway into Bradenton. U.S. 19 is the major north–south artery. Traffic can be heavy, and there are many lights, so U.S. 19 should be avoided on lengthy trips.

The bay and beaches offer two distinct communities to visit.
5 Let's start with a trip over the **Sunshine Skyway.** A $1 toll will carry you across the causeway and to the top of a sparkling new suspension bridge for a bird's-eye view of the islands and of ocean freighters and sailboats plying Tampa Bay. You can also see what's left of the original twin span that collapsed and killed more than 30 people when a ship hit it in 1980. Across the bridge, you can picnic, toss in a fishing line, or turn around and mount the summit of the bridge again. This time, you'll get a view of a series of small islands that dot the bay, and you'll see St. Petersburg Beach as you head north.

When you reach the north end of the causeway, turn left on 54th Avenue South (Rte. 682), and follow it to Rte. 679. Turn left and cross the islands you saw from the Sunshine Skyway.
6 You'll end up eventually at **Fort DeSoto Park** at the mouth of Tampa Bay. Here you can roam the fort that was built to protect Gulf sea lanes during the Spanish-American War or wander the beaches of any of the islands that make up the park. *Mullet Key, 34th St. S. No admission charge, but tolls totaling 85¢ will be charged on the Bayway to the islands.*

Head back up the Bayway and turn left toward the beaches and then right on Gulf Boulevard (Rte. 699). The colossal pink Don CeSar Resort Hotel is off to the left. Head through St. Petersburg Beach and Treasure Island to Madeira Beach. Stop here
7 at **John's Pass Village and Boardwalk** (12901 Gulf Blvd.), a collection of shops in an old-style fishing village, where you can shop and eat at a variety of restaurants or pass the time watching the pelicans cavorting and dive-bombing for food.

When pelicans become entangled in fishing lines, locals some-
8 times carry them to the **Suncoast Seabird Sanctuary,** a nonprofit organization whose facilities are open to the public. Drive up Gulf Boulevard to Indian Shores. *18328 Gulf Blvd., tel. 813/391–6211. Open daily 9–5:30. Admission free, but donations welcome.*

9 Ready to get off the road and out on the water? **The Admiral** is the place to relax and enjoy dinner and a little dancing while sightseeing on Clearwater Harbor. *Up Gulf Blvd. to Clearwater Beach Marina, tel. 813/462–2628. Open year-round. Boarding at 6:30 PM. Reservations required. Fare is $9.50, dinner is extra.*

For a second day in St. Petersburg, you'll enjoy a change of pace
10 along the cosmopolitan bayfront. Begin at the **Salvador Dali Museum.** To get there, take I-275 and then follow I-175 toward the bay. At 3rd Street South, turn right. The museum is on the left, about two blocks ahead. Inside you'll find a large collection of paintings of melting watches, colorful landscapes, and thought-provoking works of the late Spanish surrealist. *1000 3rd St. S, tel. 813/823–3767. Open Tues.–Sat. 10–5, Sun. noon–5. Admission: $4 adults, $2.50 students and senior citizens.*

Head up 3rd Street and turn right on 2nd Avenue. You're now
11 heading for the bayfront and **The Pier,** which looks as though a hurricane has turned it upside-down. The unusual building, a five-story inverted pyramid, was recently renovated and now contains a number of shops and eateries. *800 2nd Ave. NE. Open daily 10–9. Admission free.*

12 It's a short walk to the **Museum of Fine Arts,** the large building to your right along Beach Drive as you're returning from The Pier. French impressionists highlight the collection, but the museum also has outstanding examples of European, American, pre-Columbian, and Far Eastern art, as well as photography exhibits. *225 Beach Dr. NE, tel. 813/896–2667. Open Tues.–Sat. 10–5, Sun. 1–5. Suggested donation: $2.*

From here, it's a short drive to one of Florida's most colorful
13 spots, **Sunken Gardens.** To get there, take 4th Street North (a right turn) to 18th Avenue North. Visitors can walk through an aviary with tropical birds, stroll among more than 50,000 exotic plants and flowers, and stop to smell the rare, fragrant orchids. *1825 4th St. N., tel. 813/896–3186. Open daily 9–5:30. Admission: $6.95 adults, $4 children 3–11.*

To end the day, drive to U.S. 19, head north to Rte. 60, turn
14 right, and stop for dinner at **The Kapok Tree** (*see* Dining, below).

For visitors spending several days in the Tampa Bay area, there are a couple of worthwhile excursions just to the north: the pristine Crystal River area and rustic Cedar Key.

Exploring the Manatee Coast and Cedar Key

Manatee Coast The area from Weeki Wachee Spring to Crystal River can aptly be called the Manatee Coast. The springs, rivers, and creeks are among the best spots to view these endangered animals, also called sea cows. Only 1,200 manatees remain. It's believed ancient mariners spun tales of mermaids based on these curious mammals related to elephants.

U.S. 19 is the prime route through manatee country, but this highway is free-flowing, unlike the stop-and-go traffic on U.S. 19 in St. Petersburg.

Heading north on U.S. 19 out of St. Petersburg about 60 miles,
15 you'll see **Weeki Wachee Spring** at the junction of Route 50.
Here, an underwater theater presents mermaid shows and a nature trail through the subtropical wilderness, plus a jungle boat cruise to view local wildlife. Allow at least three hours to see everything. *At U.S. 19 and Rte. 50, Weeki Wachee, tel. 904/596–2062. Open daily 9–6. Admission: $10.95 adults, $6.95 children 3–11.*

About 15 miles further north on U.S. 19 is another of Florida's
16 natural wonders: **Homosassa Springs Nature World.** Turn left
on County Road 490-A and follow the signs to the attraction at Fish Bowl Drive. Here you may see manatees, but the "Spring of 10,000 Fish" is a main attraction, where you seem to mingle with the inhabitants in a floating observatory. A walk along the park's paths will lead you to reptile, alligator, and exotic bird shows. Jungle boat cruises on the Homosassa River are available across Fish Bowl Drive from the park's main entrance. *One mi west of U.S. 19, Homosassa Springs, tel. 904/628–2311. Open daily 9–5:30. Admission: $6.95 adults, $3.95 children 3–11; 20% AARP discount with current card if presented before purchasing ticket.*

17 The **Yulee Sugar Mill State Historic Site** is just a short drive from Homosassa Springs. The site of a ruined sugar plantation built by the state's first U.S. senator, this is a good spot for a picnic. *From Homosassa Springs Nature World, turn left on C.R. 490-A. Open daily. Admission free.*

18 The last stop could be a half-day or an all-day event. **Crystal River** is a U.S. Fish and Wildlife Service sanctuary for manatees. The Kings Bay area of the river is set aside to prevent human intrusion, but wide stretches are open for people to watch and swim with the sea cows. The main spring feeds crystal-clear water into the river at 72 degrees year-round. During winter months, when manatees congregate around the spring, you may rent a boat for a half or full day and view the animals from the surface. You may also opt to don a wet suit, snorkel, and fins (all available as rentals), as manatee enthusiasts do. You may be able to pet the leathery mammals (they've been known to roll over like puppies when petted)—just remember, don't chase or harrass them. During warmer months when manatees scatter, the main spring still makes an interesting swim. *Go north on U.S. 19 into the town of Crystal River, turn left on C.R. 44. Two marinas with boat and snorkel rentals are Port Paradise, tel. 904/795–7437 and Plantation Golf Resort, tel. 904/795–4211. Admission to refuge free.*

Cedar Key

Up in the area known as the Big Bend, Florida's long curving
coastline north of Tampa, you won't find many beaches. But you
will find an idyllic island village tucked in among the marshes
and scenic streams feeding the Gulf of Mexico. From U.S. 19,
19 take Route 24 until the highway ends. This is **Cedar Key.**

Once a strategic port for the Confederate States of America, Cedar Key today is a commercial fishing center. Historical photographs dating to 1800 and exhibits that focus on the development of the area, visit **Cedar Key Historical Society Museum** *at Rte. 24 and Second St., tel. 904/543–5549. Open Mon.–Wed. 10–5, Thurs.–Sun. 9–5. Admission: $1 adults, 50¢ children 6–12.*

Cedar Key State Museum offers another look at Cedar Key's history with household articles and dioramas on display. *Follow signs from Rte. 24 north for 1¾ miles. Tel. 904/543–5350. Open Mon., Thurs.–Sun. 9–5. Admission: 50¢ adults, children under 6 free.*

Bradenton and Sarasota

Numbers in the margin correspond with points of interest on the Sarasota/Bradenton Area map.

Sarasota is a city of two tales. Situated on the water, it is unquestionably a beach resort. But it also has a thriving cultural community, making it a suitable destination for those with a taste for the arts. Much of the credit for the city's diversity is due to the late John Ringling, founder of the now Ringling Brothers Barnum & Bailey Circus, who chose to make Sarasota the winter home of his circus and his family.

For those who like statistics, here are a few: Sarasota County has 35 miles of Gulf beaches, 2 state parks, 22 municipal parks, and 44 golf courses, many of them open to the public.

Nearby Bradenton maintains a lower profile, but also has its share of sugar-sand beaches, golf courses, and historic sites dating back to the mid-1800s.

To the south is Venice, with its multitudinous canals crisscrossing the city. Besides being the winter home of the circus, the city contains the world's only clown college. And, though shell collecting is quite good, the beaches of Venice are best known for the wealth of shark teeth to be found.

Bradenton Bradenton is on a finger of land enclosing the southern end of Tampa Bay; the Manatee River also borders the city's north side. The barrier island, Anna Maria, lies off the mainland and fronts the Gulf of Mexico. The combined U.S. 41 and 301 cuts north-south through the center of the city. I-75 is to the east, and Rte. 64 connects the interstate to Bradenton and Anna Maria Island.

Hernando de Soto, one of the first Spanish explorers, set foot in Florida in 1539 near what is now Bradenton. Take Rte. 64 to
1 75th Street NW, turn north, and drive to **DeSoto National Memorial,** where park employees dressed in costumes of the period demonstrate various 16th-century weapons and show how the explorers who roamed the southeastern United States prepared and preserved food for their journeys through the untamed land. Films, demonstrations, and a short nature trail are on the grounds. *75th St. NW, tel. 813/792–0458. Open daily 8–5:30. Admission: $1 per person.*

Head back to the center of the city, to 10th Street West. A few
2 blocks from the river is the **South Florida Museum,** where you can find artifacts on Florida's history, including displays of Indian culture and an excellent collection of Civil War memorabilia. The museum is also home to "Snooty," the oldest living manatee (or sea cow) in captivity. In the wild, manatees

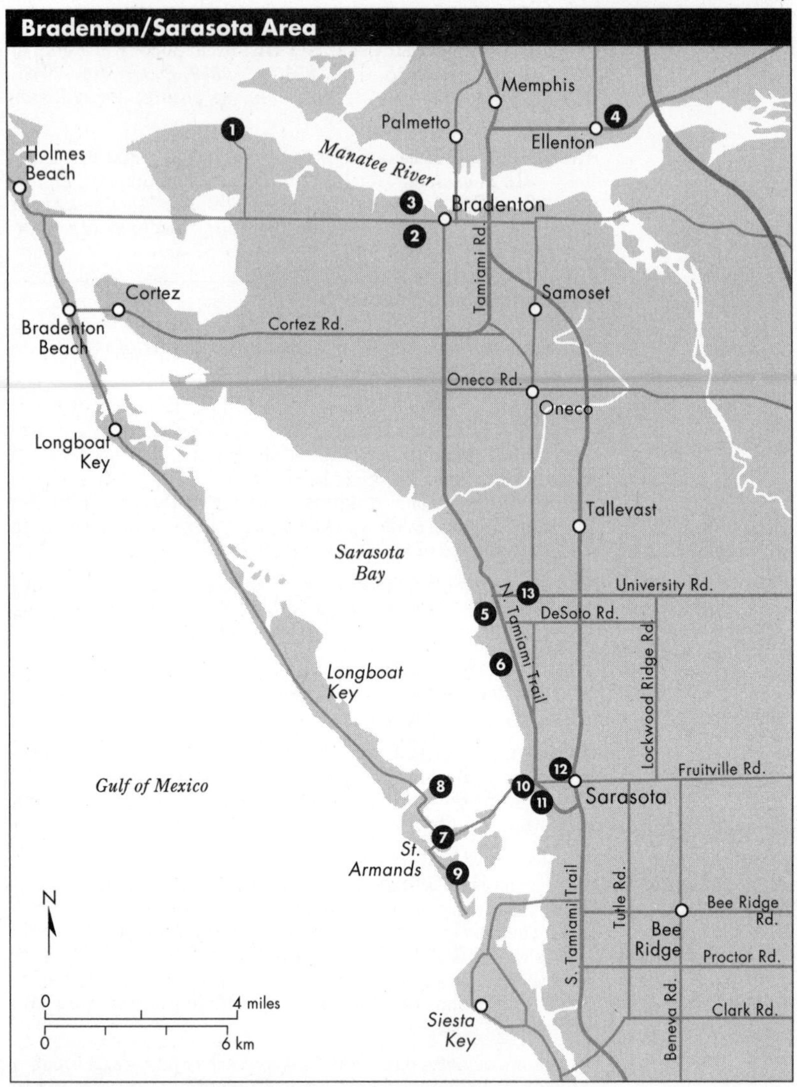

Bellm's Cars & Music of Yesterday, **13**
Bishop Planetarium, **3**
Desoto National Memorial, **1**
Downtown Art District, **12**
Gamble Plantation, **4**
Marie Selby Botanical Gardens, **11**
Marina Jack II, **10**
Mote Marine Science Center, **8**
Ringling Museums, **5**
St. Armand's Key, **7**
Sarasota Jungle Gardens, **6**
South Florida Museum, **2**
South Lido Park, **9**

are endangered, but here Snooty likes to shake hands and perform other tricks at feeding time. *201 10th St. W, tel. 813/746–4132. Open Tues.–Sat. 10–5, Sun. 1–5. Admission: $4 adults, $3 children and students.*

3 Also part of the museum is the **Bishop Planetarium,** where, inside a domed theater, you can see star shows and special-effects laser light displays. *Tel. 813/746–4131. Admission: $3 adults, $2 children and students; "Laser Fantasies" admission: $4 adults, $2 children. Star show Tues.–Sun. at 1:30 and 3 PM. plus Fri. and Sat. at 7:30 PM.*

Time Out **The Pier Restaurant.** Take a lunch break on fresh-caught seafood and alligator and enjoy a view of the Manatee River in an old Spanish-style building. *At the foot of 12th St. on Memorial Pier, tel. 813/748–8087. Open daily from 11:30 AM.*

Cross the river on U.S. 41 and turn right when U.S. 301 splits
4 off. On the left, three miles ahead, is the **Gamble Plantation State Historical Site.** The mansion, built in 1850, is the only pre-Civil War plantation house surviving in south Florida. This is where the Confederate secretary of state took refuge when the Confederacy fell to Union forces. Some of the original furnishings are on display in the mansion. *3708 Patten Ave., Ellenton, tel. 813/722–1017. Admission: $1. Open Thurs.–Mon. 9–5; closed Tues. and Wed. Tours of the house begin on the hour; no tours from noon to 1 PM.*

Sarasota The City of Sarasota sits on the eastern shore of Sarasota Bay. Across the water lie the barrier islands of Siesta Key, Longboat Key, and Lido Key, with myriad beaches, shops, hotels, condominiums, and houses. U.S. 41 is the main north-south thoroughfare in the city; further east, I-75 carries traffic past the city to Tampa or Fort Myers. Four state roads run west from the interstate highway into Sarasota.

Long ago, circus tycoon John Ringling found Sarasota an ideal spot to bring his clowns and performers to train and recuperate during the winter. Along the bay, Ringling also built himself a fancy home, patterned after the Palace of the Doges in Venice,
5 Italy. Today, the **Ringling Museums** include that mansion, as well as his art museum (with a world-renowned collection of Rubens paintings) and a museum of circus memorabilia. Also situated on the property is the Asolo State Theater. *Located ½ mile south of the Sarasota-Bradenton Airport on U.S. 41, tel. 813/355–5101. Open Mon.–Wed. and Fri.–Sun. 10–6, Thurs. 10–10. Combined admission $6 ($1.75 for children 6–12) is good for the mansion and both museums.*

From the Ringling museums, head south on U.S. 41 about 1½
6 miles to **Sarasota Jungle Gardens.** Here you can stroll through 10 acres of tropical plants and watch the bird and reptile shows. *3701 Bayshore Rd., tel. 813/355–5305. Open daily 9–5. Admission: $5.95 adults, $2.95 children 3–12.*

Time Out **St. Armand's Circle.** It's time to swing out across the bay. Continue south on U.S. 41 to Rte. 789. Turn right, and cross the Ringling Causeway to the small island of St. Armand's Key, where you'll find this chic little circle of shops and restaurants.

---

7 8 Just up the road from **St. Armand's Key** is the **Mote Marine Science Center.** On display in the aquarium are sharks, rays, fish,

and other marine creatures native to the area. A huge outdoor shark tank lets you see its inhabitants from above and below the water's surface. To get there from Harding Circle, turn north on Ringling Boulevard. Before you reach the bridge leading to Longboat Key, turn right at the sign for City Island and Mote Marine Lab. *1600 City Island Park, tel. 813/388-2451. Open daily 10–5. Admission: $5 adults, $3 children 6–17.*

9 You now have an option. One choice is to either head back south, past the public beach at Lido Key, to **South Lido Park,** where you can try your luck at fishing, take a dip in the waters of the bay or Gulf of Mexico, roam the paths of the 130-acre park, or picnic as the sun sets through the Australian pines into the Gulf. *Admission free. Open 8–sunset.*

10 The alternative is to turn back east across Sarasota Bay and turn right into the Marina Plaza along U.S. 41. Here you can enjoy an evening on the water in style, with a sunset dinner cruise on board a stern-wheel paddleboat, the ***Marina Jack II.*** *Marina Plaza, Island Park, tel. 813/366-9255. Cost: $4 plus dinner. Reservations required.*

11 Start out your second day of exploring Sarasota at **Marie Selby Botanical Gardens,** which are near the Island Park yacht basin. Here you can stroll through a world-class display of orchids and wander through 14 garden areas along Sarasota Bay. *800 S. Palm Ave., off U.S. 41, tel. 813/366-5730. Open daily 10–5 except Christmas. Admission: $4 adults, free for children under 12 when accompanied by an adult.*

12 In the heart of Sarasota, you'll discover a **downtown art district,** with galleries such as Art Uptown (1367 Main St.), Adley Gallery (1620 Main St.), Corbino Galleries (69 S. Palm Ave.), Apple & Carpenter Gallery of Fine Arts (1280 N. Palm Ave.), and J. E. Voorhees Gallery (1359 Main St.).

13 On the road to the airport (U.S. 41) is **Bellm's Cars & Music of Yesterday.** The display includes 130 classic cars, such as Pierce Arrows and Auburns, and 2,000 old-time music makers, such as hurdy-gurdies and calliopes. *5500 N. Tamiami Trail, tel. 813/355-6228. Open Mon.–Sat. 8:30–6, Sun. 9:30–6. Admission: $6 adults, $3 children 6–12.*

Fort Myers/Naples Region

Numbers in the margin correspond with points of interest on the Fort Myers/Naples Region map.

Lee County has a split personality. Its inland communities—Fort Myers and Cape Coral—are primarily commercial and residential. Its Gulf-front communities are beach resorts filled with people who are working mainly on relaxing and cultivating tans.

Fort Myers gets its nickname, the City of Palms, from the hundreds of towering royal palms that inventor Thomas Edison planted along a main residential street, McGregor Boulevard, on which his winter estate stood. Edison's idea caught on, and there are now more than 2,000 royal palms on McGregor Boulevard alone, with countless more throughout the city.

Along the county's western border are the resort islands of Estero, Sanibel, and Captiva. Estero contains Fort Myers

Beach, a laid-back beach community favored by young singles and those who want to stay on the Gulf without paying the higher prices on Sanibel or Captiva. A few miles farther off the coast are Sanibel and Captiva, connected to the mainland by a mile-long causeway. In recent years development has threatened the charm of the islands. However, island dwellers have staunchly held the line on further development, keeping buildings low and somewhat farther apart than on the majority of Florida's barrier islands. Sanibel has long been a world-class shelling locale, with fine fishing, luxury hotels, and dozens of restaurants. You will not be able to see most of the houses, which are shielded by tall Australian pines, but the beaches and tranquil Gulf waters are readily accessible.

Naples is often likened to Palm Beach for its ambience. Fifth and Third avenues south are lined with exclusive boutiques, shops, and restaurants. Here, first-time visitors and long-time members of the city's society mingle.

For those to whom beaches are important, Naples far outstrips Palm Beach with its abundance of public beach accesses—41 miles of beach are open to the public. The yen to go shelling, sunning, and fishing can be indulged to excess on the sun-drenched white shores.

South of Naples is yet another resort island, Marco. Here, high-rise condominiums and hotels line much of the waterfront, but many natural areas have been preserved, including the tiny fishing village of Goodland, where Old Florida lives on.

Fort Myers–Lee County

1

Fort Myers is the heart of the county, but only a few major roads lead through it. I-75 runs north-south, as does the more commercial thoroughfare, U.S. 41 (called Cleveland Avenue in Fort Myers). McGregor Boulevard runs from downtown Fort Myers southwest to Sanibel-Captiva. Summerlin Road runs southwest from Colonial Boulevard in South Fort Myers to Sanibel-Captiva and Fort Myers Beach. Rte. 78 (Pine Island-Bayshore Rd.) leads from North Fort Myers through north Cape Coral onto Pine Island.

If you are headed downtown from the beaches, drive at least part of the way on palm-lined McGregor Boulevard (from College Parkway north into town is the most scenic).

Thomas Edison's Winter Home, containing a laboratory, botanical gardens, and a museum, is open for guided tours. The property straddles McGregor Boulevard (Rte. 867) about a mile west of U.S. 41 near downtown Fort Myers. The inventor spent his winters on the 14-acre estate, developing the phonograph and teletype, experimenting with rubber, and planting some 6,000 species of plants from those collected throughout the world. A recent addition to the Edison complex is **Mangoes,** the winter home of the inventor's long-time friend, automaker Henry Ford. The 3-acre grounds and renovated home opened to the public in early 1990. *2350 McGregor Blvd., Fort Myers, tel. 813/334–3614. Open daily except Thanksgiving and Christmas. Tours 9–4 daily except Sun. 12:30–4. Admission to the Edison home: $5 adults, $1 children 6–12; admission to the Ford home: $3; combined ticket $7.*

Just a few blocks east is the **Fort Myers Historical Museum,** which is housed in a restored railroad depot. Its displays depict the area's history dating back to 1200 BC. *2300 Peck St., Fort*

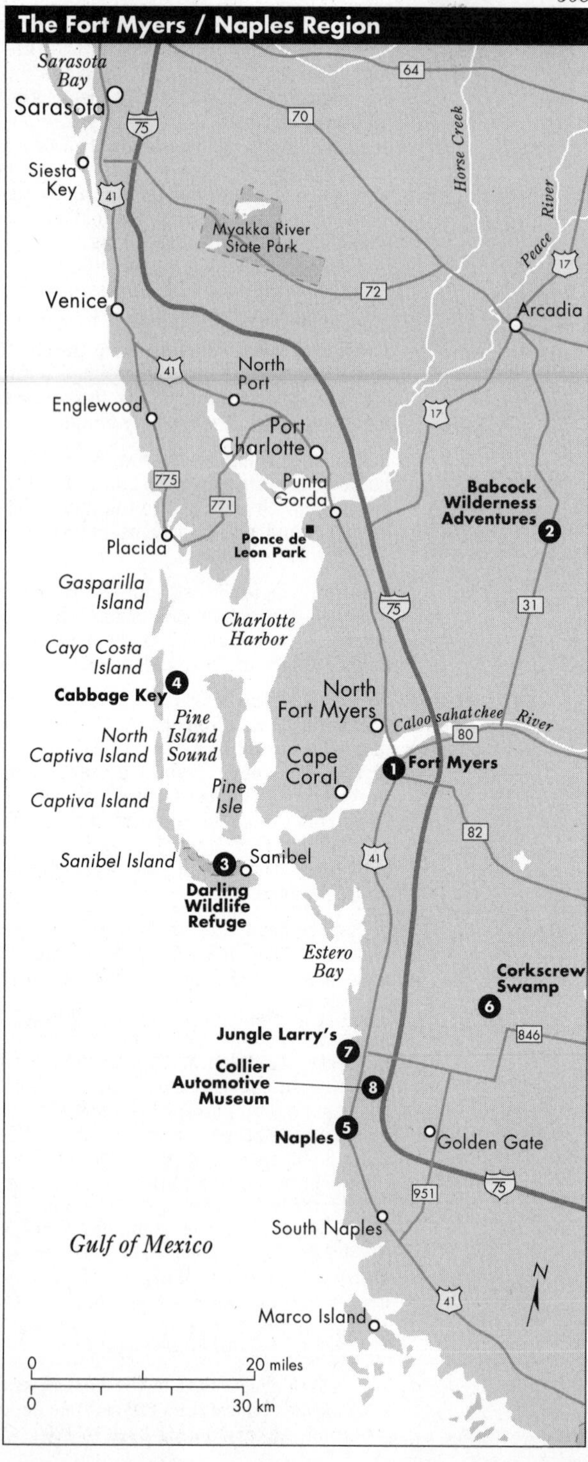
The Fort Myers / Naples Region
Sarasota Bay
Sarasota
Siesta Key
Myakka River State Park
Horse Creek
Peace River
Venice
Arcadia
North Port
Englewood
Port Charlotte
Punta Gorda
Babcock Wilderness Adventures
Placida
Ponce de Leon Park
Gasparilla Island
Charlotte Harbor
Cayo Costa Island
Cabbage Key
Pine Island Sound
North Captiva Island
North Fort Myers
Caloosahatchee River
Cape Coral
Fort Myers
Captiva Island
Pine Isle
Sanibel Island
Sanibel
Darling Wildlife Refuge
Estero Bay
Corkscrew Swamp
Jungle Larry's
Collier Automotive Museum
Naples
Golden Gate
South Naples
Gulf of Mexico
Marco Island
N
0
20 miles
0
30 km
64
70
75
41
72
17
775
771
31
80
82
846
951

Myers, tel. 813/332–5955. Open Mon.–Fri. 9–4:30, Sun. 1–5. Admission: $2 adults, 50¢ children 2–12.

Head northwest to Edwards Drive, which borders the Caloosahatchee River. The **City Yacht Basin** has tour boats that offer sightseeing and luncheon cruises on the river. Also on Edwards Drive, you can find a plethora of shuffleboard courts that weather heavy use on all but the hottest days. Adjacent to the courts is the **Hall of 50 States,** where the Fort Myers Chamber of Commerce dispenses information. *1365 Hendry St. Open weekdays 9–4.*

Time Out Walk another block in from the river to First Street, which runs through the heart of downtown Fort Myers. Stroll past the shops and have lunch at one of several eateries, including **Casa De Guerrero** (2225 First St., tel. 813/332–4674), **French Connection Café** (2282 First St., tel. 813/332–4443), and **April's** (2269 First St., tel. 813/337–4004).

To see what Florida looked like centuries ago, reserve a place
2 on **Babcock Wilderness Adventures',** 90-minute swamp buggy excursions through the Telegraph Cypress Swamp on the 90,000-acre Babcock Crescent B Ranch, south of Punta Gorda. Among the inhabitants you are likely to see are turkey, deer, bobcats, alligators, cows, and a herd of bison. From downtown Fort Myers, head east on Route 80 (Palm Beach Blvd.) past the I-75 interchange, then look for Route 31. Make a left and drive until you see the entrance for Babcock Wilderness Adventures on your right. *Tel. 813/656–6104. Reservations required; not recommended for children under 6. Four tours daily, weather permitting. Closed Mon. Admission: $12 adults, $8 children.*

3 On Sanibel, explore the **J. N. "Ding" Darling National Wildlife Refuge**—by car, foot, bicycle, or canoe. The 5,014-acre refuge is home to some 290 species of birds, 50 types of reptiles, and various mammals. A 5-mile dirt road meanders through the sanctuary. An observation tower along the road is a prime bird-watching site, especially in the early morning and just before dusk. *Tel. 813/472–1100. Admission: $3 per car or $10 for a duck stamp (which covers all national wildlife refuges).*

4 Board a boat to visit **Cabbage Key,** which sits at Marker 60 on the Intracoastal Waterway. Atop an ancient Calusa Indian shell mound on Cabbage Key is the friendly inn that novelist and playwright Mary Roberts Rinehart built in 1938. Now the inn offers several guest rooms, a marina, and a dining room that is papered in thousands of dollar bills, signed and posted by patrons over the years. *Lunch and dinner tours available through Captiva's South Seas Plantation (tel. 813/472–5111), and Fishermen's Village in Punta Gorda (tel. 813/639–0969).*

Naples **Naples** and surrounding suburbs are squeezed between the
5 Gulf of Mexico and the wilderness of the Big Cypress National Preserve, which stretches to the Everglades. I-75 and U.S. 41 lead from the north. Alligator Alley and U.S. 41 cut through the Everglades to bring travelers from the east coast.

To get a feel for what this part of Florida was like before humans began draining the swamps, take a drive out Rte. 846 to
6 the **Corkscrew Swamp Sanctuary.** The National Audubon Society manages the 11,000-acre tract to help protect 500-year-old trees and endangered birds, such as the wood storks that nest

high in the bald cypress. Visitors taking the 1¾-mile self-guided tour along the boardwalk can glimpse alligators, graceful wading birds, and unusual "air" plants that cling to the sides of trees. *16 mi east of I-75 on Rte. 846, tel. 813/657-3771. Open daily 9–5. Admission: $4 adults, $2 students, children under 6 free.*

7 If you want to monkey around, head for **Jungle Larry's African Safari Park.** Drive south on U.S. 41 past Mooringline Drive until you see the big sign for Jungle Larry's, then turn left. Here you can see a tiglon—a cross between a tiger and a lion—and other exotic wildlife in a junglelike park. The kids will also enjoy the petting zoo. *1590 Goodlette Rd., tel. 813/262-4053. Open 9:30–5:30; shows at 11:30, 2, and 4. Closed Mon., May–Nov. Admission: $9.95 adults, $5.95 children 3–15.*

Antique car enthusiasts should head to Naples' newest tourist
8 attraction, the **Collier Automotive Museum,** where 75 antique and classic sports cars now enjoy a splendid retirement. *2500 S. Horseshoe Drive, Collier Park of Commerce, off Airport-Pulling Road, tel. 813/643-5252. Open Wed.–Sun. 10–6. Admission: $6 adults, $3 children under 12.*

Head back to U.S. 41 and go south to **Third Street South** or **Fifth Avenue South,** Naple's fashionable shopping areas.

Head south on U.S. 41 to the **Old Marine Market Place at Tin City** (1200 5th Ave. S). In a collection of former fishing shacks along Naples Bay, entrepreneurs and artisans have set up 40 boutiques, studios, and shops offering everything from scrimshaw to Haitian art.

Time Out **Merriman's Wharf** (1200 5th Ave. S, tel. 813/261-1811), in the Old Marine Market Place, is a good bet for a drink or a seafood lunch—either along the dock or indoors in air-conditioned comfort.

What to See and Do with Children

Adventure Island is a water wonderland in the heart of Tampa, complete with water slides and pools with man-made waves. There are also changing rooms, snack stands, a gift shop, and a video arcade. *1 mi northeast of Busch Gardens. 4545 Bougainvillea Ave., tel. 813/971-7978. Open daily; closed Jan. and Feb. Admission: $13.95 per person, children under 2 free.*

Busch Gardens (*see* The Tampa Bay Area, above).

Great Explorations! is a museum where you will never be told, "Don't touch!" Everything is designed for a hands-on experience. The museum, which opened in late 1987, is divided into theme rooms, such as the Body Shop, which explores health; the Think Tank, which features mind-stretching puzzles and games; the Touch Tunnel, a 90-foot-long, pitch-black maze you crawl through; and Phenomenal Arts, which displays such items as a Moog music synthesizer (which you can play) and neon-filled tubes that glow in vivid colors when touched. *1120 4th St. S, St. Petersburg just off I-275, tel. 813/821-8885. Open weekdays 10–3, Sat. 10–5, Sun. noon–5. Admission: $4.50 adults, $3.50 children 2–17, $4 senior citizens.*

Sarasota Jungle Gardens (*see* Bradenton and Sarasota, above).

Circus Galleries, Ringling Museum (*see* Bradenton and Sarasota, above).

301 Raceway, go-cart rides and a video game room. *4050 N. Washington Blvd. (U.S. 301), Sarasota, tel. 813/355–5588. Open Sun.–Thurs. 11–10, Fri. and Sat. 11–11.*

Babcock Wilderness Adventures (*see* Fort Myers/Naples Region, above).

Nature Center of Lee County and Planetarium offers frequently changing exhibits on wildlife, fossils, Florida Indians, and native habitats. An aviary is home to a variety of permanently disabled birds, including hawks, owls, and bald eagles. There are 2 miles of nature walks through the cypress swamps. The planetarium offers star and laser light shows and Cinema-360 films. *3840 Ortiz Ave., Fort Myers, tel. 813/275–3435. Open Mon–Sat. 9–4, Sun. 11–4:30. Nature Center admission: $2 adults, 50¢ children; Planetarium admission: $3 adults, $2 children under 12.*

Everglades Wonder Gardens captures the flavor of untamed Florida with its exhibit of native wildlife and natural surroundings. *U.S. 41, tel. 813/992–2591. Open daily 9–5. Admission: $5 adults, $3 children 5–15.*

The DeSoto National Memorial. (*see* Bradenton and Sarasota, above).

Southwest Florida for Free

Bradenton

Manatee Village Historical Park. An 1860 courthouse, 1887 church, 1903 general store and museum, and 1912 settler's home are situated here, as is the Old Manatee Cemetery, which dates back to 1850 and contains the graves of early Manatee County settlers. (Appointments necessary to tour the cemetery.) *Rte. 64, 1 mi east of U.S. 41, tel. 813/749–7165. Open weekdays 9–4, Sun. 2–5 Sept.–June. Closed Sun. the rest of the year.*

Fort Myers/ Naples Area

Youth Museum of Charlotte County. Mostly animal specimens from Africa and North America, plus dolls, shells, and a variety of programs, are displayed here. *260 W. Retta Esplanade, Punta Gorda. Open weekdays 10–5.*

St. Petersburg

Fort de Soto Park. This 900-acre park is composed of six keys: Mullet, Bonne Fortune, Cunningham, Madeleine, St. Christopher, and St. Jean. Fort de Soto, begun during the Spanish-American War, is on the southern end of Mullet Key. *Reach it via 34th St. S, U.S. 19, and the Bayway. Open sunrise to sunset.*

Sarasota

Ringling Museum of Art. This is one of three museums on the grounds of the John and Mable Ringling Estate. A stipulation in the wealthy circus owner's will requires the art museum to be open free every Saturday. *On U.S. 41, 3 mi north of downtown, tel. 813/355–5101. Open Mon.–Wed. and Fri.–Sun. 10–6, Thurs. 10–10.*

Tampa

Villazon and Co. cigar factory. Free 30-minute guided tours are offered. You'll see the process from the selection of tobacco through the wrapping, banding, and packaging of the cigars. *3104 Armenia Ave., tel. 813/879–2291. Open weekdays 9:30–5. Closed holidays, late Dec.–mid-Jan., and late June–mid-July.*

Shrimp Docks. By late afternoon, the shrimp boats pull in at the 22nd Street Causeway to unload their catches.

University of Tampa. Tour the administration building, built as a luxury hotel in 1890, which served as Theodore Roosevelt's headquarters during the Spanish-American War. *Tel. 813/253–6220. Reservations required. Tours Tues. and Thurs. at 1:30, Sept.–May. Closed holidays.*

Tampa Bay Downs and Turf Club. Women are admitted free here on Thursdays. *Rte. 580 (Hillsborough Ave.) in Oldsmar, tel. 813/ 855–4401. Races Dec.–mid-Mar.; post time 1 PM. Parking $1.*

Tampa Jai Alai Fronton. This fast-paced and strenuous game is popular among Floridians, even those who don't like to bet (South Dale Mabry Highway and Gandy Boulevard, tel. 813/ 831–1411). Men are admitted free to Wednesday noon matinees; women to Saturday noon matinees; senior citizens to Monday matinees. No one under age 18 admitted. Pari-mutuel betting.

The Suncoast Seabird Sanctuary. This refuge and rehabilitation center for injured birds houses brown pelicans, cormorants, white herons, ospreys, and many other species. Many are on exhibit for public viewing. *18328 Gulf Blvd., tel. 813/391–6211. Admission free, but the nonprofit center accepts donations. Open daily 9–5:30.*

Tampa Bay Area

Railroad Historical Museum. Once a railroad station for the Orange Belt Railroad system, this place dates back to 1889. Drawings and relics from the Scottish community are on display. Maps for self-guided walking tours of historic areas are available. *341 Main St., Dunedin, tel. 813/733–4151. Open Wed. and Sat. 10–noon, Thurs. 9:30–11:30. Closed June 1–Oct. 1.*

Heritage Park and Museum. A collection of restored pioneer homes and buildings is spread on a 21-acre wooded site. The museum is the park's centerpiece, with exhibits depicting Pinellas County's pioneer lifestyle. Spinning, weaving, and other demonstrations are held regularly. *11909 125th St. N, Largo, tel. 813/462–3474. Open Tues.–Sat. 10–4, Sun. 1–4.*

Suncoast Botanical Gardens. Small by public botanical-garden standards, but all 60 acres are populated with cacti, eucalyptus trees, palms, crepe myrtle, and other flora of the Sunshine State. *10410 125th St., Largo, tel. 813/595–7218. Open daily daylight hours.*

Off the Beaten Track

Boca Grande

Before roads to southwest Florida were even talked about, the wealthy boarded trains to get to the Gasparilla Inn on **Boca Grande.** The small community continues to be a haven for the monied who seek to stay out of the limelight. The grand inn, built in 1912, remains in operation. From U.S. 41 in northern Port Charlotte head southwest on Rte. 776, then south on Rte. 771 into Placida, where a causeway runs out to the island.

While condominiums and other forms of modern sprawl have begun to creep up on Gasparilla, much of Boca Grande looks as it has for a century or more. The mood is set by the old Florida homes, many made of wood, with wide, inviting verandas and wicker rocking chairs.

At the island's southern end is Old Lighthouse Beach, where a historic wooden lighthouse still stands and where there is ample parking and lots of Gulf-front beach space. At mid-island is Banyan Street, so named for the huge trees that send down hundreds of shoots, shading the residential street, so that it appears to be twilight much of the day.

There is generally sleepy ambience to the island, except in the spring, when the tarpon fishermen descend with a vengeance on Boca Grande Pass, considered among the best tarpon-fishing spots in the world.

Everglades City Nestled amidst the 10,000 Islands, this tiny fishing village is the western gateway to Everglades National Park. From here, you can get a close look at the Everglades, sometimes called the river of grass. **Wooten's** offers airboat and swamp buggy rides through the swamps. Some 200 alligators are on display at Wooten's, too. *35 miles east of Naples on U.S. 41, tel. 813/394–8080. Rides depart about every 30 minutes.*

Fort Myers **Eden Vineyards Winery and Park** opened to the public in late 1989 claiming to be the southernmost bonded winery in the United States. The family-owned winery offers tours, tastings, picnics, and tram rides. *On the right side of Rte. 80, 10.2 mi east of the I–75 interchange. Open daily 10–6. Admission free; tastings $2.50.*

North Fort Myers **ECHO** (Educational Concerns for Hunger Organization) is a small active group striving to solve the world's hunger problems. The group offers tours of its gardens that feature collections of tropical food plants, simulated rain forests, and fish farming. *17430 Durrance Rd., tel. 813/543–3246. Tours Fri. 10 AM or by appointment.*

North Port An early-morning journey in a **hot-air balloon** gives the adventurous a bird's-eye view of a portion of southwest Florida (the portion depending on the prevailing winds). Rides commence (from North Port, south of Venice) early enough to watch the sunrise and are followed by leisurely breakfasts of quiche and champagne. *Contact Trans-America Balloons, North Port, tel. 813/426–7326. Cost: $99 per person, maximum of 3 people.*

Palmdale You aren't likely to happen upon Palmdale, a speck of a town about 40 minutes east of Punta Gorda, unless you make a point of visiting either of two singular attractions. You know you're approaching the **Cypress Knee Museum** when you see spindly hand-carved signs along Rte. 27 with sayings such as Lady, If He Won't Stop, Hit Him on Head with a Shoe. If you are younger than 6 or older than 80, you get in free; otherwise, you pay $2 for entry to Tom Gaskins's world of cypress knees. In the museum are thousands of cypress knees, the knotty, gnarled protuberances that sprout mysteriously from the bases of some cypress trees and grow to resemble all manner of persons and things. There are specimens resembling dogs, bears, ballet dancers' feet, an anteater, Joseph Stalin, and Franklin D. Roosevelt. Many require Gaskins's handwritten explanations, such as Lady Hippopotamus Wearing a Carmen Miranda Hat.

After touring the museum, walk the narrow boardwalk through three-quarters of a mile of cypress swamp to see the knees and trees in an unspoiled setting. The diminutive, barefoot man wandering amid the cypress is apt to be the 80-year-old Gaskins, who has appeared twice on Johnny Carson's "Tonight" show to display—what else?—his cypress knees. *1 mi south of the U.S. 27 and U.S. 29 junction, tel. 813/675–2951. Open daily 8 AM–dusk. Admission: $2 adults, $1 children 6–12.*

Just two miles southeast on U.S. 27, **Gatorama's** 1,000 alligators and assorted crocodiles await visitors, smiling toothily. Visitors who want to take a good long gander at gators can get their fill here, where a variety of species and sizes cohabit. It's also a commercial gator farm, so you'll see how the "mink" of the leather trade is grown for profit. *Tel. 813/675–0623. Admission: $4.50 adults, $2.50 children 2–11. Open daily sunrise–sunset.*

Shopping

Most visitors eventually get their quota of sun, sand, and surf and find themselves in need of something else to do. For many, that something is shopping.

Gift Ideas It is a rare vacationer who does not leave the state with at least one sack of oranges or grapefruit. Most produce stands are open during the citrus season (Dec.–Mar.). You cannot take citrus out of state without a USDA inspection sticker, so make sure you take only those sacks that are properly sealed.

In Tarpon Springs, natural sponges are plentiful and reasonably priced. Many shops along Dodecanese Boulevard, the town's main street, sell a variety of locally harvested sponges.

Tampa's Ybor City is a thriving Cuban community where the art of cigar making lives on. There are many small cigar shops in the area on Tampa's east side.

Shell items—jewelry, lamps, plant hangers, and such—are among the more kitschy commodities found in abundance in the region. Sanibel Island, one of the world's premier shelling grounds, has numerous shops that sell shell products (including two named **She Sells Seashells,** at 1983 and 1157 Periwinkle Way). **The Shell Factory** in North Fort Myers claims to have the world's largest display of seashells and coral. *2787 N. Tamiami Trail (U.S. 41). Open daily 9–6.*

Fine Shopping Those who gravitate toward exclusive boutiques have a wealth of them to explore in southwest Florida. In Sarasota, St. Armand's Key (just west of downtown Sarasota) has Harding Circle, a circular string of shops and restaurants that cater to consumers seeking out-of-the-ordinary items and willing to pay high prices for them.

In Fort Myers, there are two such centers—**Bell Tower** (U.S. 41 and Daniels Rd., South Fort Myers) and **Royal Palm Square** (Colonial Blvd., between McGregor Blvd. and U.S. 41). Both have about 36 shops and restaurants. Both are worth visiting if just to look at the elegant tropical landscaping, which includes parrots that stand sentry from perches among the palms. Neither center is enclosed, but both have covered sidewalks. In Naples, 3rd Street South and 5th Avenue South are lined with fine boutiques and restaurants.

Flea Markets **Wagonwheel** is 100-plus acres containing some 2,000 vendors and a variety of food concessions. Parking costs $1. There is a tram from the parking lot to the vendor area. *7801 Park Blvd., Pinellas Park, tel. 813/544–5319. Open weekends 8–4.*

Red Barn has the requisite big red barn, in which vendors operate daily except Mondays. The number of vendors increases to about 1,000 on weekends. *1707 1st St. E, Bradenton, tel. 813/747–3794. Open Wed., Sat., and Sun. 8–4.*

Dome has sheltered walkways under which can be found dozens of stalls selling new and recycled wares. *Rte. 775, west of U.S. 41, Venice, tel. 813/493–6773. Open Fri.–Sun. 9–4; closed Aug.*

Ortiz also features covered walkways and hundreds of vendors selling new and used items. *Ortiz and Anderson avenues, east of Fort Myers, tel. 813/694–5019. Open Fri.–Sun. 6–4.*

Beaches

You can't drive on them like you can in Daytona. And the scantily attired college-age revelers who pack Fort Lauderdale each spring are not found in abundance here. But there are myriad reasons why a growing number of Florida-bound beachgoers are heading to the southwest coast. For sun worshipers, there are beaches on which to bask in relative solitude; for singles, there are sands on which to see and be seen; for shell collectors, there is treasure to unearth. And not one beach offers less than a spectacular sunset.

Charlotte County (Punta Gorda Area)

Englewood Beach, near the Charlotte-Sarasota county line, is popular with teenagers, although beachgoers of all ages frequent it. In addition to a wide and shell-littered beach, there are barbecue grills, picnic facilities, and a playground.

Collier County (Naples Area)

Bonita Springs Public Beach is 10 minutes from the I-75 exit at Bonita Beach Road, on the southern end of Bonita Beach. There are picnic tables, free parking, and nearby refreshment stands and shopping.

Delnor-Wiggins Pass State Recreation Area is at the Gulf end of Bluebill Avenue, off Vanderbilt Drive in North Naples. The well-maintained park offers miles of sandy beaches, lifeguards, barbecue grills, picnic tables, a boat ramp, observation tower, rest rooms with wheelchair access, lots of parking space, bathhouses, and showers. Fishing is best in Wiggins Pass at the north end of the park. *Admission: Florida residents pay $1 for the operator of a vehicle, plus 50¢ per passenger; out-of-state drivers pay $2, $1 per passenger. Boat launching costs $1. No alcoholic beverages allowed.*

Lowdermilk Park stretches along Gulf Shore Boulevard in Naples. There are 1,000 feet of beach plus parking, rest rooms, showers, a pavilion, vending machines, and picnic tables. No alcoholic beverages or fires permitted.

Tigertail Beach is on Hernando Drive at the south end of Marco Island. Singles and families congregate here. Facilities: parking, concession stand, picnic area, sailboat rentals, volleyball, rest rooms, and showers.

Lee County (Fort Myers Area)

Estero Island, otherwise known as **Fort Myers Beach,** is 18 miles from downtown Fort Myers. It has numerous public accesses to the beach, which is frequented by families and young singles. In most areas, you are never far from civilization, with houses, condominiums, and hotels nestled along the shore. The island's shores slope gradually into the usually tranquil and warm Gulf waters, affording a safe swimming area for children.

From Fort Myers, it is reached via San Carlos Boulevard; from Naples and Bonita Springs, via Hickory Boulevard.

Lynn Hall Memorial Park is on Estero Boulevard, in the more commercial northern part of Fort Myers Beach. Singles can be found playing in the gentle surf or sunning and socializing on shore. A number of night spots and restaurants are within easy walking distance. A free fishing pier adjoins the public beach. Facilities: picnic tables, barbecue grills, playground equipment, and a bathhouse with rest rooms.

Carl E. Johnson Recreation Area is just south of Fort Myers Beach. The admission of $1 per adult, 50 cents per child includes a round-trip tram ride from the park entrance to Lovers Key, on which the park is situated. Shelling, bird-watching, fishing, canoeing, and nature walks in an unspoiled setting are the main attractions here. There are also rest rooms, picnic tables, a snack bar, and basic showers.

Sanibel

Sanibel and **Captiva** islands are about 23 miles from Fort Myers and are reached via a toll bridge on the Sanibel Causeway. Though the $3 round-trip toll may seem steep, avid shell collectors and nature enthusiasts are apt to get their money's worth. Sanibel beaches are rated among the best shelling grounds in the world. For the choicest pickings, get there as the tide is going out or just after a storm. Windsurfers need go only as far as the Sanibel Causeway to find a suitable place to set sail.

Gulfside Park, off Casa Ybel Road, is a lesser-known and less-populated beach, ideal for those who seek solitude and do not require facilities.

Lighthouse Park, at Sanibel's southern end, attracts a mix of families, shellers, and singles. Rest rooms are available. One of the draws is a historic old lighthouse.

Bowman's Beach is mainly a family beach on Sanibel's northwest end, but nudists have been known to bathe unabashedly in more secluded areas of the beach.

Manatee County (Bradenton Area)

Anna Maria Island, just west of the Sunshine Skyway Bridge, boasts three public beaches. **Anna Maria Bayfront Park,** at the north end of the municipal pier, is a secluded beach fronting both the Intracoastal Waterway and the Gulf of Mexico. Facilities include picnic grounds, a playground, rest rooms, showers, and lifeguards. At mid-island, in the town of Holmes Beach, is **Manatee County Beach,** popular with all ages. It has picnic facilities, a snack bar, showers, rest rooms, and lifeguards. At the island's southern end is **Coquina Beach,** popular with singles and families. Facilities: picnic area, boat ramp, playground, refreshment stand, rest rooms, showers, and lifeguards.

Egmont Key lies just off the northern tip of Anna Maria Island. On it is Fort Dade, a military fort built in 1900 during the Spanish-American War, and Florida's sixth-brightest lighthouse. The primary inhabitant of the 2-mile-long island is the threatened gopher tortoise. The only way to get to the island is by boat. Shellers will find the trip rewarding. An excursion boat makes trips on Tuesday, Thursday, and Sunday. The *Miss Cortez* departs from Cortez, just west of Bradenton (tel. 813/794–1223).

Cortez Beach, on the mainland, just north of Coquina, is on Gulf Boulevard in the town of Bradenton Beach. This one's popular with those who like their beaches without facilities—nothing but sand, water, and trees. The Palma Sola Causeway takes Manatee Avenue on the mainland to Anna Maria Island and also offers beachgoers a long, sandy beach fronting Palma Sola Bay. There are boat ramps, a dock, and picnic tables.

Greer Island Beach is at the northern tip of the next barrier island south on Longboat Key. It's accessible by boat or via North Shore Boulevard. The secluded peninsula has a wide beach and excellent shelling, but no facilities.

Pinellas County (Gulf Coast west of Tampa)

Tarpon Springs has two public beaches: **Howard Park Beach,** where a lifeguard is on duty daily 8:30–6 Easter through Labor Day, and **Sunset Beach,** where there is similar lifeguard duty as well as rest rooms, picnic tables, grills, and a boat ramp.

Caladesi Island State Park lies 3 miles off Dunedin's coast, across Hurricane Pass. The 600-acre park is one of the state's few remaining undeveloped barrier islands. It's accessible only by boat. There is a beach on the Gulf side and mangroves on the bay side. This is a good spot for swimming, fishing, shelling, boating, and nature study. A self-guided nature trail winds through the island's interior. Park rangers are available to answer questions. Facilities: boardwalks, picnic shelters, bathhouses, a ranger station, and concession stand. A ferry runs hourly 10–5 between Caladesi Island and Honeymoon Island to the north but it runs in good weather only. *Ferry admission: $3.75 adults, $2.10 children 2–10. Park admission extra. Call for ferry information (tel. 813/734–5263).*

Clearwater Beach is another popular, more accessible island beach. It is south of Caladesi on a narrow island between Clearwater Harbor and the Gulf. It is connected to downtown Clearwater by Memorial Causeway. Facilities: marina, concessions, showers, rest rooms, and lifeguards.

St. Petersburg Area

The St. Petersburg beaches are numerous and wide-ranging in character.

Bay Beach (North Shore Dr. and 13th Ave. NE, on Tampa Bay) charges 10¢ admission. It has showers and shelters.

North Shore Beach (901 North Shore Dr. NE) charges $1 admission. Facilities: pool, beach umbrellas, cabanas, windbreaks, and lounges.

Maximo Park Beach (34 St. and Pinellas Point Dr. S) is on Boca Ciega Bay. There is no lifeguard. There is a picnic area with grills, tables, shelters, and a boat ramp.

St. Petersburg Municipal Beach (11260 Gulf Blvd.) is a free beach on Treasure Island. There are dressing rooms, metered parking, and a snack bar.

Pass-a-Grille Beach, on the Gulf, has parking meters, a snack bar, rest rooms, and showers.

Fort DeSoto Park consists of the southernmost beaches of St. Petersburg, on five islands totaling some 900 acres. Facilities: two fishing piers, picnic sites overlooking lagoons, a waterskiing and boating area, and miles of beaches for swimming. Open daily until dark. To get there, take the Pinellas Bayway through three toll gates (cost: 85¢).

Sarasota County The county contains 10 beaches, ranging from 5 to 113 acres. **South Lido,** at the southern tip of Lido Key, is among the largest and best beaches in the region. The sugar-sand beach offers little for shell collectors, but the interests of virtually all other beach lovers are served on its 100 acres, which probably accounts for the diverse mix of people it attracts. Facilities: fishing, nature trails, volleyball, playground, horseshoes, rest rooms, and picnic grounds.

Siesta Beach is on Beach Road on Siesta Key. The 40-acre park contains nature trails, a concession stand, soccer and softball fields, picnicking facilities, play equipment, rest rooms, and tennis and volleyball courts.

Turtle Beach is farther south on Siesta Key's Midnight Pass Road. Though only 14 acres, it includes boat ramps, horseshoe courts, picnic and play facilities, a recreation building, rest rooms, and a volleyball court.

North Jetty Park is at the south end of Casey Key, a slender barrier island. It's a favorite for family outings. Amenities include rest rooms, a concession stand, play and picnic equipment, fishing, horseshoes, and a volleyball court.

Nokomis Beach is just north of North Jetty on Albee Road. Its facilities are similar to those at North Jetty, except that it has two boat ramps and no horseshoe court.

Caspersen Beach, on Beach Drive in south Venice, is the county's largest park. It has a nature trail, fishing, picnicking, rest rooms, plus lots of beach for those who prefer space to a wealth of amenities. Along with a plentiful mix of shells, observant beachcombers are likely to find sharks' teeth on Venice beaches, washed up from the ancient shark burial grounds just offshore.

Manasota Key spans much of the county's southern coast, from south of Venice to Englewood. It has two choice beaches: *Manasota*, on Manasota Beach Road, with a boat ramp, picnic area and rest rooms; and *Blind Pass*, where you can fish and swim but will find no amenities.

Participant Sports

Biking Call the nearest chamber of commerce or bike store for the best bike paths. Two of the best are at Boca Grande and Sanibel Island.

Tampa Bay. There are many places to rent bikes, but not much in the way of bike paths. Rental stores include **St. Petersburg:** *The Beach Cyclist* (7517 Blindpass Rd., tel. 813/367–5001) and *Village Bike Shops* (2236 62nd Ave., tel. 813/867–6667); **Largo:** *D & S Bicycle Shop* (12073 Seminole Blvd., tel. 813/393–0300); and **Tarpon Springs:** *BiSick* (tel. 813/937–3030).

Sarasota/Bradenton. No bike paths. Rental shops include **Bradenton:** *Bicycle Center* (2610 Cortez Rd., tel. 813/756–5480); **Sarasota:** *Mr. CB's* (1249 Stickney Point Rd., tel. 813/349–4400), and *Pedal N Wheels* (Merchants Pointe Shopping Center, 2881 Clark Rd., tel. 813/922–0481); and **Venice:** *The Bike Doctor* (291 Trott Circle, tel. 813/426–4807); and *Bicycles International* (1744 Tamiami Trail S, [U.S. 41], tel. 813/497–1590).

Fort Myers/Naples. There are several bike paths in the area. **Boca Grande,** an hour's drive from Fort Myers or Sarasota, has good bike paths. **Fort Myers:** The best choice here is the path along Summerlin Road. For rental, try *Trikes & Bikes* (3224 Fowler St., tel. 813/936–4301). **Sanibel:** The island's extensive bike path is well used. It is in good condition and runs throughout the island, keeping bikers safely apart from the traffic and allowing them some time for reflection on the waterways and wildlife they will encounter. Rent bikes at *Finnimore's Cycle Shop* (1223 Periwinkle Way, Sanibel, tel. 813/472–5577) and *Jim's Bike & Scooter Rental* (11534 Andy Rosse La., Captiva, tel. 813/472–1296). **Naples:** *Pop's Bicycles* (4265 Bonita Beach Rd., Bonita Springs, tel. 813/947–4442) and *The Bicycle Shop* (813 Vanderbilt Beach Rd., Naples, tel. 813/566–3646); **Marco Island:** *Scooterville* (855 Bald Eagle Dr., tel. 813/394–8400).

Canoeing For those who like to travel slowly and under their own power, canoe rentals abound. Among them are **Art's Swap Shop** (9608 Nebraska, Tampa, tel. 813/935–4011), canoe and car racks for rent; and **Myakka River State Park,** 15 miles south of Sarasota near Venice (tel. 813/924–1027), canoes, paddles, and life vests for rent. **Canoe Outpost** offers half-day, full-day, and overnight canoe-camping trips from a number of southwest Florida locations, including Little Manatee River (18001 U.S. 301 S, Wimauma, just south of Tampa, tel. 813/634–2228) and Peace River (Rte. 7, Box 301, Arcadia, 25 miles northeast of Port Charlotte, tel. 813/494–1215). **Lakes Park** in Fort Myers (tel. 813/481–7946) rents canoes on waterways where you can see the carp swimming, and, if you are quiet enough, some herons and osprey flying overhead; **Canoe Safari** (Arcadia, tel. 813/494–7865) has half- and full-day trips, plus overnighters including camping equipment; **Parkland Ventures** (Fort Myers, tel. 813/482–1328) has guided nature treks in canoes or kayaks; and **Tarpon Bay Marina** (Sanibel, tel. 813/472–8900) has canoes and equipment for exploring the waters of the J. N. "Ding" Darling National Wildlife Refuge. **Estero River Tackle and Canoe Outfitters** (20991 Tamiami Trail South, Estero, tel. 813/992-4050) has canoes and equipment for use on the meandering Estero River.

Fishing Anglers flock to southwest Florida. You need very little to get started—a rod and reel will suffice. Just wander out to a bridge and cast off. Tampa Bay and its inlets are known for yielding tarpon, kingfish, and speckled trout. Snapper, grouper, sea trout, snook, sheepshead, and shark are among the species to be found throughout the region. You can also charter your own boat or join a group on a party boat for full- or half-day outings.

Party boats in the area include **Flying Fish** (Marina Jack's, U.S. 41 and bay front, Sarasota, tel. 813/366–3373), **L-C Marine** (215 Tamiami Trail S., [U.S. 41], Venice, tel. 813/484-9044), **Kingfisher Charter** (Fishermen's Village, Punta Gorda, tel. 813/639–0969), **Deebold's Marina** (1071 San Carlos Blvd., Fort Myers, tel. 813/466–3525), **Gulf Star Marina** (708 Fisherman's Wharf, Fort Myers Beach, tel. 813/765–1500), **Deep Sea Charter Fishing** (Old Marine Market Place, Naples, tel. 813/263–8171).

Golf Courses open to the public include **Apollo Beach Club** (Tampa, tel. 813/645–6212), **Babe Zaharias Golf Course** (Tampa, tel. 813/932–4401), **Rocky Point Golf Course** (Tampa, tel. 813/884-5141), **Clearwater Golf Park** (Clearwater, tel. 813/447–5272),

Dunedin Country Club (Dunedin, tel. 813/733–7836), **Manatee County Golf Course** (Bradenton, tel. 813/792–6773), **Bobby Jones Golf Course** (Sarasota, tel. 813/955–8097), **Forest Lake Golf Course** (Sarasota, tel. 813/922–1312), **Bird Bay Executive Golf Course** (Venice, tel. 813/485–9333), **North Port Golf Course** (North Port, tel. 813/426–2804), **Deep Creek Golf Club** (Charlotte Harbor, tel. 813/625–6911), **Burnt Store** (Punta Gorda, tel. 813/332–7334), **Bay Beach Club Executive Golf Course** (Fort Myers Beach, tel. 813/463–2064), **Cypress Pines Country Club** (Lehigh Acres, tel. 813/369–8216), **Fort Myers Country Club** (Fort Myers, tel. 813/936–2457), **The Dunes** (Sanibel, tel. 813/472–2535), **Wildcat Run** (Estero, tel. 813/936–7222), **Pelican's Nest Golf Course** (Bonita Springs, tel. 813/947–4600), **Hibiscus Country Club** (Naples, tel. 813/774–3559), and **Oxbow** (LaBelle, tel. 813/334–3903).

Motorboating Much of southwest Florida's charm lies beyond its shoreline. Fortunately, there are many concerns that rent boats of all sizes.

On Nokomis Beach, **Don and Mike's Boat and Ski Rental** (tel. 813/485–7345) has water skis, jet skis, Windsurfers, wavejammers, plus instruction in windsurfing and waterskiing.

Lakes Park Marina (7330 Gladiolus Drive, Fort Myers, tel. 813/481–6563) rents paddleboats, canoes, and fishing gear.

Boat House of Sanibel (Sanibel Marina, tel. 813/472–2531) rents powerboats.

Getaway Bait and Boat Rental (18400 San Carlos Blvd., Fort Myers Beach, tel. 813/466–3200) rents powerboats and fishing equipment and sells bait.

Brookside Marina (2023 Davis Blvd., Naples, tel. 813/263–7250) rents 16- to 25-foot powerboats.

Sailing Sailing schools and guided or bare-boat rentals are plentiful. Spend a week learning the ropes or a few hours luxuriating on a sunset cruise.

O'Leary's Sarasota Sailing School (near Marina Jack's, U.S. 41 and the bay front, Sarasota, tel. 813/953–7505); **Southwest Florida Yachts** (3444 Marinatown La. NW, Fort Myers, tel. 813/656–1339 or 800/262–7939); **Fort Myers Yacht Charters** (Port Sanibel Yacht Club, south Fort Myers, tel. 813/466–1800); **Adventure Sailing Escape** (Fort Myers, tel. 813/489–0344); **CSA Charters** (110 Gulf Shore Blvd. N, Naples, tel. 813/649–0091); and **Marco Island Sea Excursions** (1281 Jamaica Rd., Marco Island, tel. 813/642–6400).

Scuba Diving Dive shops are found all over the region. However, most make excursions to the Florida Keys or the east coast of Florida rather than dive in this area.

Tennis Many hotels and motels in Florida have outdoor tennis courts, some lighted for night use. For those who are motivated to find other courts, a list of public ones follows:

City of Tampa Courts (59 Columbia Dr., Davis Islands, Tampa, tel. 813/253–3782), **Cedar Tennis Club** (Longboat Key, tel. 813/383–6461), **Port Charlotte Tennis Club** (22400 Gleneagles Terr., Port Charlotte, tel. 813/625–7222), **Bay Beach Racquet Club** (120 Lenell St., Fort Myers Beach, tel. 813/463–4473), **Lochmoor Country Club** (3911 Orange Grove Blvd., North Fort

Myers, tel. 813/995–0511), **The Dunes** (949 Sand Castle Rd., Sanibel, tel. 813/472–3522), and **Forest Hills Racquet Club** (100 Forest Hills Blvd., Naples, tel. 813/774–2442).

Windsurfing **Watersports Inc.** (17624-312 San Carlos Blvd., Fort Myers Beach, tel. 813/466–SURF) offers Windsurfer rentals and lessons.

Spectator Sports

Baseball The season comes early to Florida with the annual convergence of the Grapefruit League—17 major league teams offer exhibitions in March and April. These teams hold their spring training in southwest Florida. For information on all the teams, tel. 904/488–0990. Home bases for area teams are Bradenton: **Pittsburgh Pirates** (McKechnie Field, 9th St. W and 16th Ave., tel. 813/748–4610); Clearwater: **Philadelphia Phillies** (Jack Russell Stadium, Seminole and Greenwood Ave., tel. 813/442–8496); Dunedin: **Toronto Blue Jays** (Grant Field, 311 Douglas Ave., North of Rte. 88, tel. 813/733–0429); Fort Myers: **Minnesota Twins** (at press time, stadium under construction at the intersection of Six Mile Cypress and Daniels roads); Port Charlotte: **Texas Rangers** (Charlotte County Stadium, Rte. 776, tel. 813/625–9500); St. Petersburg: **St. Louis Cardinals** (Al Lang Stadium, 1st St. and 2nd Ave., tel. 813/822–3384); Sarasota: **Chicago White Sox** (Payne Park, U.S. 301 and Ringling Blvd., tel. 813/953–3388); and Tampa: **Cincinnati Reds** (Plant City Stadium, Park Road, Plant City, tel. 813/752–7337).

The Senior Professional Baseball Association (for major leaguers 35 or older) plays in Florida November–February. Home bases for area teams are Bradenton: **Explorers** (McKechnie Field, 9th St. W and 16th Ave., tel. 813/748–4610); Fort Myers: **Sun Sox** (Terry Park, Palm Beach Blvd., tel. 813/332–0909); and St. Petersburg: **Pelicans** (Al Lang Stadium, 1st St. and 2nd Ave., tel. 813/822–3384).

Football NFL football comes in the form of the **Tampa Bay Buccaneers,** who play at Tampa Stadium (4201 N. Dale Mabry Hwy.). For information, tel. 813/461–2700 or 800/282–0683.

Soccer The lone competitor in the area is the **Tampa Bay Rowdies** (tel. 813/877–7800). The team plays April–September indoors at the Bayfront Center (400 1st St., St. Petersburg) and outside at Tampa Stadium in Tampa.

Gambling Casino gambling has yet to find its way into the state, but the odds are that there are more than enough alternatives to suit bettors. There is **horse racing** at Tampa Bay Downs (Race Track Rd. off Rte. 580, Oldsmar, tel. 813/855–4401, with Thoroughbred races December–mid-April). **Dog racing** occurs somewhere in the region all year: January–May at Derby Lane (10490 Gandy Blvd., St. Petersburg, tel. 813/576–1361); Sept.–Jan. at Tampa Greyhound Track (8300 N. Nebraska Ave., Tampa, tel. 813/932–4313); May–Sept. at the Sarasota Kennel Club (5400 Bradenton Rd., Sarasota, tel. 813/355–7744); and year-round at the Naples–Fort Myers Kennel Club (10601 Bonita Beach Rd., Bonita Springs, tel. 813/334–6555). **Jai alai** is offered at the Tampa Jai-Alai Fronton (S. Dale Mabry Hwy. and Gandy Blvd., Tampa, tel. 813/831–1411) Jan.–Sept. Big-time **bingo** can be found at the singular Seminole Bingo Hall

(5221 Orient Rd., Tampa, tel. 800/282–7016), run by the Seminole Indians. Jackpots regularly exceed $60,000.

Dining and Lodging

Dining As in most coastal regions, fresh seafood is plentiful. Raw bars, serving just-plucked-from-the-bay oysters, clams, and mussels, are everywhere. The region's ethnic diversity is also well represented. Tarpon Springs adds a hearty helping of classic Greek specialties such as moussaka, a ground meat and eggplant pie, and baklava, delicate layers of pastry and nuts soaked in honey. In Tampa, the cuisine is Cuban. Standard menu items include black beans and rice and paella, a seafood, chicken, and saffroned-rice casserole. In Sarasota, the accent is on the Continental, both in food and service. Heading toward Fort Myers and Naples, seafood reigns supreme, especially the succulent claw of the stone crab, in season October 15–May 15. It's usually served with drawn butter or a tangy mustard sauce. There are some people who proclaim its flavor superior to that of lobster.

The most highly recommended restaurants in each price category are indicated by a star ★.

Category	Cost*
Very Expensive	over $60
Expensive	$40–$60
Moderate	$20–$40
Inexpensive	under $20

**per person, excluding drinks, service, and 6% sales tax*

The following credit card abbreviations are used: AE, American Express; CB, Carte Blanche; DC, Diners Club; MC, MasterCard; V, Visa.

Lodging There are old historic hotels and ultramodern chrome-and-glass high rises, sprawling resorts and cozy inns, luxurious waterfront lodges and just-off-the-highway budget motels. In general, inland rooms are considerably cheaper than those on the islands. The most expensive accommodations are those with waterfront views. Rates are highest mid-December–mid-April. The lowest prices are available May–November. Many apartment-motels are springing up in the area and can prove economical for families that wish to prepare some of their own meals or for groups who can share an apartment. Price categories listed below apply to winter rates. Many drop to a less expensive category at other times of the year.

Category	Cost*
Very Expensive	over $120
Expensive	$90–$120
Moderate	$50–$90
Inexpensive	under $50

**per person, double occupancy, without 6% state sales tax and nominal (1%–3%) tourist tax.*

Bradenton
Dining

Charlie Brown's. Lots of antiques and collectibles here create a turn-of-the-century decor. A menu laden with steaks and fresh seafood poses a difficult choice for diners. *7051 Manatee Ave. W, tel. 813/794–3138. Dress: casual. Reservations advised for parties of 10 or more. AE, CB, DC, MC, V. Moderate.*

Lodging

Holiday Inn Riverfront. A Spanish Mediterranean-style motor inn near the Manatee River. *100 Riverfront Dr. W 34205, tel. 813/747–3727. 153 rooms. Facilities: pool, whirlpool, restaurant, lounge. AE, CB, DC, MC, V. Moderate.*

Cape Coral
Dining

Cape Crab House. Crabs are served Maryland-style—with mallet and pliers and heaped on a tablecloth of newspaper—or in the more refined atmosphere of a second dining room with linen tablecloths and a piano player. *Coralwood Mall, Del Prado Blvd., tel. 813/574–2722. Dress: casual. Reservations accepted. AE, MC, V. Moderate.*

★ **Siam Hut.** Thai music pings and twangs in the background while the dishes do the same to your tastebuds. Get it fiery hot or extra mild. Specialties: *pad thai* (a mixture of noodles, crushed peanuts, chicken, shrimp, egg, bean sprouts, and scallions) and crispy Siam rolls (spring rolls stuffed with ground chicken, bean thread, and vegetables). *1873 Del Prado Blvd. (Coral Pointe Shopping Center), tel. 813/772–3131. Dress: casual. No reservations. AE, MC, V. Inexpensive.*

Venezia. A small, neighborhood restaurant serving straightforward Italian food including pastas, pizza, chicken, veal, and fresh seafood. *1515 SE 47th Terr., tel. 813/542–0027. Dress: casual. No reservations. MC, V. Moderate. No lunch.*

Lodging

Cape Coral Inn & Country Club. A resort for golf and tennis enthusiasts who also seek economy. Understated decor reflects the sporty atmosphere. *4003 Palm Tree Blvd. 33904, tel. 813/542–3191. 100 rooms. Facilities: pool, golf, driving range, tennis, baby-sitting, restaurant, lounge. AE, CB, DC, MC, V. Moderate.*

Quality Inn. Conveniently located in downtown Cape Coral. *1538 Cape Coral Pkwy. 33904, tel. 813/542–2121. 146 rooms. Facilities: pool; pets accepted. AE, CB, DC, MC, V. Moderate.*

Cedar Key
Dining

The Heron Restaurant. The specialty at this island restaurant is seafood, served in Victorian comfort. *S.R. 24 and 2nd St., tel. 904/543–5666. Dress: neat but casual. Reservations advised. AE, MC, V. Moderate.*

The Captain's Table. This is a dockside seafood restaurant with a fine view of anglers on the pier and artists along the seawall. Broiled seafood is the house specialty, but there are chicken and steak dishes as well. *On Dock St., tel. 904/543–5441. Dress: casual. Reservations advised for Sat. dinner. MC, V. Inexpensive.*

Lodging

Historic Island Hotel. Located in the historic district, this bed-and-breakfast hotel features 1850 Jamaican architecture and gourmet natural foods. *Main and B sts. 32625, tel. 904/543–5111. 10 rooms. Facilities: cafe, bicycle built for 2. MC, V. Moderate.*

Island Place. One- and two-bedroom suites that sleep four are available at this small two-story condominium complex. The roof is tin, and the decks offer a view of the busy dock. *Box 687 32625, tel. 904/543–5307. 25 suites. Facilities: pool, sauna, Jacuzzi, laundry. MC, V. Moderate–Expensive.*

Clearwater
Dining

The Kapok Tree. A cluster of dining rooms serving steak and seafood overlook tropical gardens. A strolling minstrel performs. *923 McMullen Booth Rd., tel. 813/726–0504. Dress: casual. Reservations advised. AE, CB, DC, MC, V. Moderate.*

Bob Heilman's Beachcomber. Southern-fried chicken and mashed potatoes with gravy have long been the Sunday staple at this 40-year-old restaurant. Also known for its seafood, homemade desserts, and hearty portions. *447 Mandalay Ave., Clearwater Beach, tel. 813/442–4144. Dress: casual. Reservations advised. AE, DC, MC, V. Moderate.*

Lodging

Belleview Biltmore Hotel & Spa. This large, historic resort on Clearwater Bay has extensive facilities and transportation to the beach. *25 Belleview Blvd. 34616, tel. 813/442–6171. 350 rooms. Facilities: pools, whirlpools, saunas, golf, tennis, bicycles, playground, fishing, sailboats, restaurant, lounge. AE, CB, DC, MC, V. Very Expensive.*

Adam's Mark Caribbean Gulf Resort. Situated on the Gulf shore, this modern resort offers comfort. A taste of the islands is provided by the steel-drum band that plays poolside. *430 S. Gulfview Blvd. 34630, tel. 813/443–5714. 205 rooms. Facilities: beach, pool, wading pool, whirlpool, restaurants, lounge. AE, CB, DC, MC, V. Expensive.*

Sheraton Sand Key Resort. A resort for those who want lots of sun, sand, and surf. Balconies and patios overlook the Gulf and well-manicured grounds. *1160 Gulf Blvd., Clearwater Beach 33515, tel. 813/595–1611. 390 rooms. Facilities: pool, wading pool, beach, whirlpool, playground, tennis courts, windsurfing, sailboats, restaurant, lounge. AE, CB, DC, MC, V. Expensive.*

Radisson Inn. This is a comfortable, unpretentious motor inn near the airport and Tampa Bay. *3580 Ulmerton Rd. (Rte. 688) 34622, tel. 813/573–1171. 116 rooms. Facilities: pool, whirlpool, fitness center, restaurant. AE, CB, DC, MC, V. Moderate.*

Fort Myers
Dining

Peter's La Cuisine. The quiet elegance of this downtown restaurant blends perfectly with the fine Continental cuisine served within. The menu changes every few weeks but usually includes a fresh salmon dish, chateaubriand, and duck or some other exotic meat. *2224 Bay St., tel. 813/332–2228. Dress: neat but casual. Reservations advised. AE, DC, MC, V. Expensive.*

★ **The Prawnbroker.** Its ads urge you to scratch and sniff. There is no odor, says the ad, because fresh fish does not have one. What there is is an abundance of seafood seemingly just plucked from Gulf waters, plus some selections for landlubbers. Almost always crowded. *6535 McGregor Blvd. tel. 813/489–2226. Dress: casual. Reservations accepted. AE, MC, V. Moderate. No lunch.*

Sangeet of India. Indian melodies waft through the air mingling with fragrant spices used in traditional dishes of India. Buffet lunch served weekdays. *Villas Plaza, U.S. 41 and Crystal Dr., tel. 813/278–0101. Dress: casual. Reservations accepted. AE, MC, V. Moderate.*

Smitty's Beef Room. An old and reliable local restaurant, offering an assortment of steaks, prime rib, and seafood. A great meat-and-potatoes place that is popular with locals and visitors. *2240 W. 1st St., tel. 813/334–4415. Dress: casual. AE, CB, DC, MC, V. Moderate.*

The Veranda. Within a sprawling turn-of-the-century home is served an imaginative assortment of American regional cuisine. This is a popular place for business and governmental bigwigs to rub elbows. *2122 2nd St., tel. 813/332–2065. Dress: stylishly casual. AE, CB, DC, MC, V. Moderate.*

Miami Connection. If you hunger for choice chopped liver, lean-but-tender corned beef, and a chewy bagel, this kosher-style deli can fill the bill. The sandwiches are huge. It is, as the local restaurant critic aptly said, "the real McCohen." *11506 Cleveland Ave., tel. 813/936–3811. Dress: casual. No reservations. No credit cards. Inexpensive. No dinner.*

Woody's Bar-B-Q. A no-frills barbecue pit featuring chicken, ribs, and beef in copious amounts at bargain-basement prices. *6701 N. Tamiami Trail (U.S. 41), North Fort Myers, tel. 813/997–1424; and 17105 San Carlos Blvd., tel. 813/454–0454. Dress: casual. No reservations. MC, V. Inexpensive.*

Lodging

Sanibel Sonesta Harbour Resort. This high-rise apartment hotel sits on the east side of the Sanibel Causeway, not quite in Fort Myers, not quite on Sanibel. It overlooks San Carlos Bay and has a full complement of amenities. *17260 Harbour Pointe 33908, tel. 813/466–4000. 240 rooms, 100 condominiums. Facilities: pools, health club, tennis, whirlpool, restaurant, lounge. AE, DC, MC, V. Very Expensive.*

Sheraton Harbor Place. This modern high-rise hotel commands a dominant spot on the downtown Fort Myers skyline, rising above the Caloosahatchee River and Fort Myers Yacht Basin. *2500 Edwards Dr. 33901, tel. 813/337–0300. 437 rooms. Facilities: pool, tennis, a game room, whirlpool, dock, exercise room. AE, DC, MC, V. Expensive.*

Best Western Robert E. Lee Motor Inn. Rooms are spacious, with patios or balconies overlooking the Caloosahatchee River. *6611 U.S. 41N, North Fort Myers 33903, tel. 813/997–5511. 108 rooms. Facilities: lounge, pool, dock. AE, CB, DC, MC, V. Moderate.*

Crystal River

Dining

The Oyster Bar. This popular, no-frills seafood spot features locally caught fish, oysters, crab claws, and lobster. Only beer and wine served. *224 U.S. 19 N, tel. 904/795–3949. Dress: casual. MC, V. Inexpensive.*

Lodging

Plantation Golf Resort. Set on the banks of Kings Bay, this is a colonial-style resort with many outdoor amenities. *C.R. 44, tel. 904/795–4211. 136 rooms. Facilities: lounge, pools, golf, saunas, canoes, rental boats, fishing, tennis, scuba rental, dining room. Pets permitted. AE, CB, DC, MC, V. Expensive.*

Econo Lodge Crystal Resort. This cinder block roadside motel offers proximity to Kings Bay and its manatee population. There's a marina within steps of the motel, with dive boats departing for scuba and snorkeling excursions. The only rooms that view the water are 114 and 128. *U.S. 19, 32629, tel. 904/795–3171. 94 rooms. Facilities: pool, waterfront restaurant. AE, CB, DC, MC, V.*

Fort Myers Beach

Dining

★ **The Mucky Duck.** Slightly more formal than its waterfront sister restaurant on Captiva, this restaurant concentrates on fresh, well-prepared seafood. A popular dish is the bacon-wrapped barbecued shrimp. *2500 Estero Blvd., tel. 813/463–5519 and Andy Rosse Lane, Captiva, tel. 813/472–3434. Dress: casual. Reservations for large parties only. AE, MC, V. Moderate.*

Snug Harbor. Casual, rustic atmosphere is evident at this seafood restaurant on the harbor at Fort Myers Beach. *645 San*

Carlos Blvd., tel. 813/463–4343. Dress: casual. No reservations. AE, MC, V. Moderate.

Lodging **Seawatch-on-the-Beach.** A modern seven-story hotel with two-bedroom suites. Each has a whirlpool, kitchen, and a view of the Gulf. *6550 Estero Blvd. 33931, tel. 813/481–3636 or 800/237–8906. 42 rooms. Facilities: beach, pool, tennis, baby-sitting. AE, MC, V. Very Expensive.*

The Boathouse Beach Resort. A nautical theme pervades this all-suite time-share resort, with lots of teak and brass throughout. *7630 Estero Blvd. 33931, tel. 813/481–3636 or 800/237–8906. 22 units. Facilities: kitchen, beach, pool, whirlpool, shuffleboard. AE, MC, V. Expensive.*

Sandpiper Gulf Resort. Gulf-front apartment-motel. *5550 Estero Blvd. 33931, tel. 813/463–5721. 63 rooms. Facilities: pools, beach, whirlpool, playground, shuffleboard. MC, V. Moderate.*

Homosassa Springs

Dining **K.C. Crump on the River.** An 1870 Old Florida residence on the Homosassa River., K.C. Crump was restored in 1986, then opened as a restaurant in 1987. There is a marina on the river, lounge, and outdoor dining, plus large, airy dining rooms serving meat and seafood. *3900 Hall River Rd., tel. 904/628–1500. Dress: neat but casual. Reservations advised. AE, CB, DC, MC, V. Expensive.*

Lodging **Sheraton-Homosassa Springs Inn.** This is a simple motor inn that accepts pets and has a playground for the kids. *On U.S. 19 and 98 at C.R. 490A West, tel. 904/628–4311. 104 rooms. Facilities: pool, tennis, restaurant, lounge. AE, DC, MC, V. Moderate.*

Marco Island

Dining **Marco Lodge Waterfront Restaurant & Lounge.** Built in 1869, this is Marco's oldest landmark. Fresh local seafood and Cajun entrees are features, as is live Dixieland jazz Sundays at 2. *1 Papaya St., Goodland, tel. 813/394–3302. Dress: casual. Reservations suggested. AE, DC, MC, V. Moderate.*

★ **European Cafe Restaurant.** A small and intimate European-style cafe specializing in seafood and Continental cuisine. Pompano is prepared in a multitude of ways. All fish comes from the family-owned fish market. Owned and operated by Kare DeMartino, a generation Marco Islander. *918 N. Collier Blvd., tel. 813/394–7578. Dress: casual. Reservations accepted. MC, V. Inexpensive.*

Lodging **Eagle's Nest Beach Resort.** This time-share resort contains one- and two-bedroom villas (with French doors opening onto screened patios) clustered around a large tropical garden and a high rise with two-bedroom suites overlooking the Gulf. *410 S. Collier Blvd. 33937, tel. 813/394–5167 or 800/237–8906. 96 rooms. Facilities: kitchen, beach, pool, whirlpool, sauna, exercise room, tennis, racquetball, sailing, windsurfing. AE, MC, V. Very Expensive.*

Marco Bay Resort. An all-suite motor inn on Marco Bay. *1001 N. Barfield Dr. 33937, tel. 813/394–8881. 320 rooms. Facilities: kitchens, pools, whirlpools, dock, fishing, putting green, transportation to beach, tennis, restaurant, lounge. AE, CB, DC, MC, V. Very Expensive.*

Marriott's Marco Island Resort. Large rooms with balconies surrounded by lush, tropical grounds right next to the Gulf. *400 S. Collier Blvd. 33937, tel. 813/394–2511. 736 rooms, 86 suites. Facilities: pools, beach, whirlpool, waterskiing, sail-*

boats, windsurfing, tennis, bicycles, golf, exercise room, restaurants, lounge. AE, CB, DC, MC, V. Very Expensive.

Radisson Suite Resort on Marco Island. All 214 one- and two-bedroom suites in this medium high-rise resort contain kitchens fully equipped with utensils to give a home-away-from-home touch. The casual decor of the suites contrasts sharply with the marble floors and chandelier in the lobby. Built in 1986, the resort faces a large beachfront. *600 S. Collier Blvd., Marco Island 33937, tel. 813/394–4100 or 800/333–3333. 214 rooms. Facilities: pool, beach, whirlpool, exercise room, game room, water sports equipment, restaurant, lounge. AE, CB, DC, MC, V. Very Expensive.*

Naples

Dining

★ **The Chef's Garden.** A mixture of Continental, traditional, and California cuisines has consistently won this restaurant awards over the past decade. Some daily specials include Scottish smoked salmon with avocado and caviar, roast rack of lamb, and spinach and fresh mango salad with toasted cashews and honey vinaigrette. *1300 3rd St. S, tel. 813/262–5500. Jacket required during winter season. Reservations advised. AE, CB, DC, MC, V. Expensive.*

Cafe La Playa. The soul is French, and from it comes classic offerings such as pâté de fois gras, veal in a Dijon mustard sauce, and vichyssoise. The view is of the Gulf, either indoors or from the broad-screened patio. *9891 Gulfshore Dr., tel. 813/597–3123. Dress: neat but casual. Reservations advised. AE, MC, V. Moderate.*

★ **St. George and the Dragon.** A long-lived seafood-and-beef restaurant, with a decor reminiscent of an old-fashioned men's club—heavy on brass, dark woods, and deep-red tones. Among the specialties are conch chowder, various cuts of prime rib, and shrimp steamed in beer. *936 5th Ave. S, tel. 813/262–6546. Jackets and ties suggested. No reservations. AE, CB, DC, MC, V. Closed Sun. and Christmas. Moderate.*

Truffles. The less-formal bistro upstairs from The Chef's Garden. A wealth of ethnic specialties appears on the frequently changing menu. Exceptional desserts such as chocolate-peanut butter pie, banana cream pie, and chocolate-mousse cake. *1300 3rd St. S, tel. 813/262–5500. Dress: casual. No reservations. AE, CB, DC, MC, V. Moderate.*

Lodging

Edgewater Beach Hotel. An all-suite Gulf-front hotel on fashionable Gulf Shore Drive, long an elegant address in Naples. Close to downtown. *1901 Gulf Shore Blvd. N 33940, tel. 813/262–6511, or 800/821–0196; in FL, 800/282–3766. 124 rooms. Facilities: restaurant, beach, pool, exercise room. AE, CB, DC, MC, V. Very Expensive.*

The Registry Resort. This modern, luxurious high-rise resort is a half mile from the beach and offers a wealth of amenities, including a shuttle through the mangrove wetlands to the beach. *475 Seagate Dr. 33940, tel. 813/597–3232. 50 tennis villas, 29 suites, 395 rooms. Facilities: pools, whirlpools, bicycles, tennis, health club, restaurants, lounge. AE, DC, MC, V. Very Expensive.*

Ritz-Carlton Hotel. Opulence reigns from its sweeping palm-lined driveway and through every inch of this Mediterranean-style resort on the Gulf. *280 Vanderbilt Beach Rd. 33941, tel. 813/598–3300. 463 rooms. Facilities: beach, pool, saunas, whirlpool, tennis, bicycles, exercise room, golf, children's program, windsurfing, restaurants, lounge. AE, CB, DC, MC, V. Very Expensive.*

Comfort Inn. Modern motel on the banks of the Gordon River. *1221 5th Ave. S 33940, tel. 813/649–5800 or 800/228–5150. 101 rooms. Facilities: pool. AE, CB, DC, MC, V. Moderate.*

Port Charlotte/ Punta Gorda

Dining

Salty's Harborside. Seafood is served from a dining room that looks out on Burnt Store Marina and Charlotte Harbor. *Burnt Store Marina, Burnt Store Rd. Punta Gorda, tel. 813/639–3650. Dress: casual. Reservations advised. AE, CB, DC, MC, V. Moderate.*

Mexican Hacienda. Tex-Mex of a high order is presented in humble surroundings. The building matches its well-worn neighbors; inside are well-interpreted guacamole dip and tacos made with tender shredded beef. *123 E. Retta Esplanade, Punta Gorda, tel. 813/639–7161. Dress: casual. Reservations: parties of 6 or more. MC, V. Inexpensive.*

★ **Ria's Ristorante.** This small, hard-to-find establishment serves a range of pastas (lasagna, spaghetti, stuffed shells), seafoods, and meats. *Olean Plaza, 21202 Olean Blvd., Port Charlotte, tel. 813/625–3145. Dress: casual. Reservations accepted. MC, V. Inexpensive.*

Lodging

Burnt Store Marina Resort. For golfing, boating, and getting away from it all, Burnt Store can fill the bill. One- and two-bedroom modern apartments are situated along a relatively undeveloped stretch of vast Charlotte Harbor. Two-bedroom units available only on a weekly or monthly basis. *3150 Matecumbe Key Rd., Punta Gorda 33955, tel. 813/639–4151. 46 1-bedroom condominiums. Facilities: kitchens, pool, golf, marina, boats, tennis, restaurant, lounge. AE, CB, DC, MC, V. Expensive.*

Days Inn of Port Charlotte. A modern mid-rise motel on Charlotte County's major business route. *1941 Tamiami Trail (U.S. 41), Port Charlotte 33948, tel. 813/627–8900. 126 rooms. Facilities: pool. AE, CB, DC, MC, V. Moderate.*

St. Petersburg

Dining

King Charles Room. Quiet elegance, attentive service, and soothing harp music are to be found in this restaurant on the fifth floor of the Don CeSar Beach Resort. Continental specialties include beluga caviar on ice and smoked salmon stuffed with crab mousse. *3400 Gulf Blvd., tel. 813/360–1881. Dress: dressy. Reservations advised. AE, CB, DC, MC, V. Very Expensive. No lunch.*

★ **Peter's Place-Cafe International.** Small, elegant dining rooms with subdued lighting and fresh flowers atop crisp linen tablecloths offer Continental food that is seasoned and served with flair and imagination. Specials change daily. Favorites include breast of capon in a honey-lemon sauce and roast duckling with brandied peaches and just a suggestion of Amaretto. *208 Beach Dr. NE, tel. 813/822–8436. Reservations advised. Jacket and tie advised. AE, MC, V. Closed Sun. and Mon. Expensive.*

The Wine Cellar Restaurant. The decor is Swiss chalet; the food, classic French. This popular spot is usually crowded. *17307 Gulf Blvd., North Redington Beach, tel. 813/393–3491. Jacket and tie advised. Reservations advised. AE, CB, DC, MC, V. Closed Mon. Expensive.*

★ **Ted Peters Famous Smoked Fish.** The menu is limited to mackerel and mullet, but both are smoked and seasoned to perfection and served with heaping helpings of German potato salad. All meals are served outdoors. *1350 Pasadena Ave. S, Pasadena, tel. 813/381–7931. Dress: casual. No reservations. No credit cards. Closed Tues. Inexpensive. No dinner.*

Lodging

Tradewinds on St. Petersburg Beach. Old Florida ambience is offered here, with white gazebos, gondolas gliding along canals, and hammocks swaying on 13 acres of beachfront property. *5500 Gulf Blvd., St. Petersburg Beach 33706, tel. 813/367–6461. 365 rooms. Facilities: kitchens, pools, wading pool, beach, sauna, whirlpools, boating, dock, fishing, tennis, racquetball, bicycles, playground, exercise room, scuba instruction, waterskiing, windsurfing, restaurant, lounge. AE, CB, DC, MC, V. Very Expensive.*

Don CeSar Beach Resort. This palatial, pink-rococo resort sprawls along the Gulf front. A favorite of author F. Scott Fitzgerald in the 1920s and '30s. *3400 Gulf Blvd., St. Petersburg Beach 33706, tel. 813/360–1881. 277 rooms. Facilities: pool, whirlpool, beach, saunas, tennis, children's program, exercise room, sailboats, parasails, jet skis, restaurants, lounge. AE, CB, DC, MC, V. Expensive.*

Colonial Gateway Resort Inn. This Gulf-front hotel is family-oriented, with half of its 200 rooms equipped with kitchenettes. The resort was recently remodeled to give it a contemporary look for young families. *6300 Gulf Blvd., St. Petersburg Beach 33706, tel. 800/237–8918 outside FL, 800/282–5245 in FL. 200 rooms. Facilities: beach bar, pool, water sports, restaurants, lounge. AE, CB, DC, MC, V. Moderate.*

Sanibel/Captiva

Dining

The Bubble Room. It's hard to say which is more eclectic here, the atmosphere or the menu. Waiters and waitresses wearing Boy Scout uniforms race amid a dizzying array of Art Deco, while music from the 1940s sets the mood. The aged prime rib is ample enough to satisfy two hearty eaters—at least. Chances are you'll be too full for dessert, but it can be wrapped to go. *Captiva Rd., Captiva, tel. 813/472–5558. Dress: casual. No reservations. AE, CB, DC, MC, V. Expensive.*

The Greenhouse. Though the kitchen is in full view of the diminutive dining area, all is calm and quiet as you wend your way through the day's specials. Chef-owner Danny Melman changes his Continental-style menu every four to six weeks. Each menu features fresh seafood and game among its selections. *Captiva Rd., Captiva, tel. 813/472–6066. Dress: neat but casual. Reservations advised. No credit cards. Expensive. No lunch.*

★ **Jean Paul's French Corner.** French food, finely seasoned with everything but the highfalutin attitude often dished up in French establishments. Salmon in a creamy dill sauce, sautéed soft-shell crabs, and roast duckling in fruit sauce are among the few but well-prepared choices on the menu. *Tarpon Bay Rd., tel. 813/472–1493. Dress: casual. Reservations advised. MC, V. Expensive. No lunch.*

McT's Shrimphouse and Tavern. Somewhat of a departure from most Sanibel establishments, McT's is lively and informal, featuring a host of fresh seafood specialties, including all-you-can-eat shrimp and crab. *1523 Periwinkle Way, Sanibel, tel. 813/472–3161. Dress: casual. No reservations. AE, CB, DC, MC, V. Moderate.*

Truffles at Thistle Lodge. A New Orleans-style mansion in the midst of the mangroves, it serves the same fine quality Continental fare as the Naples Truffles, including wondrous desserts. *Casa Ybel Resort, 2255 W. Gulf Dr., Sanibel, tel. 813/472–9200. Dress: neat but casual. Reservations advised. AE, MC, V. Moderate.*

Lodging

Casa Ybel Resort. This time-share property features contemporary one- and two-bedroom Gulf-front condominium villas on

23 acres of tropical grounds, complete with palms, ponds, and a footbridge. *2255 W. Gulf Dr., Sanibel 33957, tel. 813/481–3636 or 800/237–8906. 40 1-bedroom units, 74 2-bedroom units. Facilities: kitchens, pool, whirlpool, biking, tennis, sailing, playground, shuffleboard, game room, baby-sitting, restaurant, lounge. AE, CB, DC, MC, V. Very Expensive.*

South Seas Plantation Resort and Yacht Harbour. Virtually an island unto itself, South Seas lies on the northernmost 330 acres of Captiva Island. There are villas and cottages clustered at various secluded spots throughout the grounds. *South Sea Plantation Rd., Captiva 33924, tel. 813/472–5111 or 800/237–1260. 600 rooms. Facilities: kitchens, boat docking, beauty parlor, baby-sitting, fishing, golf, game room, playground, pools, sailboats, sailing school, tennis, waterskiing, windsurfing, windsurfing school, restaurants, lounges. AE, CB, DC, MC, V. Very Expensive.*

Sundial Beach & Tennis Resort. The largest all-suite resort on the island; many suites look out upon the Gulf of Mexico. *1246 Middle Gulf Dr., Sanibel 33957, tel. 813/472–4151 or 800/237–4184. 200-plus suites. Facilities: kitchens, pools, beach, bicycles, tennis, sailboats, recreational program, children's program, baby-sitting, game room, shuffleboard, restaurants, lounge. AE, CB, DC, MC, V. Very Expensive.*

Sarasota
Dining

★ **Cafe L'Europe.** Located on fashionable St. Armand's Key, this greenery- and art-filled cafe specializes in fresh veal and seafood. Menus change frequently, but might include fillet of sole Picasso, Dover sole served with a choice of fruits, wiener schnitzel sautéed in butter and topped with anchovies, olives, and capers. *431 St. Armand's Circle, tel. 813/388–4415. Dress: neat but casual. Reservations advised. AE, CB, DC, MC, V. Expensive.*

Marina Jack. Have a dinner cruise on the *Marina Jack II* or eat fresh seafood overlooking Sarasota Bay. *2 Marina Plaza, tel. 813/365–4232. Dress: neat but casual. Reservations advised. No credit cards. Expensive.*

★ **The Bijou Cafe.** Wood, brass, and sumptuous green carpeting surround diners in this gas station turned restaurant. Chef Jean Pierre Knaggs's Continental specialties include crispy roast duckling with tangerine brandy sauce or cassis and blackberry sauce, rack of lamb for two, and *crème brûlée*, a custard with a carmelized brown-sugar topping. *Corner of 1st and Pineapple Sts., tel. 813/366–8111. Dress: neat but casual. Reservations advised. AE, MC, V. Moderate.*

Whisper Inn. Next to the K Mart in south Sarasota sits this small but choice Continental restaurant. The house specialty is charred prime rib. Other entrees include veal, fresh seafood, and rack of lamb. *8197 S. Tamiami Trail (U.S. 41), tel. 813/922–6400. Dress: casual. Reservations advised. AE, MC, V. Moderate.*

Lodging

Hyatt Sarasota. Recently renovated, the Hyatt is contemporary in design and conveniently located in the heart of the city. Some rooms overlook Sarasota Bay. *1000 Blvd. of the Arts 34236, tel. 813/366–9000. 297 rooms. Facilities: pool, sauna, sailing, health club, dock, restaurant, lounge. AE, CB, DC, MC, V. Very Expensive.*

The Meadows VIP Program. This all-suite resort is a bit removed from downtown, but it is like a small city unto itself, including 54 holes of golf and 16 lighted tennis courts. *3101 Longmeadow Dr. 34235, tel. 813/378–6660. 12 1-bedroom* *suites. Facilities: pool, sauna, golf, tennis, bicycles, children's program, restaurants, lounge. AE, CB, DC, MC, V. Expensive.*

Days Inn Sarasota-Siesta Key. Modern, built in 1986, with earth-tone rooms, this inn is one mile from the beaches. *6600 S. Tamiami Trail (U.S. 41) 34231, tel. 813/924–4900. 132 rooms. Facilities: pool, whirlpool. AE, CB, DC, MC, V. Moderate.*

Hampton Inn Sarasota Airport. On the main drag, convenient to beaches and downtown. Budget prices. *5000 N. Tamiami Trail (U.S. 41) 34234, tel. 813/351–7734. 100 rooms. Facilities: pool. AE, CB, DC, MC, V. Moderate.*

Tampa

Dining

★ **Bern's Steak House.** Specialties include aged prime beef and an extensive wine list—some 6,000 choices, with selections ranging in price from $10 to $10,000 a bottle. The vegetables are grown on owner-chef Bern Lexer's organic farm. Upstairs are the dessert rooms: small, glass-enclosed rooms where sumptuous desserts are served. Each room is equipped with a control panel for TV, radio, or listening in to the live entertainment in the lounge. *1208 S. Howard Ave., tel. 813/251–2421. Dress: neat but casual. Reservations advised. AE, CB, DC, MC, V. Expensive. No lunch.*

CK's. This revolving restaurant sits atop Tampa International Airport's Marriott Hotel. An eclectic Continental menu includes stir-fried shrimp and red snapper. Champagne brunch on Sunday. *Marriott Hotel, tel. 813/879–5151. Dress: neat but casual. Reservations accepted. AE, CB, DC, MC, V. Moderate.*

Colonnade. The wharfside location of this popular restaurant is reflected in its nautical decor. Seafood—particularly grouper, red snapper, and lobster—is a specialty, but steak and chicken are also served. *3401 Bayshore Blvd., tel. 813/839–7558. Dress: casual. No reservations. AE, CB, DC, MC, V. Moderate.*

★ **Columbia.** A Spanish fixture in Tampa's Ybor City for more than 80 years, this restaurant has several airy and spacious dining rooms and a sunny atrium with tile decor. Specialties include the Columbia 1905 salad—lettuce, ham, olives, cheese, and garlic; and paella—saffron rice with chicken, fish, and mussels. Flamenco dancing. *2117 E. 7th Ave., tel. 813/248–4961. Dress: casual weekdays, semidressy weekends. Reservations accepted. AE, CB, DC, MC, V. Moderate.*

Selena's. New Orleans Creole food served here with some Sicilian dishes as well, in antique-filled dining rooms. Shrimp scampi and other fresh seafood featured. *1623 Snow Ave., tel. 813/251–2116. Dress: casual. Reservations advised. AE, CB, DC, MC, V. Moderate.*

★ **Bella Trattoria.** Brightly lit, slightly noisy, and filled with the smells of such Italian fare as *capelli di l'Angelo*—smoked salmon and caviar tossed with spinach and angel-hair pasta in a vodka and cream sauce—and *Bella! Bella!*, a truffle torte of bittersweet, semisweet, and white chocolates. Crayons and paper tablecloths afford a public outlet for frustrated artists. *1413 S. Howard Ave., tel. 813/254–3355. Dress: casual. No reservations. AE, MC, V. Inexpensive.*

Lodging

Wyndham Harbour Island Hotel. Elegant ambience, with lots of dark wood paneling, substantial furniture, and attentive service. *725 S. Harbour Island Blvd. 33602, tel. 813/229–5000. 300 rooms. Facilities: pool, dock, sailboats, tennis, health club, restaurant, lounge. AE, CB, DC, MC, V. Very Expensive.*

Saddlebrook. This modern tennis and golf resort on sprawling, heavily wooded grounds is 15 miles north of Tampa. A variety of accommodations and amenities. *100 Saddlebrook Way, Wesley Chapel 34249, tel. 813/973–1111. 501 rooms. Facilities: kitchenettes, pools, wading pools, whirlpools, saunas, fishing, golf, tennis, bicycles, health club, restaurants, lounge. AE, CB, DC, MC, V. Very Expensive.*

Guest Quarters. Modern all-suite hotel midway between Tampa International Airport and downtown Tampa. *555 N. Westshore Blvd. 33609, tel. 813/875–1555. 221 rooms. Facilities: pool, whirlpool, sauna, exercise room, transportation to airport, restaurant, lounge. Pets allowed. AE, CB, DC, MC, V. Expensive.*

Hyatt Regency-Downtown. A large, elegant high-rise hotel with a modern, mirrored ambience. *2 Tampa City Center 33602, tel. 813/225–1234. 517 rooms. Facilities: pool, whirlpool, sauna, exercise room, restaurant, lounge. AE, DC, MC, V. Expensive.*

Holiday Inn Busch Gardens. A family-oriented motor inn just 1 mile west of Busch Gardens. *2701 E. Fowler Ave. 33612, tel. 813/971–4710. 399 rooms. Facilities: pool, sauna, exercise room, restaurant, lounge, transportation to Busch Gardens. AE, CB, DC, MC, V. Moderate.*

Tahitian Inn. This family-run motel offers comfortable rooms at budget prices. *601 S. Dale Mabry Hwy. 33609, tel. 813/877–6721. 79 rooms. Facilities: pool. AE, CB, DC, MC, V. Inexpensive.*

Tarpon Springs
Dining
★

Louis Pappas' Riverside Restaurant. The decor consists mainly of wall-to-wall people who pour into this waterfront landmark for all manner of Greek fare, especially the Greek salad, made with lettuce, feta cheese chunks, onions, and olive oil. *10 W. Dodecanese Blvd., tel. 813/937–5101. Dress: casual. Reservations advised. AE, CB, DC, MC, V. Moderate.*

Lodging

Innisbrook Resort. There are deluxe rooms and suites here, some with balconies or patios at this get-away-from-it-all resort on 1,000 wooded acres. *Box 1088, U.S. 19 34689, tel. 813/942–2000. 1,200 rooms. Facilities: golf, tennis, racquetball, pools, health club, children's program (May–Sept.), miniature golf, saunas, dining rooms, nightclub. AE, CB, DC, MC, V. Very Expensive.*

Venice
Dining

Sharky's on the Pier. Gaze out on the beach and sparkling waters while dining on grilled fresh seafood. *1600 S. Harbor Dr., tel. 813/488–1456. Dress: casual. Reservations advised. MC, V. Moderate.*

Lodging

Holiday House. Comfortable rooms in motor inn on the main business route through town. *1710 S. Tamiami Trail (U.S. 41) 34293, tel. 813/493–4558. 72 rooms. Facilities: pool, restaurant, lounge. Pets allowed. AE, MC, V. Moderate.*

Veranda Inn-Venice. A landscaped pool is the focal point of this small but spacious inn. All rooms look out on the pool and courtyard. *625 S. Tamiami Trail (U.S. 41), tel. 813/484–9559. 37 rooms. Facilities: pool, restaurant. AE, DC, MC, V. Moderate.*

The Arts

Not too many years ago, southwest Florida was content to bask in the warmth of the sun and leave cultural matters to others.

But as the population has boomed, a growing number of transplanted northerners have been unwilling to sacrifice the arts for nature. Hence, there are curtains going up at performing-arts centers throughout the region.

If you are interested in cultural events while staying in Florida, it's a good idea to purchase tickets before you arrive, especially during the busy winter tourist season. Most halls and theaters accept credit-card charges by phone. The area chambers of commerce (*see* Important Addresses and Numbers, above) can supply schedules of upcoming cultural events.

The **Tampa Performing Arts Center** (1010 W. C. MacInnes Pl., Box 2877, tel. 813/222–1010) occupies nine acres along the Hillsborough River and is said to be the largest such complex south of the Kennedy Center in Washington, DC. The festival hall, playhouse, and small theater accommodate opera, ballet, drama, and concerts.

Ruth Eckerd Hall (1111 McMullen Booth Rd., Clearwater, tel. 813/791–7400) also plays host to many national performers of pop, classical, and jazz music; ballet; and drama.

Sarasota's **Van Wezel Performing Arts Hall** (777 N. Tamiami Trail, tel. 813/953–3366) is easy to find. Just look for the purple shell rising along the bay front. It offers some 200 performances each year, including Broadway plays, ballet, jazz, rock concerts, symphonies, children's shows, and ice skating. For tickets and information, contact the box office.

Fort Myers's center for the arts is the **Barbara B. Mann Performing Arts Hall** (Edison Community College/University of South Florida campus, 8099 College Pkwy., tel. 813/489–3033), a 1,770-seat theater that opened in 1986. Plays, concerts, and ballets by local, national, and international companies perform here. For more information, contact the box office.

The **Naples Philharmonic Center for the Arts** (5833 Pelican Bay Blvd., tel. 813/597–1111) comprises two theaters and two art galleries offering a variety of plays, concerts, and exhibits year-round.

Theater

Tampa Bay

The **Tampa Theater** (711 N. Franklin St., tel. 813/223–8981) presents shows, musical performances, and films. Area dinner theaters include the **Encore Dinner-Theatre** (1850 Central Ave., St. Petersburg, tel. 813/821–6676), and the **Showboat Dinner Theatre** (3405 Ulmerton Rd., Clearwater, tel. 813/223–2545). All offer dinner and a variety of Broadway and off-Broadway shows throughout the year.

Sarasota/Bradenton

The **Asolo State Theater** (Drawer E, tel. 813/355–5137) offers productions nearly year-round. Located in the new $10 million Asolo Performing Arts Center, this Sarasota theater is known for its well-rounded repertoire. The theater's company of actors performs about 10 plays per season (Dec.–Aug.). For tickets or information, contact the theater.

Florida Studio Theatre (1241 N. Palm Ave., Sarasota, tel. 813/366–9796) is a small professional theater that presents contemporary dramas, comedies, and musicals.

Golden Apple Dinner Theatre (25 N. Pineapple Ave., Sarasota, tel. 813/366–5454) combines a buffet dinner with musicals and comedies.

The **Players of Sarasota** (U.S. 41 and 9th St., tel. 813/365–2494), a long-lived troupe, provided opportunities for then-unknowns Pee-Wee Herman, Montgomery Clift, and Polly Holiday. The community theater features volunteer actors and technicians and performs comedies, thrillers, and musicals.

Theatre Works (1247 1st St., Venice, tel. 813/952–9170) presents professional, non-Equity productions at the Palm Tree Playhouse.

Venice Little Theatre (corner of Tampa and Nokomis aves., Venice, tel. 813/488–1115) is a community theater offering comedies, musicals, and a few dramas during its October–May season.

Fort Myers/Naples **The Naples Dinner Theatre** (Immokalee Rd., halfway between U.S. 41 and the I-75 interchange, tel. 813/597–6031) is open October–August and features professional companies performing a variety of mostly musicals and comedies. Admission includes buffet.

The **Naples Playhouse** (Harbour Town Shopping Center, 399 Goodlette Rd., tel. 813/263–7990) has winter and summer seasons. The winter shows often sell out well in advance.

Concerts

Tampa Bay Area The **Florida Orchestra** (tel. 813/221–2365) performs throughout Tampa Bay each fall, at Clearwater's Eckerd Hall, St. Petersburg's Bayfront Center, and the Tampa Performing Arts Center.

Sarasota/Bradenton The **Florida Symphonic Band** (Van Wezel Hall, 709 N. Tamiami Trail [U.S. 41], Sarasota, tel. 813/955–6660) includes 50 players, many of whom are full-time musicians. The group performs monthly concerts.

Florida West Coast Symphony Center (tel. 813/953–4252) consists of a number of area groups that perform in Manatee and Sarasota counties regularly. Included are the *Florida West Coast Symphony*, *The Florida String Quartet*, *Florida Brass Quintet*, *Florida Wind Quintet*, and *New Artists String Quartet*.

Sarasota The **Sarasota Opera** (61 N. Pineapple Ave., tel. 813/953–7030) operates from its home in a historic theater downtown at the corner of 1st and Pineapple streets. The company's season runs from February to March. Internationally known singing artists perform the principal roles, supported by a professional apprentice chorus—24 young singers studying with the company.

Dance

Tampa Bay Area The **St. Petersburg Concert Ballet** performs periodically throughout the year, mostly at the Bayfront Center in St. Petersburg.

The Tampa Ballet performs at the Tampa Bay Performing Arts Center.

Film All areas have conveniently located commercial movie houses. Check the local newspapers for shows, times, and locations.

Sarasota The **Sarasota Film Society** operates year-round, showing foreign and nonmainstream films on weekends at the Plaza Theatre (Crossroads Shopping Center, tel. 813/388–2441).

Nightlife

Bars and Nightclubs

Harbour Island Hotel (Harbour Island, Tampa, tel. 813/229–5000). Great view of the bay, large-screen television, and thickly padded, comfortable chairs.

Coliseum Ballroom (535 4th Ave. N, St. Petersburg, tel. 813/892–5202). Ballroom dancing Wednesday and Saturday night.

The Patio (Columbia Restaurant, St. Armand's Key, tel. 813/388–3987). A casual lounge with live music nightly.

Marina 31 Restaurant and Lounge (17281 Rte. 31, Fort Myers, tel. 813/694–1331). Live bands playing Top-40 hits.

'Tween Waters Inn (Captiva Rd., Captiva, tel. 813/472–5161). Live entertainment and large-screen TV catering to casual, over-30 crowd.

Harp & Thistle (650 Corey Ave., St. Petersburg Beach, tel. 813/360–4104). Live Irish music Wed.–Sat.

Jazz Clubs

Most offer jazz several nights a week. Call for details.

Baxters (714 S. Dale Mabry Hwy., Tampa, tel. 813/879–1161).

Cha Cha Coconuts (City Pier, St. Petersburg, tel. 813/822–6655). Overlooks the water from atop the pier.

Maestro's (14727 N. Florida Ave., Tampa, tel. 813/961–5090).

The Beach Room (10650 Gulf Blvd., Treasure Island, tel. 813/360–5531).

Hurricane Lounge (807 Gulf Way, Pass-a-Grille Beach, tel. 813/360–9558).

Victoria Pier (2230 Edwards Dr., Fort Myers, tel. 813/334–4881).

Upstairs at Peter's (2224 Bay St., Fort Myers, tel. 813/332–2223).

Drillers (Island Park Shopping Center, 16520 Tamiami Trail, South Fort Myers, tel. 813/482–0303).

Rock Clubs

Volley Club (15212 N. Nebraska Ave., Tampa, tel. 813/972–0176). Live rock-and-roll rings from the rafters Wednesday–Monday.

The Barn (13815 Hillsborough Ave., Tampa, tel. 813/855–9818). Plays '50s and '60s hits.

306th Bomb Group (8301 N. Tamiami Trail, Sarasota, tel. 813/355–8591). Amid World War II gear, a DJ spins Top-40 tunes for a generally over-25 clientele.

Club Yesterdays (2224 S. Tamiami Trail, Venice, tel. 813/493–2900). Top-40 is king every night at this club popular with the under-30 set.

Flashbacks (Metro Mall, 2855 Colonial Blvd., Fort Myers, tel. 813/275–4487). Oldies from the '50s and '60s nightly.

Edison's Electric Lounge (Holiday Inn, 13051 Bell Tower Dr., Fort Myers, tel. 813/482–2900). Top-40 tunes, usually live bands, rock nightly.

Country-Western

Joyland Country Night Club (11225 U.S. 19, St. Petersburg, tel. 813/573–1919).

Dallas Bull (8222 N. Hwy. 301, Tampa, tel. 813/985–6877).

Carlie's (5641 49th St., St. Petersburg, tel. 813/527–5214).

Comedy Clubs

Comedy Corner (3447 W. Kennedy Blvd., Tampa, tel. 813/875–9129).

Coconuts Comedy Club at Barnacle Bill's (Howard Johnson's, 6110 Gulf Blvd., St. Petersburg, tel. 813/360–4575).

Ron Bennington's Comedy Scene (Rodeway Inn, 401 U.S. 19 S, Clearwater, tel. 813/799–1181).

Bijou Comedy Club & Restaurant (McGregor Point Shopping Center, Fort Myers, tel. 813/481–6666).

Dr. Al's Comedy Clinic (The Spanish Main, Cleveland Ave., Fort Myers, tel. 813/936–2414).

Discos

Club Paradise (1927 Ringling Blvd., Sarasota, tel. 813/366–3830). A rock-and-roll palace, complete with extensive light show, music videos, a DJ, and several bars. Especially popular with the younger set.

Norma Jean's (4797 U.S. 41, Fort Myers, tel. 813/275–9997) packs in the singles (21 and up) with such events as hot legs and lip-sync contests, hot-tub night, live bands and disc jockeys.

10 The Panhandle

Introduction

Part-time Northwest Florida resident Ann Hughes is associate editor of Indiana Business *magazine and a contributing editor to other travel and trade publications.*

Because there are no everglades or palm trees here, some call northwest Florida "the other Florida." Instead, magnolias, live oaks, and loblolly pines flourish, just as they do in other parts of the Deep South. When the season winds down in south Florida, it picks up here (beginning in May). Northwest Florida is even in a different time zone: Crossing the Apalachicola River means an hour's difference between eastern and central times.

Others call this section of the state "Florida's best-kept secret." It was, until World War II when activity at the air bases in the area began to rev up. Also known as the Panhandle—because of the region's long, narrow shape—northwest Florida is nestled between the Apalachicola River, the Gulf of Mexico, and the Alabama state line.

By the mid-1950s, the 100-mile stretch along the Panhandle coast between Pensacola and Panama City was dubbed the "Miracle Strip" because of the dramatic rise in property values of this beachfront land that in the 1940s sold for less than $100 an acre. Today, property fetches millions. But the movers and shakers of the area felt this sobriquet fell short of conveying the richness of the region, with its white sands and forever-green sparkling waters, swamps, bayous, and flora. And so the term "Emerald Coast" was coined.

This little green corner of Florida that snuggles up to Alabama is a land of superlatives: It has the biggest military installation in the Western Hemisphere (Eglin Air Force Base); the oldest city in the state (Pensacola, claiming a founding date of 1559); and the most prolific fishing village in the world (Destin). Thanks to restrictions against commercial development imposed by Eglin AFB and the Gulf Islands National Seashore, the Emerald Coast has been able to maintain several hundred linear miles of unspoiled beaches.

The Panhandle is also an ideal tourist destination. It has resorts that out-glitz the Gold Coast's and campgrounds where possums invite themselves to lunch. Lovers of antiquity can wander the many historic districts or visit archaeological digs. For sports enthusiasts, there's a different golf course or tennis court for each day of the week; and for those who decide to spend time with nature, there's a world of hunting, canoeing, biking, and hiking. And anything that happens on water happens here, from surfboarding and scuba diving to fishing off the end of a pier or casting a line from a deep-sea charter boat.

Getting Around

By Plane Both **Panama City-Bay County Airport** and **Fort Walton Beach/Eglin AFB Airport/Okaloosa County Air Terminal** are served by Continental Express (tel. 800/525–0280), ASA-The Delta Connection (tel. 800/282–3424), Eastern Metro Express (tel. 800/327–8376), and Northwest (tel. 800/225–2525). **Pensacola Regional Airport** is served by Continental, Delta, Eastern, Northwest Airlink (tel. 800/225–2525), and USAir (tel. 800/428–4322).

Accommodations for corporate jets, private planes, and charter services are offered by **Miracle Strip Aviation** (tel. 904/837–6135) in Destin and at **Bob Sikes Airport** (tel. 904/682–6395) in Crestview.

By Car The main east-west arteries across the top of the state are Interstate 10 and U.S. 90. I–10 tends to be monotonous, but a drive along U.S. 90 piques your interest by taking you down the main streets of several county-seat towns. Along the coast, U.S. 98 snakes eastward, forking (into 98 and 98A) at Inlet Beach before becoming U.S. 98 again at Panama City and continuing down to Port St. Joe and Apalachicola. Major north-south highways that weave through Florida's Panhandle are (from east to west) U.S. 231, U.S. 331, Rte. 85, and U.S. 29. The Emerald Coast is also accessible to yachtsmen and sailors from the Intracoastal Waterway, which turns inland at Apalachicola and runs through the bays around Panama City to Choctawhatchee Bay and into Santa Rosa Sound.

By Taxi or Car Service At the Panama City airport, **DeLuxe Coach Limo Service** (tel. 904/763–0211) provides van service to downtown Panama City for $5–$8 and to Panama City Beach for $10–$16.50. **Yellow Cab** (tel. 904/763–4691) taxi service charges about $14 to the beach area, depending on where your hotel is. A ride from the Fort Walton airport via **Yellow Cab** (tel. 904/244–3600) costs $10 to Fort Walton Beach and $18 to Destin or Niceville/Valparaiso. **Airport Limousine** (tel. 904/244–5638) charges $8–$10 to Fort Walton Beach and $13 to Destin. A trip from the Pensacola airport to downtown via **Yellow Cab** (tel. 904/433–1143) costs about $7 and $15 to Pensacola Beach.

By Bus The principal common carrier throughout the region is the **Greyhound/Trailways Bus Line** with stations in Crestview (tel. 904/682–6922), DeFuniak Springs (tel. 904/892–4847), Fort Walton Beach (tel. 904/243–1940), Panama City (tel. 904/785–7861), and Pensacola (tel. 904/476–4800).

Scenic Drives

Route 399 between Pensacola Beach and Navarre Beach takes you down Santa Rosa Island, a spit of duneland that juts out into the turquoise and jade waters of the Gulf of Mexico. It's a scenic drive if the day is clear; otherwise, it's a study in gray.

The view of the Gulf from **U.S. 98** can leave you oohing and ahhing, too, if the sun's out to distract you. If not, the fast-food restaurants, sleazy bars, and tacky souvenir stores along the Miracle Strip Parkway are a little too noticeable.

The panorama of barge traffic and cabin cruisers on the twinkling waters of the Intracoastal Waterway will get your attention from **U.S. 331**, which runs over a causeway at the east end of Choctawhatchee Bay between Route 20 and U.S. 98.

Guided Tours

Right This Way, Pensacola (311 E. Intendencia St., tel. 904/434–6367) offers tours by reservation and tailors them according to individual preferences and interests.

Important Addresses and Numbers

Tourist Information

Crestview Chamber of Commerce. *502 S. Main St., tel. 904/682–3212. Open weekdays 9–5.*
Destin Chamber of Commerce. *Stahlman Ave., tel. 904/837–6241. Open weekdays 9–5.*
Fort Walton Beach Chamber of Commerce. *34 Miracle Strip Pkwy., U.S. 98, tel. 904/244–8191. Open weekdays 8–5.*
Niceville/Valparaiso Chamber of Commerce. *170 John Sims Pkwy., tel. 904/678–2323. Open weekdays 9–4:30.*
Panama City Beach Visitors & Convention Bureau. *12015 W. U.S. 98A, tel. 800/PCBeach. Open Oct.–Apr., daily 8–5; May–Sept., daily 8–7.*
Pensacola Convention & Visitor Information Center. *1401 E. Gregory St., tel. 904/434–1234 or 800/343–4321. Open daily 8:30–5.*
Walton County Chamber of Commerce. *W. Baldwin Ave., tel. 904/892–3191. Open weekdays 8–noon and 1–5.*
Walton County Chamber of Commerce Welcome Center. *U.S. 331 at U.S. 98, tel. 904/267–3511. Open weekdays 8–4, Sat. 9–4.*

Emergencies

Dial 911 for **police** and **ambulance** in an emergency.

Hospitals

Emergency rooms are open 24 hours at the following northwest Florida hospitals: **North Okaloosa Medical Center** (151 S.E. Redstone Ave., Crestview, tel. 904/682–9731), **Walton Regional Hospital** (21 College Ave., DeFuniak Springs, tel. 904/892–5171), **White-Wilson Medical Center/Destin** (1000 Airport Rd., Destin, tel. 904/837–3848), **Humana Hospital-Destin** (996 Airport Rd., Destin, tel. 904/654–7600), **Humana Hospital-Fort Walton Beach** (1000 Mar-Walt Dr., Fort Walton Beach, tel. 904/862–1111), **HCA Twin Cities Hospital** (2190 N. Rte. 85, Niceville, tel. 904/678–4131), **HCA Gulf Coast Hospital** (449 W. 23rd St., Panama City, tel. 904/769–8341), **Bay Medical Center** (615 N. Bonita Ave., Panama City, tel. 904/769–1511), **Baptist Hospital** (1000 W. Marina St., Pensacola, tel. 904/434–4011).

24-Hour Pharmacy

The **North Hill Pharmacy** (1015 W. Moreno St., Pensacola, tel. 904/432–3479) provides emergency pharmaceutical services around the clock.

Exploring Northwest Florida

Numbers in the margin correspond with points of interest on the Panhandle map.

Pensacola, with its antebellum homes and historic landmarks, is a good place to start your trek through northwest Florida. After a browse through its museums and a stroll through the preservation districts, begin heading east on U.S. 98. Don't overlook the deserted beaches along the Gulf of Mexico, where the sugar-white quartz-crystal sand crunches underfoot like snow on a sub-zero night. The next point of interest is Fort Walton Beach, the Emerald Coast's largest city and the hub of its vacation activity, with shops and restaurants galore. From Fort Walton, swing north on Rte. 85 to Niceville/Valparaiso, on Choctawhatchee Bay, considered to be one of the world's most beautiful "sandboxes." The explorer's itinerary calls next for a run up Rte. 85 to Crestview, then to I–10 to DeFuniak Springs and down U.S. 331 to its junction with Rte. 20 at Freeport. A drive along Rte. 20, a two-laner that twists along Choctawhatchee Bay and through the piney woods past bait shacks and catfish restaurants, is a great way to see the other Florida. Proceed on Rte. 20 to Rte. 79 just beyond Ebro, then head south to Panama City Beach, a resort community with a wealth of varied leisure activities. Consider making this a base for some interesting side trips. Afterward, circle back toward Destin, but take time for a meander through the backwaters and byroads that spur off the main drag.

1 Pensacola

Spanish conquistadors, under the command of Don Tristan de Luna, made landfall on the shores of Pensacola Bay in 1559, but, discouraged by a succession of destructive tropical storms and dissension in the ranks, De Luna abandoned the settlement two years after its founding. In 1698, the Spanish once again established a fort at the site. During the early 18th century, control jockeyed back and forth between the Spanish, the French, and the British and ultimately, in 1819, landed in the hands of the United States. During the Civil War, Pensacola came under the governance of the Confederate States of America, so by the time the 20th century rolled around, the flags of five different nations had flown over this fine, old southern city; hence its nickname, the City of Five Flags.

Today, historic Pensacola consists of three distinct districts—Seville, Palafox, and North Hill—though they are easy to explore as a unit. Stroll down streets mapped out by the British and renamed by the Spanish, such as Cervantes, Palafox, Intendencia, and Tarragona. Be warned, though, that it is best to stick to the beaten path; Pensacola is a port town and can get rough around the edges, especially at night.

The best way to orient yourself is to stop at the **Pensacola Convention & Visitors Information Center** (1401 E. Gregory St., tel. 904/434–1234 or 800/874–1234). Located at the foot of the Three-Mile Bridge over Pensacola Bay, it's easy to find. You can pick up maps of the self-guided historic district tours and other information.

Approaching from the east, the first historic district you reach is **Seville**—the site of Pensacola's first permanent Spanish colonial settlement. Its center is Seville Square, a live oak-shaded park bounded by Alcaniz, Adams, Zaragoza, and Government streets. Park your car and roam these brick streets past honeymoon cottages and bay-front homes. Many of the buildings have been restored and converted into restaurants, commercial offices, and shops where you can buy anything from wind socks to designer clothes.

Continue west to Palafox Street, the main stem of the **Palafox Historic District.** This was the commercial and government hub of old Pensacola. On Palafox Place, note the Spanish Renaissance-style Saenger Theater, Pensacola's old movie palace; and the Bear Block, a former wholesale grocery with wrought-iron balconies that are a legacy from Pensacola's Cre-

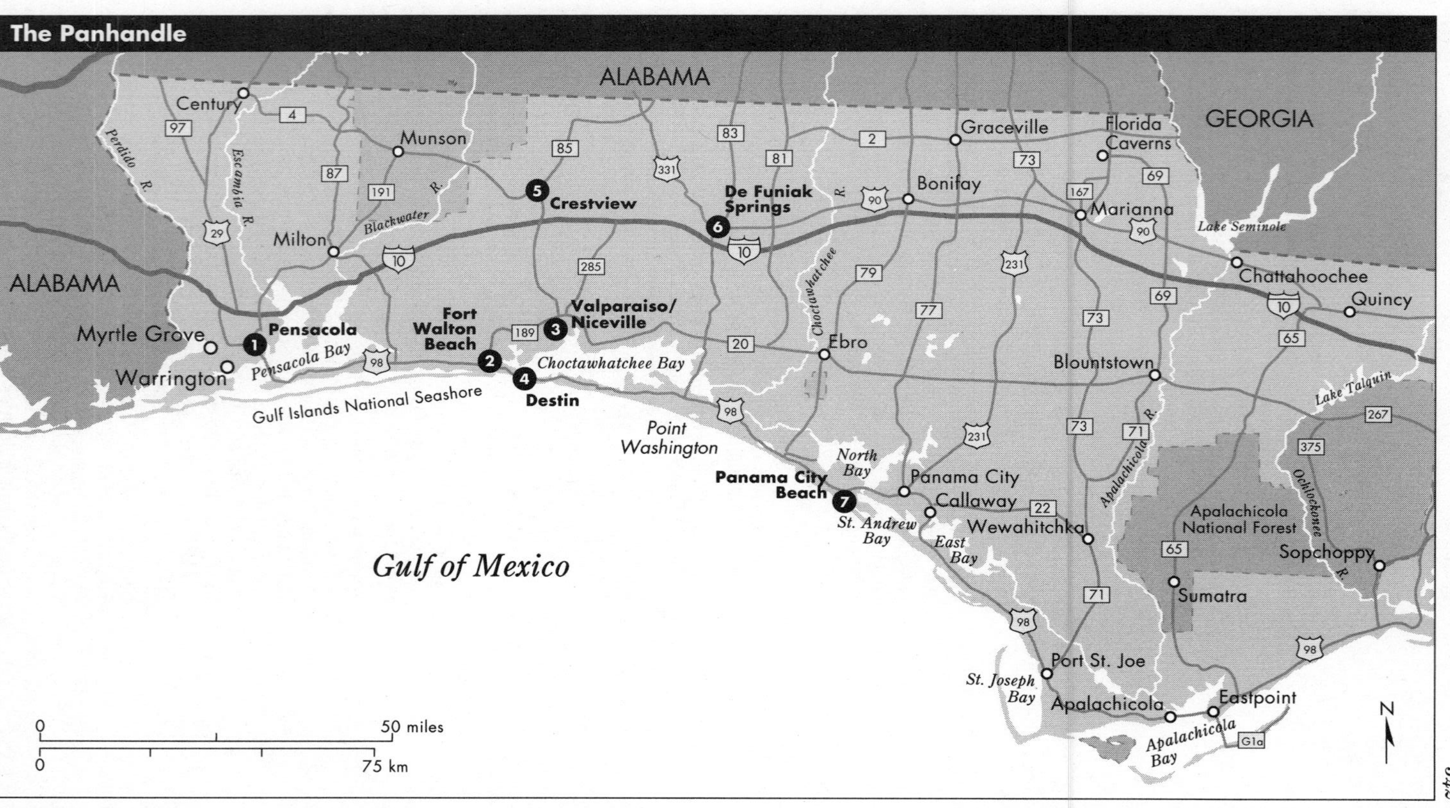
The Panhandle
ALABAMA
GEORGIA
ALABAMA
Century
Munson
Crestview
De Funiak Springs
Graceville
Bonifay
Florida Caverns
Marianna
Lake Seminole
Chattahoochee
Quincy
Milton
Myrtle Grove
Pensacola
Warrington
Pensacola Bay
Fort Walton Beach
Valparaiso/ Niceville
Destin
Choctawhatchee Bay
Gulf Islands National Seashore
Ebro
Blountstown
Lake Talquin
Point Washington
North Bay
Panama City Beach
Panama City
Callaway
Wewahitchka
St. Andrew Bay
East Bay
Apalachicola National Forest
Sopchoppy
Sumatra
Port St. Joe
St. Joseph Bay
Apalachicola
Eastpoint
Apalachicola Bay
Gulf of Mexico
Perdido R.
Escambia R.
Blackwater R.
Choctawhatchee R.
Apalachicola R.
Ochlockonee R.
N
0
50 miles
0
75 km

ole past. Though the San Carlos Hotel has been closed for many years, in its heyday the Mediterranean-style building at Palafox and Garden streets was the proper place for business tycoons and military officers to savor their cigars and brandies and where Pensacola's elite dined after the theater and introduced their daughters to society. Nearby, on Palafox between Government and Zaragoza streets, is a statue of Andrew Jackson that commemorates the formal transfer of Florida from Spain to the United States in 1821.

Palafox Street also funnels into the **North Hill Preservation District,** where Pensacola's affluent families, many made rich during the turn-of-the-century timber boom, built their homes on ground where British and Spanish fortresses once stood. To this day residents occasionally unearth cannonballs while digging in their gardens. North Hill occupies 50 blocks that consist of more than 500 homes in Queen Anne, neoclassical, Tudor Revival, and Mediterranean architectural styles. Take a drive through this community, but remember these are private residences not open to the public. Places of general interest in the district include the 1902 Spanish mission-style Christ Episcopal Church; Lee Square, where a 50-foot-high obelisk stands as Pensacola's tribute to the Old Confederacy; and Fort George, an undeveloped parcel of land at the site of the largest of three forts built by the British in 1778.

From the North Hill district, go south on Palafox Street to Zaragoza Street to reach the **Historic Pensacola Village,** a cluster of museums between Adams and Tarragona. The **Museum of Industry,** housed in a late 19th-century warehouse, hosts permanent exhibits dedicated to the lumber, maritime, and shipping industries—once mainstays of Pensacola's economy. A reproduction of a 19th-century streetscape is displayed in the **Museum of Commerce,** while the city's historical archives are kept in the **Pensacola Historical Museum**—what was once Old Christ Church, one of Florida's oldest churches. Also in the village are the **Julee Cottage Museum of Black History, Dorr House, Lavalle House,** and **Quina House.** *Pensacola Village Information Center, tel. 904/444–8905. Open Mon.–Sat. 10–4; Pensacola Historical Museum, tel. 904/433–1559. Open Mon.–Sat. 9–5, Sun. 9–4:30. Admission: $3 adults, $2 children over 12.*

In the days of the horse-drawn paddy wagon the two-story mission revival building housing the **Pensacola Museum of Art** served as the city jail. *407 S. Jefferson St., tel. 904/432–5682. Open Tues.–Fri. 10–5, Sat. 10–4. Admission free.*

Pensacola's 1908 old City Hall has been refurbished and reopened as the **T. T. Wentworth Jr., Florida State Museum.** The Wentworth displays some 150,000 artifacts ranging from Civil War weaponry to bottle caps. Representing more than 80 years of collecting, the assemblage is worth over $5 million. *333 S. Jefferson St., tel. 904/444–8905. Open Mon.–Sat. 10–4:30, Sun. 1–4:30. Admission: $3 adults, $2.50 senior citizens, $2 children over 6.*

Double back on Palafox Street five blocks to the Port of Pensacola, downtown. Here, the oldest operational aircraft carrier in the world, the USS *Lexington,* is berthed. Now a training vessel used to qualify student pilots, the *Lady Lex* is open for the public to tour. *Tours weekends and holidays 9–3. Children under 8 not permitted on board. Admission free.*

From the port, take Palafox Street to U.S. 98 (Garden St.) to reach the **Pensacola Naval Air Station** (tel. 904/452–2311). Established in 1914, it is the nation's oldest such facility. On display in the **National Museum of Naval Aviation** are more than 100 aircraft that have played an important role in naval aviation history. Among them are the NC-4, which in 1919 became the first plane to cross the Atlantic by air; the famous World War II fighter, the F6F *Hellcat;* and the *Skylab Command Module.* Thirty-minute films on aeronautical topics are shown, June–August. Call for details. The National Park Service-protected **Fort Barrancas,** established during the Civil War, is also located at the NAS. Nearby are picnic tables and a half-mile woodland nature trail. *Navy Blvd. (off U.S. 98), tel. 904/452–3604. Open daily 9–5. Admission free.*

❷ Fort Walton Beach

Fort Walton Beach dates from the Civil War years when patriots loyal to the Confederate cause organized Walton's Guard (named in honor of Colonel George Walton, one-time acting territorial governor of West Florida) and made camp on Santa Rosa Sound, the site that would come later to be known as Camp Walton. In 1940, fewer than 90 people lived in Fort Walton Beach, but thanks to the development of Eglin Field during World War II, and New Deal money spent for new roads and bridges, within a decade the city became a boom town. Today, Greater Fort Walton Beach has over 78,000 residents, making it the largest urban area on the Emerald Coast. The military is Fort Walton Beach's main source of income, but tourism runs it a close second.

Eglin Air Force Base encompasses 728 square miles of land, has 10 auxiliary fields, including Hurlburt and Duke fields, and a total of 21 runways. Jimmie Doolittle's Tokyo Raiders trained here, as did the Son Tay Raiders, a group that made a daring attempt to rescue American POWs from a North Vietnamese prison camp in 1970. Tours leave from the officers club at the base. The main gate is on U.S. 98 northeast of Fort Walton Beach. Tour tickets, which are free, may be picked up at the local chambers of commerce. *Tel. 904/678–2323 or 904/244–8191. Tours Jan.–Mar. and June–Aug., Mon., Wed., and Fri. 9:30–noon.*

Just outside Eglin's main gate on U.S. 98, is the **Air Force Armament Museum,** with an uncluttered display of more than 5,000 articles of Air Force armaments from World Wars I and II, and the Korean and Vietnam wars. Included are uniforms, engines, weapons, aircraft, and flight simulators; larger craft such as transport planes and swept-wing jets are exhibited on the grounds outside the museum. A 32-minute movie about Eglin's history and its role in the development of armaments is presented continuously throughout the day. *Rte. 85, Eglin Air Force Base, tel. 904/882–4062. Open daily 9:30–4:30. Admission free.*

Artifacts reflecting the cultural, artistic, technological, and spiritual achievements of the many prehistoric peoples who have inhabited northwest Florida during the past 10,000 years are on exhibit at the **Indian Temple Mound Museum.** Of special interest are the funerary masks and weaponry of these pre-Columbian tribes. The museum is adjacent to the 600-year-old National Historic Landmark Temple Mound, which is a large earthwork built over saltwater. *139 Miracle Strip Pkwy. (U.S. 98), tel. 904/243-6521. Open Sept.–May, Mon.–Sat. 11–4; June–Aug., Mon. to Sat. 9–4. Admission: 75¢ adults, children 12 and under free.*

A two-mile jaunt east on U.S. 98 will bring you to the **Gulfarium**—a great way to spend a few hours when bad weather drives you off the beach. The Gulfarium's main attraction is its "Living Sea" presentation, in a 60,000-gallon tank, that simulates conditions on the ocean bottom. There are performances by trained porpoises, sea lion shows, and marine life exhibits featuring seals, otters, and penguins. There's also an extensive gift shop where you can buy anything from conch shells and sand-dollar earrings to children's beach toys. *U.S. 98E, tel. 904/244–5169. Open May–Sept., daily 9–6, Oct.–Apr. daily 9–4. Admission: $5 adults, $3.50 children 11 and under.*

3 Valparaiso/Niceville

There aren't many places in the country where you can find people who were involved in the city's chartering activities and who are alive and well and currently serving on the local boards of directors. You can in **Valparaiso** and **Niceville,** however. The Twin Cities, as they are often called, are still in their youth, having been granted their charters in 1921 and 1938, respectively.

Niceville evolved from a tiny fishing hamlet called Boggy, whose sandy-bottomed bays were rich in mullet. Valparaiso, on the other hand, didn't evolve. An entrepreneurial Chicagoan named John B. Perrine envisioned Valparaiso as an ideal city by the sea, or "vale of paradise." Together, the cities have maintained an uncomplicated and serene existence, one relatively untouched by the tourist trade farther south. But that may change as word gets out about the abundance of opportunities to water-ski, fish, and sail.

The history of the Twin Cities and surrounding counties is on display in Valparaiso's **Historical Society Museum.** Take a step back in time among 8,000-year-old stone tools and early-20th-century iron pots and kettles. A rarity on display here is a steam-powered, belt-driven cotton gin. The museum also maintains a reference library of genealogical and historical research materials and official Civil War records. *115 Westview Ave., tel. 904/678–2615. Open Tues.–Sat. 11–4. Admission free.*

East of Niceville, off Rte. 20 on Rocky Bayou, are 50 excellent picnic areas, nature trails, boat ramps, and uncrowded campsites with electrical and water hookups in the **Fred Gannon State Recreational Area** (tel. 904/897–3222). It's quiet and secluded, yet easy-to-find, and a great venue for serious bikers.

4 Destin

A fishing village since the mid-1830s, Destin was founded by Leonard A. Destin, a New London, Connecticut, sea captain who sailed in and settled his family near the strait that connects

Choctawhatchee Bay with the Gulf of Mexico. Life remained calm here until the strait, or East Pass, was bridged in 1935. Then, recreational anglers discovered its white sands, blue-green waters, and the abundance of some of the most sought-after sport fish in the world. More billfish are hauled in around Destin each year than from all other Gulf fishing ports combined. But you don't have to be the rod-and-reel type to love Destin. You could stay in Destin for a month and still not try every gourmet restaurant in the area. There's also plenty to entertain the sand-pail set as well as seniors who ask for nothing more than a chance to sprawl in the sun and soak up its rays.

The Destin Fishing Museum has a dry aquarium where lighting and sound effects create the sensation of being underwater. You can get the feeling of walking on a sandy bottom that's dotted with sponges while viewing the species of fish indigenous to the Gulf of Mexico. *39 U.S. 98E, tel. 904/654–1011. Admission: $1 adults, children under 12 free. Open Wed.–Sun. noon–4.*

Drive east on U.S. 98 for about 8 miles to the **Museum of the Sea and Indian,** where there are exhibits on marine life in the Gulf of Mexico as well as the seven seas of the world. Artifacts from both North and South American Indian tribes also are displayed here. *4801 Beach Hwy. (off U.S. 98), tel. 904/837–6625. Open summer, daily 8–7; winter, daily 9–4. Admission: $3.25 adults, $1.75 children.*

In the **Eden State Gardens,** 25 miles east of Destin on U.S. 98, an antebellum mansion, with colonnaded porticoes and upstairs galleries that wrap the entire house, is set amid an arcade of moss-draped live oaks and is open to the public for touring. Furnishings in the spacious rooms date from several periods as far back as the 17th century. The surrounding gardens are beautiful year-round, but they're nothing short of spectacular in mid-March when the azaleas and dogwoods are in full bloom. *County Rte. 395, Point Washington, tel. 904/231–4214. Open daily 8 AM–sunset. Mansion tours Thurs.–Mon. 9–4 (hourly). Admission to gardens free; mansion tour $1.*

Seaside has all the features of Cape Cod, right here in Florida. "A new town with the old ways," Seaside, with its Victorian fretwork, white picket fences, and captain's walks, is contrived. But the pastel paint jobs, latticework, and Adirondack chairs also make this community stunning. Open-air markets for shoppers and old-fashioned ice-cream parlors for the kids add up to a memorable way to spend a tranquil afternoon. *County Rte. 30A (off U.S. 98), 25 mi east of Destin, tel. 904/231–4224.*

5 6 Crestview/DeFuniak Springs

By linking Crestview and DeFuniak Springs to neighboring cities, the railroads did for these landlocked Panhandle towns what the military did for the settlements along the Gulf shore. When the Louisville & Nashville Railroad Company completed a line through northwest Florida in 1882, its surveyors dubbed the area **Crestview** because, at 235 feet above sea level, it had the highest altitude in the state. **DeFuniak Springs,** on the other hand, was so named to flatter the then-prominent L & N official Ernest A. DeFuniak.

The Okaloosa county seat of Crestview is also known as the Hub City of northwest Florida because of its location at the junction of three major highways. Crestview makes no bones about being a small town where folks enjoy going roller-skating, playing softball, or packing a picnic lunch and taking off to the woods. But it is not without its cultural accomplishments. It brags about its **Robert L. F. Sikes Public Library** and research center that houses more than 44,000 volumes within a stately Greek Revival building.

DeFuniak Springs brags about its culture, too. In 1885 it was chosen as the location for the New York Chautauqua's winter assembly. It was also the site of the Knox Hill Academy, the only institution of higher learning in northwest Florida for more than half a century after its founding in 1848. The Chautauqua programs were discontinued in 1922, but DeFuniak Springs attempts to revive them, in spirit at least, with a county-wide Chautauqua Festival it sponsors every May.

Another legacy from the Chautauqua era is the **Walton-DeFuniak Public Library,** by all accounts Florida's oldest library continuously operating in its original building. This tiny library, measuring 16 by 24 feet, opened in 1887 to make reference and recreational reading material available to the Chautauqua crowd. At present, it contains nearly 28,000 volumes, including rare books, many of which are older than the building itself. The collection has grown over the years to include an impressive display of European armor that can easily compete with similar exhibits twice its size. *100 Circle Dr., tel. 904/892–3624. Open Mon. 9–7, Tues.–Fri. 9–6, Sat. 9–3.*

7 Panama City Beach

A vacation spot with mass appeal, Panama City Beach is about 5 miles south and to the west of Panama City proper. In spite of shoulder-to-shoulder condominiums, motels, and amusement parks that make it seem like one big carnival ground, Panama City Beach has a natural beauty that excuses its overcommercialization. The incredible white sands, navigable waterways, and plentiful marine life that attracted Spanish conquistadors and gave sustenance to the settlers early on, are a lure to today's family-vacation industry. Peak season for Panama City is June–September, and during spring break.

Time Out **Pineapple Willie's** brings together the best elements of a discotheque and a Wild West saloon, and caters to the 25- to 40-year-old crowd. If you feel overwhelmed by the live entertainment, you can escape to the serenity of a seaside deck. *On Beach Blvd. at Thomas Dr., tel. 904/235–0928. AE, MC, V.*

At the eastern tip of Panama City Beach is the **St. Andrews State Recreation Area,** which comprises 1,038 acres of beaches, pinewoods, and marshes. There are complete camping facilities here, as well as ample opportunities to swim, pier fish, or hike the dunes over clearly marked nature trails. You can board a ferry to **Shell Island**—a barrier island in the Gulf of Mexico that offers some of the best shelling north of Sanibel Island.

About 40 miles southeast of Panama City Beach on U.S. 98 at **Port St. Joe** is the spot where Florida's first constitution was drafted in 1838. Most of the old town, including the original hall, is gone—wiped out by hurricanes—but the exhibits in the **Constitution Convention State Museum** recall the event. There are also provisions for camping and picnicking in a small park surrounding the museum. *200 Island Memorial Way, tel. 904/229–8029. Open Thurs.–Mon. 9–5. Closed noon–1. Admission: 50¢ per person, children under 6 free.*

From Panama City, head north for a two-hour drive on U.S. 231 to Rte. 167 to visit the 1,783-acre **Florida Caverns State Park.** Take a ranger-led spelunking tour to see an array of stalactites, stalagmites, and "waterfalls" of solid rock. If the underground bit isn't your thing, the park also has hiking trails, campsites, and areas for swimming and canoeing on the Chipola River. *Rte. 167, tel. 904/482–3632. Open daily 8 AM–sunset; cavern tours 9–4:30. Admission to park: $1 per vehicle and driver, 50¢ each additional person, children under 6 free; admission to caverns: $2 adults, $1 children 6–12.*

Falling Waters State Recreation Area is about an hour's drive north on Rte. 77 from Panama City. One of Florida's most recognized geological features is the Falling Waters Sink, a 100-foot-deep cylindrical pit that provides the background for a waterfall. There's an observation deck for viewing this natural phenomenon. *Rte. 77, tel. 904/638–4030. Open daily 8 AM–sunset. Admission: $1 driver, 50¢ per passenger over age 8.*

What to See and Do with Children

Fast Eddie's Fun Center (W St. at Michigan, Pensacola, tel. 904/433–7735) features kiddie rides, a video room, air hockey, and basketball.

The Zoo (5801 Gulf Breeze Pkwy., Gulf Breeze, tel. 904/932–2229) is home to plants, animals, and 30 acres of ponds, lakes, and open plains.

Island Golf Center (1306 Miracle Strip Pkwy., Fort Walton Beach, tel. 904/244–2612) has 36 holes of miniature golf, a nine-hole par-three course, pool tables, and video games.

Museum of the Sea and Indian (4801 Beach Hwy., Destin. tel. 904/837–6625) (*see* Destin, above).

The Track (1125 U.S. 98, Destin, tel. 904/654–4668) is a special theme park with go-cart tracks and rides.

Big Kahuna (U.S. 98, Destin, tel. 904/837–4061) is a water park with miniature golf and an amphitheater.

Shipwreck Island (12000 U.S. 98W, Panama City Beach, tel. 904/234–2282) features 6 acres of water rides for kids and adults of all ages.

Miracle Strip Amusement Park (12000 U.S. 98W, Panama City Beach, tel. 904/234–5810) has 30 rides, including a roller coaster with a 65-foot drop.

Gulf World (15412 U.S. 98A W, Panama City Beach, tel. 904/234–5271) performers include a bottle-nosed dolphin, porpoises, seals, otters, and sea lions.

Snake-A-Torium (9008 U.S. 98W, Panama City Beach, tel. 904/234–3311) treats reptile lovers to exhibits and shows starring live rattlesnakes, water moccasins, and giant pythons.

Off the Beaten Track

Take I–110 from downtown Pensacola to I–10. About 40 miles northeast is **Blackwater River State Park** (tel. 904/623–2363), in Holt. Park the car, stretch your legs, and take advantage of what is regarded as one of the cleanest rivers in the country. Don't be fooled by the dark color of the Blackwater River, though. It's the result of the tannic acid that leaches into it from the cypress trees along its banks. The river's shallow waters offer the best canoeing in the area; the largest, whitest sandbars; plus the scenic beauty of the magnolias and cedars in the surrounding Blackwater River State Forest. Canoeing fans will enjoy the special challenges of a paddle up Sweetwater/ Juniper Creek, whose sandbars and cliffs call for more maneuvering and technical skill. Okay—so you didn't bring your own canoe. Not to worry. **Blackwater Canoe Rental** (U.S. 90E, Milton, tel. 904/623–0235) provides complete round-trip service (*see* Participant Sports, below). These friendly folks will meet you at the end point of the trip, transport you upstream, and launch you on your way. The river winds around so that you'll end up back at your car, where you simply beach your canoe, without having to wait or load the gear yourself.

Back on U.S. 98, head east over the 3-mile-long Pensacola Bay Bridge and cross the bridge to Santa Rosa Island. This barrier reef offers more than seascapes and water sports. It's also a must-see for bird-watchers. Since 1971 more than 280 species of birds from the common loon to the majestic osprey have been spotted here. Two caveats for visitors: "Leave nothing behind but your footprints," and "don't pick the sea oats" (natural grasses that help keep the dunes intact). At Santa Rosa Island's western tip is **Fort Pickens National Park,** where there are a museum, nature exhibits, aquariums, and a campground with more than 180 campsites, many with electrical hookups. Fort Pickens's most famous resident was Apache Indian chief Geronimo. Legend has it that he became a fairly likable fellow before he was transferred to Oklahoma's Fort Sill for his final incarceration. *Ranger station at Fort Pickens Rd., tel. 904/934–2600 or 904/932–9994. Admission: $3 per car. Open daily 8:30–4.*

Proceed along Rte. 399 from Fort Pickens to **Navarre Beach,** a small, relaxed niche without the traffic and congestion common to most resort areas, but with amenities ranging from luxury condominiums to unspoiled campgrounds. It's the halfway point between Pensacola and Fort Walton Beach. To reach Fort Walton Beach, cross over the Navarre Bridge to U.S. 98.

Shopping

Cordova Mall (511 N. Ninth Ave., Pensacola, tel. 904/477–7562) is anchored by four department stores in addition to its specialty shops and a food court with 13 fast-food outlets. **Harbourtown Shopping Village** (913 Gulf Breeze Pkwy., Gulf Breeze, tel. 904/932–9198) has trendy shops and the ambience of a wharfside New England village. There are four department stores in the **Santa Rosa Mall** (300 Mary Esther Cut-off, Mary Esther, tel. 904/244–2172), as well as 118 other shops and 15 bistro-style eateries. Stores in the **Manufacturer's Outlet Centers** (127 U.S. 98W, Fort Walton Beach, and 105 W. 23rd St., Panama City, tel. 904/234–0840) offer well-known brands of clothing and accessories at a substantial discount. **The Market at Sandestin** (5494 U.S. 98E, tel. 904/654–5588) has 27 upscale shops that peddle such wares as gourmet chocolates and designer clothes in an elegant minimall with boardwalks. **The Panama City Mall** (U.S. 231 and Rte. 77, Panama City, tel.

904/785–9587) has a mix of more than 100 franchise shops and national chain stores.

Participant Sports

Biking Some of the nation's best bike paths run through northwest Florida's woods and dunelands, particularly on Santa Rosa Island where you can pedal for 50 miles and never lose sight of the ocean. Routes through Eglin AFB Reservation present cyclists with a few challenges, but biking here requires a $3 permit, which may be obtained at **Jackson Guard Forestry** (tel. 904/882–4164). Rentals are available from **Bob's Bicycle Center** (Fort Walton Beach, tel. 904/243–5856) and at **The Wheel Works** (Fort Walton Beach, tel. 904/244–5252).

Boating There are niches for boaters of all classes in northwest Florida's sheltered inlets and lazy rivers, as well as in the open waters of its bays and the Gulf of Mexico. You can rent powerboats for fishing, skiing, and snorkeling at **Club Nautico** (320 U.S. 98E, Destin, tel. 904/837–6811, and U.S. 98E, Santa Rosa Beach, tel. 904/267–8123). Pontoon-boat rentals for the more laid-back water enthusiast are available at **Consigned RV's** (101 W. Miracle Strip Pkwy., Fort Walton Beach, tel. 904/243–4488).

Canoeing Both beginners and veterans will get a kick out of canoeing the Florida Panhandle's abundance of rivers and streams. The shoals and rapids in the Blackwater River in the Blackwater River State Forest will challenge even the most seasoned canoeist, while the gentler currents in the sheltered marshes and inlets are less intimidating. Canoe rentals are readily available from **Blackwater Canoe Rental** (U.S. 90E., Milton, tel. 904/623–0235) and at **Adventures Unlimited** (12 mi north of Milton on Rte. 87, tel. 904/623–6197). Rentals can be obtained for a paddle up the out-of-the-way Shoal River at **Sasquatch Canoes, Inc.** (U.S. 90, 3 mi east of Crestview, tel. 904/682–3949). For a trip down Econfina Creek, "Florida's most beautiful canoe trail," rentals are supplied by **Econfina Creek Canoe Livery, Inc.** (north of Rte. 20 on Strickland Rd., tel. 904/722–9032).

Diving A breathtaking world of adventure and beauty awaits below the water's surface where you can observe colorful fish and marine life or, if you're in the Panama City Beach area, investigate the wreckage of sunken tanker ships, tugboats, and cargo vessels. For snorkelers and beginning divers, the jetties of St. Andrews State Recreation Area, where there is no boat traffic, are safe. Wreck dives are offered by **Diver's Den** (3603 Thomas Dr., tel. 904/234–8717) or **Panama City Dive Center** (4823 Thomas Dr., tel. 904/235–3390). In the Destin-Fort Walton Beach area, you can arrange for diving instruction and excursions through **Aquanaut Scuba Center, Inc.** (24 U.S. 98W, Destin, tel. 904/837–0359) or **The Scuba Shop** (348 Miracle Strip Pkwy., Fort Walton Beach, tel. 904/243–1600).

Fishing Northwest Florida's fishing options range from fishing for pompano, snapper, marlin, and grouper—in the saltwater of the Gulf of Mexico—to angling for bass, catfish, and bluegill in the freshwaters of the region. All fisherfolk, except Florida residents 65 years or older, children under 16, and anyone fishing from a licensed charter boat, must have fishing licenses, which are available at tackle shops, and hardware and sporting-goods stores where fishing tackle is sold. You can buy bait and tackle at **Stewart's Outdoor Sports** (4 Eglin Pkwy., Fort Walton Beach, tel. 904/243–9443; 1025 Palm Plaza, Niceville, tel. 904/678–4804), at **Port Panama City Beach Pier Tackle Shop** (16101 U.S. 98W, Panama City, tel. 904/235–2576), or at **Penny's Sporting Goods** (1800 Pace Blvd., Pensacola, tel. 904/438–9633). If your idea of fishing is to drop a line off the end of a pier, you can fish from **Old Pensacola Bay Bridge** or from the 3,000-foot-long **Destin Catwalk,** along the East Pass Bridge. For $2 adults, $1.50 children, $1 observer, you can also fish from Panama City Beach's **city pier.**

Deep-Sea Fishing Charters

When planning an excursion, be advised that rates for renting deep-sea fishing boat are usually quoted by the day (about $550) or half day (about $350). This is an immensely popular pastime on the Emerald Coast, so there are boat charters aplenty. Among them are **Miller's Charter Services**/*Barbi-Anne* (off U.S. 98 on the docks next to A.J.'s Restaurant, Destin, tel. 904/837–6059), **East Pass Charters** (at East Pass Marina, U.S. 98E, Destin, tel. 904/837–1918), **Paper Tiger** (U.S. 98E, Destin, tel. 904/654–5860), **Lafitte Cove Marina** (1010 Ft. Pickens Rd., Pensacola Beach, tel. 904/932–7954), **The Moorings Marina** (655 Pensacola Beach Blvd., Pensacola Beach, tel. 904/932–0305), and **Holiday Lodge Marina** (6400 U.S. 98W, Panama City Beach, tel. 904/235–2809).

Party boats that carry as many as 100 passengers at $35–$40 per head are the cheapest way to go, offering everything from half-day fishing excursions to dinner cruises. The old standbys are ***Capt. Anderson's*** (Captain Anderson Pier, 5558 N. Lagoon Dr., Panama City Beach, tel. 904/234–3435) and *Her Majesty II* (U.S. 98E, Destin, tel. 904/837–6313).

Golf

The Gulf is northwest Florida's number one asset; golf is number two. **Perdido Bay Golf & Country Club** (One Doug Ford Dr., Pensacola, tel. 904/492–1223) has an 18-hole layout with four sets of tees, making it virtually four different courses. **Tiger Point Golf & Country Club** (1255 Country Club Rd., Gulf Breeze, tel. 904/932–1333) offers 36 holes of golf overlooking the natural wonderland of Santa Rosa Sound. **The Club at Hidden Creek** (3070 PGA Blvd., Gulf Breeze, tel. 904/939–4604) has 18 holes that wind through woods of hickory, magnolia, oak, and pine. Ranked among the Southeast's top 50, the 18-hole course at the **Shalimar Pointe Golf & Country Club** (2 Country Club Dr., Shalimar, tel. 904/651–1416) presents a professional challenge, but is forgiving enough for players of all levels. Long, well-groomed fairways rank the 18-hole **Fort Walton Beach** golf course (Rte. 189, Fort Walton Beach, tel. 904/862–3314) one of the state's finest municipal routes. Heavily wooded and enhanced by water and rolling terrain, **Bluewater Bay**'s (Rte. 20, 6 mi east of Niceville, tel. 904/897–3613) 27 championship holes combine to make three different 18-hole courses. **Shoal River Golf & Country Club** (1104 Shoal River Dr., Crestview, tel. 904/243–7664) has lakes, well-placed bunkers, and lush woods that provide a scenic backdrop as well as a good test of skill. **Indian Bayou Golf & Country Club**'s (Airport Rd. off U.S. 98, Destin, tel. 904/837–6191) bunkered, undulating greens make this 7,000-yard course one of the most interesting on the Emerald Coast. **Baytowne Golf Club** (Emerald Coast Pkwy., Destin, tel. 904/267–8155) at the Sandestin Beach Resort is gentler than its sister course, the sticky **Sandestin Links** (Emerald Coast Pkwy., Destin, tel. 904/267–8144), but is no pushover. Tight fairways, cavernous sand traps, and water hazards make the 18-hole course at **Santa Rosa Golf & Beach Club** (County Rte. 30A, Santa Rosa Beach, tel. 904/267–2229) provoking yet memorable. Water, water everywhere and island fairways make the **Lagoon Legend** (100 Delwood Beach Rd., Panama City Beach, tel. 904/234–3307), at Marriott's Bay Point, northwest Florida's answer to the Blue Monster at Doral. Bruce Devlin and Bob von Hagge designed this one to punish the big boys; its complement, the **Club Meadows** (100 Delwood Beach Rd., Panama City Beach, tel. 904/234–3307) course, is kinder and gentler.

Sailing Jet skis and sailboats are available at **Holiday Boat Rentals** (Hathaway Bridge at U.S. 98, Panama City Beach, tel. 904/234–0609). The **Hobie Shop** (12705 U.S. 98A W, Panama City Beach, tel. 904/234–0023) rents Hobie Cats. Sailing instruction as well as rentals are offered by **Friendship Charter Sailing** (500 U.S. 98, Destin, tel. 904/837–2694). **Patrick's Water Sports** (U.S. 98E, Fort Walton Beach, tel. 904/244–5222) rents equipment for jet skiing, parasailing, sailing, and sailboarding. **S&S Sailing** (1350 Miracle Strip Pkwy., Fort Walton Beach, tel. 904/243–2022) operates a sailing school as well as a charter service. Sailboat rentals come in a range of classes at **Cove Marina at Bluewater Bay** (300 Bay Dr., Niceville, tel. 904/897–2821). Renting sailboats, jet skis, or catamarans from **Bonifay Water Sports** (460 Pensacola Beach Blvd., Pensacola Beach, tel. 904/932–0633) includes safety and sailing instructions. Hobie Cats, Sunfish, jet skis, Windsurfers, and surfboards are available at **Key Sailing** (400 Quietwater Beach Blvd. or 410 Pensacola Beach Blvd., Pensacola Beach, tel. 904/932–5520).

Tennis At **Marriott's Bay Point Resort**'s (100 Delwood Beach Rd., Panama City Beach, tel. 904/234–3307) tennis center there are 12 Har-Tru clay tennis courts. **Sandestin Resort** (U.S. 98E, Destin, tel. 904/267–8150), one of the nation's five-star tennis resorts, has 16 courts with grass, hard, or Rubico surfaces. **Destin Racquet & Fitness Center** (995 Airport Rd., Destin, tel. 904/837–7300) boasts 10 courts. The **Municipal Tennis Center** (45 W. Audrey, Fort Walton Beach, tel. 904/243–8789) has 12 lighted Laykold courts and four practice walls. You can play tennis day or night on nine courts at the **Ft. Walton Racquet Club** (23 Hurlburt Field Rd., Fort Walton Beach, tel. 904/862–2023). There are 21 courts (18 lighted) featuring three different playing surfaces at **Bluewater Bay Resort** (Tennis Center, Bay Dr., Niceville, tel. 904/897–3679). Tennis courts are available in more than 30 locations in the Pensacola area, among them the **Pensacola Racquet Club** (3450 Wimbledon Dr., Pensacola, tel. 904/434–2434).

Spectator Sports

Auto Racing Billed as the fastest half-mile track in the country, **Five Flags Speedway** (7450 Pine Forest Rd., Pensacola, tel. 904/944–0466) features action-packed racing every Friday with top-name stock-car drivers and special draw events such as the Snow Ball Derby and Super National Enduro.

Dog Racing Rain or shine, year-round, there's racing with pari-mutuel betting six nights a week and afternoons on Friday, Saturday, and Monday at the **Pensacola Greyhound Track.** Lounge and grandstand areas are fully enclosed, air-conditioned, and have instant-replay televisions throughout. *U.S. 98 at Dog Track Rd., W. Pensacola, tel. 904/455–8598. Open Mon.–Sat.; post time: 7:45 PM.*

There's pari-mutuel betting and greyhound racing six nights a week at the **Ebro Dog Track.** *Rte. 20 at Rte. 79, Ebro, tel. 904/535–4048. Open May–Labor Day, Mon.–Sat.; post time: 8 PM.*

Beaches

Pensacola Beach (tel. 904/932–2258). To get to Pensacola Beach, which is 5 miles south of Pensacola, take U.S. 98 to Gulf Breeze, then cross the Bob Sikes Bridge over to Santa Rosa Island. Beachcombers and sunbathers, sailboarders and sailors keep things going at a fever pitch in and out of the water. In season, no particular demographic group has a lock on Pensacola Beach. Off season, conventioneers keep things hopping.

Gulf Island National Seashore (tel. 904/932–5302). This 150-mile stretch of pristine coastline runs all the way from Gulfport, Mississippi, to Destin. Managed by the National Park Service, these beach and recreational spots include the **Fort Pickens Area,** at the west end of Santa Rosa Island; the **Santa Rosa Day Use Area,** 10 miles east of Pensacola Beach; and **Johnson's Beach** on Perdido Key, about 20 miles northwest of Pensacola's historic districts. Check with the National Park Service for any restrictions that might apply.

John C. Beasley State Park (no phone). Located on Okaloosa Island, this is Fort Walton Beach's seaside playground. A boardwalk leads to the beach where you'll find covered picnic tables, changing rooms, and freshwater showers. Lifeguards are on duty during the summer. In the winter, the desolate, nostalgic quality is peaceful.

Eglin Reservation Beach (no phone). Situated on 5 miles of undeveloped military land and located about 3 miles west of the Brooks Bridge in Fort Walton Beach, this beach is a favorite haunt of local teenagers and young singles.

Crystal Beach Wayside Park (tel. 904/837–6447). With something to appeal to just about everyone, this Gulf-side sanctuary is located just 5 miles east of Destin and is protected on each side by undeveloped state-owned land.

Grayton Beach State Recreation Area (tel. 904/231–4210). Sandwiched between Santa Rosa Beach and Grayton Beach, this is one of the most scenic spots along the Gulf Coast. Located about 30 miles east of Destin on Rte. 30A, this recreation area offers blue-green waters, white-sand beaches, salt marshes, and swimming, snorkeling, and campground facilities.

St. Andrews State Park (tel. 904/234–2522). On the eastern tip of Panama City Beach, this is Florida's most visited park. An artificial reef creates a calm, shallow play area that is perfect for young children.

Panama City Beaches (tel. 800/PC–BEACH). These public beaches along the Miracle Strip combine with the plethora of video-game arcades, miniature golf courses, sidewalk cafes, souvenir shops, and shopping centers to lure people of all ages.

Dining and Lodging

Dining Since the Gulf of Mexico is only an hour's drive from any spot in the Panhandle, menus in restaurants from modest diners to elegant cafes feature seafood, most of which will be hauled out of the water and served that same day. Native fishes such as grouper, red snapper, amberjack, catfish, and mullet are the regional staples.

Restaurants are organized geographically. Unless otherwise noted, they are open for lunch and dinner.

Category	Cost*
Very Expensive	over $60
Expensive	$40–$60
Moderate	$20–$40
Inexpensive	under $20

**per person, excluding drinks, service, and 6% sales tax*

Lodging Northwest Florida offers everything from posh seaside resorts to modest roadside motels. The rule of thumb is: The closer you are to the water, the more you can expect to pay. If you're planning a lengthy stay, a condominium rental is a good idea. Most accept walk-ins, but to be on the safe side, reserve a spot through a property management service.

Category	Cost*
Very Expensive	over $120
Expensive	$90–$120
Moderate	$50–$90
Inexpensive	under $50

**All prices are for a standard double room, excluding service charge.*

The most highly recommended restaurants and lodgings are indicated by a ★.

The following credit card abbreviations are used: AE, American Express; CB, Carte Blanche; DC, Diners Club; MC, MasterCard; and V, Visa.

Crestview *Lodging*

Crestview Holiday Inn. Within this simple brown-wallpapered motel is typical Florida decor: shell-shape ceramic lamps, seashell-print bedspreads, and oceanic art on the walls. It's right on the main drag and is the in place for local wedding receptions and high school proms. *Rte. 85 and I–10, Box 1355, 32536, tel. 904/662–6111. 121 rooms. Facilities: pool, restaurant, lounge. AE, CB, DC, MC, V. Inexpensive.*

Destin *Dining*

Captain Dave's. This beachfront restaurant comprises three dining rooms: a central room with a glass dome overlooking the Gulf; a sports room filled with bats, helmets, jerseys, autographed baseballs, and photographs of professional atheletes; and finally, a more intimate dining area with small dim lights and potted plants. The hearty menu offers seafood entrées such as fillet of snapper sprinkled with crabmeat and covered with shrimp sauce and Parmesan cheese; and a medley of broiled seafood served with celery, onions, bell peppers, tomatoes, and topped with black olives and mozzarella cheese. Children's plates are available. Dancing and live entertainment are featured in the downstairs lounge. *3796 Old Hwy. 98, tel. 904/837–2627. Dress: casual. No reservations. AE, MC, V. No lunch. Inexpensive.*

★ **Flamingo Cafe.** Two types of atmosphere are presented at the Flamingo Cafe; the black, white, and pink color scheme, with waiters and waitresses dressed in tuxedos with pink bow ties, shouts nouveau; while a panoramic view of Destin harbor can be seen from every seat in the house, or from a table on the full-length porch outside. Chef specialties are veal *Magenta* (baby white veal sautéed with lobster and shrimp, finished with raspberry beurre blanc and garlic butter) and grouper Flamingo (broiled with butter, Madeira wine, and bread crumbs, topped off with sautéed mushrooms and artichoke hearts in lemon-butter sauce). *414 U.S. 98E, tel. 904/837–0961. Jacket advised. Reservations advised. No lunch. AE, DC, MC, V. Inexpensive–Moderate.*

Vaccaro's. Black ashtrays and gray napkins on pink tablecloths cap off the art deco appointments in this restaurant's striking interior. Italian foods are featured, from pizza made with sun-dried tomatoes, roasted shallots, and mushrooms to *pollo saltimbocca* (sautéed breast of chicken with prosciutto, mozzarella, and tomato sauce). Have the happy hour on the rooftop deck and watch the sun set over Destin harbor. *Morena Plaza, U.S. 98, tel. 904/654–5722. Jacket advised. Reservations accepted. AE, DC, MC, V. No lunch. Inexpensive–Moderate.*

Lodging

★ **Sandestin Beach Resort.** This 2,600-acre resort of villas, cottages, condominiums, and an inn seems to be a town unto itself. All rooms have a view, either of the Gulf, Choctawhatchee Bay, a golf course, lagoon, or bird sanctuary. This resort offers something for an assortment of tastes, from simple to extravagant. Special rates October–March. *Emerald Coast Pkwy., 32541, tel. 904/267–8100 or outside FL 800/874–3110. 175 rooms, 400 villas. Facilities: miles of private beach, several pools, 2 golf courses, 16 tennis courts, tennis and golf pro shops, marina, 5 restaurants, shopping mall. AE, DC, MC, V. Expensive–Very Expensive.*

Summer Breeze. White picket fences and porches or patios outside each unit make this condominium complex look like a summer place out of the Gay Nineties. One-bedroom suites have fully equipped kitchens and can sleep up to six people in queen-size beds, sleeper sofas, or bunks. It's halfway between Destin and Sandestin and is across from a roadside park that gives it the feel of privacy and seclusion. *3885 U.S. 98E, 32541, tel. 904/837–4853. 35 units. Facilities: pool, outdoor Jacuzzi, barbecue. MC, V. Moderate.*

Village Inn. This Best Western property, only minutes away from the Gulf, was built in 1983 with families in mind. A variety of amenities, including entertainment, are provided to occupy each member of the family in some way. Rooms have serviceable dressers and queen- or king-size beds. Senior discounts are available. *215 U.S. 98E, 32541, tel. 904/837–7413. 100 rooms. Facilities: pool, free HBO, 24-hr restaurant, lounge. AE, DC, MC, V. Moderate.*

Fort Walton Beach

Dining

★ **Liollio's.** Spicy Greek seafood somehow doesn't seem right in a restaurant with an Italian name—unless it's Liollio's. Dishes such as snapper (seasoned with Greek spices, tomatoes, green peppers, onions, and garlic) or Athenian-style shrimp (broiled with spices in garlic butter and topped with Parmesan cheese) make a memorable meal. Every table enjoys a view of Santa

Rosa Island, and owner John Georgiades is always around to schmooze with customers. *14 Miracle Strip Pkwy., tel. 904/243–5011. Dress: casual. Reservations accepted. AE, CB, DC, MC, V. Inexpensive–Moderate.*

Seagull. In addition to an unobstructed view of Brooks Bridge and the sound, this waterside restaurant has a 400-foot dock for its cruise-minded customers. Decorated with pictures from Fort Walton in the 1940s, and dimly lit, the Seagull is a comfortable place to dine. Choose between no-frills steak and prime rib or fancier fare such as fillet of snapper topped with almonds and Dijon mustard sauce. After the family business clears out, things liven up a bit when one of two bands provide live soft rock music. *U.S. 98E, by the Brooks Bridge, tel. 904/243–3413. Dress: casual. Reservations advised. AE, DC, MC, V. No lunch. Inexpensive–Moderate.*

Lodging

Holiday Inn. This U-shape hotel consists of a seven-story tower flanked on either side by three-story wings. The rooms are done in pastel green and peach, with flowered bedspreads complimenting striped draperies. Rooms face either the Gulf or the pool, but even the poolside rooms have at least some view of the Gulf. There are four floors of suites in the middle tower, each with a spacious sitting area and access to an extensive veranda overlooking the Gulf. The lobby has an upscale, contemporary design, featuring glass elevators, colored banners hanging from the ceiling, wicker furniture, and tiled floors. *1110 Santa Rosa Blvd., 32548, tel. 904/243–9181 or outside FL, 800/465–4329. 385 rooms. Facilities: 3 pools, 800-foot beach, tennis courts, exercise room, restaurants, lounge. AE, CB, DC, MC, V. Moderate–Expensive.*

Ramada Beach Resort. A 1988 renovation gave the Ramada lobby and entrance a slick new look with black marble and disco lights—what some locals feel is too much like the Las Vegas strip. Guest rooms were refurbished, too. Activity here centers around a pool with a five-story grotto, a swim-through waterfall, and along the 800-foot private beach. *U.S. 98E, 32548, tel. 904/243–9161 or outside FL 800/2–RAMADA. 454 rooms. Facilities: pools, whirlpool, tennis courts, game room, exercise room, restaurants, lounges. AE, MC, V. Moderate–Expensive.*

Valparaiso/Niceville

Dining

Heidelberg Haus. Enjoy the best of the wurst with gemütlichkeit on the side, and don't be surprised if the couple at the next table is tête-à-têting in a foreign tongue. The biergarten atmosphere, as well as the food in this German-European restaurant, attracts visitors from overseas who are seeking such back-home specialties as schweinebraten, sauerbraten, or *rouladen* (sliced top sirloin rolled and stuffed with bacon, pickles, and herbs and served with *spätzle*). Consider starting with a glass of German beer or wine and ending with *Schwarzenwalder kirschtorte* (Black Forest cherry cake). *4400 Rte. 20E, Niceville, tel. 904/897–3338. Dress: casual. Reservations accepted. AE, MC, V. Inexpensive.*

Lodging

★ **Bluewater Bay Resort.** This upscale residential resort is carved out of 1,800 acres of pines and oaks on the shores of Choctawhatchee Bay. It's still woodsy around the edges, but showcase homes are surrounded by tenderly manicured gardens. Rentals run the gamut from motel rooms to villas, some with fireplaces and fully equipped kitchens, to patio homes. Check-out information in the rental units is translated into

German for the benefit of the international visitors who flock to this golf course–rich region. *Rte. 20E., Box 247, Niceville, 32578, tel. 904/897–3613 or outside FL 800/874–2128. 134 units. Facilities: 2,000-ft private beach, several pools, 27 holes of golf, 21 tennis courts, marina, playground, exercise room, 2 restaurants, lounge. AE, MC, V. Expensive.*

Panama City Beach

Dining

Boar's Head. An exterior that looks like an oversize thatch cottage sets the mood for dining in this ever-popular ersatz-rustic restaurant and tavern. Prime rib has been the number one people-pleaser since the house opened in 1978, but broiled shrimp with crabmeat and vegetable stuffing, and native seafood sprinkled with spices and blackened in a white-hot skillet are popular, too. For starters, try escargot in mushroom caps or a shrimp bisque. There's a special menu for the junior appetite. *17290 U.S. 98A W, tel. 904/234–6628. Dress: casual. Reservations accepted. AE, CB, DC, MC, V. No lunch. Inexpensive–Moderate.*

Capt. Anderson's. Come early to watch the boats unload the catch of the day, and be among the first to line up for one of the 600 seats in this noted eatery. The atmosphere is nautical, with tables made of hatch covers. The Greek menu isn't limited to feta cheese and shriveled olives; charcoal-broiled fish and steaks have a prominent place on the menu, too. *5551 N. Lagoon Dr., tel. 904/234–2225. Dress: casual. No reservations. No lunch. AE, DC, MC, V. Closed Sun. and Dec.–Jan. Inexpensive–Moderate.*

Montego Bay. Queue up with vacationers and natives for a table at any one of the three restaurants in this local chain. Service is swift and the food's good. Some dishes, such as red beans and rice or oysters on the half shell, are no surprise. Others are quite a treat, such as shrimp rolled in coconut and served with a honey mustard and orange marmalade sauce, or steak doused with Kentucky bourbon and presented with a bourbon marinade. *4920 Thomas Dr., tel. 904/234–8686; 9949 Thomas Dr., tel. 904/235–3585; The Shoppes at Edgewater, tel. 904/233–6033. Dress: casual. No reservations. MC, V. Inexpensive.*

Lodging

★ **Edgewater Beach Resort.** Luxurious one-, two-, or three-bedroom units in beachside towers or golf-course villas are elegantly furnished with wicker and rattan and done in the seaside colors of peach, aqua, and sand. The centerpiece of this resort is a Polynesian-style lagoon pool with waterfalls, reflecting ponds, footbridges, and more than 20,000 species of tropical plants. *11212 U.S. 98A, 32407, tel. 904/235–4404 or outside FL 800/874–8686. Facilities: golf, 12 tennis courts, game rooms, health club, shuffleboard, restaurants, lounge. AE, MC, V. Expensive–Very Expensive.*

★ **Marriott's Bay Point Resort.** Sheer elegance is the hallmark of this pink stucco jewel on the shores of Grand Lagoon. Wing chairs, camel-back sofas, and Oriental-patterned carpets in the common areas re-create the ambience of an English manor house, which is sustained by the Queen Anne furnishings in the guest rooms. Gulf view or golf view—take your pick. Kitchen-equipped villas are a mere tee-shot away from the hotel. *100 Delwood Beach Rd., 32407, tel. 904/234–3307 or outside FL 800/874–7106. 400 rooms, suites, or villas. Facilities: 5 pools, including indoor pool with Jacuzzi, 2 golf courses, 12 lighted Har-Tru tennis courts, 145-slip marina, sailboat rentals, fishing charters, riverboat cruises, 5 restaurants, lounges. AE, MC, V. Moderate–Expensive.*

Miracle Mile Resort. A mile of beachfront is awash with hotels (Sheraton, Gulfside, Sands, Barefoot Beach Inn). These older properties target the family and convention trade. *9450 S. Thomas Dr., 32407, tel. 904/234–3484 or outside FL 800/874–6613. 632 units. Facilities: pools, tennis courts, restaurants, lounges. AE, CB, DC, MC, V. Inexpensive–Moderate.*

Pensacola

Dining

★ **Jamie's.** This is one of a handful of Florida restaurants that are members of the prestigious Master Chef's Institute. Dining here is like spending the evening in the antiques-filled parlor of a fine, old southern home. If a visit to Florida has you fished-out, try the liver pâté flavored with herbs and cognac and served with currant and citrus sauce. Follow it with almond-coated breast of chicken accompanied by a champagne cream sauce and seedless grapes. The wine list boasts more than 200 labels. *424 E. Zaragoza St., tel. 904/434–2911. Jacket required at dinner. Reservations advised. AE, MC, V. Inexpensive.*

McGuire's Irish Pub. Drink cherry beer brewed right on the premises in copper and oaken casks, and eat your corned beef and cabbage while an Irish tenor croons in the background. Located in an old firehouse, the pub is replete with antiques, moose heads, Irish Tiffany lamps, and Erin go bragh memorabilia. More than 36,000 dollar bills signed and dated by the pub's patrons flutter from the ceiling. McGuire's also has a House Mug Club with more than 2,000 personalized mugs. The waitresses are chatty and aim to please. Menu items run from kosher-style sandwiches to chili con carne to Boston cream pie. *600 E. Gregory St., tel. 904/433–6789. Dress: casual. No reservations. AE, MC, V. Inexpensive.*

Perry's Seafood House & Gazebo Oyster Bar. This vintage 1858 house, known locally as "the big red house," was a residence, a tollhouse, and a fraternity house before Perry purchased it in 1968 and turned it into a restaurant. Native fish are broiled with Perry's secret sauce and garlic butter, or baked and topped with garlic sauce and lemon juice. The menu varies depending on weather conditions, fishing boat schedule, and what was caught that day. *2140 Barrancas Ave. tel., 904/434–2995. Dress: casual. No reservations. AE, MC, V. Closed Tues. Inexpensive.*

Cap'n Jims. Get a table by a picture window and gaze at Pensacola Bay while you savor a house special such as snapper Chardonnay (served with lobster-based wine and cream sauce, scallions, and mushrooms) or snapper Dean'o (broiled and served with fresh tomatoes, spring onions, and lemon butter sauce). *905 E. Gregory St., tel. 904/433–3562. Dress: casual. Reservations advised. AE, MC, V. Closed Sun. Inexpensive.*

Lodging

Perdido Sun. This high rise is the perfect expression of Gulfside resort living. After a stay here, you'll know why the Spanish explorers of 300 years ago called the area the "Lost Paradise." One-, two-, or three-bedroom decorator-furnished units all have seaside balconies with spectacular views of the water. You can choose to make this your home away from home —accommodations include fully equipped kitchens—or you can pamper yourself with daily maid service. *13753 Perdido Key Dr., 32507, tel. 904/492–2390 or outside FL 800/227–2390. 93 rooms. Facilities: glass-enclosed pool, outdoor pool, spa, health club, restaurant. AE, MC, V. Expensive–Very Expensive.*

Pensacola Hilton. The Hilton's lobby is in the renovated L & N train depot. Ticket and baggage counters are still intact and old railroad signs are reminders of the days when steam locomotives chugged up to these doors. The old train station connects via a canopied two-story galleria to a 15-story tower. Here's where the spittoons and hand trucks give way to upholstered furniture and deep-pile carpet. Standard doubles are up-to-date and roomy. Bilevel penthouse suites have snazzy wet bars and whirlpool baths. The hotel is adjacent to the Pensacola Civic Center and only few blocks away from the historic districts. *200 E. Gregory St., 32590, tel. 904/433–3336 or 800/HILTONS. 212 rooms. Facilities: heated pool, restaurants, lounges, complimentary airport limo. AE, CB, DC, MC, V. Moderate–Expensive.*

Holiday Inn/Pensacola Beach. This property enjoyed its finest hour during the filming of *Jaws II*, when the cast made this its headquarters. Inside, the lobby is simple, with potted plants, floral arrangements, and a coral–colored decor. Outside, the Holiday Inn has its own 1,500 feet of private beach. From the ninth-floor Penthouse Lounge, you can watch the goings-on in the Gulf, especially when the setting sun turns the western sky to lavender and orange. *165 Ft. Pickens Rd., Pensacola Beach, 32561, tel. 904/932–5361 or 800/HOLIDAY. 150 rooms. Facilities: heated pool, tennis courts, restaurant, lounge. AE, CB, DC, MC, V. Moderate.*

★ **New World Landing.** This is Pensacola's little hotel, where celebrities who visit the city are likely to stay. Photos of dozens of the inn's famous guests (Lucille Ball, Shirley Jones, Charles Kuralt) hang behind the front desk in the lobby. The exquisite furnishings in the guest rooms take their inspiration from the five periods of Pensacola's past and are French or Spanish provincial, early American, antebellum, or Queen Anne. The baths are handsomely appointed with brass fixtures and outfitted with oversize towels. *600 Palafox St., 32501, tel. 904/432–4111 or outside FL 800/258–1103. 14 rooms, 2 suites. Facilities: 3 restaurants, lounge. AE, DC, MC, V. Moderate.*

Ramada Inn. All the guest rooms at this hotel have been recently renovated. Suites have game tables and entertainment centers; some have whirlpools. This Ramada is conveniently located close to the airport. *6550 Pensacola Blvd., 32505, tel. 904/477–0711 or outside FL 800/2–RAMADA. 106 rooms. Facilities: pool, restaurant, lounge, courtesy airport transportation, complimentary Continental breakfast. AE, MC, V. Inexpensive.*

Seaside
Dining

★ **Bud & Alley's.** This roadside restaurant grows its own herbs—rosemary, thyme, basil, fennel, and mint—in a garden visible from the restaurant. The inside room has a unique, down-to-earth feel, with hardwood floors, ceiling fans, and six-foot windows looking out onto the garden. There is also a screened-in porch area with a view of the Gulf. The Gorgonzola salad with sweet peppers is a delightful introduction to one of the entrées, perhaps the seared duck breast with caramelized garlic, wild mushrooms, and Cabernet sauce. *County Rte. 30A, tel. 904/231–5900. Dress: casual. Reservations accepted. AE, MC, V. Closed Tues. Inexpensive.*

Lodging

★ **Seaside.** Two- to five-bedroom porticoed Victorian cottages are furnished right down to the vacuum cleaners. Although there's no air-conditioning, the Gulf breezes blowing off the water will cool rooms and remind you of the miles of unspoiled beaches so nearby. *County Rte. 30A, 32459, tel. 904/231–4224 or outside FL 800/636–0296. 38 cottages. Facilities: pool, tennis court,* *croquet, badminton, bicycles, Hobie Cats, and beach equipment rentals. AE, MC, V. Expensive.*

The Arts and Nightlife

The Arts Broadway touring shows, top-name entertainers, and concert artists are booked into the **Marina Civic Center** (8 Harrison Ave., Panama City, tel. 904/769–1217) and the **Saenger Theatre** (118 S. Palafox St., Pensacola, tel. 904/438–2827).

Concerts **Okaloosa Symphony Orchestra** (tel. 904/862–2418) performs a series of concerts featuring guest artists at the Fort Walton Beach Civic Auditorium (107 Miracle Strip Pkwy.) **Pensacola Symphony Orchestra** (tel. 904/435–2533) presents a series of five concerts each season at the Saenger Theatre (118 S. Palafox St.).

Dance **The Northwest Florida Ballet** (1201 Quail Lake Blvd., Fort Walton Beach, tel. 904/837–4945) has a repertoire of the classics and performs in communities throughout the Panhandle.

Theater **The Pensacola Little Theatre** (186 N. Palafox St., tel. 904/432–8621) presents plays and musicals during a season that runs from fall through spring.

Nightlife Northwest Florida's nightlife falls on the scale somewhere between uptown Manhattan supper clubs and Las Vegas–style dinner shows. There are places that cater especially to the night owls, but some of the family restaurants also take on a different character when the sun goes down. A good way to find out what's hot and what's not is to ask locals.

Bars and Nightclubs **Pineapple Willie's** (9900 Beach Blvd., Panama City Beach, tel. 904/235–0928) alternately features big-band and rock music and caters to the post-college crowd. After dark, **McGuire's Irish Pub** (600 E. Gregory St., Pensacola, tel. 904/433–6789) welcomes anyone of legal drinking age, particularly those of Irish descent. If you don't like crowds, stay away from McGuire's on Friday nights and nights when Notre Dame games are televised. **Mesquite Charlie's** (5901 N. W St., Pensacola, tel. 904/434–0498) offers good, ol' down-home pickin' and grinnin' with live entertainment and singin' up a storm. Pensacola's **Seville Quarter** (130 E. Government St., tel. 904/434–6211) with five fabulous bars featuring music from disco to Dixieland is this city's equivalent to the New Orleans French Quarter. Find the **Palace Oyster Bar** (tel. 904/438–9453) and take it from there. **Trader Jon's** (511 Palafox St., Pensacola, tel. 904/438–3600) is officially recognized as the second home for Navy aviators as well as the preferred pub for all pilots. **Tickets** at the Pensacola Hilton (200 E. Gregory St., tel. 904/433–3336) is the spot for those who dip when they dance but still like to boogie. The Hilton's **L & N Lobby Bar** (*see* Lodging, above) is where the Baby Boomers gather after a hard day's work. Catch the action at **Cash's Faux Pas Lounge** (106 Santa Rosa Blvd., Fort Walton Beach, tel. 904/244–2274) where anything goes. **Jamaica Joe's** (790 Santa Rosa Blvd., Fort Walton Beach, tel. 904/244–4137) features live show bands and $3 pitchers of beer that appeal to younger pub crawlers. **Nightown** (140 Palmetto St., Destin, tel. 904/837–6448) has a dance floor with laser lights and a New Orleans–style bar with live band music.

11 Northeast Florida

Introduction

Janet and Gordon Groene are a full-time writer and photographer team. They are contributing editors of Family Motor Coaching Magazine and co-writers of Living Aboard Your Recreational Vehicle. *Janet's most popular book,* Cooking on the Go, *is considered an outdoor-cooking classic.*

When Orlando's new cinema industry scouts for filming locations, it can find almost any setting it needs in Northeast Florida. Towering, tortured live oaks, plantations, and antebellum-style architecture symbolize the Old South, and the mossy marshes of Silver Springs and the St. Johns River look today as they did generations ago when Tarzan movies were filmed in the jungles here. Jacksonville is a modern metropolis abounding with skyscrapers; Tallahassee, a brave Confederate capital; Payne's Prairie, near Gainesville, looks like it's a lost prehistoric stomping ground; while county seats such as De Land and Green Cove Springs are reminiscent of Thorton Wilder's *Our Town*.

Fishing villages of Big Bend country along the Gulf have a ramshackle, New England look. And the beaches, spreading in shimmering, sandy glory south from Fernandina, vary in likeness from the stony shores of the North Sea in Great Britain to the deep, hot sands of the Caribbean. In this chapter, we'll take you east from Tallahassee to Jacksonville, and south to New Smyrna Beach on the east coast.

Getting Around

By Plane

Daytona Beach Regional Airport is served by Delta (tel. 904/252–9661), Eastern (tel. 800/327–8376), American (tel. 800/433–7300), USAir (tel. 800/428–4322), and Continental (tel. 904/253–6300).

Taxis meet every flight; fare to beach hotels is about $10. Taxis include **Yellow Cab** (tel. 904/252–5536), **City Shuttle** (tel. 904/255–8422), **Checker Cabs** (tel. 904/255–8421), *AAA Cab* (tel. 904/253–2522), and **City Cab** (tel. 904/253–0675).

Gainesville Regional Airport is served by USAir (tel. 800/428–4322), Eastern (tel. 904/376–4411), Comair (tel. 800/354–9822), and ASA (tel. 800/282–3424).

Taxi fare to the center of town is about $10. Some hotels provide free airport pickup.

The main airport for the region is **Jacksonville International.** It is served by American (tel. 800/433–7300), Continental (tel. 800/525–0280), Eastern (tel. 800/327–8376), TWA (tel. 800/221–2000), United (tel. 800/241–6522), and USAir (tel. 800/428–4322).

Vans from the airport to area hotels cost $15 per person. Taxi fare is about $17 to the downtown area, $32 to the beaches, and $38 to Amelia Island. Among the limousine services, which must be booked in advance, is *AAA* **Limousine Service** (tel. 904/751–4800 for Jacksonville and beaches, tel. 904/ 277–2359 for Amelia Island). The charge is $30 for one or two persons to downtown, $35 for one or $40 for two to the beaches, and $30 for one or $15 each for multiple passengers to Amelia Island.

Tallahassee Regional Airport opened its new terminal in 1990. It is served by Delta (tel. 800/221–1212), USAir (tel. 800/368–5425), and Eastern (tel. 800/327–8376).

Taxi fare to downtown is about $12. Taxis include **Capitol** (tel. 904/656–9442), **City Taxi** (tel. 904/893–4111), **Tallahassee Cab** (tel. 904/576–2227), and **Yellow Cab** (tel. 904/222–3070). Some hotels provide free shuttle.

By Car East–west traffic travels the northern part of the state on I–10, which is a cross-country highway stretching from Los Angeles to Jacksonville. Farther south, I–4 rambles east from Tampa to Orlando, then northeast to the sea. Signs indicate this east–west orientation, which can be confusing when you're driving north (signs say east) from Orlando to Daytona Beach. Chief north–south routes are I–95 along the east coast, and I–75, which enters Florida south of Valdosta, Georgia, and joins the Sunshine Parkway toll road at Wildwood. If you want to drive as close to the Atlantic as possible, and are not in a hurry, stick with A1A (although the name changes several times along the way). Where there are no bridges across inlets, cars must return to the mainland. Where there are bridges, openings and closings cause unexpected delays. While I–75 is the fast route from Georgia to Tampa and points south, U.S. 19–98 takes you closer to the Gulf, for quick forays into coastal communities, beaches, and fishing villages.

Car Rentals Rental cars include **Alamo** (tel. 904/576–6009), **Avis** (tel. 904/576–4133), **Budget** (tel. 904/575–9191), **Hertz** (tel. 904/576–0155), and **National** (tel. 904/576–4107).

Private Services **My Brother's Limousine** (tel. 904/437–5466), based in Bunnell, serves Flagler, Volusia, and St. Johns counties. Chauffeured limousines cost $35 per hour, with a two-hour minimum. The firm is also a General Rent-a-Car center.

By Train **Amtrak** (tel. 800/USA–RAIL) schedules stops in Jacksonville, De Land, Waldo (near Gainesville), Ocala, and Palatka. The Auto Train serves Sanford from the Washington, D.C., area. Schedules vary depending on the season.

By Bus **Greyhound/Trailways** serves the region, with stations in Jacksonville (tel. 904/356–5521), St. Augustine (tel. 904/829–6401), Gainesville (tel. 904/376–5252), Tallahassee (tel. 904/222–4240), Daytona Beach (tel. 904/255–7076), and De Land (tel. 904/734–2747).

Daytona Beach has an excellent bus network, **Votran** (tel. 904/761–7600), that serves the beach area, airport, shopping malls, and major arteries. Exact fare is required.

DOTS Transit Service (tel. 904/257–5411) has scheduled service among the Daytona Beach Airport, Orlando International Airport, the Palm Coast Sheraton area, De Land, De Land's Amtrak station, and Deltona. Fares to the airport in Orlando are $20 one way and $36 round trip from Daytona; $12 each way from De Land or Daytona. DOTS also has trips three times weekly (Monday, Wednesday, and Friday), departing at 7:45 AM from Daytona Beach to the Orlando attractions area for $21 plus $3 for pickup at your home or hotel. Reservations are essential.

Taltran (tel. 904/574–5200) system provides service throughout the city limits of Tallahassee.

By Water Taxi Connecting the banks of the St. Johns River to different points of interest in the downtown Jacksonville area, this system makes many attractions within reach of one another. Fare is $3 round-trip adult, $2 senior citizens; $1.50 one way. Water taxis run every 15 minutes.

Scenic Drives

The **Buccaneer Trail** (Rte. A1A) on the Atlantic Coast goes from Mayport (where a ferry is part of the state highway system), through marshlands and beaches into Fort Clinch State Park, with its massive brick fortress, then into the 300-year-old seaport town of Fernandina Beach.

Rte. 13 takes you up one side of the St. Johns River, through has-been hamlets. **U.S. 17,** which was once the main highway between Miami and New York, travels the west side of the river, passing through Green Cove Springs and Palatka, where Ravine State Gardens' mountains of spring azaleas bloom.

S.R. 19 runs north and south through the Ocala National Forest, giving a nonstop view of stately pines and bold wildlife. Short side roads lead to parks, springs, picnic areas, and campgrounds.

Riverside Drive, where New Smyrna Beach's grand old homes line the Intracoastal Waterway is a good bicycle path, in addition to being a picturesque thruway.

Guided Tours

Northeast Florida **Suwannee Country Tours** (White Springs, tel. 904/397–2349) organizes bicycle and canoe trips on some of the state's most unspoiled and unique roads and waters. Stay overnight in country inns, picnic in ghost towns, eat at country churches, and explore forgotten sites.

Daytona Beach Sightsee aboard a seaplane from **Braunig Aeromarine** (tel. 904/761–7310). Helicopter flights are booked at **Space Coast Helicopter Services** (tel. 904/724–4191) in Palm Bay. For a sightseeing flight, try **Flagler Aviation** (tel. 904/437–4547) at Bunnell. **Dixie Queen Riverboat Cruises** (tel. 904/255–1997) runs lunch, brunch, dinner, and specialty cruises throughout the Daytona Beach area.

Jacksonville City tours of Jacksonville are offered by **Gray Line Tours** (tel. 904/730–2232) and **Jacksonville Historical Society Tours** (tel. 904/384–0849). **Europa Cruise Line Ltd.** (tel. 800/852–7529) sails daily from Mayport to "nowhere," wowing the entire family with boffo buffets, floor shows, games, dancing, and other cruise ship hoopla. For grown-ups only, there is casino gambling.

Riverwalk Cruise Lines, Inc. (tel. 904/743–6843) offers you a chance to see the quickly changing Jax skyline from the St. Johns River. Sightseeing, lunch, dinner, and dancing cruises depart Tuesday–Sunday from the Chart House on the Riverwalk.

Important Addresses and Phone Numbers

Tourist Information **Amelia Island-Fernandina Beach Chamber of Commerce.** *102 Centre St., tel. 904/261–3248. Open weekdays 9–5.*

Apalachicola Chamber of Commerce. *128 Market St., tel. 904/653–9419. Open weekdays 9–5; closed noon–1.*

Destination Daytona! *126 E. Orange Ave., tel. 904/255–0415 or 800/854–1234. Open weekdays 9–4.*

Gainesville Chamber of Commerce. *300 E. University Ave., tel. 904/336–7100. Open weekdays 8:30–5.*

Jacksonville and Its Beaches Convention & Visitors Bureau. *6 E. Bay St., Suite 200, tel. 904/353–9736. Open weekdays 8:30–5.*

Ocala-Marion County Chamber of Commerce. *110 E. Silver Springs Blvd. tel. 904/629–8051. Open weekdays 8:30–5.*

St. Augustine Visitor Information Center. *10 Castillo Dr., tel. 904/824–3334. Open daily 8:30–5:30.*

Tallahassee Visitor & Convention Bureau. *100 Duval St., tel. 904/224–8116 or 800/628–2866. Open weekdays 8:30–5.*

Emergencies Dial 911 for **police** or **ambulance** assistance in life-threatening situations.

Hospitals Emergency rooms are open 24 hours at the following: In Gainesville, **Alachua General** (801 S.W. 2nd Ave., tel. 904/372–4321); **North Florida Regional Medical Center** (S.R. 16 at I–75, across from the Oaks Mall, tel. 904/333–4000); **Shands Hospital** (at the University of Florida, tel. 904/395–0111). **Physician Care** (tel. 904/385–2222) has three locations in Tallahassee, all open seven days a week. In Ocala, **Munroe Regional Medical Center** (131 S.W. 15th St., tel. 904/351–7200). In Daytona, **Halifax Medical Center** (303 N. Clyde Morris Blvd., tel. 904/254–4100); **Atlantic Shores Hospital** (841 Jimmy Ann Dr., tel. 904/258–1055) is a private psychiatric hospital with two hotlines for psychiatric emergencies, including drug and alcohol abuse. **Hotline** numbers are 800/237–0835 or 800/345–2647.

24-Hour Pharmacies The only 24-hour pharmacy in the area is **Eckerd Drug** (4397 Roosevelt Blvd., Jacksonville, tel. 904/389–0314).

Exploring Northeast Florida

Numbers in the margin correspond with points of interest on the Northeast Florida map.

Tallahassee

Interstate 10 rolls over the timid beginnings of the Appalachian foothills and through thick pines into the state capital,
1 **Tallahassee,** with its canopies of ancient oaks and spring bowers of azaleas. Among the best canopied roads are St. Augustine, Miccosukee, Meridian, Old Bainbridge, and Centerville. Country stores and antebellum plantation homes still dot these roads, much as they did in earlier days.

In the heart of the city, stop at the **Tallahassee Visitors and Convention Bureau** to pick up information about the capital and the surrounding area. The bureau, housed in **The Columns,** is the city's oldest structure, built in 1833 and moved in 1970 to its present location. *100 N. Duval St., tel. 904/224–8116 or 800/628–2866. Open weekdays 8:30–5.*

The downtown **Capitol Complex area** is compact enough for walking, but is also served by a free, continuous shuttle trolley. It's a pleasant walk to the **Old Capitol,** originally a pre–Civil War structure. It has been added to and subtracted from but now has been restored to the way it looked in 1902, with its jaunty awnings and combination gas-electric lights. *Monroe St. at Pensacola St., tel. 904/488–1673. Admission free. Self-*

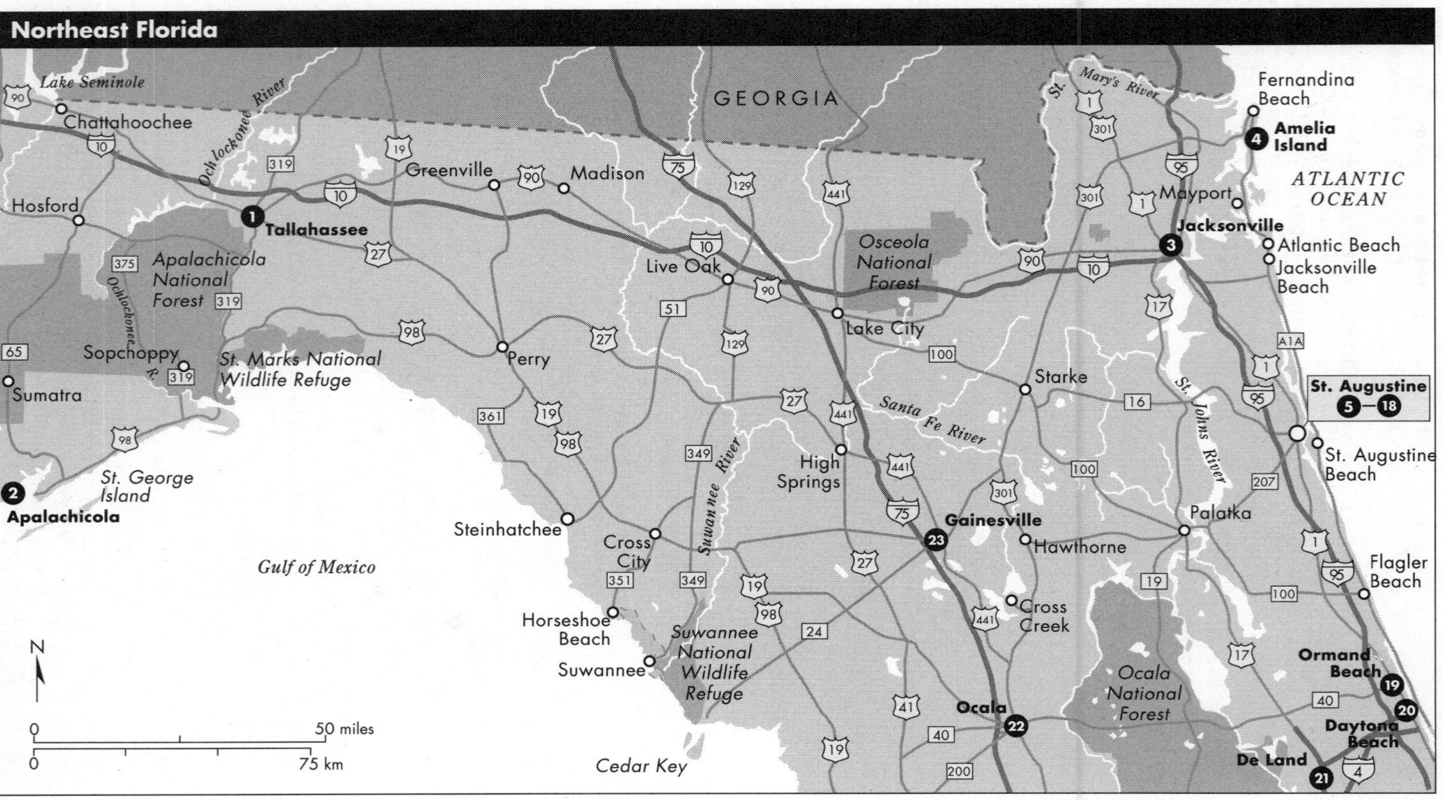
Northeast Florida
GEORGIA
Lake Seminole
Chattahoochee
Ochlockonee River
Hosford
Tallahassee
Greenville
Madison
Live Oak
Osceola National Forest
Lake City
St. Mary's River
Fernandina Beach
Amelia Island
ATLANTIC OCEAN
Mayport
Jacksonville
Atlantic Beach
Jacksonville Beach
Apalachicola National Forest
Ochlockonee R.
Sopchoppy
St. Marks National Wildlife Refuge
Sumatra
Perry
Starke
Santa Fe River
St. Johns River
St. Augustine
St. Augustine Beach
St. George Island
Apalachicola
High Springs
Suwannee River
Steinhatchee
Cross City
Gainesville
Hawthorne
Palatka
Gulf of Mexico
Cross Creek
Flagler Beach
Horseshoe Beach
Suwannee
Suwannee National Wildlife Refuge
Ocala National Forest
Ormand Beach
Ocala
Daytona Beach
De Land
Cedar Key
N
50 miles
75 km

guided or guided tours weekdays 9–4:30, Sat. 10–4:30, Sun. noon–4:30.

The **Union Bank Building,** built in 1833, is Florida's oldest bank building. Since the time it closed in 1843, it has played many roles, from ballet school to bakery. It's been restored to what is thought to be its original appearance as a bank. *Monroe St. at Apalachee Pkwy., tel. 904/488–1673. Admission free. Open Tues.–Fri. 10–1, weekends 1–4.*

At the **Museum of Florida History,** the long, intriguing story of the state's role in history—from prehistoric times of mastodons to the present, with the launching of space shuttles—is told in lucid and entertaining ways. *500 S. Bronough St., tel. 904/488–1673. Admission free. Open weekdays 9–4:30, Sat. 10–4:30, Sun. and holidays noon–4:30.*

On a clear day, from the 22nd floor of the **New Capitol,** you can catch a panoramic view of Tallahassee and its surrounding countryside. *Monroe St. at Apalachee Pkwy., tel. 904/488–6167. Admission free. Hourly tours of the New Capitol, weekdays 9–4, weekends 11–3.*

San Luis Archaeological and Historic Site focuses on the archaeology of 17th-century Spanish mission and Apalachee Indian townsites. In its heyday, in 1675, the Apalachee village here had a population of at least 1,400. Threatened by Creek Indians and British forces in 1704, the locals burned the village and fled. *2020 W. Mission Rd., tel. 904/487–3711. Admission free. 1-hr guided tours weekdays noon, Sat. 11 and 3, Sun. 2.*

A short drive north of Tallahassee, off U.S. 27 is **Lake Jackson,** a resource bass fishermen hold in reverence. Sightseers view, along the shores of the lake, Indian mounds and the ruins of an early-19th-century plantation built by Colonel Robert Butler, adjutant to General Andrew Jackson during the siege of New Orleans. *Indian Mound Rd., off U.S. 27, tel. 904/562–0042. Admission free. Open 8 AM–sunset.*

Five miles north of town on U.S. 319 is the magnificent **Maclay State Gardens.** In springtime the grounds are afire with azaleas, dogwood, and other showy or rare annuals, trees, and shrubs. Allow at least half a day for wandering the paths past the reflecting pool, into the tiny walled garden, and around the lakes and woodlands. The Maclay residence, furnished as it was in the 1920s, as well as picnic grounds, and swimming and boating facilities, are open to the public. *3450 Thomasville Rd. (1 mi north of I–10), tel. 904/487–4556. Admission: $1/driver plus 50¢ per passenger, May 1–Jan. 1; free rest of year. Open daily 8 AM–sunset.*

Lafayette Vineyards, a mile west of exit 31-A off I–10, is a gleaming, modern winery set among timeless vineyards. In 1812, these lands were granted by President Monroe to the Marquis de Lafayette in gratitude for his role in the American Revolution. French settlers planted the vines, and today award-winning wines catch the attention of oenophiles nationwide. Engage in the entertaining slide show, winery tour, and wine tastings (juice is also available). Wines are sold by the case or bottle at discount prices. *Tel. 904/878–9041 or 800/768–WINE. Admission free. Open Mon.–Sat. 10–6, Sun. noon–6.*

In 1865, Confederate soldiers stood firm against a Yankee advance on St. Marks. The Rebs held, saving Tallahassee—the only southern capital east of the Mississippi that never fell to the Union. The **Natural Bridge Battlefield State Historic Site,** about 10 miles southeast of the capital, marks the victory, and is a good place for a hike and a picnic. *Natural Bridge Rd. (Rte. 354), off U.S. 363 in Woodville, tel. 904/925–6216. Admission: $1/driver plus 50¢ per passenger. Open daily 8 AM–sunset.*

Wakulla Springs, about 15 miles south of Tallahassee on Rte. 61, is one of the deepest springs in the world. The wilderness remains untouched by the centuries, retaining the wild and exotic look it had in the 1930s, when Tarzan movies were made here. Aboard glass-bottom boats, visitors probe deep into the lush, jungle-lined waterways to catch glimpses of alligators, snakes, waterfowl, and nesting limpkin. Nature guides are available at the lodge to help you explore the trails around the springs. More than 154 bird species can be spotted in a teeming wilderness that also hosts raccoon, gray squirrel, and an encyclopedia of southern flora. *1 Springs Dr., Wakulla Springs, tel. 904/222–7279. Admission: $1/driver plus 50¢ per passenger. Boat tours $4 adults, $2 children. Tours daily 9–5:30. Springs open daily 8 AM–sunset.*

Time Out The **Wakulla Springs Lodge and Conference Center** (tel. 904/224–5950), located on the grounds, serves three meals a day in a sunny, spartan room that seems little changed from the 1930s. Schedule lunch here to sample the famous bean soup, home-baked muffins, and a slab of pie.

About 25 miles south of Tallahassee along the coast is the **St. Marks Wildlife Refuge and Lighthouse.** The once-powerful Fort San Marcos de Apalache was built here in 1639. Stones salvaged from the fort went into building the lighthouse, which is still in operation today. Exhibits are on display at the visitor center. *C.R. 59 (3 mi south of the Newport and U.S. 98 intersection) in St. Marks, tel. 904/925–6121. Admission: $3 per car. Refuge open sunrise–sunset; visitor center open weekdays 8–4:15, weekends 10–5.*

A scenic 90-minute drive west along U.S. 98, will bring you to
2 **Apalachicola,** the state's most important oyster fishery. Visit the **Raney House,** circa 1850; **Trinity Episcopal Church,** built from prefabricated parts in 1838; and the **John Gorrie State Museum.** In this museum, the physician who is credited with inventing ice-making and air-conditioning is honored. Exhibits of early Apalachicola history are displayed here as well. *John Gorrie State Museum, Ave. C and Sixth St., tel. 904/653–9347. Admission: 50¢ adults, children under 6 free. Open Thurs.–Mon. 8–5.*

If hiking and the outdoors are an important part of your travels, explore **Fort Gadsden State Historic Site,** on the river north of Apalachicola at Sumatra, and **St. George Island State Park.** St. George is reached by a causeway from Eastpoint, where you can drive toward the sea along the narrow spit of land with its dunes, sea oats, and abundant bird life. *Fort Gadsden, tel. 904/670–8988. St. George Island State Park, tel. 904/670–2111. Admission: FL residents, $1/driver plus 50¢ per passenger; out-of-state, $2/driver plus $1 per passenger; children under 6 free. Open 8 AM–sunset.*

Spreading north of Apalachicola and west of Tallahassee is the **Apalachicola National Forest** where you can camp, hike, picnic, fish, or swim. Just above the forest, on the east bank of the Apalachicola River south of I–10, is **Torreya State Park,** with campsites, hiking trails, and an antebellum mansion. *Torreya State Park, tel. 904/643–2674. Admission free. Open daily 8 AM –sunset.*

Jacksonville/Jacksonville Beach

One of the oldest cities in Florida, in area the largest city in the
United States, and an underrated tourist destination,
3 **Jacksonville** continues its battle against the stench of the sulfur
pulp mill that keeps many travelers speeding straight on
through. Improvements have been made, and winds shift, so
stay and give it a try.

Culturally and scenically the city is on a par with the best of the South. It has neighborhoods with a solid look and heritage and a strong business base. Its residents have a great love for the outdoors as well as the arts, and some of the best beaches in the state are located here.

Stop off in Jacksonville and savor remnants of the Old South that continue to flavor the city, and the sense of subtropical paradise for which Florida is famous. Because the city was settled around the river, many attractions are on or near one riverbank or the other. To avoid crossing back and forth, you may want to sit down with a map and plan your trip carefully. Some attractions can be reached by water taxi, but for others, a car is necessary.

On the south side of the river, the **Jacksonville Art Museum** brings together contemporary and classic arts. Especially noteworthy are the Koger collection of Oriental porcelains and the pre-Columbian collection of rare artifacts. Special exhibits, film and lecture series, and workshops make this destination worthy of more than one visit. Travel by car. *4160 Boulevard Center Dr., tel. 904/398–8336. Admission free. Open Tues., Wed., Fri. 10–4, Thurs. 10–10, weekends 1–5; closed Mon.*

The **Cummer Gallery of Art,** situated on the northwest side of the river, amidst leafy formal gardens, occupies a former baron's estate home. The permanent collection of more than 2,000 items includes one of the nation's largest troves of early Meissen porcelain as well as the works of some impressive Old Masters. Travel by car. *829 Riverside Ave., tel. 904/356–6857. Admission free. Open Tues.–Fri. 10–4, Sat. noon–5, Sun. 2–5; closed Mon.*

Jacksonville's Museum of Science and History (originally the Children's Museum) presents hands-on exhibits, live animals, temporary displays, and a planetarium with free astronomy programs. Devote an entire day to this museum, and lunch in the cafe. Located downtown on the south bank, the museum can be reached by water taxi. *Riverwalk, downtown, tel. 904/ 396–7062. Admission: $3 adults, $2.50 senior citizens, $2 children, children under 4 free. Open Mon.–Thurs. 10–5, Fri. and Sat. 10–10, Sun. noon–5.*

The **Alexander Brest Museum,** located on the campus of Jacksonville University, has a small but important collection of Stueben glass, Boehm porcelain, ivories, and pre-Columbian artifacts. The home of composer Frederick Delius is also on the campus and is open for tours, upon request. Travel by car. *N. University Blvd., east bank of the St. Johns River, tel. 904/744–3950, ext. 3374. Admission free. Open weekdays 8:30–4:30 during school year; closed holidays.*

To experience some of Jacksonville's natural resources, start with the ferry to **Mayport,** 12 miles east of A1A. Dating back more than 300 years, Mayport is one of the oldest fishing villages in the United States. Today it's home to a large commercial shrimp boat fleet and is the Navy's fourth largest home port. *Ferry tel. 904/246–2922. Ferry admission: $1.50 per car, 10¢ pedestrians. Ferry runs daily 6:20 AM–10 PM, every half hour. Naval Station tel. 904/246–5226. Admission free. Open Sat. 10–4:30, Sun. 1–4:30.*

Travel south on A1A to State Route 10 for about 2 miles to Girven Road; follow signs to the replica of **Fort Caroline National Monument.** The original fort was built in the 1560s by French Huguenots who were later slaughtered by the Spanish. The site, which is the scene of the first major clash between European powers for control of what would become the United States, maintains the memory of a brief French presence in this area. Today, it's a sunny place to picnic (bring your own food and drink), stretch your legs, and explore a small museum. *12713 Fort Caroline Rd., tel. 904/641–7111. Admission free. Museum open daily 9–5. Closed Christmas and New Year's.*

Take Fort Caroline Road west to Rte. 9A for 3 miles, crossing the N.B. Brovard Bridge (locally known as Danes Point Bridge). Take the first exit (S.R. 105) and drive northeast for about 12 miles to Fort George Island, where signs will lead you to the **Kingsley Plantation.** Built by an eccentric slave trader, the Kingsley dates to 1792 and is the oldest remaining plantation in the state. Slave quarters, as well as the modest Kingsley home, are open to the public. *Tel. 904/251–3122. Admission: $1 adults, children free. Open daily 8–5. Guided tours Mon.–Thurs. 9:30, 11, 1:30, and 3.*

Driving northeast on A1A for about 5 miles will take you to **Little Talbot Island State Park**—a picturebook paradise of sand dunes, endless beaches, and golden marshes that hum with birds and bugs. Come to picnic, fish, swim, snorkel, or camp. *Tel. 904/251–3231. Admission: FL residents, $1 driver plus 50¢ per person; out-of-state, $2/car and driver plus 50¢ per person. Open daily 8 AM–sunset.*

Jacksonville's sensational beaches spread south from Mayport, but casual tourists can miss the boundaries between, as well as the distinctions among, the beaches.

Atlantic Beach was another Henry Flagler project, developed in 1901 with the building of a hotel. A condo now stands on the site of the once-grand Atlantic Beach Hotel, built in 1929. Neighboring **Neptune Beach** is a quiet bedroom community, while **Jacksonville Beach,** once Ruby Beach and later Pablo Beach, was already a tent city in 1884 and was soon served by a narrow-gauge railway. Today it's a solid resort community, with new beach hotels replacing the original 350-guest resort hotel that burned in 1890. **Ponte Vedra Beach,** now the home of the Tournament Players Club and American Tennis Professionals, has been golfing since 1922 when the National Lead Company built a 9-hole course for its workers to play.

4 Before heading on to St. Augustine, plan a visit to **Fernandina Beach,** which lies north of Jacksonville on **Amelia Island,** across the border from St. Marys, Georgia. Take A1A east off I–95. Or, for a more fun and leisurely approach, drive north on A1A from the Jacksonville beaches, take the Mayport ferry across the St. Johns River, then drive the Buccaneer Trail (A1A).

Once an important political and commercial stronghold and now merely a quaint haven for in-the-know tourists, Fernandina Beach offers a wide range of accommodations from bed-and-breakfasts to Amelia Island Plantation, a sprawling landmark resort.

Fernandina's 30-block historic district includes the old cemetery where names on gravestones reveal the waves of immigrants who settled here—Spanish, French, Minorcan, Portuguese, and English. In **Old Town** you'll see some of the nation's finest examples of Queen Anne, Victorian, and Italianate mansions dating back to the town's glory days of the mid-19th century.

Begin your self-guided walking or driving tour of the historic district with a visit to the old railroad depot, originally a stopping point on the first cross-state railroad. Now the **Amelia Island-Fernandina Beach Chamber of Commerce,** this is a good place to pick up leaflets and information on the area. *102 Centre St., tel. 904/261–3248. Open weekdays 9–5.*

Follow Centre Street (which turns into Atlantic Avenue) for about 8 blocks to **St. Peter's Episcopal Church.** Founded in 1859, the church once served as a school for freed slaves.

Continuing on Atlantic, you will reach the bridge. From here you can see the **Amelia Lighthouse,** built in 1839. It's a great background for photos, but is not open to the public for touring.

A couple of blocks farther is the **Fort Clinch State Park,** home to one of the best-preserved and most complete brick forts. Built around the rim of Florida and the Gulf states, the fort served to protect against further British intrusion after the War of 1812 and was occupied in 1847 by the Confederacy; a year later it was retaken by the north. During the Spanish-American War it was reactivated for a brief time but for the most part was not used. Today the park offers camping, nature trails, carriage rides, swimming, surf fishing, picnicking, and living history reenactments showing life in the garrison at the time of the Civil War. *Tel. 904/261–4212. Admission: FL residents, $1/driver plus 50¢ per passenger; out-of-state, $2/driver plus $1 per passenger. Open daily 8 AM–sunset.*

Time Out **The Palace Saloon** (117 Centre Street, tel. 904/261–9068) is the state's oldest continuously operating watering hole, still sporting swinging doors straight out of Dodge City. Stop in for a cold drink and a bowl of boiled shrimp. The menu is limited, but the place is unpretentious, comfortable, and as genuine as a silver dollar.

St. Augustine

Numbers in the margin correspond with points of interest on the St. Augustine map.

5 To reach **St. Augustine,** take U.S. 1 south and head straight for the **Visitor Information Center** (10 Castillo Dr., tel. 904/824-3334). The center has loads of brochures, maps, and information about the nation's oldest city.

6 The massive **Castillo de San Marcos National Monument** hunkers over Matanzas Bay, looking every century of its 300 years. Park rangers provide an introductory narration, after which you're on your own. This is a wonderful fort to explore, complete with moat, turrets, and 16-foot-thick walls. The fort was constructed of coquina, a soft limestone made of broken shells and coral, and it took 25 years to build it. Garrison rooms depict the life of the era, and special artillery demonstrations are held periodically on the gun deck. *1 Castillo Dr., tel. 904/829-6506. Open daily 9-5:15. Admission: $1 adults, children under 16 and senior citizens free.*

7 The **City Gate,** at the top of St. George Street, is a relic from the days when the Castillo's moat ran westward to the river and the Cubo Defense Line (defensive wall) protected the settlement against approaches from the north. Today it is the entrance to the popular restored area.

8 The **Museum Theatre** screens two 30-minute films several times daily. One tells the story of the founding of the city in 1565, and the other depicts life in St. Augustine in 1576. *5 Cordova St., tel. 904/824-0339. Open daily 9:30-5:30. Admission: $2 adults, $1.50 children under 15; combination ticket for both films; $3 adults, $2.50 children.*

The **Oldest Wooden Schoolhouse** (14 St. George St.) is a tiny 18th-century structure that, because it was the closest structure to the city gates, served as a guardhouse and sentry shelter during the Seminole Wars.

San Agustin Antiguo is a state-operated living-history village with eight sites. You can wander through the narrow streets at your own pace. Along your way you may see a Colonial soldier's wife cooking over an open fire; a blacksmith building his shop (a historic reconstruction); and craftsmen busy at candle dipping, spinning, weaving, and cabinetmaking. They are all making reproductions that will be used within the restored area. *Entrance at Triay House, 29 St. George St., near the Old City Gate, tel. 904/824-6383. Open daily 9-5. Admission: $3.50 adults, $2 students 6-18; $8 family ticket.*

Time Out **Spanish Bakery,** behind Casa de Calcedo on St. George Street, has meat turnovers, cookies, and fresh-baked bread made from a Colonial recipe. *No credit cards.*

9 **Basilica Cathedral of St. Augustine** has parish records dating back to 1594, the oldest written records in the country. Following a fire in 1887, extensive changes were made to the current structure, which dates from 1797. It was remodeled in the mid-1960s. *40 Cathedral Pl., tel. 904/824-2806. Open weekdays 5:30-5, weekends 5:30 AM-7 PM. Admission free, but donations requested.*

10 **Plaza de la Constitution,** at St. George Street and Cathedral Place, is the central area of the original settlement. It was laid out in 1598 by decree of King Philip II, and little has changed since. At its center there is a monument to the Spanish constitution of 1812; at the east end is a public market dating

Basilica Cathedral, **9**
Castillo de San Marcos, **6**
City Gate, **7**
Flagler College, **15**
Flagler Memorial Church, **16**
Fountain of Youth, **17**
Lightner Museum, **14**
Mission of Nombre de Dios, **18**
Museum Theatre, **8**
Oldest House, **13**
Oldest Store Museum, **12**
Plaza de la Constitution, **10**
Ximenez-Fatio House, **11**

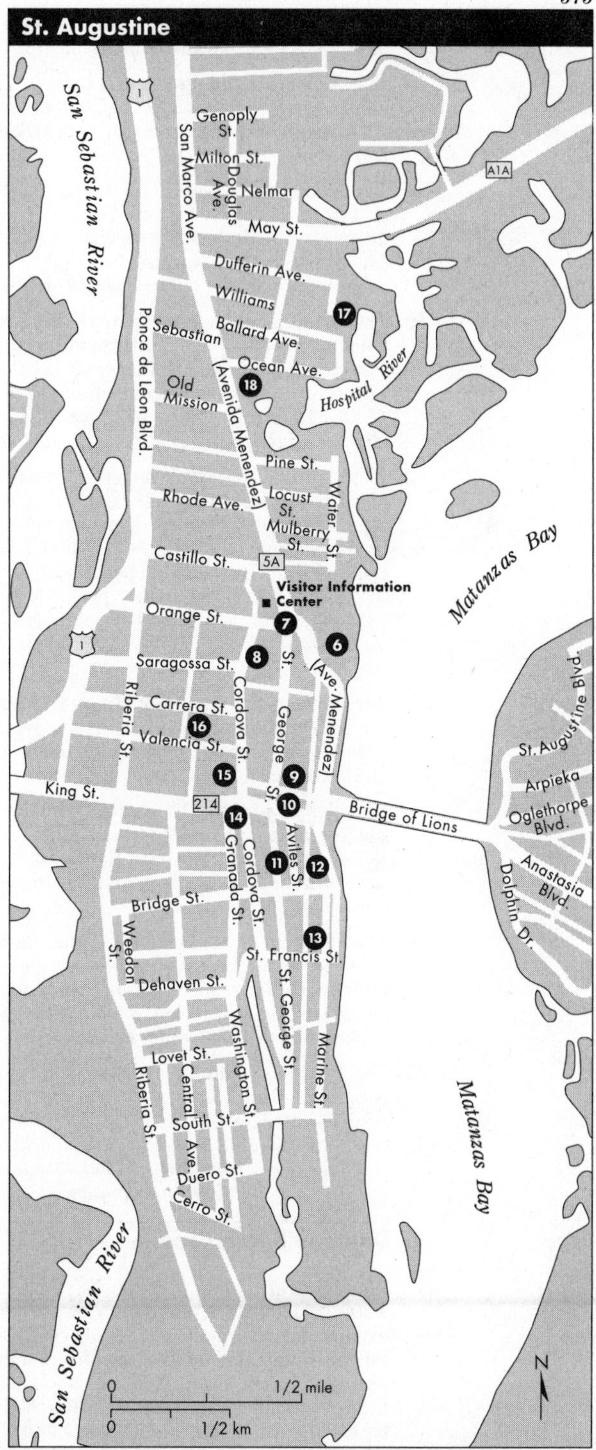

from early American days. Just beyond is a statue of Juan Ponce de León, who discovered Florida in 1513.

11 The **Ximenez-Fatio House** was built in 1797, and it became a boarding house for tourists in 1885. *20 Aviles St., tel. 904/829–3575. Open Mar. 1–Aug. 31, Sun.–Thurs. 1–4. Admission free.*

12 The **Oldest Store Museum** re-creates a turn-of-the-century general store. There are high-button shoes, lace-up corsets, patent drugs, and confectionery specialties. *4 Artillery La., tel. 904/829–9729. Open Mon.–Sat. 9–5, Sun. noon–5. Admission: $3 adults, $2.50 senior citizens, $1.50 children 6–12.*

13 The **Oldest House,** operated by the Historical Society, reflects much of the city's history through its changes and additions, from the coquina walls built soon after the town was burned in 1702 to the house's enlargement during the British occupation. *14 St. Francis St., tel. 904/824–2872. Open daily 9–5. Admission: $3 adults, $2.75 senior citizens, $1.50 children.*

14 The **Lightner Museum** is housed in one of two posh hotels built in 1888 by railroad magnate Henry Flagler, who wanted to create an American Riviera. The museum contains a collection of ornate antique music boxes (ask about demonstrations!), and the Lightner Antique Mall perches on three levels of what was the hotel's grandiose indoor pool. *75 King St., tel. 904/824–2874. Museum open daily 9–5; mall open Wed.–Sun. 10–5. Admission to museum: $4 adults, $1 students, children under 12 free.*

15 Across from the Lightner Museum, **Flagler College** occupies the second of Flagler's hotels. It's a riveting structure replete with towers, turrets, and arcades and decorated by Louis Comfort Tiffany. The front courtyard is open to the public.

At Valencia and Sevilla streets, behind Flagler College, the
16 **Flagler Memorial Presbyterian Church,** which Flagler built in 1889, is a splendid Venetian Renaissance structure. The dome towers more than 100 feet, and it is topped by a 20-foot Greek cross. *Open Mon.–Sat. 9–5.*

17 The **Fountain of Youth** salutes Ponce de León. In the complex there is a springhouse, an explorer's globe, a planetarium, and an Indian village. *155 Magnolia Ave., tel. 904/829–3168. Open daily 9–4:45. Admission: $3.50 adults, $2.50 senior citizens, $1.50 children 6–12, under 6 free.*

18 The **Mission of Nombre de Dios** commemorates the site where America's first Christian mass was celebrated. A 208-foot stainless-steel cross marks the spot where the mission's first cross was planted. *San Marco Ave. and Old Mission Rd., tel. 904/824–2809. Open daily 7 AM–8 PM summer; 8–6 winter. Admission free, but donations requested.*

Daytona Beach Area

Like most of coastal Florida, Daytona sprang up around the water, so its waterfront offers views of historic homes between expanses of natural marsh. As you venture along the Intracoastal Waterway, take note of the different names assigned to the passage. In the Daytona area, it's called the Halifax River, though it is not actually a river, but a tidal waterway that flows between the mainland and the barrier islands.

Numbers in the margin correspond with points of interest on the Northeast Florida map.

A good place to begin touring Daytona environs is along a segment of Old Dixie Highway. From I–95 north of Ormond Beach, take Exit 90 and travel east.

The first left off Old Dixie Highway (Kings Hwy.) will take you to the entrance of **Bulow Plantation Ruins State Historic Site,** built in 1821. From the entrance, a winding dirt road cuts through tangled vegetation and leads to a picnic area and day-use facilities facing Bulow Creek. All that remains of the plantation are the massive ruins of the sugar mill, which may be reached either by auto or bicycle along a one-way loop road, or on foot via a scenic walking trail from the picnic area. *Tel. 904/439–2219. Open daily 9–5. Admission: $1 per car.*

Continue southeast on Old Dixie Highway through a tunnel of vine-laced oaks and cabbage palms. Next stop is **Tomoka State Park,** site of a Timucuan Indian settlement discovered in 1605 by Spanish explorer Alvaro Mexia. Wooded campsites, bicycle and walking paths, and guided canoe tours on the Tomoka and Halifax rivers are the main attractions. *North Beach St., Ormond Beach, tel. 904/677–3931. Open daily 8 AM–sunset. Admission: June 1–Dec. 31, $8 per day; Jan. 1–May 31, $17 per day; electricity, $2 per day.*

Time moves forward and the canopy begins to thin as you travel
19 east on Old Dixie Highway to **Ormond Beach.** Auto racing was born on this hard-packed beach back in 1902, when R. E. Olds and Alexander Winton staged the first race. **Birthplace of Speed Antique Car Show and Swap Meet** is an annual event, attracting enthusiasts from across the nation. Sportsmen and socialites flocked to Ormond Beach each winter and made the massive Ormond Hotel their headquarters. The grand old wooden hotel (built in 1888 to pamper Flagler's East Coast Railway passengers) still stands watch on the east bank of the Halifax, but it is now vacant and no longer entertains guests.

Across the street from the hotel is **The Casements,** the restored winter retreat of John D. Rockefeller, now serving as a cultural center and museum. The estate and its formal gardens, on the National Register of Historic Places, are the setting for an annual lineup of special events and exhibits. Tours of the estate also are offered. *25 Riverside Dr., Ormond Beach, tel. 904/673–4701. Open weekdays 9–5, Sat. 9–12. Admission free; donations accepted.*

From the Casements go two blocks east to the **Birthplace of Speed Museum.** Devoted to the most exciting moments in America's long love affair with the automobile, the museum exhibits a replica of the Stanley Steamer, old Model T and Model A Fords, and a wealth of auto racing memorabilia, including a commemoration to auto-aero pioneer Glenn Curtis. *160 E. Granada Blvd., Ormond Beach, tel. 904/672–5657. Admission: $1 adults; 50¢ children under 12. Hours vary depending on race events.*

Take A1A about 8 miles south to Beach Street, on the mainland. In the old downtown section is the **Halifax Historical Society Museum.** Photographs, Indian artifacts, and war memorabilia relevant to this area's fascinating, varied past are on display here. You can also shop for gifts and antiques. *252 S.*

Beach St., tel. 904/255-6976. Admission free. Open Tues.-Sat. 10-4.

Pick up Volusia Avenue and drive west to Nova Road. Go two blocks south and follow signs to Museum Boulevard and the **Museum of Arts and Sciences.** This competent little museum has two blockbuster features: One is a large collection of pre-Castro Cuban art; the other is a complete and eye-popping skeleton of a giant sloth. The sloth remains, found near here, are the most complete skeleton of its kind ever found in North America. *1040 Museum Blvd., tel. 904/255-0285. Admission: $2 adults, 50¢ children, students, senior citizens, and members; Wed. and Fri. free. Open Tues.-Fri. 9-4, Sat. noon-5.*

20 To reach the famous beaches of **Daytona Beach** go east to A1A and follow signs to beach ramps, which lie for miles both north and south. During spring break, race weeks, and summer holidays, expect heavy traffic along this strip of garishly painted beach motels and tacky souvenir shops.

Several miles south of the Marriott, on A1A, is **Ponce Inlet,** which is frequented by locals and visitors who are familiar with the area. A manicured drive winds through low-growing shrubs and windblown scrub oaks to parking and picnic areas. Boardwalks traverse the delicate dunes and provide easy access to the wide beach. Marking this prime spot is a bright red century-old lighthouse, now a historic monument and museum. *Token admission. Open daily 10-5.*

Time Out **Lighthouse Landing** (4931 Peninsula Dr., tel. 904/761-1821), only yards from the historic light, is a good place for sipping cocktails and watching the sunset.

A 20-mile drive west on U.S. 92 (International Speedway) will
21 take you to little **De Land,** home of **Stetson University.** The **Gillespie Museum of Minerals,** on the stately campus, houses one of the largest private collections of gems and minerals in the world. *Michigan and Amelia aves., tel. 904/822-7330. Admission free. Open Mon.-Sat. 9-noon and 1-4; call before visiting on Sat.*

Drive 4 miles south on 17-92, toward Orange City. Follow signs to the **Blue Spring State Park,** one of the best places to spot manatees. February is the top month for sightings, but you're likely to see one almost any time. The park, once a river port where paddle wheelers stopped to take on cargos of oranges, also includes a historic homestead that is open to the public. Park facilities include camping, picnicking, and hiking. *Off U.S. 17-92 in Orange City, tel. 904/775-3663. Admission: $1.50 car and driver plus 50¢ per passenger. Open 8 AM-sunset.*

Ocala

22 To reach **Ocala,** take any of three Ocala exits off I-75. The city is on State Route 40, an east-west artery that runs from Yankeetown on the Gulf of Mexico to Ormond Beach. Once known only as the home of Silver Springs and the Ocala National Forest, the city has become a center for thoroughbred breeding and training. Along with the horses have come a new generation of glitterati, with their private jets and massive estates surrounded by green grazing grasses and white fencing.

As Ocala matures from country to gentry, its tourist appeal becomes more upscale. Trendy hotels and inns now dot the city; restaurants serve more innovative, international fare; and the Appleton Museum of Art is turning into a complex for all the arts, including theater, dance, and music.

Silver Springs, the state's oldest attraction (established 1890), is a National Landmark that centers on the world's largest collection of artesian springs. Today, the park features wild animal displays, glass-bottom boat tours in the Silver River, a jungle cruise on the Fort King Waterway, Jungle Safari, an antique and classic car museum, and walks through natural habitats. A multimillion-dollar project is recapturing the look and atmosphere of the 1890s. The attraction promises visitors a journey to the wild kingdom above and below the water. *Rte. 40, 1 mi east of Ocala, tel. 904/236–2121. Open daily 9–5. Admission to all attractions: $15.95 adults, $9.95 children 3–11.*

Next door is Silver Springs's **Wild Waters,** a water theme park with a giant wave pool and seven water-flume rides. *Open late Mar.–June 7, daily 10–5; Aug., daily 10–7; Sept. 4–30, weekends only 10–5. Admission: $8.95 adults, $7.95 children 3–11.*

Farther east on Rte. 40 is the entrance to **Ocala National Forest,** a 366,000-acre wilderness with lakes, springs, rivers, hiking trails, campgrounds, and historic sites. Area residents recall the filming of *The Yearling* at several sites within the forest. The **Visitor Information Center** (tel. 904/625–7470) on the left just over the bridge, is the site of old-fashioned sugar-cane grinding and cane-syrup making during the first two weeks of November each year. The syrup is bottled and sold on the premises.

Lake Waldena Resort & Campground (tel. 904/625–2851), several miles farther east into the national forest on Rte. 40, features a white-sand bathing beach and crystal-clear freshwater lake. Noncampers pay day-use fees for picnicking and access to the beach.

South of Rte. 40 (via Rte. 314-A) is **Moss Bluff,** on the Oklawaha River, which forms the southern boundary of Ocala National Forest.

Three major recreational areas are found in the national forest: **Juniper Springs,** off Rte. 40, featuring a picturesque stone waterwheel house, campground, natural-spring swimming pool, and hiking and canoe trails; **Salt Springs,** off Rte. 40 (via Rte. 19 North), featuring a natural saltwater spring, where Atlantic blue crabs come to spawn each summer; and **Alexander Springs,** off Rte. 40 (via Rte. 445 South), featuring a swimming lake and campground.

Just outside the eastern boundary of the forest, at the crossroads of Rte. 40 and U.S. 17, are **Barberville** and the **Pioneer Settlement for the Creative Arts, Inc.** A bridge house, moved from the St. Johns River at Astor, forms the entrance to the museum. On the grounds are an old-time caboose, a railroad depot, the commissary store of a turpentine camp, and a newly constructed "post-and-beam" barn, built of wood milled on the premises. During the first weekend in May and November each year, the museum hosts a Country Jamboree, which features arts, crafts, folk music, and country cooking. *U.S. 17 and Rte.*

40, Barberville, tel. 904/749–2959. Open weekdays 9–4. Admission: $2.50 adults, $1 children 3–12.

North of Barberville on U.S. 17 is another 1800s steamboat stop, **Crescent City,** where the historic **Sprague House Inn** (125 Central Ave., Crescent City, tel. 904/698–2430) traces steamboat-era history through the inn's collection of stained-glass windows. The three-room bed-and-breakfast inn also features a full-service restaurant.

South on U.S. 17 is **DeLeon Springs State Recreation Area,** promoted as a fountain of youth to 1889 winter tourists. Today, visitors come to picnic, swim, fish, and hike the nature trails. *Tel. 904/985–4212. Open daily 8 AM–sunset. Admission: $2 per car and driver, $1 per passenger.*

Gainesville

The University of Florida and its beloved Gators football games
bring most visitors to this city, so styles and prices are geared
primarily to modest budgets. In addition to the excellent theater, concerts, film series, and other activities typical of campus
23 life, tourists come to the **Gainesville** area for its strange geological features.

During the 1600s, the largest cattle ranch in Spanish Florida flourished on these great savannas. The area, written about in Marjorie Kinnan Rawlings's *The Yearling* and made more famous by the film *Cross Creek,* is a place of great vitality and energy—to be discovered by the diligent hiker. Be warned, though, that the shimmering heat can be stupefying to even the most knowledgeable outdoorsperson.

The **Florida State Museum,** on the campus of the University of Florida, will be of interest to the entire family. Explore a replica Mayan palace, see a typical Timucuan household, and walk through a full-size replica of a Florida cave. There are outstanding collections from throughout Florida's history, so spend at least half a day here. *S.W. 8th Ave. at Newell Dr., tel. 904/392–1721. Admission free. Open Mon.–Sat. 9–5, Sun. and holidays 1–5; closed Christmas.*

About 11 miles south of Gainesville on U.S. 441 is the village of **Micanopy** (micka-*no*-pee), where Timucuan Indians settled. There was a Spanish mission here, but little remains from before white settlement, which began in 1821. Today, the streets are lined with antiques shops and live oaks. Browse the shops on the main street, or come in the fall for a major antiques event involving 200 dealers.

Paynes Prairie, situated between I–75 and U.S. 441 in Micanopy, is a strangely out-of-context site that attests to Florida's fragile, highly volatile ecology. Evidence of Indian habitation dated as early as 7,000 BC has been found on this 18,000-acre wilderness that was once a vast lake. Only a century ago, the lake drained so abruptly that thousands of beached fish died in the mud. The remains of a ferry, stranded here in the 1880s can still be seen. In recent years buffalo lived here; today persimmon trees, planted by settlers long ago, flourish, and wild cattle and horses roam. Swimming, boating, picnicking, and camping are permitted in the park. *Tel. 904/836–4281. Admission: $1 per car. Open daily 8 AM–sunset.*

At the **Marjorie Kinnan Rawlings State Historic Site,** Rawlings's readers will feel her presence. A typewriter rusts on the ramshackle porch; the closet where she hid her booze during Prohibition yawns open; and clippings from her scrapbook reveal her legal battles and marital problems. Bring lunch and picnic in the shade of one of Rawlings's trees. Then visit her grave a few miles away at peaceful Island Grove. *S.R. 325 at Hawthorn, southeast of Gainesville, tel. 904/466–3672. Admission free. Open Thurs.–Mon. 10–11:30 and 1–4:30; closed Thanksgiving, Christmas, and New Year's day. Tours every half hour.*

The **Devil's Millhopper State Geological Site** is a botanical wonderland of exotic, subtropical ferns and trees, with a waterfall. The state geological site is situated in and around an enormous 1,100-foot-deep sinkhole. *Off U.S. 441 north of Gainesville, tel. 904/336–2008. Admission: $1 per car. Open daily 9 AM–sunset.*

Off the Beaten Track

About 55 miles south of Jacksonville in Palatka is **Ravine State Gardens,** which began during the depression as a WPA project, and blossomed into one of the area's great azalea gardens. The ravines are atypical in flat Florida. They're steep and deep, threaded with brooks and rocky outcroppings, and floored with little flatlands that make for a perfect intimate picnic. Although any month is a good time to hike the shaded glens here, the azaleas are in full bloom February and March. The gardens can be easily reached from Gainesville and St. Augustine. *Off Twig St., from U.S. 17S, tel. 904/329–3721. Admission free. Open daily 8–5:30.*

Perry, 26 miles south of I–10 between Tallahassee and Jacksonville, was once the largest single source of naval stores in the world and the home of a 1929 sawmill that was the largest one east of the Mississippi. The **Forest Capitol Museum,** on U.S. 19–98 a mile south of the city, includes lively, likeable forestry exhibits, a picnic area, and a pioneer homestead typical of this area. *Tel. 904/584–3227. Admission: $1. Open Thurs.–Mon. 9–5; closed noon–1 and major holidays.*

Far off the beaten byway, on Dog Island, is the **Pelican Inn** (tel. 904/697–2839), with pristine beaches, an eyeful of bird life, and peacefulness that can't be matched. Reached only by plane or boat, the inn provides a guaranteed island get-away. The kitchen is furnished, you supply the food and cook it yourself.

What to See and Do with Children

Castle Adventure is a slick update of an old-style family fun park, where you can play miniature golf, wander through a giant maze, explore waterfalls, caves, and lush tropical landscaping. *200 Hogen Terr., Daytona Beach, on U.S. 92, tel. 904/238–3887. Admission: $7 adults, $6 children and senior citizens. Golf alone or maze alone, $4.50 and $3.75 adults, $3.50 children. Open daily 10–10.*

Jacksonville Zoo is best known for its rare white rhinos and an outstanding collection of rare waterfowl. On a 7-acre veldt, see 10 species of African birds and animals. *I–95 north to Heckhsher Dr. E., Jacksonville, tel. 904/757–4463. Admission: $4 adults, $2 children 5–18, $1.50 senior citizens. Open daily 9–4:45.*

Marineland, one of the first of such attractions in the United States is still a magic place. Dolphins grin, sea lions bark, and seals slither seductively to everyone's delight. *South of St. Augustine on A1A, tel. 904/471–1111 or in FL, 800/824–4218. Admission: $12 adults, $7 children 3–11. Open daily 9–5:45, shows continuously.*

The Fred Bear Museum displays archery artifacts dating to the Stone Age, and a wealth of natural history exhibits all seeable in a one-hour guided tour. *Fred Bear Dr. at Archer Rd., Gainesville, tel. 904/376–2327. Admission: $2 adults, $1 children 5–11. Open Wed.–Sun. 10–6.*

At the **Florida Sports Hall of Fame** children can see mementos of more than 100 of their favorite sports heroes. *601 Hall of Fame Dr., off U.S. 90 W., Lake City, tel. 904/755–5666. Admission: $5 adults, $3 children and senior citizens. Open Mon.–Sat. 9–9, Sun. 10–7.*

Tallahassee Junior Museum features a collection of old cars and carriages, a red caboose, nature trails, a snake exhibit, and a restored plantation home. *3945 Museum Dr., Tallahassee, tel. 904/576–1636. Admission: $4 adults, $2 children. Open Tues.–Sat. 9–5, Sun. 12:30–5.*

Shopping

Souvenirs unique to northeast Florida include stuffed manatees, citrus fruits, gems and minerals from De Land, beach and surf-theme merchandise from along the coast, award-winning Lafayette wines from Tallahassee, and auto racing items from Daytona Beach.

For specialty shops, roam around **Jacksonville Landing,** downtown at the Main Street Bridge.

Brand-name items are sold at discount prices at the **Daytona Beach Outlet Mall** (2400 S. Ridgewood Ave., South Daytona, tel. 904/756–8700). Daytona's **Flea Market** is one of the South's largest (I–4 at U.S. 92).

Beaches

Beaches in northeastern Florida are the most varied in the state, ranging from the rocky moonscape of Washington Oaks State Park, just below St. Augustine, to the slick sands of Daytona.

Daytona, which bills itself as the "World's Most Famous Beach," permits cars to drive right up to your beachsite, spread out a blanket, and have all your belongings at hand; this is especially convenient for elderly or handicapped beachgoers. Be warned, however, that accidents occur in which sunbathers are run over, so you may want to consider this when deciding on a beach.

Flagler Beach is a vast, windswept swath of sand with easy access.

Jacksonville Beach is the liveliest of the long line of Jacksonville Beaches. Young people flock to the beach, where there are all sorts of games to play and also beach concessions, rental shops, and a fishing pier.

Neptune Beach, adjoining Jacksonville Beach to the north, is more residential and offers easy access to quieter beaches. Surfers take to the waves, and consider it one of the area's two best surfing sites.

Atlantic Beach, north of Neptune Beach, is the other favored surfing area. Around the popular Sea Turtle Inn, you'll find catamaran rentals and instruction. Five areas have lifeguards on duty in the summer 10–6.

Kathryn Abbey Hanna Park, near Mayport, is the Jacksonville area's showplace park, drawing families and singles alike. It offers beaches, showers, and snack bars that operate April–Labor Day.

Fort Clinch State Park, on Amelia Island's northern tip, includes a municipal beach and pier. That's where Fernandina Beach's city beaches are, meaning you pay a state-park entrance fee to reach them. But the beaches are broad and lovely, and there is parking right on the beach, bathhouses, picnic areas, and all the facilities of the park itself, including the fort.

Amelia Island's lower half is mostly covered by the Amelia Island Plantation resort. However, on the island's extreme southern tip you can go horseback riding along the wide, almost deserted beaches.

St. Augustine has 43 miles of wide, white, level beaches. The young gravitate toward the public beaches at St. Augustine Beach and Vilano Beach, while families prefer the Anastasia State Recreation Area. All three are accessible via Rte. A1A: Vilano Beach is to the north, across North River, and Anastasia State Park and St. Augustine Beach are both on Anastasia Island, across the Bridge of Lions.

Participant Sports

Biking Serious cyclists tour central Florida's hilly countryside on their sleek racers; others prefer pedaling the coastal flatlands on a beach bike. In Daytona Beach, bicycle concessions set up shop along the beach year-round. Near New Smyrna Beach, try **Swift Cycles-Beach Concession** (1803 12th St., Edgewater, tel. 904/427–2413).

Boating
Rentals Pontoon boats, houseboats, and bass boats for the St. Johns River are available from **Hontoon Landing Marina** (De Land, tel. 800/248–2474). Boats for the Tomoka River are offered by **Daytona Recreational Sales & Rentals** (Ormond Beach, tel. 904/672–5631). **Club Nauticos** rents boats to members and nonmembers (Amelia Island, tel. 904/261–6998; Daytona Beach, tel. 904/252–7272; Jacksonville, tel. 904/388–2628; Jacksonville Beach, tel. 904/241–2628). Other rentals are available from **The Boat Club** (Daytona Beach, tel. 904/255–0864). Explore the silver waters of the St. Johns River system with its many springs, lakes, and tributaries, aboard **Three Buoys Houseboats** (De Land, tel. 904/736–9422).

Rental boats and motors for fishing the St. Johns are available from **Highland Park Fish Camp** (De Land, tel. 904/734–2334), **Blair's Jungle Den Fish Camp** (near Astor, tel. 904/749–2264), **Tropical Apartments & Marina** (De Land, tel. 904/734–3080), **Halls Lodge** (Astor, tel. 904/749–2505), and **South Moon Fishing Camp** (near Pierson, tel. 904/749–2383).

Canoeing Float down sparkling clear spring "runs" that may be mere tunnels through tangled jungle growth. To canoe the Wakulla River near Tallahassee, contact **TNT Hideway** (St. Marks, tel.

904/925–6412); the 7-mile Juniper Springs run in the Ocala National Forest (tel. 904/625–2808); the Sante Fe River at High Springs (tel. 904/454–1853).

Fishing Your options range from cane-pole fishing in a roadside canal or off a fishing pier, to luxury charters. On the cheaper end of the scale, **Jacksonville Beach Fishing Pier** extends 1,200 feet into the Atlantic, and the cost for fishing is $3 for adults, $1.50 for children and senior citizens, or 50¢ for watching.

Charters Deep-sea fishing charters are provided by **Critter Fleet Marina,** (Daytona Beach, tel. 904/767–7676 or in FL, 800/338–0850) and **Cindy Jay Charters** (Ponce Inlet, tel. 904/788–3469).

For sportfishing, charter the *Sea Love II* (St. Augustine, 904/824–3328) or from **Critter Fleet Marina** (Daytona Beach, tel. 904/767–7676). One of the savviest guides to St. Johns River bass fishing is **Bob Stonewater** (De Land, tel. 904/736–7120). He'll tow his boat to whatever launch ramp is best for the day's fishing, and meet clients there.

Golf Florida is famed for its golf facilities, and no section of the state has better courses than the Northeast.

In Daytona Beach, the **Indigo Lakes Course** (tel. 904/258–6333) is now developing a headquarters course and golfing community for the LPGA (tel. 800/854–1234). The **Tournament Players Club at Sawgrass** (tel. 904/285–2261) in Ponte Vedra is home to the championship of that name; the Central Classic is held yearly at **Killearn** (tel. 904/893–2186) in Tallahassee; **Spruce Creek Golf & Country Club** (tel. 904/756–6114), near Daytona, has 18 holes of championship golf and its own fly-in runway for private planes.

At **Amelia Island Plantation** (tel. 904/261–6161), three stunning oceanfront holes are true "links" in the old Scottish golf tradition.

Ocala's **Golden Ocala Course** (tel. 904/622–0198) is rated among the state's top 25. Each of its holes is modeled after one of the world's most famous, from St. Andrews to Troon.

Horseback Riding Ocala's bluegrass horse country can be explored during trail rides organized by **Oakview Stable** (S.W. 27th Ave., behind the Paddock Mall, tel. 904/237–8844).

Skydiving Anybody who wants to jump out of an airplane when it's thousands of feet up in the air can do so with the help of **Skydive De Land** (tel. 904/738–3539) or **Titusville Parachute Center** (tel. 407/267–0016). Open weekends 9 AM–sunset.

Tennis Resorts especially well known for their tennis programs include **Amelia Island Plantation** (tel. 904/261–6161), site of the nationally televised WTA Championships; the **St. Augustine Beach and Tennis Resort** (tel. 904/471–9111); **Ponce de Leon Lodge and Country Club** (tel. 904/824–2821); the **Ponte Vedra Club** (tel. 904/285–6911); and the **Marriott at Sawgrass** (tel. 904/285–7777).

Water Sports
Rentals Most larger beachfront hotels offer water sports equipment for rent. Other sources for renting sailboards, surfboards, or boogie boards include **The Surf Station** (1002 Anastasia Blvd., St. Augustine Beach, tel. 904/471–9463); **Aloha Sports** (100 N. Atlantic Ave., Daytona Beach, tel. 904/257–3843); **Sandy Point Sailboards** (1114 Riverside Dr., Holly Hill, tel. 904/255–4977);

and **Too Hip** (2108 S. Atlantic Ave., Daytona Beach, tel. 904/255-2399).

For jet ski rentals try **J&J** (841 Ballough Rd., Daytona Beach, tel. 904/255-1917) or **Jet Ski Headquarters** (3537 Halifax Dr., Port Orange, tel. 904/788-4143).

Diving/Snorkeling Northeast Florida offers, in addition to ocean diving, a wide range of cave diving and snorkeling over spring "boils." For information about scuba diving in springs and caves, instruction, and rental equipment, call **Scuba World II** (1941 S. Woodland Blvd., De Land, tel. 904/734-3483) or **Drive & Tour Inc.** (1403 E. New York Ave., De Land, tel. 904/736-0571).

Scuba equipment, trips, refills, and lessons are available from **Family Discount Diving** (3948 S. Peninsula Dr., Daytona Beach, tel. 904/756-9123), **Adventure Diving** (3127 S. Ridgewood Ave., S. Daytona, tel. 904/788-8050), and **Capt. Jim's Divers Cove** (1676 E. Ridgewood Ave., Holly Hill, tel. 904/673-5363).

Spectator Sports

Auto Racing The massive **Daytona International Speedway** on U.S. 92 (Daytona Beach's major east-west artery) is home of year-round auto and motorcycle racing including the annual Daytona 500 in February and Pepsi 400 in July. Twenty-minute narrated tours of the historic track are offered daily 9-5 except on race days. For racing schedules, call 407/253-6711.

The Gatornationals of the **National Hot Rod Association** (tel. 818/914-4761) are held each year in late winter in Gainesville.

Baseball The **Jacksonville Expos,** a Class A Southern League professional team, play home games in Wolfson Park, Gator Bowl complex (1400 E. Duval St., Jacksonville, tel. 904/358-2846).

Football The blockbuster event in Northeast Florida is Jacksonville's **Gator Bowl** (tel. 904/396-1800). Other major events include **Florida Gators** games in Gainesville and the **Florida State Seminoles** in Tallahassee.

Golf The Tournament Players Championship is a March event at the **Tournament Players Club** (near Sawgrass in Ponte Vedra Beach, tel. 904/285-7888), which is national headquarters of the PGA Tour.

Greyhound Races During the summer, you can bet on the dogs every night but Sunday at the **Daytona Beach Kennel Club** (on U.S. 92 near the International Speedway, tel. 904/252-6484).

Greyhounds race year-round in the Jacksonville area, with seasons split among three tracks: **Jacksonville Kennel Club,** May-September (1400 N. McDuff Ave., tel. 904/646-0001); **Orange Park Kennel Club,** November-April (U.S. 17 at I-295, tel. 904/264-9575); and **Bayard Raceway,** March and April (18 mi south on U.S. 1, tel. 904/268-5555).

Jai Alai The speediest of sports, jai alai is played January-March and June-September at **Ocala Jai-Alai** (Rte. 318, Orange Lake, tel. 904/591-2345), October-May at the **Big Bend Fronton** (off I-10 south of Quincy and west of Tallahassee, tel. 904/442-4111), and February-July at **Daytona Jai Alai** (U.S. 92, across from the Daytona International Speedway, tel. 904/255-0222).

Tennis The top-rated Women's Tennis Association Championships is held in April, and the Men's All-American Tennis Championship in September, both at **Amelia Island Plantation** (Amelia Island, tel. 904/387–5497).

Dining and Lodging

Dining The state is embraced by the Atlantic Ocean and the Gulf of Mexico and is laced with waterways, which means that seafood is prominently featured. In coastal towns, the catches often come straight from the restaurant's own fleet. Shrimp, oysters, snapper, and grouper are especially popular.

Restaurants are organized geographically. Unless otherwise noted, they serve lunch and dinner.

Category	Cost*
Very Expensive	over $60
Expensive	$40–$60
Moderate	$20–$40
Inexpensive	under $20

**per person, exclusive of wine, service, or 6% sales tax*

Lodging Accommodations range from splashy beachfront resorts and glitzy condominiums to cozy inns and bed-and-breakfasts nestled in historic districts. As a general rule, the closer you are to the center of activity in the coastal resorts, the more you'll pay. You'll save a few dollars if you stay across from the beach rather than on it, and you'll save even more if you select a place that's a bit removed from the action.

Category	Cost*
Very Expensive	over $120
Expensive	$90–$120
Moderate	$50–$90
Inexpensive	under $50

**per double room, exclusive of 6% state sales tax and nominal tourist tax*

The most highly recommended restaurants and lodgings are indicated by a star ★.

The following credit card abbreviations are used: AE, American Express; CB, Carte Blanche; DC, Diners Club; MC, MasterCard; and V, Visa.

Amelia Island
Lodging
★ **Amelia Island Plantation.** One of the first "environmentally sensitive" resorts, Amelia Island's grounds ramble through ancient live-oak forests and behind some of the highest dunes in the state. A warm sense of community prevails; some homes are occupied year-round, and accommodations range from home and condo rentals to rooms in a full-service hotel. The resort is best known for its golf and tennis programs, but hiking and biking trails thread through the 1,300 acres. Restaurants range from casual to ultraelegant. *3000 First Coast Hwy.*

32304, tel. 904/261-6161; in FL, 800/342-6841; outside FL, 800/874-6878. 125 rooms in the inn; 475 villa apartments; home rentals by arrangement. Facilities: private indoor pools in honeymoon villas, water sports, 25 tennis courts, golf courses, fishing, racquetball, fitness center, instruction, pro shops, children's activities, restaurants, shopping, entertainment. AE, CB, DC, MC, V. Expensive.

Daytona Beach

Dining

Gene's Steak House. Gene's is located west of town, in the middle of nowhere, but this family-operated restaurant has long upheld its reputation as the place for steaks. The wine list is one of the state's most comprehensive, and there are seafood specialties, but it's basically a meat-and-potatoes paradise for power beef-eaters. *U.S. 92, 4.5 mi west of the I-95/I-4 interchange, tel. 904/255-2059. Dress: neat but casual. Reservations advised. AE, DC, MC, V. Closed Mon. Expensive.*

★ **Top of Daytona.** Especially dazzling at sundown, this 29th-floor supper club has a 360° view of the beach, Intracoastal, and the city. It's a project of television personality and cookbook author Sophie Kay, who is famous for her shrimp dishes, chicken inventions, and delicate veal recipes. *2625 S. Atlantic Ave., tel. 904/767-5791. Jacket and tie suggested. Reservations advised. AE, DC, MC, V. Moderate.*

Cap'n Coty's. Locally popular, this seafood and steak center, with a cozy bar, is known for its eye-popping, 70-item Sunday brunch. Ask about the daily specials, which depend on the day's catch. *333 Beville Rd., S. Daytona, tel. 904/761-1333; other location is at 601 W. Granada Blvd., Ormond Beach, tel. 904/672-2601. Dress: casual. Reservations accepted. AE, CB, DC, MC, V. Inexpensive.*

Lodging

Captain's Quarters Inn. It may look like just another mid-rise hotel, but inside, it's like a home away from home. An antique desk, Victorian love seat, and tropical greenery greet guests in the lobby of this beachfront inn. Fresh-baked goodies and coffee are served in The Galley, which overlooks the ocean and looks like grandma's kitchen with a few extra tables and chairs. Each guest suite features rich oak furnishings, a complete kitchen, and private balcony. *3711 S. Atlantic Ave., Daytona Beach Shores 32019, tel. 904/767-3119. 25 suites. Facilities: pool, sunbathing deck. AE, MC, V. Expensive.*

Daytona Beach Hilton. A towering landmark, this Hilton is situated on a 22-mile beach. Most rooms have balconies; some have a kitchenette, patio, or terrace. Convenient touches include an extra lavatory in every room, hair dryer, lighted makeup mirror, and a bar with refrigerator. *2637 S. Atlantic Ave. 32018, tel. 904/767-7350 or 800/525-7350. 214 rooms. Facilities: heated pool, children's pool, putting green, exercise room, sauna, game room, playground, gift shop, laundry. AE, DC, MC, V. Expensive.*

★ **Daytona Beach Marriott.** The location is a bombshell: The Ocean Center is in one direction and the best of the beach, boardwalk, and band shell is in the other. Fresh and flowery pastels set a buoyant tone for a beach vacation. Every room views the ocean. *100 N. Atlantic Ave. 32018, tel. 904/254-8200. 402 rooms. Facilities: indoor-outdoor pool, 2 whirlpools, children's pool and playground, poolside bar, 2 restaurants, 30 specialty shops. AE, DC, MC, V. Expensive.*

Howard Johnson Hotel. Straight out of the glamour films of the 1930s, this 14-story hotel on the beach is an oldie that has been brought back to the splendor of its Deco years. Kitchenette suites are available. *600 N. Atlantic Ave. 32018, tel. 904/255-4471 or 800/767-4471. 320 rooms. Facilities: heated pool, golf privileges, restaurant, lounge with live entertainment and dancing. AE, CD, DC, MC, V. Moderate.*

★ **Indigo Lakes Resort & Conference Center.** Home of the Ladies Professional Golf Association, this sprawling inland resort offers sports galore. The championship golf course measures 7,123 yards and has the largest greens in the state. Rooms are light and lavish in Florida tones. *U.S. 92 and I-95, Box 10859, 32120, tel. 904/258-6333; in FL, 800/223-4161; outside FL, 800/874-9918. 212 rooms, 64 condo suites. Facilities: Olympic-size pool, racquetball, tennis, golf, archery, pro shops, restaurant, courtesy transportation to airport and around resort, in-room coffee, nonsmoker and handicapped rooms available. AE, MC, V. Moderate.*

Perry's Ocean-Edge. Long regarded as a family resort, Perry's enjoys one of the highest percentages of repeat visitors in the state. Spacious grounds are set with picnic tables. Free home-made doughnuts and coffee—a breakfast ritual here—are served in the lush solarium, a good way to get acquainted. *2209 S. Atlantic Ave. 32018, tel. 904/255-0581; in FL, 800/342-0102; outside FL, 800/447-0002. 204 rooms. Facilities: heated indoor pool, whirlpools, golf privileges, planned activities, cafe open for breakfast and lunch, shops. AE, CB, DC, MC, V. Moderate.*

Aku Tiki Inn. Located right on the beach, the family-owned inn has a Polynesian theme inside and out. You can bake by the large heated pool or snooze under a shady tree on the spacious grounds. *2225 S. Atlantic Ave. 32018, tel. 904/252-9631, 800/AKU-TIKI, or 800/528-1234. 132 rooms, some with efficiencies. Facilities: pool, shuffleboard, game room, restaurant, 2 lounges with live entertainment, pool bar, gift shop, laundry. AE, CB, DC, MC, V. Inexpensive-Moderate.*

De Land

Dining

★ **Karlings Inn.** This facility is best described as a Bavarian Brigadoon set beside a forgotten highway near the has-been hamlet of DeLeon Springs and decorated like a Black Forest inn. Karl Caeners personally oversees preparation of the sauerbraten, red cabbage, succulent roast duckling, sumptuous soups, and tender schnitzels. Ask to see the dessert tray. *4640 N. U.S. 17, tel. 904/985-5535. Dress: neat but casual. Reservations required. MC, V. Closed Sun. and Mon. Moderate.*

★ **Pondo's.** You lose a couple of decades as you step into what was once a romantic hideaway for young pilots who trained in De Land during the war. The owner/chef specializes in whimsical veal dishes, but he also does fish, beef, and chicken—always with fresh vegetables, a platter-size salad, and oven-baked breads. The old-fashioned bar is "Cheers"-y, and a pianist entertains. *1915 Old New York Ave., tel. 904/734-1995. Dress: neat but casual. Reservations advised. AE, MC, V. Moderate.*

Rose Room. A quiet, multilevel corner of the Hilton offers seating at tables or in romantic booths. In addition to the blackboard dinner specials are a Mediterranean concoction called Grouper De Land, boneless breast of chicken, pasta du jour, and a couple of steak items. Come here for breakfast, too. *De Land Hilton, 350 International Speedway Blvd. (U.S. 92), tel. 904/738-5200. Dress: neat but casual. Reservations accepted. AE, MC, V. Moderate.*

Holiday House. This, the original of what has become a small chain of buffet restaurants in Florida, is enormously popular with senior citizens, families, and college students. Patrons can choose from three categories: salads only, salads and vegetables only, or the full buffet. *740 N. Woodland Blvd., tel. 904/734–6319. No reservations. Dress: neat but casual. MC, V. Inexpensive.*

Lodging

De Land Country Inn. This home replete with spacious verandas and glowing hardwoods, was built in 1903 and is furnished in an eclectic blend of restored antiques and reproductions. Hosts Raisa and Bill Lilley serve a complimentary Continental breakfast to start your day. *228 W. Howry Ave. 32720, tel. 904/736–4244. 4 rooms, with 2 baths. Facilities: pool. AE, MC, V. Moderate.*

De Land Hilton. Picture a snazzy, big-city hotel in a little college town, run by friendly, small-town folks with city savvy. An enormous painting by nationally known local artist Fred Messersmith dominates the plush lobby. Rooms are done in subdued colors and styles; prestige suites have housed the likes of Tom Cruise and the New Kids on the Block. *350 International Speedway Blvd. (U.S. 92) 32724, tel. 904/738–5200. 150 rooms. Facilities: pool, tennis and golf privileges, restaurant, nightclub, bar. AE, MC, V. Moderate.*

University Inn. For years this has been the choice of business travelers and visitors to the university. Located on campus, and across from the popular Holiday House restaurant, this motel is in a convenient location, has clean, comfortable rooms, and offers a Continental breakfast each morning. *644 N. Woodland Blvd. 32720, tel. 904/734–5711. 60 rooms, some with kitchenette. Facilities: pool. AE, CB, DC, MC, V. Inexpensive.*

Flagler Beach

Dining

★ **Topaz Cafe.** An unexpected treasure on a quiet stretch of the beach highway, this intimate restaurant is operated by two sisters who do all their own cooking and baking: vegetables are bright and appealing and meats and fish are artistically presented. The menu changes weekly. Though the selection is limited, there are always enough choices, including a vegetarian entrée. The decor is a whimsical combination of enamel-top tables, unmatched settings and linens, and wildflowers. *1224 S. Ocean Shore Blvd. 32136, tel. 904/439–3275. Dress: neat but casual. Reservations advised. MC, V. Closed Mon., Fri. lunch only. Moderate.*

Lodging

★ **Topaz Hotel.** This lovingly restored 1920s beach house is lavishly furnished in museum-quality Victoriana. It's a popular beachfront honeymoon hideaway—romantic and undiscovered. *1224 S. A1A, 32136, tel. 904/439–3301. 48 units, including efficiencies. Facilities: pool, restaurant, laundry. MC, V. Moderate.*

Flagler Beach Motel. If you yearn for the mom-and-pop motels of old Florida, at 1950s prices, this is it in plain vanilla. It's on a quiet stretch of beach, away from the Daytona crowds, and dressed with old-fashioned informality and friendliness. *1820 Ocean Shore Blvd. 32136, tel. 904/439–2340. 23 units, including efficiencies, cottages, and apartments. Facilities: pool, shuffleboard, cable TV. MC, V. Inexpensive.*

Gainesville

Dining

Sovereign. Crystal, candlelight, and a jazz pianist set a theme of restrained elegance in this 1878 carriage house. The veal specialties are notable, particularly the *saltimbocca* (veal sautéed with spinach and cheese). Duckling and rack of baby lamb are dependable choices as well. *12 S.E. Second Ave., tel. 904/378–*

6307. Jacket required. Reservations advised. AE, MC, V. Expensive.

Fiddler's. This rooftop restaurant is a celebration spot for locals and a dependable place for travelers who are looking for a good meal. The superb view, classic Continental cuisine, and mellow background music make for a relaxing evening. The pastries and breads are home-baked; duckling with orange and cherry sauce is a specialty. Sunday brunches are served, too. *University Centre Hotel, 1535 S.W. Archer Rd., tel. 904/371–3333. Jacket and tie requested. Reservations advised. AE, DC, MC, V. Moderate.*

The Yearling. Marjorie Kinnan Rawlings would have been proud of this country restaurant with city savvy. On the menu are quail, frogs' legs, alligator, and "cooter"—the local name for turtle. For dessert, try the frozen lemon pie laced with Bacardi rum. *Rte. 3, Box 123, Hawthorne, tel. 904/466–3033. Dress: casual. Reservations accepted Tues.–Thurs. only; wait can be long on Sunday. MC, V. Closed Mon. Inexpensive.*

Lodging

Herlong Mansion. Adorned with old relics at every turn, this late-19th-century home screams out its antiquity. Continental breakfasts and evening cordials with petit fours, provided by caring hosts, strengthens the appeal. Although the nearest restaurants are in Gainesville, this inn has much to offer. There's no street address; just look for the big, brick house on the short main street of Micanopy. *Tel. 904/466–3322. 6 rooms, some with private bath. Facilities: library, parlor with TV. MC, V. Expensive.*

Holiday Inn University Center. An upbeat, casual look sets the scene for business, medical, and vacation travelers. It's downtown and near the university and football stadium, jogging paths, and tennis courts. *1250 W. University Ave. 32601, tel. 904/376–1661 or 800/HOLIDAY. 167 rooms. Facilities: rooftop pool, remote control TV, rental cars on property, restaurant, lounge, airport transportation. AE, CB, DC, MC, V. Moderate.*

Residence Inn by Marriott. Studios and two-bedroom suites with kitchen and fireplace make a cozy pied-à-terre. Cocktails, Continental breakfast, and a daily paper are part of the hospitality. The central location is convenient for the university or business traveler. *4001 S.W. 13th St., (at U.S. 441 and S. R. 331) 32602, tel. 904/371–2101 or 800/331–3131. 80 suites. Facilities: pool, whirlpool, exercise equipment, restaurant, lounge, microwave, laundry, free transport to airport or bus station. MC, V. Moderate.*

Cabot Lodge. Included in the room rate is a Continental breakfast and a chummy two-hour cocktail reception. Spacious rooms and a clublike ambience make this a favorite with business and university travelers. *3726 S.W. 40th Blvd. 32608, tel. 904/375–2400 or in FL, 800/331–8215; outside FL, 800/843–8735. Facilities: satellite TV. DC, MC, V. Inexpensive.*

Jacksonville/ Jacksonville Beach

Dining

Cafe on the Square. This 1920 building, the oldest on San Marco Square, is an unpretentious place for an after-theater meal, tête-à-tête dining, or Sunday brunch. Dine indoors or out and choose from a menu ranging from steak sandwiches to quiche, marinated chicken, or pasta—all choices with a Continental flair. *1974 San Marco Blvd., Jacksonville, tel. 904/399–4848. Dress: casual. Reservations accepted Mon.–Thurs. AE, DC, MC, V. No lunch. Moderate.*

Crustaceans. With the Intracoastal in the background, hearty hard-shell crabs or juicy grilled fillet will taste all the better. The menu also offers steak and homemade bakery specialties. It's especially festive on summer weekends when there's live entertainment. *2321 Beach Blvd., Jacksonville Beach, tel. 904/241–8238. Dress: casual. Reservations advised. AE, MC, V. No lunch. Moderate.*

Ragtime. A New Orleans theme threads through everything from the Sunday jazz brunch to the beignets. It's loud, crowded, and alive with a sophisticated young bunch. If you aren't into Creole and Cajun classics, have a simple po-boy sandwich or fish sizzled on the grill. *207 Atlantic Blvd., Atlantic Beach, tel. 904/241–7877. Dress: casual. Reservations advised. AE, MC, V. Moderate.*

Angelo's. A cozy, inelegant, hospitable family spot where you can dive into mountainous portions of southern Italian standards, including a socko eggplant parmigiana. House specials change daily. *2111 University Blvd. N, Jacksonville, tel. 904/743–3400. Dress: casual. Reservations accepted. MC, V. Inexpensive.*

Beach Road Chicken Dinner. If down-home chicken, potatoes, and biscuits are your comfort food, this is the place. It's the best of basic roadside diner stuff at Depression-era prices. Eat in or take out. *4132 Atlantic Blvd., Atlantic Beach, tel. 904/398–7980. Dress: casual. Reservations accepted. No credit cards. Inexpensive.*

Crawdaddy's. Take it Cajun or cool, this riverfront fish shack is the place for seafood, jambalaya, and country chicken. Dig into the house specialty, catfish—all you can eat—then dance to a fe-do-do beat. Sunday brunch served. *1643 Prudential Dr. (just off I–10 at I–95) Jacksonville, tel. 904/396–3546. Dress: casual. Reservations accepted for parties of 7 or more. AE, CB, DC, MC, V. Inexpensive.*

★ **Homestead.** A down-home place with several dining rooms, a huge fireplace, and country cooking, this restaurant specializes in skillet-fried chicken, which comes with rice and gravy. Chicken and dumplings, deep-fried chicken gizzards, buttermilk biscuits, and strawberry shortcake also draw in the locals. *1712 Beach Blvd., Jacksonville Beach, tel. 904/249–5240. Dress: informal. Reservations accepted for parties of 6 or more. AE, DC, MC, V. Inexpensive.*

The Tree Steakhouse. You select your steak and watch the staff cook it over a charcoal fire. Charbroiled chicken is also on the list, and there are several seafood dishes, too. The atmosphere is low-key and casual. *942 Arlington Rd., in Arlington Plaza, Jacksonville, tel. 904/725–0066. Jacket required. No reservations. AE, CB, DC, MC, V. Inexpensive.*

Lodging

Jacksonville Omni Hotel. The city's newest hotel is a 16-story, ultramodern facility with a splashy lobby atrium and large, stylish guest rooms. All rooms have either a king-size or two double beds. You'll feel pampered anywhere in the hotel, but the extra frills are to be found in the two floors of the concierge level. *245 Water St., Jacksonville 32202, tel. 904/355–6664. 354 rooms. Facilities: heated pool, restaurant, lounge, exercise room, nonsmoker rooms, cable TV. AE, DC, MC, V. Expensive.*

Sheraton at St. Johns Place. This five-story luxury hotel, connected to the Riverwalk complex, has modern rooms with either a king-size or two double beds. It's located right in the center of things, and the hotel bustles with activity inside and out. Rooms overlooking the St. Johns River command the highest prices. *1515 Prudential Dr., Jacksonville 32207, tel. 904/396–5100. 350 rooms, 18 suites. Facilities: concierge, pool, 2 lighted tennis courts, 2 restaurants, lounge, shopping arcade, privileges at Downtown Athletic Club, nonsmoker rooms, facilities for handicapped persons. AE, CB, DC, MC, V. Expensive.*

Comfort Suites Hotel. Located in bustling Baymeadows, central to the currently "in" restaurants, nightclubs, and shops, this all-suites hotel is an unbeatable value. Suites, which are decorated in breezy, radiant Florida hues, include refrigerators, remote control TV, and sofa sleepers. Microwaves and VCRs come with master suites. Complimentary Continental breakfast and cocktail hour are included in rates. *8333 Dix Ellis Trail, Jacksonville 32256, tel. 904/739–1155. 128 suites. Facilities: outdoor pool, heated spa, laundry, free transportation within 5 mi. AE, MC, V. Moderate.*

House on Cherry St. This early 20th-century treasure is furnished with pewter, oriental rugs, woven coverlets, and other remnants of a rich past. Carol Anderson welcomes her guests to her riverside home with wine and hors d'oeuvres and serves full breakfast every morning. Walk to the parks and gardens of the chic Avondale district. Call for restrictions. *1844 Cherry St. Jacksonville 32205, tel. 904/384–1999. 4 rooms, each with private bath. Facilities: free use of bicycles. MC, V. Moderate.*

Sea Turtle Inn. Every room in this inn has a view of the Atlantic. Let the staff arrange special outings for you: golf, deep-sea fishing, or a visit to a Nautilus fitness center. You'll be welcomed each evening with a complimentary cocktail reception, and in the morning you'll be awakened with hot coffee and a newspaper. *One Ocean Blvd., Atlantic Beach 32233, tel. 904/249–7402. 198 rooms. Facilities: oceanfront pool with cabana bar, restaurant, lounge with live entertainment, room service, unlimited local phone service, free airport shuttle. AE, DC, CB, MC, V. Moderate.*

New Smyrna Beach

Dining

★ **Cuda's Old Style Florida Eatery & Sports Bar.** This is where the Mets hang out when they are in town, watching a sports event on one of Cuda's nine big television screens. Come for drinks, appetizers, and the raw bar. You can also come for the big menu that starts with soup and salad and ends with a steaming steak-and-scallops platter. *540 N. Dixie Hwy., tel. 904/427–3289. Dress: neat but casual. No reservations. AE, DC, MC, V. Moderate.*

The Skyline. Watch private airplanes land and take off at the New Smyrna Beach airport as you dine on secretly seasoned Tony Barbera steaks, veal, shrimp, chicken, and fish. A tray will be brought for your selection: order steaks by the ounce, cut to order if you wish. House specialties include the *zuppa di pesce*, served in a crock; fresh homemade pastas; and a New England clam chowder that took first place in the 1988 Chowder Debate. The building, once an officers club for American and RAF pilots, is filled with aeronautical nostalgia. *2004 N. Dixie Freeway, tel. 904/428–5325. Dress: neat but casual; no jeans or T-shirts. Reservations advised. AE, DC, MC, V. No lunch. Moderate.*

Riverview Charlie's. Look out over the Intracoastal Waterway while you choose from a menu loaded with local and imported fish, all available broiled, blackened, or grilled. The shore platters are piled high; landlubbers can choose steaks and chicken dishes instead. *101 Flagler Ave., tel. 904/428–1865. Dress: neat but casual. Reservations required Sun.–Thurs.; on weekends for parties of 6 or more. AE, DC, MC, V. Inexpensive–Moderate.*

Blackbeard's Inn. An array of seafood comes in fresh from the nearby docks. It's hard to beat the shrimp Louie, which is served at lunchtime, the stuffed grouper, or mountainous combo platters, but the inn is also known for its prime beef and barbecues. *701 N. Dixie Hwy., tel. in Daytona, 904/788–9476; outside Daytona, 904/427–0414. Dress: casual. No reservations except for parties of 15 or more. AE, CB, DC, MC, V. No lunch weekdays. Inexpensive.*

Franco's. Begun as a pizza joint in 1983, Franco's has become a high-voltage Italian specialty house. Light concoctions include spinach or broccoli pies, pasta salads, and what could possibly be the best Greek salad you've ever had. There's a long list of fish, Italian classics, including a captivating zucchini parmigiana, seven styles of veal, and gourmet pizzas. *1518 S. Dixie Freeway (U.S. 1, ½-mi south of S.R. 44), tel. 904/423–3600. Dress: casual. Reservations advised. AE, DC, MC, V. No lunch Sun. Inexpensive.*

Goodrich Seafood & Restaurant. For those who like mullet, this is a piscatorial Shangri-la. Gorge on steamed oysters, fried fish, hush puppies, clams, shrimp, and chowders. Fresh and frozen seafood is also sold over the counter. *253 River Dr., tel. 904/345–3397. Dress: casual. Reservations required for all-you-can-eat buffet (Sept.–May). No credit cards. Closed Sun. Inexpensive.*

Lodging

Riverview Hotel. A landmark since 1886, this was once a bridge tender's home. Verandas look over the Intracoastal, dunes, and marshes, while inside, Haitian prints and wicker furniture add to a feeling of island getaway. Complimentary Continental breakfast is served in your room, on the balcony, or poolside. *103 Flagler Ave. 32069, tel. 904/428–5858. 18 rooms with private bath. Facilities: restaurant, pool. AE, CB, DC, MC, V. Moderate.*

Sea Woods Resort Community. Get the best of the beach plus 50 acres of rolling dunes and hammocks. A true community of homes, condos, and villas, this has a rhythm of doing, going, and playing. Most people rent by the week, month, or season, but nightly rates are available. *4400 S. Atlantic Ave. 32169, tel. 904/423–7796 or 800/826–8614. 350 units. Facilities: racquetball, tennis, Nautilus fitness center, planned activities in winter. No credit cards. Moderate.*

Ocean Air Motel. One of those modest little "finds," this motel is operated by a caring British couple who, in the English manner, groom the grounds as carefully as they do the neat and commodious rooms. It's only a five-minute walk from the beach. *1161 N. Dixie Freeway 32069, tel. 904/428–5758. 14 rooms. Facilities: pool, picnic tables. AE, CB, DC, MC, V. Inexpensive.*

Ocala

Lodging

Ocala Hilton. A winding, tree-lined boulevard leads to this nine-story pink tower, nestled in a forested patch of countryside just off I–75. The marble-floor lobby, with piano bar, greets you before you enter your spacious guest room, decorated in deep, tropical hues. *3600 S.W. 36th Ave. 32674, tel. 904/854–1400. 200 rooms. Facilities: outdoor heated pool and Jacuzzi, tennis courts, restaurant, pub, live entertainment. AE, DC, MC, V. Expensive.*

Seven Sisters Inn. This showplace Queen Anne mansion is now a bed and breakfast. Each room has been glowingly furnished with period antiques; each has its own bath and fireplace. Rates include a gourmet breakfast. *820 S.E. Fort King St., 32671, tel. 904/867–1170. 5 rooms; wicker-furnished loft sleeps 4. Moderate. MC, V.*

Ormond Beach
Dining

Shogun II. The largest of this area's Japanese steak and seafood houses, this is the place for flashy tableside food preparation, a sushi bar, and a tropical bar. It's a fun, family place; call ahead if you want to celebrate a special occasion in traditional Japanese style. The steak and shrimp are stellar, but the lobster and chicken are also tempting. *630 S. Atlantic Ave. (A1A), in the Ellinor Village Shopping Center, tel. 904/673–1110. Dress: casual. Reservations accepted. AE, MC, V. Inexpensive.*

Ponte Vedra Beach
Dining

The Augustine Room. For a very special night out, come here not just to dine but for a look at the Marriott Sawgrass's emerald exterior and grounds filled with lagoons and waterfalls. Gaze at pleasing original paintings and enjoy the fresh flowers on your table while pondering a menu of fine steaks, native seafood, and veal specialties. The wine list is one of the area's most comprehensive. *1000 TPC Blvd., tel. 904/285–7777. Jacket and tie required. Reservations advised. AE, CB, MC, V. Closed Sun. Very Expensive.*

Lodging

The Lodge at Ponte Vedra Beach. The look of this plush new resort is Mediterranean villa grand luxe, aimed at serving an elite clientele whose passions are golf and tennis. The PGA Tour, Tournament Players Club, and Association of Tennis Professionals are based here. Rooms, designed with a country-French flair, have private balconies and cozy window seats. *607 Ponte Vedra Blvd. 32080, tel. 904/273–9500. 42 rooms, 24 suites, some with private whirlpool and fireplace. Facilities: 54 holes of golf, water sports, deep-sea fishing, two beachside pools with bar and grill, exercise room, restaurant, lounge. AE, DC, MC, V. Very Expensive.*

Marriott at Sawgrass. A tropical design is conveyed throughout this luxury hotel. Pick a room with a fireplace or private balcony. Fine details, from the private lounge and special services on the concierge level to the mood set by the lagoon and waterfall in the complex, enhance this resort. *1000 TPC Blvd. 32082, tel. 904/285–7777 or 800/872–7248. 512 rooms, 48 villas. Facilities: 5 heated pools, children's program and pool, lighted tennis courts, 99 holes of golf and complete golf program, bicycling, croquet, boating, exercise facilities, restaurants, valet, gift shop, airport pickup, private beach. AE, CB, MC, V. Very Expensive.*

St. Augustine
Dining
★

Columbia. An heir to the cherished reputation of the original Columbia founded in Tampa in 1905, this one serves time-honored dishes including *arroz con pollo*, *filet salteado*, shrimp and scallops Marbella, and a fragrant, flagrant paella. The Fiesta Brunch on Sunday is a Spanish gala. *98 St. George St., tel. 904/824–3341 or 800/227–1905. Dress: neat but casual. Reservations advised. AE, MC, V. Moderate.*

La Parisienne. Tiny and attentive, pleasantly lusty in its approach to honest bistro cuisine, this little place is a true find—and weekend brunches are available, too. Save room for the pastries. *60 Hypolita St., tel. 904/829–0055. Dress: neat but casual. Reservations required. MC, V. Closed Mon. Moderate.*

Le Pavilion. The Continental approach spills over from France to Germany with a wow of a schnitzel with spätzle. Hearty soups and good breads make a budget meal, or you can splurge on the rack of lamb or escargot. *45 San Marco St., tel. 904/824–6202. Dress: neat but casual. Reservations advised; required for 5 or more. AE, MC, V. Moderate.*

★ **Raintree.** The oldest home in this part of the city, this building has been lovingly restored. The buttery breads and pastries are baked on the premises. Try the brandied pepper steak or the Maine lobster special. The Raintree's Madrigal or Champagne dinners are especially fun. The wine list is impressive, and there are two dozen beers to choose from. Courtesy pickup is available from any lodging in the city. *102 San Marco Ave., tel. 904/824–7211. Reservations advised. Dress: neat but casual. AE, CB, MC, V. No lunch. Moderate.*

Santa Maria. This ramshackle landmark, run by the same family since the 1950s, perches over the water beside the colorful city marina. Seafood is the focus, but there are also steaks, chicken, prime rib, and a children's menu. Have drinks first in the salty lounge or feed the fish from the open-air porch. *135 Avenida Menendez, tel. 904/829–6578. Dress: casual. AE, DC, MC, V. Inexpensive–Moderate.*

Zaharias. The room is big, busy, and buzzing with openhanded hospitality. Serve yourself from an enormous buffet instead of, or in addition to, ordering from the menu. Greek and Italian specialties include homemade pizza, a big gyro dinner served with a side order of spaghetti, shish kabab, baked *mostaccioli*, steaks, seafood, and sandwiches. *3945 A1AS, tel. 904/471–4799. Dress: casual. Reservations accepted. MC, V. Inexpensive.*

Lodging

The Old Powder House Inn. Part of an 1899 Flagler development of winter cottages for the rich, this inn stands on the site of an 18th-century Spanish gunpowder magazine. Imaginative decor makes every room, from "Granny's Attic" to "Queen Anne's Lace," unique. Try the two-night package, which includes a romantic room, full breakfast and high tea daily, wine and hors d'oeuvres nightly, and a moonlight carriage ride with champagne. *38 Cordova St., tel. 904/824–4149. 6 rooms, with private bath. Facilities: bicycles. MC, V. Very Expensive.*

★ **Sheraton Palm Coast.** This is a bright, nautical-style resort hotel near the beach, thanks to the newly built bridge nearby. Rooms have private patios that overlook the Intracoastal. *300 Club House Dr., 32037, tel. 904/445–3000 or 800/325–3535. 154 rooms, suites. Facilities: 2 heated pools, children's pool, marina, 16 tennis courts, 3 championship golf courses, whirlpool, exercise equipment, sauna, restaurant, bar, shops, refrigerators, free transportation around resort and to beach. AE, CB, DC, MC, V. Very Expensive.*

★ **Casa Solana.** A hushed air of yesteryear hangs over this gracious, antiques-filled, 225-year-old home where you'll be welcomed like an old friend. Complimentary sherry and chocolates and a breakfast of fresh fruits and homemade specialties further convey the mellow but comfortable tone of this inn. *21 Aviles St. 32084, tel. 904/824–3555. 4 suites with private bath. Facilities: bicycles. AE, MC, V. Expensive.*

★ **Ponce de Leon Resort & Convention Center.** Pick your site to loll in the sun from the 350 lavishly landscaped subtropical acres or seek the shade of century-old live oaks in spacious contrast to the narrow streets and crowding of the old city. Insiders reserve well in advance to stay here for special events occurring in and around the area. *4000 U.S. 1N 32085, tel. 904/824–2821; in FL 800/228–2821; outside FL, 800/824–2821. 200 rooms, 25 condos. Facilities: pool, tennis, 18-hole championship golf course, 18-hole poolside putting course, volleyball, horseshoes, restaurant. AE, CB, DC, MC, V. Expensive.*

★ **Kenwood Inn.** For more than a century this stately Victorian inn has been welcoming wayfarers, and the Constant family continues the tradition. Located in the heart of the historic district, the inn is within walking distance of restaurants and sightseeing. A Continental breakfast of home-baked cakes and breads is included. Call for restrictions. *38 Marine St. 32084, tel. 904/824–2116. 10 rooms, 3 suites with bath. Facilities: walled-in courtyard with pool, fish pond, street parking and off-street parking 1 block away. MC, V. Moderate.*

Beacher's Lodge. An all-suites hotel on the dazzling white beach of Anastasia Island provides complimentary coffee, juice, newspaper, and a glimpse of the sun rising over the Atlantic. *6970 A1AS 32086, tel. 904/471–8849; in FL, 800/654–1450; outside FL, 800/527–8849. 132 suites. Facilities: pool, fully equipped kitchen, laundry. MC, V. Inexpensive–Moderate.*

Carriage Way Bed and Breakfast. A Victorian mansion grandly restored in 1984, this B&B is within walking distance of restaurants and historic sites. Innkeepers Karen Burkley-Kovacik and husband Frank see to welcoming touches such as fresh flowers and home-baked breads. Special-occasion breakfasts, flowers, picnic lunches or romantic dinners, or a simple family supper can be arranged with advance notice. *70 Cuna St. 32084, tel. 904/829–2467. 7 rooms with bath. Facilities: bicycles. MC, V. Inexpensive–Moderate.*

St. Francis Inn. If only the walls could whisper, this late-18th-century house would tell tales of slave uprisings, buried doubloons, and Confederate spies. The inn, which was a boarding house a century ago, now offers rooms, suites, an apartment, and a cottage. Rates include Continental breakfast. *279 St. George St. 32085, tel. 904/824–6068. Facilities: pool, some fireplaces, bicycles. MC, V. Inexpensive–Moderate.*

Tallahassee
Dining

★ **Andrew's 2nd Act.** Part of a smart complex in the heart of the political district, this is classic cuisine: elegant and understated. If you like pub hopping, there's Andrew's Upstairs, and the Adams Street Cafe (also by Andrew) is next door. For dinner, the veal Oscar is flawless or choose a chef's special from the chalkboard. You can't go wrong. *102 W. Jefferson St., tel. 904/222–2759. Jacket and tie suggested. Reservations advised. AE, DC, MC, V. Expensive.*

Anthony's. Often confused with Andrew's, but a different and equally deserving restaurant, this is the locals' choice for uncompromising Italian classics. Try one of the Italian-style grouper or salmon dishes. *1950 Thomasville Rd., tel. 904/224–1447. Dress: casual. Reservations advised. AE, MC, V. Moderate.*

Nicholson's Farmhouse. The name says a lot about this friendly, informal country place with its outside kitchen and grill. If you've never tried amberjack, discover this unusual, meaty fish—a specialty of the house. *Turn off Hwy. 27 to Hwy. 12 toward Quincy; follow signs, tel. 904/539–5931. Dress: casual. Reservations advised. MC, V. BYOB. Closed Sun. and Mon. Moderate.*

★ **Barnacle Bill's.** Don't be put off by the slummy decor. The seafood selection is whale-size and it's steamed to succulent perfection before your eyes, with fresh vegetables on the side. This popular hangout is famous for pasta dishes and home-smoked fish, too. Choose from complete weight-loss menus and daily chalkboard specials. Children eat free on Sunday. The full menu is available for carryout. *1830 N. Monroe St., tel. 904/385-8734. Dress: casual. Reservations required for large groups. AE, MC, V. Inexpensive.*

Lodging ★ **Governors Inn.** Only a block from the Capitol, this plushly restored historic warehouse is abuzz during the week with politicians, press, and lobbyists. It's a perfect location for business travelers involved with the state, and on weekends, for tourists who want to tour the Old Capitol and other downtown sites. Rooms are a rich blend of mahogany, brass, and classic prints. The VIP treatment includes airport pickup, breakfast, cocktails, robes, shoe shine, and a daily paper. *209 S. Adams St. 32301, tel. 904/681-6855 or in FL, 800/342-7717. 41 units. Facilities: restaurant, lounge. AE, DC, MC, V. Expensive.*

Las Casas. The quiet courtyard with its own pool and the darkly welcoming cantina where a complimentary Continental breakfast and evening cocktail are served convey the look of old Spain. Rooms are furnished in heavy Mediterranean style. *2801 N. Monroe St. 32303, tel. 904/386-8286 or outside FL, 800/521-0948. 113 rooms. Facilities: heated pool. AE, CB, DC, MC, V. Moderate.*

Tallahassee Hilton. Bustling and upscale, the hotel hosts heavy hitters from the worlds of politics and media who can walk from here to the Capitol. *101 S. Adams St. 32301, tel. 904/224-5000. 246 rooms. Facilities: pool, 2 restaurants, lobby bar, lounge with entertainment, gift shop, valet service. AE, DC, MC, V. Moderate.*

The Arts and Nightlife

The Arts Broadway touring shows, top-name entertainers, and other major events are booked at the **Tallahassee-Leon County Civic Center** (Box 10604, Tallahassee, tel. 904/487–1691), the **Florida Theater Performing Arts Center** (128 Forsyth St., Jacksonville, tel. 904/355–5661), the **Jacksonville Civic Auditorium** (300 Water St., Jacksonville, tel. 904/633–2900), and **The Ocean Center** (101 N. Atlantic Ave., Daytona Beach, tel. 904/354–4545 or 800/858–6444).

For information on the arts scene in Jacksonville, call 904/353–5100 for the latest news on art, music, and theater productions.

Concerts **Peabody Auditorium** (600 Auditorium Blvd., Daytona Beach, tel. 904/255–1314) is used for many concerts and programs throughout the year.

Florida State University School of Music (tel. 904/644–4774), in Tallahassee, stages 350 concerts and recitals a year.

The **Tallahassee Symphony Orchestra** (tel. 904/224–0461) performs at Florida State University, September–April.

The **Jacksonville Symphony Orchestra** (tel. 904/354–5479) presents a variety of concerts and hosts visiting artists.

The **Capitol City Band** (tel. 904/385–2809) has been brandishing its brass in Tallahassee since 1924.

Opera The **Monticello Opera House** (tel. 904/997–4242) presents operas in the restored, gaslight-era playhouse, near Tallahassee.

Theater The **Florida State University** (tel. 904/644–6500) presents 15–20 productions a year.

Seaside Music Theater (901 6th St., Holly Hill, tel. 904/274–2200) presents professional musicals January–March and June–August.

Alhambra Dinner Theater (12000 Beach Blvd., Jacksonville, tel. 904/641–1212) offers professional theater and competent menus that change with each play.

Nightlife

Bars and Nightclubs **Finky's** (640 N. Grandview, Daytona Beach, tel. 904/255–5059) brings in name entertainers you've seen on the Nashville Network and MTV. **Waves** in the Daytona Beach Marriott (100 N. Atlantic Ave., tel. 904/254–8200) is the area's hot, upscale place to drink, dance, and nosh while you listen to Top 40 and mellow standards. **Ocean Pier** (1200 Main St., Daytona Beach, tel. 904/253–1212), located on the ocean, has two rock 'n' roll bands, four bars, and one of the biggest dance floors in town.

In St. Augustine, **Richard's Jazz Restaurant** (77 San Marco Ave., tel. 904/829–9910), **Scarlett O'Hara's** (70 Hypolita St., tel. 904/824–6535), the **White Lion** (20 Cuna St., tel. 904/829–2388), and **Trade Winds** (Charlotte St., tel. 904/471–0113) offer live music from bluegrass to classic rock. Call for information on specific performances.

In Tallahassee, stop by **Andrew's Upstairs** (228 South Adams St., tel. 904/222–3446) to hear contemporary, jazz, and reggae music.

Comedy Clubs **Mac's Famous Bar** (2000 S. Atlantic Ave., Daytona Beach Shores, tel. 904/252–9239) features comedians who have already made their television debuts.

Index

Personal Itinerary

Departure *Date*

Time

Transportation

Arrival *Date* *Time*

Departure *Date* *Time*

Transportation

Accommodations

Arrival *Date* *Time*

Departure *Date* *Time*

Transportation

Accommodations

Arrival *Date* *Time*

Departure *Date* *Time*

Transportation

Accommodations

Personal Itinerary

Arrival *Date* *Time*

Departure *Date* *Time*

Transportation

Accommodations

Arrival *Date* *Time*

Departure *Date* *Time*

Transportation

Accommodations

Arrival *Date* *Time*

Departure *Date* *Time*

Transportation

Accommodations

Arrival *Date* *Time*

Departure *Date* *Time*

Transportation

Accommodations

Personal Itinerary

Arrival *Date* *Time*

Departure *Date* *Time*

Transportation

Accommodations

Arrival *Date* *Time*

Departure *Date* *Time*

Transportation

Accommodations

Arrival *Date* *Time*

Departure *Date* *Time*

Transportation

Accommodations

Arrival *Date* *Time*

Departure *Date* *Time*

Transportation

Accommodations

Personal Itinerary

Arrival *Date* *Time*

Departure *Date* *Time*

Transportation

Accommodations

Arrival *Date* *Time*

Departure *Date* *Time*

Transportation

Accommodations

Arrival *Date* *Time*

Departure *Date* *Time*

Transportation

Accommodations

Arrival *Date* *Time*

Departure *Date* *Time*

Transportation

Accommodations

Personal Itinerary

Arrival *Date* *Time*

Departure *Date* *Time*

Transportation

Accommodations

Arrival *Date* *Time*

Departure *Date* *Time*

Transportation

Accommodations

Arrival *Date* *Time*

Departure *Date* *Time*

Transportation

Accommodations

Arrival *Date* *Time*

Departure *Date* *Time*

Transportation

Accommodations

Addresses

Name

Address

Telephone

Name

Address

Telephone

Name

Address

Telephone

Name

Address

Telephone

Name

Address

Telephone

Name

Address

Telephone

Name

Address

Telephone

Name

Address

Telephone

Name

Address

Telephone

Name

Address

Telephone

Name

Address

Telephone

Name

Address

Telephone

Name

Address

Telephone

Name

Address

Telephone

Name

Address

Telephone

Name

Address

Telephone

Addresses

Name	*Name*
Address	*Address*
Telephone	*Telephone*
Name	*Name*
Address	*Address*
Telephone	*Telephone*
Name	*Name*
Address	*Address*
Telephone	*Telephone*
Name	*Name*
Address	*Address*
Telephone	*Telephone*
Name	*Name*
Address	*Address*
Telephone	*Telephone*
Name	*Name*
Address	*Address*
Telephone	*Telephone*
Name	*Name*
Address	*Address*
Telephone	*Telephone*
Name	*Name*
Address	*Address*
Telephone	*Telephone*

Notes

Notes

Notes

Fodor's Travel Guides

U.S. Guides

Alaska
Arizona
Boston
California
Cape Cod
The Carolinas & the Georgia Coast
The Chesapeake Region
Chicago
Colorado
Disney World & the Orlando Area
Florida
Hawaii
The Jersey Shore
Las Vegas
Los Angeles
Maui
Miami & the Keys
New England
New Mexico
New Orleans
New York City
New York City (Pocket Guide)
New York State
Pacific North Coast
Philadelphia
The Rockies
San Diego
San Francisco
San Francisco (Pocket Guide)
The South
Texas
USA
The Upper Great Lakes Region
Virgin Islands
Virginia & Maryland
Waikiki
Washington, D.C.

Foreign Guides

Acapulco
Amsterdam
Australia
Austria
The Bahamas
The Bahamas (Pocket Guide)
Baja & the Pacific Coast Resorts
Barbados
Belgium & Luxembourg
Bermuda
Brazil
Budget Europe
Canada
Canada's Atlantic Provinces
Cancun, Cozumel, Yucatan Peninsula
Caribbean
Central America
China
Eastern Europe
Egypt
Europe
Europe's Great Cities
France
Germany
Great Britain
Greece
The Himalayan Countries
Holland
Hong Kong
India
Ireland
Israel
Italy
Italy's Great Cities
Jamaica
Japan
Kenya, Tanzania, Seychelles
Korea
Lisbon
London
London Companion
London (Pocket Guide)
Madrid & Barcelona
Mexico
Mexico City
Montreal & Quebec City
Morocco
Munich
New Zealand
Paris
Paris (Pocket Guide)
Portugal
Puerto Rico (Pocket Guide)
Rio de Janeiro
Rome
Saint Martin/ Sint Maarten
Scandinavia
Scandinavian Cities
Scotland
Singapore
South America
South Pacific
Southeast Asia
Soviet Union
Spain
Sweden
Switzerland
Sydney
Thailand
Tokyo
Toronto
Turkey
Vienna
Yugoslavia

Special-Interest Guides

Bed & Breakfast Guide to the Mid-Atlantic States
Bed & Breakfast Guide to New England
Cruises & Ports of Call
A Shopper's Guide to London
Health & Fitness Vacations
Shopping in Europe
Skiing in North America
Sunday in New York
Touring Europe